Lead Us Not into Temptation

BOOKS BY JASON BERRY

The Spirit of Black Hawk: A Mystery of Africans and Indians

Lead Us Not into Temptation

Up from the Cradle of Jazz: New Orleans Music since World War II
(with Jonathan Foose and Tad Jones)

Amazing Grace: With Charles Evers in Mississippi

Lead Us Not into Temptation

CATHOLIC PRIESTS

and the

SEXUAL ABUSE

of

CHILDREN

Jason Berry

Foreword by
Andrew M. Greeley

UNIVERSITY OF ILLINOIS PRESS

URBANA AND CHICAGO

Library of Congress Cataloging-in-Publication Data
Berry, Jason.
Lead us not into temptation : Catholic priests and the sexual abuse of children /
Jason Berry ; foreword by Andrew M. Greeley.
p.   cm.
Originally published: New York : Doubleday, c1992.
Includes bibliographical references and index.
ISBN 0-252-06812-2 (pbk. : alk. paper)
1. Child sexual abuse—Religious aspects—Catholic Church.
2. Catholic Church—Clergy—Sexual behavior.
3. Child sexual abuse by clergy.
I. Title
BX1912.9.B47   2000
253'.2—dc21   99-057760

P 5 4 3 2

For Lisa,
and for my brothers, Lamar and Jack

"Whosoever shall offend one of these little ones that believe in me, it is better that a millstone were hanged around his neck and he were cast into the sea."

MARK 9:42

Contents

Introduction to the Illinois Paperback Edition

The publication of this book in 1992 coincided with a storm of news coverage about Catholic priests who had sexually abused young people and an entrenched pattern of bishops who concealed the perpetrators, shuffling many of them on to new assignments. Civil lawsuits provided the documentation on most of the cases I wrote about. The statistics I cited—four hundred priests accused in the preceding decade, $400 million paid out by dioceses in legal and medical expenses—became a stock paragraph in many reports; the book became a reference work in newsrooms. As a national scandal unfolded I gave scores of interviews, and watched with a sense of exhausted closure as the story I had worked years to bring to light surged across the media grid.

Lead Us Not into Temptation is less a study of sexual abuse than a political anatomy of clerical culture. Sexual secrecy is honeycombed through the rungs of ecclesiastical governance; the chronicle of abuse cover-ups is an account of how two institutions of democracy, the court system and a free press, trained a spotlight on the inner workings of a culture premised on celibacy and sexual conflicts tearing at its central nervous system.

On a deeper level, this is a book about journalism, a profession much maligned by tabloid obsessions at century's end, most strikingly seen in the media feed over President Clinton's reckless conduct with Monica Lewinsky. The hurdles I faced in the early phases of research, beginning in 1985, seem antique now. I wrote the book as a freelance writer. Convincing editors that there was a national story about sexual crimes in priestly life required a major time investment. I cultivated ties with editors at far-flung newspapers and spent many hours explaining how the civil litigation and rarer criminal prosecutions were creating a baseline of information that warranted scrutiny in the press. The Internet was not yet available; fax machines were a cutting edge tool. I made endless photocopies of the initial articles for the *Times of Acadiana* and the *National Catholic Reporter* in contacting editors as the investigation took on a nationwide scope, and advanced research by gathering legal documents and exchanging information with other reporters who were covering similar cases.

How much money has the church lost in legal and medical expenses due to the abuse scandals? "Close to a billion dollars," states the Rev. Thomas P. Doyle, a canon lawyer who worked at the Vatican Embassy in the mid-eighties and coauthored a prophetic report that warned the bishops of the impending crisis in 1985 (see Chapter VI). The National Conference of Catholic Bishops has never released a reliable accounting of financial losses, perhaps out of fear that donations to the church would fall off in protest.

Doyle has since become an ironic exile, demanding accountability of the bishops he once advised. In his odyssey from clergy loyalist to whistle-blower (he received a Cavallo award for moral heroism), Doyle became an Air Force chaplain, a position that protected him from potential retribution by the church hierarchy. By the mid-nineties he had become an advocate of abuse survivors and witness for plaintiffs in lawsuits against dioceses. He has followed hundreds of cases.

How widespread is the phenomenon of child molestation among Catholic clergy? Rev. Andrew M. Greeley, the noted sociologist who has written extensively on the church, using data from the Chicago archdiocese as a statistical baseline, estimated in the March 20, 1993, issue of *America,* the Jesuit magazine, that 2500 priests, or some six percent of the U.S. clergy, had abused 100,000 children in the last generation. Sylvia Demarest, a plaintiffs attorney in Dallas who spent years in litigation with that diocese, amassed a database on public accusations "in excess of a thousand priests," she says. Many cases have been settled through out-of-court negotiations in which the perpetrator is not publicly identified.

In March of 1993 the CBS TV newsmagazine *Sixty Minutes,* following leads I provided, reported accusations by three young women from New Mexico that Archbishop Robert F. Sanchez of Santa Fe had engaged in sexual activities with them; with each one it began when they were teenagers. Sanchez, who had recently served as secretary of the National Conference of Catholic Bishops, resigned from his archdiocesan position in disgrace, though he remained a priest. Some two dozen other clerics of the archdiocese were the subject of civil suits which resulted in negotiated settlements.

Pope John Paul II "saw the publicity as more damaging than the crime," wrote Jonathan Kwitny in *Man of the Century* (Holt, 1997; p. 639), a largely favorable biography. The Pope's response seemed to equate sin on both sides: he asked the faithful to pray for "our brother from Santa Fe" and "the persons affected by his actions." As for Sanchez, "a person's fall, which in itself is a painful experience, should not become a matter for sensationalism. Unfortunately, however, sensationalism has become the particular style of our age."

Sensationalism indeed pervades the American media culture; yet the notion of "a person's fall" evades an ethical position on what it means when an archbishop pursues sexual gratification from vulnerable young females, while covering up for other priests who abused children. Sanchez's "fall" coincided with a rash of lawsuits in New Mexico surrounding the Servants of the Paraclete, an obscure religious order that specialized in treating pedophile priests. "At least twenty priests had done part-time parish work while in treatment, and reoffended," states Bruce Pasternack, the attorney who litigated most of the cases in New Mexico.

Several factors made "pedophile priests" a national story. The tide of litigation against church dioceses revealed so many cover-ups that survivors—adults who as children had been molested by priests—began speaking out. A sense of moral outrage surrounded the issue that many newsrooms had approached reluctantly if at all just a few years earlier. In the fall of 1992 two groups formed, Victims of Clergy Abuse Linkup and SNAP—Survivors Network of those Abused by Priests. Between them, the groups eventually drew about six thousand members; their leaders became vocal, sometimes high-profile critics in news coverage and on talk shows.

Barbara Blaine was the founder of SNAP. When I met her in 1990, she was living in a Catholic Worker house on the South Side of Chicago, working with homeless people, gathering the courage to confront church officials about what had been done to her and others. "We have a right to be treated as good people, not as enemies of the church," said Blaine. "The church is not the property of the bishops. It belongs to the People of God. Survivors are demanding respect and justice." Blaine, who has since become an attorney in Chicago, was a catalytic figure in putting the survivors' issues in the public square.

Entwined with the devastating accounts of the abuse survivors was the issue of medical treatment for the perpetrators and whether they should remain as priests. "Priests can do anything they damn well please to lay people, and feel pretty confident they can get away with it," Father Greeley told a gathering of survivors in 1992.

Many such clerics were never criminally prosecuted, even as the dioceses negotiated settlements with their victims. Bishops were looking to treatment centers for advice on whether to allow a given cleric to remain a priest. "I don't think exile is the answer," the Rev. Canice Connors, director of St. Luke Institute, a clergy psychiatric facility, told me for a June 13, 1993, article in the *Los Angeles Times Magazine*.

"I would never, ever, recommend putting a pedophile back into ministry," Connors continued. "He should be removed from any activity with children. But removal from the priesthood has a parallel with incest. I can never cancel out [an abusive parent's] relationship to that child. You're still that child's father . . . Are we saying that this is the one unforgivable sin?"

The issue outside of clerical culture was not sin but whether the church should function as a safe house for men who had committed sexual crimes and suffered serious pathologies. Connors argued that it was more responsible to keep them within the church and monitor them; he was building on the treatment model established by Rev. Michael Peterson, founder of the Institute, whose career is chronicled in the book. A combination of support groups and use of Depo-Provera, the synthetic hormone reputed to reduce testosterone levels in sex offenders, was a cornerstone of St. Luke's approach.

An unofficial group of therapists at several clinical facilities had begun exchanging information as the crisis worsened. With the bishops unwilling to provide definitive data on priest perpetrators, the psychotherapists were dealing with a complicated institutional client to say the least. Dr. Leslie Lothstein, a clinical psychologist at Institute of Living in Hartford, Connecticut, had treated ministers of various faiths. He was skeptical of the support-group philosophy espoused by St. Luke, which often recommended that its clerical patients return to the priesthood, albeit on the condition that they not have contact with children. Lothstein felt that the bishops were unable to address the scope of the crisis or search for genuine solutions. "It seems that a part of them doesn't want to know," he said.

The politics of treatment for sexually abusive clerics will haunt the church until some future pope insists that offenders be summarily removed. There is a linkage here with celibacy; but it has to do with the political dynamics of the church rather than human sexuality per se. Clerical celibacy, an unmarried life that assumes chastity, does not cause aberrant sexual behavior any more than the institution of marriage can be blamed for incest. Most sex offenders have conflicts rooted in childhood. But celibacy is central to the governing of the church, an institution ruled by unmarried men. What we have seen in the late twentieth century is an ecclesiastical culture that has become a magnet to men with pathological problems, as well as a great number of homosexuals. I am not here suggesting an equation between gay men and pedophiles; the distinctions are made clear in the book. But the power structure of the church is inseparably bound with the dynamics of a gay clergy culture that shrouds reality from the public. This hypocrisy was a target of plaintiff lawyers who uncovered patterns of active homosexual clergymen participating in cover-ups of criminal behavior by child molesters, among other sexual behavior patterns. The obsession with secrecy and avoiding scandal bred a mentality of criminal deception.

There is no greater sign of the cultural schizophrenia that grips the church than the spreading presence of homosexuals within the priesthood. Many gay priests are good men who strive to serve their parishes; but the power structure is so addled with hypocrisy and the larger clerical culture so distorted by the absence of women and a heterosexual equilibrium as to render the medieval logic of celibacy—to prevent the offspring of priests from inheriting church property—a concrete boot on the People of God.

Cycles of media coverage can swing like a pendulum. In late 1993 the issues raised by abuse survivors and church critics hit a brick wall when Cardinal Joseph Bernardin, the archbishop of Chicago, was accused in a civil lawsuit of sexual abuse. The plaintiff, Steven Cook, a young man dying of AIDS, alleged that he had had sex with Bernardin and another priest in the mid-seventies as a seminarian in Cincinnati, when Bernardin was archbishop there.

Cardinal Bernardin is a central figure in the final section of this book. When I interviewed him in 1991—well before the lawsuit against him was filed—he struck me as a man of Hamlet-like complexity, unable to reconcile his loyalty to a labyrinthine clerical culture, rife with sexual corruption, and the church's moral responsibility to people in the pews, especially the victims. I would qualify that view to a certain degree now. The review board he empaneled in the Chicago archdiocese eventually did achieve some reforms; and Bernardin was the rare church leader to release figures to the media about the number of perpetrators and financial losses caused by the crisis. Yet there was a Machiavellian quality about Bernardin that troubled me before Steven Cook's controversial case. Bernardin's "reforms" came only after intense pressure driven by news coverage, survivors, and attorneys with suits against the archdiocese. As his moves garnered good press, and helped turn a tide of damaging publicity, Bernardin also sanctioned a strategy of legal counterattacks against plaintiffs, charging them with character defamation for having filed suit in the first place.

Steadfastly denying Steven Cook's charges, without attacking Cook, the cardinal emerged a heroic figure in the media for showing grace under pressure as the case made international headlines. The case turned on delayed, or repressed, memory—the idea that trauma victims will bury recollections too painful to deal with on a daily basis, and come to terms with them gradually, or in some spontaneous recall, years later. The accusations against Bernardin unleashed a torrent of media coverage that equated repressed memory with false accusations. Father Greeley, who had gone from being a critic of Bernardin's handling of the abuse cases to a supporter of the cardinal's reforms, denounced the charges, adding: "It's become open season on priests."

When the qualifications of a therapist who had treated Cook became suspect, the young man said he could not trust his memory and withdrew the lawsuit against Bernardin, which never should have been filed. The second defendant, Ellis Harsham, was removed from his position as a chaplain and a settlement eventually negotiated with Cook. The Bernardin case was like a lightning rod. Almost overnight, the scandal of bishops harboring child molesters was transmogrified into a collective media parable on false memory. The media prism filled with accounts of conflated stories planted in the minds of vulnerable clients by quack therapists; unprovable cases of Satanic conspiracies, a culture of victimage shorn of rational bearings.

There were indeed abuses within the culture of therapy; but the backlash against the survivors' movement obscured the hard work done by diligent therapists in treating people who had suffered genuine traumas.

In this climate the civil lawsuit of the Doe family, whose ordeal concludes the book, ended in a trial that found the defendant priest and school principal not guilty. I had moved on to other projects by then and did not attend the trial, though I followed it through news accounts and conversations with reporters, observers, and others who attended. The well-financed church legal team ran over the plaintiffs like a steamroller: the parents, after years of anguish, made poor witnesses; the boy who was seven when he told his parents and legal authorities that he had been abused was now a tall young adolescent, trying to put the past behind him. The family settled the priest's countersuit out of court.

The second family with a child alleging abuse by the same priest subsequently withdrew the allegations. The Chicago archdiocese had proven its ability to fight a civil case for years and spare no expense. The attorney for the second family, Jeffrey Anderson of St. Paul, Minnesota, was a tenacious force in advancing legal claims for clergy molestation. Anderson has represented some five hundred clients against two hundred priests, and litigated several high-profile trials that won large verdicts. Reflecting on the legal terrain in an interview for this edition, he said: "The patriarchy has not changed, the power structure has not changed, so the extent to which they draw a certain number of misfits is unlikely to change without some fundamental structural change. But they can't get away with what they did in times past . . . For business reasons, not any fundamental moral reasons, there's been a heightened awareness."

The tide of civil lawsuits has slowed considerably, according to Anderson, because church officials now "do everything to avoid litigation. In the past they did everything to avoid exposure, scandal, or accountability. I'm not saying their motives have changed—it's still self-protection and survival—but they definitely respond to it differently. When the legal system got involved they had to answer on a level they never had to before, and that caused them to change the way they do business."

A reaction also occurred in many state legislatures, which have stiffened the statute-of-limitations laws, making it harder to seek legal redress. "The doors that were kicked open in the late eighties and early nineties have definitely been shut," says Anderson. "It's a backlash."

When Bernardin died of cancer, his funeral in Chicago was a virtual affair of state with eloquent remembrances from elected officials, commentators, and leading citizens. In his final months he had spoken of being at peace, prepared to meet his maker. A journal he kept became a posthumous best-seller. In death he became a public saint, a Prince of the Church whose final lesson was to teach the living how to die with dignity. This, coupled with his resolve against the Cook lawsuit, elevated him to a near-mythical standing. And yet the money and legal power Bernardin had long put at the disposal of pedophile priests, and the tactics he allowed church lawyers to use in Chicago, makes my skin crawl as I think of it even now.

It was inevitable that an issue so searing would fade from the radar screen of national news. A priest arrested for sexual abuse is just another crime story in many places now. That's not what happens when high-profile cases go to trial, as in the summer of 1997 when a Dallas jury returned a staggering $120 million verdict to eleven victims of Rudy Kos, a priest who had been admitted to the seminary despite his ex-wife's warning church officials of his bizarre behavior. Father Kos was shuffled to new parish work after other priests complained about his activities with minor boys to Bishop Charles Grahmann. Grahmann's detached attitude toward those complaints in a time when "pedophile priests" was an issue of great discussion among the National Conference of Catholic Bishops is more remarkable for its stupidity than arrogance. After the trial, with the diocese facing bankruptcy, the two sides negotiated a $30.6 million settlement, according to Sylvia Demarest, the attorney who represented three of the victims. She estimates that seventy percent of the settlement was borne by insurance carriers, although the diocese did have to sell property to satisfy its share of the burden.

Father Tom Doyle, who was a pivotal witness in the Kos case, had had a bitter falling-out with Bernardin over his handling of cases in Chicago. Today, Doyle considers clerical culture "a subworld, and I was part of it, and I got out of it. I still see terrible abuse. Society is being bamboozled in thinking it's not a problem within the church." Although many dioceses have adopted policies pledging compassionate treatment of victims and prompt removal of priests when accusations arise, Doyle remains skeptical because "the pope is a disbeliever about the meaning of the problem. God bless him, but I'm not mesmerized by John Paul II any more . . . He's the head of the institutional church."

Although the pope has made statements expressing compassion for victims of clergy sex abuse, the actions of the hierarchy reflect an approach of defending priests as an interest symmetrical with defending the church. There is no more striking example of Pope John Paul's attitude toward "the problem" than his handling of Rev. Marcial Maciel Degollado, founder of the Legionaries of Christ, an ultraconservative religious order and one of the richest organizations in the Roman Catholic Church.

The problem of Father Maciel entered my life after the wave of coverage about clergy abuse had subsided. For several years I kept turning down requests by lawyers and victims to write about their cases; in many instances I simply did not return calls. But there was something more compelling about the group of men from Mexico City who contacted me, wanting to expose Maciel, the man they said had sexually abused them as young seminarians in the 1950s and 1960s. They provided written statements with chronologies of their lives and the alleged abuse. They wanted to get their message to Pope John Paul II.

As I was weighing all that, Gerald Renner, the religion editor of the *Hartford Courant*, called from Connecticut, wondering if I knew anything about the Legionaries of Christ (also known as the Legion.) Renner, who interviewed me several times in his coverage of the clergy pedophilia crisis, had done a long report in the June 10, 1996, issue of the paper about the Legion's "tightly controlled, boot camp-like training program" at a seminary in the town of Chesire. Renner's report quoted several seminarians who had left in disgust. The Legionaries operated elite prep schools in several countries, and had recently purchased two weekly papers, the *National Catholic Register* and *Catholic Twin Circle*.

"The order also runs a sophisticated direct-mail fund-raising campaign out of its U.S. headquarters in Orange [Connecticut]," Renner had reported on March 24, 1996. "'Lottery sweepstakes' offering cash prizes of up to $5000 for a $5 donation for a book of 10 tickets accompany moving pleas for money to train seminarians."

Gerry Renner was one of the best religion reporters in the country; he had good contacts in the hierarchy and access to officials in Rome. Like me, he was a Georgetown graduate; he also had a good newspaper behind him.

The founding of the Legion was a strange story. When Maciel was only twenty, he gathered a group of teenage boys and young men in Mexico to follow him on the religious path; yet he had failed to pass muster at a Jesuit seminary. Since two of his uncles had been bishops, his rise through the ecclesiastical culture seemed distinctly baroque. How he amassed the early financial support to travel and cultivate Vatican officials was a mystery; but he had become a financial powerhouse in the global church, much vaunted by the pope, and a symbol of resurgent orthodoxy. As Renner and I shared information, we kept looking at Maciel, wondering *who is this man?* A guardian of church tradition who had traveled with Pope John Paul II and clearly had his favor (a full-page letter from the pope praising Maciel and endorsing the Legionaries had appeared in several Mexican newspapers)—was he also a man who had molested seminarians, while building a quasi-empire?

Embarking on a joint assignment with Renner for the *Courant*, I flew to Mexico City in the fall of 1996 for lengthy interviews with the accusers, among them a literary scholar, an attorney, an engineer, and an instructor with the U.S. Defense Department School of Linguistics in Monterey, California. In all, nine men made on-the-record accusations against Maciel (and named others). The Mexicans were in their fifties and sixties, from middle- or upper-middle-class backgrounds, with solid jobs and careers. They had not filed legal actions. They didn't want money. They wanted Pope John Paul II to acknowledge their accusations and to remove Maciel from his powerful position in Rome as head of the Legionaries of Christ.

As Jose de J. Barba Martin, a professor of literature with a doctorate from Harvard, put it: "The pope has reprimanded Germans for lack of courage during the Nazi era. We are in a similar situation. For years we were silent. Then we tried to reach authorities in the church. This is a statement of conscience."

Renner interviewed sources within the church, including Rev. Felix Alarcon, a

63-year-old priest in Florida who had left the Legionaries in the late 1970s, after reporting to Rome that he had been abused by Maciel as a youth. So had Juan Vaca, a college guidance counselor in Holbrook, New York, who had been a priest and president of the Legionaries in the U.S. from 1971 to 1976. Vaca had sent a letter detailing accusations of Maciel abusing him and other seminarians to Pope John Paul II when he left the priesthood in 1978.

Renner confirmed from an official in the Diocese of Rockville, New York, that Vaca's letter—and a supportive letter from Alarcon—had gone by diplomatic pouch from the Vatican Embassy in Washington, D.C., to the Holy See in Rome in 1978, and that its receipt had been acknowledged. Beyond that, nothing was known about the pope's response.

The article Renner and I wrote appeared in the February 23, 1997, *Hartford Courant.* Father Maciel refused to be interviewed; a spokesman for the Legionaries denied the accusations, as did Maciel's Washington, D.C., law firm, Kirkland and Ellis, which provided affidavits of several churchmen who disparaged the men we interviewed. The Legionaries' position was that the Mexicans had a personal vendetta against Maciel. On March 2, Maciel issued a statement calling the accusations "defamations and falsities . . . never in any way did I commit those acts with them, nor did I make any such advances to them . . . During the time that these men were in the Legion of Christ I spared no sacrifice to help them as much as I could."

The accusers had been "apostolic schoolboys" who left Mexico in their early adolescence to study for ordination in the Legion's minor seminary in Spain, and from there to major studies at a seminary in Rome. They had been taught that Father Maciel was a living saint, a man on a crusade to purify the church against communism and sin. He also had abdominal problems, which made him seem all the more valiant. In interviews they recounted a succession of teenage boys who had been summoned to the founder's darkened room where they described sexual grooming rituals that began with masturbation.

Some tried to resist and weren't invited back. Vaca said that he eventually became Maciel's lover. As pubescent boys, an ocean away from their homes and families, mesmerized by a charismatic figure, living in harsh dormitory environments, they had no real power, an issue that haunted them for years.

"He said that he had a personal dispensation from Pope Pius XII to do these sexual acts because of his pain," stated Arturo Jurado Guzman, who taught Spanish in the Defense Linguistics school in Monterey. Jurado said that he submitted to Maciel's designs about forty times, and when he resisted Maciel's attempts at anal penetration, the priest summoned another boy.

The men also stated that Maciel was addicted to painkillers. Jurado said he was dispatched to Salvator Mundi hospital in Rome on a dozen occasions to obtain morphine and that "I gave him injections many times in the forearm." Ironically, it was the realization of his addiction that softened their attitudes toward his sexual abuse of them.

In 1956 accusations against Maciel reached the Vatican, and he was suspended from his position as superior of the Legionaries. An ecclesiastical investigation ensued. This plunged the boys into a fearful moral drama. Jurado recalled the seminary headmaster in Rome telling them that the Vatican investigators were "evil people" and that the boys did not have to tell the truth. The students were in a terrible position, having to balance their own years of study—and the likelihood of being kicked out, losing the chance to become priests, if they told the truth—against the interests of Maciel, for whom they had deeply conflicted feelings.

When an investigator asked Jose Barba what he thought of Maciel, the young Mexican answered: "He is a saint"—as they had been told for years.

"I retreated," the literary scholar reflected, many years later, in Mexico City. "I was scared . . . I didn't tell him about my experiences."

Others lied for similar reasons. "For me it was obedience," said Jurado.

In a letter dated December 12, 1996, that was provided by the Legion's law firm, retired Bishop Polidoro Van Vlieberghe of Illapel, Chile, who had been part of the investigation, stated that the charges were "meritless" and "part of a methodically organized campaign to discredit Father Maciel and the Legionaries" by two clerics in the Legion, a pair of Mexican bishops, and the Jesuits. In a strange twist, the bishop also said there had been no accusations of sexual abuse. Why then was Maciel investigated?

The Vatican's response to Gerry Renner's requests for comment was exactly nothing. Not a word—neither defending Maciel nor denying the allegations.

The March–April 1997 issue of *Inside the Vatican* came to Maciel's defense. The headline read "Another Bernardin?" But Bernardin had been accused by a man unsure of his memory, and the Mexicans who accused Maciel said they had never forgotten.

The Maciel story brought the scandal of sexual abuse to the papal doorstep. I had expected some sort of defense of Maciel; the disappointment came when the investigation on which Renner and I had worked so hard, with considerable support from the *Courant*, made little dent in the news. The networks never picked up on the story, and although the wire service of the *Los Angeles Times* (whose parent corporation owned the *Hartford Courant*) carried an abbreviated account, the newsweeklies and major daily papers ignored it. There are many reasons why some reports don't reach a critical mass in the national media; sometimes length means an imposing task for editors at the wire services, and some papers shy away from summarizing long investigative accounts about controversial topics done by other publications—a sort of "it's their story" attitude. Whatever the reason, the vacuum into which the Maciel story disappeared reminded me of the national media environment I had encountered in writing the first reports on clergy pedophilia from Lafayette, Louisiana, twelve years earlier. In many respects, "the problem" is still one that many people don't want to think about, and perhaps it always will be.

It is often said that the Roman Catholic Church thinks in centuries, not in years. Perhaps then Pope John Paul's response was comparatively swift, for in 1998 he named Maciel as a special representative to a Synod of Bishops in Rome.

Foreword to the Illinois Paperback Edition
Andrew M. Greeley

The problem of abusive priests must be seen against the background of the widespread (and apparently old) problem of the abuse of children. It would appear that seventeen percent of the American population has been sexually abused during the years before puberty, equally men and women. Moreover, half the men were abused by women older than they were. Priest abusers then represent the tip of the iceberg of abuse—a fact which does not make their behavior any less objectionable.

The general tendency among those who write about abuse by priests is to see it as a psychological problem—the pedophile priest is someone with an acute and apparently incurable personality disorder. However, Professor Anson Shupe of Purdue University has argued persuasively that the problem is social structural or sociological. The abuser, he suggests, is almost always someone for whom there is an "asymmetric" relationship with the victim, a father or a stepfather with a daughter, a baby-sitter with a child, a teacher with a pupil, a cleric with a parishioner, especially a young parishioner. In such relationships the preponderance of power or even a monopoly of power is with the abuser. The alarmingly high rate of abuse suggests that there are many personality types in the population who are prone to abuse sexually those who in one way or another fall under their power. One must of course strive to search out those whose personality inclines them to abuse and to eliminate them from the priesthood. This is not enough, however. One must also tilt the playing field so that the dependent person has a fighting chance to complain effectively and fight back. Potential abusers are likely to have second thoughts if they realize that there is a good chance of getting caught.

I was asked by an Irish bishop before the problem of clerical pedophilia hit Ireland like an Atlantic hurricane what responses I would recommend to the Irish church when it had to face the problem. I said bishops and superiors should not try to cover the situation up; they should take response out of the hands of lawyers; they should apologize immediately; they should promise new policies; and, above all, they should not leave the judgment about clerical abuse to other priests. The bishop nodded wisely. Shortly thereafter the abuse problem exploded in Ireland and all my advice (which I'm sure others had passed on to the Irish bishops and which they could have derived from reading American newspapers) was ignored. The result? A virtual drying-up of vocations to the priesthood in Ireland.

In the mid-eighties, Jason Berry stumbled against a stone. When he turned the stone over he found an incredible mass of corruption. Most of us would have been tempted to turn the stone back. However, he resisted the temptation and dug into the corruption, into what may be the greatest scandal in the history of religion in America and perhaps the most serious crisis Catholicism has faced since the Reformation.

Progress has been made since Berry wrote his painful and critically important book. However, the problem of clerical abuse has not gone away. Some bishops still fight every charge in court. Others still stonewall. Priests still sit in judgment on other priests (even, according to Berry's new research, it would seem in the Vatican) and their judgments lack all credibility. The parents of the victims and the victims themselves are still brutalized by church lawyers. Worst of all, perhaps, most priests still deny the problem, at least in every specific case that arises. The organized priesthood is utterly unwilling to police itself.

Jason Berry, a troubled but enduring Catholic, discovered the problem almost by chance. He has been motivated through all the years of his work by the desire to protect children from terrible harm. If anything, he underestimates the extent of the problem.

His book is more important than ever.

Prologue

The coming of a couple's first child is a precious experience. In October 1984, when my wife was seven months pregnant, a Catholic priest was indicted for sexually abusing altar boys near her Louisiana hometown. Although we lived many miles away in New Orleans, I just couldn't get that priest out of my mind.

This book investigates child molestation in the North American clergy and the impact of those behaviors on the larger community of believers. It is also a report, of sorts, on other sexual issues dividing the Roman Catholic Church in the United States—particularly the rule of celibacy. At root, this book is about politics: how sexual scandals have compromised the authority of men in high places of the oldest church in Christendom.

The Rev. Thomas P. Doyle, an American who served five years as canon lawyer at the Vatican Embassy in Washington, D.C., has called the pedophilia scandals "the most serious problem that we in the church have faced in centuries."

Between 1983 and 1987, more than two hundred priests or religious brothers were reported to the Vatican Embassy for sexually abusing youngsters, in most cases teenage boys—an average of nearly one accusation a week in those four years alone. In the decade of 1982 to 1992, approximately four hundred priests were reported to church or civil authorities for molesting youths. The vast majority of these men had multiple victims. By 1992, the church's financial losses—in victims' settlements, legal expenses, and medical treatment of clergy—had reached an estimated $400 million.

Reports of these cases—and how bishops handled them—raise stark questions about the psychological dynamics of clerical governing. For seven years it has been my strange lot to travel long distances, interviewing countless sources, gathering legal documents and church reports, reading theology, psychology, and studies of human sexuality. In my travels I sought an objective account of changes tearing at the central nervous system of the church. In time this line of inquiry ran up against an older memory of faith and the tension caused me quite a struggle. It has left the Catholic in me with a certain sense of urgency.

In *A Secret World*, an insightful recent study on celibacy and the priesthood,

A. W. Richard Sipe estimates that two percent of U.S. Catholic priests are pedophiles—men sexually fixated on young children—with an additional four percent who are sexually drawn to older youths. Although church officials challenged Sipe's percentages, Father Doyle—who advised many bishops as cases broke—has estimated that 3000 American priests may be so inclined, a figure that would support Sipe's estimates.

Most cases of child sexual abuse occur within the home. Celibacy does not cause priests to molest youngsters any more than marriage can be faulted for the greater number of men who commit incest. The roots of abusive behavior more often lie in an offender's own childhood or in neurological abnormalities. Experts say that the vast majority of homosexuals, like most heterosexuals, do not molest children. According to David Finkelhor, an authority in the field, "The evidence suggests that a great number of the men who victimize young boys are not self-identified homosexuals. . . . [M]any abusers of boys appear to be married and have lengthy heterosexual histories."

Child abuse became a major issue in the 1980s, a decade also marked by a resurgence of religious worship in America. People of many professions violate children, including ministers of varied denominations. The crisis in the Catholic Church lies not with the fraction of priests who molest youngsters but in an ecclesiastical power structure that harbors pedophiles, conceals other sexual behavior patterns among its clerics, and uses strategies of duplicity and counterattack against the victims.

In that clerical milieu, honeycombed with secrecy, I set out to report tangled conflicts of sex and power. My primary sources were transcripts of civil testimony given under oath by bishops and priests in lawsuits across the country.

For some eight hundred years celibacy—the promise or vow by priests and nuns to remain unmarried and to abstain from sex—has been a cornerstone of church governance. St. Paul called celibacy a "gift from God." At its purest, this tradition stands as a timeless ideal of self-sacrifice, a concept that grew after the dawn of Christianity.

But celibacy, as an institutional tradition, has a more complex political history. In the early church it was a convention often breached. In the eleventh century Pope Gregory VII ordered strict prohibitions against priestly marriage and introduced the standard of celibacy which has lasted to the present day. The human toll of what historians call the Gregorian Reforms was a sobering discovery for me. Married priests had their marriages and families destroyed. Pressed at one side by an emperor demanding the power to appoint local bishops, Gregory also felt threatened from below, by priests' families who could potentially lay claim to church holdings through inheritance. In Gregory's push for mandatory celibacy, property was a major concern.

These harsh new regulations created an ironic by-product: tolerance of clergy homosexuality. Historian John Boswell has marshaled impressive evidence of gay clergy writings in medieval monasteries. The magnitude of clerical homosexuality, historically, is unclear. But the issue has become a factor now. A recent stream of apologist writings about gay priests has shaken American clerical life.

Richard Sipe's study also stirred up controversy because of his estimates that less than half of American priests honor the vow of celibacy and that twenty percent of American clergy are homosexual, a figure other researchers would

double. The dispute over percentage estimates is itself an extension of concealment strategies. Without a random probability sample of priests, their sexual orientation and activity cannot be definitively gauged. And bishops wouldn't dream
of sponsoring a study on the possibility of the many failures of those professed to
be celibate. Thus a logical trap closes upon itself: if there are no numbers, it
cannot be true. Yet church leaders face a growing priest shortage, while the *National Catholic Reporter* found in 1988 that many religious orders were requiring HIV
tests for candidates. Today, most men have to prove they do not have the AIDS
virus before becoming priests.

Chastity is the core concept in Catholic teaching on sexuality—priests and
nuns called to sexual abstinence, married couples to chaste (i.e., faithful) lives. All
other sexual activities—including masturbation, homosexual sex, and genital relations between unmarried adults—are considered immoral. For generations, most
Catholics accepted these strictures. Today, most of the American laity ignore
church prohibitions on using birth control devices. Celibacy, divorce, the rights
of women and of homosexual persons now occupy the works of theologians. In
the widening gulf between the hierarchy and the laity, psychologist Eugene Kennedy has openly criticized an "asexual dynamic" among Vatican and American
church officials, men who in the absence of intimacy seek to regulate private
lives, often in demeaning ways.

The Catholic Church's history of monarchical rule, grounded in celibacy,
stands at a painful crossroads. The conflicts here recorded—involving families of
abuse survivors, fallen priests and their bishops; attorneys for both sides; admira-
ble priests and Vatican diplomats; therapists; insurers; nuns; gay activists; seminarians; theologians; journalists and editors—amount to variations of a central
theme: religious power in conflict with morality.

Lead Us Not into Temptation is divided into three parts. The first follows the child
molestation scandal from Louisiana to Washington, as abuse cases and cover-ups
began breaking nationwide. Part Two explores the political dynamics of celibacy
and gay-straight tensions in clerical culture. The final section chronicles the hierarchy's reaction to escalating abuse cases, and also depicts a countermovement by
a burgeoning group of women and men challenging the bishops.

I have employed pseudonyms for certain families or individuals to protect
anonymity. Legal considerations barred me from identifying several priests, as
noted in the text. Others who spoke at length about their lives did so on condition of anonymity. Otherwise, the majority of sources are identified. I have taken
small liberties with the language (but not the factual content) of dialogue passages. These are mainly changes of tense and the distillation of longer statements
given under oath or to me. The dialogue is based on deposition transcripts and
hundreds of interviews.

Finally, this is a book about faith—my own, and that of others drawn into a
maelstrom much larger than ourselves. The journey of this troubled believer was
slowly engulfed by the agonizing quest for justice of people from as far afield as
Newfoundland and Hawaii. Pulled along by currents of their lives, I witnessed
courage and grace in ways that humble me still.

Acknowledgments

My parents, Mary Frances and Jason, Sr.—to whom previous books are dedicated—have given me love and career encouragement in countless ways. For that and much more, my loving thanks.

The Rev. Andrew M. Greeley provided critical advice and seasoned insights about this work before either of us anticipated his role in events chronicled in the final chapter. I thank him for the friendship but, more so, for the courage of his convictions.

I am profoundly grateful to the Rev. Thomas P. Doyle, O.P., the late Rev. Michael Peterson, and Ray Mouton for the time they gave in helping me.

I owe a lasting debt to the faculty of Jesuit High School, New Orleans, 1963–67, particularly Fathers Kenneth Buddendorf, Francis Coco, Robert Donnelly, William Hill, Patrick Koch, Hervé Racivitch, and the late Roy Schilling. I would also like to thank the Rev. George Lundy, S.J., and the Rev. Neil Hurley, S.J.

My literary agent, Don Congdon, saw the potential of this work at an early stage and stuck with me through the long haul, an act of faith I will long remember. I appreciate the help of his colleagues, Michael Congdon and Susan Ramer, as well.

Thomas Cahill, director of the religious books division at Doubleday, has been a pleasure to work with. David DeCosse edited the work with exceptional care. I have profited by his expertise.

Journalist David Hechler, an authority on child sexual abuse, provided a perceptive critique of the manuscript, as did Jeffrey Gillenkirk and Marcus Smith. Frederick Barton, William Griffin, Richard Hart, and Lucian K. Truscott IV read early chapters in draft; A. W. Richard Sipe and Elisabeth Tetlow read several later chapters.

This book could not have been written without the assignments that supported research or afforded outlets for my work. Some individuals now at different jobs are listed at the positions they held when we met. In more or less chronological order, I wish to thank: Steve and Cherry Fisher May, publishers of *The Times of Acadiana*, editors Linda Matys and Richard Baudouin, staffers Geoff

O'Connell and Kirkland Ropp. At the *National Catholic Reporter*, editor Thomas Fox, Arthur Jones, Vincent Golphin, and Tim McCarthy. At the *Los Angeles Times*, the late Art Seidenbaum, an editor dearly missed by Opinion-page contributors, and Gary Speicker. At the *Cleveland Plain Dealer*, editors Thomas Greer, William Woestendiek, Jack Murphy, Diane Carmen, Robert Snyder, reporter Karen Henderson, and a special thanks to Gloria Millner of the Sunday Perspective section. At the *Baltimore Sun*, op-ed editor Hal Piper, reporters Frank Somerville and Doug Struck. At the *Washington Post*, Outlook editors David Ignatius and Jodie Allen, and religion reporter Laura Sessions Stepp. At the *Washington Times*, Patrick Boyle, Charlotte Hayes, and Larry Witham. At the *Atlanta Journal-Constitution*, Perspective editor Paul Bernstein. Sandy Shilstone, of *New Orleans Magazine* (1985), and Clancy DuBos, editor of *Gambit*, the city's newsweekly, were most helpful.

Michael Lenehan, editor of the *Chicago Reader*, helped shape my final report, and his geniality made exacting work more pleasant. Special thanks to Carl M. Cannon, a Washington reporter with Knight-Ridder, and Jon Standefer, an investigative journalist who worked at the *San Diego Union*. Both gave generously of their time and shared research that had bearing on mine.

I am also grateful to Charles Sennott for sharing insights from his reporting on Bruce Ritter, contained in the book *Broken Covenant*.

The following reporters and editors provided information or insights that assisted me: Debbie Abe, *Idaho Statesman*; Eleonor Bergholz, *Pittsburgh Post-Gazette*; Bonnie Britt, *Asbury Park Press* (N.J.); Barbara Dolan, *Time Magazine*, Chicago; Jeff Fleishman, *Allentown Morning Call* (Pa.); David Firestone, *New York Newsday*; Jim Franklin, *Boston Globe*; Michael Harris, publisher-editor, and Philip Lee, *Sunday Express*, St. John's, Newfoundland; Jim Holman, *San Diego Reader*; Paul Likoudis, *The Wanderer*; Dorothy Lipovenka, *Toronto Globe and Mail*; Ann Rodgers-Melnick, *Pittsburgh Press*; syndicated columnist Michael McManus, Bethesda; Joanna Morgan, *Toronto Star*; Clark Morphew, *St. Paul Pioneer Press Dispatch*; Mike Murphey, *Spokane Spokesman-Review*; Judy Rakowski, *Providence Journal*; Marie Rohde, *Milwaukee Journal*; Joe Rigart, *Minneapolis Star Tribune*; Joe Stephens, *State Journal-Register* (Springfield, Ill.); James Gill and Sheila Grissett, *New Orleans Times-Picayune*; and author-journalist Civia Tamarkin of Chicago.

The following television reporters or producers helped me: Mary Ann Ahern, WMAQ, Chicago; Richard Angelico, WDSU, New Orleans; Jim Baronet and Dee Stanley, KLFY, Lafayette, La.; Rory Bennett, KCST, San Diego; Mike Conway, WJWT, Cleveland; Bill Elder, WWL, New Orleans; Chris Harper, "20/20"; Penny Price, "The Geraldo Rivera Show"; Gary Reels, WUSA, Washington, D.C.; Dale Russell, WAGA, Atlanta; Dennis Smith, WLBT, Jackson, Miss.; Mark Stendal, KOMO, Seattle; and the staff of Shirley Solomon, CTV, Toronto.

A great many attorneys facilitated my research, some as background sources. Those I can name, and to whom I am most grateful, include: Jeffrey R. Anderson, Mark Reinhardt, and Mark Wendorf, St. Paul; Mark Bello and Alan Kaufman, Southfield, Mich.; Raul Bencomo, Richard Ducote, David Fine, Oliver Houck, and Michael Simpson, New Orleans; James B. Brincefield, Alexandria, Va.; Peter T. Cahill, Maui, Hawaii; Charles E. Davis and Sheldon Stephens, Orlando; Thomas D. Decker, Chicago; Allen B. Ellis, Boise; Paul Englander, Phoenix; Anthony Fontana and Paul Hebert, Abbeville, La.; Philip J. Freeburg, Antigo, Wis.; Jack Harris, St. John's, Newfoundland; Pamela Klebaum, Ventura, Calif.; Roland

Lewis, Jackson, Miss.; Ray Mouton, J. Minos Simon, J. Nathan Stansbury, and Bob F. Wright, Lafayette, La.; Alice Richmond, Boston; and Jonathan Turley, Washington, D.C.

Among psychiatrists, psychologists, therapists, and sexual behavior researchers: Marianne Benkert, Fred Berlin, Anne Brown, Fran Ferder, David Finkelhor, John Heagle, Eugene Kennedy, Jeannine Gramick, Kenneth Lanning, Robert Nugent, John Money, the late Michael Peterson, Glodys St.-Phard, Gary Schoener, Richard Sipe, and Tim Smith.

Theologians who shed light on my reporting include Charles Curran, Vernon Gregson, Anthony Kosnik, Richard P. McBrien, William McFadden, S.J., John Harvey, John J. McNeill, Anthony Padavono, Elisabeth Tetlow, and John Yockey.

For various forms of assistance: Jeffrey Anderson, Barry Jean Ancelet, Jack Berry, Lamar D. Berry, and the staff of International Marketing Systems; Barbara Blaine and the Catholic Worker community at St. Elizabeth's, Chicago; Raymond Blanco, John Ed Bradley, Howard Bray, Mark Brooks, Gary Bullert, Ted Campbell, Floyd Campisi, Hodding Carter, Kenny M. Charbonnet, Len Cooper, Linda Cumberland, Charles and Kent Davis, Patt Derian, Adele Doran, Terry Dosh, Shane Earle, David Figueroa, the Rev. Charles Fiore, Glenn and Faye Gastal, Ellen Gilchrist, Richard Godin, Philip Gould, Art Harris, Joe Izzo, Robert Blair Kaiser, Michael Kennedy, Bill and Jarvan Kienzle, Steve Knipstein, Mary Kotecki, Edward F. LeBlanc, Evelyn LeBlanc, Michelle LeBlanc, Jeanne Liuzzi, Lou Martinelli, John MacIsaac, Jeanne Miller, Pat Morley, Tom Phillips, Lawrence Powell, Robert Putnam, Gary Raymond, Carie Reardon, Liz Reilly, Elizabeth Rickey, June Rosner, the late Katherine Salmon, Michael Schwartz, Maryalyce Ebert Stamatiou, Charles Wilson, and Ken Wooden.

In the long journey that this book entailed, many people opened their lives to me. Of those who cannot be named, three stand out as valued sources: John and Jane Doe of Chicago, and Roy Robichaux.

Finally, I thank Gilbert Gauthe for sharing details of his life with the hope that some good might come of these revelations. I too hope that will be the case.

SNAP (Survivors Network of those Abused by Priests) can be contacted at P.O. Box 6416, Chicago, IL 60680, phone (312) 409-2720, or <www.snap-net.org/>.

The Linkup (Survivors of Clergy Abuse) can be contacted at 1412 W. Argyle St. #2, Chicago, IL 60640, phone (773) 334-2296 or

PART ONE

Anatomy of a Cover-up

◆

What is a rebel?

A man who says no:

but whose refusal does not

imply a renunciation.

ALBERT CAMUS, *THE REBEL*

Pronunciation of most Cajun names is on the first syllable.

Plaintiff Families in Vermilion Parish, Louisiana: Roy and Ella Robichaux (pseudonyms); Glenn and Faye Gastal; Ted Campbell.

Clergy and Church Officials in the village of Henry: Rev. Gilbert Gauthe, pastor, St. John the Evangelist. In the town of Abbeville: Monsignor Richard Mouton, pastor, St. Mary Magdalen. In the city of Lafayette: Bishop Gerard F. Frey; Monsignor H. Alexandre Larroque, vicar-general; Monsignor Harry Benefiel, vicar of finance; Mr. Gerald Dill, vicar of education. In New Orleans: Archbishop Philip M. Hannan.

In Washington: Archbishop Pio Laghi, papal pro-nuncio, apostolic nunciature [Vatican Embassy]; Rev. Thomas P. Doyle, canon lawyer. In the diocese of Cleveland, Ohio: Auxiliary Bishop A. James Quinn, canon lawyer and civil lawyer, special emissary of Pio Laghi.

Unofficial adviser to Bishop Frey: Raymond Blanco, vice-president for student affairs, University of Southwestern Louisiana.

Psychologists and Psychiatrists: Ken Bouillion, Lafayette; Ed Shwery, New Orleans; Fred Berlin, M.D., and John Money, Sexual Disorders Clinic, Johns Hopkins Hospital, Baltimore. Rev. Michael Peterson, M.D., St. Luke Institute, Suitland, Maryland.

Attorneys: For various plaintiff families: Paul Hebert, Abbeville, and Raul Bencomo, New Orleans; J. Minos Simon, Lafayette; Tony Fontana, Abbeville. For the Lafayette diocese: Bob F. Wright. For diocesan liability insurers: Robert F. Leake, Charles Schmidt III, New Orleans. For the New Orleans archdiocese: Thomas Rayer. District attorney of Lafayette: Nathan Stansbury. For criminal defense of Gilbert Gauthe: Ray Mouton, Lafayette.

Journalists: Jim Baronet, news director, KLFY-TV, Channel 10, Lafayette; Dee Stanley, reporter, KLFY; Steve May, publisher, Linda Matys and Richard Baudouin, editors, *The Times of Acadiana*, Lafayette; Tom Fox, editor, *National Catholic Reporter*, Kansas City, Missouri; Arthur Jones, Washington bureau chief, *NCR*; Jason Berry, free lance, New Orleans.

i.

Pleadings

In the beginning wild horses roamed the Attakapas, a soft, green prairie named after the Indian tribe who lived there and along arterial bayous crossing the land. To the east, the Chitimacha tribe lived around Atchafalaya swamp. The name means "long river," a tributary of the Mississippi. Towering cypress trees loom across the swamp basin; hundreds more shadowed seventeenth-century explorations by Frenchmen into the interior. The Chitimacha have a reservation now; the Attakapas are long since extinct. But the memory of Indians is stamped upon the topography of South Louisiana. Between the prairie and the swamp flows the Bayou Teche, lined by palmetto and hyacinths, curling past elegiac plantation houses in New Iberia, draining into marshes of the Gulf of Mexico. Indians believed the bayou came from a mighty silver snake: stung by arrows, crushed by clubs, his death twists cut grooves into the earth and with rainfall rose the Teche.

Today the region of Louisiana where the pedophilia scandals first broke is called Acadiana. The poet Virgil coined the word Arcadia to mean "earthly paradise." In the early 1600s, emigrants fleeing religious strife in central France settled in Nova Scotia and called that island Acadie. In 1755 *le grand dérangement* began when a ruthless British warlord herded 10,000 Acadians onto ships, while crown troops burned their homes. Tossed over chilly sea lanes, some to die in prisons or as serfs in British ports, the exiles wandered nine years before reaching New Orleans, from where they moved deeper inland, claiming prairie and bayou country. They carried a deep Catholic religion and the resilience of farming folk. In time, with terse patois cadences, they became known as Cajuns.

The lush soil of this semitropical environment allowed many Cajuns to lift themselves out of poverty. In the 1950s the regional economy began to accelerate with oil and gas drilling. By 1980, Louisiana's oil patch was booming; fortunes were made in the hub city of Lafayette. Yet the land held a primordial allure.

In the forest, duns and green mingle with shawls of moss, gray as smoke, that drape the cypress and ancient oaks. Winters in the marsh dawn to pumping shotguns, the bay and slosh of hounds retrieving teal and mallard and geese. Most hunters reside in towns now, but there are still families in hamlets, harvesting crawfish, stalking muskrat and nutria as their forebears did.

In summer, when rice fields are greenest, tropical clouds darken the sky and drench the land. In autumn, the towns come alive with festivals celebrating prize livestock and crop yields. In Abbeville, seat of Vermilion Parish (as counties are called in Louisiana), there is even a competition for the most beautiful baby, which my brother-in-law won in 1952.

Vermilion, from old French, means "brilliant scarlet red"—the color found in bluffs and shoulders of the bayou by explorers long ago. It is a polluted river now, laden with barges bearing chemical waste from oil drilling rigs out in the Gulf.

Cajun culture has a pronounced *joie de vivre*. The cuisine has lately followed the export trails of Cajun ensembles and zydeco bands, finding aficionados in such remote latitudes as Manhattan Island. Long before that, cut off by geography and language from the urban Creole aristocracy, the Cajuns were an insular people, bonded to a code of absolute values: land, faith, and family.

Roy Robichaux* had a farm in a cove of the bayou. He was forty that spring of 1983, married twenty years to Ella,* whose family had lived in Esther community longer than his own. An hour's drive west, out in the marsh, they had a camp that his grandfather built before Roy was born. The late Bishop Jules Jeanmard, who founded the Lafayette diocese, went hunting there when Granddaddy was alive; Roy saw the shotgun with grooves on the butt, a gift from Bishop Jeanmard. He remembered that good man, small and genial as each child knelt to kiss his ring. Then parents and grandparents, siblings, cousins, aunts, and uncles took seats and bowed heads as Bishop Jeanmard said grace.

His casual air was buffered by a regal presence. Roy had seen him on the altar of the cathedral, wearing robes of watered silk, as hundreds answered prayers in Latin down the pews. Around the bishop bloomed the one, holy, Catholic, and apostolic church like a garden greened by rains along a line of the equator.

In 1983, Jeanmard was long since buried beneath the altar of the cathedral next to his successor, who had built more schools and churches. Robichaux's large family was not acquainted with the present bishop. But in Father Gilbert Gauthe, pastor of St. John Parish in the village of Henry, they found a church with a warmth that made them feel at home.

Gauthe was thirty-eight, lean and slight of build, with dark hair and two visible passions: the wilderness and young people. Flocks of them followed him on outings to the marsh. He was not a priest wrapped in piety. The man rode horseback with Roy on a cattle drive, and when Ted Campbell loaned him his .357 Magnum, chuckles spread with the tale of Father Gauthe, perched in the church belfry, blasting geese in low flight on foggy dawns.

Gauthe could be charming, especially with older ladies. He spoke to people on their own level. Nobody forgot his sermon about crime. The oil boom was on. When vandals hit several churches, Father asked the congregation to think about the kind of people coming into Vermilion Parish. Roughnecks, people without local ties. When strangers come, crime follows. "The Lord expects us to *protect* ourselves," he said. He put iron burglar bars on rectory doors and windows, and yellow floodlights that lit up the carport at night like a spaceship.

---

* Asterisks denote pseudonyms for this family and other persons as indicated in the text.

With a powerful car radio he intercepted police messages, dashing to the scene of accidents, aiding people who were hurt. Once he saved a man's life by pulling him out from an upended tractor. Another parishioner gave Father use of his camp on Forked Island; on Friday afternoons he made the rounds in his van, picking up kids for overnight trips.

Robichaux's older boys no longer served Mass. But the rectory was a magnet for youngsters. Years of hard drinking had begun to blur Roy's appreciation of Gauthe's appeal. In May 1983 the whole family came apart and Robichaux went off to a substance abuse clinic. Three weeks later his wife arrived with the children. "Alcoholism is a family disease," Roy told them. "I drank and y'all got hurt." He knew now that breaking his own denial was crucial to his family. "I accept the responsibility for what I did wrong. We have to be open—can't deal with anything by keepin' secrets."

He stayed another week: drank volumes of coffee and was attentive in group, read Alcoholics Anonymous literature, prayed each day and night as he had not done in years. Then he went home. After Mass one day he spoke to Father Gil outside church, proposing a parish AA chapter. Gauthe frowned. He told Roy that, while AA had been important for him, "it cannot take the place of the church." Roy explained that through AA people gained spiritual strength to keep sober. AA was nondenominational, Gauthe replied, and *that* concerned him.

June was nearly over now. It was bedtime, and Ella sat on the bed next to Pete.* The nine-year-old muffled sobs in his pillow. "Daddy said we are not supposed to have secrets." She told him that Daddy meant keeping his drinking a secret. The boy said his secret was bad: "God doesn't love me."

"Why shouldn't God love you?" she gently prodded.

He told her he had done bad things. She asked what things. He said Father Gauthe did it too. "What did Father do?"

The little, halting words came out—things a child his age would never say. "Don't tell Daddy," the boy entreated.

When his wife entered their bedroom Roy saw a look of nausea on her face. "Pete says Gauthe molested him."

Roy went immediately to his son's bedside. "What's wrong, Pete?" The child sat up in the large presence of his father. "I love you, son. Do you want to talk about it?" The child's cheeks were soaked. Slowly, he shook his head no. Roy peered into eyes of pain such as he had never seen. "This is something I need to know, son. It sounds like Father Gauthe is a very sick man." As the child spoke, it tore into Roy Robichaux's heart. *Oh, my boy, my baby boy.* Tears brimming, the boy's whole body began to shake. Roy gathered his son in his arms and slowly rocked him back and forth on the bed. The child was sobbing. Roy Robichaux began crying too. "Son," he croaked, "I respect you for telling me this. It's wrong what he's been doin'. And it's good you brought it out to me. Now we can do something to stop it."

When Ella returned to the boy's room, Roy left, plotting how he would kill the son of a bitch. *I can break his body with my hands. Twist his neck and make him die slowly.* In his bedroom he dropped to his knees. *Dear God, with You I stopped drinking. I don't know what to do. I've never killed anybody. Help me, Lord. Help me.*

The child's past behavior suddenly made sense. The year before he had gone through a stretch of crying spells, worried that the Devil would get him, made the sign of the cross all the time. A psychologist had tested him and said he was suffering a loss of self-esteem, which Roy blamed on his drinking. Then the symptoms had subsided. Roy was on his feet when Ella returned again to their bedroom. "I should have known," he brooded. "Nobody hangs around kids that much, so many weekends."

Grim-faced, his wife recalled the first time Pete returned from the rectory and said: "Father and me have a secret. It's a secret just between Father and the altar boys."

That was two years ago.

"Pete said his cousin was involved." Roy swallowed.

Ella asked if they should tell the parents—their neighbors, their kin, people they had known since they were kids. "I don't know," muttered Roy. The thought sent a shudder through his limbs. "We can't overreact."

Early the next morning he took his older sons for a drive in the pickup truck. Jim,* seventeen, was the quieter of the two. Hank,* fifteen, had more beef and muscle.

"Pete got real upset last night," Roy announced. "He says Gauthe's been molesting him."

Fields floated past. Jim stared out the window. Hank said: "I told you not to let Pete go near that son of a bitch."

The profanity jolted Roy. He saw Jim cover his brow with his hand. *Please God,* prayed Roy: not Jim.

"What acts took place?"

Seconds passed. Roy waited.

"Everything," Hank muttered glumly.

"What you mean by everything?"

Hank said that Father made them take their clothes off and showed porno films. Roy wanted to shout, *Why didn't you tell me?*—but the memory of drinking possessed him in a cavity of guilt.

"Well, what happened?"

"Well, everything."

A dead feeling lodged in Roy's intestines. "What the hell. Did he suck people off?"

"Yeah."

Disgusting images multiplied in Roy's thoughts. He told his sons that before he could do anything he had to know what had taken place. It made him feel like a dentist using pliers. "So, did he—screw people in the ass?" No one spoke. "Hank?"

"That was goin' on with some of 'em. I told you not to let Petie get near that son of a bitch."

No one had ever called Father Gauthe that. But Roy remembered Hank complaining when Pete became an altar boy. The past was twisting into a different shape. His older sons had complained about serving Mass. Roy insisted that they participate—to better themselves, be a credit to the family. Jim was an A student until he turned twelve, when Father arrived as pastor. Since then he had struggled for C's. Hank's moods, anger flashes, ugly arguments over petty points of discipline suddenly made sense now. Jim stared at the fields.

Roy stopped the truck on the side of the road and all three of them got out to talk. Roy addressed a fidgety Hank. "How often did it go on?"

"All the time."

"Where?"

"Everywhere."

Early heat was beginning to break. "Jim, what do you think about all this?" The boy would not meet his eyes. Roy spoke softly. "I know it hurts, son. Just tell the truth."

Jim said that Father did it to them in the marsh and the rectory. Roy winced. *My firstborn, too. God, give me strength.* Then he said: "It's good you're tellin' me this, Jim. And you too, Hank. This is hard to talk about, but I have to know."

Hank glared at his father. Jim stared off.

"Did it happen in church?"

"Yeah," said Hank.

"Other kids involved?"

"Yeah."

"Yeah."

"How many?"

Hank said that everyone who spent the night was involved. If you didn't blend in, you were not invited back. He weeded people out. Roy asked for names. No one spoke.

"Well?"

Slowly the boys opened up—one name, then another, another, another and another—boys whose parents Roy had known for years, some since childhood, sets of siblings and cousins, a litany of names that punctured his conscience like a needle in the skin. *Jesus Christ,* he thought, *altar boys! When people find out, someone will kill him. I pray it is not me. I must get help—someone higher up.*

ii.

Paul Hebert was raised to be a gentleman. At thirty-three he reflected this training; however, it was not the sort taught in fancy schools. Born in the port town of New Iberia, the middle child of five, he had patience bred into him by the example of his parents, who expected people to be kind. The family attended Mass together; there had even been Good Fridays when all seven made the stations of the cross. In 1960 the Heberts supported John Kennedy, whose picture still hung in Paul's parents' living room, equal in size to that of the Sacred Heart. The 1767 passenger list of Acadian exiles arriving in Louisiana included Heberts. But neither Paul's grandfather, who presided over the police jury when they built the courthouse, nor his father, who owned a feed and seed store, knew where the kin source lay. Grave markers in floral cemeteries bear primal names of Acadia—Broussard, Robichaux, LeBlanc, Mouton, Landry—and, like them, Heberts had multiplied across the generations.

In New Iberia he would always be the son of the man who owned the store, so Hebert established his law practice twenty-one miles away in the Vermilion

Parish seat of Abbeville, a town of ten thousand with a tall brick church on the banks of the Vermilion River. His life was reflected neatly in the triangle of home, church, and office on St. Victor Street, behind the white-pillared courthouse that faced Mary Magdalen Square, behind which stood the church. He dealt with accident injuries, civil disputes, and commercial contracts. Nothing he had done prepared him for the presence of his friend Roy Robichaux saying that Father Gauthe had molested his three sons. "And if I cross that man I'm gonna kill him, Paul."

It was eleven in the morning, Tuesday, June 27, 1983, and Paul Hebert, communicant Catholic, was stunned. He began writing on a legal tablet. When Robichaux was done, they reviewed Hebert's notes. Then Hebert dialed the chancery in Lafayette. "Bishop Frey, please. This is urgent."

The receptionist put him through to Monsignor Henri Alexandre Larroque. "Good morning, Monsignor, this is Paul Hebert in Abbeville. Roy Robichaux is in my office and we have a very serious problem." As an attorney, Hebert chose his words cautiously. "I suspect Father Gilbert Gauthe has sexually abused several of his children."

"Mmm," intoned Monsignor Larroque—an echo of priestly response to confessions Hebert had made as a boy and youth and young man: no sin so great as to elicit scolding, the tone a register of mankind's perpetual misconduct. "Yes, I understand."

"We want to see Bishop Frey, Monsignor."

Larroque explained that Bishop Gerard Frey was in Bay St. Louis, Mississippi. As vicar-general, Larroque was in daily communication with Frey and acted for the bishop in his absence. "I know Mr. Robichaux," Larroque said.

"We want Father Gauthe removed from Henry immediately."

That could not be done on the basis of a phone call, Larroque averred, and asked if they could meet him at the chancery. Hebert set the appointment for 2 P.M. Robichaux felt small hope. Larroque had officiated at his wedding.

"I think we're on the right track," Hebert replied. "The church needs to take control, get Gauthe out."

That afternoon, as Robichaux drove the twenty-two-mile stretch into Lafayette, Hebert brooded. *Children make up stories,* he reflected: *maybe Gauthe took some disciplinary action, got 'em mad. I have never dealt with this before. A priest does not molest altar boys.* "Are we positive about this, Roy? How positive?"

"I know my sons. They aren't lying."

"Right." Hebert resisted the urge to loosen his tie. "You don't take on your parish priest unless it is something like this. I just can't understand how the guy could have done it."

"Me neither. The man came to our house for dinner—many times, Paul." He stared at the road. "Many times."

"How is Ella taking it?"

"Not good."

Traffic into Lafayette slowed on Johnston Street, a garish concourse of Taco Bell, McDonald's, and car lots. They passed the green lawns of the University of Southwestern Louisiana. Neither man had ever been to the diocesan chancery, which was next to the cathedral. Hebert spoke with the receptionist, and they sat down to wait. Roy remembered Larroque from high school. One night at a speech tournament upstate, the boys bought liquor and drank with girls from another school in the hotel room. The next morning, a pal dumped an empty bottle out of the school bus. Sister Bartholomew, the trip chaperone, greeted them at the tournament with a singsong voice: "Must have been one hell of a party."

Back in Abbeville, the nun who was principal summoned Roy to her office, asking, "Who bought the booze?" He refused to answer. This went on every day until he exploded: "I got enough of this shit! You know I was involved. Quit askin' me questions!"

"*Father Larroque!*" cried the sister. "Come in here, please."

A teacher of religion as well as parish pastor, Larroque said: "Follow me, Mr. Robichaux." Roy marched behind the priest to his office down the hall. Larroque pulled out a pack of cigarettes. "Me?" said Roy. "Sure," said Larroque. The boy took the light. "You know," said Larroque, "she's getting kind of up there, Roy. She's going through her life change. You shouldn't be so hard on her." And Roy Robichaux laughed.

The receptionist said: "You can go back now." Their heels clacked along a corridor adorned with murals of saints. At the end of the hall a lady showed them to the vicar-general's door.

Alex Larroque greeted them warmly. He was a courtly man, somewhat stout, with wavy silver hair beginning to thin. Declining coffee, Robichaux and Hebert took seats. "Thank God I'm not drinking," Roy said. "I would have killed Gauthe already."

"I know what you're talking about," Larroque commiserated, volunteering that he too was a recovering alcoholic.

Robichaux told him what his sons had said. Larroque listened somberly. Then he said, "We've known that Father Gauthe had a problem for some time, but we thought it had been resolved."

The words hit Paul Hebert like a slap in the face.

The diocese had received a report some time ago, Larroque continued, terming it "a case of misguided affection." This was more serious. He asked if he could speak with Robichaux's older boys. "We're talking about ruining a man's career," said Larroque, referring to the implications of charges against a priest.

Robichaux agreed on six-thirty at the bishop's house.

"This really strikes me as *strange*," said the attorney.

It was, said Larroque, but Gauthe had had problems in the past. "At one time I believe he was seeing a psychiatrist."

"This man shouldn't be a priest," Hebert said. "What can be done?"

Laicization, explained Larroque, was a complex procedure. Only the Holy Father could authorize dispensation, which removes a man from the clerical state. Canon law allowed a bishop to suspend a priest from administering the sacraments.

"Who makes the decision to suspend?" asked Robichaux.

Only the bishop, and he would return on Thursday.

"I think you oughta encourage him to get back sooner," Hebert pressed.

The church had to get rid of this guy, Robichaux fumed. "I fear I'm going to do something totally uncontrollable."

"I understand, Mr. Robichaux," said Larroque, asking him to take it one step at a time. First he had to talk with the boys.

A shower fell as they left the chancery. As they moved into late afternoon traffic, Robichaux said, "What do you make of that 'misguided affection'?"

Hebert admitted that he too had trouble believing that the priest might have molested boys earlier in his career. "But we both heard him say it," he told his client. "Let's put that aside for now. We have other things to deal with."

Driving back that evening, the farmer told his two sons to tell Larroque everything. L'Évêché, the bishop's residence, was a two-story house on a lawn with magnolia trees next to the cathedral. Larroque led them up a stairwell. "Let me speak with the boys, Mr. Robichaux, and after that you and I will talk."

After meeting with each son one on one, Larroque met alone with the father and told him the boys had been honest. The boys were able to discuss things. He felt things would be fine.

"I don't see how you can say that when I find out my three boys have been sexually abused!"

"Mr. Robichaux, I believe this is very minimal."

Robichaux wasn't sure what he meant by that. The anger in him rose again. "I want Gauthe removed *now.*"

"These things take time."

Roy Robichaux glared.

The next morning Alex Larroque drove four hours with Monsignor Harry Benefiel and Sister Joanna Valoni to brief Bishop Gerard Frey in Bay St. Louis, a Mississippi fishing village where the Frey family had a summer compound by the bay. As finance vicar, Benefiel wrote checks and kept the books. As chancellor, Sister Joanna's purview included record keeping and scheduling events. There was no doubt among them that Father Gauthe had to go, but they wanted to avoid scandal.

As vicar-general, Alex Larroque had great latitude. Frey had come to depend heavily on Larroque as his alter ego in church governance. In the 1970s Larroque had undergone treatment for alcoholism and Frey had stood by him in those troubles. Once back, Larroque had spoken of his ordeal at a meeting of priests; many were moved by his candor. A man of surpassing intelligence, Larroque had long ties to many priests and prominent families.

Frey came from a New Orleans family whose wealth was built on a meat-packing business. He had arrived in Lafayette in 1973 by way of Savannah, his first bishopric. In 1983 he was sixty-nine, a product of the old school: he entered seminary in ninth grade and later became a New Orleans pastor, followed by a teaching stint at Notre Dame, the city's major seminary. He had a brother who was also a priest. In another time, Lafayette might have been Gerard Frey's way station to becoming prelate of his native city. But Philip M. Hannan, archbishop of New Orleans since 1965, was a commanding presence and well liked in Rome, a fact ensuring him a long stay in the prelate's chair.

Hannan, who came from a large Washington family, had known John F. Kennedy personally and given the eulogy at the President's funeral Mass. His background held a certain prestige in heavily Catholic New Orleans. Although a liberal on civil rights, he moved with seamless ease through linings of a conservative society. An adroit fund raiser, he expanded Associated Catholic Charities, built a solid program of housing for the elderly and poor, and launched an archdiocesan PBS station.

Frey by contrast was more retiring, even shy. Hints of this surfaced after his Lafayette investiture in 1973. The retiring bishop, Maurice Schexnayder, was quite at home in the house on Cathedral Street. Frey quietly moved into a home of his own. After Schexnayder passed away, he preferred to live in the Immaculata complex, site of the defunct diocesan seminary, on the outskirts of town. Larroque and several priests lived in L'Évêché.

Frey's philosophy was to delegate power and govern quietly. In the spirit of Vatican II, he encouraged lay people's involvement in parish councils and diocesan programs, particularly religious education. But by 1983 the bishop's reserve had given way to detachment. Although he visited outlying churches, spending the night in rectories and meeting parishioners at Mass, he was spending three- and four-day stretches in Bay St. Louis. Some felt that he was drinking more than his health could afford.

Many months after that fateful day, Benefiel would recall the sadness of the drive to Bay St. Louis. The car was quiet as a crypt. "We were," he sighed, "like three zombies—wondering how in the world is this man going to take it?" Nothing in his life had prepared Gerard Frey for what was to come. When the news broke his face crumpled like a paper bag. "I just can't believe he would do that," the bishop said, shaking his head. Then he grew angry. "I warned him after the Abbeville incident that if there was *ever* any more problem, that would be the end of it!" He shook his head. "I just can't believe he would do it."

Frey gave Larroque the task of suspending Gauthe from priestly duties in accordance with canon law, of which he was resident authority. While the trio drove back to Lafayette, Frey stayed on in Bay St. Louis.

Paul Hebert had arranged for the Robichaux boys to be screened by a Lafayette psychologist, Ken Bouillion. Robichaux's anger worried the lawyer. Ella worried about other boys, wondering should she contact their parents. Wait, Hebert advised: the church should contact other parents. Larroque called Hebert on Wednesday night, June 28, to say that Frey had authorized Gauthe's suspension. Larroque would inform Gauthe the next day at the chancery, having felt it unwise to confront him on the phone.

"How soon will he clear out, Monsignor?"

"Quickly—within twenty-four hours."

"Another day?"

Larroque explained that Gauthe had belongings to pack. And when he left, he had to go *somewhere*. "This is not easy."

Hebert asked if the diocese would pay for the Robichaux boys' therapy. Larroque said they would consider it. Hebert asked for a commitment in writing. "I don't know if I can give you that at this time," Larroque averred.

"Well, I'm going to send the bills on."

From what the Robichaux boys had told the psychologist, many altar boys had regularly spent the night at the rectory. Hebert urged Larroque to canvass other families, find out how many kids were involved. Larroque's immediate concern was Father Gauthe. He asked Hebert to discuss the situation with his pastor, Monsignor Richard Mouton of Abbeville.

Ever since seminary days, Gilbert Gauthe had felt discomfort in the presence of authority figures. His passion for young boys matched his love of woodlands and bayous, where a man could hunt and fish. The bishop made him nervous. Gauthe's salary, a modest $590 per month, was augmented by honoraria for weddings, funerals, baptisms. He also received a hundred here, a hundred there, from ladies whose generosity enlarged his income to some $18,000.

Bookkeeping was on his mind that last day of June 1983. The parish in Henry had been in debt when he arrived in 1977; five and a half years later it had $45,000 in bank accounts, thanks to the oil boom and Gauthe's own hard work. Gray flecks dotted his dark brown hair. Entering Larroque's office, he fretted about the ledger sheet to which he was late in attending, knowing that the best response was to remain silent, ask forgiveness, and pledge swift remedy to the lapse.

"Gil," said Larroque gravely, "we have a big problem."

Father Gauthe said nothing.

"It's with young boys." Stern-faced, Larroque did not reveal his sources. "Lots of young boys, Gil. The bishop is very angry with you and wants you out of the parish right now."

And then it came, the years of sin and a thousand secrets of sex—the lies he would later admit having told a psychiatrist and the bishop and Monsignor Mouton in Abbeville, the chain of nocturnal beds with sweet youths he had taken in and loved in a way that others would never understand. At that moment the upright image of his priesthood broke beneath the weight of his superior's words and Gilbert Gauthe began to weep.

Alex Larroque sat next to the younger priest, trying to give comfort. Gauthe was terrified. "I—I need some help. Is there any place you can send me?" Larroque told him not to go home or to other rectories. Perhaps in Baton Rouge they could arrange treatment. "That's too far away," blurted Gauthe.

Larroque told him to check into a hotel in Opelousas and to contact no one but Lafayette psychologist Alan Campo, a consultant to the diocese. Then Larroque handed him papers and said, "Sign." Gauthe obeyed.

"Get out of Henry within twenty-four hours, Gilbert."

It was June 30. The document, dated July 1, 1983, read:

> Certain and undenied evidence has been brought against Father Gilbert Gauthe, Pastor of Saint John Parish, Henry, that he engaged in sexual acts on several occasions with minors (Canon 2359, 2). These actions have come to public attention of the parents of these minor children. Grave scandal has been given and the danger of public scandal is imminent.
>
> Father Gauthe has been warned in the past when confronted with such indiscretions which were less of a public nature.
>
> Whereas, Bishop Frey according to the norms of Canon 2190 has reviewed the

*evidence that the delict has actually been perpetrated, he is constrained by law to
invoke the penalty of suspension on Father Gilbert Gauthe.*

   *Father Gauthe is therefore declared to be suspended a Divinis. (Canon 2279,
2, 2) This penalty is incurred at the present time and for an indefinite period of time.
With evidence of graver and more widespread scandal, more stringent penalties may
be invoked.*

*By mandate of the Most
Reverend Ordinary
H.A. Larroque
Vicar-General*

Acknowledged: Gilbert Gauthe

Driving back to Henry, Gauthe's mind went blank; his memory of that night
would be opaque. He packed some things and slept on the couch. The next
morning he said First Friday Mass and was on his way to Mass at the chapel in
Esther with communion for the shut-ins when he pulled over on the road and was
sick. He returned to the rectory, finished packing, scribbled a note to the housekeeper that he was going away, and loaded his van with clothing, a small television, an Atari video game, two pistols, three shotguns, and two rifles. The rest he
left behind: files, clothing, plaques, fishing gear, and other items in two trunks.

Opelousas is forty-four miles from Abbeville. Gauthe found a motel and met
with Alan Campo, a specialist in child sexual abuse. That night, in his motel, he
called Larroque and left his phone number. Fearing that someone might find him,
he peeled decals off his van and lay down with a loaded gun on the bedside table.
Nothing happened. The next day, sitting in a restaurant with the pistol strapped
to his ankle, he ate a salad but couldn't hold that down when he returned to the
room. He spent vacant hours staring into space, with jumbled prayers and
thoughts of the kids. Larroque told him to be patient and pray. After a final
meeting with Campo he drove to his parents' house in Napoleonville, an Assumption Parish town on Bayou Lafourche.

Ten days later he went back to Henry to gather the rest of his belongings. He
called ahead and found his oldest victim, a fifteen-year-old, with time to spare.
They met outside town and when they finished having sex Gauthe drove back to
Napoleonville where he would wait out the summer at his family home.

iii.

The first person who asked Roy Robichaux about their pastor was Ted Campbell,
a strapping man who was parish council president. Campbell's fourteen-year-old
had been an altar boy for five years. Gauthe's abrupt departure made Campbell
suspicious, and he asked Robichaux, a neighboring farmer, if he knew anything.
Robichaux gave it to him straight: "Talk to your boy, Ted. He might deny it." If
he flinched or turned red, Roy suggested contacting Hebert and Dr. Bouillion.

Campbell had a crop-dusting business. Three airplanes crisscrossed the area,
spraying rice fields on a contract basis. He had come far from a childhood on

nearby Forked Island, where sanitation consisted of an outhouse behind the dwelling, and the kids took sponge baths at twilight. At night they gathered around coal-oil lamps and a battery-powered radio. His daddy, a day laborer in the fields, spoke Cajun French and little English. In 1956, when Ted was six, the house got electricity.

Hobo was his daddy's nickname, and he avoided church. As Ted grew older, the old man operated the ferry that crossed the Vermilion bayou connecting Esther and Henry. Father Leon Perras crossed the bayou frequently. "Hey, Hobo," Perras would say, *"comment le temps depuis t'a fait à la masse et confesser* [How long since your last Mass and confession]?" And Hobo would grunt: *"Vingty-un ans, Père.* [Twenty-one years, Father]" *"Vingty-un! Mais, Hobo!"* They went around like that for a couple of years until the old man said one night: "Well, it's gonna snow. Perras talked me into goin' to Mass."

The morning after his talk with Robichaux, Campbell rose as usual at four-thirty and drove to the airstrip. Days began with coffee and small talk among pilots as the planes were fueled. For months Campbell's only son, fourteen, had kept distance from the men. The office was empty now, save father and son. Ted asked if he knew why Gauthe had left. His son said no. "He was sexually mo-lestin' some kids," Ted said, "and I was wonderin'—well, did that happen to you?"

His son looked down, face flushed red. "Yeah."

A lump built in Ted Campbell's throat. "That's all right, m' boy. It's not . . . your fault. We'll take care of this."

Ted Campbell stepped out of the hangar into the dawn light. He clenched his fist in a rage that would consume him for years and stared at the heavens, waiting for a message from God.

On Sunday, July 3, 1983, Monsignor Harry Benefiel went to Henry and said Mass. A portly, balding man, he donned vestments in the sacristy while three boys with nervous grins, hovering, asked about Gauthe. Benefiel feigned igno-rance. "Father Gauthe has been relieved of his pastorship," he said in his sermon. After Mass parishioners confronted him, seeking an explanation for Gauthe's re-moval. "He's been relieved of his duties," said the finance vicar. "That's all I know."

Rumors spread like brushfire. Father had a nervous breakdown. Father quit the priesthood. Father ran off with a woman.

Meanwhile, Paul Hebert opened discussions with the pastor of Mary Magda-len Church in Abbeville. Richard Mouton, tall, with gray hair and a scholarly air, had studied in Rome and was acting at Larroque's behest. If the church wanted Mouton to be his liaison, that was fine with Hebert, provided he got results. Several years earlier, when the Heberts had asked permission for a young priest from a neighboring town to baptize their son, Mouton denied them use of the church, saying that he had received thirteen days' notice instead of the requisite fourteen. Hebert called Larroque, who said: "That's ridiculous." The next day Mouton called to say they could hold the baptism, whining, "If the rule is changed for one, it has to change for all."

With Gauthe gone, attorney and pastor sipped coffee in the rectory. What was Monsignor planning to tell people about Gauthe's departure? "For medical reasons," Mouton replied. But that wasn't accurate, Hebert countered. Moreover, Dr. Bouillion was emphatic: other families besides his clients had boys who had been molested by Gauthe. It was a tragic situation, Mouton conceded; but he wanted to avoid rumors.

"I understand the church will pick up medical expenses for the Robichaux boys," Hebert said.

Mouton replied that he could not agree to that without knowing the cost. Hebert said he would be happy to meet with higher officials to review the cost of therapy; however, Larroque had told him to meet with Mouton. "Just tell me who, Monsignor."

"That would be the diocese."

When was the church going to contact families with other altar boys? "If they want something done, tell them to come see me," responded the pastor.

But the situation was quickly worsening. Based on his initial screenings of the Robichaux boys, the psychologist estimated that Gauthe had molested thirty or more youngsters, and Bouillion was not optimistic about swift therapeutic success. "Send the bills to my office," Hebert had told him. "And keep me posted."

Civil lawsuit bells began ringing in his thoughts. For plaintiffs with serious personal damage, you consult medical or psychological experts and project long-term expenses. Hebert's mind raced through the legal possibilities, but his faith held him back from plunging into litigation against the church, an act which in a Catholic stronghold like Abbeville could become a scandal in itself. Better to resolve it privately without exposing families and church to bitter strife.

Meanwhile, Ella Robichaux had spoken with mothers on nearby farms: of six boys she knew had been molested, only her three were seeing the therapist. Hebert asked Monsignor Mouton to meet with Dr. Bouillion.

"I don't think I can do that," the pastor said. His orders were to communicate with Hebert.

"Look, I am really getting heat," said the lawyer. "Y'all are not telling the people what happened. Several others have called me with concerns about *their* children. Don't you think you oughta do something?"

Mouton said that he would say Mass at Henry that weekend, with a message to be put in the parish bulletin.

"You better make it good. Because they're waiting."

First, however, Monsignor Mouton invited Roy Robichaux over to the rectory in Abbeville for a chat. He told him that the church would cover his children's therapy bill. Robichaux thanked him and asked about the other children. The pastor explained that he was the only parent to come forward. "As far as we can tell, your children are the only ones involved."

"There *are* other children. I've started notifying parents."

Should anyone get hurt from this, Mouton admonished, the guilt would rest on Roy for making it public. Then Mouton said something that nearly knocked Robichaux out of his seat: "Imagine how Gauthe's mother would feel."

"How in the fuck do you think the mothers of these kids feel?" Undaunted by profanity, the pastor repeated the offer of therapy for Robichaux's sons. "That's not enough!" the farmer snapped. After Larroque's remark about a previous case of

Gauthe's "misguided affection," Robichaux had been talking with people. Now, steadying his nerves, he told Mouton: "This is not the first time Gauthe messed with kids, Monsignor. I understand it happened right here in Abbeville."

"Oh," said Mouton—who admitted that in 1976, when Gauthe was an assistant pastor in Abbeville, two fathers had reported him to the pastor for kissing their sons. Mouton had ordered him to move into an upstairs bedroom in the rectory. The final straw had come when Gauthe brought a child to the dining room. "And I will not have a child at table," said the pastor. *At table?* thought Robichaux, wondering if that meant a child's presence elsewhere in the rectory was all right. He thought that the man was from another planet.

The boys were young, Mouton said gently. They would bounce back and get over these things. The next day he telephoned Robichaux, offering to hear the boys' confession.

"My sons do not need confession! *They* did nothing wrong."

The pastor made the same offer to Ted Campbell, who also rejected it. Without revealing that his son was now in therapy, Campbell was fanning out, asking neighbors: "Hey, you heard why Gauthe left?" "We heard he got sick." "No, man, he was a child molester." "No, it can't be." He asked one friend if his son, a Biddy Basketball player, had ever been alone with Gauthe. The man called back: "He says Gauthe checked him once for hernias."

"Why don't you bring him to a psychologist, just get him evaluated? It can't hurt."

"Not my boy. He's fine."

On July 24, Monsignor Mouton celebrated Mass in Henry. Roy and Ella Robichaux sat pensively as he read a prepared statement.

"In announcing Father Gauthe's resignation three weeks ago, your Church leaders made a very short statement. In effect, it said that Father was resigning for reasons of health. That was and is true. It obviously did not say everything that could be said. At this time, because of the excessive talk, the false accusations and the general sense of consternation and frustration, the Diocese judges it is necessary to broaden its statement."

Robichaux's heartbeat quickened. *Now, get it all out—*

"Father Gauthe was asked to resign the pastorate because of grievous misconduct of such an immoral nature that he could no longer serve as your Pastor. This statement is hard and painful to make; it is hard and painful to accept. The statement is made only after a thorough investigation of the facts was conducted by Monsignor H. A. Larroque. The complaint of grievous misconduct was not in any way contested by Father Gauthe. Let it also be stated that Father's condition did not invalidate all that he did as pastor. He was a person beloved by many parishioners whom he willingly and eagerly served. Personal testimonies bear witness to this. The service of Father Gauthe's remains to his credit.

"At the same time, Father's conduct has brought harm to the community and to some of its members. Rather than concentrating on his serious failure we need to contain the harm and curtail it. Efforts will be made to achieve this goal. Each of us can do his part by refraining from gossip and speculative talk which does no one any good."

Roy Robichaux stared at the priest, still not satisfied with the roundabout talk. "Scripture clearly admonishes us, 'Brothers, do not slander one another. . . .

There is only one law giver and he is the only judge. Who are you to give a verdict on your neighbor?' "

Robichaux slumped in his seat. He wouldn't level with them, thought Robichaux with gathering disgust.

Monsignor Mouton announced that a new pastor would take Father Gauthe's place. "Let me congratulate you," he concluded, "for the brave way you have faced the tragic and sorrowful happening of the past few weeks. You are a fine and wholesome people. Let that truth be ever more clearly demonstrated now at this important moment in the history of your wonderful parish."

The statement was posted on the bulletin board.

Six angry parents gathered in Paul Hebert's office a week after the sermon. Gauthe was at his parents' home in Napoleonville. They wanted him behind bars. Questions came so fast, Hebert could not distinguish one voice from another. "When they gonna come down here and talk straight, Mr. Paul? . . . They hidin' this thing, Mr. Paul! . . . What about these kids of ours?"

To file criminal charges, he explained, they would have to meet with the Lafayette district attorney. The civil sphere of the court system was something else. The children had just begun a long road of therapy. Beyond medical fees, they had rights to compensatory damages. But no one in their world had ever sued the church. All agreed that the attorney should make one last attempt with Monsignor Mouton to see if the church would admit Gauthe's crimes and offer all victims psychological help.

"I can't control these people," Hebert told the pastor. With the number of victims mounting, the church's response was leaving no alternative but legal action. Monsignor Mouton's eyebrows arched. Did Hebert realize what a lawsuit would do to the children—to the community? Mouton's tone shifted to paternal chiding. "Why, you're a good ole Catholic High boy, Paul. And a Catholic High boy wouldn't do that."

Five weeks of frustration came down in a slam of his hand on the table. *"I'm not gonna sit here and let you batter me with guilt!* And I'm not stupid enough to go into this all by myself."

Raul Bencomo and Paul Hebert had been friends since law school at LSU. Lean, mustachioed, with a penchant for elegant suits and alligator suspenders, Bencomo had left Cuba as a child. He was a graduate of Jesuit High School in New Orleans, the city where he now practiced law. When Hebert's call came, Bencomo quietly listened as his friend discussed the case, interlacing his tale with reflections about the spiritual pain it was causing him. Suing the church seemed the only route left. "Raul, if I make a mistake, this is the biggest screw-up of my life."

"Paul, this thing is a goddamn outrage. A tort is a tort."

They agreed that the premise behind the tort, or legal wrongdoing, was *respondeat superior*, which means that a company can be held liable for crimes committed by an employee on company time. The church paid no federal taxes but had a corporate status. Catholic dioceses also carried insurance policies. A handful of states prohibited civil action against religious or charitable entities. Louisiana is not among them.

After enlisting Bencomo as cocounsel for civil action against the Lafayette diocese, Hebert contacted prosecutor Nathan Stansbury, who met with the parents, pledging full cooperation. For indictment he would need the boys' testimony before a grand jury. Stansbury doubted that an indictment would result in an immediate guilty plea. The church would provide Gauthe with a good lawyer, who would need time to prepare a defense. Conviction would hinge on the boys' testimony. That troubled everyone. Gauthe had been gone five weeks; their sons had only begun therapy. Stansbury was sympathetic. He would be ready when they were.

Several days later Paul Hebert received a letter from Bishop Frey, dated August 12, 1983.

> Mr. Nathan Stansbury, District Attorney, conferred yesterday afternoon with Monsignor Larroque after his meeting with you and concerned parents from Saint John Parish, Henry. Monsignor Larroque outlined for Mr. Stansbury the steps which the Diocese of Lafayette had taken in the matter of Father Gilbert Gauthe and what the Diocese would do on behalf of the young people who were affected by his actions. These steps were clear from the beginning in my own mind and in the minds of my representatives, particularly Monsignor Larroque and Monsignor Mouton. I regret very much that these steps may not have been adequately communicated to those concerned.

And then, in language suggesting the cover-up into which the diocese was sinking, the letter stated:

> The caution which has been exercised throughout may have impeded the proper communication of the actions taken by the Diocese. This caution was necessary not simply to avoid scandal and harm to the Church, but primarily to avoid further injury or trauma to the young people and their families, or other innocent parties.

Gauthe would be going to House of Affirmation, a clergy treatment center in Massachusetts. The bishop offered assistance to "those affected" and proposed meeting with "a core group" of parents and psychologist Alan Campo. "I request, therefore, that you contact Monsignor Larroque at my office to set up such a meeting." But by then the die was cast. Bencomo wrote the bishop requesting copies of diocesan insurance policies and asked that the diocese cease direct communication with his clients.

Public perception of liability for child sex abuse was not associated with names like Gallagher-Bassett; Lloyd's of London; Fire and Casualty Insurance; Houston General Insurance; Pacific Employees Insurance; Interstate National Insurance; Centennial Insurance—carriers of Lafayette diocesan policies. Robert Leake, who represented Preferred Risk, the insurance carrier with the largest exposure, wanted no business played out in public. All firms wanted to settle the civil cases before a criminal indictment, which augured heavy media coverage and the possibility of more victims.

Nor did Thomas Rayer, counsel to the archdiocese of New Orleans, need to convince Bencomo that Archbishop Hannan—who was named among the defendants—wanted to avoid scandalous news. By New Year's, 1984, nothing had surfaced in the media.

No matter the human damage, a lawsuit needs expert witnesses. Jurors can see a quadraplegic in court and pity his immobility. But a physician's limb-by-limb testimony quantifies the suffering. Bencomo wanted an analysis of Bouillion's findings in language that would send insurance claims adjusters sprinting to their corporate coffers. Bencomo wanted to know the number of visits each child made to the rectory, specific acts, how many times. Ramifications of Gauthe's crimes gave the legal claims greater weight. How much did two years of oral sex with a given child add up to in compensatory damages? Here were altar boys violated by a priest. How much money would compensate for the loss of innocence? What is a lost religion worth? How much for fractured bonds between parents and child, and lost affection between spouses caused by their emotional or psychological hurt? ·

Ken Bouillion counseled the families using a model of incest treatment. Under this approach, therapists seek to reconstitute the family if at all possible, striving to rebuild the offender as well as the victims. This can only work if the offender is not a fixated pedophile and the victim (or victims) not shorn of all trust. Pathologies behind sexual abuse can vary. Many offenders reenact abusive practices suffered by them as children. For others, child molesting can be spurred by drug or alcohol abuse that alters brain chemistry, or by intense depression or psychotic break. The saddest and most revealing axiom of incest family treatment is that children may forgive abusive parents because they fear losing the only family they know.

To Gauthe's victims, the church was like an extended family, with the priest as surrogate father. For parents and boys alike, Bouillion's procedure was fraught with painful awakenings. The Catholic Church as institution had betrayed them. Now the hand of behavioral science entered their lives, demanding a new and awesome kind of faith.

Bouillion treated boys whose sexuality had been prematurely awakened by a strange combination of surrogate father and older brother. Gauthe lost interest in most boys once they reached puberty. Some played computer games while he played with younger boys in other rooms. He ate dinner in homes of the boys' families, ingratiating himself with parents, who allowed the priest to become a convenient baby-sitting service.

Why did boys keep going back? Children often do not understand the feelings aroused and manipulated by nonaggressive sexual advances. Many do not know how to resist or even that they should.

Erotic impulses are a natural part of childhood. Kids "play doctor" in rehearsal games, prefiguring a sexual awareness that sprouts in puberty and ripens in young adulthood. The latent sensuality of a child awakens to touches, caresses, and ostensibly tender overtures by an adult. Moreover, children are capable of "enjoying" sexual sensations, even amid confusions of arousal. However bewildered a child may be, if a pedophile does not use extreme force, the body transmits messages of pleasure. The great damage is psychological.

Some of the boys with Gauthe were escaping dysfunctional families or tensions with their fathers. Robichaux was not the only alcoholic parent. Other children were drawn into the mysteries of dawning physical pleasure. Gauthe made the rectory into a kind of toyland, with video games and pornographic tapes. He would never accuse them of being bad; he was their confessor. He avoided force. Those who shunned his advances were not invited back. Dozens of boys passed through the rectory. By adolescence their choice was to move on with life, confused, insecure, afraid of telling parents something they couldn't confess to the priest—or to continue, as some did, visiting the rectory.

By July 1, 1983, he had been at it five and a half years in Henry. When he disappeared, the boys beneath his sway were dumped into a lonely sea. Tossed between faith and family, most had to fend for themselves. Repercussions from the more than three dozen young victims in the community did not immediately surface.

Each family moved at its own pace to a point when the child could tell his parents what Gauthe had done. Bouillion advised one father to visualize Gauthe's deeds. Raised in a rural culture with crusty machismo, the man hated such mental imagery. His wife became frigid at the sight of her husband in the nude.

Bencomo and Hebert wanted Bouillion to quantify his treatment forecast so that Bob Leake and the insurance lawyers would understand therapy costs with specificity. Because these were national insurance companies, the plaintiff attorneys selected a consultant, Edward Shwery, a clinical psychologist in New Orleans who had often testified at sex abuse trials, counseled victims and offenders, and consulted with law enforcement authorities. He was skeptical about rehabilitation for a fixated pedophile, especially one who had taken hundreds of pornographic pictures, as Gauthe had. Bencomo wanted Shwery's expertise to strengthen his case for settlement purposes or for testimony before a jury.

Shwery requested a $200-an-hour fee. Blue-chip attorneys earned as much, but Bencomo needed a document to jar his adversaries into a large financial settlement, and so agreed. Two more families had now gone to Hebert's office, raising the ante to nine youngsters in six families.

While Bencomo negotiated with lawyers in New Orleans, the listless February fields intensified Ted Campbell's frustration: he wanted the priest brought to justice. Gauthe was tucked away in some church tank and Bishop Frey had yet to visit the parish. The diocese had not told the people what Gauthe had done. Many people had heard through scuttlebutt, yet few outside of Hebert's clients understood the long-term impact. And the idea of other families, blind to their children's suffering, gnawed away at Campbell. Seven months of therapy had gotten his family to break through ugly secrets, but communication was hard; his boy spent long stretches alone in his room while his moods swung back and forth like a pendulum. Father and son avoided Mass.

One afternoon, in his cousin Glenn Gastal's feed store, Campbell made small talk. A short, wiry man, Gastal had a son and daughter by his wife Faye and three daughters from a previous marriage. Although divorce was forbidden by the church, Gauthe had accepted Gastal as a parishioner. Now Gastal was fuming because his ex-wife did not spend enough time with those girls. Ted asked when he last had a heart-to-heart with the boy.

"I talk to my boy all the time. What are you drivin' at?"

"Gauthe molested altar boys," Campbell muttered.

The year before, in March 1983, the Gastal boy, then nine, had entered the hospital with a case of rectal bleeding. Father Gauthe had come to visit with a model car kit. Faye thanked him in the hallway and asked him to visit the child's room. "Not now," said Father. "I'm too busy." On hearing Gauthe's voice, the boy scampered out of the room and down the hallway, out of the priest's sight. Father asked Faye how he was doing. She said the doctor thought it might be intestinal problems, but that tests had revealed nothing. Gauthe promised to see him later.

The Gastals met with Paul Hebert. Faye took the boy to Dr. Bouillion, conferring alone with the therapist after her son's session, and her heart began to crumble. Therapy would take time, Bouillion said. Let the boy come forth at his own pace; don't force him. Driving back, she asked the boy if there was anything he wanted to talk about. He shook his head no. She wanted to tell him she understood, that she loved him all the more, that Father had done him wrong. The boy hated being touched. His nightmares and nervous floor-pacing at night made sense now.

"They're treatin' *us* like criminals!" Glenn bristled to his wife. "All this silence, like *we* done somethin' wrong." Pressure inside him whistled like a teapot. Thinking about the church, his anger got worse. "We need to tell people, Faye. This community has got to know."

In her agony Faye Gastal prayed, trying to comprehend for what reason God would let a priest sodomize *her* little boy.

Paul Hebert told them that the first nine cases were moving, and if they spoke to the press it would jeopardize the good-faith bargaining for the others. The Gastals' case was among four new ones Hebert was preparing to file. Once the first nine were resolved, Hebert assured them, prosecutor Stansbury would indict Gauthe. That would put the church in the media spotlight; their suit would eventually be settled too. But it took time. Bouillion advised the couple that if they went public it would hurt the boys. Anger ate like acid through the Gastals' lives.

As the days of Lent in 1984 unrolled toward Easter, Bencomo was clashing with Bob Leake, point man for the insurance defense. Leake, who sang in the choir at Trinity Episcopal Church in the New Orleans Garden District, had negotiated many insurance settlements in his long career. He was offering a $19 million package. Less than $3 million would be paid up front; the rest would be paid out to each plaintiff in a structured annuity—long-term, high-yielding accounts that provided an escalating payment shelf: say, $20,000 up front with $1500 a month till age eighteen; then $30,000 for college (or other uses) with a monthly hike to $2000; at age twenty-five, a $50,000 lump, and so on. To reduce cash losses, insurers would purchase annuities from other insurers or holding companies for a fraction of their final yield. In this case, insurers were willing to pay $3 million to yield the $19 million in annuities. Bencomo wanted a single, larger cash settlement which his clients could then invest.

In June 1984 they agreed on $4.2 million spread among six families with nine victims. It was the largest civil damage settlement for sex abuse claims of which lawyers or insurers had any knowledge. Psychologist Shwery earned $20,000 for his psychological evaluation work. After the fees to Shwery and Bouillion, Hebert and Bencomo split one third of the settlement figure, somewhere in the $1.3 million range. Although case sums varied, the average settlement of $455,000 (before attorneys' fees) was far in excess of what families of lower-middle-class incomes had ever received in one sum. The money was for therapy and compensation for damages suffered; however the agreement did not restrict the use of funds. Hebert brought in a financial consultant to brief each couple on tax shelters and investment packages. The parents also met with Bouillion and Shwery to discuss each child's progress.

How much were the damages really worth? It is no small question in view of the precedent set by the first reported settlements against the church, and in view of how this precedent affected pedophilia torts getting under way in other states. For some reason the defense did not question Shwery under oath. Nor was Bouillion's deposition taken. The defense did not attack the expert testimony supporting Bencomo's high demands. That may not have mitigated injury, but as a means to challenge multimillion-dollar demands it was simply not used. In 1986, Lafayette diocesan counsel Bob Wright said: "I think there's a feeling that [the defense] gave away the cart before the horse."

On June 4, 1984, driving to Hebert's office, Ted Campbell told his wife: "I just don't want to sign. [The boy] deserves his money, but we lose our rights to sue for damages as parents." He was angry and wanted to fight on in court for more money. The agreement would prevent him from doing that. The year had drained Cedina, who still attended Mass in the little church which her son and husband had abandoned. In Hebert's office Ted insisted on retaining his right to sue the church.

"They're not going to pay this amount to settle your boy's case without settling yours," said Hebert.

"Ted," said Cedina wearily, "let's sign."

Reluctantly, he signed.

The Robichaux received roughly $1.2 million, which after attorneys' fees came to about $800,000. The diocese paid roughly $800,000 as its deductible of the $4.2 million package. The rest was borne by the insurers. The Campbells received $405,000 before attorneys' fees, with a $30,000 lump sum to the parents.

Money was rough balm to the wounds of the faithful. Spiritually distraught, the families wanted to meet with the bishop. In an effort to rebuild bridges, Paul Hebert asked Larroque for a weekend retreat with the six couples, Frey, and the vicar-general. The retreat was set when Larroque called to say that, because of litigation with four new families, a retreat was legally impossible. Hebert took that to mean that church officials feared that anything they might say could be used against them in lawsuits.

iv.

Gauthe had been gone eleven months when the news broke.

State law required filing the settlement agreements in court. Hebert briefed Judge Allen Babineaux, who ordered a seal on the documents, prohibiting public access. As a precaution, Hebert blacked out all names and omitted the settlement sums.

The next morning a court clerk called Dee Stanley of KLFY, the CBS television affiliate in Lafayette. The sketchy details quickened the reporter's pulse. If a priest was molesting kids, call the district attorney. Nathan Stansbury, the D.A., agreed to talk off the record: "The problem is all worked out. The kids won't have to talk for the civil cases."

"What about criminal prosecution?"

"No comment."

"*Nathan*, you're not prosecuting a child molester?"

"I didn't say that." The prosecutor explained the pivotal position of the youngsters: when they were ready to give testimony to the grand jury, he would have nails to hammer out an indictment, but not until then. When the boys testified was up to the parents and their attorney. Stansbury told Stanley to call Paul Hebert. "There really is no story," Hebert told the reporter, refusing further comment.

Stanley had the skeleton of a story—no names, verbal confirmation of a settlement, presumably with the church. And nothing to support it on paper. A quick sounding of Abbeville sources confirmed that a priest had left the summer before.

"Do not use his name," ordered news director Jim Baronet. "We don't know all the facts. We could get our asses sued."

Baronet was troubled. Child abuse stories were erupting nationwide, and if there was a big one in his yard he wanted to report it. Baronet had contacts with the local hierarchy. However, all he could confirm was that Gauthe had been removed.

Then a strange thing happened. Edmund Reggie, who lived in the nearby town of Crowley, a hub of the regional rice market, called Baronet from, of all places, his summer house on the Massachusetts island of Nantucket. Reggie had once been a city judge in Crowley, and many people called him Judge. Judge Reggie had long supported the Kennedys, his 1960 support of JFK (who carried Louisiana) carrying through to Senator Ted Kennedy's 1980 presidential race in the Democratic primaries.

Reggie was a rich man and a generous church benefactor. In a "60 Minutes" profile of Louisiana's Edwin Edwards (who was later indicted while governor), reporter Ed Bradley asked why Reggie had loaned $300,000 to the governor's 1983 campaign. Reggie said: "Just the excitement of having him back in again." Edwards had begun his career with Reggie in Crowley, where news director Jim Baronet grew up.

In the casual tone of one homeboy to another, Reggie downplayed the situation as a small problem involving a priest who was away in treatment and a few families being cared for. If suits were filed, then do a story. To do so now would only harm those people involved. Heretofore, Jim Baronet had never given much thought to Reggie's Catholicism. His call from Nantucket convinced Baronet that the hierarchy must be upset.

It also convinced him to air a story, but to proceed cautiously. The first report featured Stanley in front of the Abbeville courthouse, informing viewers that Channel 10 had learned the identity of a priest who had molested children but was withholding it until the legal situation became clear. Then, on June 27, 1984, Paul Hebert filed four suits in the courthouse on behalf of new families, including the Gastals. This was the first record of actual litigation. Stanley's source called back. But when the television truck arrived in Abbeville, Stanley found that the file read: *Not Available vs. Not Available.*

Russell Gaspard, the Vermilion Parish Clerk of Court, was seasoned in the folkways of Cajun politics. Reporters passed through his life with little tension; providing documents was part of his job. Stanley asked for copies of the suits. "Can't give it to you, Dee. Judge Babineaux sealed 'em."

"I want a copy of the order sealing the suits."

"I can't give you that. Paul Hebert has it."

"It's our First Amendment right. If you don't give it to me I'll put this on the news and then we'll sue your ass."

An hour later Gaspard gave Stanley a copy of the protective order sealing the file. Stanley called Baronet and Baronet called Babineaux. The judge explained the logic of the seal: to preserve the anonymity of minor children. The result was a shutout: no names, not of the children, the defendants, or the perpetrator. The station would have to file its own suit to determine who was suing whom.

"Call the station lawyers," Stanley entreated his boss. "Break the seal. They're covering it up."

But Baronet, a veteran anchorman with good ratings, had second thoughts. No other media had touched the story KLFY had broken. Challenging Babineaux's seal would pit the station against the privacy requests of families with abused kids. And that troubled Baronet, even with the First Amendment on his side. The first report had assured viewers that TV 10 would not divulge victims' names; Baronet did not want to hurt children merely to get a story. A Catholic, he was also not eager recklessly to take on the church.

But Stanley's first report brought forth calls from people wanting to know which priest and from others who knew Gauthe had left but had never known why. Stanley's follow-up report identified Gilbert Gauthe and said he was in treatment out of state.

Few callers complained about the reports, allaying the newsmen's concerns of angry viewer protest. The station fed a print summary to the AP and UPI bureaus in New Orleans. But without substantiating documents, the wire services ran nothing. By July, with ten-year-old Pete Robichaux gone to a psychiatric hospital in Texas, the story hung in abeyance.

When Glenn Gastal saw the Channel 10 reports, he was fuming over Paul Hebert's strategy. Gastal didn't want his boy's suit filed under seal; he wanted to speak out against Bishop Frey and Hebert wouldn't let him do that. So the couple drove to Lafayette and met with J. Minos Simon (pronounced *My*-nus *See*-mon), a lawyer who had cut a large swath through courtrooms of Louisiana. Simon advised Hebert that his clients had secured new counsel and promptly filed a motion to break the protective seal on Hebert's lawsuits.

On August 19, 1984, Monsignors Larroque and Benefiel asked Lafayette attorney F. Ray Mouton, Jr.—no relation to the Abbeville monsignor—to defend Father Gauthe on criminal charges soon to be filed. This set the stage for a conflict between two of the most brilliant and unorthodox attorneys in the state. Minos Simon lived for courtroom battle as General Patton had lived for war. As the crusty Simon crashed his way toward sensitive documents, Ray Mouton, a generation younger and one of the first Cajun lawyers to defend drug dealers, was about to take the toughest case of his career: the defense of a pedophile priest. Like Simon, Mouton was a hard-charger in the legal arena. But Ray Mouton had no glimmer of the seismic scandal under way and how it would batter his religious beliefs in the months and years to come.

ii.

Ethics of an Exposé

My home was in New Orleans, 150 miles east, but I knew Vermilion Parish well as my wife, Lisa LeBlanc, had grown up in Abbeville. No one close to her family had been abused by Gauthe; however the community was fraught with rumors. His crimes were magnified by his vocation. As a priest he occupied vaunted status: a server of ritual and symbol of trust, confessor to parent and child, the hand of God baptizing infants, confirming youngsters, performing weddings, burying the dead.

As Lisa entered the final term of pregnancy, the unfolding news stalked me like a shadow in the sun. For, after years of irregular church attendance, I had drawn back to the moorings of the faith. At some point, most young Catholics reckon with the guilty yoke of sex. I had been devout in childhood, adolescence, and college. In time, the church's prohibitions of premarital sex became a source of confusion to me. Sex was part of human nature. Adultery was immoral; but was all sexual intimacy outside of marriage sinful? As a bachelor, unable to reconcile myself intellectually, I drifted away from the church.

After we married, the monolithic rule made no more sense to me than before; but now my sex life was valid, so to speak. The larger change was a spiritual undertow pulling me back to a church that was greater than the sum of its rules. Like millions of Catholics, my wife and I did not accept the church's stance on birth control. But I found a memory and clarity in the gospels, a possibility of grace amid the violence and madness of the world. For the church had also become a potent instrument for freedom. In Poland it stood with Solidarity as a bulwark against Communism; in the Philippines and Haiti it helped topple decadent tyrants. In Latin America liberation theology and Christian base communities planted hope in lives of the landless and oppressed. If the church could shift in political realms, so might one hope for nuanced changes in its sexual teaching.

In the early 1980s I wrote about oil waste dumping in Cajun country, a process facilitated by deputy sheriffs, bureaucrats, and a cynical governor. On October 24, 1984, Gilbert J. Gauthe, Jr., was indicted in Lafayette on thirty-four criminal counts. *Politicians rape the land,* I thought—*and now a priest violates children.*

One charge—rape of a minor child—carried a mandatory sentence of life imprisonment under Louisiana law. On November 9 the *New Orleans Times-Picayune* cited sworn testimony by Gauthe and Monsignor Mouton in the Gastals' $12 million lawsuit against the church. Reporter John Pope's story began:

> *Abbeville, La.—Catholic Church officials knew for almost seven years about the Rev. Gilbert Gauthe's sexual activities with boys at churches in southwest Louisiana, according to two depositions filed this week in a court case.*
>
> *Even though the second-ranking church official in Gauthe's diocese knew that the fathers of two Abbeville boys had complained about Gauthe in 1976, the priest was appointed pastor of a church in Henry in late 1977 according to a deposition. . . .*
>
> *Gauthe, who has pleaded innocent by reason of insanity, is being held without bond in the Lafayette Parish jail. No trial dates have been set.*

When the story appeared, Gauthe's attorney, Ray Mouton, announced that he was filing a $40 million libel suit against the newspaper, saying, "There is absolutely no evidence which indicates that anyone in the Catholic Church had any knowledge that Gilbert Gauthe was sexually involved with any child or children."

The year before, Mouton and I had met at a party in New Orleans. He radiated an intensity one appreciates in latitudes such as these—an unabashed liberal, witty, well read, with a passion for bullfights. Now he was threatening suit against a newspaper whose reporter I respected. Over the telephone, after an exchange of amenities, I accused him of assaulting the First Amendment. "You don't have any grounds to sue. Pope's story says your client admitted under oath to molesting thirty-seven children."

"That's *my client's* admission," Mouton retorted. "Pope wrote that church officials knew about Gauthe's sexual activities for seven years, okay? Nothing—I repeat, nothing—in those two depositions John Pope cited proves prior knowledge by church officials of *sexual* contact. The only reference Monsignor Mouton makes is to my client kissing two boys inside a camper. Kissing—not molesting, got it?"

"That's really splitting hairs."

"Sure it is. I want to freeze that newspaper so they pull off the story. Libel suits drag on forever."

"*That smells.*"

"Does it smell any more than some reporter saying the bishop left a child molester in a country church?"

"Well, how did that priest do it all those years?"

"The guy is *deranged*, Jason. I just shipped him back to a treatment center up North."

"When's the trial?"

"Nine months, maybe a year. I need a shrink to convince a Catholic jury he belongs in a hospital instead of the pen."

The Gastals' attorney had attacked Mouton's position in a motion on their personal injury claim. J. Minos Simon wanted to strike Mouton's pleadings on factual grounds so that Mouton could not bring any insanity issues before a civil jury. Mouton was trying to exculpate his client—and, by extension, the bishop. A boxer in his youth, Minos Simon at sixty-three brought to cases large and small a pugilist's spoiling for the fight. No court had designated the priest insane, he argued, and if he was insane he could not have hired counsel.

Alternatively [the Simon motion read], if indeed Gauthe is sane and thus competent, then by asserting the defense of insanity he is guilty of knowingly asserting a falsehood and raising an unprovable defense. Such a false defense is unworthy of judicial cognizance and makes a mockery of justice.

But the motion was never heard by a judge. Sensing that Mouton's position was for public relations more than legal merit, Simon let the matter hang in abeyance. Mouton recognized the warning shot, realizing that Simon would fight him hook and claw should the insanity defense threaten the Gastal suit. In fact, Mouton was buying time in the criminal prosecution of Gauthe.

Louisiana is one of a handful of states in which the insanity statute restricts legal responsibility to the sole question of an offender's mental state *at the time the crimes were committed.* His client, Mouton told reporters, "is in a large institution in the Northeast under maximum security. [He] had a compulsion to deceive [and] hide from everyone all around him—including himself—the very grave sickness he held in the deep recesses of his disordered mind. Suicide is a real threat."

The libel suit against the *Times-Picayune* was never filed. But Ray Mouton got what he wanted. The state's largest newspaper pulled back, resorting mainly to wire service copy of scattered legal developments, printed in back pages, for the next year.

In December my wife gave birth to a daughter, Simonette, named after a maternal great-grandfather whose name had been feminized as it proceeded down the generations. The household shifted to a new rhythm of bottles, baths, and diapers. On trips to the store, I stared at milk cartons with faces of missing children and thought of Cajun altar boys. "I hope you don't write about it," Lisa said one night. "The research—"

"—would not be pleasant."

Now a father, I felt the malleability of children in a new way. In the tender epiphanies of those early weeks, the emotional prospects of such reporting cast a cold light. *Of all the stories,* I brooded, *why this—and why now?*

In January 1985 the Associated Press in Boise, Idaho, reported that a Rev. Mel Baltazar had been sentenced to seven years in the Idaho penitentiary after pleading guilty to a reduced charge of lewd behavior with a minor. According to the *Idaho Statesman*, a presentence investigation of church records found a history of Baltazar's sexual contact with youths over twenty years. Judge Alan Schwartzman stated: "I think the church has its own atonement to make as well. They helped create you and hopefully will help to rehabilitate you." That made me sit up. No judge gratuitously criticizes a church. Schwartzman declined to be interviewed. The *Statesman* reported that the presentence investigation also found that Baltazar had been discharged from duties as a naval chaplain in 1979 for adult homosexual conduct—and later dismissed as chaplain in a California hospital for molesting "a dying youth on a dialysis machine. . . . Translations of Latin passages revealed that the priest's superiors knew of other complaints against him but took no action."

My thoughts reversed along a grid of years to the memory of priests at Jesuit High School in New Orleans, sturdy intellects who taught a manly, rigorous code. "Sound of mind, sound of body" was their philosophy, with a premium placed on "mind over matter." Now thirty-five, I thought of those priests. One man, quite effeminate, left the Jesuits and was openly gay. Of the others, none had struck me as homosexual. No student I knew had ever been sexually approached. The school was pervaded by an intense masculinity. As a freshman, we followed Caesar's Gallic wars under Kevin Trower, a layman and scholarly basketball coach whose brow furrowed as he pounded home Latin declensions: "*Think, boys. . . . Think!*" His team won the state championship that year.

As a writer I had grown to cherish the Socratic method of Jesuit teaching. Question leads to answer, answer triggers new questions, and so the cycle turns. Now I had all kinds of questions about priests and sex in Lafayette and Idaho.

A January 23, 1985, AP report from Lafayette cited a new pretrial deposition in which Bishop Frey called Gauthe a "very unique person. He's got a Dr. Jekyll and Mr. Hyde personality . . . and he certainly deceived me." More startling was Frey's admission that he first learned in 1974 that Gauthe had molested a boy. So John Pope was right: they did have prior knowledge of Gauthe's behavior. I called Ray Mouton, who said brusquely: "The evidence quoted in Pope's article did not exist when he wrote it."

"Well, it exists now."

"I have nothing to say about that."

Mouton grumbled that Simon was throttling the diocese by taking his case to the local television stations. "He gives depositions to every reporter who walks in the door."

When I telephoned Simon, he was blunt: "This is the biggest scandal to hit the church in four hundred years. Talk about a cover-up!"

Raul Bencomo was miffed that Simon had called his legal strategy a cover-up. "Minos hasn't gotten a dime for the Gastals yet, and he inherited the pleadings that Paul Hebert and I filed," said Bencomo. "We obtained settlements without the victims' names ever appearing in the media or the kids having to testify, and making sure they received psychological care from the outset. We took the same approach with the Gastals, but they got restless. Glenn Gastal wanted to attack the bishop. That's his business, but if it was my kid, I wouldn't do it that way."

Bencomo and I had gone to Jesuit High together. "You're the first reporter I've agreed to talk to," he said, nibbling on an unlit cigar. "I think Ray Mouton has a basic conflict of interest. He represents Gauthe criminally and he was ready to sue on behalf of the church, which is a civil client. The libel threat on the *Picayune* was bullshit. I was an altar boy and once considered the priesthood myself. We wanted to get to upper councils of the church to say, 'You're not running a good clean house.' They've been totally remiss toward their flock. They should be offering psychological counseling to all afflicted families."

Simon had inherited a second suit from Bencomo-Hebert—that of Ted Campbell, who wanted to file his own suit against the church. That was precluded by the settlement. So Campbell went to Simon, who filed a writ with the Louisiana

Supreme Court asking that Campbell be allowed to return the $30,000 he had received and sue for harm to himself as a parent. Simon also sued Paul Hebert for malpractice in representing Campbell.

The malpractice charge was a hip shot. I was intrigued by the settlement figure of $405,000 to the Campbell family in the record. That was just one case. The implications were staggering. In the wave of sex abuse reports I found none that dealt with personal injury litigation. Lexis, the computerized registry of court decisions, recorded no such case, which did not mean there had been no settlements. Here was a new field of civil torts linked to, of all institutions, a Catholic diocese. These details had not appeared in print.

I thought it was an extraordinary story. My contact at the *New York Times Magazine* returned my proposal, saying, "The editors feel we need to do a child abuse story but not in the context of the Catholic Church." The *Washington Post* balked at assigning an investigative story to a nonstaffer. *Rolling Stone* said simply, "Sorry, not for us." *Vanity Fair, The Nation,* and *Mother Jones* followed suit. Nobody wanted to touch it. Had the scandal occurred in New York or Washington, coverage would have been heavy. By media lights, Lafayette was backwater South, a city of 90,000 with no NBC affiliate. The *Daily Advertiser,* owned by the conservative Thomson chain, had given meager coverage.

The more I learned, the greater grew my determination to report the events. If one researched and wrote well, a solid report would move. I felt for those anguished parents before I met them. Regardless of Gauthe's sickness, the legal drama showed a breakdown in church governing. Twenty suits had now been filed. How many other kids were out there? After four months of preliminary research, I called Linda Matys, editor of Lafayette's weekly, *Times of Acadiana,* and broached the story idea. "I am absolutely interested," said Matys, a *Time* stringer. "There's an eerie silence in this town. Channel 10 has run some stories but the legal picture is confusing."

Linda offered a month's salary and expenses, allowing me to publish reports in national outlets after they appeared in the *Times of Acadiana.* "I am interested in the kids," she said. "If there are boys out there needing help, we should report that. But we can't go barging into people's lives."

Meanwhile, Minos Simon provided the name of a Pittsburgh attorney who had clients who had been molested by a Pennsylvania priest. When I called, the lawyer refused to give details: "Everything is under a court-ordered seal which the church attorneys requested." Now there were cases in three states involving multiple victims. Idaho and Louisiana had a common trait: dioceses shuffling the perpetrator from parish to parish, with parents unaware. I wanted a budget for research in Washington, where the National Conference of Catholic Bishops and U. S. Catholic Conference were headquartered. How were high church officials reacting to these events?

Before leaving for Lafayette to do the Gauthe research, I called Tom Fox, editor of the independent weekly, the *National Catholic Reporter,* which is published in Kansas City, Missouri. "We've found information similar to what you have," said Fox, "though not in any systematic way. There was a case in Portland some time ago. We've been following a situation in San Diego, though it doesn't involve child abuse." A young man who left the seminary had filed a lawsuit claiming he was forced out by gays.

I asked if he thought homosexuality was very prevalent in the priesthood. "It's there," said Fox, "but you have to treat it in the context of celibacy." A priest who was homosexual and chaste occupied equal ground with a heterosexual celibate. I asked if the Portland case suggested a cover-up; he said it had. He cautioned me to remember that bishops acted according to an ecclesiastical tradition: priests could fall, pick up, and carry on. The church was not subject to the same checks and balances as a government. But, he said, if child abuse had crept into that tradition and could be proven, *NCR* would report it.

Fox had degrees from Stanford and Yale and had reported from Vietnam for the *New York Times* before becoming editor of *NCR.* "This is an important story," he continued, "but as a loving critic of the church, I want it done in a way that will spur the hierarchy to act responsibly. We don't have to pull punches, but there has to be a motive beyond sheer exposé."

"The families are important," Fox said. "But I'm also interested in the illness. What causes men to do this?" One could expect a knee-jerk reaction of people blaming celibacy, which he did not rule out "as potentially one factor, among others. But these cases stem from a pathology we don't adequately understand. I want our readers to understand it."

The baby was four months old as we prepared to leave for Lafayette. Lisa's resistance to the assignment had lessened but she had a growing strain of hostility toward the church. "I can't believe they were sick enough to harbor a man like that," she bristled.

"We don't know all the facts," I replied, and mentioned Fox's notion: a loving critic of the church.

"You wouldn't be a loving critic if it was our child," she said.

"No, I probably wouldn't."

Before we left, in search of deeper insight, I visited a Jesuit of long acquaintance. He had seen news reports but knew nothing of the inner workings of the Lafayette diocese. I asked: "How do you account for a guy like Gauthe slipping through the cracks—or getting ordained in the first place?"

"It's hard to predict sexual deviance. Psychological testing can denote spots and then you deal with those areas in an individual. The Jesuits use the Minnesota Multi-Phasic Personality Inventory as a screening procedure. It's a tough question: how do you screen reliably? The problem with deviant behavior is that it tends to be secret."

And how, I asked, should one weigh questions of deception on the part of church authorities? He said, "Remember something: those men can argue that they were trying to protect the reputation of the church, the victims, and other priests. They're handling it the way scandals are always handled: covertly. Given the tradition of heavy reliance by diocesan officials on their lawyers, a key issue is whether the defendants besides Gauthe may be victims of their attorneys."

Sitting across from a priest and friend, I felt embarrassed. The assignment I had sought now troubled me. In fits and starts I confessed a reluctance—wondering if by subjecting the church to hard scrutiny I would end up hurting the faith. He listened carefully. His gaze narrowed. "Write it! In the long run the church will profit by it. These things should not be covered up."

iii.

Mouton for the Defense

Minimizing evil intent is crucial to criminal defense law. F. Ray Mouton, Jr., believed in psychological evidence to explain why some people commit terrible crimes. His command of such stratagems was not the only reason why the diocese considered him to represent the priest. He had also done well at personal injury suits. But the revolution in Ray Mouton's life was owed equally to social pedigree. He was a linear descendant of Lafayette's founder, Jean Mouton, who in 1821 donated land on which the cathedral stands today, and his father, a contractor, built Our Lady of Fatima Church, raising much of the funds with a coterie of friends. All of that sent comforting signals to Monsignor Larroque and Bishop Frey.

At thirty-seven, Mouton had it all—an attractive wife, three children he adored, and a large brick house on lush acreage a dozen miles west of Lafayette. A few steps off the guest cottage was a pond where his daughter fed the ducks.

In court he functioned like a heat-seeking missile. As a young lawyer, he represented the city police chief who accused Mayor Ken Bowen of trying to curb his powers. In heated civil service hearings, some of which were televised live, Mouton, whose family had supported Bowen in the mayoralty, accused him of building a fiefdom. The *Daily Advertiser*, in support of the mayor, blasted Mouton. Bob Wright, whose clients included the paper, represented the mayor. Mouton won, but the chief suffered a stroke. So Mouton again targeted Bowen, sinking $10,000 into a campaign that led to his defeat. It was not full justice, because the chief was a broken man, but a form of justice just the same.

Mouton was amiable, chain-smoking, willing to attack the press. Defending a monster in a no-win situation, he was one of the most complex men I have ever met. "Always I totally drown myself this way," he explained. "An old lawyer in Shreveport, after watching me try a case for a few weeks, knocked on my hotel door as I was packing. 'Boy,' he said, 'you got about ten years, no more. You finished that argument in there and they could have wiped you off the floor, put you in the trash. There was nothing left in you.' I won that case four years ago. He may be right."

A symbiosis often develops between journalists and lawyers in a high-profile case. I was reading heavily about child sexual abuse and interviewing specialists by long-distance phone. "You're the only guy I've met in this town who uses the word 'pedophilia,' " he groused through a haze of smoke. I didn't believe him, but let it pass as we discussed the sexual pathology. Mouton kept calling Gauthe "tragic"—one of the most overused words in journalism. But many months later, when the prosecution of Gauthe was done, Mouton revealed parts of a second story more dramatic than the first. As the two narratives converged, with the help of other sources I found an essence of tragedy. It came first in the person of Gilbert Gauthe; however, that too would change in time.

Built in 1913, St. John the Evangelist Cathedral stands in the heart of Lafayette, with twin cupolas that rise out of a Romanesque body made of red brick. Behind the terrace bridging chancery and church, row upon row of white sarcophagi and mausoleums of marbled gray fan out toward a ridge of trees, with floral wreaths ennobling concourses of the city's prominent dead.

On August 19, 1984, Mouton attended a luncheon hosted by Monsignor Larroque in L'Évêché, the handsome diocesan residence. Bishop Frey was absent. The group included Monsignor Benefiel, Sister Valoni, education vicar Gerald Dill, New Orleans archdiocesan counsel Tom Rayer, and Edgar "Sonny" Mouton —Ray's cousin, an older man and former state senator. Benefiel and Sonny Mouton were convinced that Channel 10's reports would cease if District Attorney Nathan Stansbury did not indict Gauthe. Ray Mouton, who had only sketchy details of the allegations, felt that if crimes were serious Stansbury would indict. "And if Nathan indicts," he added, "CBS is gonna land on your lawn in a helicopter."

"Not a chance, Ray," laughed Benefiel. The meeting ended with no consensus on a public stance for the church if Gauthe were indicted and with Mouton unsure whether or not he had a client. Larroque subsequently called and formally asked him to represent Gauthe. Mouton agreed to fly to Massachusetts and meet the priest. Shortly after 9 A.M. on August 24, he met with Larroque, who gave him literature on the House of Affirmation. Hands trembling, the vicar-general also gave him a psychological report on nine boys and copies of the civil suits. Then Mouton dashed to his first appointment with the district attorney.

Nathan Stansbury's prosecutorial turf covered Lafayette, Vermilion, and Acadia parishes, a good swath of political real estate. A lean man with chiseled features, Stansbury loved to hunt and fish; he stood rock solid in Democratic Party politics. He was feeding tropical fish in an aquarium when Mouton entered his office. "Do you represent Gilbert Gauthe?" asked Stansbury.

Mouton liked Stansbury. In past cases they had gotten on well in the conflicts between prosecutor and criminal defense counsel. "Help me, Nathan. I don't know what he did. I don't even know who he did it to." Gazing at the fish, Stansbury spoke without emotion. "There's no defense, Ray. If we work a pre-indictment deal, it spares the kids from going to the grand jury."

"Don't beat up on me," Mouton joshed. He had not even met with his client. "You've got your job to do, I've got mine. Let's just keep the lines of communication open."

"We're open," murmured Stansbury. On the desk Mouton saw a stack of documents and the same psychological report on the boys Larroque had given him minutes earlier. He had yet to read the dossier but realized now that Stansbury was preparing a criminal indictment. Mouton asked what Gauthe had done. "Thousands of offenses. I would not like to have to extradite him." Mouton conceded that little would be solved by that. Stansbury's gaze moved from the fish to Mouton: "Then you agree to extradition?" Mouton would not agree to anything yet. Stansbury asked if he was planning an insanity plea. Mouton was not sure, but he *thought* Gauthe was insane. "No rational human being would do the things you say you've got documented, Nathan."

Stansbury shook his hand. "Good luck, Ray."

Mouton had never defended a sex offender before. The day before he had discussed the case with Raymond Blanco, a vice-president at the University of Southwestern Louisiana, and chairman of the Bishop's Services Appeal. Blanco had recommended Mouton for the job. On the flight out of Lafayette to Boston he pored over the report on damage to the children prepared by the psychologists. Glossy photographs of nine boys accompanied a chart detailing astounding sexual perversion by the priest—repeated acts of sodomy; oral sex; instigation of sexual acts between boys; taking photographs of kids in sexual acts; showing pornographic videotapes; fondling boys' sexual organs in the confessional, in the sacristy, in the rectory, on Saturday trips to the marsh. Mouton was stunned. Most of these kids were *little boys.*

Changing planes in New Orleans, he sprinted to a pay phone and called Blanco. "*Raymond:* you would *not believe* what this guy did!" Lowering his voice, he ran down a litany of sex crimes the priest had allegedly committed *hundreds and hundreds of times!*

"It's bad," said Blanco somberly.

On the airplane, blood racing, he read further. *What am I getting into?* A few days earlier a young priest, disillusioned about Gauthe, had mumbled something to him about the Apostolic Penitentiary. Mouton asked if that was a prison where they put priests. No, the priest sighed: it was a single cardinal in the Roman Curia among whose many responsibilities was to assist inquiries into occult activities such as satanic possession. The priest knew of no inquiry by the Apostolic Penitentiary into Gauthe. As the plane circled Logan Airport in Boston, Mouton was numb. A priest who seduces a child in the sacristy, then celebrates Mass, giving the boy's mother holy communion as the child holds a plate beneath her chin—this was a portrait of absolute evil, something he had never imagined.

Peering into darkened waters of Boston Harbor, he struck a match and the flash in the window distorted his reflection into a sinister visage that frightened him so much he burned his finger. *I am going to meet Lucifer disguised as a Roman Catholic priest.*

With satchel and suit bag he walked through the airport, heavy with dread. And then, in a moment he would remember as almost sacred, he suddenly felt serene. He realized that he had been walking to this point all of his life.

ii.

In 1970, Bishop Bernard Flanagan of Worcester established a counseling center for the troubled clergy of his diocese. Founded by Sister Anna Polcino, a psychiatrist, and the Rev. Thomas Kane, a clinical psychologist, the program filled a need and expanded. In 1973 the House of Affirmation was established outside Worcester. A large house was then acquired in nearby Hopedale, and offices moved to Boston. By 1982 other Affirmation houses were operating in Montara, California; Webster Groves, Missouri; and in England.

"It is not a nesting place for those unfit for ministry," Father Kane had written. Each facility housed about twenty clergy at a time. Admission was supposedly voluntary; bishops sent many clergy for evaluation. The campus atmosphere, wrote Kane, helped residents become aware "that the day they arrive at the House of Affirmation they are being prepared to leave it."

Celibacy, wrote Kane, often "jars with the usual Freudian model of therapy." He called the facility a "psycho-theological community." He added:

> Many of the problems that have presented themselves at the House of Affirmation may be classified as deprivation syndromes and what Freud classified as the repressive neurosis. In the first case, lack of love and acceptance (lack of affirmation) has crippled the psychological functioning of the priest and religious; in the latter case, one encounters [those] who have made excessive use of the defense mechanism known as intellectualization. These individuals are not aware of their emotions and have even repressed anger in their life as celibates.

Mouton was met by Sister Miriam Ukeritis, a therapist who said that "Gil" had had a hard night. Mouton asked if Gauthe understood what he had done. Yes, she said; they had discussed it in group therapy. Gil was in the backyard, waiting.

The terrace faced placid greenery. The man on the bench wore a Banlon shirt and black pants. At five foot eleven and two hundred pounds, Mouton felt quite a bit larger than his client. "I—I'm just so scared," Gauthe blurted. His body began trembling.

Mouton sat on the bench. "You ought to be scared," he said. "I'm scared too." Gauthe stared. "Do you know why I'm here, Father? Is that what you want me to call you—Father?"

"You can call me Gil."

"Well, call me Ray."

Gil knew why he was there. He removed a contact lens from watery eyes. Mouton wanted one thing clear: if at any moment Gil did not like him—his glasses, his tie, how he spoke or reasoned—he could get another lawyer. Gauthe replied that Larroque had called him "a very good lawyer and I should listen to you."

Some lawsuits had been filed, Mouton said. Gauthe knew that, and asked if it had made the newspapers. No, said Mouton, but it soon would. He asked if Gauthe knew the district attorney. "Yeah, I know Nathan. He keeps his boat at Hazel's landing. He's real nice." Did Gil know him personally? No, he just knew him—"because of boats." Nathan was a nice man, Ray averred, thinking, *This is like talking to a nine-year-old. Come out to meet Satan and I find—this.*

"He's gonna indict you, Gil."

Gauthe began shaking. Mouton waited. Then he said there would be a grand jury.

"Which one is it?" asked Gauthe.

"Which one what?"

"Which family?"

"Man, I don't know." He told the priest about his background, emphasizing that he was an unorthodox lawyer. But he believed there was a way to make the system work—if you never got tired, held to the objective, and held your wits.

Shaken, Gauthe said: "I like things done, you know, the regular way." Then maybe he needed another lawyer. No, said Gauthe. "I like you. I want you."

"I think there's a reason why I'm meeting you. I think I'm supposed to do this. But, Father, there are limits to what my mind is capable of." He could understand a poor man stealing, or a rich man committing adultery. He understood things he abhorred, and even developed compassion for people who did things society scorned, like trafficking in drugs. "And that bothers me, Father. Because I do not have any compassion for you at all."

"It's the bell," said Gauthe in a tiny voice. "It's time for us to eat."

In the dining room men wore sports shirts and the few women wore skirts and blouses. To Mouton it seemed like a country club. In a confusion of priorities mirroring his mood, he ordered iced tea and two desserts. As Gauthe ate, Mouton excused himself and went to Sister Miriam's office. He told her he was confused about this priest, who had been like a hero in his parish; then Mouton had read reports on the children. And whom, asked the nun, had he met? Mouton did not know. "A child, didn't you?" she said. Mouton conceded that Gil seemed child-like. She pointed to a painting on the wall: a woman carrying a papoose on her back. "Look at the face of the papoose, Mr. Mouton." It resembled Gauthe, who had painted it. She told him that Gauthe was like a dependent child. Mouton cringed.

Reviewing Gauthe's medical dossier, he found a document that made him sit upright. "*What is this?*" he snapped. She explained that he would be going to Gulfport, Mississippi, to work as an emergency paramedic. He had learned skills during his months at House of Affirmation. On a trip to Gulfport an ambulance firm had offered him a job. Mouton exploded: "*Jesus Christ, lady!*" Did she know that hundreds of sex crimes had made him eligible for life at hard labor in Louisiana's penitentiary? She insisted that he was making good progress. Mouton asked for privacy and a phone.

If Gauthe took a job in Gulfport, Stansbury might have grounds to charge church officials with criminal negligence. Mouton called Larroque in Lafayette and requested authority to move Gauthe. Larroque asked where. "I don't know, just as long as it doesn't have a Catholic name and is not accessible to the press." He wanted bars to prevent Gauthe from fleeing. Larroque concurred. Gauthe said that he had been visited months earlier by archdiocesan attorney Tom Rayer. Mouton called Rayer in New Orleans, and he concurred with the decision to move Gauthe.

He rejoined Gauthe in an empty room, opened his briefcase, and told him to read every word of the boys' psychological reports and the civil suit papers. "And let's get one thing straight: if I'm gonna represent you, you're gonna do exactly what I say. You're not gonna lie to me."

"Okay."

He returned to Sister Miriam's office. He said they had no idea of the breadth of his crimes and told her to destroy all documents pertaining to discharge and the Gulfport job. The papers were discoverable—Nathan Stansbury, Minos Simon, anyone could get them on subpoena and make a bad situation worse in criminal and civil spheres. He said that Monsignor Larroque had approved Gauthe's transfer. That would be terrible, she said. He was doing well at Affirmation; he had friends and support. Mouton asked for a list of facilities. She reiterated her opposition, stopping short of an ugly argument. Mouton settled on the Institute of Living in Hartford, Connecticut. When he returned to Gauthe, he found him sitting alone, smoking a cigarette.

"You read that stuff, Gil?"

"Yep."

So it was all true? *No:* it was not all true. Gil said he never put bars on the rectory to scare people: churches were being vandalized, and priests received a directive with a list of security firms—

"Okay, Gil. They're wrong about the burglar bars."

And what he had done had nothing to do with religion, Gauthe declared. He never told anyone you had to have sex to be an altar boy. And it was wrong to blame the bishop. Frey didn't know everything Gauthe was doing. The suits said Frey and Larroque were "liable"—but they weren't. "*I'm* liable, Ray. If you're my lawyer, don't say I'm innocent. But they didn't do it."

Mouton explained that technicalities might warrant a mental illness defense. If the attorney simply said he was guilty he would spend his life in prison. Gauthe had heard that child molesters behind bars were subject to violence by other inmates. "I'll kill myself. I am not going to prison."

Ray Mouton and Gilbert Gauthe made a pact. If at any point Gil chose to take his life, he promised to first allow Ray the chance to talk him out of it. Mouton in turn promised not to interfere should Gil choose suicide as a last resort. "I will never lie to you, Gilbert." His case would change often. All big ones did. As events transpired, Ray would explain each one. Gil would never be in the dark. "I'm not strong enough to do this," Gauthe pleaded. "Promise me you'll walk every step of the way."

"I can't promise I'll give you the strength. But I will be there with you—every step of the way."

The next day, Sunday, Mouton spent hours in a rent-a-car, driving aimlessly, wondering what the hell he had gotten into.

iii.

On Monday they spent all day with a tape recorder. Of his early sexual encounters, Gauthe said: "There was a sugar cane plantation about three miles behind our house. I must have been in the fifth grade, and our family moved into one of those old houses on the plantation." A neighbor boy was older than Gil. "The houses were kinda raised; we were playing under the house and he made advances to me. He didn't really say very much. He took off my pants and underwear and began to feel me. I can't say he forced me but he was a very threatening person and I knew I'd get beat up. This happened maybe twice as best I can remember and the third time he did oral sex on me—forcing me to do the same thing to him. It didn't last very long at all. And from that point on I completely avoided him. I'd only go outside when I knew he wasn't there."

Later, in Lafayette, at USL before entering seminary, he became involved with a girl. "But I pushed love away. I've pushed love away from me that my parents and everyone has extended. I've been afraid to lose them. God, I see that as a pattern now. I guess I thought that maybe the seminary, the priesthood, would isolate me from that. I thought I'd learn. Maybe God could give me an answer. . . . I knew He wouldn't be taken away. I knew that God couldn't be hurt. I don't know if there was anything else I could have done except go to Him."

He discussed his paintings in art therapy. "This is a picture I did on December 23, 1983, the eve of my twelfth anniversary as a priest. It's just a barren tree with twelve broken ornaments. And I couldn't hang the star. . . . I thought, *Well, what is my star? What can I put at the top?* The only thing I could think of was a crown of thorns: just an awful lot of suffering. And then I have a little symbol of a broken chalice with 'Merry Christmas, Gil.'"

Mouton did not ask about his implicit identification with Jesus, who wore a crown of thorns before crucifixion. He probed further about Gauthe's sex life. Gil spoke of an affair while he was a priest with a woman in New Iberia: they had sexual intercourse but once. Mouton asked how that compared with sexual encounters with children. "The involvement with the kids was much more emotional. I really felt a sense of attachment, of protecting, of being with them, of really genuine love. I had feelings toward her, but I can't say they were feelings of love. I did trust her to be gentle with me because I was still very much a bumbling fool when it came to that. 'If we do this, would you be hurt?' 'No, I'd feel guilty but I wouldn't be hurt'—that kind of thing. I kind of talked myself into it. Very, very exciting. I was fascinated. I'd never in my life seen a grown woman undress. I climaxed outside of her. I had a real fear of pregnancy so I didn't wait. And that was it, just that one time. We sat down and really reassured each other that we were both okay."

"Did you really feel okay?"

"I didn't. I felt a lot of guilt. It was the only time I ever betrayed my priesthood—in that way."

Mouton asked if he had ever confessed his sexual activities with boys to another priest. One time, said Gauthe. Mouton asked why. "I felt a real urge to try and make a new beginning. I really thought inside that I—"

"Did you think you had sinned?"

"Yeah."

"Were you aware that you had violated criminal laws?"

"No, that didn't sink in."

"It never occurred to you?"

"What occurred to me was, *Hey, this isn't right but I can't help it.*"

"Explain this 'can't help it.'"

"I said to myself, *This is wrong. I shouldn't do this. But I want to do it again. I like it.*"

"Did you ever reach a point where you had no feelings that it was bad or wrong?"

"Yeah. It became very automatic. I didn't think about it any more—didn't look upon it as moral or immoral. It was just something I did."

"You don't think of yourself as a homosexual?"

"*No, I don't.*"

Gauthe had painted several pictures of a young boy. In one, a teddy bear was being taken from a child. Mouton asked what it meant. When he was four, said Gauthe, his sister was born. "She was the only one who had her own room. We had six boys."

Mouton asked about his relationships with women, with his mother and sister. "I've always been very respectful. These are people you just don't say bad things to, you don't hurt. Women to me are very, very delicate." And did he think he shared that delicacy with them? "Yeah, oh yeah: I know how fragile and easily hurt I am. I'm very mixed up."

Regarding the boys he seduced, Mouton asked: "Did you feel you were the child's father or the child's mother?"

"At different times, I felt the father image."

"When you engaged in sex with older children did you—"

"I felt equal."

As the questioning wore on, Mouton discerned a strange ethic in the tangled skein of Gauthe's pathology: if it came to a trial, he would admit everything in court to spare the kids from having to testify. Mouton was convinced that the behavior was clearly pathological. Said Gauthe: "Every time, every time, I just couldn't help it. I functioned like a machine in many ways. I wasn't in control. I knew there was another person acting."

"What do you mean, 'another person'?"

"It was a dark me. The underside. The part of me that was goodness, that went out of his way to break his back for his people, I saw that as making up for the guilt. That's the way I've always interpreted it: another person." Mouton asked if this dark underside was an adult. "It wasn't anything. I called it a sex monster. That's what I call it now, too." He described another painting, a gold-colored thing with two yellow eyes. "When I first got in touch with him, he was a monster. He went in and out of my mind. Two big yellow eyes: he filled up everything that I could see and I could see myself very, very small. He was powerful, more powerful than—"

"Than what?"

"More than me. He was everything, Ray."

"He was everything: you were aware of that?"

"I was aware of a force but I knew I couldn't control it. I had tried. I hated myself for what I was doing but what I hated more was that I didn't have the power to stop it."

"Did you ever convince yourself that this other force wasn't you?"

"I thought it was all me. I thought this was my makeup, the way I was born, the way I would always continue to be."

"Did you ever contemplate suicide?"

"Yes, but I didn't do it because I knew it would hurt my family and hurt the kids. That's the only thing keeping me from suicide now. I'm always watching out for others."

He recalled looking out over the congregation, "and I would see kids that I had had sex with come to communion, and I'd say, 'How can I do that?' And then I'd see other kids I'd want."

"Did that person, that monster, make decisions?"

"No, he never made decisions. But remember, Ray. There was a good functioning priest. The other was destruction. When destruction started I was just caught up in that moment—not looking beyond what it meant, not even trying to realize what it meant at the time. It was just happening."

Before departure, Mouton telephoned Nathan Stansbury, assuring him that Gauthe would return to Lafayette when the arraignment date was set. On August 31, 1984, after his attorney had returned to Lafayette, Gilbert Gauthe drove alone to Hartford. The Institute of Living, founded in 1822, was Connecticut's first hospital and one of the nation's earliest hospitals to provide exclusive care for the mentally ill. Behind the fallen priest lay nearly a year of treatment grounded in religious trust—few fetters on his movement; across the street from the Hopedale house children cavorted in a playground. For the first time in his life, Gauthe had begun to understand his awful sickness. He thought therapy was working; he knew he was not cured but felt he was gaining control. In Hartford he soon felt like a prisoner.

iv.

Turning to Raymond Blanco as a confidant was a natural move for Ray Mouton because Blanco made it his business to know everyone, and Mouton needed all the help he could get.

Blanco began each day on an early walk with his friend Bob Wright, a name partner in Lafayette's most prestigious law firm. Blanco was on a first-name basis with the governor, congressmen, sheriffs, media people, and benefactors of the university where he worked. With silver hair and Falstaffian paunch, Blanco had a quick wit and relish for politics. His wife Kathleen was a member of the state legislature; they had five children. The Blancos enjoyed a rustic little camp in the marsh where a group of judges made annual pilgrimage to shoot ducks, sup, drink, and play cards. Blanco's own net worth was minuscule but many people genuinely liked him, going out of their way to pay back his kindnesses. Once he checked into a swank Dallas hotel. The receptionist said: "Um, it says you're only supposed to pay $25. Your credit card, please?" He gave her $25 in cash. "Mr. Blanco, could I ask—*just who are you?*"

Above all, he was a defender of the faith.

Born in Birmingham, his early memory was marked by the story of Father Jim Coyle, pastor of St. Paul's Cathedral there. Catholics were a terrorized minority in Alabama during the twenties. In the spring of 1921, Ku Klux Klansmen assaulted a Catholic pharmacist, stripped him, and knocked out his teeth. On August 11, Coyle was shot dead on the rectory steps by Edwin Stephenson, a would-be Methodist minister who turned himself in with the gun still hot. Coyle had performed the wedding of Stephenson's daughter to a Puerto Rican. Stephenson was defended by a young lawyer named Hugo Black, who fed racial animosities by suggesting the groom was black. "Because a man becomes a priest does not mean he is divine," Black told the jury, arguing self-defense. "He has no more right to protection than a Protestant minister." The killer's daughter lashed out at the prosecutor for not allowing her to testify. She said her parents wanted Coyle dead and the cathedral destroyed. The acquittal moved the *Nation* to pronounce Alabama "the American hot-bed of anti-Catholic fanaticism." Black later became a liberal U.S. Supreme Court justice.

Blanco's father, a knife sharpener, would whisper to his son, "Over there"—pointing out the hack who performed weddings—"that's the man who murdered Father Coyle."

Kids called him Dago, made fun of his daddy, taunted him about tunnels where nuns, impregnated by priests, killed their babies. He was fired from a summer job in a meat market for saying "Yes, ma'am," to a black customer. His first two years of high school were in a Benedictine monastery. An elderly German monk told of an encounter with rough whites at a train depot. "I take off my hat," he wheezed, "so dey see I have no horns."

Blanco finished high school in Birmingham. He traveled with the local bishop in a pickup through dusty towns for meetings that sometimes drew three or four people. On a swing through Walker County a redneck struck the bishop and spat in his face. In contrast to such primitive hatreds, Blanco's home life was tender with warmth and marked by fidelity to the Church of Rome.

Football was his exit vehicle. After linebacking at St. Benedict's College in Kansas, he moved to New Iberia in 1959 and as head coach at Catholic High won two state championships. More than a coach, he was a molder of men. When Blanco moved to USL, first as assistant coach, then as dean of men, finally vice-president of student affairs, he kept tabs on those he had taught or coached, asking assistance in various of his projects. Blanco had coached Ken Bouillion and retained a mentor's pride in the psychologist. And Bouillion, he told Ray Mouton, understood pedophiles. Those people were criminals who could not be cured! Maybe so, said Mouton, but Gauthe was more than just a criminal.

On the last Thursday in August they drove to New Orleans for a meeting with the insurance defense. At Blanco's request, Mouton guided his Mercedes along old Highway 91, a single-lane road hugging curves of the Mississippi. Blanco loved the rustic shacks, plantation houses, and mossy oaks. He also thrived on provoking his friends. "Common good!" he announced. "You gotta think of the common good. So Gauthe does life."

"What if he kills himself?"

"So he kills himself," said Blanco, intimating that if it couldn't be helped, well . . .

"Goddamn, Raymond!" snapped Mouton to Blanco's bait.

"Common good. Common good."

But Mouton would not plead a life sentence. Blanco told him he had no shot against Stansbury. They argued all the way to the Hilton and continued after they unpacked. Blanco said he was nuts. He thought every play in his life was third down and three yards to go. Now it was fourth and sixty-five. Time to punt. "I know it's fourth and sixty-five!" snapped Mouton. "But I got time, Raymond."

They quit arguing at 4 A.M. Six hours later they joined Bishop Frey, Monsignors Larroque and Benefiel, Tom Rayer, insurance counsel Robert Leake, and others at Denechaud and Denechaud, of which Rayer was a partner. The firm rented space in the Pere Marquette Building, which was owned by the Southern Province of the Society of Jesus. Rayer was the church's link to the insurers, and in his deference to Bob Leake, a balding man whose silver sideburns conveyed an image of authority, Blanco saw how the lines of power were drawn in the church's response to the crisis. Blanco was worried about news damage. Leake said not to worry. Gordon Johnson, president of the New Orleans Country Club, represented Lloyd's of London, and he agreed with Leake. "Just say, 'No comment.'" But they did not understand the people, Blanco countered, launching into a peroration on local sentiments. Leake and Johnson listened politely. Blanco said that Cajuns could forgive, but they needed to know the truth. Mouton realized that Blanco had come to New Orleans not to argue Gauthe's fate but to gain leverage for the diocese with its insurance lawyers. Blanco wanted the bishop to speak out. Leake did not protest. Blanco asked Frey if he would say Mass in Henry that weekend with a full disclosure. "Sure," said Frey.

Mouton was delighted. The bishop was a stout, lumbering man who had said little. Blanco's idea enlivened him. But disclosure was not so simple, Monsignor Benefiel warned. The chancery closed at noon on Friday, a short time away. Disclosure meant drafting and disseminating a statement across the diocese. Mouton argued that they could do it. They had Xerox machines, cars, people. Apart from the need to strike a responsible image, the legal logic impelling disclosure was Minos Simon's motion to unseal the lawsuits Paul Hebert had filed in Abbeville. Bob Leake said that no judge would agree to that. Blanco listened as Mouton said the law was on Simon's side. Blanco believed that if the church didn't come clean on its own it would soon be forced to.

Leake insisted that Simon's attempts to publicize the civil actions would fail. With that failure, said Leake, Simon "is going to put a hatchet in my hand."

"In rebuttal," said Mouton, "he'll plant it between your eyes." Leake stared back impassively.

Blanco was experienced at political strategy sessions. He knew that the New Orleans lawyers had not taken him seriously, and that stuck in his craw. Once outside, he fumed to the bishop: "Those bastards are gonna kill us!" Frey was grim-faced. On the drive back to Lafayette, Blanco insisted again to Mouton that Gauthe should plead a life sentence, based on the common good.

Frey did not go to Henry that weekend nor issue a statement.

On Monday, September 4, Larroque hosted a lunch at the chancery. Bishop Frey was absent. Attending were Benefiel, education vicar Gerald Dill, Blanco, Tom Rayer, Ray Mouton, and Ross Brubacher, a former pro football player who had served as Lafayette's sheriff before joining Bob Wright's law firm.

Wright's presence lent weight to the moment. A wealthy plaintiff attorney, he pitched his firm in eloquent television spots. His smooth face and sandy-gray hair conveyed a calm image much in keeping with the cool, unruffled way he went about his business. In the years since their clashes over the mayor and police chief, Mouton and Wright had grudgingly acquired a mutual respect for each other. But they were as different as fire and ice. Seeing Wright, Mouton realized that Raymond Blanco had turned to new allies. Blanco could spend days with you and mask his true designs.

Lunch got down to talk of J. Minos Simon, in Abbeville that very hour pitted against Paul Hebert over the protective order which barred the Gastal suit and three others from public scrutiny. There was no chance the judge would grant Simon's motion, said Tom Rayer, echoing Leake's confidence of Friday.

Minutes later Rayer was called to the phone. Hebert reported that the judge had removed the seal on the Gastal case, clearing the way for the angry couple to give media interviews. Hebert's other suits were still protected. Ray Mouton recommended that the bishop issue a statement from Dill's office. Larroque was puzzled. So was Gerry Dill, a former coach. "Dill's out on Breaux Bridge Highway," said Mouton. "You want cameras in front of the cathedral?"

Bob Wright was less interested in media than in the law: Gauthe should plead guilty to criminal charges and take the Fifth Amendment in civil depositions. Mouton flatly disagreed: pleading guilty would mean a life sentence for a man bordering on suicide. Ross Brubacher agreed with Wright: plead guilty, and prevent a long prosecution. The civil suits could be negotiated; a drawn-out criminal case would mean protracted bad news.

"No way," Mouton told Brubacher.

"What is it that you want?" Dill asked Mouton.

He wanted a sentence in an institution where Gauthe would have medical care. Perhaps he could plea-bargain twelve years. Who, asked Dill, was going to pay for the medical care? "We are," said Mouton. Dill asked, "Who is we?"

"The church," said Mouton, turning toward Larroque, whose eyes were trained on his luncheon plate. Tom Rayer rose from his seat. The archdiocesan attorney apologized, but he had to pick up his daughter, who lived in the dormitory at USL. Mouton's mercury was rising. "Nobody knows I represent Gilbert Gauthe and before I go out on a limb I've gotta be damn sure nobody saws it off!"

Dill was insistent: What kind of care? And involving what kind of commitment by the diocese? Mouton wanted "unconditional commitment for the medical treatment this man requires."

"We absolutely cannot," Dill retorted.

"Is that right, Monsignor?" said Mouton, staring at Larroque. Larroque said nothing. Mouton jabbed an index finger toward the vicar-general. "May God have more mercy on Gilbert Gauthe than the Roman Catholic Church does!"

Bob Wright, a nominal Baptist, gazed at the ceiling. Rayer had reached the door. "*Wait a minute, Tommy!*" shouted Mouton. "*I've got to have an answer to this!*" He pounded the table with his fist. "I know the difference between right and wrong, and it's *you* people"—he pointed at Larroque and Benefiel—"who taught me that difference. Gauthe is *ours*. This guy is a priest, and we have a responsibility to him!"

The meeting ended. Rayer was out first. In the hallway Mouton exploded: "This is outrageous!"

"No, no, calm down," said Blanco. "That's why we wanted you. If we'd wanted a whore we'd have gotten someone else."

Bob Wright was gone.

Mouton and Blanco caucused in Frey's empty office. "What the fuck are we talking about, Raymond?"

"Shh, Ray. Don't talk like that."

"You're telling me don't say fuck and they're condemning a priest to death? Who's diseased, Raymond?"

Larroque entered the room. He had just spoken with the bishop: the diocese could not guarantee all of Father's medical care. Mouton resolved to change that.

As accounts of Simon's victory shot across the media grid, the diocese of Lafayette was forced into a public posture on a scandal that, as Mouton had predicted, could not be contained. That afternoon a statement issued under Bishop Frey's name said: "From the beginning, I have reached out and offered assistance to those who have been harmed or hurt. . . . We should not be shaken in our faith, for we know that the spirit helps our weakness."

The action now shifted to the civil sphere, where Minos Simon had grabbed Bob Leake's hatchet.

iv.

The Passion of J. Minos Simon

Legal documents formed the baseline on which I built my reporting. In Lafayette, Minos Simon made a mountain of them available to me—motions, depositions, even transcripts of telephone interviews with potential witnesses. A journalist never takes such largesse for granted. Simon wanted his case covered in the press. So did I—without getting used. He had a commanding presence. With graying mustache and silvered black toupee, the forehead etched with distinctive lines, his dark, arched eyebrows registered perpetual skepticism. In conversation he could argue like a debater, convinced of his intellectual rightness.

He grew up in Nunez, a village west of Abbeville where a rail depot had hooks to catch the mailbags when trains rumbled past. His parents had spoken Cajun French with snatches of English. Once a week his mother carved beef at a communal butchery, seasoned her allotted share, and buried it for cooling beneath the house. "When you are raised in an environment of illiteracy," he told me, "you carry a sense of inferiority into the literate world." Greek mythology was a staple of Acadian education; though most original Acadians were little schooled, many chose Hellenic names for their children. In the annals of ancient Crete, King Minos was known for justice.

Simon's oratory could rise to impassioned eloquence. At a crucial juncture, he said the Gastal case illustrated "what human dignity is about, an intangible quality that dignifies man and separates man from beast—that we have a creator." The creator in which Simon believed was a central force behind the universe, connecting mankind to a superseding intelligence. Twice divorced, he had long since abandoned the Catholicism of his youth. In that rupture, before he had even married, lay the roots of his passion.

When he was a student, Dale Carnegie's *How to Win Friends and Influence People* convinced him he had word-power shortage. He began keeping a notebook, jotting five definitions a day, memorizing the lot each week. Discharged from the service in World War II, he entered the University of Wisconsin and there began to read. The legend of Demosthenes, who put rocks in his mouth to enunciate more clearly, spurred an effort to improve his diction, discarding the Cajun overlay by saying *the* instead of *de, there* instead of *dere*. In that semester, the literate world opened to him, and once lit, the flame of desire for learning burned on. He returned to LSU in Baton Rouge and read Montesquieu, Hugo, Kant, Plato, Aristotle, Hegel. Upon graduation he worked at the Library of Congress and read *The Federalist Papers*. He returned again to LSU for law school, and in 1946 was admitted to the bar.

He had found a secular faith to supplant the creed of his unlettered past. It was illogical to forbid the eating of meat on Friday for fear of losing one's soul. Who were those men in Roman collars to impose such ideas on enlightened thought? Simon's business was the law, and he needed no church to guide his ways.

Lafayette in the late forties was run by a clique of well-heeled lawyers whose commerce turned on the oil business and on a system greased by political patronage. Simon began with cases in city court—whatever came in off the street—typing his own briefs. His break came in the oddest way. An old man with a sandwich shop was arrested for selling wine on Sunday. Bootleggers kept seven-day weeks in cahoots with local sheriffs; the normal procedure was to slip someone a bill, get the old geezer off with a warning. Simon read the statute and found that, if any part could be found unconstitutional, the entire statute could be scrapped. He saw no difference between a hotel restaurant that ignored the statute by serving wine on Sunday and the old man's shop. He failed to quash the indictment but the state Supreme Court upheld his appeal to show just cause for the indictment. "And that," he says, "was like Chicken Little said the goddamn sky was falling. The Knights of Columbus applied for a rehearing." The state liquor association saw a good thing and paid him $800 for a speech. At a bar convocation, a friend praised him from the floor. Of the mild applause that followed his friend's praise, says Simon: "He was talking to all those old bastards who thought me a pariah." The Supreme Court soon reversed its decision, but Minos Simon, not yet thirty, had arrived.

He took grievances against anyone—sued sheriffs, police jurors, cops, it made no difference. He quickly ran afoul of the local establishment. Two patrician attorneys sought to have him disbarred. "Talk about a raunchy conspiracy," Simon recalled. "They charged I solicited money from the liquor association, and got some guy who ran a whorehouse to sign a complaint that I solicited money from him." When Simon requested an open hearing in Lafayette, the accusers backed down, claiming it had only been a report to the bar.

In Simon's hands the law was like a fencer's foil—thrust, parry, burrow until the opponent dropped his guard. He took pleasure in enunciating complicated names of body parts, hammering home the impact of riven limbs to jurors of meager education. Come from poverty, he understood its hold, and as he grew rich he did not condescend toward jurors.

I was struck by the irony of Ray Mouton and Minos Simon, both mavericks, one a religious man defending a priest who had destroyed young lives, the other an irreligious dynamo with clients whose faith had been betrayed. More than forty years had passed since Simon broke away from the faith. In a way, he had been waiting for this case all his life.

By Simon's lights, here was a fortress of centuries: A system governing laity and clergy: prescriptions of ritual, gradations of sin, levels of hierarchy—each parish a unit in the circle of a diocese, and each diocese a unit of the universal Church of Rome. Once into his review of the Code of Canon Law, the antecedent hit him: the power of one man to batter the doors of corruption as Martin Luther had done in launching the Protestant Reformation. The insight began flashing as phone calls came from young men in New Iberia who had seen "Mr. Minos" on television. They knew things about Gauthe, some wondering if they, too, could sue for what he'd done to them back then. Simon said no, that the statute of limitations prescribed one year to file suit, unless you were a minor. But the names of others who had been molested by Gauthe in the seventies strengthened Simon's hand in accusing the diocese of longstanding negligence. A taping system recorded the calls. When I read his secretary's transcripts—Simon offering sympathy, each revelation extending a chronology of sexual plunder—the pages gave me chills.

At the Institute of Living, Gauthe was surrounded by schizophrenics, manic depressives, people who defecated on the floor—a world radically different from the House of Affirmation. Others had ready access to the grounds; he did not, because of the specter of criminal charges looming over him. He hated the place. But Ray Mouton had played his card with Stansbury: the facility had to guarantee no freedom of movement. He could have escaped—break a window, hop the fence and, once out, Hartford police would have to track him down. He whiled away hours doing needlepoint, painting, attending therapy sessions, and Mass, which helped, yet saddened him. Some of the younger people on his wing had sexual hangups, looking for action which some of them got. Gauthe moaned to Mouton that he was resisting sex and that even so his psychiatrist was still telling him he was a danger to society! *He still doesn't get it,* Mouton realized.

Gil missed the Affirmation support groups, rooted in religious values. In psychodrama sessions he had confronted himself, working hard to understand pedophilia, a word he had never known in all the years he practiced it. No one in the Lafayette chancery had wanted him indicted; but the Hartford way station averted further trouble for Bishop Frey. On his trip to Gulfport, Gauthe had found a house he wanted to rent, not far from the Frey compound in Bay St. Louis. He had called a couple of kids in Louisiana after the job was secured; he had been looking forward to Gulfport.

The daily cost for Gauthe's treatment in Hopedale was $90; in Hartford it was $300, excluding consultations with his physician and any medication—$9000 a month at a minimum. The diocese paid his expenses not covered by insurance. But Gauthe's ties to the church now existed mainly in the person of his attorney, who tried to console his client. Sometimes Mouton's warmhearted assistant, Cecile Cook, would take the calls and listen sympathetically, offering friendship and messages of hope.

In September 1984, Nathan Stansbury made his move with reporters unaware. In Abbeville, he met in a conference room of the Sonnier and Hebert law firm with eleven boys, one by one, ranging in age from nine to seventeen. After a year of therapy, some had new words in their vocabularies. With a video cameraman, Stansbury interviewed each boy alone. "Did Father Gilbert Gauthe engage in sexual contact with you?" "Yes." "Did he put his penis in your mouth?" "Yes." And so on. No child was present when the prosecutor screened tapes for the grand jury in Lafayette, which returned a thirty-four-count indictment on October 18, 1984.

Eleven counts were aggravated crimes against nature; eleven of committing sexually immoral acts; eleven of taking pornographic photographs of juveniles; and a single count of aggravated rape—sodomizing a child under twelve. The children were not identified. Mouton knew the indictment was coming. When Judge Lucien Bertrand issued the arrest warrant, Mouton was in Manhattan, en route to fetch Gauthe. He was relieved. The bill of particulars could have been longer, leaving less room for a plea bargain.

A man called Mouton's office, threatening to kill the lawyer and Gauthe. Similar threats were lodged at Channel 10. Mouton kept an unlisted home number but by late afternoon his wife Janis was worried. Alex Larroque called twice, offering any assistance the chancery might provide. Nathan Stansbury told Mouton, "When they call threatening to kill it's usually a bluff. The ones who're serious don't call first. You will have protection."

Janis Mouton was concerned about Chad, the middle child, a seventh-grader at St. Thomas More who had been harassed by classmates calling his old man a pervert and other names. A good-sized kid who played football, he had come home in tears. Early the next morning Ray called, explaining to his son in gentle tones that he had a job to do. Chad Mouton was nobody's fool. "I know you're a lawyer." Gently, his father told him, "We have a constitution, son, and Father Gauthe has the right to a defense. That's one of the major differences between America and most other countries. Sometimes it's difficult. Father Gauthe is a nice man. He's also a very sick man."

Securing Gauthe's release from the Institute involved a thicket of legal problems. Before they would release him, hospital officials needed assurance that they would not be liable if he committed suicide or escaped in transit. In their opinion, Gauthe—sedated, depressive, paranoid about jail—was incompetent to give such assurances. After a series of calls between Stansbury, Judge Bertrand, physicians at the Institute, and attorneys, Mouton drafted an agreement entrusting Gauthe to the custody of himself and two Louisiana deputy sheriffs waiting at the Hartford Hilton. They flew to Houston on a late flight, then drove to Lafayette, five hours in an unmarked car, arriving October 24 at 3:45 A.M. From the outskirts of town three squad cars escorted them on the final leg.

Surrounded by police, Nathan Stansbury, wearing blue jeans with a pistol on his hip, met them at the criminal justice building. Uniformed men formed a wedge, sweeping lawyer and priest into the building and onto an elevator which stopped at the cellblock on the fifth floor. For more than a year Stansbury had wanted Gauthe in his corral. Now he had him. As they walked down the last corridor to the cell, Stansbury's scorn turned to pity as Gauthe tremulously withdrew a cigarette, searching for a match. Stansbury handed him a lighter. "You can keep this."

"Thanks."

"See you in court."

When the prosecutor's footsteps emptied down the hall, the prisoner asked Mouton, "How long will I be in jail?"

"A week. Maybe two. Trust me: you'll get through this." He had to be arraigned on criminal charges and give civil depositions to Simon and Raul Bencomo, after which Stansbury had agreed to let him return to Hartford until the trial. A weary Mouton said, "I've gotta get home now, Gil."

Five hours later, at 9 A.M., in a courtroom bulging with journalists and spectators, Mouton and Gauthe, flanked by police, entered via the back elevator. Gauthe looked away from the crowd; Judge Bertrand read the charges. Mouton entered a plea of not guilty by reason of insanity. The hearing lasted three minutes.

With Gauthe back in his cell, Mouton met with Stansbury. Their dealings had been smooth; Mouton wanted to keep it that way. He was exhausted and had work backed up in his office.

"I want you to carry a message to the bishop," Stansbury said brusquely. "The other night vice squad officers apprehended Father Tom Bathay* for soliciting sex in the men's room of a truck stop outside town. He was not charged. That's the second time this has happened with him. You tell the bishop that if it happens again Bathay's ass is going to jail."

Mouton was dumfounded.

In his cell Gauthe could hear the cathedral bells tolling bleakly. A woman parishioner from Abbeville visited him, bringing fruit and needlepoint. Before leaving for Affirmation he had alluded to things he had done, and she had forgiven him. In prison that day he did not tell her that he had molested her son too —but then, she didn't ask.

He was at the end of a wing for female prisoners. After the nightly news, metal bars began banging, punctuated by obscenities and screams—*"You no-good white trash . . . out on the street, raping children."* He begged God for mercy.

Thirty miles away in Henry, the Gastal boy slept soundly for the first time in months.

ii.

After a lawsuit is filed, months and even years can pass while attorneys question prospective witnesses, under oath, gathering pretrial evidence. This is called the discovery phase of litigation. Minos Simon used it like a battering ram.

His strategy differed dramatically from that of Bencomo and Hebert, who held to a tight definition of their clients' interests: preserve anonymity and go for the insurers' deep pocket. Simon was going for the same pocket, only many fathoms deeper. With expanding research tentacles, his case rested on a startling premise: that church officials not only had prior knowledge of Gauthe's crimes but that they also tolerated active homosexuality among other priests in the diocese. Although sexual activity between consenting adults was a far cry from child molesting, Simon was bent on proving systemic negligence on the part of church officials who failed to enforce canonical codes that demanded celibacy.

At Mouton's request, Gauthe's deposition was scheduled for Lafayette prison on October 31. In late afternoon the day before, Simon's secretary informed Mouton that Judge Sue Fontenot (whose campaign Simon had generously sup-

ported) had ordered the depositions changed to Simon's office. The next morning, when he saw TV cameras in the parking lot, Mouton knew why.

Gauthe would be deposed in the afternoon. In the foyer, Mouton introduced
himself to Glenn and Faye Gastal, who eyed him with the wariness of rural folk
for city lawyers. "I have a boy about the age of your son," he said soothingly.
"We'll get through this the right way."

Lawyers and churchmen filed in; the group moved to Simon's conference
room. The Gastals sat at the long table opposite attorney Tom Rayer for the
church, and Charles Schmidt III and Gordon Johnson representing insurance
firms. Larroque watched as Monsignor Richard Mouton was sworn in, across from
J. Minos Simon.

Simon established that Monsignor Mouton's responsibility was to report complaints about priests to the chancery. Then he said: "Is my recollection correct
that at one point Christ said, 'Suffer little children to come unto me'? "

"He said that, yes."

Simon asked if that was considered doctrinal teaching. Mouton answered: "Of
course, the remainder of the text is: 'For such is the Kingdom of Heaven,' referring not simply to the physical child but to the childhood that all of us as such
have to enter the Kingdom, as He clarifies elsewhere." Glenn Gastal sat in his
chair, scornful of the priest composing his answers, hungry for one of the cigarettes he and his wife smoked incessantly.

"And what," continued Simon, "is 'childlike' in this context?"

"There are a number of attributes generally given by those who concern
themselves with text," said the Abbeville pastor. "Openness, for instance—docil-
ity; humility; dependence."

"It typifies innocence, a pristine personality?"

"I think innocence could very well be a quality of 'childlike,' as well," the
priest replied.

"Does the church, then, officially recognize these qualities in little children?"

"When you say 'church,' Mr. Simon, again we have to distinguish. Is there any
official teaching with regard to that? No. St. Augustine points out: 'Their members are innocent but not their wills.' In other words, their appearance is one of
innocence, but not their wills. They can be terribly rebellious."

"And misled?"

"Easily."

"Vulnerable?"

"Very."

Then the lawyer focused on responsibility in the levels of the hierarchy by
use of a soily metaphor. "You are the first pit stop in the process of bringing a
complaint to the bishop's attention?"

"That is correct."

"And you're telling us today that you have no written guidelines as to how
you're going to handle those complaints?"

"No."

"I have information to the contrary."

Ray Mouton thought he might be bluffing.

Minos Simon was reading from Scripture. "Leviticus 20, paragraph 13: 'If a

man also lie with mankind as he lieth with a woman, both of them have committed an abomination and they shall surely be put to death. Their blood shall be
upon them.' Have you ever read that?"

"Yes, sir."

"Do you understand that to be speaking about homosexuality?"

"Yes, sir."

"I now have Romans, first chapter, 26 and 27: 'For this cause God gave them
up to vile affections: for even their women did change their natural usage into
that which is against nature. And likewise also the men, leaving the natural use of
the woman and burned in their lust, one toward another, men with men.' It speaks
of lust. Do you think that has to be a necessary ingredient, or do you say it can
exist with or without an affection?"

"Well, I certainly think this: that a lot of people would call sexual activity
between two members of the same sex, regardless of affection, as homosexuality."

Midway through the deposition Glenn Gastal bolted the room, muttering
under his breath. Faye followed him into the hall.

Simon elicited testimony that in 1976 two parents had complained to Monsignor Mouton about Gauthe kissing their sons. Simon also asked why Bishop Frey
gave Gauthe his own parish in Henry in 1977. "He asked me one question," the
monsignor replied. "Had there been any other incidents?" And the pastor said no.

"And you never made any inquiry as to this potential for sexual misbehavior
either by talking to [Gauthe], or by talking to the lay people, the parents, or even
to the altar boys?"

"That is correct, sir. I tend, just personally, not to remember these things
about people. I don't gossip. And I know you are going to think I'm just saying
that. But it's the gospel truth. As a priest I am trained to forget people's sins. We
do that through our confession. That, for me, easily transfers over to a priest who
I know is as human as I am; who can fall, just like I can, and who needs help, just
like I do. But Father Gauthe had his problem. I tried to be paternal towards him,
not some person cutting him."

"Did you know he had sexually abused children in New Iberia?"

"Yes, sir."

Gauthe had been in New Iberia in 1974. Then Simon advanced a question
that would transform the scope of my investigation. Was Monsignor Mouton
aware "that complaints of sexual abuse of children" were lodged against a Father
Lane Fontenot?

"I do not have that knowledge. No, sir."

"Had you heard about it?"

"I had heard about it. Yes, sir."

"Wasn't he with Father Gauthe in New Iberia at the time?"

"I do not know, sir."

Minos is getting information from someone very close to the church, Ray Mouton
thought. Larroque had never mentioned a Lane Fontenot. Simon then asked for
the names of two other priests who had been reported to Monsignor Mouton for
homosexual conduct—making no reference to abuse of children. Archdiocesan
counsel Rayer instructed Monsignor Mouton not to answer. "The rights of privacy of these individuals would be seriously impaired, without what appears to us

to be any relevance to this litigation," said Rayer. "Now perhaps, Mr. Simon, if you want to ask him other questions about these individuals, without direct personal identification, I don't think we have any objection."

Simon asked if the two complaints about homosexual activity of priests had been confirmed. Monsignor Mouton said the diocese investigated one complaint and discovered "there was nothing to it. It was spurious." Of the second complaint Mouton said he knew nothing, and with that the morning deposition was done.

After lunch, as Ray Mouton sat in the foyer, the door swung open and two policemen swept in with Gauthe, whose head was down to avoid cameras. Mouton pushed a cameraman out while officers barred the door; he took Gauthe into an empty room. Gil wore a dark blazer with white shirt and dark tie. He was shaking. "I want a Coke, Ray."

"Sit here. Do not leave this room." When he returned with the drink Gauthe fell onto the floor. Mouton put him back in the seat and knelt on one knee next to his client. "Are you sedated?"

"The prison doctor gave me a Valium to calm me down."

"You're really calmed down."

Gauthe asked why cameras were outside the building.

"They're there because they're there. It's something you'll have to get used to."

Gauthe asked if the Gastal boy was present; Mouton said no.

Entering the conference room, Gauthe ducked his eyes to avoid the Gastals, who now sat across from him, glaring.

Ray Mouton and Minos Simon retreated to the latter's private office. Behind his chair hung the picture of a yacht and on his desk rested a bronze horse, hooves high, next to a nameplate with large letters. "Awright, Minos. I won't mess with the Fifth Amendment. You can have the truth."

"What do you want in return?"

"I don't want you trying to punish my man. Let the Court punish him." Simon had no problem with that. Gauthe still faced a deposition with Bencomo on the four new cases he and Hebert had pending. Once that interrogation was done, Mouton wanted Gauthe back in Hartford. Simon posed no objection. "The deal I want," Mouton said, "is that you do not fuck with my criminal case. If you jump on TV and start hollerin' about Gauthe's guilt, it won't work."

They shook hands and returned to the conference room.

Simon began by honing in on Gauthe's background. After a year at Immaculata Junior Seminary in Lafayette, he went to Notre Dame, the major seminary in New Orleans. Four years later he was ordained. From 1971 through mid-1973 he was assistant pastor in Broussard, a community of sugar plantations outside Lafayette. There, Gauthe testified, he had molested four boys. He had lived alone in the rectory; the pastor, an elderly Dutchman named Joseph Kemps, had lived in his own house. On a 1973 parish picnic, two parents confronted Gauthe about his activity with their sons. "With their help," he said, "I went in for psychiatric help."

That help consisted of six to eight sessions with a Lafayette psychologist, which Gauthe said that he had not reported to his superiors. Later in 1973 he moved to a parish in New Iberia, where he lived with the Rev. Joseph Bourque, the pastor, and two other clerics. "No priest ever confronted me," he said.

"You were aware that parents complained to Father Bourque?"

"No, sir."

And the priests never asked why he brought children to sleep with him? "No, sir. We lived separate lives." Simon asked him to name the children or parents of other victims in Henry besides the Gastal boy with whom he had had sexual encounters. Twenty-one names were blacked out of the transcript that I read.

Never uttering the word "pedophilia," Minos Simon asked about other priests "involved in homosexuality"—of which Gauthe professed no knowledge. Did he not know that Lane Fontenot was one of them? "No, sir, I don't. He's never talked to me and nobody has ever accused him."

Simon asked where he had met Fontenot. "The priests would get together several times during the year for studies and courses at various places. I know that we met at St. Peter's in New Iberia several times—I really don't remember."

"Was he carrying out his priestly duties at the time that you're talking about now?"

"I have no idea."

Simon asked Gauthe to identify his New Iberia victims. Gauthe balked. "Well, let me recite some names," said Simon, "and you tell me if you recognize them." As Simon began naming them—sixteen in all—Ray Mouton was astounded. *Where did he get this stuff?* Gauthe answered "Yes" to five names, and "No" or "I don't remember" to the others.

"Was the bishop aware of what you were doing?"

"I don't know."

Transferred to Abbeville in 1976, Gauthe lived in the rectory with Monsignor Mouton, Father Glenn Provost, who had since become rector of St. John Cathedral, and an elderly priest who was retired. Children from New Iberia visited him there. "They would come in late at night, leave early in the morning."

He said the diocese paid for his therapy after the 1976 kissing incident. In December 1977, Frey appointed him pastor in Henry. Simon: "He never asked if you were doing better, not doing better—never made any inquiry as to your therapy?"

"Not that I can remember."

Simon ran through a litany of sexual acts, extracting names and details. Asked about the total number of victims, Gauthe said, "It would be possibly thirty-five, thirty-six, thirty-seven, something like that."

When it was over Mouton led Gauthe into the sheriff's vehicle with cameras recording their departure in pictures that would be shown on local reports and national broadcasts over the next four years. Two days later Simon offered Channel 10 audio tapes of Gauthe's deposition. Jim Baronet declined, opting for a report by Dee Stanley citing the transcripts.

As Christmas, 1984, neared, Ray Mouton's defense of Gauthe was beset with problems. Nathan Stansbury wanted a term of life imprisonment. Simon apparently had someone feeding him information from inside the church. Frey and Larroque had still refused to level with parishioners at Henry.

Mouton was dejected about these developments when a priest who had known his family for years invited him to dinner at a restaurant. Afterward, the two men sat in the rectory. Father spoke warmly of Mouton's parents, brothers, and sisters, and wistfully recalled Ray's years as an altar boy. "Good men," said the padre, "are made of good families." The priest told him he was proud of the job he was doing, defending Gauthe. It took courage. Mouton thanked him.

"It's bad, Ray. The days of the jocks are over. You're looking at the last of the jocks."

"They're all queer—is that what you're telling me?"

"I can't tell you that. But it's bad. You're doing the right thing." The priest handed him a wooden crucifix. "I want you to have this. My mother gave it to me when I was ordained."

Mouton thanked him but refused the gift. "No," insisted the older man, pressing the cross into his palms. "You take it."

The priest murmured a blessing, then said: "Remember, your job on earth is to please *Him*"—he pointed to a picture of Jesus on the wall—"please *Him*, not *them*."

"Can't you just give me some facts?"

"You'll understand. Just keep the cross with you. Let there be a desert, because from the desert a flower of faith can grow."

The next afternoon Mouton was angry. Let a flower bloom in the desert: why wouldn't he give me facts? Larroque had twice asked him to call a Father Michael Peterson, who was supposed to be a psychiatrist somewhere in Maryland. Miffed by evasions all around, Mouton had purposely not called Peterson. Sitting in his office, with the crucifix on his desk, he felt the old Catholic guilt and placed the call to St. Luke Institute. After an exchange of pleasantries, Peterson asked about Gauthe, his past, the patterns of sexual addiction. Mouton was impressed. Then the line of questioning made an abrupt turn, resembling that of an attorney. Peterson wanted to know about the diocese. How was it run? What were Larroque's specific duties? Finally Mouton said: "What interest do you have in these things?"

Peterson wanted background on the local community and how the church had been perceived before the indictment. Well, Mouton averred, the depositions contained an awful lot on both.

"What depositions?"

Had he not read news accounts of the testimony by Gauthe and Monsignor Richard Mouton? Apologetically, Peterson explained that he had only just learned of the situation. So Mouton briefed him and promised to send copies of the two transcripts. Peterson asked about Gauthe's diagnosis at the House of Affirmation.

Mouton said that he was considered "an abnormally adjusted prepubescent male, sexually and emotionally."

"That's horseshit."

This guy is real, thought Mouton, who still cringed when he thought of Affirmation's plan to let Gauthe work in Gulfport. Then Mouton began asking questions of a general nature about pedophilia, and Peterson's answers convinced him that he knew the territory. "Father, I think I would like to meet with you."

They agreed to a meeting on January 25, 1985.

iii.

By New Year's, 1985, Simon had received no copies of diocesan insurance policies that he had requested in September. On January 3, Judge Bradford Ware presided at a hearing to address Simon's motion to compel the defense to provide information on the policies.

No attorney for the defense showed up.

Ware issued an order to the defense to answer the questions. Simon filed a motion to hold the church in contempt, buttressed by letters to Robert Leake and other lawyers demanding $300 for his January 3 appearance. The money was paid. Why would a bevy of New Orleans attorneys, with millions of dollars at risk, fail to send a single counsel to Abbeville, or ask the judge to postpone the hearing?

Rayer, the only Catholic among those attorneys, secured an order delaying testimony by Monsignor Larroque, hoping that a negotiated settlement would obviate such testimony. But the botched hearing of January 3 and the continued absence of insurance policies were like red flags fanning in front of a bullish Minos Simon, who was convinced they were stonewalling. As the order staying Larroque's deposition moved toward eclipse, Simon, who still had received no insurance policies, issued a subpoena for Bishop Frey.

Raymond Blanco had prevailed upon Bob Wright to represent the bishop. Wright asked Bob Leake, point man for the insurance defense, to stipulate liability—the legal phrase for accepting financial responsibility for the damage caused by Gauthe. That would halt Simon's discovery, leaving the amount of money to be negotiated. Bishop Frey wanted to stop the interrogations, stanch the news flow, pay claims, and start binding the wounds.

Ray Mouton also wanted to stop Simon's fusillade. His original strategy had been to portray the boys, their families, and the diocese as victims of Gauthe's pathological crimes—and finally, Gauthe himself as the victim of a terrible illness.

But Leake rejected Bob Wright's arguments. The majority of the $4.2 million paid in the Hebert-Bencomo claims had come from insurance coffers. Leake was holding fast to a standard insurance defense: delay, put as much distance as possible between the time of injury and settlement, and push for a lower loss. Accepting liability could open a Pandora's box. How many victims were out there? Those under eighteen had a year to file suit from the time parents learned of the injury. A ten-year-old might not tell his parents for several years.

Simon wanted answers from Frey and Larroque. And so to Simon's office they went on January 18, 1985, Leake, Wright, Ray Mouton, four attorneys representing insurers. In the foyer Mouton took coffee with the Gastals, chatting about Christmas gifts and kids. Then a large figure lumbered through the door, extended his hand to Glenn Gastal, and said: "Bishop Frey." Gastal stared fiercely, refusing to shake hands. The bitterness building over months hung like acid rain between the two men of different social stations. "*Fine,*" said the bishop. "If that's the way you want it"—and entered the conference room. Mouton shrank in embarrassment. Why hadn't Frey gone the extra mile and made a more conciliatory gesture? Gauthe had torn the Gastal boy's rectum. He wanted to grab Frey and shake him by the shoulders.

Larroque was sworn in. Simon asked for the insurance documents. Larroque said he did not have them. "Well," said Simon, "it's in plain language in the notice and subpoena that was served. Can you tell us why you do not have these?"

"I would presume that would have been taken care of by counsel."

Leake said they had no objection to furnishing them.

"Well, when are you going to furnish? I wanted them today."

"Well," replied Leake tartly, "I just don't have them today. I'll be glad to get them together for you promptly, if that's agreeable. If that's not agreeable I'll get them to you within thirty days."

Offended over the dilatory tactics, Simon snapped: "You don't think a subpoena is effective?"

"I'm sure it probably is. I have never seen the subpoena."

"You're counsel and I assume you have access to the records and your client—"

Leake cut him off: "I'll be glad to furnish the policy."

Larroque had studied canon law at Catholic University of America from 1962 through 1965. Simon asked if he was the "legal adviser" of the bishop. "On matters of church law," he answered.

Simon asked about the complaint process regarding sexual misconduct of a clergyman. Larroque said his role was "simply to report it to the bishop." Under canon law a serious crime involving a cleric is called a delict. As vicar-general, Larroque stated, he was "bound to discuss all complaints with the bishop." Most were handled informally, by privately interviewing the parties involved.

Larroque's answers went further, raising the curtain on an inner sanctum of church jurisprudence. He spoke of an investigative procedure for matters of serious moral transgressions—"a church court [whose] membership is composed of priests who are assigned to the position of judges, defenders, advocates. They determine the facts. The penalty would usually be stated in the law. The bishop sets up the court."

Simon asked if Larroque kept a record after a complaint was investigated. Answer: "I imagine they're usually kept." Simon asked where. Larroque: "In the files."

"In the personnel file or file of the individual priest?"

"It could be either."

"Your communication to the bishop is in writing?"

"Not necessarily."

"The gravity [of the act] has nothing to do with that?"

"No, sir."

"Who is in charge of keeping those records of complaints?"

"They are part of the chancery files."

"Your files?"

"The diocesan files, that is right."

Simon asked how many church courts had been convened in the past. "I have been in the office since 1965," said Larroque, "and, to the best of my knowledge, there has never been a formal investigation [or] judicial procedure."

Simon had established a key point. Monsignor Mouton knew Gauthe had had problems in 1974 and 1976. Why then hadn't the bishop convened a canonical court in 1983 to question Gauthe when he was suspended? With discovery powers of their own, chancery officials might have confirmed names of children as Paul Hebert had asked. They could have approached the families discreetly, offered therapy, and conceivably stopped the litigation train.

Larroque told Simon that Gauthe was never put on probation or made to face any sort of ecclesiastical censure in response to various allegations made against him.

"You're telling me that Father Bourque [in 1975] never communicated any complaints about Gauthe in New Iberia?"

"Not to me."

"Are you aware today that he did engage in sexual molestation of young boys while he was in New Iberia?"

"I have no direct knowledge of that," said Larroque, contradicting Monsignor Mouton.

"Who would have that knowledge?"

"The bishop."

Simon asked Larroque to review a letter, dated April 5, 1980, obtained under subpoena from Gauthe's diocesan file. (Roman type indicates words underlined in the original.)

> *Dear Bishop Frey:*
>
> *In view of hearsay that Father Gilbert Gauthe was taken out of New Iberia and then put on probation, we as parishioners of St. John Parish in Henry believe that it* was [sic] *our duty to report to you his progress—if any. We hope that you will read all of our letter and regret that we have to write this.*
>
> *When Father Gauthe came to Henry, he seemed to fit in fine, but when he became settled, he slowly became less and less seen around Henry. At the beginning, some Henry boys would sleep over at his house and things were going great. Then it came to where it was just Abbeville boys sleeping over at his house. Once the Abbeville boys were caught* playing on the roof of the rectory and Father wasn't there. Father *even took an Abbeville boy* out of school three times to go help him fix his *camp. At the camp is where Father stays constantly. A member of the community died when Father was taking a rest (trapping in the marsh) and almost not found. Whenever we want him we have to contact the sheriff to see where he is. . . . The other day he took four days off for a rest. When he came back from trapping in the marsh, he was more tired than when he left.*
>
> *Many adults are finding it increasingly difficult to be wholehearted about their religious faith. . . . It is with the deepest regret that we send this letter, but with the highest hope that God will answer our prayers by allowing us to become better Christians by giving us a better model to follow. It is very difficult indeed for Catholics to denounce their own Priest, but in the interest of putting an end to this before it is too late, we implore of you to at least examine in such a manner as would be less harmful to all parties involved.*
>
> *Sincerely,*
> *Concerned Parishioners [sic] of St. Johns Parish*

The letter, said Simon, referred to Gauthe having "young boys to his camp, sleeping overnight. Is that an acceptable behavior for a priest?"

"Yes, sir."

"So that type of intimate relationship between priest and young altar boys is acceptable conduct approved by the church?"

Leake interjected: "Are you referring to that which is stated in the letter?"

"I'll refer to the letter when I am speaking of it," Simon said. "I'm referring in general right now." Leake demanded that the question be made "more categorical." Simon would not budge: "I have done that." He asked Larroque: "Sleeping overnight with young boys—that's not disapproved by the church, is it?"

Protecting his client, Leake objected: "What do you mean, 'sleeping overnight with young boys'? That is not what the letter says."

"It doesn't make any difference what the letter says."

"Tell me what you're talking about."

"Mr. Leake, why don't you stop being so damned obstructive?"

"We apologize."

Larroque said: "It would not be unusual to have young people or adults sleep in the rectory. It would be unusual for people to sleep in the priest's apartment. There are guest rooms."

Was the parishioners' letter investigated? "I can only presume it was," said Larroque, adding that the files had no record of an inquiry. "I really don't know what the disposition was."

"Who would know?"

"I presume the bishop."

Simon asked when Larroque had met with Dr. David Rees, the psychiatrist who counseled Gauthe in 1976. Answer: After Gauthe's 1983 suspension. Why only then? Larroque: "Particularly to learn whether or not there had been received recommendations that we did not know about. To determine whether or not there could have been something obvious that we were overlooking."

"You were also trying to raise a defense against those [legal] claims, by using this doctor?"

"The lawyers were not involved."

"No, I'm talking about you—the lawyer for the church."

"Well then," put in Bob Wright, "we raise the lawyer-client privilege. You're putting him in the position of a lawyer."

"Nobody has to instruct me from the blind side," Simon huffed. "I know what kind of lawyer he is."

"You are suggesting that he's trying to build a 'defense,' " Wright hammered. "Your suggestion is wrong."

"Absolutely," said Simon in a swift aboutface.

"Let him assert his privilege," insisted Wright.

Simon went on, telling Larroque: "Mr. Wright has indicated what he thinks you should do. Do you have any alternative answer?"

"The church was not involved internally in church law in any defense," Larroque testified.

"Monsignor, there has been, has there not, to the church's knowledge, evidence from time to time involving sexual abnormality of some of the priests in the diocese?"

"Yes, sir."

"So these tendencies are a reality and were a reality in the Lafayette diocese—"

"And the world," interjected Bob Wright.

"—previous to the occurrence of the Gauthe matter, is that right?" concluded Simon.

"Yes, sir."

"Does the church have records of these instances?"

"Records in the sense of written documents? I don't know."

"If you have knowledge of abnormal sexual behavior of a priest and make no record of it, you die the next day and are the only one who knows—how would the church know that the person coming into contact with young people has this tendency?"

"I don't know. A person would die with it."

Bishop Frey was deposed after lunch. Again Simon requested copies of the insurance policies, which Frey said he did not have. "Is that because no documents exist," asked Simon, "or because they were otherwise produced?"

"Well, I assume that Monsignor Larroque was the one who was asked to bring the documents, which he did," Frey said, although he had been present in the morning when Larroque denied having them.

Frey discussed the selection of pastors. A personnel board of priests made recommendations but the bishop had the final word. Of Gauthe's 1973 transfer to New Iberia, Frey stated: "He was changed from Broussard, as I recall, because there was some controversy regarding canefield workers and [sugar] mill operators. He and the pastor were at odds. Two sisters there were also heavily involved, trying to organize the field workers. [Gauthe] sort of took their side. And it just became uncomfortable for him and the pastor."

"So you made a judgment in the interest of the church to transfer him?"

"That's right."

"Was there any reprimand in any way associated with that?"

"There was no need for a reprimand. It was a conflict of personalities, which happens every day, somewhere, somehow."

Questioned further, Frey said that more than a year later a man "told me that he was counseling a boy from Broussard and it came out that [the boy had] had a homosexual contact with Gauthe. So I called [Gauthe] in and discussed this with him. He's a very plausible person, as you may have found out. He said it was something that he had been sorry for; he was taking counseling and was sure it would never happen again. This is the only complaint I had during that period of his stay in New Iberia."

Who had told him this? Said Frey: "I don't know the person. I just bumped into him one day—a layman."

Frey said that he had received no complaint from the New Iberia pastor, Father Bourque. Of the decision to send Gauthe to Henry, Frey said that after the 1976 incident Monsignor Mouton, as pastor in Gauthe's church, had had nothing further to report. (Monsignor Mouton, however, in his deposition by Simon on October 31, had stated that the monitoring of Gauthe "was being done on the diocesan level," a reference to chancery officials.)

Simon continued: "You heard the questions I asked Monsignor Larroque about [Gauthe's] association with young boys and sleeping overnight at the rectory and camping places. Would your answers be substantially the same as Monsignor Larroque?"

"I think he made an important distinction. Many people would think it normal for the priest to be interested in the young people of the parish, CYO, Boy Scouts. It happens frequently that they go on camping trips. That I do not think unusual."

"Well, how about sleeping overnight in the rectory?"

"Well, it depends on where they sleep and on the reason, I guess. I was never told too much about the sleeping business. Normally, I would certainly not approve."

Simon asked if there was a special procedure designed to "guard against homosexual activity" by priests. The bishop said: "We operate on the assumption that ninety percent of our priests are very sincere, committed men, freely giving of their time and effort to the spiritual services of the people. And when an instance comes up where this is proven not to be true, we try to handle it immediately. If a man has a problem and is unsuited for the priesthood, then they leave."

Simon said he had information from Wisconsin, Idaho, and Pennsylvania of similar abuse cases. Did the church pool such information in an organized manner? Frey did not answer directly, saying that the church provided therapy to priests who "have the same psychiatric problems that are current today in our society."

Again, Simon asked about an "information pool." Frey said there was none and added: "But for a priest to leave a diocese and be accepted elsewhere, he has to get the recommendation from the bishop [he is] leaving."

Simon asked if there was a program to oversee "the priest in his relationship with young people." To which Bob Wright objected: "It's irrelevant, immaterial, and inadmissible."

But Bishop Frey insisted on speaking. "It's very important to understand that the church, which is deeply interested in the spiritual welfare of the people, is well aware of the enormity of this problem. We give instructions or information for eliminating these things as much as possible. We do what we can. I personally find this sort of thing absolutely despicable. I feel very deeply for the parents. And I certainly want to do everything I can to avoid it occurring within this diocese. I don't need to be urged to do that. That's my responsibility."

"I can understand that," said Simon. "I'm making inquiry."

However penetrating his probe, Simon failed to ask Bishop Frey about the 1980 letter from the Henry parishioners, and he never mentioned Lane Fontenot.

On February 27, 1985, Raul Bencomo took Frey's deposition on behalf of his clients, and asked about the 1980 letter. "It's very difficult to give credence to an anonymous letter," said Frey. "I get them about all kinds of things all the time." He referred it to assistants, "who reported back to me that—you know, it's a mixture of all kinds of complaints, many of them very superficial . . . nothing of a serious nature against Father Gauthe."

Larroque's answers to Simon about record keeping sent me to *The Code of Canon Law.* In the fourth century A.D. Roman civil law served as the model for church canons, with aspects of the canons also derived from Scripture. Penalties for violating celibacy stem from the Sixth Commandment—"Thou shalt not commit adultery"—and are cited in eighteen canons. Early bishops were concerned about priests who lived with unmarried women. Canon 1395 also states:

A cleric who remains in another external sin against the Sixth Commandment . . .
which produces scandal is to be punished with a suspension; and if such a cleric
persists in such an offense after having been admonished, other penalties can be added
gradually including dismissal from the clerical state.

This canon also states that a clerical offense

with force or threats or publicly or with a minor below the age of sixteen . . . is to
be punished with just penalties, including dismissal from the clerical state if the case
warrants it.

Twice reported for sexual misconduct, Gauthe had not produced "scandal"—
i.e., something public—until 1983. But his abusive behavior was persistent. Canon
392 reads:

Since the bishop must defend the unity of the universal Church, he is bound to foster
the discipline which is common to the whole Church, and so press for observance of
all ecclesiastical laws. He is bound to insure that abuses do not creep into ecclesiasti-
cal discipline. . . .

Reading further, I remembered Paul Hebert's frustration at vainly seeking to
have Larroque (who acted in the bishop's absence) canvass altar boy families.
Canon 398 is a model of simplicity: "The Bishop is to endeavour to make his
pastoral visitation with due diligence." Frey had yet to go to Henry.

The policy of record keeping was contained in Canon 489.

1. In the diocesan curia there is also to be kept a secret archive, or at least in the
ordinary archive there is to be a safe or cabinet, which is securely closed and bolted
and which cannot be removed. In this archive documents which are to be kept under
secrecy are to be the most carefully guarded.

2. Each year documents of criminal cases concerning moral matters are to be
destroyed whenever the guilty parties have died, or ten years have elapsed since a
condemnatory sentence concluded the affair. A short summary of the facts is to be
kept, together with the text of the definitive judgment.

The week after Frey and Larroque were deposed, Simon filed a notice to take
new depositions on

The existence and prevalence of homosexual activities . . . involving members
of the clergy, church personnel and seminarians inter se and with others, of the
Immaculata Seminary situated in Lafayette since 1970 to the time Immaculata was
discontinued.

He requested information on the "presence or absence of any security system"
designed to prevent abuses and protect youngsters. The sweeping discovery re-

quest demanded chancery records on treatment, therapy, or evaluation for any sexual aberrations among twenty-seven diocesan priests—all identified by name—between 1970 and 1985. Simon entered the document in the courthouse record. No church attorney moved to have it barred from public scrutiny. The list included two of the four priests whom Larroque had identified as members of the canonical court, which had never been convened. Lane Fontenot's name was also on the list.

V.

Sexual Outcasts

On March 12, 1985, I sat in the Abbeville courthouse as Simon and insurance counsel Bob Leake clashed over the list of twenty-seven priests whose personnel files Simon had requested.

Having failed to persuade the state Supreme Court to rescind Ted Campbell's $30,000 settlement, Simon was turning the Gastals' suit into a legal firestorm. The courtly Leake told Judge Bradford Ware that Simon's demands were "a hunting license to pore through records that might exist. Whether they exist, I can't say. Where is the legitimacy? The inquiry into private lives unrelated to Gauthe does not seem to us appropriate."

"We wouldn't be here today," drawled the judge, "if attorneys for the defense had been in court in January"—referring to the day when no defense attorney appeared for a scheduled hearing with Simon over production of insurance documents. Ware had been mild in his chastisement of Leake on that score.

"The failure is self-evident," Simon declared. "I submit there can't be a clearer case of contempt."

But the issue at hand was personnel files. Ware took the matter under advisement, which gave Leake some breathing room.

Dee Stanley of Channel 10 and I followed the lawyers at a polite distance as they left the courthouse. I asked Stanley if he had investigated the list of twenty-seven priests. He said no; Gauthe was one of many stories he covered. News director Jim Baronet was concerned that Simon wanted to manipulate their coverage. "When it gets to a court hearing, and not just a motion, then it's news," said Stanley.

"Minos has got to have a source," I said. "That document is too explicit. How'd he get names of twenty-seven priests?"

"I'm sure Minos does have a mole somewhere in the chancery."

Leake declined to comment and left. After Stanley finished his interview with Simon and left for Lafayette, the lawyer and I sat on a bench in the tree-lined square. I asked if innocent people might be hurt by appearing on the list. Simon cocked an eyebrow: "Innocent people? My li'l client was sodomized. The purpose of my discovery is to make the church institutionally liable. I'm showing that homosexuality is a fact of life in the church and that they did nothing to protect those kids."

"You must have someone feeding you stuff from the inside."

He sat stone-faced, speaking in deep baritone: "There is an awareness within ranks of the enormity of deception, the hypocrisy that has occurred in these matters."

I asked if his source would be willing to let me do an interview with complete assurance of anonymity. "I don't know about that," he pondered. "I could ask. I don't know what the answer will be. If his name comes out he'll be in deep trouble."

"I would never reveal his name—even under subpoena."

"They'd never do that," he growled. "They can't afford to."

On April 8, Simon and Leake were back in Abbeville, arguing over the files on twenty-seven priests. Leake claimed that disclosure would violate separation of church and state. Simon boomed: "We deal here with a violation of secular law. Church immunity does not apply. Once you get into that area, all parties stand on equal footing."

Judge Ware—"Bumpy" in the old boy network of Cajun politics—had shown unwavering lenience to the defense. Now he telegraphed a message to Leake: "I don't think the church is entitled to any privilege. 'Relevancy' is the key word."

"The sexual conduct of priests," Simon thundered, "is the risk-creating factor resulting in harm to plaintiffs' child. We believe those records will disclose instances of homosexuality for the last twelve to fifteen years. We must establish the existence of this, hence the risk factor. They failed to create a safeguard and let it proceed with full knowledge."

Leake attacked the list of twenty-seven as "indictment by innuendo."

"I still have not heard why counsel did not come forth in January regarding Mr. Simon's interrogatories," the judge remarked of the January 3 hearing that defense attorneys missed. "It rather aggravates me that the church has taken this position."

"Evidently we had too many lawyers working the case," Leake replied lamely. "Some knew about it; others didn't. Otherwise, I can only apologize to the Court."

Ware asked Simon for a brief on the personnel files, allowing Leake to explore his options. But time was running short.

If certain priests were homosexuals, I did not see it as my role to expose them. But Simon's list had to be checked on other grounds. "If other priests are pedophiles," *Times of Acadiana* editor Linda Matys insisted, "then parents of this community have a right to know." And if Simon was on a witch hunt we would expose him.

I began calling child abuse caseworkers and personal injury attorneys, asking about allegations against other priests. A lawyer with no involvement in the Gauthe suits discussed the second man on Simon's list, Lane Fontenot: "He was almost a carbon copy of Gauthe. He got young boys in Sunset and Lafayette to sleep with him. This went on for years." The source had knowledge of one family; however, they would not talk. "The Catholic Church's tentacles reach so far into all of this," he continued. "After the Gilbert Gauthe mess, they don't want a repeat of Minos Simon. They're in a quagmire, up to their neck."

Prosecutor Nathan Stansbury had no knowledge of Fontenot. But he volunteered information on another priest, one Robert Limoges. In 1984 a man from the town of Eunice told Stansbury that Limoges had molested his son. "It was not his wish to press charges," said Stansbury. "The guy was upset. I told him there was nothing I could do without someone to press charges. I sensed he wanted to get it off his chest."

A source in Eunice described Limoges as "a law-and-order type"—a police chaplain who, like Gauthe, "had a beeper and would ride through town in patrol cars. He wanted people to call him Skipper. He had a big problem with authority. He wanted people to obey him." In the public library I found an informal history of St. Anthony Parish in Eunice for which Limoges had written an autobiographical sketch. Born August 27, 1930, in Terrebonne County, Quebec, he was nicknamed Skipper as a Boy Scout. "My father's first spouse died in 1927 after bearing five children. He remarried a year later and had six more children." Along the way, the familial fabric became frayed. "I found myself in the roughest orphanage of Montreal, run by the Grey Nuns."

> *It was during my short stay there that I felt called to the Holy Priesthood (age 11). I was given the duty to assist our chaplain in the distribution of Holy Communion every morning at 6 A.M., going to the old women's floor, then to the old men's floor, carrying a lit candle all the while. I was 14 and decided to start earning my keep.*

But the priesthood's call was delayed by years of disparate jobs—grocery clerk, knitting mills worker, lumberjack, private investigator, policeman, service in the Canadian Air Force in France, England, and North Africa. Not until 1979 was he ordained, at age forty-nine, after a B.A. from St. Bernard College in Alabama, and studies at Notre Dame in New Orleans and St. Mark's in Union, Kentucky. Why had it taken him so many years to enter seminary? Of his first parish, St. Anthony's in Eunice, he wrote: "I feel very much at home in the Diocese of Lafayette which adopted me two years ago. My heart is truly Acadian."

In Eunice he lodged emotional complaints about sex education classes in public schools. In 1982, Bishop Frey transferred him to a black parish in tiny Loreauville, where he got along poorly with people. He longed for Eunice, where a family had befriended him. Stansbury referred me to another prosecutor, who explained that on a camping trip with youngsters Limoges made advances to a boy, who told his parents. "A priest was immediately called into that family," he continued, "and within an hour Limoges was in Larroque's office. They packed him off right away. The family wasn't coerced. It was handled quietly." The story was confirmed by a third attorney, who represented the family. The *Official Catholic Directory* listed him as "absent, on sick leave."

"What is *wrong* with this diocese?" Linda Matys moaned. The editor's incredulity matched my own. Each night I drove the twenty-two miles from Lafayette to Abbeville, where my wife and I were staying at her mother's home. Lisa and I decided that while there it was best not to discuss findings. Her father, a prominent attorney, died when she was fourteen; her mother was a devout Catholic already troubled by the scandal. I cherished the sprawling kinship of the LeBlanc family. The aunts would gather, doting over our four-month-old daughter and reminiscing about branches of the ancestral family tree. And there was J. B. Broussard, a charming old neighbor and cowboy in his youth who turned the mobile, causing sweet music and plastic animals to revolve over the baby. There was a tenderness in those moments that soothed my spirit. At night Lisa and I spoke about what it meant to profess faith in a town where neither of us felt comfortable attending Mass at the local church.

Her family had deep roots in the local church. One great-uncle was a Canadian priest who settled in Abbeville and after the fire of 1907 rebuilt Mary Magdalen Church on the land it occupies today. Her grandmother salvaged Confederate bills from the burning rectory, using them in later years to make paper dolls for her children. Lisa's father had done free legal work for the parish when Alex Larroque was pastor. As a girl she played the organ for weddings and Christmas midnight Mass. When the church was empty she composed songs with her favorite cousin, a girl who laced guitar lines through Lisa's organ chords. Such memories clashed with the sense that something had gone terribly wrong with the church of her youth.

ii.

Bishop Frey testified that he had transferred Gauthe to New Iberia in 1973 because of a dispute in Broussard, where he had run afoul of the pastor by siding with two nuns "who were pushing the cause of the [sugar cane] field workers."

I located the sisters in another state. They explained that Gauthe *opposed* their activism and sided with the sugar planters. But that had not been their only concern. One afternoon the young priest called a boy out of class in the parochial school. "God forgive me for what I thought when [the boy] returned to class and I saw that expression on his face," one sister told me. They made a rule never to allow children to leave school grounds for the rectory. "If most people were like me," she continued, "when they became suspicious, they were afraid to falsely accuse. I noticed how he'd have little boys spend Friday and Saturday nights in the rectory. I thought, how inappropriate—but also how sad, that a man would depend on the companionship of children. The more I worried about it, I felt caught between my growing suspicion and the need to bring the matter to others."

The nun said Father Kemps—the pastor—"had utter disrespect" for Gauthe and grumbled about "his theology being so shallow—that Gauthe was not smart and did not get good seminary training."

Rev. Vincent O'Connell had worked with the sisters during the field workers' struggle for better wages. A second nun said that back in Broussard she had asked O'Connell about Gauthe's seeming problem with children and "he responded in such a way as to imply that the rumors were true. I presumed Gauthe's change in assignment [to New Iberia] was one way in which the bishop was handling the situation."

I found O'Connell in New Orleans, a tough-minded realist and former labor organizer, now working with housing activists for the poor. On a drowsy April morning, sipping coffee in a house he shared with several other members of the Marist order, he confirmed that Gauthe had threatened the labor organizing in Broussard but denied knowing "anything about personal acts of Gauthe. But he never should have been ordained. I knew he had a problem. He was looked upon as being gay by the other priests." Then he checked himself. "I don't know of it being reported at all. The only thing I was concerned with was keeping him out of the [labor] situation. You couldn't trust him."

"You don't know about his spending time with boys?"

"No. I doubt if many knew he was. Those in authority, what they knew, I don't know."

Father Kemps, who might have known, was deceased. I asked why O'Connell thought Gauthe never should have been ordained. "His theology was weak." Then how had he graduated from seminary? O'Connell didn't know. But he was concerned about the new generation of priests. In 1968, after Gauthe left Immaculata for major studies in New Orleans, O'Connell became interim rector of the Lafayette seminary. The previous rector "started to drink. It was too much for him." O'Connell found a community split by personality disputes and questions of discipline. Age was one problem: older seminarians taking courses at USL had greater freedom than those of high school age. "There was no uniformity of policy, and six or seven ideas about [seminarians'] formation. Too much was going on—priests talking to other priests, in the chancery, taking the linen outside."

O'Connell, who had entered a Pennsylvania seminary in 1926, saw complex issues at work. Young men required more than spiritual attention. If a seminarian showed signs of stress, "he needed a psychiatrist for direction." Maurice Schexnayder, bishop of Lafayette in 1968, resisted the idea. O'Connell threatened to resign. "I told him it was too important to run the institution without that resource. The faculty agreed. It was obvious that, besides the normal emotional development of students, there were two main appetites. One was food and drink; the other is called sex, but it's really the appetite for procreation. When this is not allowed in normal circumstances, it must be dealt with."

Schexnayder relented. O'Connell hired a psychiatrist. Six seminarians were dismissed for showing homosexual proclivities. The next year O'Connell left to resume his work as a labor priest. "This tendency," he frowned, "of having people who are homosexually inclined come to seminary has increased God knows how much. Back when I was coming up, ninety percent of them were more masculine; we played football, handball. There was a noisy, rowdy spirit, full of pep. For [priests] fifty or older, you find a feeling that there are too many expressions of effeminate action and tastes among younger priests. This is a generalization. But without any hesitation, I can say it's a real problem."

"Why do you think this has happened?"

He shook his head. "It seems to be more *acceptable*. I'm not taking sides on the gay movement; but who would have ever thought, even in the open town of New Orleans, that a gay community would be recognized? In 1940, if you even identified yourself in any way whatsoever, you were on the skids. But you have this mentality. I'm not judging it: that's too complicated. I have no idea what is *the* reason—biologic, genetic?—but it is a hazard in the priesthood. You take the ordinary priest in his fifties, sixties, seventies—the guy was down to earth, we knew who he was. He had difficulties, as every human being had, in trying to live the celibate life. But you knew, ninety-nine times out of one hundred, that if he was going to give in to his emotional desires, and if it reached the point of having sexual relations, it would be with a woman."

Immaculata closed in 1977. I asked why.

"Lack of vocations."

He reminded me of priests I had known as a youth; a little gruff, but forthright and open-hearted. I asked what the Gauthe situation meant to him. His brow wrinkled. "It's sad to think that he, who was ordained to serve the people, would do so much harm. That is the horrible part about it—to have a persistent pattern, especially with youngsters. Jesus said that it is better to have a millstone tied around one's neck than to do harm to little children. I don't know anything from the inside, but it seems to me there is too much concern about what it's going to cost the church financially. This has to do with lives, and alleviating the pain with therapy for those who have suffered. And the moral therapy that's needed for families that have been afflicted. That is the key concern."

Not long after the interview with O'Connell I met with Glenn and Faye Gastal at their house in Henry. She was slender, with clear features and short brown hair; he was short, wiry, with dark hair. Said Glenn Gastal: "This whole neighborhood has a doubt in their minds [as to what Gauthe did] and ones who won't face it. I'm talking about people I wouldn't wanna hurt. The ones that settled their cases tried to explain to others, and some of 'em have been kicked out of homes."

"Just for bringing up the subject?"

They both nodded. "People don't want to face those that's seen the problem," Glenn brooded. "And we're not talkin' about parents, either. Maybe a grandchild was involved, maybe a nephew. It's like a black cloud hanging over you that's just going to fall on you any damn minute."

Their feed store, said Faye, had gone out of business.

"Because of your lawsuit?"

"Well, we can't prove it," she said. "After we went public, people just quit coming." Just then the door opened and three girls spilled in, followed by the boy who had been abused. The moment he saw me his eyes widened. He scampered to his mother's side. "Not now, son," she said. "Daddy and Momma are talking." The boy followed his sisters, but in another moment he was back in the room, waiting and watching. Said Glenn: "Y'all go play outside now. We talkin'." The children went outside. I smiled, watching him bound across the lawn. "How's he doing?"

"Some days not so bad." She sighed. "It used to be a lot worse. He's doing better now that he's seeing Dr. LeCorgne. But he still has nightmares. Paces the floor, gets in bed with us when he's scared. He slept real good when they brought Gauthe back for the indictment, knowing he was in jail."

They were only too glad when Simon said that the boy should cease therapy with Ken Bouillion, who, they felt, had not helped them strengthen ties with their son. Simon wanted a therapist untainted by the situation and paid for the boy's sessions with Lyle LeCorgne. The parents felt that their son was improving.

"I think the bishop oughta be put in jail," said Glenn.

Bishop Frey had not spoken at the parish since Gauthe's removal. The Gastals lived ten miles from the little church, now a spiritual abscess in their lives. Bitter, broke, scorned by some members of the community, they were locked in a legal system that was in no special hurry to settle the $12.5 million tort that consumed their existence.

For days I thought about the boy, hovering on the edges of his parents' conversation with a reporter, knowing that he was our topic. What about families who had not reckoned with Gauthe's impact on their young? Glenn Gastal's "black cloud" lingered in my thoughts. I placed a call to Dr. David Finkelhor, author of *Sexually Victimized Children* and *Child Sexual Abuse*, at the University of New Hampshire. "The evidence is better on girls than on boys," he explained. "We know from studies that twenty to twenty-five percent of sexually victimized girls show severe mental health impairments in the absence of treatment—depression, flashbacks, suicide attempts, psychosis. With boys there are more responses to stress: alcoholism, aggression, the possibility of homosexuality. Long-term impacts are inevitable.

"But let me caution you on interpretations. It is entirely possible that some of the children who become involved are pre-homosexual to start with. Research on homosexuality shows that there are early developmental factors—pre-utero and genetic factors. Some pre-homosexual boys could possibly enjoy the closeness. I'm speculating. But the fact that someone has been victimized does not mean that they were [homosexually] predisposed."

He had a hard-nosed attitude toward offenders. "People who have been involved with children have massive denial systems, and a difficulty in getting voluntary treatment. The only way seems to be prosecution. I think they should go to jail."

Finkelhor echoed the sentiments of countless prosecutors who were being faced with child abuse cases in record numbers. As reports poured out of the national media, a great fear was on the rise. In the McMartin preschool case near Los Angeles, seven adults had been indicted for scores of sexual crimes in what would become the longest and most costly criminal trial in California history. Meanwhile, in tiny Jordan, Minnesota, a county prosecutor was pursuing indictments of parents accused of engaging in a sexual ring with children.*

My next call was to Dr. John Money, a medical psychologist at Johns Hopkins University Hospital in Baltimore. He listened carefully to my explanation of the Vermilion situation. Then he said: "We have the potential for a witch hunt in sex abuse and child abuse. We will become so hysterical that people will be afraid to go into professions that deal with children. I know of a case in Piedmont country [West Virginia] where a boy suffering from ear and throat infections was

---

* The Jordan case later collapsed because of sloppy work by an overzealous prosecutor. An investigation by the *Minnesota Star and Tribune* concluded that key witnesses among the children exaggerated claims which became allegations. In 1986, all but two of the defendants in the McMartin case had charges against them dropped. The final two were later acquitted. In both cases, defense lawyers attacked therapists who treated the youngsters as coaching them for testimony; some therapists were later sued for civil damages. In both cases, prosecutory problems and absolved defendants disheartened certain parents and many child abuse specialists, who were convinced that true crimes went unpunished.

examined; the doctor asked him to cough and held his scrotum. This eleven-year-old told his parents the doctor played with him. The doctor was eventually cleared but his career was ruined."

But in this case, I explained, a priest had admitted abusing many children. What kind of impact could one expect on the community? "The number one trauma for children is a Catch-22," said Money. "Respect for the church and parents precludes their ever [discussing the abuse], so they have no escape. Kids are coerced into desperation because society has found no way to deal with them."

"This priest," I said, "claims he's not a homosexual."

"Of course not," said Money. "He's a pedophile."

Money had volumes to say, and was amenable to a long interview if I could get to Baltimore.

Intrigued by the deposition findings, Tom Fox of NCR agreed to cover my expenses for a research trip to Washington. Before leaving I met with Ray Mouton, whose normal ebullience was subdued. "Gilbert is complaining about the *food* now. I tell him it's worse in prison. You notice how pedophiles are so *narcissistic?* The self-obsession sometimes staggers me. Nathan's talkin' September for the trial."

"Have you found your shrink for expert testimony?"

"I found a guy who understands the illness *and* the church. He's brilliant." Mouton crumpled an empty cigarette pack and lit a new Winston. "Put a Roman collar up there and a Cajun jury thinks, *Mais, how can a priest know so much about dat wacko sex?"*

"You've got a priest who understands pedophilia?"

"There's more to it than that."

With assurance that I would not write of it until after the trial, he outlined his predicament. His early libel threat against the *Times-Picayune* had halted big city media. If he could prepare his defense with solid expert witnesses, then the chances of a plea bargain improved. He wanted to portray the church as one of Gauthe's many victims, and Gauthe, finally, as a victim of his own illness. Simon had foiled his media containment strategy by keeping the Gastal suit on local television. Then the testimony by Frey and Larroque, admitting prior knowledge of Gauthe's sexual acts, had dwarfed his strategy of portraying the church as a victim of Gauthe's secret deeds. Now, in the constellation of attorneys surrounding the church, Bob Wright advised the bishop, Bob Leake ran the insurance defense, and Mouton—the only Catholic—was odd man out. My story was rising from depositions that Mouton felt might have been prevented. When I asked about Robert Limoges, he shook his head. "Jesus Christ . . . another one."

In locating a priest who "understands the illness," Mouton had cast his net on wider waters. This priest obviously had connections. "I can't give you details now," he said, popping a Diet Coke, "but I want you to understand that what this diocese has done, the failure and stupidity here, is of serious concern to higher officials of the Roman Catholic Church. If you don't try an end run on me, I believe I can lead you to men who will talk about those concerns and their efforts to stop the scandal."

"When?"

"After Gilbert's trial."

Realizing that Mouton would reveal his activities in his own good time, I flew to Washington. The *National Catholic Reporter* office was on the twelfth floor of the National Press Building. Bureau chief Arthur Jones, an affable chap with glasses and thinning silver hair, listened over lunch at the Press Club as I laid out the story. Money's remark about Gauthe being a pedophile, not a homosexual, was an important distinction, Jones said. "But your contact Father O'Connell is onto a deeper tale, I do believe. Homosexuality in the priesthood is the biggest problem to face the church in years—much larger than most people suspect. The hierarchy hasn't a clue how to deal with it."

In his travels Jones visited parishes to chat with priests, nuns, lay workers; he had written about the loneliness of rectory life, how priests in an age of declining vocations yearned for fellowship of years past. Still, he said, "I'm bullish on the church. There's an awful lot under this big tent, y'know."

I had just read of a case in Thousand Oaks, California. Suits on behalf of four children had been filed against Father Patrick Roemer, who received psychiatric treatment in lieu of a prison sentence. I asked Jones if there might be a church official in Washington, monitoring such cases, willing to talk on background. "There might be," he chuckled, "but I doubt he'll talk. The real story should be told from legal documents. That's why your stuff is unique. It opens a window we don't often find."

I also called U. S. Catholic Conference spokesman Russell Shaw and asked about pedophilia cases. "We're just trying in a slightly disorganized way to find out what the information is," he said. "The general counsel is following the legal side. There's no report or document under way. Nobody here is soliciting information from the grass roots." I mentioned the Boise judge's remark about the church "having atonement of its own to do." Shaw claimed no knowledge of that case or the one in California. But he made passing reference to "the situation in Rhode Island."

A call to the *Providence Journal-Bulletin* yielded press clips. In Bristol, sixty-three-year-old Rev. William O'Connell (no relation to the New Orleans priest) had been charged with twenty-two counts of sexual molestation more than two years after a concerned mother reported him to Bishop Louis Gelineau of Providence. Like Gauthe, O'Connell had allegedly taken pornograhic photographs. And Gelineau—like Bishop Frey and Father Baltazar's superiors in Idaho—had failed to take safeguards despite warnings from lay people. A suit against the Los Angeles archdiocese stated that Roemer "several times informed various counselors, psychologists, and other [church] personnel" of his tendencies.

In Baltimore I took a taxi from the train station to the Johns Hopkins medical complex, where John Money worked with aberrations of human sexuality that would cause most people to recoil. Money approached his subject with the zest of a sailing enthusiast who enjoys brisk winds on the open sea. In the 1940s, as a young psychologist in his native New Zealand, Money had counseled a woman suffering from hallucinations who was scheduled for a lobotomy. In therapy she spoke of things she had written; Money read the material and recommended her to a publisher. The lobotomy was canceled. When Money left at age twenty-seven for the United States, she had won a literary prize and become a *cause célèbre*.

At Harvard, Money studied birth defects of sex organs. In 1951 he transferred to Hopkins, where he founded the Office of Psychohormonal Research and developed the concept of gender identity—the process by which human beings acquire their sense of being male or female. Money argued that a society's attitudes toward sexual behavior are shaped by cultural patterns. In a primitive Oceanian tribe pubertal boys would split off, engaging in homogenital sex before returning to the community to sire children and live as heterosexuals—a process considered decadent by Judeo-Christian values.

Money's research also focused on the role of hormones and brain cells that govern sexual behavior. This is known as psychoendocrinology. As a founder of the Gender Identity Clinic at Hopkins hospital, Money counseled men seeking sex change operations. In 1979, Dr. Jon K. Meyer, a conservative Freudian psychiatrist at the hospital, published a paper attacking the surgical practice and Money's advocacy. The two had a bitter feud. The operations were discontinued; however, Money—described by Mark Bowden of the *Baltimore Sun* as a "leveller of sexual taboos [and] an avowed bisexual"—never flinched and continued publishing articles and books.

In the 1980s Money was writing about paraphilia, the medical term for forty forms of aberrant sexual behavior. "Deviant" was not in his lexicon. His writing ranged across the dark terrain of pedophilia, voyeurism, exhibitionism, zoophilia (bestiality), and other disorders.

A taut man with gray-brown hair and wire-rim glasses, Dr. Money wore khaki pants, boots, a faded work shirt with thin tie, and a roll of keys on his belt. His foyer was lined with books and masks and totems from Africa and New Guinea. I had become a devotee of animist art on a 1983 trip to West Africa. "That's a beautiful Songe mask," I said. "Zaire pieces are so powerful."

"Mm. You collect?"

"Much more modestly."

He ushered me into his office: more books, more masks. The value of animist art is determined by age and rarity; collectors gauge each object by ritual use, its function in the religious ceremonies. Faces and forms of tribal memory surrounded Money in his work with broken sexual beings.

I asked about Gauthe's statement that he was not a homosexual. "It was his attempt to clarify something," Money replied matter-of-factly. "He doesn't have sex with other men, frequent gay bars, or identify himself as gay. Most pedophiles I've come across are people who fall in love with young people. There's something distinctly childlike in pedophiles. Psychosexual age does not keep pace with chronological age."

From the shelf behind his desk he withdrew a book, *J. M. Barrie and the Lost Boys: The Love Story That Gave Birth to Peter Pan.* "James Barrie," said Dr. Money, "was a pedophile."

"The guy who wrote *Peter Pan?*"

"That's right. And Lewis Carroll [author of *Alice in Wonderland*] was a pedophile who took photographs. It's not documented that he had body contact, but Barrie I believe did, based on peripheral information. He was the boy who never grew up; a spooky character, tragic, really, but a great contributor to civilization."

A wave of sadness swept through me—the innocence of childhood tales, suddenly soiled. Gauthe's obsession with photographs began to make sense: another form of stimulation.

"I've known pedophiles who destroyed [pornography] collections," Money continued. "They make gigantic resolutions to clean the slate, but after a few weeks or months they backslide. Collectors also destroy pictures under threat of disclosure. The remarkable thing is that they assemble so much incriminating evidence, like minutely kept diaries. You find this in all paraphilia, meticulous record keeping and total obliviousness, an attitude of incredible omnipotence. It has a lot to do with the Dr. Jekyll-Mr. Hyde association—a flight from the normal to an altered state of consciousness, like a fugue state."

I began to understand what Ray Mouton had meant in telling me that Gauthe "had no power to stop himself. Sexually he was out of control."

Pedophilia is a disorder that Money likened to "an aborted method of retaining lust in your life. It's always a one-sided love affair, and so a desperate searching. This explains the extraordinary repetitiveness of the [seduction] rituals. Many pedophiles can achieve orgasm ten times a day, which points to the central nervous system, something firing down the prostate. There's got to be excess fluid—a total functional difference in the way the sexual brain is regulating the sex organs."

Paraphilic sicknesses stem from a distorted love map, Money's metaphor for the defacing of an individual's psychosexual blueprint early in life. A person molested as a child can carry more than psychological scars; as victims advance into adulthood, for some (though by no means all) the imprinted memories of the abuse cause them to search for sexual gratification with children about the age they were when the love map was warped. The animist art that lined Money's room formed a vivid analogue: deface a carefully carved mask and the defiled visage is abused of its intended spiritual essence.

He had no use for David Finkelhor's law-and-order approach. "If you put a pedophile in jail there's not a chance he'll grow up and learn to love a woman of his own age. With a lust murderer you have no choice. If you have a pedophile who doesn't physically hurt children, we have to ask ourselves: What is better for society? Because when they get out they'll do it again. Every pedophile I know in jail says the fantasies drive them wild. It costs $40,000 a year to incarcerate a prisoner in Maryland. It's an awful lot cheaper on an outpatient basis."

Did Money think any pedophile should be incarcerated? "No. I think society should be educated about sexual illnesses."

Pedophilia has become a catchall phrase to describe child molesters; however, many do not fit the strict clinical classification of an adult sexually fixated on prepubescent children. Adults who sexually molest older adolescents are called ephebophiles. The distinction becomes more difficult when there is a narrow age gap between sexual partners. Is a twenty-three-year-old man in a consensual relationship with a seventeen-year-old girl accurately called an ephebophile? The root factor is victimization. An adult who molests a youngster abuses the trust on which the young rely in forming their values and ethics. As for Gauthe, although some of his victims were teenage boys, most were younger, prepubescent boys. Clearly, he was a pedophile.

Society, through the courts and social service agencies (such as they are), tries to protect children. The Hopkins program, prevention-based, tried to help sex offenders gain control.

The Sexual Disorders Clinic was under the direction of Dr. Fred Berlin, a psychiatrist who also had a Ph.D. in psychology. "People do not decide voluntarily what will arouse them sexually," Berlin had written. "Biology, too, can play a role in the development of sexual interests." In a study of forty-one men suffering from sexual disorders—the majority were either pedophiles or exhibitionists—Berlin found that twenty-nine of them had biochemical abnormalities. At the Sexual Disorders Clinic, he wrote, it was

> unusual to see a man who experiences recurrent pedophilic cravings in the absence of (a) a significant biological abnormality, (b) a past history of sexual involvements with an adult, or (c) both. . . .
>
> Diagnosing a person as a pedophile says something about the nature of his sexual desires and orientation. It says nothing whatsoever, however, about his temperament, or about traits of character (such as kindness versus cruelty, caring versus uncaring, sensitive versus insensitive, and so on). Thus, a diagnosis of pedophilia does not necessarily mean that a person is lacking in conscience, diminished in intellectual capabilities, or somehow "characterogically flawed." In evaluating a person who has become sexually involved with a child, one needs to try to determine whether the behavior in question was a reflection of (a) psychosis, (b) poor judgment and psychological immaturity, (c) lack of conscience, (d) diminished intellect, (e) intoxication, (f) a pedophilic sexual orientation, or (g) a combination of these plus other factors. One needs to evaluate independently the nature of an individual's sexual drives and interests, as opposed to what the person is like in terms of character, intellect, temperament, and other mental capacities.

Of men treated in the Sexual Disorders Clinic's outpatient program, said Dr. Berlin's assistant, Maggie Ryder, "most either come from extremely deprived beginnings—poverty, trauma, sexual activity imprinted too early—or you find biological problems, like brain damage."

John Money had been a pioneering advocate of Depo-Provera (medroxyprogesterone acetate), a synthetic hormone whose effect has been erroneously likened to chemical castration. Literature of the Sexual Disorders Clinic called Depo-Provera "a sexual appetite suppressant." Long used in Europe on sex offenders in lieu of surgical castration, Depo-Provera works on testosterone, the male hormone carrying messages from the brain to the genitals. Perhaps its strongest impact is its reputed ability to uproot mental imagery of children (or women, in the case of rapists) as erotic stimuli. It had not been approved by the U. S. Food and Drug Administration; however, that did not mean it was outlawed.

Under Berlin, the Sexual Disorders Clinic was treating about 150 pedophiles on an outpatient basis, with serious offenders in a restricted ward. These included serial rapists, facing long prison terms, who were receiving Depo-Provera injections and undergoing group therapy. Staffers who worked with these sex offenders used their findings to further research in the field.

Recidivism rates of offenders treated at the clinic were less than twenty percent—remarkable in light of the addictive syndrome. In the outpatient program, several priests and rabbis had been treated in the past. Average outpatient treatment included individual and group therapy. This lasted two years, several times a week initially, then lessening. About thirty-five percent received injections of Depo-Provera. It had potential side effects: weight gain, increased blood pressure, nightmares, hot flashes, cold sweats, muscle cramps, fatigue, lowered sperm count, blood clotting. A physician had to prescribe it. Patients signed a consent form, which said: "Depo-Provera has also been found to increase the frequency of malignant breast tumors in female beagle dogs and of uterine cancer in female monkeys. There have been no reports of this drug causing cancer in men."

Administrator Maggie Ryder said of the effect of the drug: "It takes a long time for a man's sex drive to return. The biggest thing is that it does quiet down the mental imagery. There's a slow increase in the sex drive after Depo is halted. Some can be weaned off it. Others will be on it for most of their lives." And for those not on the drug? "It's a question of whatever it takes to avoid temptation. For some it's smell, or TV shows, or avoiding playgrounds." I thought of the old Baltimore catechism admonition, to avoid the near occasion of sin.

As a female contraceptive, Depo-Provera had sparked controversy as a possible carcinogen; however, some U.S. physicians still prescribed it. Villa Louis Martin, a church treatment center in Jemez Springs, New Mexico, used Depo-Provera for certain clergy. (A Wisconsin prosecutor sent me a copy of the consent form priests had to sign.) VLM was run by Servants of the Paraclete, a monastic order founded in the 1940s to assist troubled clergy. Rev. Michael Foley, the director, refused to be interviewed.

But a consulting psychiatrist, Dr. Jay Feierman, testifying at the Idaho hearing of Father Baltazar, stated: "We try to get them not to act on their sexuality, and that's what's so hard."

The Vatican has condemned birth control devices. Yet here were priests taking a synthetic hormone that was not only a female contraceptive but that radically altered a man's sexual chemistry. How could such a drug be morally sanctioned? The Rev. Richard McCormick, S.J., an ethicist then at Georgetown University, told me in a telephone interview: "I'm presuming it's voluntary use of drugs. If it's for the overall good of the person, it's justifiable."

Back in Louisiana, seeking further insights, I called a Jesuit psychiatrist in Boston, who was unavailable; his secretary referred me to Father Michael Peterson, a psychiatrist at a clergy hospital in Maryland. He said that his program used Depo-Provera. I asked about moral implications. "I was a psychiatrist before I became a priest so I view these things in medical terms," he said. "Your question is based on an acceptance of *Humanae Vitae* [the 1968 papal encyclical on birth control]. I never bought that. Did you?"

"Well, no."

"Where did you go to college?"

"Georgetown."

"I taught at the medical school. When did you graduate?"

"Nineteen seventy-one."

"Did you demonstrate against the Vietnam War?"

"Yeah."

"Good for you!"

I laughed. "Tell me about pedophilia, Father Peterson."

"My impression when I came in as a clergyman was that priests are ill prepared for everyday life, especially for their own problems. Before Vatican II priests were supposedly perfect. We were not supposed to have sexual feelings. So suddenly, in the last few years, sexual abuse of children has emerged as a national issue. Let's put it in some perspective. Most pedophiles are parents: this seems to happen mostly in families. It's difficult to get good data, though, because so much of it is unreported. We've only begun to get a true picture. Imagine you're a bishop and someone says, 'This priest molested my boy.' He thinks, *I can't believe it*. It's that kind of milieu.

"I deal almost exclusively with chemically dependent clergy," he continued. "I'm amazed at the numbers who were abused as children. That's not dissimilar when viewed against pedophilia. The church is as perplexed about this as society. Sex is such a difficult area for the church to talk about."

Did these cases reflect pressures caused by celibacy? "It's not a problem of celibacy. It's a problem in early childhood. They may not be aware of the proclivity till they're older. I'm quite sure biological factors are involved as well. In my opinion, the only way to try and understand if a man is well motivated, a good role model, is to live with him. Get to know him in a religious environment, see how he interacts."

The next morning Ray Mouton's voice exploded through the coils of South Central Bell: *"I told you not to go behind my back!"*

"What are you talking about?"

"Why the hell did you call Michael Peterson?"

"Why the hell not? Am I supposed to get a request form from you for my interviews? A lady in Boston gave me his name."

"See you next year, Berry."

"Oh, come off it."

Shortly thereafter, over a drink, Mouton explained that Dr. Peterson was the priest he was considering as an expert witness. *Use him*, I said: the guy was fantastic. Mouton shook his head. "Nathan will get him to talk about degenerate priests, the jury will go gaga, and Gilbert gets life in the pen."

I realized that Peterson was giving him valuable advice. Mouton was such a mercurial man; I was never sure when to press for information or tilt to an innocuous subject like bullfighting. He asked about my impressions of the Johns Hopkins program, confiding that Peterson had suggested Dr. Fred Berlin as an expert witness in Gauthe's behalf. Peterson also wanted Gauthe on Depo-Provera and asked to have him sent to St. Luke. But Mouton needed a court order to get Gauthe there. "Peterson does brain tests on each patient, and I sure would like to know what Gilbert's brain is like."

"How'd you hook up with Peterson?"

He paused. "I will tell you if you agree not to use it in print before the trial." I gave him my word.

"Peterson treats more than alcoholics." Bishops were calling the priest-psychiatrist for advice as abuse cases erupted.

"Kind of an emergency politician?" I said.

He nodded. "The hierarchy hasn't felt the legal weight yet. They look at Louisiana as a management disaster but they have no idea of the financial repercussions. Bencomo and Hebert got huge sums and lawyers around the country know that."

Then everything tilted. A *Dallas Morning News* editor called Linda Matys inquiring about Gauthe. His paper had received depositions of the Gastal case with an anonymous cover letter accusing the Catholic Church of a cover-up. The letter was addressed to the *Washington Post*, CBS, and a dozen other news agencies. Dallas was sending a reporter to Lafayette.

"They can't scoop us," Linda said reassuringly. "You've worked two and a half months. Any reporter will need at least a week just to figure out where the pieces fit. But I think you better start writing."

The only person I knew of with a motive for sending out the depositions was the source feeding information to Minos Simon. I telephoned the lawyer immediately. "Minos, I have got to talk to the guy."

"I think he's ready."

iii.

"We have to be clear on one thing," Linda Matys insisted. "Whatever this man tells you *must* be substantiated by other sources. We have no way of knowing whether the stuff he gave Simon is legitimate. He could have all kinds of reasons for leaking information. Do you know his name?"

"Not yet."

Linda drew an analogy with the reporting of the Watergate scandal. The identity of Bob Woodward's source, Deep Throat, had been known to reporter Carl Bernstein but to none of the *Washington Post* editors. "I don't need to know your source's name," she said. "If by some chance we get hauled into court I will truthfully testify that I do not know his identity. But I must know that *you* know. If push comes to shove, you'll have to stand on the First Amendment and refuse to reveal your source."

It was not a consoling thought, but such pressure seemed remote. Matys was emphatic: "*Nothing* can be used until you know who he is—and the information checks out." She smiled chipperly. "What's our code name for this clerical whistle blower?"

"The Chalice."

I sat in my cubicle at the paper, reviewing notes, waiting. I ate lunch at my desk, told the receptionist to interrupt any call should a man say he was referred by Minos Simon. The call came at 5 P.M. "I can't talk now," he said in a low voice. "Will you be at this number tonight?"

"Yes. Tell me what time."

"Eight o'clock."

The office was empty when he called that night. I asked if he wanted any assurances about what I planned to do. He said: "I think I have a pretty good idea about what you're going to do."

There was something haunting in those first syllables—a soft, lyrical cadence of the patois: a voice too sweet, in some way, for what he had to say. I tape-recorded the call, took copious notes, and began with the mistake of asking two questions at once: "Besides Gilbert Gauthe, to the best of your knowledge, how many priests have been removed for committing pedophilia acts? I know of Lane Fontenot. Is that correct?"

"Mm-*hmmm*," he said, meaning yes.

"I don't know anything about your background. Have you been a priest?" Answer: "No." I asked about another name on the list. Was Father X a pedophile? Answer: "Yes."

"Do you know how many children were affected?"

"No, I don't have that number. You're asking for specific information that would be quite sheltered."

No lawsuits had been filed against Father X, who Chalice said had been relieved of his post. If the information was correct, this meant four priests had been removed. Yet I had only his word to go on. Father X was now in his early forties. Dripping sarcasm, Chalice said: "From his seminary days he boasted of his conquests of virile males."

"Were these adults or youngsters?"

"Oh, they were all ages."

"How did you become aware of this? Did he boast of it to you?"

"What is the purpose of your question?" he chuckled. "You want to know if it's fact? It's fact."

"Well, it's not that I doubt you but, as you may know, there's a difference between established fact and hearsay. And what someone says he heard—"

"Let's put it this way. It's common knowledge by all priests who were in his class. I was in New Orleans two weeks ago and met up with a priest"—he laughed —"ha-ha, and even *he* knew how active he had been."

He said that Father X had gone to Notre Dame Seminary in New Orleans, but he was not sure if he had gone to Immaculata.

"Is there anyone else who can give me more information?"

"Willing to speak? Oh no, they're scared to death."

What triggered Father X's removal? Chalice said that in 1984 a young man at a retreat had blurted news of his encounters with the priest. The shocked retreat master contacted Bishop Frey. Father X was shipped off for treatment. (A priest later told me that he had gone to Villa Louis Martin in New Mexico.)

Chalice said, "Shit."

"I can tell you've been living with this for a long time."

"Ah, why don't you ask questions? I'm already depressed." Again came the cynical chuckle. Was he enjoying this, or did the laughter cover bottomless contempt? I wanted to keep him talking, and asked about reports on these men in chancery files. He speculated that files had been destroyed but admitted he had no proof. I asked how he knew about these various priests.

"How does someone in the Pentagon know that hammers cost $5000?" he said, not answering the question. I let it pass.

"Obviously, everything you're telling me I am taking down. But I'm going to have to corroborate. . . . I can't just say, 'A source said . . .' I certainly run a risk, as does this newspaper—"

"Of libel. Certainly."

"So I'm trying to find out how you have gotten information."

"It's like a club, my good man. And those in the club share the information with other people."

I asked about Lane Fontenot's departure. "Lane Fontenot got reported by parents in Lafayette and a settlement was made in the hundreds of thousands." Before I could respond, he said: "What percentage, do you think, of priests are gay?"

"Well, my guess would be"—pulling a number out of nowhere, trying to seem in the know—"about forty percent."

"I think you're about thirty percent off. I think sixty to seventy percent."

"Uh, is that based on your knowledge of this diocese and New Orleans?"

"Yes." Homosexuality, he insisted, was intrinsic "to the training." But he had no data to back this up. As he talked on, about youths going into seminary, ignorant of their sexuality, falling prey to older men, I tried to imagine this person, how he knew so much. And how much was true? He mentioned photographs of naked men that had been taken at Immaculata Seminary.

"This is mind-boggling," I said. "Was there much of a concerted effort to address the problem of pedophilia by the bishop, or was it something he just got swamped in?"

"It's the normal practice of the average parish priest who has homosexuality as the pervasive part of his behavior."

"Now wait, we're talking about pedophilia—"

He repeated what he had just said, word for word—an assertion that would not be supported by authorities like Finkelhor, Money, Berlin, or Peterson. But I saw no use in arguing. Chalice's loaded statements seemed to be leading somewhere.

"Because it's easier to get to kids than adults?" I said.

"Right! It's more dangerous—but also more stimulating."

"Who are the other priests who have been removed?"

"How about *recycled*? It's a better word." And then: "Everyone on the list."

"All twenty-seven on the list have been recycled for sexually molesting children?"

"For sexual misconduct. I can't say with children. Those include men only. You haven't touched the mendacity." He went down some of the names—citing drunken sexual outbursts here, a transfer after compromising positions there, angry lovers' quarrels, another priest cruising at night by the bus station, dragged into police headquarters—story upon story accumulating like a tropical depression. I knew that certain specific details could not be used in the newspaper, yet if even half were true, what a picture of clerical life run amok! Why, I asked, had he gone to Minos Simon?

"When I saw him on TV, and what they were doing to him, it offended me."

"Aren't you afraid of getting caught?"

"I'm not by myself in this. I have people in every office and they will go to their graves before they sneeze."

He said he was tired and had to go. "Sure, okay. Uh, look, before I use any of this, I have to know your name."

"Let me think about that."

"Is there some way I can reach you?"

"I will call you. G'bye."

I began calling men who had left Immaculata Seminary before ordination. A businessman in his thirties, who left in 1969, said he had been twice propositioned by older students but did not think it typical of the environment. Said another man, who left a little later on: "I can't say I saw [genital] activity, but homosexuality certainly presented itself. These people were quite different from guys I hung around with growing up."

"Was that why you left?"

"No, it was more the problem with celibacy. I just couldn't live that way."

Through a half dozen other interviews, I found similar reflections. Hints of behavior, suggestions of sexual activity—but not an environment of open promiscuity.

The first five priests I called hung up on me. Then I found a priest who said: "The seminary went through a period when younger priests were getting close to the kids, palsy, a whole different world than when I went through. Later on it got scandalous. A parish priest was sexually involved with younger men. [Pornographic] pictures were found of college-age males." After a period of psychological treatment the priest returned—to live at Immaculata!

How extensive was homosexuality among Lafayette clergy? "It exists. But unless you're one of them, it's hard to say how widespread." Lane Fontenot, he said, "gave youth retreats. He was very outgoing with kids. I was never friendly with him. He had an air of independence, a kind of know-it-all. He worked exclusively with kids."

Another priest knew more. He said that in 1978 Fontenot was living at Our Lady of Mercy in Opelousas. "He molested many kids. I've been told that on certain days he got boys into the rectory and up into his bedroom and molested them." The person who told him was a boy's mother. I asked if they had filed a lawsuit. He said no. I asked if she might agree to an interview, with written assurance that her identity would be concealed.

"No, no. These people are afraid."

Fontenot and Limoges had been identified as pedophiles by three sources each. I still wanted something on paper. I found it in the depositions that Raul Bencomo had taken of Frey and Larroque, on February 27, 1985, as part of his litigation with minor plaintiffs who had not been identified in the media.

Bencomo asked the vicar-general if he had had "occasion to discipline Father Fontenot." Yes, said Larroque, "a little over a year ago." Chalice was right on the date.

"It also involved young children?" Answer: "Yes." And was Fontenot also in a House of Affirmation? "Not any longer," Larroque replied. When Bencomo asked if other priests had been censured for similar offenses prior to June 1983, Larroque said yes, in the early part of that year—fitting the time frame of Limoges's offense, as the two prosecutors had told me. Attorney Wright objected to Bencomo's questions about further identifications.

Bishop Frey testified that Fontenot was suspended.

Bencomo asked why, on October 27, 1975, Frey had appointed Gauthe chaplain of the Lafayette Boy Scouts. "I conducted an inquiry with members of the personnel board, who knew him better than I. And Monsignor [Jude] Speyrer, who was chancellor at the time, assured me that he was the logical choice for the position."

"Why was he the logical choice?"

"Because he had been carrying on the work of the chaplain for a few years prior to [that priest's] resignation."

"Did you at that point say, 'Monsignor Speyrer'—I am paraphrasing—'this man has had a previous homosexual incident with a young man. I don't think we ought to place him in a position where he might sin again'?"

"Speyrer was aware of that," said Frey. "The position does not of itself place the man in contact with Boy Scout troops. He works with Scout chaplains, with the office, things like that. He's not in charge of a troop is what I'm saying."

Speyrer in 1980 had become bishop of Lake Charles, Louisiana.

Bencomo asked why, after the 1976 Abbeville kissing incident, Gauthe was given a parish in Henry, instead of working with the aged or in adult education. Frey was revealing. "The simple answer is that we do not have the luxury of appointing people to be in charge of the aged and these special jobs. We are desperately in need of priests to serve immediate needs of the people."

"Regardless of their qualifications or suitability?"

"I did not say that. Please do not put words in my mouth."

Bencomo also subpoenaed Gauthe's transcript from Notre Dame Seminary. His standing had been assessed by the holy orders review board chairman, Alexander O. Sigur, who had since become pastor of a parish in Lafayette. In a March 10, 1971, document, Sigur wrote:

> *Mr. Gauthe is a "B" student who works hard and gives of himself. He has done pastoral work at Little Flower which has been satisfactory. As a radio ham and Scout leader he has perhaps overextended himself in a compulsive fashion. He shows little humor and worries others. At times he has seemed threatened and not quite with it.* However, he is steady, constant and was ordained Subdeacon January 16, 1971.

On October 11, 1971, Sigur reported the board's unanimous recommendation of Deacon Gauthe:

> *He has worked effectively with the young, sometimes seemingly over-involved but personally assured that his Scouting effort is not a burden, but a help, not a distraction but a development.*
>
> *He is eager to deepen his personal prayer life and his theological depth, to see the joys of the Priesthood not only the anguish, and has found parish experience quite good with his perspective enlarged.*
>
> *The Board acknowledges his honest awareness of some inadequacies, as in theology, his intense interest in performance, but was impressed by his honest self-evaluation.*
>
> *He should make a devoted and hard-working priest for the Diocese of Lafayette.*

His seminary transcript showed that Gauthe failed classes in Ethics, General Metaphysics, Sacrament of Penance, and Human Knowledge of Christ. His 1.5 average put him on academic probation. He twice failed his Master of Divinity exams before passing.

In interviews with former seminarians and faculty who had known Gauthe at Notre Dame, I found no evidence that his sexual proclivities were known. "Gilbert never really hung around anyone in particular," said a former classmate. "He was very popular with families. Gil was really a charismatic person for those kids. It's incredible, the more you think about it."

That a failing student "not quite with it" was ordained testifies to the pressure on seminaries to produce priests. Had he gone through seminary in the early 1950s, when enrollments nationwide were at a record high and intellectual standards more rigorous, it's doubtful he would have lasted. By the early seventies, seminaries were undergoing wrenching changes.

Father Gauthe was no accident of history; he was one product—albeit an extreme one—of a clerical environment that in 1971 had already begun to decay.

vi.

Men in High Places

Washington

The Vatican Embassy—in church parlance, the apostolic nunciature—is a three-story structure of Florentine design across the street from the official residence of the Vice-President of the United States. Built in 1939 when America and the Vatican State did not exchange ambassadors, it was well situated on Massachusetts Avenue's "Embassy Row." In countries where the Vatican has no diplomatic ties, the papal envoy to the nation's church is called the apostolic delegate. Where the church has diplomatic ties, the delegate is called the papal pro-nuncio —Latin for ambassador.

In 1980, Pope John Paul II appointed Pio Laghi, an Italian archbishop fluent in four languages, to Washington's nunciature. Laghi's first posting had been in Nicaragua under the Somoza regime; he subsequently served in India, Jerusalem, and Cyprus. In 1974, Pope Paul VI sent Laghi to Argentina, where the military government paid the salaries of Catholic bishops. The regime systematically tortured and killed thousands of people suspected of leftist or dissident activities. Laghi later called it the "most thankless" task of his career. His name appeared on a hit list of death squads, while human rights activists criticized him for not denouncing generals waging "the dirty war."

In a 1985 *National Catholic Reporter* story from Buenos Aires, correspondent Penny Lernoux wrote that Laghi had spoken "infrequently and ambiguously" about military violence. An Argentine newspaper quoted a 1976 speech he gave to troops: "There are situations in which self-defense sometimes demands positions that can imply a respect for the law as far as is possible." Laghi told Lernoux he was misquoted and actually said "even in extreme circumstances, self-defense must be pursued within the limits of the law."

Whatever his words, Laghi's leverage was negligible. Argentina's conservative bishops in the 1970s criticized Marxist elements, or kept silent—despite the deaths of seventeen priests, nuns, and seminarians. Families of "the disappeared" sought help from Laghi. He told Lernoux that he raised human rights matters at private meetings with Argentine bishops who were not under his control; his comments were not made public. Lernoux wrote:

> *Father Antonio Puigjane, a Capuchin monk who risked his life to work with the families of the disappeared, supports Laghi's claim, recalling Laghi's complaints to him about the indifference of the hierarchy. "For him the bishops were not pastors but lazy people," said Puigjane. "They were not part of the church. Although he had repeatedly requested Bishop (Victorio) Bonamin (the then military vicar) to have an interview with him, Bonamin just ignored him."*
>
> *Puigjane also said Laghi told him, " 'You should be ashamed to be an Argentine and have those military men in the government. I have never encountered more cynical people in all my life.' "*
>
> *Yet Puigjane retains mixed feelings about the nuncio's role. "Knowing what he did, Laghi made no public denunciations, preferring diplomacy, even though such diplomacy was effective complicity because of its silence."*

The Rev. Thomas P. Doyle was incensed by the article. At forty, he was one of four American priests at the Washington nunciature. In 1984, Laghi had assumed ambassadorial rank when the Reagan administration and the Vatican cemented diplomatic relations. Doyle believed that Argentina was a no-win situation for Laghi and thought the article a smear job. But there was not much in *NCR* that Tom Doyle liked. To him the newspaper was marked more by dissent than by fidelity to the church.

Rugged and athletic, Doyle flew airplanes avocationally. He liked Ronald Reagan and believed in a strong military defense. He was the embassy's canon lawyer. He also had a master's in political science and a second master's, in theology, from Aquinas Institute in Dubuque, Iowa. He earned his Juris Doctor in church law at Catholic University of America (CUA), where he taught part time. In the 1136-page *Code of Canon Law: A Text and Commentary*, Doyle wrote the section on marriage. His embassy job was a career track for Vatican diplomacy or possibly becoming a bishop one day.

Laghi's staff consisted of four Italian priest-diplomats who handled correspondence, reports, and cable traffic with Rome. Laghi and his foreign secretaries had diplomatic immunity and State Department license tags for embassy cars. Of the American priest-secretaries, one wrote speeches, another was the nuncio's personal secretary and accompanied him to events. A third held the title *economo* and functioned as a quartermaster—planning menus, events, issuing checks, supervising work on the grounds.

Doyle dealt with the geography of faith: creating new dioceses as populations grew, selecting bishops, and canonical matters from around the country. He lived at Dominican House of Studies, a cavernous neo-Gothic structure on the CUA campus. Weekdays he rose early, prayed with his brother Dominicans, and drove across town to the embassy. At seven-thirty the nunciature priests celebrated Mass in a first-floor chapel lined with wooden carvings of the Stations of the Cross that Laghi had brought from Italy. Breakfast was served by French nuns who lived in a small convent behind the embassy. The staff returned to chapel for prayers; then the workday began with a *congresso,* or staff meeting. Laghi traveled frequently to various dioceses. Because of his Latin American experience, he was also Vatican observer at the Organization of American States.

Raised in New York and Canada, Doyle came from sturdy Irish stock. His father, an executive in an agrichemical firm, had fifteen siblings spread across the Midwest with whom Doyle kept close ties, flying off to weddings, reunions, and funerals. The priest who had influenced his own vocation was Monsignor R. J. MacDonald of Cornwall, Ontario. In 1966, his second year in the Chicago novitiate, Doyle's mother lay dying of cancer. MacDonald was there, day after day, and Tom Doyle never forgot it.

The priesthood had been much battered since then. Doyle had watched turmoil over the birth control encyclical cut divisions in community and parish life. Good men left the priesthood, frustrated over the 1968 encyclical and Pope Paul VI's intransigence on mandatory celibacy. Those issues and social protest movements had a devastating impact on the church's institutional authority.

More church canons were devoted to marriage than to any other subject, and Doyle was steeped in these canons as a scholar and priest. In the late seventies, he had worked on the Chicago archdiocesan tribunal, assisting men and women whose marriages had failed. Where once remarriage after a divorce had meant automatic excommunication, Vatican II reforms facilitated remarriage under certain conditions. As a tribunalist he saw the ravages wrought on children by their parents' alcoholism, violence (especially toward wives), and infidelity. He wanted those who approached the tribunal to find there more than the removal of the stigma of a divorce; he wanted them to feel a hand of faith extending hope and love. Particularly the kids. At his Chicago rectory youngsters sometimes turned up—vulnerable, hurt, wanting someone to listen and care. Tom Doyle took his title, Father, seriously.

The Dominicans—also known as Order of Preachers—were more than seven hundred years old and Tom Doyle felt that tradition in his bones. Early friars defended orthodoxy against heretics. Doyle's vocation had been strengthened by the friendship of older men who preached the gospel with deep conviction. He believed that most priests were good men. He was not an alarmist. Abuses creeping into clerical life did not surprise him. The church was human.

When a Pittsburgh coalition requested a role in selecting a local bishop, Pio Laghi wrote the fifteen priests, twenty-four nuns, and thirty lay people that "nothing resembling group consultations, canvasses and referendums may take place." Doyle's embassy work included background checks on men under consideration to become bishops. Doyle made strong recommendations to Laghi on two key appointments. And Pope John Paul named Bernard F. Law, a Missouri bishop, archbishop of Boston, and John O'Connor, a Navy rear admiral and former military vicar, archbishop of New York. O'Connor had served briefly as bishop of Scranton. In them Doyle saw durable values that the church needed. John Paul II subsequently named Law and O'Connor to the College of Cardinals.

Doyle operated confidently in an ancient governing system not unlike the military in its chains of command, with canonical codes premised on obedience to authority. But there was a strain in Doyle's molecular composition that he knew a diplomat must needs keep in check. Tom Doyle could be blunt to a fault.

In autumn, 1984, he experienced a growing sadness, wondering if Gilbert

Gauthe's victims would ever feel Christ's presence in a priest again. He grieved for the families—and for Gauthe, whom he had never met. However costly the lawsuits, the church had weathered worse scandals. But things were happening in Louisiana that Doyle didn't like. Information coming up through channels was too sketchy. And then a legal summons arrived at the embassy signaling that Minos Simon had *sued the Holy Father.*

Simon named Pope John Paul II as a defendant in his ill-fated motion to resurrect Ted Campbell's suit against the diocese. The move stemmed from a defense blunder. In the settlement papers that Campbell signed, one of the New Orleans lawyers unwittingly *added* the Pope—who had not previously been named —as a defendant to be absolved of future litigation. Thus, Simon added the Pope to his motion on Campbell's behalf. "Merely a legal technicality," he told me, deadpan. With a flourish he asked the Court to appoint local counsel for the pontiff.

A frustrated Doyle wanted to respond—not just to Simon, but to the scandal. For the first matter, he turned to Wilfred Caron, general counsel of the U. S. Catholic Conference. Caron engaged a Lafayette attorney to handle the Pope's removal as a defendant. On a trip to Lafayette to assess the situation, Caron met with various attorneys, including Ray Mouton. A balding man in his early fifties, Caron said, "This is a very clubby church, Ray. And those who respect the club get along in it." Mouton was not impressed. Simon's naming of the Pope was a media ploy and an example of his search-and-destroy tactics. Caron left for lunch with Simon. The next day Simon called Mouton in a huff, asking why the Washington lawyer had stood him up. Caron had gone to the wrong restaurant. As Mouton predicted, the Holy Father was removed as a defendant.

Doyle meanwhile was gathering information.

Father Michael Peterson's alcoholism rehabilitation program for clerics at St. Luke Institute in Suitland, Maryland, had won high marks among bishops. A year older than Doyle, Peterson was a psychiatrist with expertise in sexual pathologies. The canonist broached the topic bluntly: "So tell me about pedophilia, Mike. Are they all queer?" Peterson gave Doyle a brief backgrounder and promised to send over some literature. When he had finished the reading, Doyle felt Peterson should brief Laghi.

Peterson lived in a suburban house adorned with religious art. He devoured detective novels, loved James Bond movies, and despised Ronald Reagan. Ideological opposites, the two priests were unlikely allies in the tempest that lay ahead.

Several bishops had by late 1984 already called Peterson for advice on pedophile priests when he attended an embassy luncheon honoring a visiting nuncio from Latin America. He was appalled at the fine wines, waiters, nuns in the kitchen, and rapt silence as Laghi spoke. After the meal, Doyle walked Peterson to the door. "Does this happen every day, Tom?" Often enough, chuckled Doyle, who confided that he missed his share of lunches. Peterson wondered if he was merely being diplomatic.

Peterson saw the church as a massive force for good, despite moral teachings he considered archaic. His clinical status had given him the temerity to tell a 1981 gathering of bishops that "the chasm between the biological sciences and theological sciences continues to cause, rather than heal, much human suffering."

In the dialogue of psychiatrist and canonist, Doyle absorbed Peterson's belief that genetic as well as behavioral factors can deface the love map each soul possesses at birth. John Money's metaphor gave Doyle a way to understand the terrible moral abuses of priests like Gauthe. He was impressed by the acumen Peterson brought to such a delicate situation. Michael had a superb political mind; he knew that pedophile priests loomed as a painful, potentially explosive issue for bishops.

Peterson was amazed at the sexual ignorance among priests he treated. On admission to St. Luke, each patient wrote a sexual history. When asked to state their orientation, several did not understand. Gently, Peterson explained that it meant homosexual or heterosexual. "But, Father," one priest told him, "I *can't* be homosexual: the church forbids it."

For most of his life Peterson had run against the grain. His father was an obstetrician-gynecologist in Stockton, California. The eldest of three children, Michael was raised in a home with country club privileges and a religion he rejected. The Church of Jesus Christ of Latter-day Saints was founded in 1834 by Joseph Smith, who beheld an angel with golden tablets in upstate New York. Peterson's rebellion was, well, vintage Michael.

"When I was thirteen I opened the Book of Mormon and it was absurd," he would tell me. "I didn't see how anyone with any kind of intellectual honesty could swallow the first five pages. It's a phenomenon that could only occur in the United States; no other country could support such strange religions that don't have any tradition or roots. This guy has a vision of some angel that isn't even in the Old Testament. He just appears with the golden tablets and says, 'Don't tell too many people!' And because he told, the angel took 'em away. I told my parents I wasn't going to church. My brother and sister followed later. My parents were politically conservative and I was radical, but they mellowed."

High school class president and valedictorian, he went to Stanford University in the early sixties. Pulled by tides of campus discontent, he tilted left. But demonstrations did not sate his spiritual hunger. Studies of organic chemistry and particle physics fascinated him but were limited. Peterson sought a system of thought to bridge science and the soul.

Robert MacAfee Brown, the distinguished Protestant theologian, lectured on Martin Luther King's moral thought. Moved by that dynamic vision of Christianity and hungry for community, Peterson gravitated to the campus Newman Club for daily liturgies. The group included a Japanese scholar, future nuns and Trappist monks, and Tom Fox, future editor of *NCR*. Peterson's instructions in faith began under a Benedictine who was studying for a doctorate in classics. When he asked about sexual sins—how could masturbation be evil?—the priest said to read St. Thomas Aquinas. "You don't"—he smiled—"have to buy the whole story."

At the foot of the *Summa Theologica*, Aquinas's terraced mountain of human thought reaching toward God, Peterson was animated by the idea that faith and reason need not collide. Aquinas's medieval writing grafted Aristotelian thought onto Christian theology. To Peterson it was clean and logical. Ideas flowed smoothly. He took Aquinas's pronouncements on sex—woman as an inferior form of man, and the view that the "conjugal act impedes the acts of the mind"—in the context of an age long passed. And he saw since then a history of intellectual development within the church, a foundation. Peterson was not a Thomist but, like a moth, he was drawn to Aquinas's flame.

Then the Second Vatican Council began. And in a sermon the young catechu-
men never forgot, a French priest said that centuries of darkness were lifting. Not
since the Counter Reformation had the church embraced the challenge of a new
age. At nineteen, Peterson converted to the Catholic faith.

After graduation from the University of California at San Francisco Medical
School, he worked in Washington at the National Institutes of Health and Virol-
ogy. In 1974 he was back in San Francisco at the university hospital as a resident
in psychiatry. One day a senior colleague showed him a letter from a man who
had been found guilty of exposing himself—for the fourth time—and faced long
imprisonment. Peterson knew nothing about exhibitionism but was willing to
learn. The judge approved a visit. Two policemen escorted the man into the
hospital in an orange prison suit, handcuffed, with leg chains and manacled an-
kles. Remove the chains, said Dr. Peterson. The policemen refused. "I'm not going
to see this man unless you take those things off." They struck a compromise: the
leg irons were removed, the handcuffs stayed on.

Bill was in his early thirties, a skilled craftsman with steady work, a wife and
two children. He was not a child molester. He had sexual intercourse with his
wife on just about a daily basis, masturbated once or twice a day, and still had
need to expose himself. Like most exhibitionists, he experienced orgasm the moment he made eye contact with a stranger.

Testosterone, the hormone activating a man's sex drive, is produced by the
testes working in circuitry with the brain. Bill's testosterone level tested normal,
Peterson recalled. "All tests were normal, but there was no measurement [then] of
brain and pituitary hormones, or radioimmunoassay tests like we use today. We
convinced the judge to release Bill for observation and therapy."

Who was hurt more: the women who saw Bill flash—or Bill himself? Peterson
prescribed an antipsychotic drug, but it made Bill sick. Other pills proved futile;
so he weaned Bill from prescriptive drugs. Bill had a relapse but physicians managed to keep him out of jail. In 1974, after Peterson moved to Washington and a
research position at NIH, Bill—arrested once again—asked his support for voluntary castration. Peterson wrote the judge recommending surgical removal of the
testes. After the operation Bill's exhibitionism ceased. He remained sexually active
with his wife. (Contrary to myth, surgical castration does not automatically
render a man impotent, although it often does.)

In 1971 there was sparse medical literature on sex offenders; few psychiatrists
were interested in treating them. Peterson proposed a Gender Identity Clinic
similar to the pioneering work of John Money at Johns Hopkins University Hospital in Baltimore, and won approval. Within a month three men arrived asking
for sex change operations. The program began cautiously, with transsexuals in a
separate group. Only after a year of hormone injections could they move toward
surgery. At the hospital Peterson was met with cold stares. He told me that
obscene phone calls forced him to take an unlisted home number.

Professionally, he searched for accurate classifications. In his heart he knew
that, like schizophrenics he had treated, exhibitionists and transsexuals were crip-
pled, not criminal.

One could implant hormones in the uterus of a beagle dog and alter gender
traits of the offspring. Virtually any animal could be so manipulated. Male pup-
pies were studied through maturity as their sexual interest veered to male dogs.

Peterson was curious about the brain's programming. Could conflicts in gender identity stem from problems in the neural pathways? It was a point of scientific dispute. Money's argument in *Man & Woman Boy & Girl* (1972) impressed Peterson. Money questioned formation of gender identity. What caused men to be men, and women women? Part of the answer lay in the self-determining nature of chromosomes. Two X chromosomes in a fertilized egg normally signal a female. In males it is an XY combination.

A chromosome may be broken or otherwise distorted [Money wrote]. Even without such a mishap, the conditions in which the earliest stages of cellular and embryonic differentiation take place may be altered and atypical, so that normal masculine or feminine course of differentiation is interfered with. . . .

If the hand of God sketched the design of human life, then distorted chromosomes, deep in a woman's womb, had to be part of His plan. So reasoned Michael Peterson. Whether biological fate or, as ample case studies showed, environmental forces distorted a child's love map, sexual aberration in later life caused terrible inner suffering.

In 1975 a priest asked Peterson to lecture students at Mount St. Mary, the nation's oldest Catholic seminary in Emmitsburg, Maryland—rolling hill country near Camp David. "I was impressed by the students," he recalled. "I told myself, *You should be here. It's crazy: here you are sitting in a laboratory, shooting monkeys and mice full of viruses. Why don't you do something with your life?*" At thirty-two, with the permission of Cardinal William Baum, then archbishop of Washington, Peterson began seminary studies while residing at St. Anselm's Abbey. He also counseled priests and taught at Georgetown University medical school. Ordained in 1978, at thirty-five, he founded a hospital named for the healing disciple Luke to treat chemically dependant clergy.

ii.

On January 23, 1985, Ray Mouton bought newspapers at the Lafayette airport and cursed beneath his breath. The *Baton Rouge Morning Advocate* story citing Simon's depositions with Frey and Larroque had the glorious headline: BISHOP SAYS HE GOT WORD OF GAUTHE'S ACTIONS TEN YEARS AGO. The New Orleans attorneys hadn't tried to secure a court order sealing the documents, thus allowing Gauthe to be judged in the court of public opinion. Mouton was in a raw mood. Earlier, an ice storm had moved President Reagan's second inauguration indoors. At the Hilton, Mouton reviewed literature on St. Luke Institute before hailing a taxi.

Tall and trim with light brown hair, wearing a turtleneck shirt and sports coat, Peterson had the relaxed air of a successful college professor. The two men hit it off immediately. As he gave Mouton a tour of the three-story brick hospital, Peterson explained that patient evaluation lasted from seven days to three weeks. The therapy that followed had no time limit. St. Luke used AA group sessions, but with a theological approach. The complex also had a substance abuse outpa-

tient clinic. St. Luke's theological emphasis on healing reminded Mouton of the
House of Affirmation, but it was more sophisticated and scientific. Peterson grew
animated showing him the machines used for CAT scans, explaining that if an
alcoholic had brain damage and a psychiatrist never knew it, group therapy would
not suffice.

In Peterson's office Mouton studied the bookcase: theology, church history.
Where were the medical books? Peterson laughed. "Bishops are more relaxed in a
room with books like this. The medical texts are in another room."

After Mouton reviewed the Louisiana statutes on criminal insanity, Peterson
asked, "What are you most afraid of for Gilbert?" Mouton feared that before he
could dispose of the case the public and prosecutor would learn that his client
was not the only priest in the diocese with such sexual problems. Peterson was
startled. "There are others?" Indeed. Simon had grilled church superiors about
Lane Fontenot, and Nathan Stansbury had fumed after Tom Bathay's* brush with
officers at the truck stop.

"Where are these men now?" said Peterson.

Mouton was not sure about Fontenot, but Bathay was still a pastor. Peterson
asked about the Gauthe litigation. Mouton handed him the newspaper. Peterson
read it, then picked up the phone. "Hello, Tom? He's here. I think you should see
him now."

Driving across icy, wind-swept streets of Washington, Peterson explained that
Father Doyle, canonist at the nunciature, was concerned. Mouton nodded, wondering what "nunciature" meant. He had little respect for the canon lawyers he
had met thus far. The car headed up Michigan Avenue, past Catholic University's
whitened lawns. A majestic blue dome with radiant gold bands gleamed in the
sky. "What's that, Michael?"

"The National Shrine of the Immaculate Conception."

They parked next to a stone building with a row of steeples and a crucifix
atop the pyramidal arch above the large door. A sign said: DOMINICAN HOUSE OF
STUDIES. Peterson led Mouton to the chapel and asked him to wait. It was an
immense room with vaulted ceilings and tiers of wooden pews—a medieval ambi-
ence; a figure of Christ was nailed to a life-sized cross above the altar. Ray
Mouton prayed: *Dear God, please don't let me mess up.*

Peterson returned with Father Doyle, who wore a sweater and blue jeans.
"Thank you for coming, Mr. Mouton. Let's head up to my office." He followed
the priests down a hushed corridor, up a stairwell, and along another silent corridor. No one spoke. Doyle's office was surprisingly small. Iron shelves contained
hundreds of books and a computer terminal rested on a desk in the center of the
room. Two chairs occupied the remaining space.

Out came the cigarettes as Mouton answered Doyle's questions. Months of
frustration hit a crest; he said the cover-up was on a collision course with Minos
Simon. After detailed discussion about the path of civil and criminal actions,
Doyle said: "Are there other priests with problems in Lafayette?"

"Yes."

"How do you know?"

He repeated what he had told Peterson, who gave Doyle the Baton Rouge
paper. Then Doyle made Mouton reconstruct each step of the proceedings, with
probing questions about administration of the diocese—some of which he could

not answer—and about Frey and Larroque. When the interrogation was done, Doyle picked up the phone. "Hey, this is Tom. I need to speak to him."

Peterson gave Mouton an encouraging smile. Doyle frowned. *"I don't care if he's playing handball. Get him off the court! I need to talk to him right away."* Doyle replaced the phone, stood, shook hands, and thanked Mouton for his time. "I admire what you're doing for Gil Gauthe. I'll be talking to you again."

Peterson led Mouton through the vast silence of Dominican House. Mouton whispered, "Who is that guy?"

"He works for the nuncio."

"Who is that?"

"Archbishop Pio Laghi. He's the ambassador."

"For the Pope?" Peterson nodded. Mouton prayed to himself: *"Holy Mary, Mother of God, pray for us sinners, now and at the hour of our death. Amen."*

They drove to the Hilton. Peterson reviewed the entire chronology once again, writing quickly and precisely on page after page of a tablet. Then they discussed legal moves that would allow Peterson to screen Gauthe before his return to Lafayette for trial.

Mouton flew home. The next day Peterson briefed Archbishop Laghi at the embassy about the Lafayette situation. The nuncio listened carefully, thanked him, and in Peterson's presence called Archbishop Hannan in New Orleans, politely explaining that problems in Lafayette were more serious than previously perceived. The nuncio asked Hannan if he would please join others at a meeting in Washington.

Doyle plunged into the literature of pedophilia. Mouton sent the depositions to Peterson, who made copies for Doyle. Peterson was appalled at the duplicity of Gauthe's superiors, yet as a psychiatrist he understood their denial mechanisms. His thinking on pedophilia was broadening in the face of legal issues being shaped by Ray Mouton. "Don't put pedophiles back in ministry!" Mouton told Peterson and Doyle. "It's not only courting legal risks, it's *immoral.* You're playing with innocent lives."

Communicating such risks was on the agenda when Peterson and Doyle met on February 11, 1985, in a conference room of the Marriott Hotel in Crystal City, Virginia, with Archbishop Hannan, Bishop Frey, Monsignor Larroque, and church attorneys Tom Rayer of New Orleans and Bob Wright of Lafayette.

As prelate of Louisiana's largest metropolis, Hannan was the ranking official in the room, his presence a clear sign of Laghi's concern. Doyle had great respect for Hannan; Peterson wondered if Hannan knew what Frey was up against. Doyle conveyed the nuncio's appreciation to the group for traveling to Washington. He and Father Peterson had been asked to assist them in the difficulties faced in Lafayette. Both men were struck by the smirk on Alex Larroque's face. Peterson had privately complimented the vicar on his success as a recovering alcoholic, but Larroque's expression hardly masked his contempt at having to attend this meeting.

The Washington clerics had spent days on the telephone, eliciting information about Lafayette from many contacts. But broaching these subjects with the Louisianans had to be done sensitively, showing respect. In positioning themselves as troubleshooters, they were taking a calculated risk. Bishops do not like priests—even ones with the support of the nuncio—meddling in their affairs.

Doyle reviewed canonical issues regarding a bishop's responsibility for a suspended priest. If such a cleric left his diocese for another, the original bishop was responsible for him. Where was Lane Fontenot? In Spokane, Washington, said Larroque. Lafayette was responsible for him as a matter of canon law, said Doyle, telegraphing a message: if church officials did not follow their own canons, civil attorneys could seize on that. They knew chancery records were subject to subpoena in civil litigation.

Ray Mouton had spoken highly of Bob Wright, but Peterson wondered if this man, who was not a Catholic yet had worked hard in assisting Frey, realized just how serious the situation had become. When Peterson was asked for clinical remarks, he stressed the addictive nature of pedophilia. They were concerned, Doyle continued, that if the situation got out of hand a class action suit might be filed. They knew that Minos Simon had been making noises to this effect. Was it possible? Yes, said Wright, in whom Peterson detected a mind now moving like a calculator. But Wright explained that the prescription, or statute of limitation—one year for an adult to file suit after sustaining an injury—would make such litigation a hard plaintiffs' struggle if abuse had occurred years ago. Tom Rayer echoed Wright.

Doyle voiced concern over Simon's naming the Pope in the Campbell suit. The lawyers said it was a gratuitous move that would fail. But the Holy See *was* concerned, said Doyle. "The Bishops' Conference does not like the way it was handled," he added. Peterson studied the faces. Frey, quiet, seemed way over his head, not even a part of the room. Larroque had a weird grin. Archbishop Hannan, serious as stone, listened carefully and then announced: "We must stipulate to liability"—meaning they must accept institutional responsibility for Gauthe's crimes. Mouton and Wright had long recommended this, but the insurance attorneys, fearing new cases and more losses, had refused. Hannan felt that protracted litigation was tarnishing the church, needlessly so. The Louisiana attorneys agreed; however, they cautioned that liability stipulation was Bob Leake's decision.

"We're here to help," explained Doyle. The situation was too big for the visitors alone to handle. Peterson discussed St. Luke's program. He also said the House of Affirmation had little experience in the specialized field of sexual dysfunctions.

"How many problems do you have?" Doyle asked.

It was not a major problem, Larroque countered: Gauthe and Fontenot had left the state. Peterson asked about Father Robert Limoges, who had also left Lafayette. Wasn't he in a monastery in another state? asked Peterson. Larroque said there was no need to put Limoges in treatment: the abbot had said Limoges could stay in the monastery working as a carpenter. *I don't believe it*, thought Peterson: how sick was Limoges? Could he be helped? What would a CAT scan show? But Larroque's expression gave him pause. The last thing he wanted was an argument with bishops present. Doyle entered the vacuum, saying that if a man like Limoges had a problem, then at least get him to St. Luke so Peterson could check him out. Frey said nothing. Larroque stared.

"Well," said Doyle, "what about Father Tom Bathay?"

Larroque exploded: *"How did you get that name?"*

That was not what they were here to discuss, Doyle allowed. "We're here to assist you."

"Ray Mouton gave you his name," Larroque fumed.

In one of his few utterances, Bishop Frey said that Bathay was not a problem. Doyle observed that he had been picked up at a truck stop and almost arrested: that *was* a problem.

Peterson squirmed as tension mounted. Larroque was a case of denial. Frey was withdrawn, perpetuating the denial by letting Larroque argue. But Philip Hannan's eyes registered the gravity of the moment. As a World War II Army chaplain Hannan had dropped into Cologne, Germany, in a parachute and saved the magnificent cathedral there from destruction by charging GIs. His office in New Orleans had served as a neutral zone where city officials and black activists met after policemen stormed a house, searching for a cop killer, and shot a woman dead in front of her child. Hannan helped defuse the crisis. Such a prelate, Peterson believed, with the weight of the nuncio behind him, was sure to prevail on Frey and Larroque to do the right thing.

As they departed, Peterson told Doyle, "Tom, I can't get involved in the political end." But, of course, he already was.

The irony of his new stature, gained because of his relationship with Doyle and Peterson, delighted Ray Mouton. He had sent Alex Larroque a red muffler for Christmas and had acceded to his wish by calling Michael Peterson. Yet he had often felt stymied by Frey and Larroque. Now, after frustration in Lafayette, Mouton had found men in high places who would not be passive as a disaster unfolded. At the same time, he found other men in high places who seemed to be threatened by him.

USCC general counsel Wil Caron was monitoring civil cases in other states. When Mouton offered advice on defense, Caron told him that as a criminal lawyer "that's out of your field"—unaware that Mouton had litigated a $4.2 million settlement for a man paralyzed in an automobile accident. Caron instructed Mouton to communicate with no church officials without his clearance. "I'll talk to anyone I damn well please," retorted Mouton.

Doyle began calling Mouton, sometimes three and four times a day. With cases breaking in other states, bishops were seeking Doyle's advice and Doyle wanted Mouton on the back channel for criminal and civil questions. At first bemused by this circuitous route around Caron, Mouton realized that few bishops grasped the nature of the mistakes—moral, financial, psychological—Frey and Larroque had made. Peterson was telling bishops that medical intervention was imperative, even if a priest denied the charges. Moreover, the clerical tradition of forgiving sins, on which bishops often relied in dealing with abusive priests, had its limits: compulsive sexual problems would not go away with a trip to confession. There were deeper realities at work—dark realms of the self which needed to be understood before they could be treated. Bishops could blunder into costly swamps through their ignorance or fear of reality.

The hierarchy's tradition was to handle clergy problems privately, and that concerned Doyle. Canonical codes spelled out the rights of priests. But under secular law, what was a bishop's responsibility when a priest was accused of child molesting? Could a bishop be indicted for failure to report a priest who abused a child? "You bet," said Mouton—depending on the local statute and a prosecutor's sense of public opinion.

Around the professional concerns a set of friendships was forming. Peterson began calling Mouton at night—always asking about his wife and children, about Gauthe's condition, encouraging the attorney to keep faith. He also posed hypothetical problems. Could a bishop refuse to answer questions on grounds that he had heard a pedophile priest's confession? That depended on local statutes governing religious confidentiality, Mouton explained: it was better for a bishop not to hear those confessions. As the calls multiplied, Mouton realized that Peterson was in far-off places and needed advice to pass on the next day. Michael always seemed exhausted; once he fell asleep during a phone call.

Peterson was curious about civil statutes of limitations. How could the law draw an arbitrary line at age eighteen and say that after one year (or two, depending on the state) victims could no longer sue? Abuse victims create denial mechanisms that harden with time. When therapy succeeds, buried memories surface. What then? Why didn't the time to file suit start when the victim consciously realized the source of pain embedded in the past? Wasn't that the premise behind the Agent Orange class action suits? Mouton marveled at his logic. Of course it made sense. If Minos Simon was thus animated, God help the Lafayette diocese.

As canonical, medical, and legal issues converged via phone calls, Doyle asked Mouton for something on paper—a memo, suggestions, a plan to pull out when bishops called. Mouton jumped at the idea. Well-thought-out guidelines, disseminated to bishops and order superiors, would convey the breadth of the crisis. Doyle felt that he could get the issue on the NCCB's agenda when they met at St. John's Abbey in Collegeville, Minnesota, in June 1985.

Mouton drafted the memo for Doyle. Doyle and Peterson subsequently met in Washington with Cardinal John Krol of Philadelphia. One of Pope John Paul's favored American prelates, Krol liked the draft; he wanted the bishops to take action. Laghi briefed Monsignor Daniel Hoye, secretary of the NCCB. Mouton was eager to forge ahead. But Doyle was moving at his own pace.

"Tom briefed Bernie Law," Peterson told Mouton one night. After dinner at the nunciature, the Boston cardinal had strolled the embassy grounds with Doyle. Doyle proposed an adjunct committee to Law's NCCB Committee on Research and Pastoral Practices; the group would research implications of the broadening problem. Mouton asked what bishops would do with the research. Peterson wasn't sure but, judging from the frequency with which calls and priests were coming to St. Luke, word was getting out.

Isolated in Lafayette by diocesan officials who resented him for forcing their hand with the nuncio, Mouton found in the Washington priests a support system for his own embittered faith. Then Doyle became elusive. Mouton's calls were not returned. Doyle rented a plane from a Maryland airstrip. As unanswered messages mounted, Mouton was miffed. Then Doyle called. "Just, ah, coming back from Cape Cod, Ray. It was very restful."

He had been following columns of whales over the Atlantic.

Peterson's schedule was packed with short trips. Besides conferences and lectures he visited former patients to check on their progress as recovering alcoholics. No matter where he was, Peterson managed to call, always asking about Ray, Janis, and the kids, always asking about Gauthe, his medication and mood swings. "I was amazed," Mouton later told me, "that this shrink flying all over the map was so concerned about a pedophile. He had never met Gilbert, but the guy cared. Jesus, how he cared."

Doyle wanted Frey and Larroque removed; however he knew that the Pope would not simply sack them. He asked Laghi for a formal inquiry. Laghi chose A. James Quinn, a silver-haired auxiliary bishop from Cleveland and a canonist who also held a degree in civil law. Mouton never learned the scope of Quinn's probe; but his frustration lifted when Bishop Quinn said grace at dinner with Janis and their three children—the first time a bishop had visited their home. Quinn asked the children questions about school, sports, and extracurriculars, focusing on each one with a sincerity that bathed the room in warmth.

After Quinn's departure, Mouton saw an opening: Bishop Frey had ordered Father Bathay into treatment at St. Luke for his drinking. This was the preventive approach Doyle wanted. Then a Lafayette priest told Mouton of one Father Y, in a rural parish, who had made advances to a youngster several years before. His name was not on Simon's discovery list of twenty-seven priests, whose files the defense attorneys were fighting to safeguard. No charges had been filed. Mouton asked if it was safe to leave Father Y in his parish. Without evaluating him, Peterson could not say.

With that on his mind, Mouton flew to Hartford in March. Prosecutor Stansbury had dispatched his own consultant to screen Gauthe at the Institute of Living: psychologist Ed Shwery, consultant on the report on the initial nine boys for Hebert and Bencomo. While Shwery put Gauthe through a battery of tests to determine mental stability, Mouton hit on a scheme. He would ask Shwery to screen Father Y and recommend evaluation at St. Luke. This would establish a referral procedure—and serve Mouton's defense strategy. If Shwery agreed, he would have earned fees from plaintiff attorneys, prosecutor, *and* the church. When he testified against Gauthe, Mouton would attack him for conflicts of interest. Stansbury would parry that Mouton secured Shwery's services for the diocese. Mouton would say he could have refused.

Mouton was pleased with his Machiavellian ploy. Shwery had good credentials. He could help the diocese with other priests and maybe, unwittingly, help Mouton defend Gauthe. But was he willing? Mouton was watching a basketball game when Shwery knocked on his hotel room door. As they chatted, he told Shwery about the program at St. Luke and about Quinn, the Vatican emissary. Was Shwery interested in consulting? Shwery was.

Shortly thereafter, Mouton and Shwery flew to Ohio and met with Quinn, who thought the referral procedure had merit. Then they flew to Washington and had dinner with Doyle and Peterson at the Foundry restaurant in Georgetown. Peterson asked if Shwery had much experience with therapist Ken Bouillion, who had a growing caseload of Gauthe victims. Indeed he had, said Shwery, calling Bouillion "my student." Midway through the dinner, in a statement that stunned the other three for its breach of ethics, Shwery remarked how much Gilbert Gauthe liked oral sex.

Alone with Mouton, Peterson said, "I don't trust that man."

Mouton replied glumly, "I don't believe the stuff he said."

But the meeting was set with diocesan officials in Lafayette to discuss the referral procedure. Frey and Larroque listened intently as Shwery discussed the complexities of pedophilia; however, he neglected to discuss sending Father Y for evaluation at St. Luke. After the meeting Mouton was livid. Shwery had sent a $12,000 bill for his time in Cleveland and Washington. "And you didn't push St. Luke!" Mouton thundered. Shwery apologized and soon made the recommendation. Father Y went to St. Luke, but the pipeline to the facility as Mouton had envisioned it did not materialize. Shwery began counseling Lafayette priests on a consultant basis, and participated in panel discussions for clergy conference days in Lafayette, New Orleans, and Baton Rouge with men who had legal expertise in pedophilia: Tom Rayer and Bob Wright.

Mouton consoled himself that at least he had gained some ground in his defense of Gauthe. When Shwery took the stand, Mouton would fire away. But would it make a big difference?

iii.

When spring came, Doyle asked Mouton to join him and Peterson in Chicago to hammer out a document for the bishops' use at their June conference in Collegeville, Minnesota. Coordinating their schedules, they flew to Chicago in early May and met at the Marriott Hotel adjacent to O'Hare Airport. Bishop Quinn came in from Ohio; from Los Angeles came Auxiliary Bishop William Levada, of Cardinal Law's Committee on Research and Pastoral Practices. Law's support was vital to the document.

Mouton reviewed the stages of criminal prosecution—arrest, indictment, arraignment, discovery, trial. Quinn said little, but his nods and meditative expressions seemed to register approval of Mouton's approach. Levada (who later became bishop of Portland, Oregon) said more. A technical discussion of indictments was not the best way for presenting this matter to the bishops. The report would not be well broached as a lesson in the law. "It is better," said Levada, "to pose questions"—guide bishops through questions they would be likely to ask.

It made sense to Mouton. Pose questions, then break the report into legal, clinical, and canonical findings. Levada and Quinn departed. As attorney and priests worked on revisions of their respective drafts, Mouton wondered if their expertise might prove useful to other dioceses. Why not propose themselves as a crisis intervention team—willing to fly into trouble spots with a three-pronged approach to breaking cases? On learning of abuse (a diocesan attorney could argue) the bishop would have immediately sought the best available help. The plan was a blueprint for ensuring that the morally right thing was done—reaching out to victims, removing the priest—and for establishing a solid foundation for defense should litigation ensue.

Peterson, due shortly in Australia for a month of lectures, had limited time. They worked on a typewriter borrowed from the Chicago Symphony. As Doyle honed his section, Mouton helped Peterson simplify language in the clinical portion.

In a moment alone with Mouton, Peterson said he thought the project was in trouble. Monsignor Daniel Hoye, the thirty-eight-year-old executive secretary of the NCCB, had recently told him that with Doyle involved there was little hope. Mouton asked who was putting heat on Hoye. "That's not the problem," said Peterson. Dan Hoye did not like Tom Doyle. The embassy canonist showed little deference to the NCCB bureaucracy in the selection process of new bishops. Doyle worked for Laghi but Hoye controlled the agenda for the bishops' conference three weeks hence. But Doyle had his own allies, including Cardinal Law, reasoned Mouton. Then he said: "Tom's the pilot. If he crashes, I go with him." Michael laughed, wished him luck, and was off to Australia.

Doyle and Mouton returned to Chicago in late May and worked nonstop for three days. The introduction focused on an unnamed diocese (Lafayette) which faced $100 million in pending claims. (Actual settlements then totaled $4.2 million, of which the church paid about $800,000.) The problem was national in scope. "Approximately thirty cases have been reported in the press involving approximately one hundred children." The report went on:

> *If one could accurately predict, with actuarial soundness, that our exposure to similar claims (i.e., one offender and fifteen or so claimants) over the next ten years could be restricted and limited to the occurrence of one hundred such cases against the Church, then an estimate of the total projected losses for the decade could be established with a limit of* ONE BILLION DOLLARS. . . . *At the rate cases are developing, [that] over ten years is a conservative cost projection.*

The American Bar Association and plaintiff attorney groups "are conducting studies, scheduling panel conferences, and devising other methods of disseminating information about this newly developing area of law." Then came the questions. *Can a bishop be forced to testify before a grand jury?* (Absolutely.) *Should the diocese or the priest retain a criminal lawyer?* (The priest, though the diocese can help him in doing so.) *What is the requirement in criminal law for one who has knowledge that a sexual crime has been committed to report that knowledge to authorities?* "Failure to report such information," the report noted, "is considered a criminal offense in some states.

> *To allow a priest to continue to function, endangering the health of children, following the receipt of private, confidential knowledge that this priest victimized a child is considered to be "criminal neglect" (a crime in many states.)*

Other questions, not directly answered, were posed to show the hierarchy the complexity and gravity of the unfolding crisis. What provisions in diocesan liability insurance covered civil consequences of sexual contact between priest and child? At what point should insurers be told of their exposure? Does the bishop have any rights vis-à-vis civil litigation defense? Can he reject attorneys assigned by insurers to defend a case?

On and on the questions went, sculpted from the mass of emerging problems. In the medical section, Peterson noted:

> *It is inadequate to treat a sex offender in the diocese on a private psycho-therapy model. It should be emphasized that inpatient treatment, preferably with peers, is the most preferable mode.*

There are a number of rare or more unusual disorders that can cause unusual behavior over a prolonged period of time. These include manic-depressive illness, frontal lobe dysfunction, temporal lobe epilepsy, brain tumors, etc. These problems never come to light if a priest or cleric is evaluated at a center that only looks at the psychological dynamics of the patient's family, his adult and religious life as the source of all problems.

He stressed that many priests who molested adolescents also abused drugs and alcohol, adding that "the sexual problem will [not] necessarily disappear following treatment" for sobriety.

We are dealing with compulsive sexual habits which the priest may temporarily suspend in the face of legal or canonical pressure, but not in all instances. There are many examples wherein sexual abuse took place very soon after the confrontation between the priest and his Ordinary [bishop] had taken place. The priest must clearly be seen as one suffering from a psychiatric disorder that is beyond his ability to control.

He recommended a two-page list of testing for such priests to undergo, including electroencephalogram and CAT brain scan, with well-monitored aftercare and support group programs.

Psychological help and other needed assistance should be offered to the victims and their families [the report stated].

The extent and degree of the sexual abuse, the age of the child at the time of the outset of the abuse, when it was discovered and finished, the manner in which it was discovered, any other dimensions of relationship of the priest with the family . . . these are all factors involved in treating the victims and their families. Special mental health professionals, trained and competent in this particular area, should be called on. . . . to provide help and support as soon as is feasible. This is also a healthy preventive measure with respect to civil litigation since most families are eager to help their children and themselves in these embarrassing and complex psychosocial problems.

One question cut to the core: what should the bishop look for in asking whether a priest could ever return and function in the diocese? In a sense, the 92-page report was an extended answer: future reassignments were fraught with risk. An accused priest should be suspended from sacramental duties until the medical evaluation was complete; bishops must report allegations to local authorities. Doyle's section stressed the importance of a pastoral response to the victims. The report also stated:

The idea of sanitizing or purging files of potentially damaging material has been brought up. This would be in contempt of court and an obstruction of justice if the files had already been subpoenaed by the courts. Even if there has been no such subpoena, such actions could be construed as a violation of the law in the event of a class action suit. On a canonical level, to sanitize the personnel files could also pose a problem of continuity from one diocesan administration to another.

One other suggestion regarding files has been to move them to the Apostolic Nunciature where it is believed they would remain secure, in [diplomatically] immune territory. In all likelihood such action would ensure that the immunity of the Nunciature would be damaged or destroyed by the civil courts.

Canon law speaks of secret archives. Are these safe from civil discovery whereas ordinary files might not be? Thus far it appears that the secret archives afford no more security from discovery than regular diocesan archives.

In stressing the need to reach out as pastors and offer the healing hand, legal strategy was framed in moral terms.

When I received a copy of the document from Tom Fox in 1986, I realized that Mouton's advice on media relations had been written in the spring of 1985, when I was discovering the first signs of a cover-up. Mouton had written:

The first objective, of which one must never lose sight, is to maintain, preserve and seek to enhance the credibility of the church as a Christian community. The church should be presented as a sensitive, caring and responsible entity which gives unquestioned attention and concern to the victims. . . .

Adopt a policy which in all cases will carefully control and monitor the tonal quality of all public statements made about particular cases or the general problem. All statements including written legal pleadings must be entirely consistent and aligned with the image of the church in the minds of the general public, the Catholic community, the juror, judges, prosecutors and plaintiffs. The church cannot step out of character at any stage of the process including the action of legal counsel.

The church must remain open and avoid the appearance of being under siege or drawn into battle. All tired and worn policies utilized by bureaucrats must be cast away. In this sophisticated society a media policy of silence implies either necessary secrecy or cover-up.

Finishing at a breakneck pace, Doyle and Mouton made fourteen copies of the report on the hotel Xerox machine before it ran out of paper; then they flew to Cleveland with a package for Bishop Quinn. He worked out of a modest office in a nearby town wracked by industrial decline. Quinn's personal apostolate was with retarded adults, whose photographs hung in his office. *This is what a bishop should be,* thought Mouton: a man serving those in need. Never certain of how much Quinn had learned in Lafayette—or of what he reported to Laghi—Mouton was pleased as the bishop turned the pages, murmuring ". . . yes . . . mmm . . . this looks good." Mouton flew home on a wave of optimism; Doyle stopped in Pittsburgh to brief Bishop Anthony Bevilacqua.

Shortly after Mouton's return, the USCC general counsel telephoned his office. "Where is he?" demanded Wil Caron. Cecile Cook explained that Mr. Mouton was expected back in the office soon. Then Caron let loose a stream of bellowing about this report on pedophilia that had landed on his desk and what did Ray Mouton think he was doing? When Caron hung up she broke out in tears. Mouton did not return the call.

vii.

Rumblings in the Fourth Estate

In a heavily Catholic region, I was concerned that my reports might trigger a backlash against the *Times of Acadiana* or myself. The specter of scandal among Catholics can arouse a long memory of bigotry toward the faith. An 1855 Texas newspaper cited "the notorious fact that the Monarchs of Europe and the Pope of Rome are at this very moment plotting our destruction and threatening the extinction of our political, civil and religious institutions."

As the late historian Richard Hofstadter wrote: "Anti-Catholicism has always been the pornography of the Puritan."

In Louisiana that mentality thrived in Jimmy Swaggart, the superstar of a pentecostal belief system spreading through the South. A typical Swaggart statement held that for "every *one* [Catholic] who is saved, *scores* of others are trusting in a false sense of salvation, which will, sad to say, cause them to be eternally lost." Swaggart's booming television ministry and Bible college outside of Baton Rouge bespoke a powerful presence. In 1985—three years before Swaggart's encounters with a prostitute began his downfall—I occasionally found myself, coffee in hand, dazzled and appalled by his Sunday TV fulminations about sins of the flesh. I shuddered to think of what he might say after my story broke.

The only journalistic precedent for such coverage I found was the *Chicago Sun-Times*'s 1981 series about Cardinal John Cody's financial blunders and questionable relationship with a female cousin. With Cody's death, the U.S. attorney closed an investigation. Linda Matys took a no-nonsense approach to local reactions: "Some people will complain because they don't want any bad news about the church. The majority of readers will accept the stories if the tone is fair and we justify our decision to publish the material." With associate editor Geoff O'Connell, she began work on an editorial statement to precede the articles.

The *Times of Acadiana* occupied a two-story brick building on Jefferson Street, two doors down from the *Lafayette Daily Advertiser*. Owned by the conservative Thomson chain, a Canadian corporation, the *Advertiser* was short on serious digging, long on stories of meetings and social functions. The *Times* was a different story. The weekly had come of age during the region's surging oil economy,

which provided a sturdy advertising base. The *Times*'s computerized operation
with video terminals did $1 million in annual billing.

Once isolated from mainstream America, Cajun country was moving into the
nation's cultural and economic flow. The Council for the Development of French
in Louisiana—CODOFIL—had spawned language classes and foreign exchange
programs. Cajun and zydeco musicians were traveling far, exporting regional idi-
oms to match the rising chic status of Cajun cuisine. The *Times* had been a catalyst
in this larger movement. Published in tabloid format, the paper struck a sensitive
balance between cultural celebration and measured criticism of local institutions.
James Edmunds of New Iberia, who founded the paper in 1980, was a *Newsweek*
stringer. By 1984 the *Times* was reaching 40,000 readers on a free-distribution
basis, rivaling circulation of the daily.

Under publisher Richard D'Aquin and managing editor Charles Lenox, the
Daily Advertiser had two abiding passions: promoting business and attacking communism. Columnist Bob Angers knew all the movers and shakers; he also fired a
steady fusillade of criticism against Fidel Castro, the Sandinistas, and the Soviet
Union. Many local leaders depended on the New Orleans and Baton Rouge dailies to keep abreast of events within the state.

James Edmunds introduced a magazine style that stood out in bas-relief from
the daily. Every so often, when the *Times* popped a politician favored by the daily
or exposed some local fiasco, the *Advertiser* bristled, as when Lenox wrote, "We
didn't arrive in Lafayette a few years ago, rent a typewriter, desk and office and
set ourselves up as experts."

The *Advertiser* prided itself as the voice of business. Yet when Steve May, with
a background in weekly publishing in New Orleans and Baton Rouge, approached
Edmunds with a buyout offer, wealthy locals encouraged May to start a competing daily. Instead, with several investors, he purchased the *Times*, retaining Edmunds as a columnist, and hired Linda Matys as editor.

The *Advertiser* had given the Gauthe affair sparse coverage. As a policy the
daily did not credit stories broken by the weekly and rarely cited news breaks by
the TV stations. May's curiosity about the scandal had grown because of the
Advertiser's unwillingness to report it. May was not the sort to use his pages arbi-
trarily, but beneath the smooth businessman's veneer ran a feisty streak. As my
series took shape, he braced for reader complaints. "Just let the facts speak," Linda
told me. If problems arose, she would deal with May.

Meanwhile, in Kansas City, Tom Fox was waiting for my story, which would
be a condensation of the three-part series in Lafayette and would focus primarily
on Gauthe.

In early May reporters from the *Washington Post* and *Dallas Morning News* arrived in Lafayette, armed with depositions that Chalice had sent. A week had
passed since I had heard from the source. As my deadline neared, he finally called.
"We have got to meet," I said. "I have to know who you are."

That night at his home, he showed me his driver's license and other identification materials that confirmed his employment. He was not a priest, but his work
put him in contact with many clergy and religious. He also confided that he had
been sexually abused by a custodial figure as a child, which explained to me his
outrage over the events at hand.

Again we reviewed names on the list, which I was checking against depositions and clergy sources. Some things I simply could not confirm. He asked if I
had spoken with Lane Fontenot. "Larroque testified that he left House of Affirmation," I said.

"He's in Spokane, Washington."

"Are you sure?"

"Oh yes. Word of these things travels. He's made trips to Louisiana since he
left." He had gone to Affirmation in 1983.

"Where in Spokane?"

"Gonzaga University. He took courses there before."

Late that night, lying in bed, I wondered about Fontenot. Abhorring what he
had done, I still felt pity for the man. I had never tracked a priest the way one
goes after politicians. Why had the diocese let him relocate in Spokane? I had
never confronted a pedophile before. That night I said a prayer: *Lord, I'm not trying
to hurt people. Please grant me compassion. . . .*

The 1984 *Official Catholic Directory* listed Fontenot as "on leave" at Spokane
University, a Jesuit institution. I called the university and was put through to the
religious community residence, where a Father Frank Costello answered. I asked
about circumstances of Fontenot's arrival. Costello said that Fontenot had studied
at Spokane in the past, receiving a master's in spirituality. "He has been identified
in legal documents in Louisiana," I said. "Did you know he was removed from this
diocese for alleged sexual involvements with young people?"

After a pause, Costello said: "No, not to my knowledge. . . . He's in residence here, between assignments."

"Well, is he subject to any supervision?"

"He's not under any restriction. He can come and go as he pleases."

"May I speak with him?"

"Well . . . Let me see if he is here." The sound of footsteps receded from the
receiver and for two minutes I heard air. Costello returned: "I'm sorry. He's not
available." I left my number. Fontenot did not return that call or my other messages.

Before Gonzaga, Fontenot had been treated at House of Affirmation. I telephoned the director, Father Thomas Kane, who said that he could not discuss any
patient because Massachusetts law protected patient privacy. By what standards, I
asked, was it acceptable to release any pedophile into a community? "In many
cases our recommendations are that a person not return to a situation where
they're involved with children," Kane said.

"Let me pose a hypothetical question, Father. Should a priest, any priest,
alleged to have sexually molested a child, be placed in an unsupervised situation,
without psychotherapy?"

"I have been a strong advocate for laws that protect youth," Kane replied. "If
someone breaks the law, he should suffer the consequences. But justice also has a
compassionate side. People with emotional illnesses should not be incarcerated
without treatment." As for Fontenot's unsupervised status at Gonzaga, Kane said
that state law prohibited him from commenting.

In the meantime, Linda Matys wrote the Lafayette chancery, requesting interviews with Bishop Frey and Monsignor Larroque, explaining that the paper had

questions about sexual misconduct of priests other than Gauthe. Bob Wright, attorney for the diocese, wrote back that his clients were "inhibited by contractual insurance arrangements." He also said:

> A press interview on matters in litigation could result in the Church being denied insurance coverage. . . . Please be assured that the Church and its officials have always been concerned about the interests of the individuals and families affected and will continue to do all things possible, both legally and morally, to rectify-mitigate any damages and to protect as best it can against future occurrences.

The first *Times* story ran on May 23, 1985. Matys wanted to convey the message that families who sued were not traitors to be scorned. That was the crux of an editorial statement Linda wrote with Geoff O'Connell and me, preceding the report. "The price of blindness can be high indeed," the editorial said; it went on:

> A sex abuse researcher for the U. S. Senate Permanent Committee on Investigations in Washington, Bruce Selcraig, told The Times: "Many victimized kids are walking around with a terrible time bomb ticking inside them, feeling incredible guilt."
>
> We do not feel the public is served by knowing their names. Nevertheless, interviews with well-placed sources convince us that there are still walking time bombs ticking. Victims are in an agonizing quandary: Guilt haunts their memories, yet if they come forward, communities may well view them as a reality too harsh to contemplate or as harsh critics of a cherished institution. The victim is victimized again.
>
> The Acadiana community has also suffered under the veil of secrecy that surrounds the case of Gilbert Gauthe. Although Bishop Gerard Frey has issued several general pastoral statements about the case, no church authority has talked specifically about it with the media. It seems the legal exigencies of insurance companies outweigh the more visceral needs of a community to discuss the matter with full knowledge of the facts—to have a catharsis—and wipe the slate clean.

At Linda's insistence, the term "cover-up" was not used.

In the week following the first installment, a small number of readers and callers registered strong disapproval; but the consensus of reader support was unmistakable. As Steve May had thought from the outset, people wanted to know.

The *Times-Picayune*, which had been silent on the topic for months, ran an abbreviated AP account of the Gauthe affair that appeared on May 26 and was based on what the *Dallas Morning News* had reported. Nothing appeared in the *Advertiser*. Since the *Times of Acadiana* was not a subscriber to the wire services, our reports would not move beyond Lafayette unless we did the moving. Matys and I compiled a mailing list, with advance calls to the wire services.

On May 28 the *Picayune* and *Baton Rouge Morning Advocate* ran AP and UPI stories, respectively, citing our coverage. UPI led with Hebert's statement that the number of Gauthe's victims "could well exceed 70 children, many of whom are now over 18." The longer AP account included the nuns' statements about

Gauthe's activities in 1973. Both wires quoted Father O'Connell saying that Gauthe never should have been ordained. On May 29—six days after my first installment—an *Advertiser* story credited "staff and wire reports" in summarizing what had appeared in the New Orleans and Baton Rouge dailies, omitting reference to the next-door weekly that broke the story.

On June 7, NCR published a package of articles on the pedophile priest scandal nationwide, with references to a dozen cases. Of the cases spotlighted in NCR, the most tragic involved the 1979 suicide of a twelve-year-old boy in Teaneck, New Jersey, who swallowed a bottle of liniment. Molested by a Franciscan brother, Edmund Coakley, the boy told a hospital nurse that life "was not worth living." Coakley left the order and avoided prosecution because the numb-struck family had delayed too long before reporting him to authorities. The parents, promised therapeutic help by the Franciscans, sued when the order reneged on its oral agreement. A Franciscan spokesman had told the *Bergen County Record* that payment to the family for whatever purposes "would assume some belief on our part that he was guilty." Furthermore, because New Jersey law prohibited litigation against institutions with charitable, tax-exempt status, the family's lawsuit was thrown out. Coakley was reportedly in Arizona. The impact of the child's death destroyed the parents' marriage.

My second report for the *Times* explored ramifications of the civil lawsuits. Editing the series had taken long hours of Linda Matys's time. With a backlog of other stories, she decided to skip a week before the final installment. Exhausted, I went to Mississippi for a weekend at my parents' summer place. I was introducing my daughter to the wonders of a swimming pool when my father noticed a UPI report in the *Times-Picayune*: a Jesuit priest, Norman Rogge, had been extradited from a town in northern Louisiana to Inverness, Florida, to face charges of molesting a fourteen-year-old boy. His accomplice, Michael Betancourt, had a previous arrest record for child sexual abuse. After several calls I located a Florida police detective who confirmed that Rogge had a prior record of sexual abuse, in 1966, in Tampa.

Tom Fox felt that NCR's coverage had struck the right tone. Most of the letters and calls to the paper were opposed to the subject being covered, he said. That is often the case with reporting on sensitive topics. But those opposed were *very* opposed. Some 300 readers would cancel subscriptions—not a huge dent to a newsweekly with 55,000 subscribers, yet a clear sign of the subject's volatility.

"These are serious and damaging matters," editorialized Fox.

> *But a related and broader scandal rests with local bishops. Frequently, local bishops exhibit little concern for the traumatic effects these molestation scandals have on the boys and their families—even though mental disturbances, and, in one recent case, suicide have followed such molestations. Only legal threats and law suits seem capable of provoking local bishops into taking firm actions against the priest.*

NCR subscribers include bishops, cardinals, diocesan workers, and religion editors at publications across the country. The Vatican Embassy sent issues by diplomatic pouch to Rome.

When I returned to Lafayette, Matys and I again reviewed Minos Simon's list.

Linda wanted a legal opinion about identifying the priest who had been accused of sexual abuse by a young man at a retreat. David Fine, a New Orleans attorney experienced in First Amendment questions, said: "The word 'allegedly' does not buy us much. I would not use his name." Matys decided on a paragraph saying that "at least two [priests] and possibly a third, are no longer serving because of sexual misconduct with children." The issue included a sidebar on cases in other states and quoted Fox's *NCR* editorial that recommended forming parish monitoring boards.

In an overview editorial, Matys explained the logic behind coverage of Fontenot and Limoges by name: parents had a right to know if their children had been exposed to the priests.

Although the twenty-seven priests whose files Minos Simon had requested were not all pedophiles, his strategy—linking homosexuality and pedophilia as "risk-creating" factors—was germane to coverage of a legal story. Matys wrote:

> Our reporter found allegations of homosexuality in cases of 16 priests on the list and three whose names do not appear. We chose not to report the names. . . . [Homosexual activity] is a matter for the Church and individual conscience. As a coda to this investigation, the editors asked reporter Berry for his personal reflections:
>
> "I must confess to a divided heart. The Catholic in me recoils from what I have learned about homosexual priests—because of the hypocrisy with respect to celibacy and certain things told me that would shock even the most jaded.
>
> "How many tragedies, written in Latin, lie in musty vaults or have gone to the graves of bishops with scandals hidden in their heads? Four months ago I'd never have dreamed of posing such questions. Now I have no choice but to wonder.
>
> "Nevertheless, my greatest concern is that these articles not give rise to a witch hunt mentality of vicious rumors or mean suspicions. To me the final measure of Church morality is that priests and nuns were willing to speak with me. Many felt anguish, and spoke because their conscience dictated it. In a strange way, the sadness of all this brings one closer to a message of the Gospels—a legacy of love and forgiveness. As a journalist I have no doubt that the Church has a deeply rooted problem concerning human sexuality. As a Catholic I think finally of that precious word metanoia—from the ancient Greek meaning a radical conversion of will."

Several callers asked for copies of Simon's list. The receptionist referred them to the Abbeville courthouse. One caller complained that the motion was no longer in the record.

NCR's coverage put the issue into the national media. The editorial was cited in a *Washington Post* story on Gauthe of June 9 and in a *New York Times* story on June 20. *Time* magazine devoted a July 1 religion column to priests accused of "pederasty"—focusing on Gauthe, with references to fifteen cases nationally. But none of those reports identified Limoges or Fontenot, or alluded to Lafayette priests other than Gauthe. The AP and UPI bureaus in New Orleans had not identified the other two. "We don't have documents to back up your reporting," said Kent Prince of AP. The bureau did not undertake investigative projects. *The Times* did not subscribe to the wire service. Unless an AP subscriber—in other words, a daily paper—published the allegations, Prince felt that the New Orleans bureau was exposed to a legal challenge. This was the same position in which KLFY-TV found itself after breaking the story on Gauthe a year earlier.

With the Gauthe story moving nationally, crucial questions remained. How widespread was the problem? How had other bishops responded to the families? What were the causes of the problem? Was pederasty somehow linked to a gay priest subculture?

On June 16, 1985, the *Sunday Advertiser* published a front-page editorial: "In the Gauthe Affair: The Catholic Church Is Not on Trial!" Sources at the paper said the editorial was written by Bob Angers at the publisher's behest. With a swipe at "vultures of yellow journalism," the paper announced: "It's time to call a halt to the exploitation of the Gauthe affair." Church leadership had learned "an agonizing lesson" and was "now taking strong, corrective action"—no example of which was given.

> *Now, will those who thrive on the misery of others permit the matter to rest, content to let the judicial system work, or will they turn it all into some extrava- ganza exploiting pornography while condemning the Catholic Church and all the priests who serve it?*
>
> *. . . Let's offer a special prayer for the resolution of the affair that has rocked the Acadiana community and ask the forgiveness of any unscrupulous individuals who for one reason or another attempt to blacken the reputation of our entire religious community.*

By not naming the *Times*, the daily was baiting the weekly to identify itself in responding, which Steve May wisely chose not to do. Jim Baronet of KLFY-TV told me: "I called [*Advertiser* managing editor] Charlie Lenox and told him I thought it was a chicken shit thing to print. He told me he was opposed to it, and it could have been a lot worse."

Judge Reggie of Crowley, who had failed to get Baronet to halt Channel 10's coverage the year before, fired off a letter to the *Times:* "You have done a serious injustice to the holy priesthood by sensationalizing [and] debased us all by your series. I believe the jury of public opinion convicts you of journalistic malfea- sance." The *Daily Advertiser* ran several letters championing its editorial. A letter from attorney David S. Cook, lector at St. John Cathedral, did not agree:

> *To suggest that your competition has been guilty of "yellow journalism" smacks of rank commercialism; your prayer for forgiveness of those who have dared to shed some light on this terrible subject is self-serving and pretentious.*
>
> *While it is indeed time to begin to put this tragedy behind us, and while the task of rebuilding the faith in the Church may not be an easy one, I am grateful to your competitor for having had the courage to provide the public with the information needed to make a responsible decision. I am confident that the Church and her people will overcome these recent events, and that they will be stronger for having dealt with the truth, rather than having avoided it.*

In mid-June the National Conference of Catholic Bishops gathered at St. John's Abbey in the green hills ninety miles north of Minneapolis—three hundred bishops, half as many reporters. The main issue on their agenda was the Conference's pastoral letter on the U.S. economy, an unprecedented and liberal critique of the American economy in the light of Catholic social thinking. Though not due for publication until 1986, the letter promised to become a major religious event. Milwaukee Archbishop Rembert Weakland, who was supervising the letter's writing, had discussed the draft with dozens of business leaders. Many were openly skeptical. "My brother bishops," said Weakland with a smile, "having faced Wall Street, you're easy."

George Will accused the bishops of believing "that God subscribes to the liberal agenda." New York Times and Washington Post editorials, never friendly to supply-side economics, were more approving. The Times deemed the 60,000 word draft "a plea that America give priority to the human condition." The letter addressed mounting Third World poverty, unemployment in America's rusting industrial belt, the breakdown of inner-city families, and the morality of merger acquisitions and corporate expansion fed on junk bonds.

Circulating among reporters in Collegeville, Eugene Kennedy had more than economics on his mind. A clinical psychologist and former priest, Kennedy, now married, taught at Loyola University of Chicago. He had close ties among many bishops. By virtue of his novels and insightful books about Catholicism, Kennedy was often called by reporters seeking comment on major stories involving the church. At Collegeville, press speculation focused on the German cardinal, Joseph Ratzinger, prefect of the Congregation for the Doctrine of the Faith, who had said that a collegial body of bishops should be "a limited structure, without juridical dimension," a judgment having the effect of giving more power to the Pope and not bishops. Ratzinger was also putting pressure on the Rev. Charles Curran, a prominent moral theologian at Catholic University, to revise his writings on sexual ethics.

From his knowledge of the church's moral teaching, and as a psychologist to many of the clergy, Kennedy viewed sexual morality as the surface issue in the Ratzinger-Curran dispute. The root conflict was power—the Vatican's desire to maintain its authority to restrict theological debate. At the same time, Kennedy saw a more profound and powerful shift under way.

Pastors—from the Pope down to parish priests—were becoming demythologized in the eyes of lay people grown more skeptical of church authority since the 1968 letter banning artificial methods of birth control. Kennedy viewed the reports of pedophilia cover-ups as a sign of the hierarchy's inability to shake off the comforts of power and to confront sexual realities. Few bishops were willing to discuss openly psychological and emotional problems of celibacy. A 1970 survey of clergy by Andrew Greeley and the National Opinion Research Center had found loneliness to be a problem. From his own case studies, Kennedy had become troubled by the eroding fabric of clerical culture. In the post-Watergate era, as American society lost faith with authority figures—doctors, lawyers, politicians —the priesthood too had been suffering a loss in its esteem.

The secret report on pedophilia was sinking into ecclesiastical myopia. After delivering the report to Auxiliary Bishop Quinn in Ohio, Tom Doyle had flown to Montreal for the baptism of a niece. He was at his sister's house when Bill Levada, the Los Angeles auxiliary, called to say that Cardinal Law's Committee on Research and Pastoral Practices would not be handling the issue but that it would be discussed in Collegeville.

Back in Washington, Doyle went about his embassy duties and followed news accounts of the Lafayette debacle. After Gauthe's picture appeared in the *Washington Post*, he wondered if the long effort with Peterson and Mouton had been worth it. He gave Laghi a copy of the report; the nuncio was impressed, remarking, "I certainly hope they'll do something." Laghi's relationship with the conference was cordial. But Ratzinger's signals from Rome about the limited jurisdiction of episcopal bodies did not sit well with NCCB leaders. This threatened to put Laghi, the Vatican delegate, in something of an adversarial role with bishops.

Monsignor Daniel Hoye was general secretary of the NCCB. "He ran the conference's day-to-day operations," Doyle recalled, "and believe me, that meant an awful lot. When you have something as big as the NCCB, the staff makes a major difference." Because of the peace pastoral, bishops were being courted by Reagan administration officials, anxious to soften their views.

Dan Hoye was tightly allied with the bishops who shaped the conference's earlier, 1983 pastoral letter on war and peace, another progressive document that had called, among other things, for the United States to abandon its first-strike nuclear policy. These men—Archbishop John Roach of Minneapolis; Cardinal Joseph Bernardin of Chicago; Bishops James Malone of Youngstown, Ohio, and Thomas Kelly of Louisville, Kentucky—had worked with Hoye to frame the conference's decisions, appointments, and committees. Tom Doyle was not their favorite guy. "The whole outfit over there was opposed to most of the appointments [of new bishops] we supported," Doyle remarked of his embassy work.

Doyle then had two strikes against him in getting the bishops to address the pedophilia report seriously: his alliance with Laghi and his opposition to the peace pastoral. Michael Peterson had carefully trod his own path, cultivating ties with Hoye and letting various bishops know of his own genuine support for the conference's antinuclear agenda. But by the middle of June neither priest had been asked to discuss their report. Despite his shaky standing with the NCCB, Doyle was waiting to be asked. Finally he asked Laghi to call Hoye about the pedophilia discussion. Laghi reported back that Hoye had told him someone else was handling it.

Two nights before the Collegeville meeting, Hoye telephoned Doyle: "I want to talk about pedophilia."

"Wonderful."

"I understand you've been talking to bishops."

"That's true. This is the United States of America."

Hoye asked why they had not made the document public. Because of litigation, Doyle explained—a concern that it not heighten civil liability. If it became known that the bishops had such a document, plaintiff attorneys would request it by subpoena. On that note the conversation ended. Having braced himself for the disappointment of being excluded from the Collegeville presentation, Doyle began simmering anew.

Hoye made certain the pedophilia briefing was off limits to the press. But Bishop James Malone, the conference president, subsequently revealed that a session had been held. Richard Issle, a consulting psychologist to the archdiocese of

Chicago, addressed clinical issues. Auxiliary Bishop Kenneth Angelle of Providence, Rhode Island, spoke from the vantage point of one who had such problem priests. And USCC general counsel Wil Caron discussed legal problems.

A puzzled Pio Laghi returned from the conference, wondering why Doyle, after so much work, had not appeared at the briefing. "You should have been there," he told Doyle. "Why weren't you?"

"You tell me and we'll both know," came the cryptic reply.

The Doyle-Mouton-Peterson document had referred to thirty priests—twice the number reported in *Time*. As summer wore on, Doyle became more frustrated over the NCCB's failure to embrace a national response plan. Bishops continued to call him for advice, which he readily gave. On a trip to the Midwest, Doyle met with Pittsburgh Bishop Anthony Bevilacqua, a friend. Doyle asked if any headway was being made on a pedophilia policy. Bevilacqua said that it had been given to a committee headed by retired Bishop Michael Murphy of Erie, Pennsylvania. Several weeks later Bevilacqua told Doyle that the issue had been tabled.

Archbishop Roach, in reference to the peace pastoral, had once stressed "the consistency with which moral principles are defended across a range of moral issues." If the bishops could speak out on nuclear warheads, Doyle wondered, why couldn't they adopt a policy to defend kids from being molested by their own priests?

Mark Chopko, who succeeded Caron as USCC general counsel, later told me: "There was a feeling that those guys"—Mouton, Doyle, Peterson—"wanted to set themselves up for work."

Ray Mouton, however, said that his concern had not been over who should be involved, only that *something* should be done: "The church could have done it with other people. That's not my quarrel. Given the cases that followed, there's no way we could have put out all those fires. To bishops and bureaucrats, a damage control effort with bad news potential would not further a clerical career. To seek a remedy means you're admitting the existence of a problem, and people were afraid of that. It was killed by the politics of inertia."

Of the 1985 report, Eugene Kennedy said: "The medical section was flawed. Among other things, Peterson overemphasized possible genetic factors in pedophilia. The real problem was that the bishops didn't know what to make of the document. But it was an important attempt. Someone had to do something to sensitize the hierarchy. The tragedy is that the hierarchy had no coherent policy."

Several weeks after Collegeville, Doyle and Peterson had dinner at a restaurant in Washington. "Sometimes," Doyle said somberly, "I feel ashamed to be a priest."

In Chicago, Gallagher-Bassett, an insurer for nearly half of the nation's dioceses, saw the looming possibility of huge losses from pedophilia litigation. And so the decision was made that, beginning January 1, 1986, cases of sexual misconduct by clergy would no longer be covered. Priests, like psychiatrists, were now considered bad insurance risks for malpractice.

As of July 4, 1985, insurance attorneys for the Lafayette diocese had still not accepted financial liability for Gauthe's crimes. The strategy of delay, and bargain, seemed set in stone when a twenty-eight-year-old man from Opelousas met at KLFY-TV with Jim Baronet and Dee Stanley and accused his pastor, Father

Lloyd Hebert (no relation to attorney Paul Hebert) of having molested him through adolescence. Channel 10 refused to air a report unless the victim identified himself. The young man then met with J. Minos Simon, who immediately issued a subpoena for the priest's deposition. The chancery announced that Hebert was taking a vacation before a new pastoral assignment. The *Opelousas Daily World* published a glowing tribute to Hebert's thirteen years as pastor. When that happened, Channel 10 reported the victim's allegations. Father Hebert went to live with relatives and reportedly entered therapy. He did not resume priestly duties. In an interview, the emotionally fragile young man told me how his life had been wrecked by the years when Hebert molested him. A childhood friend of the victim, who had moved to another state, told me in a background interview how "Hebert wrecked [the victim's] life. There was a time when I wanted to kill that priest." The statute of limitations had passed in the criminal and civil spheres.

Meanwhile, in New Orleans, Raul Bencomo was proceeding with his four cases and issued subpoenas to depose Archbishop Hannan and Father O'Connell, who had known Gauthe at his 1973 parish. On July 7, 1985, Bob Wright, the attorney for the Lafayette diocese, stated in court in Abbeville that the defense accepted institutional liability—that is, financial responsibility for Gauthe's deeds —thus ending the discovery onslaught of the plaintiffs' attorneys.

By then, four priests had been removed from the diocese under accusations of sexually molesting boys.

viii.

Prosecution

In late summer of 1985, Minos Simon rejected a settlement proposal by the insurance attorneys, offering the Gastal family structured payments over thirty years with an ultimate value of $3 million. The Gastals and their attorney wanted a lump sum well over $1 million. And so, on August 21, the child was deposed in Simon's office with seven attorneys present. Therapist Lyle LeCorgne stood beside him throughout the deposition.

"It was a way of reassuring him," said LeCorgne. "To the credit of the lawyers, there was a significant amount of tenderness, a consideration of what the boy went through. I think he came away feeling he did the right thing by telling the truth. It was not easy but I don't think it was traumatic for him." Nevertheless, on therapeutic grounds, LeCorgne wanted no further testimony. "I see no purpose served for this child to go into open court. Let's just get the damn thing settled."

The child was caught between conflicting forces. Therapy aims at rebuilding trust, strengthening bonds, restoring dignity. After months of counseling, would his answers convey his suffering and strengthen the case? Yet if therapy had achieved some success, would the boy's renewed confidence reduce prospects for a large settlement? Charles Schmidt III, one of the insurance attorneys, asked most of the questions—about family, school, friendships—the subtler skein of which sought to see just how badly the plaintiff had been hurt. In one exchange, the boy used "pee-pee" as an anatomical noun in stating that Gauthe had performed oral sex on him.

> Q: Did you think there was anything wrong with that at the time?
> A: No. I thought the priest knew what he was doing.

When asked how many sexual encounters had occurred in a given month, the fourth grader said: "I don't remember. I just know he did a lot."

A crucial issue was when the boy told his parents. If that was done much before Gauthe's July 1983 suspension, then the one-year legal period for filing suit would have expired, as Paul Hebert had filed the Gastal suit in mid-1984. After

Gauthe left the area, he testified, his mother asked if the priest "was doing something to me. . . . The first time she had asked me I told her nothing was going on." Schmidt asked why. "Because he said he would come back and hurt my daddy if I told."

When Schmidt asked about explicit acts, the boy told of a series of them, using "pee-pee" in descriptions of anal and oral sex of several variations. From time to time Simon interrupted to say, "Take your time, just relax." Simon completed the session with questions about photographs that Gauthe had taken. The child said they portrayed "all kinds of bad things" and added, "Taking those pictures naked, he said that he was going to give them to us when we got old so that we will know how we looked when we were a little baby."

The boy's innocent language left me feeling angry, something I worked hard to contain lest emotions prejudice my reporting. Nothing I had ever written so challenged the basic premise of fairness. Gauthe was clinically sick, yet what he had done was so monstrously wrong. How should one view his superiors? At Mass in New Orleans churches, I wondered what people in the pews would think had they known what I knew. My reports had received little mention in the *Times-Picayune;* Lafayette was a world away.

I was not always certain of my motives in returning to Mass. The years I spent detached from the church were not ones of hard rupture. I had benevolent memories of priests and nuns. Catholicism, a belief in Christ, social concern and forgiveness, were part of me. In my mid-twenties I had drifted away, single, with a foot planted in bohemia. Why was the Mass now pulling me back? Was it to alleviate guilt—to tell myself that I was not hurling rocks at a glass temple but rather embracing a church whose corruption assaulted my troubled faith?

In my heart I felt another impulse drawing me toward communion and liturgy —a sense of community one did not feel on muggy afternoons when churches were empty and I could pray alone. In those reveries I kept thinking of Albert Camus's idea of the absurdity one faces between "human need and the unreasonable silence of the world." Although I revered Camus's work, faith to me was a search for God's voice amid human suffering. Praying for strength and compassion was one way of processing the wretched behavior surfacing through the legal record. I needed the Mass for its sacrificial essence, to believe again in redemption, mystery, and hope. In the parish where we lived a black choir sang soaring gospel refrains, reminding me of black Baptist churches I visited in rural Mississippi in 1971. Then I had been an idealist, fired by a belief in civil rights. Now I sought sanctuary, an essence of spirit. The institution, at least in Lafayette, might be in the hands of blundering men, perhaps even corrupt men, but faith transcended mortal flaws.

ii.

As civil cases dragged on, the criminal trial was slated for October 14 in Lafayette. Ray Mouton confided, "My major concern is keeping Gilbert alive. Michael Peterson thinks he will try to kill himself when he's brought back to Lafayette.

Gil's called me twice at home, at night. He wanted to give my daughter a teddy bear. I said fine, send it."

The district attorney of Lafayette had his own major concern: putting Gauthe behind bars for the rest of his life.

The violence in nature gave Nathan Stansbury feelings of tranquillity. Roaring thunderclaps, jagged electrical lines cracking the sky, the strong winds advancing rain all served to calm him. As a Tulane law student in 1965 he headed for Lake Pontchartrain, the vast water body bordering New Orleans, when Hurricane Betsy hit. Waves drenched his car as convicts stacked sandbags along the sea wall which girded the lake. Policemen made him leave. Years later, a fishing partner recalled Stansbury's motorboat tearing across a bay, "the sky turning black, that boat bouncing like a cork, me scared and Nathan with this weird grin on his face. I mean, he was *enjoying* it." It rained so hard the day he was born that the doctor never made it to delivery. It was 1932, a small house across from a Lafayette nunnery, since demolished, where City Hall stands today. As a kid he dreamed of thunderstorms, himself in a tent up on a mountain; when it really rained he opened the windows and got spanked after showers dampened the beds.

He had a traditional Catholic upbringing. Many years later he would fondly remember the Latin incantations of his service as an altar boy. His great-aunt, a nun at the Academy of the Sacred Heart in Grand Coteau, a bucolic village near Lafayette, sang the praises of the priesthood. Stansbury entered Immaculata Seminary in the ninth grade but lasted only a year. "I found myself thinking about girls," he chuckled.

In high school he served Mass for Bishop Jeanmard at the Carmelite convent, a cloistered order with a screen separating the tabernacle from the pews. While the bishop gave the Eucharist to sisters at the communion rail, Nathan knelt on the altar, craning his neck for a glimpse of nuns whose faces he never saw.

No one doubted he was tough. In 1972, his first year as district attorney, he was driving home late one night when headlights flashed in his eyes and a shotgun blast shattered his windshield. He hit the brakes and rolled onto the floor. From that moment he had diminished hearing in his left ear. He lay across the floorboard, heart pounding, and when he finally gazed up, taillights of a pickup truck dissolved in the night. He drove fast the other way till he saw a police car. Stumbling out of his vehicle, he asked the cop: "Is my nose still there?" The officer assured him that it was. All that blood, from a nick by glass that would leave no discernible scar. The squad car took him to the hospital while others searched for the assailant. A man called the sheriff: "We just shot the D.A."

Stansbury recalled: "Two years later the driver of the vehicle told his lawyer, in an unrelated case, who shot at me. The lawyer wouldn't identify his client. He just wanted me to know who fired the shot. It was a guy I tried for murder. A dopehead; crazy man. He got twenty-one years for manslaughter, ten for LSD. He'd gotten out of jail; they later caught him in a pharmacy with a pillowcase full of drugs. I spent six months with bodyguards. I carry a gun now but I've never had to use it. In the penitentiary I'm not poorly thought of. I am active in penal reform. A man I put away for life made a leather visor with my name on it."

He was frustrated by legal leeway given to criminals. Put a man in the pen and ten jailhouse lawyers were ready to advise him how to flood the system with writs, looking for loopholes, challenging procedural rulings, anything to get out.

Criminal lawyers did their share too. "Gloria Aucoin killed her eleven-year-old daughter," he said. "Stabbed her, beat her with a tire tool, could not kill that child. So she ran over her with a Pontiac. At a hearing her lawyer said, 'Man, she's served ten years. Can't you agree to a commutation?' I said, 'I'll agree when Shawn [her deceased daughter] does.'"

Even before the Gauthe scandal Stansbury had come to view priests more as men of rules and less as carriers of spiritual tradition. A cleric from the chancery had contacted him in the early eighties, asking whether he realized that his first wife had had their marriage annulled so that she could remarry within the church. No, he did not know. Stansbury had remarried well after the divorce. He thought that by Catholic law he was excommunicated for having remarried and was thus forbidden to receive the sacraments.* The priest who came to his office explained that the church now viewed failed marriages more compassionately, that the diocesan tribunal studied cases of those seeking church approval to dissolve a marriage; if certain prescriptions were met, the annulment was issued and permission was granted to remarry without severance from the faith.

The possibility tugged at his spiritual core. The divorce had long troubled him. *God understands,* he had told himself about his divorce and remarriage—wondering if he was rationalizing a sin for which God would make him pay on Judgment Day. The tribunal priest, having studied his case, felt it could be changed to an annulment, thus restoring his legitimacy as a Catholic. But his second wife was a Methodist and that would require more canonical footwork. The priest produced a questionnaire and said the annulment process cost $600. "I can't believe you want me to pay to get back in the church!" Stansbury snapped. The priest backed off a beat: well, the money might not be a problem. "I can afford it, Father. I just feel uncomfortable paying for it."

He promised to think it over. The form required that his second wife answer questions about their sex life before their marriage. *That's nobody else's business,* he thought. Ironically, his Protestant wife sometimes attended Mass with his mother. Stansbury threw the form away, preferring not to endure the indignity of what seemed to him a contrived process. (His instincts were correct—see footnote below—but they were only instincts.) Still, the possibility of an annulment ate at him for months. As he told me: "It's the men of the church who make the rules and change the rules. They say I can't receive the sacraments because I was divorced. I won't go against that for fear it is the correct rule. I go to church when there is a reason, like a wedding or funeral. I feel bad that I can't receive the Holy Eucharist. I grew up in a time when church and faith were extremely strong. And I still have that faith. But after the divorce—go to church for what?

"It's all changing now. The Latin Mass is gone. That meant something to me. It was different, set the church apart. I perceive the church is looking for numbers at the expense of the one universal and apostolic church. So what if First Baptist is getting bigger? In the old days, if I ate meat on Friday I went and confessed it to the priest. I've always wondered: did God send men to hell for eating meat on

* In fact, annulment practices had been greatly liberalized, though the priest did not tell him so. When I asked canonist Rev. Thomas Doyle, a specialist in marriage issues, about the offer put to Stansbury, he said that his former wife's petition of an annulment to the diocesan tribunal meant that Stansbury was thereby a beneficiary of the same annulment.

Friday? It was a mortal sin. After they changed the rule, did He take them out of hell? I hope so. We are talking about men who make these rules and those men *kicked me out of the church.*

"I feel uncomfortable with the church but comfortable with my values. They may change the rules again, which will let me return without having to compromise on that form business. It is hard for me to imagine God saying, '*Stansbury, these are the rules: they are not the Ten Commandments, they are the man-made rules of the church.* Either that priest's approach was wrong or the procedure is wrong. I may change my mind. I may get scared enough to go back. Because I believe that if I die with a mortal sin, not in a state of grace, I will go to hell."

In autumn of 1985 he was immersed in the Gauthe case, the most vexing prosecution of his career. In a pretrial interview I asked what kind of pressure he had felt from the local political establishment. "Not a single word," he said. "Nothing."

The object of Ray Mouton's defense was not to gain Gauthe's freedom but to have him secure in a facility where he would be safe and receive treatment. Stansbury agreed that Gauthe was sick; he just wanted him behind bars. Mouton, figuring on an insanity plea, proposed a life sentence at the state mental hospital. Stansbury said no. One Joe Breland had violently murdered his wife. His attorney argued that multiple sclerosis had contributed to a psychotic break. The jury found Breland not guilty by reason of insanity. Since 1979 there had been three hearings for Breland's release. Doctors said he was no longer a danger. To Stansbury it was a mockery of the insanity ruling.

At conferences in the prosecutor's office, Mouton and Stansbury drank coffee, smoked cigarettes, argued, and seven days before trial were in a stalemate. Mouton felt that his leverage would be the D.A.'s reluctance to put the boys through an agonizing public trial on the witness stand. Stansbury excused himself to go to the john. As he urinated, Mouton struck: "I'm gonna subpoena all those kids *and* their parents, Nathan."

"Your fucking client's insanity is your problem," Stansbury shot back, brushing off the threat.

"I'll put 'em all on the witness stand. It won't be pretty."

"He's going to prison," said Stansbury, giving no ground.

Both attorneys faced a gauntlet of problems. If Stansbury questioned the kids, the emotional tonnage of words, whimpers, pained nuances would portray Gauthe as a monster. But might such questioning bolster the insanity defense? Stansbury knew that if Mouton did not contest Gauthe's crimes, it would alleviate the need for the boys to testify. In that scenario, the trial would then hinge on expert witnesses: Ed Shwery vs. Fred Berlin.

Shwery carried heavy baggage because of money earned from Bencomo, the church, and the prosecutor's office. Having worked all sides, Shwery would be vulnerable on cross-examination. Stansbury had read Berlin's writings on pedophilia but had no idea of his potency as a witness. He also knew that he needed the graphic testimony of those kids as an evidentiary sledgehammer.

When Stansbury met with the victims, he could feel their jagged edges. One child trembled as he coached them on questions they might expect and reviewed answers they had already given but would have to give again. He consulted

Shwery and Bouillion, whose emphatic opinion on the kids' behalf was that the trial should be avoided if at all possible. Stansbury could protect minors from facing Gauthe by using closed circuit television for their testimony; but the four boys who were now over eighteen would have to testify in the room with Gauthe present.

When Ray Mouton issued a subpoena to Paul Hebert, Stansbury sensed the scenario. After grim testimony by the boys, Mouton would call Hebert as a witness who would say, "Yes, we secured six-figure settlements for these boys." So the jury would know the victims were receiving more than care. Reviving the litany of sexual monstrosities (now equated for the jury with money), Mouton would present Gauthe's acts in numbing detail with the view, as he had told Stansbury from the outset, that no sane man would do those things. Then he would put Shwery through a meat grinder, questioning his overlapping interests, and keep his own expert, Berlin, on the stand as long as possible with a prolonged seminar on pedophilia. If Mouton could sway just three jurors to the opinion that, however sordid his crimes, Gauthe was mentally incompetent—bingo! A mistrial.

Would it work?

Stansbury was skeptical. Still, years of combat with high-paid defense attorneys left a bad feeling in his gut. He knew Mouton was trying to back him into a corner.

Meanwhile, in Louisiana and Washington, church officials fretted as state marshals planned the conversion of a Lafayette conference room into a media center to accommodate an anticipated crush of reporters. Searching for a place to put Gauthe, Mouton proposed Villa Louis Martin in New Mexico. When Stansbury broached it to the families, they immediately said no. Gauthe belonged behind bars, said Ted Campbell, "not in some country club run by the church."

When Mouton and his paralegal, Cecile Cook, flew to Washington to visit the Sexual Disorders Clinic, the attorney was in a sullen mood. Bob Wright had told him the diocese was strapped for funds after already paying out more than $1 million for its share of civil settlements and medical expenses.

"Well," said Mouton on meeting his comrades, "how are you, Tom?"

"Suicidal," grunted Doyle.

Michael Peterson laughed.

Doyle was concerned about Father Lloyd Hebert, whose abrupt departure from Opelousas in July had given Simon the final piece of damning information with which to force the defense to accept financial liability. Why hadn't Frey and Larroque sent the priest to St. Luke? Mouton explained that Hebert was being seen by Ed Shwery.

Over dinner, Doyle explained that their report on the pedophilia crisis had failed to win the backing of key bishops; Peterson said that several bishops wanted the trio to address clergy conference days. Mouton agreed to participate. After Peterson left, Doyle, Mouton, and Cook had a nightcap at F. Scott's in Georgetown. Doyle was depressed. Dan Hoye of the NCCB had told Pio Laghi that pedophilia was not a major problem. Doyle knew of forty-eight cases around the country—and if that wasn't a problem, what was? There was one glimmer of hope. Doyle had recently met with Cardinal William Baum, formerly archbishop of Washington and now Vatican prefect for the Congregation for Catholic Education. Baum was ashen after the briefing. The situation was terrible, he allowed; it was important to pursue the issue, Baum said, even though there was no mandate to do so from the American bishops.

With his friends in Georgetown that night, Doyle brooded, "I think I'm gonna get sacked." The embassy would not fire him; but, with his appointment term nearing its end, he knew that his aggressive stance on the issue was a sure career-choker.

The trial was less than two weeks away and Nathan Stansbury was staying up late reading Berlin's literature while Mouton was searching for a foolproof strategy. Mouton was back in Louisiana when Tom Doyle called from Washington. "Rome does not want this trial," he confided. "They think you're the problem." Bishop Quinn was meeting at that moment with Pio Laghi; phone lines had been buzzing among Archbishop Hannan and Rayer, Bishop Frey and Bob Wright. "They're going to cut your money," said Doyle.

Cut my money? Mouton was outraged. He thanked the embassy canonist for the tip and thirty minutes later, when Wright asked him to please come to Bishop Frey's office, he said sure. Polite as ever, Wright opened the session with a nod toward the bishop. Frey stumbled through a small speech about the diocesan finances and held out computer printout sheets. Mouton refused to take them. Confused by the refusal, the bishop said: "We have no money." The diocese could not continue paying Mouton's fees or cover Berlin's expenses as an expert witness.

"I understand," said Mouton. "I'm glad you weren't in that position when Monsignor Larroque needed support for alcoholism."

The vicar-general managed a wry smile.

Mouton turned to Bob Wright. "Next Tuesday I will need Bishop Frey and Archbishop Hannan in court and I will issue subpoenas for them." To try the case as an indigent's defender, he would need their testimony in a pretrial hearing to prove that his client was a pauper. "And I will telephone the *New York Times*, CBS, ABC, and others in advance of the hearing." He turned to Larroque. "The church is trying to create a climate to have troubled priests come forth for treatment. This move will destroy that effort and make them just dig in deeper."

Later that day he informed Wright that, if he did not have a written statement committing the diocese to pay Gauthe's legal expenses within twenty-four hours, he would issue the subpoenas. The next morning Wright provided the agreement.

In spite of their differences, Mouton had grown to like the older attorney. Wright had a silk-smooth approach in closed-door sessions that Mouton rather envied. Even if sparks flew, once the doors opened Wright maintained the amiability of a gentlemen's club confederate. Now Wright drew Mouton into his confidence at a meeting in his well-appointed office. "Hannan wants to know if we can control Mouton," he said matter-of-factly. "I told him, 'All Ray wants is twenty years with guarantee of treatment.'" Mouton was pleased: maybe church officials would now try to help him. But Wright offered more information: Archbishop Hannan had made plans to fly to Hartford where he would visit Gauthe at Institute of Living and review his obligations to the church and priesthood. Mouton slumped in his chair. "You mean he's going to tell him to plead to life to avoid the bad publicity?"

Wright's stone-face silence said, *Draw your own conclusion.* Back in his office,

Mouton telephoned Peterson, whose concern over Gauthe's suicidal tendencies had grown as the trial date neared. Peterson had arranged his calendar to spend time in Lafayette during and after the trial to counsel Gauthe. Mouton told him about Hannan's plan and said, "I want Gilbert moved immediately to the Sexual Disorders Clinic at Johns Hopkins." Peterson agreed to provide a driver, and Mouton secured the transfer papers.

Later that day Larroque called Mouton. "Where is Father Gauthe?" Said Mouton: "He's safe."

Larroque laughed nervously. "This isn't funny. Where is he?" Safe, came the reply. "It seems that Archbishop Hannan wants to pay a pastoral visit," said Larroque to Mouton's silence. The vicar asked him to please hold. After a brief interregnum he came back on the line. "The archbishop is very angry." Mouton said he would reveal Gauthe's whereabouts and allow Hannan to visit only when he was convinced they would not discuss any aspect of the criminal proceeding.

"We understand," sighed Larroque.

Peterson, meanwhile, after conferring with Fred Berlin, provided Mouton with a new alternative: Patuxent Institute in Jessup, Maryland—a prison with a special program for sex offenders. Berlin was a consulting psychiatrist at Patuxent, which was close enough to St. Luke to allow for Peterson's therapeutic presence in Gauthe's years behind bars. Peterson was committed to treating Gilbert as long as needed.

Then Archbishop Hannan called Peterson, asking if he could talk some sense into Mouton. Peterson said no—and broached the Patuxent plan, which pleased Hannan, who recognized how Patuxent helped Mouton's bargaining position with Stansbury. If all parties accepted Patuxent there would be no trial, and Hannan had marching orders from Rome: *stop the trial.* From the Vatican to the apostolic nunciature in Washington to the chanceries in New Orleans and Lafayette, every churchman knew that the news coverage of a trial, no matter the verdict, would be a disaster for the church.

Mouton again met with Stansbury. Two issues still divided them: how many years Gauthe would do time, and where. Mouton served subpoenas on victims represented by Tony Fontana in Abbeville. A message was filtering out: it's going to be an ugly trial. He thought the pressure was working on Stansbury when a phone call interrupted their meeting: Monsignor Larroque for Mouton. Stansbury sat across from him as Larroque's voice came through the receiver: "Ray, the archbishop would like to speak with you."

Mouton took the call in another room.

Stansbury had learned from Raymond Blanco that church superiors felt Mouton was enjoying the attention the case had drawn. Stansbury hated the attention. A complex murder trial fired his intellect. Reading about child molesting depressed him.

At his end of the line Mouton tried not to simmer. Until that moment he had never spoken with Philip Hannan. Now, of all times to be interrupted, in the middle of a meeting with his adversary—but the prelate was brief. "Ray, tell me there is a way to avoid this trial."

"I am working on it, Archbishop. But I cannot promise that."

Diplomatically, Hannan acknowledged his hard work; but now, he added, for the good of all concerned, an agreement had to be reached. "I'm working on it, Archbishop," Mouton repeated, suppressing his irritation. Hannan asked if Stansbury had agreed to Patuxent. Mouton said not yet.

"What will you need?" asked the archbishop.

He needed the consent of the state Department of Corrections to allow the prisoner to serve his sentence in another state and a transfer agreement with the state of Maryland; agreement between the two governors; and commitment of the church to cover the daily cost of Gauthe's care and incarceration in Maryland, since the state of Louisiana would not.

Hannan said he would make some calls.

Mouton returned to his meeting with Stansbury and put the Patuxent proposal on the table. Would it do? "So long as it's behind bars," said Stansbury, "I don't care what kind of treatment he gets." Mouton left to meet his wife for lunch with hope fluttering in his heart.

Nathan Stansbury's next meeting was with Hannan and Frey. "Don't forget to genuflect and kiss the archbishop's ring," his secretary teased. When they arrived, Stansbury shook hands with the two bishops. He knew that eleven horrible stories on the witness stand would be awful for the church. Frey said nothing. To Stansbury he seemed like a bump on a log. Hannan was tough and crusty. "That guy Mouton," the archbishop said, "has got to let this man plead guilty. Is there any way you can think of so we can talk to Gauthe?"

Stansbury conceded that Mouton did not want them talking with Gauthe. He left unspoken the reason why: Mouton wanted no church superiors strong-arming his client into a plea that would send him to the penitentiary for life. By now Stansbury accepted Gauthe's suicidal tendency as fact. *Ray is the only one who won't spit on Gauthe,* he thought. He told the bishops that he had no problems with a sentence served at Patuxent.

"Is there anything I can do?" asked Hannan.

"Yeah," said the prosecutor. "Help Ray."

When they left, Stansbury sensed that Mouton had a problem. Fred Berlin's résumé and writings had all the earmarks of an honest doctor. He wondered how a man of such knowledge about sexual disorders could possibly diagnose Gauthe as insane. . . .

Mouton flew to Baltimore to facilitate Gauthe's first meeting with Michael Peterson. Shuttled among three facilities and a prison that year, the fallen priest sat hunched in his chair at the Sexual Disorders Clinic, waiting for another doctor to inspect him. Peterson entered the room and opened his arms: "Gilbert Gauthe, I love you as a brother in Christ." Mouton nearly cried. His client had wrecked families, cost his church millions; his bishop did not want to pay for his defense. And Michael gave him a bear hug.

Mouton's defense indeed hinged on Dr. Berlin, who was at the clinic when Mouton arrived. Under Louisiana law, the sole test for legal responsibility for a crime is restricted to whether a defendant at the time of the act knew the difference between right and wrong. After a year of expensive hospitalization, Gauthe's present state of mind was not at issue. The insanity defense turned on how he had thought and functioned during the years in which he committed the criminal acts.

Berlin was a stout, cordial man, blunt in his opinion: "I don't know what you want to talk about, but you don't have a case." Gauthe was a pedophile but he was not insane.

For the first time since they had met, Michael Peterson realized, Ray Mouton was speechless. His careful legal strategy was going up in smoke. Patuxent became all the more critical as leverage with Gauthe, who was scared stiff about the looming trial and doing time as a child molester in the Louisiana State Penitentiary. But even Gauthe's willingness to go to Patuxent did not allay Mouton's and Peterson's concerns about how his suicidal tendencies might be provoked there.

Then Hannan went to Baltimore, having assured Mouton that he would not discuss the criminal matter with Gauthe. His arrival at the Sexual Disorders Clinic sent a buzz through the staff. Many sex offenders had been treated there; never had an archbishop paid a visit. When Hannan met Gauthe, the priest fell to his knees, apologizing profusely. Hannan gently assured him that he would not be abandoned and told him in soothing tones that the legal resolution was best for all concerned. Gauthe agreed.

Mouton was back in Lafayette when Larroque informed him that Archbishop Hannan had discussed Patuxent with Governor Edwin Edwards, the flashy Cajun who at that time was standing trial in federal court in New Orleans on racketeering charges (of which he was eventually acquitted). Edwards approved the deal, Larroque told Mouton.

On October 9, Mouton and Stansbury drove to Abbeville for a procedural conference with Judge Hugh Brunson. Mouton told his adversary that his client and the psychiatrists were in accord. Mouton wanted ten years. Stansbury insisted on thirty. "You know, Nathan," Ray said, "this is a trial nobody wants."

"Where he serves is irrelevant to me so long as it is a prison at hard labor," Stansbury replied. Hard labor in Louisiana does not mean working on rock piles: legally, it means without benefit of parole.

They kept talking all the way to the judge's chambers.

By legal custom, the district attorney chose the trial date. Because the judges' calendars, rotating among three civil parishes, were set in advance, the prosecutor could choose the judge by selecting a date when only that judge was available. A lumbering man, Brunson had risen through the old boy ranks with Stansbury's political and fund-raising support.

Stansbury knew that Mouton planned to attack that relationship and demand that Brunson recuse himself. If Brunson refused, Mouton felt, the judge would be handing him nails with which to hammer out an appeal. (Several years later the Louisiana Supreme Court sided with an indigent's attorney on just such an appeal and abolished the practice of allowing the prosecutor to pick a judge.) This final prong of Mouton's attack rested tacitly among the three men as they met in the circuit judge's Abbeville office. Mouton had reached his decision: Stansbury said that counsel had agreed to a term of twenty years at hard labor. Though it was not spelled out in the plea bargain, the prosecutor was amenable to time served out of state, provided the defense arranged the details.

"Have you talked to the families?" asked Brunson.

"I will, your honor," Stansbury said.

That night Stansbury met one group of families in the courtroom. He could see the tension in the boys. Then, carefully, he explained the proposed plea bargain—twenty years in prison without parole. The church had the option of covering Gauthe's expenses in a Maryland facility. But whether in Louisiana or Maryland, he would serve his time in a prison. Heads began to nod. Stansbury woke up at four o'clock the next morning, wondering if he should go through with it. Convinced now that he could put Gauthe away for life, he could see lights flashing on his political scoreboard. But what would a trial do to the kids? Five hours later he called Mouton: the deal was on, pending approval of the remaining families, with whom he would meet the next day. Mouton, convinced now that Gauthe would receive ongoing medical attention, called Fred Berlin, who authorized his first injection of Depo-Provera. On Saturday in Abbeville, Stansbury briefed the other families, who gave approval. After the hearing, Gauthe would remain in Lafayette Parish Prison until transfer arrangements were done.

On Tuesday morning, October 14, Gauthe, wearing black suit, white shirt, and dark tie, emerged from a door in the rear of the courtroom, accompanied by Mouton, to face Judge Brunson. He pleaded guilty to thirty-three charges; Stansbury reserved the right to reimpose a life sentence should Gauthe violate the plea.

The hearing was brief. Gauthe returned to the cellblock. Reporters filled up Stansbury's office. "He'll be a guinea pig," said the D.A., referring to Depo-Provera as "the chemical castration drug. . . . That's what I call it, but I'm not a medical person."

Later that day Ted Campbell told me: "I think in a way the kids come out a winner. But the church comes out a winner by avoiding the trial. And Gilbert Gauthe comes out a winner for [still] being a priest. I told Nathan, 'After twenty years I'm glad it's on your conscience if he goes back to molesting kids.' I guess justice was partially done." But the words of lasting resonance, moved by wire services across the country, were those of Judge Brunson in sentencing Gauthe:

> *"Your crimes against your child victims have laid a terrible burden on those children, their families and society—indeed, your God and your church as well. It may be that God in His infinite mercy may find forgiveness for your crimes, but the imperative of justice, and the inescapable need of society to protect its most defenseless and vulnerable members, the children, cannot."*

Tom Doyle was in an airport when he saw Gauthe's picture in a *Time* article on the verdict. He stared at the face of the man he had never met, a fellow priest for whom he felt immense pity, despite the terrible crimes. With a shudder of sorrow and a wave of embarrassment he went to meet his flight.

The timing of Gauthe's transfer to Patuxent hinged on progress of the civil suits and the church making preparations to place him there. Tony Fontana advised Mouton that he expected to depose Gauthe. Meanwhile, more suits were being filed.

Michael Peterson's last appointment before journeying to Lafayette had been in Dallas. He woke up in his hotel with numbing pain, unable to walk. A medical examination determined vertebra damage in his upper back. A St. Luke staffer flew to Dallas and assisted him on a return flight to Washington. Surgeons went to work on the injury, using a bone graft from the hip as donor site. After months of intense work on behalf of Gauthe, whom he had only just met, Peterson was laid out in a hospital, unable to assist Gauthe in his transition to penal life.

Although Michael Peterson made a recovery, it did not last long enough to facilitate transfer to Maryland where he was to serve as Gauthe's therapist. Peterson's immune system was breaking down, a secret he would keep from his friends for months.

Gauthe's fate took a hard turn when television reporter Dee Stanley decided to do a story on the fact that he was still in the Lafayette jail, where the prison doctor complained about the responsibility of Depo-Provera injections. Administering it was something he had never done, and the drug wasn't in anybody's budget. Gauthe had more depositions to give in Louisiana when the Lafayette sheriff, reacting to Stanley's story, washed his hands of the inmate and remanded him to the state corrections department. Gauthe went to the medium security Wade Correctional Facility in Homer, a small town in northern Louisiana. When I interviewed him there in August 1986 he said he felt safe and accepted by other inmates. He was no longer on Depo-Provera but felt he was getting better. The warden said he was a model prisoner.

Gauthe's relationship with Mouton ended shortly thereafter, when the prisoner sought assistance from a federal district judge, Henry J. Politz of Shreveport, a family friend and native of his hometown, Napoleonville. Politz made the unusual move of requesting a transcript of the verdict adjudication, and began questioning Stansbury and Mouton about plea bargain details over which he had no jurisdiction. By then Peterson was gravely ill and church officials were making no move to arrange Gauthe's transfer to Maryland, which was nonbinding to the plea bargain. With Politz entering the picture on Gauthe's behalf, Mouton withdrew in exasperation, correctly assuming that the judge was in no position to move Gauthe, who in the final measure had found prison life less threatening than he had imagined. The physical proximity to his family was one advantage over Patuxent.

iii.

In autumn, 1985, Richard Baudouin became editor of the *Times of Acadiana*, replacing Linda Matys, who founded a weekly paper in San Antonio. A practicing Catholic with two children, Richard was offended by the church's cover-up yet relieved that the heavy coverage was done. If Simon took his case to trial, the *Times* would cover that when the time came. Then Tony Fontana called. He was a maverick figure in Abbeville, known for clashing with politicians on various issues. A native of the town, he had been an altar boy for Alex Larroque during his years as pastor. "There's another priest," Fontana said. "I'm getting ready to file a suit against the diocese. His name is John Engbers. He molested five sisters."

Was he certain these girls were telling the truth? "They're adults now. Yeah, I'm certain. We've talked it over. They've agreed to an interview if you want."

A transplanted Dutchman in his sixties, Engbers had been pastor in Leroy, a town outside Lafayette. An avocational artist, he gave painting lessons to children, one of whom was Fontana's oldest daughter. "Father John just loves her," his wife had told him. "He wants to give her private lessons."

Fontana did contract work for a woman whose daughter also studied art with Father John. When the client, "Beverly"*—she agreed to be interviewed without her real name used in print—told her friend Bonnie about the art lessons, Bonnie began to cry: she told Beverly that Father John had molested her as a child. Beverly had seen photographs of little girls in the rectory. Engbers told Beverly he favored little girls over little boys. "He also asked whether my husband and I gave any sex education to our kids, which I thought strange," Beverly told me.

In December 1984, Bonnie, thirty-five, met with Fontana, who withdrew his daughter from art classes and made an appointment with Larroque. When Bonnie told her story Larroque offered therapy on the spot. He told her and Fontana that Engbers had been controversial; at every parish half the people loved him and the other half couldn't stand him, but never had he been reported for sexual misconduct.

Engbers was visiting relatives in Holland over Christmas. Larroque promised to take action when he returned. Meanwhile, Bonnie broached the subject of Father John to the youngest of her four sisters, Chantelle, twenty, who admitted that she had been fondled by him as a child. In January 1985 the two women and Fontana returned to the chancery. Larroque said Engbers was "undergoing evaluation." Art lessons had been halted.

On January 15, 1985, Father John arrived at Fontana's office. Bald, bespectacled, and plump, he nervously offered to pay Bonnie "any kind of money" to stop her having him removed from Leroy. Fontana expressed concern for other children. Engbers said it was an isolated incident with Bonnie years ago. "I knew he was lying," Fontana continued. By then, Bonnie had separately spoken with her four sisters, each in turn saying that Engbers had molested her. Bonnie and Fontana went back to Larroque, who said that Engbers "minimized" his problem, and claimed he was healed. The diocese, Larroque assured them, was keeping him "under evaluation" with a therapist. From January to June 1985, as the Gauthe scandal unfolded, Engbers remained in Leroy, with parishioners unaware he was "under evaluation." Fontana said: "We just wanted to get John Engbers out. In July he was still in. I explained to my clients the legal difficulties [civil statute of limitations having elapsed since they were all adults], what their lives would be exposed to. They said, 'File the suit.'"

Puffing on a pipe in his office, Fontana told me that when he informed Larroque of his legal intentions the vicar-general invited him to the chancery on July 18. "The bishop," continued Fontana, "told me this was malicious, lawyers filing suits were just out to hurt the church. His collar was loosened; he rambled— yelled one minute, talked softly the next. He said people were saying he didn't know what he was supposed to do, and that was a damn lie. He was doing everything he could."

According to Fontana, Frey sarcastically asked if they should sell the cathedral and church properties to pay the civil losses. "I said, 'Bishop, we've had problems all through the ages but the church has survived. Yeah, people are talking about you, that you're not doing everything, and there are a lot of good reasons for that.' I named the attorneys not showing up in court. . . . I said, 'This is just completely asinine.'

"He started yelling: 'That's not us! That's insurance company lawyers. We've been on 'em *from the very beginning* to accept liability and they're the ones that have been dragging us through all this stuff.' I said, 'Well, fire your lawyers.' 'We can't do that.' *'Bull* you can't do that. If you document that they're not even showing up in court, you have a right to demand new representation.' 'Well,' Frey said, 'no one ever explained that to me.' "

Larroque asked if they could resolve the dispute. Fontana agreed to discuss it with his clients. "Frey told me, 'You hold all the cards. You can do with us what you want.' " As he left, Larroque said that Engbers had "involuntarily retired."

Shortly thereafter, Fontana and Bonnie returned to the chancery to discuss the impasse with Frey and Larroque. Gently, Larroque asked if they could settle the dispute without legal action. "Unlike Monsignor Larroque," Bonnie recalled, "the bishop was harsh. He said we only wanted revenge against the church. I told him, 'We are talking about changes to avoid *future* pain, not past pain. We don't want this man walking around molesting children. Man, don't you understand what has happened to me and my sisters? I am talking about *horror stories!* ' "

When she finished the bishop said: "You don't understand. This is the hardest thing I've ever done. I've suspended him from the priesthood and it has ruined his life." Fontana said he thought Bonnie "would come out of the chair and kill him. But that's the first time he said suspension. The day before it was involuntary retirement."

In the meantime, Engbers fled to Holland.

When I briefed Richard Baudouin, the hefty, bearded editor sat grim-faced. "Is Fontana trying to use us?"

"I think he feels betrayed. If he doesn't file a suit, we shouldn't run a story. If he files, I think we should do it."

Baudouin consulted with the publisher. Steve May said that if the lawsuit was filed the paper would run two installments: one on the suit, and then on what the women had to say.

iv.

John Engbers had written a biographical sketch for a history of Vermilion Parish. Born April 3, 1922, in Oldenzaal, a Dutch village near the German border, he was one of fifteen children, "thrifty and exceptionally handy with their hands." His father, a postmaster, also repaired shoes. At age fourteen the boy failed in school.

His father's punishment was one year's confinement to his room for study each day. During this time John Engbers began to draw. . . . This went on until his father caught him in the act. His father praised him when he discovered the quality. . . . He mixed his own paint, used old worn brushes. He copied the masters and sold them to earn money to purchase food and supplies during World War II. His longing to serve mankind helped him find his way to seminary. Due to ill health he was refused a foreign missionary post. This did not stop him. . . . In November 1947 he . . .

continued his studies at Notre Dame in New Orleans. He was ordained on June 11,
1949, and [began ministering] in the Lafayette diocese.

On November 7, 1985, I met with Fontana and the five sisters, maiden name Butaud, in Bonnie's home. They ranged in age from thirty-five to twenty. Bonnie was an accountant. Lois, an office manager, was a divorced mother. Shirleen was a housewife; Marguerite, a waitress, was also divorced with children; and Chantelle, the youngest, unmarried, an office worker. Six younger siblings did not figure into the allegations.

They had grown up in a coastal community at the edge of Cajun country, straddling the Gulf of Mexico. Their father was a chemical plant worker; their mother came from a family of Chitimacha Indians near Weeks Island. St. Helena Parish encompassed Weeks Island, Louisa, and Cypremort Point.

"In 1957," said Bonnie, who had dark hair, "Hurricane Audrey hit Cypremort Point and turned everything into matchsticks. Shirleen was the baby then. Our home was totally gone. Father John invited our parents to move into the rectory. We stayed there approximately a year. I was about six years old when John Engbers began molesting me. Cypremort Point had only about eleven families. Grownups would be together almost nightly, play dominoes, socialize. In the rectory Father John baby-sat. My father and relatives rebuilt the house. After that Father John had dinner at our home almost every night. We all felt like he was a member of the family."

She recalled the beginning of the abuse: "I don't remember my words, but there was fear. I was told that I had been chosen by God to help him with his studies of sex because *he* was responsible for helping adults and he didn't know anything about it. After that it was very consistent—every time he could get me alone. . . . He never threatened or used bodily force. Now that I'm an adult, I can see the purpose. After each, uh, incident, he would go to the restroom for several minutes." To masturbate.

He did not rape her. "He did want to when I was fourteen. That's when I became so terrified I told my sister Lois, and she said, 'Me too, Bonnie.' We went to our grandmother and she became very upset and told us we must never say this again. We made a deal: 'You just make sure we never have to go over there alone, and we will not tell anyone.' She was afraid our father would find out. After that, not another word was said for twenty years."

Married at seventeen, Bonnie had long since divorced. Chantelle, the youngest, looked down. The sisters were receiving therapy, paid for by the diocese. Shirleen, twenty-eight, with fair skin and lighter hair than Bonnie, said: "I was five or six. I used to go to the rectory. He built frames for his oil paintings. He'd give me a dollar, say that I was working for him. He would tell me I could pretend to be his puppet, like the man that built Pinocchio. He would take my clothes off and lay me on his bed and start forming my body like he was carving out a Pinocchio. I was scared numb.

"One day he went into the bedroom and all of a sudden he came out with his pants down around his knees and I freaked out 'cause I'd never seen anything like that. It was sickening when you're little; he wanted me to touch him, but I couldn't. I was shakin'. He said, 'It's not wrong. God made the body to be beautiful—for each of us to share it.' But I never did touch him. I couldn't."

At thirteen she began to date, and broke away from Father John. "He was always telling my parents the guy wasn't any good and I shouldn't date. Whenever he'd get me alone, he'd say, 'All they want to do is hurt you and do things to you that are wrong. I'm supposed to take care of you and teach you.' The last time he tried anything with me I was eighteen."

At the time she was working in Lafayette and needed a car. "He said he could help with the down payment. He'd sell two of his paintings. Well, I knew it was wrong but I was desperate. I needed a car to get to my job. So I went over to therectory, in Gueydon [where he had since moved], and said, "I'll take it"— a car down payment—"but as a loan.' Later that night in bed, I was kinda scared—"

"You agreed to stay in the rectory?"

"Well, I guess I was wrong to be alone with him but I felt I could take care of myself. He came into my room and I screamed: 'Don't touch me! If this is the way you're gonna give me a loan I don't want it!' So he left the room. The next day I was leaving early. He said, 'Don't worry. I'll send a check and put in my will that if I die you won't have to pay me back.' "

She repaid the loan in $50 monthly installments.

Chantelle was pacing the floor.

I asked Shirleen what happened when Engbers heard her confession. "I mean, he didn't think [sex with us] was wrong so I couldn't confess it. I'd just make up stuff, 'cause that"—sexual encounters with him—"was the only thing that was wrong when I was a kid. The first person I told was my husband when I got married eight years ago—until January when Bonnie started calling around."

Had Bonnie ever told another priest? Yes. In 1968 she spoke with Father T. J. Hebert in Lydia, who told her not to press it; no one would believe her. (When I called the priest he said, "I have no idea what you're talking about.") Years later, her marriage on the rocks, Bonnie met with Father Jimmy Broussard for counseling. "And he did say, 'Bonnie, you must go to the bishop and tell him of this.' But at the time I was getting a divorce and I said, 'Well, I cannot think of this now.' " (Broussard, no longer a priest, was a counselor with the public schools. When I read him her statement, he said: "The matters you talk about were confidential at the time and remain so. I have no further comment.")

Sheets of cigarette smoke covered the room. The pained women fidgeted, stood, sat, paced. Marguerite, doe-eyed, was about to break. Gently, I told her: "I sense that you're uncomfortable. You don't seem at ease discussing this."

She turned her head. I hated to press her for answers, she seemed so woeful. "Just so I can be correct . . ." I said.

She was crying. No one spoke. In the fog of cigarettes, Bonnie nodded at me, as if to say, *Ask your questions.*

"Is it correct to say you were molested by this priest?"

"Yeah," said Marguerite.

"Is it correct to say you were quite young, between the ages of six and ten?"

"I would say four to fourteen," she replied softly.

Had he physically harmed her? "No." Had she ever tried to tell anyone? "No." How frequently would it happen? "From my memory, almost every day."

"For ten years?"

"No, until he moved to Gueydon. Then only when I'd go to visit."

"He must have had you under quite a hypnotic influence for you to go over there after it all happened."

Marguerite bolted out of the room.

I felt awful. "It sounds bad," blurted Shirleen, cutting through the tension. "But we were raised to trust this person. And when he'd ask for us to go over, we'd have to come up with reasons and who in the hell wanted to say *that?* Y-you know, s-so we do look like a bunch of little bitches because w-we kept going back." Her voice broke. "Who wanted to tell anybody that God had chosen you to be a little whore? It's gonna look bad. *Why the hell did we keep going back?*"

"Please don't think I'm trying to criticize you," I said. "I'm just trying to understand what happened."

Shirleen was sobbing.

Each sister made first communion under Father John. Chantelle recalled driving down back roads with Father John, looking for arrowheads. She was four or five when he "made me lay down on the seat and took my clothes off."

Marguerite returned to the table.

After nuns left the parish, the Ladies' Altar Society taught catechism. "In my childhood," I said, "I remember being taught about immoral thoughts and actions. Was there ever a time when a teacher would say something like that? I mean, it was almost like a mirror to what was going on. . . ."

"No," said Shirleen. "They always talked about Christ."

Bonnie: "We would have been very hesitant to speak about this man."

"I myself," said an ostensibly composed Marguerite, "personally loved this man and always did."

"You loved him?" I asked. "Fell in love?"

"I guess."

Searching her face, I said: "How old were you when you stopped seeing him?"

"I don't know. When I stopped going to Gueydon. Fourteen."

"Did he take pictures of you?"

"All the time. And when we were alone, it was naked pictures, every way."

The three middle sisters claim he took hundreds of nude photographs of them as children. One setting was the church sacristy in Louisa where he would have each girl, legs open, hold a communion wafer. What happened to the pictures? No one knew. Marguerite: "He would always tell me that I was very special to him and we did these things because that's how we showed our love. He would tell me, 'This is our secret, girl.' He was always buying me stuff. We developed pictures together."

He made her promise not to marry till she was nineteen. "With every boy, he always said they were not good for me and would treat me bad." At fifteen she gave birth to a child but did not marry the father, himself a teenager.

"Do you think that because of what Engbers did that you started having intercourse? Do you think one is the result of the other?"

"I don't know."

"Why did you decide to become part of the lawsuit?"

"Because—just because I know it's right."

"Do you feel he betrayed you?"

"Mm-hmmm," she said, nodding. "Because I did think I was special. I didn't look at him as a sick man till I found out what he had done [to the others]. And then, I didn't want—I mean, he wrote me a letter after he was not supposed to contact any of us, and I wrote him back. But I never did mail it. I wanted to warn him [about legal action] but I respected Bonnie enough and all of 'em 'cause I knew what they were doing was right. But I don't want to hurt him either. And it's hurting me."

His letter said that friends never turn their backs on friends in time of trouble. "It's just put a guilt trip on me. I've always been a guilty little person."

Marguerite was crying. Shirleen was crying. I was crying.

Fontana said: "In July, when the church had not removed him from Leroy, it was Marguerite who said, 'Well, what can we do?' And I said, 'There's nothing else we can do but file a suit to force 'em to get something done.' I had my reservations all through and I told the girls it would be a difficult thing."

"He could go anywheres and molest a little girl," said Marguerite. "It's not like the bishop is gonna tell the parishioners, 'Look, y'all, stay away from this man because he's a child molester.' They all loved him. They thought he was wonderful!"

"Marguerite," I said, "you just used the term 'child molester.' When did your attitude toward this man change?"

"When I started getting therapy. And because I trusted my sisters and Mr. Fontana."

"Do you feel you hate John Engbers now?"

"No, I don't hate anybody."

"I hate him," said Shirleen.

"Me too," said Bonnie.

"I hate what he's done," said Marguerite. "And I hate the pain I feel now. Because I stopped seeing him when I got scared and now I have to bring it all out again. And people are gonna look at me like I'm crazy, a freak, you know?"

When Lois, the second oldest, arrived, her story conformed to the same pattern. A heavy woman, she spoke with a sad frown. She was six when he asked her to help him with his "experiments, as he put it—and [saying] that I was special, chosen by God to help him." Only Lois charged that Engbers had engaged in sexual intercourse with her—weekly, from the time she was ten until she was twelve. That was when Bonnie asked her, and the two sisters confronted their mother, striking the "deal"—silence—which failed to protect the younger sisters.

"After that he never came near me until my husband and I separated. But I'd see him at my parents' house all the time from [age] twelve to eighteen, when I got married. He officiated at my wedding." How could she allow him to perform her marriage ceremony? "I buried it all. I pretended this man never even came near me. I saw him as a priest, the friend of my family. That's what I wanted to see. I didn't want to remember the other stuff."

How could the parents have been so blind? The sisters described a bitter marriage, with tensions between mother and children. Their mother worshiped Father John and spent hours herself at the rectory. Consider too the vaunted position of an educated European priest—an artist to boot—in an enclave of poorly educated Cajuns and Indians. In the 1950s there was no sex education in schools, and for the girls in this family sex was a taboo subject. It was, in short, a pedophile's ideal environment—a dysfunctional family he could befriend and influence, with ample young prey.

Shirleen said her mother believed that "she's not here to judge. When we all told her, she said she might have to give up her religion 'cause what she believed in hadn't been true. And we said, 'Not all priests are creeps like that.'"

Their mother had been president of the Ladies' Altar Society and, said the sisters, continued visiting Father John after he moved on to other parishes. Several nights later I spoke with her by telephone. "I'm not going to say anything because I don't remember anyone saying anything to me," she said. "I don't know. I do believe he did it because they say it, but I don't have any comments to say."

The sisters' story raised new questions about the diocese's handling of child molesters. With Fontana preparing his lawsuit, Richard Baudouin wrote Bishop Frey and Monsignor Larroque, requesting an interview, which Bob Wright denied. If Fontana filed, Wright told me, a suit "with prescription problems like that"— meaning more than a year since the injuries were sustained—it might result in a countercharge of malicious prosecution—a suit brought for legally untenable purposes.

On November 13, Fontana filed two lawsuits seeking financial compensation. One was on behalf of the five sisters; a second was under protective seal, because the alleged victim was a child of one of the sisters. My initial story summarized the allegations, quoting Fontana and Bonnie on their meetings at the chancery. Richard Baudouin did not feature the article on the cover; that was devoted to a satiric piece on the opening of the Cajundome, a $60 million facility plagued by cost overruns and suspect profit projections.

The following night Fontana called me. He had just heard from a woman fifty miles south who read a wire account in the *Lake Charles American Press*. "She says Engbers molested her when she was a kid. Her mother reported it to church officials in Lake Charles, and they shipped Engbers out. That was in 1952!"

He thought the woman would speak with me; he was meeting her the next day. "This is incredible, Tony. Five pedophiles in the same diocese." I wondered aloud whether Frey, bishop since 1973, or Larroque, vicar-general since 1965, may not have had prior knowledge about Engbers. Under canon law, if the late Bishop Jeanmard had a file on Engbers, he could by 1962 have destroyed it, presuming there were no further accusations.

"Maybe so," conceded Fontana. "But canon law was broken all through Gauthe. The point is, Larroque and Frey knew for seven months before they let him run back to Europe."

"How do you see Larroque's role in all of this?"

"Larroque," said Fontana, "is Machiavelli."

The victim was willing to talk. Brenda Andrepont Gossett, thirty-six, lived in Lake Charles. She said that in 1952 Father John would take her on trips to the woods with other children. "I remember him fondling me. I thought I was special to him." She was three then. One day her mother discovered her fondling another little girl. "Jesus doesn't love little girls who do that," Haddie Andrepont told her daughter. "Sure he does," Brenda replied. "Father John does it all the time."

In a separate interview, Brenda Gossett's mother told me that she, her husband, and several relatives had met with Monsignor George Bodin and Engbers at St. Margaret's Church in Lake Charles. "My husband wanted him shipped back to Holland, but Monsignor Bodin told us they were going to send him to an institution for treatment. Father John asked me not to prosecute; he begged forgiveness."

The couple did not press charges. Mr. Andrepont was now deceased. Monsignor Bodin, getting on in years, lived in the cathedral rectory in Lafayette. When I called at night he was off guard. "I don't recall such a meeting. Someone complained about him once, which I reported to the dean [head of priests in a given diocesan locale]. That was Monsignor Boudreaux. He is deceased."

I told him what Mrs. Andrepont had said. "This is so long ago," he answered. "I don't remember the details."

Less than a month after the confrontation, said Mrs. Andrepont, "we went to a wedding in Eunice and Father John performed it. How can anyone get healed overnight? He came back to our neighborhood and visited another family once or twice. I just blocked it off." Her husband was furious but took no action.

Brenda discussed the effects on herself. "I don't remember having a childhood. I couldn't stand to be touched, or hugged, or kissed. I can recall dreams from adolescence; I'm running and a man is chasing me, or I'm tied up and I'm being raped."

After the news of Gauthe's indictment, she began thinking about the priest she could remember only as Father John. In January 1985 she asked Monsignor Irving DeBlanc at her church in Lake Charles to help her find the priest: she wanted to confront him, to tell him what his acts had done to her. DeBlanc told her he knew of no Father John and could not help without a last name. Then the AP account of my story appeared in her local paper, and she called Fontana. DeBlanc did not return my calls.

In the meantime, the Butaud sisters provided copies of two letters Father John had written before he fled to Holland. After his January meeting with Fontana, Engbers wrote Bonnie: "I realize that I did hurt you." He begged her not to hurt her mother, adding that, since he had left the old parish, "I have done my best to improve myself and had no recurrence of the faults you accuse me of. . . . My main work in this parish has been working with children who need love and attention in the right way." To Marguerite, he mentioned in his letter money he had given needy people over the years, and appealed to her compassion.

On Sunday, November 17—before the second installment with the sisters' harrowing story appeared—the *Lafayette Daily Advertiser* took another potshot at the *Times of Acadiana*. Charles Lenox attacked the weekly's tongue-in-cheek story about the Cajundome. But Lenox's anger seemed to be directed at another source of reporting. "Citizens can stop the cancer by cutting off the money supply," read the headline. The editor's column went on:

> As for the sophomoric approach from the negativists at the end of Jefferson Street, what can you expect from a group which lists as its highest accomplishment in five years of operation the sensational scoop of where to find the best hamburger in town?
>
> There is only one way to stop a cancer—you remove it. The people who support this offensively negative force in our community are the ones who can stop it. If you, the people of the community have finally seen the light, it is time to tell the advertisers

you support Lafayette, first and foremost, and that you definitely do not support the
exponents of yellow journalism or the detractors of your community.

Calling for the boycott of another publication appeared illegal under fair trade statutes. "Suing would take months and be expensive," said May. "And I'd lose my underdog status."

As May pondered his status, I was finishing the second installment of the Engbers story. Late at night, working on my computer in the apartment we had taken, reading words of the five women, a surge of anger rose in me. "Damn you, John Engbers!" I hissed at the screen. "Damn you to hell."

It was 4 A.M. I left the study and gazed at my wife asleep in the bed, our daughter snug in her crib.

I went back to the computer and as words of the sisters rolled down the screen, years of torment in silent yellow letters, I began to cry. *How could they just let him leave?* Maybe Larroque was Machiavellian. If so, he was a sorry prince. Did Frey know all the secrets Larroque knew? I shut off the computer and stared at the ridge of scarlet rising in the east. Then I sank to my knees and asked God's forgiveness for cursing John Engbers. I prayed to control my anger, and for the Butaud sisters. As the fatigue hit, I prayed for Frey and Larroque.

ix.

Monarchy vs. Democracy

Times of Acadiana editor Richard Baudouin was weighing his Catholicism and journalistic instincts. In editing the second Engbers report, he reflected on the clerical
hypocrisy foisted on his parents' generation. "What would they think if they knew
all this? It's *their* church too." Richard's radical phase as a Tulane undergraduate
had moderated into a neoconservative mold akin to that of the *New Republic*. He
became editor after several newspaper jobs. I had been a freelance for twelve
years, writing books on the side. We both knew that when I returned to New
Orleans he would have to live in Lafayette in the aftermath of a hard exposé.

One night after an editing session we went to dinner, our first conversation
outside the office. Sharing a bottle of wine, we marveled at the eccentricities of
the Cajun establishment. However tragic the Gauthe events, there was a lighter
human strain—Raymond Blanco pitting Bob Wright against Ray Mouton; Minos
Simon's fulminations against "those goddamn lawyers in New Orleans"; even the
rah-rah boosterism in Lenox's *Advertiser* attack. Then a mood descended on the
table, matching the darkness of Baudouin's beard and eyebrows. "I want to know
how bad it is," he said. "Tell me everything you know or suspect."

I began with Father X, whose name appeared on Simon's discovery list. I had
two sources—Chalice, and the priest now at X's old rectory, whose sleep had
been broken by my 10 P.M. call: was it true Father X had sexually molested
youngsters? "Yes, yes," said the priest. "He's gone away for treatment. I can't say
more." A nun subsequently corroborated what I had learned, in greater detail.

I had come to see the molestation cases as symptomatic of a larger breakdown
in ecclesiastical life. If there were four (as reported) or six (now certain) priest-
child molesters, that was a question of degree. Playing musical chairs with such
men stemmed from a denial mentality I was only beginning to fathom. The
church's contorted views of sexuality folded into a mindset that tolerated both
pedophiles and sexually active gay priests. Two men who would have sat in judgment of Gauthe, had Frey convened a canonical court, were known to be active
homosexuals, according to sources. Secrecy was the glue that bound priests to-

gether when the church was under attack—while other priests vented their outrage by leaking information to me.

Every publication has its limits. It was nearly December. With the second
Engbers story, about the sisters' abuse, about to run, I knew that the *Times* would
pull off the subject until the new year. Was Steve May committed to a more
systemic story on the larger cover-up involving six priests who had been removed? "He's gone out on a limb further than any other publisher in this state
would dare," said Baudouin. "At some point we have to think about overkill."

"Have you thought about an editorial?" I asked. Baudouin nodded. "The term
'cover-up' has yet to appear," I said.

"I think we've struck a good balance avoiding language like that," he replied.
"What do you think an editorial should say?"

"Call on Frey and Larroque to resign."

His eyebrows arched. "I've never written anything like that."

"Richard, *no one* has ever written an editorial like that."

We had again sought an interview with Frey, who deserved the fullest chance
to respond to the outcry sure to arise from the Engbers story. But church officials
had again refused our written request. In a preface to the Engbers piece, Baudouin
wrote of soul searching "on the part of the editor, the publisher and the reporter
himself." He continued:

> [M]any of the allegations against Engbers took place literally decades ago. We
> were concerned about matters of taste: the interview contained passages of a raw and
> emotional nature.
>
> Finally, there was a real concern for fairness. Although we have been unable to
> determine Engbers' whereabouts—the diocese and its attorneys have declined to clar-
> ify his status—he deserves the right to have his day in court. The [sisters'] claims
> . . . are at this point only allegations in a legal sense. . . . They have summoned
> the rare courage to come forward, knowing they would be publicly identified—and
> talked about—to bear witness to events in their past. . . .
>
> Why did [the diocese] take so long to dismiss the priest and under what circum-
> stances did he leave? Could he still be in a position to commit the kinds of acts he has
> been accused of? And, perhaps most critically, if John Engbers has been falsely
> accused, why did the chancery not come to his defense?

On November 25, three days before Thanksgiving, the chancery announced
that Frey would make a statement that afternoon but take no questions. "If one
reporter asks a question," I argued, "others are bound to follow suit."

"We've smoked them out," said Baudouin. "But this is their forum, not ours." If
I lobbed a question, other media could portray the paper in the role of aggressor.
All Frey had to say to avoid a question—and keep a measure of opinion in his
favor—was that litigation prevented him from answering.

When I arrived at the chancery, reporters waited outside Frey's office. A priest
embittered by the cover-up had given me minutes of a recent meeting of local
clergy, which said that Monsignor Alexander Sigur (who had recommended

Gauthe's ordination years earlier) had proposed letters supporting Frey to the Pope and Pio Laghi. I introduced myself to Sigur. He raised index and middle finger in a V, the peace sign of the 1960s. I smiled. "You were active in civil rights, weren't you, Monsignor?"

"Yes indeed."

I asked if the letters had been sent to the Pope and Laghi. "Oh, yes," said Sigur. "We haven't received a response."

As camera crews took positions, Gerald Dill, the diocesan spokesman, disseminated copies of the bishop's statement. I sat in a corner, thinking of Frey. We had met in September in the Abbeville courthouse with a waiting jury pool while Hebert and Bencomo negotiated with defense attorneys behind closed doors. In Frey's politeness I sensed magnanimity. I complimented him on a distinction he had recently made between faith Catholics and cultural Catholics—the latter being those who retained a basic Christian view but did not partake of sacraments. He thanked me and we made small talk. The civil case had been settled without trial.

Frey stepped around wires and TV lights, sat behind his desk, put on his glasses and read at medium pitch: "In the past weeks, the church has again received a great deal of negative publicity. I feel an obligation to make the following statement." As a shepherd, he always felt "an obligation to reach out pastorally to those who have been hurt in any way." Engbers had been a diocesan priest for twenty-four years before Frey arrived as bishop, with "no evidence of any kind to indicate that [he] needed special supervision. If there were allegations in the past made to my predecessors . . . I am confident that they acted according to what they considered the best thing to do."

Jeanmard and Schexnayder were deceased.

In thirteen years as bishop, Frey continued, he had received no complaint of Engbers "in the area of moral behavior. The first such report I had was in January 1985."

Fontana and Bonnie had met with Larroque in December 1984.

"I acted promptly by investigating the allegations and placing Father Engbers under psychiatric evaluation. He was under observation during the time it took for the evaluation and treatment." He continued: "At the conclusion of the evaluation, I asked Father Engbers to resign and continue therapy. He did resign and moved back to his native Holland. I was, of course, deeply concerned about the women who may have in any way been victims of his actions. . . . I am informed by the church's legal advisors that the church has no liability under the law for Father Engbers's actions which allegedly occurred many years ago."

Frey said he had "reached out as I have in the past whenever need arose" in providing therapy to the women. The language had clearly gone through a legal sieve, but his parting words sounded a more pastoral note: "It is difficult to respond to sensitive situations without sounding defensive. I hope that what I have just shared with you will help you to better understand my position and the position of the diocese at this time. . . . I deeply regret and am distressed by the suffering that has taken place because of the tragic events in the diocese over the past several years."

He laid the paper on his desk. I was chomping at the bit: *Why did you let him leave? Are church officials in Holland monitoring him?* Dill said the bishop had another meeting. Frey left with not a single question asked. The next day's AP headline in the *Baton Rouge Morning Advocate* said: "BISHOP ASKS FOR 'PRAYERS, UNDERSTANDING.' "

Several days later Bob Wright filed a motion to dismiss the sisters' grievance, suggesting the possibility of a counterclaim in asking the Court to "immediately dismiss this improperly and wrongfully instituted suit, so that all parties involved may then pursue any and all legal rights they may possess." On December 5, Fontana held a press conference in his office. With four of the five sisters seated at a table, wearing long faces, he said: "What these women are doing in exposing the wrongdoing of the church is right—morally right. What the church is doing in ignoring the truth of their accusations is wrong—morally wrong."

Television news became a battleground. Wright and Dill responded to Fontana with prepared videotaped statements. Dill stressed that Frey had immediately offered counseling for the women: "They accepted his offer and this help continues at diocesan expense." Wright gave the bishop's legal defense. "It's been dredged up from too far back," he said, advising viewers that he had told Fontana "of the harassment nature of such a suit and that it would be nothing but malicious prosecution. Now, if he wants to take that as a threat of a lawsuit—[let him] have his day."

In an interview Fontana blasted Wright's stance as "very inconsistent with the public relations campaign they're trying to put across, that the bishop is a compassionate person. They want the word to get out . . . 'you better not fool with Holy Mother the church. If you do we're gonna sue you.' " Therapy, Fontana added, had "nothing to do with compassion: that's their moral obligation."

The media countercharges made for dismal theater. Ray Mouton naturally had an opinion: "I couldn't believe Wright would say something like that. Fontana has a point: attacking the women makes no sense as a P.R. ploy. Sure the suit is a long shot. But look at what they're claiming! Still, I never would have dragged those poor women before cameras if they were my clients. I don't see any way that will help them psychologically."

Back in New Orleans that December, my favored jazz haunts seemed a sanctuary. I spent a long afternoon in the museum, gazing at tribal masks in an attempt to shed the weights of Lafayette. The season of Advent had arrived, and with it a profound feeling of relief for me. For nearly a year I had journeyed through the dark channels of an institution whose decay became more appalling as I plunged deeper into the story. What did it mean to be a loving critic of the church? Camus wrote that, in rebelling against something wrong, one also acknowledges that there are beliefs, boundaries, principles that must be preserved. In this way, wrote Camus, the rebel "says yes and no at the same time."

So many priests had shaped my ethics. How it must have pained the many like them to read of pedophiles in their midst. They endured, they believed, their faith held firm against the stone, pushing up the hill. What right had I to abandon faith?

ii.

When we returned to Lafayette in January 1986, Minos Simon was pitched for battle: "I *want* to try this case," he declared. His clients were ready as well. Since September, Faye Gastal had called me every week or so. Ostracized by many in her community, emotionally spent by the long wait, she wanted to understand the configuration of forces at work. Sometimes she would simply say, "What are you hearing?" People were calling the Gastals, passing on rumors, hints of strange activity in their communities, or expressing support as the days peeled away toward trial. "The good Lord is holding me through this," she said. "We have seen some hard times, believe you me."

I always asked about the boy. Some days he was fine, she said; other days the nightmares and mood swings worsened. When Gauthe was convicted, she described a collective acting-out among his classmates: "A number of kids started throwing things, fighting. What happens to the rest of these kids Gauthe molested?"

Meanwhile, a lawsuit filed in New Iberia alleged that Gauthe and Lane Fontenot shared sexual encounters with the same minor in 1974. An Abbeville deputy sheriff provided more insight: Gauthe had been pastor of Henry for more than five years. In two and a half years since his departure, the deputy had watched certain kids start making advances to younger boys. He had seen uncommon hostilities toward parents, teachers, guardian figures. He knew men whose sons had been molested. "There's a cryin' need for help to these kids." How many had Gauthe molested, I asked—one hundred? "Easy. In this [civil] parish alone."

According to one study, a regressive pedophile will have sexual encounters with an average of 265 youngsters in a lifetime. Michael Peterson later told me that Gauthe's inability to feel guilt was the telling sign of a sociopath.

Meanwhile, a source with knowledge of the Lafayette chancery's inner workings approached me with information—and with reference to a second insider, who also agreed to talk. They spoke of a young priest who had recently been sent to St. Luke after sexual episodes with teenage boys—Father Y, a friend of Lane Fontenot since Immaculata Seminary days. He had once held an archdiocesan position. "He rationalized celibacy by saying it meant being single and not having a wife," said one who knew him.

Now there were seven priests who had been removed.

Among journalists with whom I exchanged information, Joe Stephens of the *State Journal-Register* in Springfield, Illinois, had spent months researching Father Alvin Campbell, sixty, of nearby Morrisonville. In October 1985 he was sentenced to seven years. On the basis of Campbell's psychiatric evaluation, Stephens reported that the former military chaplain—a star athlete in high school—had molested at least one hundred boys. Like the Lafayette priests, he had been repeatedly transferred after accusations. Stephens also reported:

A housekeeper told investigators that a statue of a man and boy embracing was plainly displayed in the rectory. Among items agents later found . . . were pornographic magazines, 231 photographs of boys, sexually explicit videocassette tapes,

and love letters apparently written by now-grown men with whom Campbell had had
affairs in Vietnam.

"A swarm of emotions engulfed the people," wrote Joe Stephens, describing the reaction to the news of Campbell's sexual abuse of youths—"anger, revulsion, fear, embarrassment, hate, numbing shock. But no one approached the police." Instead, suspicious parents knocked on Campbell's door one night, demanding that he explain or leave. The next day he was gone.

I was reading Stephen's story by the coffee maker when Steve May sat down. He had black, gray-streaked hair and a genial smile. A major stockholder in *Gris-Gris*, a Baton Rouge monthly, May liked making money. He also had no small strain of feistiness. He lit a cigar. "Minos really going to court?"

"Looks that way," I replied.

"What else?"

I showed him Stephens's story. He read for a time, then muttered: "This guy was another Gauthe."

"Are you getting heat from advertisers?"

He said there had been some rumbles, but most advertisers with whom he spoke approved of the paper's stance. He was satisfied that the coverage had strengthened the paper, and in the long run that would outweigh a lost account or two.

The next day I mentioned the editorial to Baudouin, who had been talking to a priest friend of long standing. "I'll tell you when I've made a decision," he said curtly.

Recycling child molesters stemmed in part, it appeared, from a long tradition in the church of seeing the worst and yet assuming that life can go on. Catholic doctrine stresses forgiveness, the idea that a sinner, even a priest, can repent and be given a second chance. How far should one take that premise when it ran counter to findings on sexual pathology? And when it so clearly was blinding the church to the suffering of victims? If Frey had not known of Gauthe's early instances of molesting, he had ample notice with Engbers: for months Fontana and Bonnie pleaded to have Engbers removed as pastor. Yet during that time Engbers remained at his parish—until he fled the country.

Article 25 of the Louisiana Criminal Code defines accessory after the fact as

any person who, after the commission of a felony, shall harbor, conceal, or aid the
offender, knowing or having any reasonable ground to believe that he has committed
the felony, and with the intent that he may avoid or escape from arrest, trial,
convictions or punishment.

Oliver Houck, a Tulane University Law School professor and former federal prosecutor, explained that the statute "does not require that the offender be arrested or convicted. What [a supervisory figure] knew and when he knew it is a question of criminal negligence; what he should have known is the realm of civil negligence." As Gauthe had become a Boy Scout chaplain in 1975, *after* Frey knew of his problems in Broussard, so Lane Fontenot was a youth minister *after* a family said they complained about his sexual activities in New Iberia in 1976. A chancery source said that Larroque was told of Fontenot's advances to boys as late as 1983 but dismissed the suggestion out of hand. A priest told me that Fontenot as a deacon (the last step before priesthood) had made advances to a youth, which the priest reported to Frey, threatening to quit his parish if Fontenot wasn't transferred. Frey moved Fontenot but still ordained him in 1975.

My final story was nearly done when I learned that Father X, after several months' treatment out of state, was now in a parish in another Louisiana diocese. Frey had refused to take him back in Lafayette, so another bishop accepted him. When I told Baudouin he scowled. "Why don't they just kick the guy out?"

Four sources had confirmed Father X's transgressions. He had spent lavishly decorating his previous rectory; boys spent the night there. When a young man finally leveled an accusation in 1984, Frey shipped Father X off for treatment. No charges were pressed; there was no lawsuit that I could find. But the priest's sexual behavior was well known in the chancery and among certain clergy. One source claimed to have reported Father X to the chancery more than a year *before* his abrupt departure. When I called Father X at his new parish and asked him for comment, he said, "I do not wish to be interviewed," and hung up.

Once again, chancery officials refused to be interviewed.

On January 23, Bishop Frey sent a letter to diocesan employees announcing a $500,000 deficit, salary cuts, and a shorter work week. The letter also said:

> *Even with these changes, it will also be necessary to reduce the present number of central office personnel. . . . In expressing my gratitude to each and every one of you, I want you to know that I am sensitive to the fact that your personal needs may make it necessary for you to seek employment elsewhere. To you and to those whose positions are terminated, I say that I have asked the Vicars to assist you in whatever way they can to find employment elsewhere.*

On Saturday, January 25, Alex Larroque telephoned the Lafayette police: someone had broken into the bishop's office. With Bob Wright in New Orleans, Larroque called Ray Mouton, who drove to the chancery at 9:30 A.M. Police searched the office with Frey and Larroque present. Files had been searched in the offices of both men. The next morning the *Sunday Advertiser* published photographs of the window and open cabinets beneath the headline BISHOP FREY'S FILES RIFLED. The story, without a by-line, quoted Wright: "It clearly indicates to us that the person or persons involved in the burglary were obviously attempting to obtain what they thought might be confidential information relative to pending and threatened litigation . . . involving child molestation cases."

The diocesan attorney made no mention of potential suspects. The Gastal case was set for February 4. "City police had no additional details," the *Advertiser* concluded.

When I called Mouton he was in a cynical mood. "For months I was persona non grata. Then Alex wakes me up and I rush over for a new crisis. It's almost as though they wanted me present when the police came. I invited the cops to interview me at my office. Told them they should consider you a prime suspect."

"What the hell did you do that for?"

"Just being truthful."

"But I would never do something like that."

"Of course you wouldn't. And if they think you don't have anything to hide, you won't have any problems."

Monday morning I was summoned to police headquarters. Curley Dartez, a heavyset veteran detective, and the office captain asked most of the questions. They advised me of my rights to not answer without an attorney present, that anything I said might be used against me in court. I agreed to talk with the understanding that I would not identify my sources. They asked if I had broken into the office.

"No. I have no need to gather information illegally." The burglary made no sense, I continued: no attorney would pay a thief when he could obtain documents through the normal channels of a lawsuit. Besides, I noted, the Gastal trial would focus on harm to the plaintiffs, not on the actions of other priests. Since the insurance companies and the diocese had accepted financial liability, Simon could not put forth his theory about actively homosexual priests and a risk-creating factor. The trial was about damages to the boy and his family, not about other priests.

They asked whether, if stolen documents were offered to me, I would report the source to police. If I knew the documents were stolen, I would. Did sources providing me information on priests give written documents? I replied that legal documents had come my way from Simon and lawyers; church sources—most of them clergy—had provided me with verbal information. Dartez conceded that the case baffled them. "In fact," he said, "we're wondering if a burglary occurred at all. The window was opened from the inside. Nothing has been found missing."

In fact, the police investigators were wondering why, if there was no burglary, the church would try to make it appear like one. The case was subsequently closed as not having been a crime. Later, a police source told me of speculation in the department that someone had faked the break-in.

By now information was hemorrhaging out of the diocese. "They knew something was up with Gauthe," a diocesan insider confided, "but thought it would never come out. They thought they could instill the fear in people [who might sue] that they were up against the church, that they were doomed. The attitude was, 'We don't have to say anything.' They feel they're impervious because of people's faith."

"Frey hates confrontations," another diocesan source revealed. "In the past, they called in people [when a priest molested a child], provided counseling, made a settlement with the family, swore them to secrecy, and moved the priest. I think the bishop did a lot of things wrong by moving people repeatedly. [But] he has to believe that a priest is being straight with him when he says he'll behave. You don't have enough priests to go around. He can't automatically say, 'I'm sending you off for treatment.'"

What had church leadership's response been to news coverage? The bishop said little of which the sources were aware; however Larroque, when the subject was raised at a meeting, replied: "The media can't touch us."

And so they erected a wall of silence, offering scant explanation to the faithful. In so doing the bishop and vicar-general engaged in a cover-up. However, it was an anachronistic one, a sort of monarchical attempt at spin control in an impatient, democratic world. In failing to extend the pastoral hand to Gauthe's victims at the outset—and to deal candidly with laity and clergy alike—Frey and Larroque hid behind their lawyers. The result was destructive silence. Blunders by some of those lawyers—adding the Pope as defendant, failing to show up in court —and bad strategic moves, like allowing Engbers to flee, deepened the stain of scandal around the chancery. In dollar terms the cover-up was a disaster—$5.5 million compensating nine families and thirteen children as of February 1, 1986.

More important than money, dozens of youngsters had been molested and many families hurt by the strategy of silence. Seven priests—Gauthe, Fontenot, Limoges, Engbers, Lloyd Hebert, Father Y in treatment, and Father X now in a new diocese—had left Lafayette. The child-molesting map encompassed the towns of Broussard, New Iberia, Abbeville, Henry, Esther, Lake Charles, Louisa, Opelousas, Eunice, Gueydon, Sunset, Leroy, and Lafayette. Of the seven, only Gauthe and Fontenot were known to have been suspended, and even they had not been formally defrocked, a decision only the Vatican at that time could make.

The cover-up shattered against two pillars of democracy: the court system and a free press. The issue around which all others pivoted was the rights of children. In that respect the church betrayed her own historic commitment to the fostering of families. Frey and Larroque never realized that. Instead they held fast to a notion that "the church" must be spared a scandal and thus created an even greater scandal. In their myopia they became tragic figures, drawing focus onto themselves. And when others who knew too much felt the outrage mount, the wall of silence began to crack.

Such was the language of my last major article for the weekly, on the long cover-up involving seven priests. Baudouin shared it with May, and on Monday night, January 27, the three of us met in the publisher's office. May read the piece, nodded approvingly, and then, in an uncharacteristic flash of anger, he said: "I wanna know what gives them the right to think they can get away with this! Who are they to think they're above the law? This stuff is outrageous!"

I raised the subject of an editorial. Baudouin was leaning toward it, but unsure of its repercussions.

"Do it," said May. "We'll go up four pages"—meaning that the edition would be longer to accommodate the extra space.

What Richard wrote manifested a courage rarely found at newspapers of any size. JUSTICE MUST BE DONE, read the headline. The long statement tersely summarized findings about the pedophilia cases and sought to establish empathy with a specific category of readers—those of his parents' generation.

In every parish, there are a dozen laymen and women, maybe a few dozen, maybe hundreds, who are different. Not because they are exceptionally pious, or holy, or even wise in the ways of their religion. No, their particular brand of faith is marked by a sense of service to the community which is their church. . . .

Here's Mrs. Breaux, who's spent every Saturday since she was a young wife preparing the altar for mass: cutting fresh flowers, never too busy to help out. When Sister needs a ride to Lafayette these people drop everything to go. When Father

announces a fund drive to build a new church, they knock on the doors and ask for
money, even though their basic shyness makes that a most painful experience.

Without influence over clergy placements, such people relied on the bishop, whose word "is virtual gospel."

Is the unquestioned devotion of all the Mr. Thibodeauxs and Mrs. Breauxs to be abused as well, taken for granted, assumed as a given?

As a secular newspaper, we are mindful of the limitations under which we must operate when we venture into the arena of commenting on a religious group. Had the events which transpired within the Diocese of Lafayette taken place at, say, USL, or in the public school system, we would have been justified in calling for the resignation long ago of those in a leadership position. It has been much more difficult to come to such a conclusion with respect to the Church.

We must insist on the principle of justice, that officials of the Church are not above the law, not above basic moral and ethical standards of the areas which they serve. The bishops of this country have seen fit to interject themselves into debates over abortion, nuclear war, economic policy and the like. With that adoption of a public agenda comes a responsibility to be accountable to the community at large.

This newspaper, for one, will not stand silent at the outrages that have been perpetrated upon the people of this region. Children have suffered, families have been torn apart, the faith of the laity has been tested, and now even the accused priests have to endure punishment for their offenses. The bishop and his vicar general owe it to their church, yes to South Louisiana as a whole, to resign their positions immediately so that the process of healing within this community can take place. And if they refuse, we call upon the Vatican, through its official representative to the United States, Pio Laghi, to force such action.

The day the issue was put to bed, seven astronauts died when the *Challenger* exploded after liftoff. An eerie pall filled the paste-up room as television showed the tragedy again and again. Psychologists went to the New Hampshire school of the first teacher to voyage into space, counseling children who had been primed for a patriotic celebration and instead saw the death of a dream. I thought of the terrible impact on local children whose church had become not a sanctuary but a place of abuse. The story and editorial came out two days later.

Tom Fox said it was the only instance he knew of a newspaper calling for a bishop's resignation. Ted Campbell said: "The church ain't gonna take it lyin' down."

Local television stations quoted the editorial and Gerald Dill's rebuttal, which accused the *Times* of "fabricating" information and promised a longer statement. KLFY news director Jim Baronet said: "It won't make 'em resign because the church is the church. But I was damn proud of y'all for taking the stand. Maybe it'll shake 'em into cleaning house."

Edmund Reggie did not agree. The retired Crowley judge and church bene-factor called Steve May at home and said he should retract the editorial. May said no. Reggie said the editorial was a mistake: Frey had been considering retirement "but now you've put his feet in cement." May stood his ground.

"Boy," said Reggie, "you just shit in your messkit."

Bob Wright orchestrated his response by summoning Charlie Lenox, managing editor of the *Advertiser*, and a staff reporter to his office. The February 2 *Sunday Advertiser* featured page 1 interviews with the attorney and bishop in parallel columns. "My mistake," said Frey, "[was] not being able to recognize the depth of [Gauthe's] mental illness. His personality was such that he skillfully masked his condition." Since then, with knowledge of the disease, Frey said his office "made every effort to express our concerns to those involved. We have extended financial support from the very beginning."

He called the cover-up charge "an irresponsible statement" and cited constraints to explain the church's reluctance to be very public about the scandal. "Because of the need for confidentiality to protect the young people involved, we were told that they would be severely damaged if this affair became public and we believed their physicians," he said. Insurance attorneys, he said, had not exacted his silence. "It was the attorney for the plaintiffs who warned me not to have any dealings with them," he said, apparently in reference to Raul Bencomo.

Asked if he would resign, Frey said: "I have never run away from a problem in my life and I don't intend to begin now." The *Advertiser* asked if, after the Gauthe indictment, an investigation had been conducted of other priests. "Well, I think we're all very much alerted to the fact that there may be a problem," said Frey. He went on:

> *Now this doesn't mean that those seven priests are in treatment for pedophilia. There were a variety of causes. We have several priests who were treated for severe depression . . . and such problems as alcoholism or chemical dependency. The diocesan policy was to immediately investigate complaints and put a man in treatment if necessary.*

The interviewer for the *Advertiser* then said: "It must be very trying. . . . How do you manage to get through this?" Frey said that "the past two and a half years have been the most difficult . . . in my life as a priest and I will have been a priest forty-eight years in May. There is an element of harassment in this that I feel is very difficult to live with, but I manage." He cited support of priests and laity. "I feel that the Church will come through this critical period much better and much stronger than it was before." The bishop did not say why he had not yet visited Gauthe's parish.

Bob Wright struck right at the *Times*'s reporting, which he charged was marked by "some very inflammatory, inaccurate and unfair statements." Attacking the notion of a cover-up, he reviewed Gauthe's 1974 and 1976 episodes, saying that Frey was unaware of Gauthe's illness but had since recognized that "he made a mistake in letting the fellow go back." Wright did not say why Engbers had stayed so long after the first accusations were made.

Wright then characterized as "absurd" the editorial's statement that pedophile priests had been placed in positions with access to children. He said:

It is one thing for us to admit that Bishop Frey erred in evaluating Gauthe, but it is ludicrous to impugn the integrity of Bishop Frey and the institution of the Catholic Church by stating that they would knowingly subject any human being, much less . . . a defenseless child, to the risk of sexual abuse or harm.

Most of Wright's statement reiterated the diocese's legal position on Gauthe and Engbers, and avoided discussing the cumulative reality of seven abusive priests.

Wright said that Minos Simon, "contrary to the advice of . . . medical experts" had unsealed the Gastals' suit. "For the first time the name of a defendant child was made public"—which led to "the commotion that has been stirred up by the media." The *Advertiser* asked about "any move to take any kind of legal action over [*The Times*] articles?" Wright said the diocese would "evaluate the situation and make a decision at the appropriate time."

Asked about the *Time's* suggestion of criminal misconduct by Frey and Larroque, Wright called it "ludicrous. . . . If I aid and abet someone, I'm going to assist them in the perpetuation of their ongoing activity. What the church has done is absolutely contrary to that suggestion. They have done everything they can legally do to take any suspects or people who are even questionable out of their positions of responsibility."

As Bob Wright spoke those words, Lane Fontenot was about to flee Spokane, Washington, where as a substance abuse counselor he had been molesting teenage boys at the Nancy Reagan Care Unit of Deaconess Hospital.

X.

Verdict and Counterattack

To Abbeville, with its high-steepled brick church and courthouse of broad white pillars, they came that first week of February 1986—attorneys, church officials, tight-lipped insurance representatives, reporters, farmers, townsfolk, parents of other youngsters molested by Gauthe, and friends of the plaintiffs, Glenn and Faye Gastal and their minor child.

Opposite the church on tree-shrouded Mary Magdalen Square, pigeons scattered off the statue of the town's founder, Abbé Megret. In the year since my reporting began I had been drawn to the tranquillity of this spot many times. On a crisp afternoon the previous fall Ted Campbell sat on a bench, sad in his divorce from the faith, confiding that he still had trouble sleeping. "There's nothing wrong with anger as long as you direct it on the right path," he brooded. "I just want the truth to be laid out."

Now it would be laid out by J. Minos Simon in a town founded by a priest. In his bulldog tenacity, Simon shared at least one trait with the first Abbevillian.

Abbé Megret was an outspoken French priest whose demands for greater church power put him at odds with authorities in Paris. In 1842 he left Bordeaux by ship and landed in New Orleans, where an ugly dispute was under way. The St. Louis Cathedral laymen's council, known as *marguilliers*, had accused certain priests of making passes at girls in confessional. Now the *marguilliers* were challenging the archbishop's choice of a new pastor. The dispute was headed for the Louisiana Supreme Court when the archbishop dispatched Megret to Vermilionville, as Lafayette then was known.

There he first triggered a backlash by showing himself a racial moderate in issuing a sympathetic "Instructions for Colored People." Rumblings with lay people over control of the parish treasury made matters worse. Megret was beaten on the street in full view of the sheriff, who as chairman of the church trustees is reported to have laughed. Like the *marguilliers* in New Orleans, those in the future diocese of Lafayette did not take to their new pastor. Megret retaliated with his own kind of power: he quit saying Mass and headed down the Vermilion River to preach the Word among more hospitable folk.

Twenty-five miles south he found a bluff overlooking the bayou and decided
to build a church. People proposed naming the town after him—Ville de l'Abbé.
But landowners ten miles upriver at Pont Perry wanted the church built near
them. And they had the support of two young priests. Megret fired off a letter to
the archbishop in New Orleans:

> I am impelled to tell you again what's what. . . . Abbeville is the center of
> Catholicism. Pont Perry is the center of Protestantism. . . . They are making offers
> to you at Pont Perry—how could [the young priests] ever bring them to [that]
> realization? They don't even have an inch of ground. They are all as poor as Job.

The letter swayed the archbishop. Megret purchased land on the bluff, established a rectory and cemetery, selling off surplus property to finance construction
of Mary Magdalen Church. In the meantime, the Supreme Court upheld the
archbishop's right to appoint pastors of his choice. Marguilliers in both towns were
defeated. With new lay leaders Megret got along better.

He was a prototype of the mid-nineteenth-century Louisiana priest: European,
authoritarian, vastly better educated than his flock. Class and culture differences
caused many Cajun communities to bristle with anticlericalism. In 1853, Megret
became embroiled in another controversy: he sued Vermilion officials to void an
election that chose Pont Perry as the parish seat. Then a yellow fever epidemic
struck and he went among the people to anoint the dying. In 1854, after Megret
himself died of yellow fever, the legislature reversed the choice of the parish seat
and gave Abbeville the honor. Even in death, Abbé Megret triumphed over civil
authorities.

The road leading Glenn and Faye Gastal to the Vermilion Parish courthouse
stretched back across months of rising anger. Before, they had chafed at the slow
pace of litigation under Paul Hebert. Since then, beginning with their first utterances on television in August 1984, the couple had slowly moved into the center
of an appalling story. Their faces and names made concrete the effects of
Gauthe's sexual crimes in the consciousness of a public that went well beyond the
villages and oil patches of South Louisiana. As reporters from distant places kept
calling, Glenn and Faye told the story again and again, attacking Bishop Frey and
the cover-up while the boy waited, informed by his parents or his attorney, Mr.
Simon, as to each new development.

Negotiations between Simon and the defense attorneys had collapsed. The
family braced for a trial before a jury of their peers. Out-of-court settlements had
averaged $420,000 per victim. Simon insisted that this grievance was worth much
more. For their suffering, Glenn and Faye Gastal wanted more.

They had also violated an article of faith to which many therapists of sexually
abused children held fast: protect anonymity, avoid making the child relive traumatic events as a witness. Other families had filed suit, their identities known only
to relatives or friends. The Gastals shielded their son from local reporters; his first
name was ritually omitted in stories. But to countless people in Acadiana, the
Gastals were the people who sued the church.

Church and insurance carriers' financial responsibility was not at issue. Bob
Wright had already agreed to that. The jury would decide how much money in

compensatory damages would reflect the degree of harm to parents and child. With cases now being filed in other states, attorneys and insurers across the country realized that the monetary verdict would set a precedent. No case like this had ever been tried.

Perhaps as a reminder of this, the *Sunday Advertiser* on February 2 published an editorial entitled, "Lawsuits Costing Local Taxpayers." Without mentioning the trial it criticized "useless, frivolous—and costly lawsuits" for driving up insurance costs, and went on:

> *Reform is long overdue . . . write letters to the editor (your legislator will see them and take heed); get involved in grass-roots organization.*
> *Remember, it's not "those insurance companies" that are paying the bill for these outrageous claims. It's you.*

One had to wonder what potential jurors thought.

The courtroom was drab—beige walls, holes scattered through the ceiling, and brown stains running down the wall from rain leakage. Judges' portraits lined the wall behind the bench.

Bob Wright would argue the church's case. Flanked by insurance attorneys Charles Schmidt III and Gordon Johnson, he sat at the table across from Simon. In Wright, the diocese had a skilled speaker. Behind him sat Bishop Frey, Monsignor Benefiel, and Monsignor Richard Mouton, pastor of Mary Magdalen Parish. The Gastals sat at the table with Simon. Gauthe was behind bars at the far end of the state, his testimony unnecessary because the responsibility of the church for his acts had already been stipulated.

Judge Ware, an easygoing man with sandy hair, smoked cigarettes from the bench as jury selection began. Religious attitudes in the jury pool were crucial to the attorneys.

Wright, wearing bifocals and a dark blue suit, had a cool, scholarly air. Simon, in a white suit and red tie, might have been a politician on the hustings. "In your mind," he asked a potential juror, "if a minister or priest had violated the law and must give an accounting, just like anyone else, can you hold and make a judgment?"

"I could," said the man.

"Would you tend to reduce that amount just because a church or priest is involved?"

"I wouldn't reduce it."

A smiling maternal lady in her fifties acknowledged that she would have trouble awarding a monetary verdict. Judge Ware politely dismissed her. As she left, the lady patted Bishop Frey on the shoulder, which sent a mild titter through the crowd.

"During the course of this trial," Simon told members of the jury pool, "you will hear very explicit statements regarding homosexual activities and a young boy. Some of these details will be graphic. Would you be offended to hear evidence of this kind?" Judge Ware expanded: "Would it offend you so much that you couldn't render a verdict?" Several said yes and were dismissed. Others said no. To a laboratory technician, Catholic, married with two children, Simon said:

"I respect your religion, sir, and your beliefs. But as attorney for plaintiffs, I must ask, do you attend Mass?"

"Not regularly."

"Would you feel uncomfortable looking Bishop Frey in the eye if you rendered a large verdict?"

"No."

To a Catholic mother of five, Simon put similar questions. Could she evaluate evidence about homosexuality? Yes. Could she award a $10 million verdict? "No, I could not." Simon: "I thank you for being honest." Ware relieved her of jury duty.

Reporters and attorneys studied the faces and verbal nuances of prospective jurors. The case had received extensive coverage; the community was divided, the trial itself something of a blight on the town. Simon asked a Mr. Meaux: "Could you be objective?"

"If it was me," fumed Mr. Meaux, "I just think that if it was my child—"

"You don't think you could handle it," retorted Simon.

"I'm telling you my mind would be made up!"

Wright posed a general question to the pool. "Have you made up your minds about what it would take to compensate this young man?" He explained that Gauthe would not be present nor paying any of the judgment himself. "I'm having difficulty finding out, Mr. Meaux, if you're angry at this fella."

"I don't know if I could sit here and listen to what happened to this young boy," said Mr. Meaux.

"The Court will tell you," Wright calmly continued, "that you can't award punitive damages." (Unlike many other states, Louisiana law did not allow for punitive judgments.) Wright continued: "It must be fair and reasonable for the damages sustained." Speaking of Mr. Meaux, Wright said, "He told us exactly how he felt. So I'd like everybody to look me in the eye: no matter how you feel, you can't be punitive. You can't punish. That's not your job in this case."

Judge Ware reiterated that the verdict was only to compensate for plaintiff suffering, not to be punitive. Mr. Meaux was excused.

It was an ironic position for Bob Wright, whose television spots pitching his firm for personal injury cases made him a celebrity lawyer of sorts. South Louisiana juries were known for awarding seven-figure verdicts to oil workers badly hurt on the job. Would this jury see the church as a comparable institution? Wright cited a Houston jury's recent verdict of $10 billion against Texaco for its takeover attempt of Pennzoil. "You realize," said Wright, "that this case should not send a message to the world—but compensate young Gastal?"

Judge Ware questioned jurors about their ability to be fair, dismissing several who did not seem impartial. "I get the opinion," drawled Simon, "that to be impartial you're supposed to be a machine or a robot. If you are revolted or repulsed by what you hear, are you w illing to consider that the child was equally revulsed? If this is a test, to the effect that among the problems he's got today—"

"Your honor," cut in Bob Wright.

"Let me finish my question," demanded Simon.

"No! I don't want you to finish your question," snapped Wright. "May we approach the bench, your honor?"

The attorneys huddled with the judge, the exchange typifying the hostility that had long been building between Simon, the iconoclast, and Wright, the quintessential establishment lawyer. Each man would have earned a fortune wherever he had chosen to practice. In Lafayette they were two large egos in the same small pond.

And so it went: Wright seeking assurance of fairness, Simon wondering if jurors would feel intimidated by Bishop Frey, who sat quietly behind his attorneys, trying not to show discomfort. A young woman, who volunteered that her second cousin was a priest, said: "I don't feel the church should have to pay for one man's mistake." Ware excused her.

In jury selection each side had six peremptories—the right to strike a potential witness, pending the judge's approval. A former housekeeper at an area rectory, now a parish trustee, worked on financial reports for her pastor. Simon asked if the reports went to the bishop. Answer: "I guess they do." Simon: "You believe in confession and absolution as a way to everlasting life?" "Yes." Would she have any problem awarding a large judgment? "No." Simon asked that she be excused. Ware did so.

As the jury ranks thinned, Wright asked potential witnesses if any had direct relationships with the Gastals, moving to strike those who did. Ware concurred. The final twelve consisted of nine women and three men—eight Catholics in all. Ware's instructions regarding outside influences were lax: "If you want to watch TV news, fine—but don't view a TV program concerning the trial"—which was the biggest story in the territory. "If you read the newspaper, don't read any articles about this."

Richard Baudouin and I had agreed that my story on the trial would conclude *Times of Acadiana* coverage of the scandal. With the verdict, the story would have run its course. In the wake of Edmund Reggie's threat to Steve May about recanting the editorial, there were increased stirrings of an advertisers' boycott. Monsignor Alexander Sigur, a longtime friend of Reggie, had asked the board chairman of a hospital to pull his account. A car dealership had already canceled. "We're not sure whether this thing is going to grow," said Baudouin. Phone calls and letters to the paper regarding the editorials were running favorably, but even threatened boycotts can chill a publisher's veins.

ii.

The Gastal suit filed by Paul Hebert asked $12 million in damages. Settlements negotiated by Hebert and Bencomo had included payments to parents. In this case, the jury would decide how much to award the boy—and whether the parents should receive compensation for their own suffering and loss. If the latter claim was rejected, pending suits would be weakened.

Simon's argument turned on a concept of faith that touched the soul of Acadiana: that to gain salvation a Catholic must follow faith, and that loss of that faith, because of Gauthe's crimes, was the fundamental damage requiring compensation. Simon wanted his clients to hold up mirrors to the jury. The Gastals, he began, were bred of a "God-fearing" environment and taught to trust priests. "God gave them a fragile boy, born premature. The father worked as a farmer. This li'l boy was raised Catholic 'cause his parents believed this was the key to heaven and everlasting life."

Faye Gastal was a slender woman of thirty-seven; she had a lean face, pretty features framed by short brown hair. Born and raised in nearby Maurice, where her daddy drove a milk truck, she had three brothers and a sister. The family, she would testify, was "as Catholic as they come."

Where Faye absorbed suffering, Glenn, who was four years older, exuded it. The etchings of his brow made him seem much older, and his anger was immense: no one who spent much time with him could escape it. As Simon spoke, the Gastals sat at the plaintiffs' table, smoking cigarettes, a world removed from the bishop and the two monsignors a few feet away. Gerard Frey's silence filled the space around him, projecting a thick sadness. However difficult his life had lately become because of his errors, he was about to endure still another awful experience.

Litigation is built less on truth than on versions of reality. Simon spoke as if relating a parable: "This li'l boy was about to make his first communion, to assure everlasting life, the eternal hope of *every human being* in Western civilization. At the age of seven his mother wanted him to be altar boy. You'd have thought an angel was spreading joy in their lives. They said, 'Son, you must trust the priest and obey the priest. We're proud of you.' "

To Gauthe, he told jurors, the parents said: "This is my child—take my child, teach him." But the priest, "in his own inimitably evil way, began fondling him, playing with his private parts . . . he sodomizes him." The jury sat stone-faced as Simon said it happened "in the rectory, behind the confessional, in his car." Soon Gauthe "had the child sodomizing him . . . and made him sodomize other children. He told him, 'If you tell, I will hurt your daddy.' "

Simon ticked off signs of damage in the child and summarized the parents' relationship with psychologist Kenneth Bouillon. "This doctor tells them, 'Do not talk to the child. When the time comes, I will get you all together.' Don't talk! It's a secret! They soon become hostage to the terrorism of silence."

Bouillon had refused press interviews; hence his version of his instructions to the Gastals had never been made public.

"The dam of human tolerance broke from tears of grief," said Simon. "They wanted to reach out to people of their community. They wanted other parents to know so there would not be another little person victimized by secrecy. So they hired me . . . that's when the veil of secrecy was lifted. They embraced the child, they cried and washed away the doubt. At last he knew his momma and daddy loved him.

"So you're here," he concluded, "to make a judgment of how much compensation is necessary." He explained life-cycle forecasts as they related to child abuse victims: how traumatic memories often arose at the onset of puberty, that most pedophiles were themselves abused children, that medical care must continue. "Once you hear the evidence, I think that ten million dollars is right for everything he's suffered in the past and in his future."

Simon had sketched the ugly depths of suffering; now it was Wright's turn to soften the surface. Born in Indiana, Wright had gone to Centenary College in Shreveport on a basketball scholarship, then to Tulane Law School before settling in Lafayette. He spoke in flat Midwestern cadences. He also had a flair one could not help liking. After blasting me in the *Advertiser*, Wright greeted me on the courthouse steps several mornings later with a smile and pumping handshake, conveying a message of no hard feelings.

The trial had a personal side for Bob Wright. A key plaintiff witness was his brother-in-law, Lyle LeCorgne, the therapist now treating the boy. Gay—Bob's wife, Lyle's sister—a graduate of Ursuline Academy in New Orleans, sat in the audience.

It was no secret that Wright and his clients felt the trial was unnecessary, that it should have been settled. Perhaps in frustration, Wright had spoken the boy's name to newsmen on the courthouse steps. It was beeped out by television stations on the evening broadcast.

"You, ladies and gentlemen," Wright addressed the jury, "have unfortunately been brought to this courtroom to decide damages in a reasonable, fair amount. Ten million for this young man—and $2 million for his parents?

"Dr. Bouillion," he continued, "told the family that this young man needed psychological care. They decided to go public directly contrary to the doctor's advice. The doctor will tell you, yes, this young man was damaged but it could have been overturned within two years—without subjecting him to the ridicule and embarrassment in the community he sustained."

The law entitled a person to recovery of damages, Wright said, but had the family handled this properly by going public? "Was it in the best interests of [the boy]? Part of the damage has been the result of putting this out in the open."

The first witness was Monsignor Mouton of Abbeville, tall, with close-cropped silver hair. Simon asked whether a person acting contrary to faith was in a schism. In a mild professional manner, the local pastor said: "We make a distinction between one, heresy; two, schism; and three, excommunication." A heretic disagreed with church doctrine. Schism was a break from papal authority. Excommunication was formal expulsion from the church.

Simon then moved into a long exploration of traditions established by the church through divine revelation as given to the apostles; the exploration almost put the jury to sleep. He grilled Mouton about the fate of a soul who, under the old rules, ate meat on Friday. "If one is separated from God," replied the priest, "and dies in this state, he remains separated, which we call hell." Hell: there, he had said it. But to what end? The jury seemed bottomlessly bored at Simon's theological probe.

"Why do you have to obey a priest?" asked Simon.

"Because you want to," said Monsignor Mouton.

"Can you give me an example?" Then the witness asked for context. "No," snapped Simon, "you give *me* an example!"

Wright dryly interjected that the line of questioning, "while fascinating, has [not] any iota of relevance."

Ware chastised Simon and told him to move on with his examination. Simon asked if homosexuality was a violation of apostolic tradition. After a long pause, Mouton said: "Yes." If a child was an altar boy, could the parents expect this to make him better understand the faith?" Mouton said: "Are you referring to Father Gauthe?"

"No, I'm referring to priests in general."

"It depends upon the priest. You could have a priest in the parish interested in formation of altar servers. Others would have other interests."

Wright did not cross-examine Monsignor Mouton. Judge Ware announced lunch break. Simon, it seemed, had browbeaten the witness to no useful end.

Faye Gastal, born just up the road in Maurice, was sworn in that afternoon. In style and substance she was a home girl with whom jurors could identify. Simon asked of her faith. She said: "Getting absolution [from sins] was the only way to get to heaven."

The boy was born in 1974, two months premature; Glenn was working as an oilfield dispatcher. They lived in a trailer near Lake Charles before moving to Esther, where they lived on a farm in her husband's family. She recounted her enthusiasm when the child became an altar boy amid Gauthe's assurances of his religious fitness. "He was a very lovable boy," she said, voice faltering. "I never had any discipline problems. He was never afraid . . . he said his prayers. He was happy."

She spoke of his Erector set. A woman in the jury looked bereaved. The happy child's behavior began to change, Faye continued. "He wasn't loving any more. He wasn't kissing us. He didn't play with his sisters like he used to. He didn't sleep at night, he walked the floors, checking doors. He'd just tell me he was scared. I asked him what he was scared of. He couldn't answer."

In March 1983 he entered the hospital with a case of rectal bleeding. When Gauthe visited with a model car, the child scampered down the hall. His mother said she suspected nothing. In time the boy withdrew even more, refusing to eat, became "rebellious, sassy. We tried to discipline him. He goes wild."

She recounted Bouillion's instructions to keep silence and how on trips back from the therapist she wanted to hug the boy and tell him it was all right, she understood—but held back. Her voice rose: "I wanted to tell him what happened wasn't his fault. I felt we were being treated as if we were criminals and we should have been treated as victims. I wanted my neighbors to know my little boy wasn't a homo and to tell them so they'd protect their children."

Then, with the faintest hint of suggestiveness, Simon said, "When you look at Bishop Frey here, what goes through your mind?"

Staring at the bishop, voice rising, hitting words for emphasis, she said: "When I look at Monsignor Mouton and Bishop Frey, I think of Gauthe *sticking* his penis in my child's mouth, *ejaculating* in his mouth, putting his penis in his rectum —*that's* what I think about!"

Monsignor Mouton looked down. The bailiff saw the bishop go white as her words hit like hammer strokes in the stunned room.

In cross-examination Wright was gentle. "It's my responsibility to question you about some things. I hope you understand my obligation." He led her through questions about the boy's charges. When he misbehaved, what did she do? "I put him on his knees and made him pray," said she, as many a Cajun momma would do.

Asked about Bouillion, she said the therapist told them that "if we went public the news media would track us down. He said it would hurt the child. But I'd like to make a point. The only time my son's name was mentioned in public was when you did it yesterday, twice. The news media never mentioned his name."

"Why did you stop going to see Dr. Bouillion?"

"Because I saw no improvement."

Under Lyle LeCorgne, she testified, the boy had improved. He was now play- ing baseball. Wright asked if he seemed all right outside the home. "As far as I can see," she replied. "I know there are squabbles at school."

Wright asked who she thought was treating her like a criminal. Answer: "I felt like Ken Bouillion and Paul Hebert were covering this thing up."

The next witness, Dr. Perry Sudduth, had treated the boy in the hospital in 1983 for rectal bleeding. The physician—who at the time had no inkling of Gauthe's activities—said that he thought bruises in the area were from an enema. Simon returned to graphic details, questions about "ingestation of semen" and "the penile invasion" to which the physician replied that yes, such acts were harmful. Simon continued in this way, booming out the vocabulary of sex in questions that washed through the courtroom like a fetid odor. Several women jurors looked down.

As Simon bore down on anatomical details, Wright held his bifocals, eyes closed, cupping his chin with his fingers. Attorney Schmidt stared at the door. Gordon Johnson slumped in his chair. The clerics seemed frozen in their seats.

In cross-examination Wright asked, "As far as you know, the child had full recovery?"

"From gastrointestinitis, yes," said the doctor. Although he could not, as a statement of fact, say that the rectal bleeding was caused by sodomy, the implica- tion hovered starkly in the courtroom.

With the physician's testimony, the second day concluded. In the hallway friends comforted Faye Gastal. The bishop and two monsignors filed silently past. An insurance representative who had refused my interview request muttered to a lawyer: "This trial never should have been held."

The next morning Glenn Gastal testified that praying the rosary had been one way of "repenting your sins and becoming closer to God." Again, Simon was drawing the line between faith before Gauthe and faith after. Through pen- ance, Gastal said, "I would be free of sin and worthy of the body and blood of Christ."

"Did you feel through that process that you could control your ultimate destiny?" And Gastal said: "Yes, sir."

When his attorney asked about Gauthe, Gastal said: "We trusted him as a man of God," responding to requests for help "when there was a drive for repairs, the church parking lot to be paved, whatever it might take to make it be a good church."

His voice choked. "Gauthe was an *evil* man." Wavering, he spoke of wanting his son to grow "and to understand—" and then he began to sob, one wave of tears spilling out of another, covering his eyes with his hands as faces in the jury box went frail with sadness. The judge called a ten-minute recess.

Glenn Gastal was a small, wiry man with graying black hair. When testimony resumed he was still fighting back tears. Simon asked what his hopes and wishes for the boy had been. "I feel," he choked, "I had the same wishes for my son of every parent in this courtroom."

"Your honor," said Wright gently, "in deference to all concerned, we all agree
that Mr. Gastal loved his boy. The questioning is becoming repetitious."

The judge agreed but did not sustain. When Simon resumed, Gastal offered
the most painful testimony of the trial. "We were a close, loving family—still are,
except when it comes to the relationship which I can't have with my son as a
young child. He is unable to tolerate physical displays of affection."

And then he came apart again. Several women in the jury wiped away tears of
their own. "After Gauthe," sobbed Gastal, "he kissed me only if I demanded it
before he went to bed."

Until the break with Bouillion, Gastal insisted, they did not know the extent
of their son's molestation. How, asked Simon, had going public with their accusations affected the father? "I think I've gotten support from my community—that
my child was a victim. But every touch to my son by anybody has become a bad
touch. . . . He's a child, in a child's body, yet I think that spiritually he's no
longer a child. That part of his life has vanished. I've been denied and he's been
denied."

Wright objected that Simon was leading the witness, asking questions designed to elicit specific answers. The judge sustained the objection. Glenn Gastal
said: "Mr. Simon, Mr. Wright, it's necessary for me to tell you the actual things
that my child has told me. I would not put it in the bounds of hearsay."

"I didn't say it was hearsay," said the judge kindly. "I just sustained the questions as leading."

"I think the loss of the greatest thing that any man could ask for is the
relationship of father to son, and the relationship between my church and my
God," said Glenn Gastal.

As Wright began his cross-examination, the witness was distraught. Judge
Ware said: "Are you all right, Mr. Gauthe?"

"Gastal—please," the witness shot back, causing the courtroom to erupt in
laughter, breaking the awful tension. Gastal managed a smile.

"Mr. Gastal," began Wright, "we've spoken before. You express personal ani-
mosity toward Bishop Frey, Monsignor Mouton."

"Yes, sir."

"Do you realize that priests are men, human beings?"

"Definitely."

"Have you always been of the frame of mind that there are certain evil forces
among men and certain good forces among men?"

"Yes, sir. I have tried to teach that to my child, that you don't victimize. Since
the day my child was victimized I was only victimized by priests and nuns."

"You feel that all priests and nuns are bad?"

He nodded yes. Wright asked if he had ever before received psychological
evaluation—knowing the answer, which Gastal gave, that he had been screened
during a custody dispute after his first marriage ended in divorce. Wright did not
pursue the matter, and left unspoken the implication that Gastal had broken
canon law by remarrying after his divorce without obtaining an annulment.
Whether jurors sensed this is unclear.

Moving on another track, Wright asked whether, in surrendering his child to
Gauthe, "you knew about his personal character?"

"I trusted his personal character to church authorities such as Bishop Frey."

Wright was trying to show that the family should have had a sense of something wrong while the boy remained under Gauthe's tutelage. The single sign, said Gastal, was at Mass one day when the boy received holy communion and put the wafer in his pocket, rather than eating the wafer. "We talked to Father Gauthe about it." The priest told them he was a good boy, not to worry.

"The child had very marked changes," Wright resumed, "and you didn't seek counseling?"

Simon objected. Wright withdrew the question. "Let's go into your background. You ran a feed store." Gastal testified that in 1982, before the store went under, he drew $1000 a month income, his wife $500—$18,000 a year between them. The line of questioning was subtle but the implication was clear: should a family once earning $18,000 be compensated in the millions for a priest's crimes?

"You're now farming?" Wright asked.

"I am crawfishing."

"Have you not gone to church since seeing Paul Hebert [in March 1984]?"

"Yes, sir. I visit the church on a weekly basis, as a moment of meditation, to kneel down, to pray to God, but not when any existing priest is on the altar. At this point in my life I'm not sure about anything. My religious belief has been destroyed."

Wright shifted again, asking about the original lawsuit filed by Hebert and meetings with Bouillion. Gastal echoed his wife's testimony, that Bouillion told them not to discuss the molestations with their son. Alluding to results of therapy, Wright said: "You now see pride in what [the boy] comes to believe, that he was a victim. Mr. Gastal, personally, I want you to know that's how we feel."

"Objection!" thundered Minos Simon.

But with that the morning testimony was done.

Returning to the courthouse after lunch, I saw Lyle LeCorgne, the boy's therapist. As teenagers we played on the same Dixie League baseball team and attended Jesuit High together. He introduced me to a plump man with graying hair and beard: Ken Bouillion. Once again I requested an interview. Bouillion said no, he never gave interviews because of client confidentiality. "You'll get what you need from my testimony," he said airily.

He had a doctorate from Texas Tech and nine years' clinical practice in Lafayette, most of it with children. On the witness stand he told Simon that his first session with the boy was on March 13, 1984; after that there were ten sessions in all, the last on July 5, 1984. "At the conclusion of my first interview, I told the parents it was clearly my opinion that their son had been involved with Father Gauthe. I told them I would get more details and give them the full picture."

Bouillion discussed explicit sexual acts Gauthe had performed with other children as well, and photographs the priest had taken of the boys. The jurors stared grimly. "Contrary to Mr. Gastal's testimony," said Bouillion, "I explained to the parents that the child needed love, comfort, and understanding. I addressed the issue of homosexual fears. I assured them that this was not the child's fault. They were visibly upset, obviously, as all parents have been. I talked to them about their own anger. I was concerned about their ability to handle [the boy's] feedback."

Simon digressed with questions about homosexuality, eliciting more details of graphic sexual acts. When he turned to the advice Bouillion had given the parents, the therapist said: "To the best of my knowledge, I did not tell them not to talk to the child about it. I told them I would sit with them at a later time and discuss details with them."

Bouillion catalogued the boy's problems—insecurity, poor self-esteem, feelings of anger and aggression—"even his body language, he'd put his head down . . . all of that was very negative. He was also very fearful." His sense of right and wrong was impaired. "But the largest obstacle to overcome was loss of trust."

Quantifying a monetary amount to compensate for the child's damage turned in part on forecasts of the professional care he would need—care that would be "monitoring his sexual feelings, how he viewed himself as a male or deals with females," said Bouillion. Simon asked if he would need continuing psychological monitoring to guard against becoming a child molester himself.

Bouillion replied that by working with a youngster, teaching him positive skills, the chances of such behavior would be reduced. "The availability of counseling should be there throughout his lifetime," he stated.

Exactly how much therapy was needed? Bouillion estimated one hundred sessions over a three- to five-year period. The financial forecast to cover this treatment he estimated to be forty to fifty thousand dollars—a pittance of the millions requested in the lawsuit.

Under cross-examination, Wright returned to what Bouillion told the Gastals. "My advice to them and to others was to try and separate out the legal parts and prevent public knowledge of the child's name, of who the child was. I discussed with them what I observed in other children . . . the bad effects of publicity. I said it would interfere with my work with the child," Bouillion said.

The image of family innocence changed when Wright asked about the boy's concerns, and Bouillion said: "This youngster was fairly fearful of his dad. The boy was afraid of his father's temper."

Was Bouillion aware that the boy was now getting better grades? "I was not aware, no."

"That's a pleasant thing to know, isn't it?" said Wright, and Bouillion agreed that it was.

Driving back to Lafayette that evening, I wondered whether Simon's strategy was working—filling the courtroom with images of graphic sexual deviance. The boy was set to testify the following morning. Would Simon put him through a grinder, make him break down and cry? Wright had only one witness, Dr. Mark Forman, a child psychiatrist on the Tulane medical faculty; he had examined the family. The verdict, I felt, would be a gauge of Simon's personality.

My wife and daughter were out when I entered the apartment. The phone rang as I opened the refrigerator. A man from Spokane, Washington, asked if I was the reporter who had written about the church scandals. I said yes. He said: "We've just learned that Lane Fontenot molested our teenage boy."

I stared at the open refrigerator. The man said his son was in treatment for substance abuse at the Nancy Reagan Care Unit of Deaconess Hospital, where Fontenot had been a counselor. He asked for information. I recounted events that had been reported. He told me they were contacting a lawyer. I took his phone number and promised not to reveal his name.

A few moments later a reporter named Mike Murphey with the *Spokane Spokes-*

man-Review called, wanting information. I gave him the substance of what I had reported. Murphey had a tip from police sources that Fontenot was going to be charged but had already fled Spokane. I agreed to send my stories by Federal Express. He said that at least three boys in the substance abuse clinic had been molested by Fontenot, who had the nickname "Huggy Bear." (Eight minor victims would eventually file suit.) Murphey thought the story would break in two days, on Friday—the day the jury would render its verdict on the Gastal case. He promised to send his story in time for my Monday deadline. I called Richard Baudouin at home and gave him the news. "Jesus Christ," he muttered. "Where does this thing stop?"

Baudouin was worried. Monsignor Sigur was stepping up his boycott pressure, having asked a bank president to withdraw his advertisements because of the editorial; the man had refused, but Sigur was calling other businesses. The paper was facing serious revenue losses if advertisers pulled their accounts. "I can't put another story like this on the cover," said Richard, likening such coverage to "salt on a festering wound."

I proposed giving the Spokane leads to Dee Stanley of Channel 10, who had first reported news of Gauthe's departure in August 1984. "Let him break it on television, and I'll simply mention it at the end of my trial story." Baudouin agreed, provided the station not air a story about the boycott. Steve May wanted to handle things in his own way.

The next morning I arrived early at the Abbeville courthouse, drew Stanley aside, and explained the situation. "This is amazing," he said, staring at the church beyond the square. KLFY news director Jim Baronet wanted to air a story about the boycott, but at Baudouin's urging had agreed to hold back. "They let a pedophile run loose in Spokane," said Stanley, "and in Lafayette they try to kill a newspaper."

When testimony resumed shortly thereafter, a beleaguered Glenn and Faye Gastal entered the courtroom. The boy was set to testify when, at Lyle LeCorgne's request, the judge ordered spectators out. David McCormick of the Associated Press asked that the press be allowed to stay, lest the public record be incomplete. Ware concurred.

Minos Simon, in white jacket and gray pants, escorted the child to the witness stand with a hand on his shoulder, gazing at the jury as he walked.

He was a lithe boy, now eleven, with light brown hair, wearing slacks and a shirt. Jurors smiled as he answered Simon's questions—his age, names of his momma and daddy, how many siblings he had, where he went to school, and whether he played any sports. "Football," said the boy, with a modest grin.

He could have been anyone's son, sitting up there trying to do his best, a good-looking kid whose sufferings had dominated the previous witnesses' testimony while he had been in fifth-grade classes. And how old had he been when he became an altar boy? "Seven." What did his parents say? His voice tensed: "My momma said, 'Good.' "

Simon: "How long after your first communion did you meet Gauthe?" The boy couldn't answer. Simon persisted in a paternal tone. "You went to get training?" Sniffling, the child said: "Yes, sir. He come and pick me up."

Simon walked the youngster through questions about his visits with Gauthe and about when the priest left the parish. The boy answered correctly, fidgeting. Then: "What did he do?"

"He played with my pee-pee."

"You talk about your private parts?"

"Yes, sir."

Faye Gastal's hands covered her eyes as her son recounted instances of sexual abuse already well documented, using "pee-pee" and "behind" as anatomical nouns. Simon extracted more, stockpiling graphic details. Then he asked if the boy had understood why the abuse was happening. "I thought he was doing the right thing because he was a priest."

"When you think of how you feel—reach down in your heart—how do you feel about priests?"

He looked down. He stole a quick glance at the bishop—did the child really understand all of this?—and then said softly: "Real sad." And how did he feel about Gauthe? The boy said nothing. Wright remained quiet as Simon pushed the witness with leading questions, asking if he felt "sad? angry?" The boy shrugged. "Kinda angry, and kinda sad."

And how did he feel about his daddy?

"When he hugs me I feel funny."

The boy rubbed his eyes, sniffling but not crying, breathing deeply as Simon concluded. He had clearly been coached but the power of his testimony lay simply in his presence in the room.

Bob Wright was brief in his cross-examination, wanting to show the jury his— and the church's—sensitivity toward the child and his plight. He asked what position he played on the baseball team (left field) and whether he liked school all right. "Yes, sir." To which the defense attorney replied: "Real good. Good to see you again—Thank you for coming."

With the boy's departure one felt a catharsis. Spectators filed back into the courtroom. Lyle LeCorgne was sworn in and assessed the boy's problems and the therapeutic help he would require. LeCorgne's primary concern was that "he is soon to become an adolescent . . . [and] likely to have for the first time [sexual] longing." The risks of depression and aberrant behavior "grow into adulthood and sexuality," he said.

"This boy tries very hard to get along as well as he can," stated LeCorgne. "He struggles most of every day, trying to be normal. His life has been speeded up, if you will—compelled to resolve in some way things beyond the purview of normal childhood."

How long, asked Simon, would the basic disorder last? "I think he's going to be wrestling with this for the rest of his life."

Simon asked how much therapy he would need and LeCorgne said forty to fifty visits a year and "twenty to thirty years of consistent assistance." Outpatient medical costs he estimated at $75,000 to $150,000, not including "more severe reactions, breakdowns," medical assistance, psychiatric hospitalization. Lost in the massive needs-assessment was the fact that therapy diminishes as the patient improves. Was the boy who testified so bravely destined to become a mental patient in perpetuity?

The parents needed sustained treatment as well, LeCorgne explained. Who doubted that? Their lives had been ripped open on the witness stand. Bob Wright had a rubber band laced over his fingers, pulling and loosening it. Simon asked if the public airing of the suit had given comfort to the parents? LeCorgne assented, saying "there was a sense of somehow feeling vindicated."

And the boy—"was it good for him to know" of the public interest? Answer: "Yes." "In your opinion it was therapeutic?"

"It eliminated," said LeCorgne, "a great deal of his fears."

Now it was Bob Wright's turn to cross-examine his brother-in-law. Where Bouillon had opined $50,000 in psychological fees, LeCorgne had more than tripled that estimate—and without quantifying the plethora of medical possibilities. But Wright was in a pickle of his own making: on the day LeCorgne and Simon had arrived at his office for the therapist to be deposed, no one from the defense showed up. The deposition was never taken. LeCorgne had no previous testimony for Wright to use as leverage in cross-examination. Instead Wright referred to a copy of LeCorgne's notes from therapy sessions with the Gastals.

Thirty-five therapeutic visits had taken place (paid for by Simon). Studying LeCorgne's notes, Wright said: "You recall making the quote, 'The more publicity there is, the more he's teased at school, for instance being called a 'queer'?"

"That was in reference to Gilbert Gauthe," said LeCorgne.

Why had the child not received more therapy? "There were access problems in his schedule. Appointments were sometimes made considerably in advance. Efforts were made at all times."

Wright cited an October 29, 1985, notation: "The boy was restless, discussed the interview with CBS." (The family allowed the child to be interviewed by "West 57th Street" with his face shadowed. Production was continuing during the trial.)

Wright asked if LeCorgne had suggested to Mrs. Gastal that they allow the child to be interviewed. No, he said. "Did you suggest that was best for her child?" hammered Wright.

"I knew nothing about it."

Wright then referred to the press being in the courtroom for the boy's testimony: Simon had requested that all parties be removed. "Did you talk to Minos Simon and suggest that [the request be made]?" LeCorgne admitted that he asked Simon to make the request to the judge, explaining: "My wish was to have that safeguard against the possibility of anything negative for the boy. We operate on mental images. My impression was that it would be better for him to recollect talking only to the jury."

Wright was trying to corner LeCorgne with his conflicting statements about the impact of "publicity" on the boy. "Would you agree that for the sake of [the boy] that your treatment would have been more effective if his private affairs had not been made public?"

Wright had him in a box now. But LeCorgne, with dark pensive eyebrows and pregnant pauses, was an agile witness. "I don't know if I can really answer that. In this particular case the public nature of it was a *fait accompli* before I got involved. Yet I have seen several positive aspects verbalized by the child. I can't point to any damaging or deteriorating effects."

Was the publicity healthy for the boy?

LeCorgne knew Simon's strategy. The therapist testified: "To continue to perpetrate a veil of secrecy is tantamount to the restraints and prohibitions perpetrated on these boys by Gilbert Gauthe."

And so Wright's gambit failed. At the break after testimony, Wright stood alone in the hall, gazing at the ceiling, simmering.

The sole defense witness, Dr. Forman, had screened all three Gastals. He felt that weekly sessions for the boy for one to two years would suffice, and recommended weekly family therapy sessions for the parents in the same time span. He estimated the cost of those services at $15,000. Simon cross-examined Forman with restraint. He then took the physician's report and in his deep stentorian drawl read the entire document for twenty-nine minutes—reiterating the sad dirty facts once again, now in the words of a psychiatrist, using a defense document to buttress his case.

In his closing argument Simon said the boy had "an evil genie swirling around in his mind." For a final time he went through the litany of graphic sexual crimes. The damages were incalculable, the boy had lost his spiritual estate, the "hope of eternal life. It gives us courage to live our lives in an exemplary manner . . . to worship God. That is the one hope that sustains us and he has lost it forever." This, from a man whose case had been built on pummeling the clerical estate. One sensed the irony did not register with the jurors. "We don't have a magic wand that says, I hereby restore your spiritual health," Simon continued. "The only morally certain thing we do have is money as a medium of compensation." The amount, he believed, "must be very, very substantial."

When Bob Wright rose for summation his challenge was to reduce the loss. He remarked that "the events in this community were tragic" and laid a great burden on the jury. Beyond the community, the whole state has been hurt. The jurors stood as the conscience of the community. "You don't punish, you attempt to repair. That's what we ask you to do. The church is doing only what the law allows us to do."

Mrs. Gastal, he said, "is a fine young lady." Yet she had "surrendered" the boy, "as Minos Simon has constantly suggested," to the priest. "I do not surrender my seven-year-old child to another for as much as one third of the time of his formative years. I don't mean to sound too critical."

Wright's subtle design was unfolding: how much fault did the parents bear for letting their child spend so much time away? "I swear to goodness I don't know where Dr. Bouillion said, 'Don't hug your child.' He said don't dwell on ugly acts. . . . They have told us they went public [wanting] everyone to know 'we aren't criminals' . . . and to help other children. But where was the rationale to suggest that [Hebert's lawsuit] made them criminals? I don't follow the reasoning." In effect, he was telling the jury that a dispute with their first attorney had turned into a big case for Simon, whom he called "one of the best attorneys in Lafayette, if not the world." Then he said, "The *Times of Acadiana* came out with exposés every other week."

"Objection!" barked Simon.

"I'm getting too upset," replied Wright, "and I apologize." He reviewed Dr. Forman's testimony, that the public nature of the dispute had hurt the boy and the family. Still, "a cute, beautiful little man was brought to this courtroom, instead of by video, very well prepared, I believe, and told you yes or no in response to Minos Simon's questions." The boy had achieved stair-step improvement under LeCorgne "with the exception of those times associated with publicity." At school he was near the honor roll with A's in conduct. "That young man has developed a long way. He has emotional abuse, don't get me wrong, but not to the point of being hospitalized. He's not psychotic.

"What do you want for him?" he asked the jury. "Do you want to provide, or punish the church for him? Do you want to make him rich, a stigma branding him the rest of his life? To become an instant millionaire would be the very worst thing you could do for him. It would be another crutch for the family."

The family needed money for medical security, Wright continued. What amount would compensate for the boy's emotional trauma? "Millions of dollars? Lots of new cars, lots of boats—will it make him a better person?" Would people say, "Look at him, spending all that money he got from the church?"

Provide fairly for treatment, Wright asked. An award of $200,000, properly invested, would provide the child a $20,000 annuity. "Let's tell [this boy], 'You'll get the care of this community and you will learn that the church, if you want it, is still there.' The church includes such things as compassion."

Abraham Lincoln, he said, "made a plea to people of this country" and "I hope you don't think it corny . . . 'The Almighty has His own purposes. With malice toward none, with charity toward all, let us strive to finish the work we've begun . . . to achieve a just and lasting peace.'

"Think about the dollars you're going to award. Two million dollars to Mrs. Gastal? Do you think it's fair? . . . I'm suggesting $50,000 per parent." With $100,000 in an interest-bearing account, they would derive $10,000 annual income for a long time.

Simon rose a final time, marshaling his righteousness. Bob Wright "has not walked in the shoes of these people. . . . 'If you give [the boy] what he deserves he will be a marked man,' " Simon said, paraphrasing Wright. "What logic! They destroy the child, they maul his spirit!" Of the remark about an instant millionaire, he boomed: "What a distortion!

"I think it should be several million," said Simon. "It must be in direct ratio to injuries and they are enormous and will endure a lifetime."

Eyes closed, Bob Wright sat back, with his index finger across his forehead.

The judge gave the jury final instructions and dismissed them. An hour and forty-five minutes later they returned a verdict of $1 million for the boy and $250,000 for the parents.

Afterward, reporters and photographers waited on the courthouse steps. Bishop Frey, with sadness etched across his brow, spoke slowly, enunciating each word: "The legal process has been completed. It's the American way, and I have every confidence in it. I pray now that the Lord's healing presence will be felt in our community. We all have been hurt by this and well need the peace that comes with reconciliation."

Simon expressed satisfaction. The verdict stands "all by itself. It is exceedingly unique." Wright said the defense would not appeal the verdict, and offered hope that the "young man does well with what the jury has found to be fair damages for him."

Glenn Gastal, arm around his wife, was glad they gave "a signal to the other people that, if something like this ever happens to small children, they don't need to hide as if they were criminals." Faye said she was "very well satisfied. I just hope it encourages other parents whose children may have gone through this to pursue it the way we did."

No one asked the boy what he thought. He was not there.

iii.

The night of the Gastal verdict, Dee Stanley's companion story hit the airwaves: Lane Fontenot, whereabouts unknown, was wanted in the state of Washington on charges of sexual assault.

In Spokane, Mike Murphey's reporting introduced *Spokesman Review* readers to the painful issue that had gripped Acadiana for more than a year. Murphey interviewed the Rev. Patrick O'Donnell, a priest-psychiatrist who said that, to his knowledge, the Spokane diocese had experienced no problems with pedophilia. Rev. Frank Bach, the chancellor, said, "We have been lucky in this diocese."

Mary Weathers, a psychologist, called Murphey upon reading the story. There *was* a Spokane priest with such a problem, she insisted: Father O'Donnell himself! Two years earlier, in 1984, the state Board of Psychology Examiners had restricted O'Donnell's license as a practitioner because of child sex abuse, citing him for "grossly immoral acts" and "lack of good moral character." O'Donnell had been relieved of pastoral duties in 1985, Murphey wrote, "after members of his congregation became aware of past allegations that the priest had molested boys." Nevertheless, the suspension of his psychologist's license had just been lifted. The article continued:

> "Local psychologists certainly are concerned," said Mary Weathers, president of the local association. "We are frustrated that the guy still has a license."
>
> The Board of Psychology Examiners, however, says O'Donnell has met the terms of his restriction and apparently has not had a recurrence of his problem, at least in the past two years. . . .
>
> O'Donnell voluntarily has been taking regular polygraph examinations in the past year to try to prove he is in control of the disorder.
>
> In a statement Friday, Bishop Lawrence Welsh said, "Due to the sensitivity of this entire issue, and the fact that these are confidential matters, we do not wish to say anything further at this time."
>
> According to his answering machine, O'Donnell is out of town.

Murphey called Father Bach again, to ask the chancellor about his previous comments. The article said:

> Bach's initial statement in his interviews—when asked how the diocese viewed the national problem of pedophile priests—was: "In a sense, in the past, it has been a matter out of sight, out of mind, if your own diocese has not been involved, and we have been very lucky in this diocese."

Bach said Thursday that the statement should not have been construed as a denial that the problem exists here.

"I feel we have been very lucky," he told a reporter. "You never asked me directly whether we'd ever had to deal with that problem here. If you had asked, I would have said no comment."

Lane Fontenot flew to Houston, where a friend drove him to Louisiana. After consultation with Bob Wright, he returned to Spokane, where he had the benefit of an excellent attorney, Sid Wurzburg, who negotiated a plea bargain that July. Fontenot pleaded guilty to one count of third-degree statutory rape—a felony—and four misdemeanor counts of communication with a minor for immoral purposes.

"We realize he has an illness," the parent of one victim told the Court, "but our sons have illnesses too. When we put our son into treatment, we had great hopes that he would come out and we would be a family again. But now our son is not home. He's out on the street somewhere using drugs."

In his coverage of the sentencing, Murphey wrote:

A tearful Fontenot told the court that the therapy he has received in the months since his arrest have helped him begin to "understand the nature of my behavior. . . . For this reason, I want to say that I'm sorry, because I never intended to hurt my church, or the young people involved, or my family, and because of that, I ask for a greater form of mercy."

Attorney Wurzburg responded to one family's call for a harsh sentence by blaming the Lafayette diocese for "the shame" of failing to provide Fontenot with solid treatment. "He received just under six months of counseling in Massachusetts in the kind of program that no one in this state would ever consider as an appropriate sexual offender program," said Wurzburg.

The judge agreed. Fontenot was sentenced to a year in the Spokane County Jail, followed by two years of inpatient treatment at the Jemez Springs, New Mexico, facility specializing in child-molesting priests and run by the Servants of the Paraclete.

Bishop Frey's wish for "the peace that comes with reconciliation" did not come quickly. Within a week of the Gastal verdict the *Times of Acadiana* was projecting a $100,000 revenue loss for the year if accounts by advertisers now boycotting held firm. Several readers had written letters to the paper, denouncing the boycott. But if more advertisers pulled, the paper would go under. The idea of Monsignor Sigur—who as seminary rector in New Orleans had approved Gauthe for ordination—now fomenting a boycott of the paper was appalling. The *Times* had yet to run a story about its problems and Steve May had not spoken publicly about them. I considered it an important story about freedom of the press, and told May that if we arranged an interview with the *New York Times* Sigur was bound to feel pressure from the Vatican Embassy, saying enough is enough.

May sat in his office, smoking a cigar. "If my ship is going down, I'll talk to the world. First, I'd rather save my ship—my own way."

In that effort he received an unlikely ally—Raymond Blanco, one of the bishop's stalwart supporters and a longtime friend of Sigur. Blanco was getting heat from Ray Mouton, who was outraged by the boycott. "It's the whole fucking Watergate mentality of this diocese," he told me. "I told Raymond that if he didn't get Sigur to call off the dogs I would attack the bishop and Sigur on 'West 57th Street.' "

Bluff was part of the friendship Blanco and Mouton shared. They had been threatening each other for years while sitting side by side at football games. But Blanco was driven by other concerns. Al Sigur was one of his best friends. When civil rights conflicts flared at USL, Blanco, as assistant dean, and Sigur, who was then campus chaplain, worked together to defuse tensions. Blanco believed in his heart if not his gut that Sigur would retreat from a trampling of the First Amendment.

Blanco saw greater problems building. The experience of seeing the trial, coupled with the awful news about Fontenot, had been devastating to Bishop Frey. And then Paul Hebert had sent word that several couples among his initial clients—those who had long since settled their cases—wanted the bishop to meet with them. Hebert felt the time was ripe for a reconciliation to bring these people back into the church. If the church was seen as punishing the newspaper that had given credence to these families' plight, the victims would be livid.

There was finally Blanco's own position amid the convulsions of the chancery. Facing the prospect of lawsuits being filed against his diocese by Spokane parents, the beleaguered Frey had asked Blanco, Sigur, and Judge Reggie to convene a special panel to review Simon's list of priests, as well as to review accusations about adult homosexual activity just lodged against a priest in Vermilion Parish by several parishioners. If the boycott grew into an explosive news story, Blanco's effort to help the bishop cope with aberrant clergy was bound to come out. That kind of media attention was nothing Blanco wanted, and the diocese had suffered enough bad press.

So Raymond Blanco bought a batch of ducks and invited Sigur for dinner with Richard Baudouin and his wife. Editor and priest withdrew for a private talk before the main course. "We were both a little sheepish at first," Baudouin told me. The dinner went over smoothly; however, little was resolved.

Sigur wanted an editorial retraction. That was discussed at an all-night, second meeting at Ray Mouton's office with Baudouin, Blanco, and Steve May. Backing down was not in the cards. The four men then met several days later with Sigur at his office. Copies of the *Times* were on his desk. Sigur was bristling about damage to the diocese. As a peace token Baudouin offered to write a story praising the shelter for the poor that Sigur had founded. Sigur still wanted a retraction. Steve May remained silent. Ray Mouton blew up: *"Retraction for what?"* Baudouin sat restlessly as Mouton ran down the litany of crimes and church blunders. The meeting ended with rancor building between the attorney and the pastor of the parish Mouton's father had built.

In the end Blanco prevailed. Sigur backed off. The paper absorbed some $20,000 in lost revenues. Hardest hit were the account representatives, who lost commissions.

After reviewing accusations of homosexual activity against the Vermilion priest, Blanco, Sigur, and Reggie recommended that the man undergo psychological treatment, which he did for several months at an out-of-state facility. He subsequently returned to a parish elsewhere in the diocese. In May 1986 diocesan spokesman Gerald Dill told the *Baton Rouge State-Times* that in the past three years twenty priests (out of 205) in the diocese had been accused of sexual misconduct or were "in treatment for sexual problems." He did not discuss accusations or problems by category. My estimation—based on legal documents, information from law enforcement officials, reliable lay and clerical sources—was that at least fifty priests in the diocese were homosexually active at one time or another.

The root crisis in the diocese was a climate of secrecy and denial about sexual dynamics that permeated ecclesiastical governing. Two of the tribunal priests were known to be active homosexuals. A lay employee of the diocese later told me of a third, older priest who had a row with a young male who spurned his advances on the street one night. A fourth cleric, who held a high position, had several years earlier been detained by police, but not booked, for solicitation in a public place, according to Lafayette law enforcement sources. A fifth priest was arrested in early 1986 for exposing himself in a public park.

When an organization decays from within, its secrets will eventually spill out. The nature of that decay was the second stage of my research and is treated in the following sections. In Lafayette a key conduit for the secrets was Chalice. I promised not to reveal his name. Since his death I have come to see his role in these murky events as having been exceedingly complex. More than two years after my reporting in Lafayette was done, a policeman telephoned to ask if I knew Chalice's whereabouts. "We know he was your source," said the officer. "He told one of the kids he abused." Without acknowledging that he was my source, I honestly answered that I didn't know where he was.

Facing an arrest warrant, he had fled the state. I soon learned that during the time he had provided me information on priests Chalice, through a church-related job, had been molesting teenagers in a diocesan parish. He was eventually tracked down, brought back, imprisoned, and died of AIDS. I spoke with him by phone while he was in prison; he denied the charges of which he had been convicted.

In one of our early interviews he told me that he had been brutally raped by a man in his early adolescence. Whether that is true I cannot say; but his behavior strongly suggests that it was. I remembered a troubling exchange in our first interview. He called pedophilia "the normal practice of the average parish priest who has homosexuality as the pervasive part of his personality." Although I disagreed, he stood firm. Finally I said: "Because it's easier to get to kids than adults?"

"Right!" he said. "It's more dangerous—but also more stimulating!"

I believe now that he was talking about himself, for as he leaked information to me he was taking great risks in molesting young people, including a girl. Was he homosexual? He had recently gotten married when the police set out after him. The "dangerous" appeal of his sexual crimes stemmed from the defiled love map of a child molester. That raises a more interesting question: why did he leak information? I believe he was driven by conflicting forces—a guilt over his own molestation patterns, and a twisted attempt to deflect scrutiny onto others whose sexual preferences ran a gamut from children to men. Although he was not a priest, his attachments to clerical culture exposed him to its secrets, and in revealing them, psychologically, he was trying to tell on himself.

The cleric who suffered most from the constellation of clergy child abusers was Bishop Frey, who was surrounded by gays in the chancery yet I am convinced was not one himself. How much he denied, how much he didn't know, we cannot know. He spent much of Holy Week, 1986, visiting the homes of parents in Vermilion Parish whose lawsuits had been settled. As Christ was crucified on Good Friday, so Gerard Frey saw crosses borne by families who had been violated by Gilbert Gauthe. Before the first encounter, Paul Hebert told Frey: "Don't worry. Nobody's going to hit you. Nobody's going to pull a weapon."

By all accounts the verbal battering at those visits was enormous. Parents poured out their rage, breaking down in tears. The bishop himself wept in trying to console a ten-year-old girl whose brothers had been molested. "I don't believe in the church and I don't believe in God," she told him.

"I saw the bishop when he came back from one of those meetings," sighed Raymond Blanco, "and he looked like a dying man." The emotional strain had left his face puckered with blotches that Blanco said "looked like welts."

Frey and Larroque did not resign, but the Vatican took the rare and, for Frey, embarrassing step of sending a coadjutor bishop to Lafayette six months after the editorial, in July 1986. This was Harry S. Flynn, a pastor in the Albany, New York, diocese and the former rector of Mount St. Mary Seminary in Maryland. As coadjutor, and Frey's designated successor, Flynn served alongside the bishop while making the rounds of churches, getting to know his flock, visiting sick people in hospitals, working to bind the wounds. Frey eventually retired, and Flynn replaced Larroque with Monsignor Sigur.

Contrary to Bob Wright's statement the day the Gastal trial concluded, the defense did appeal the $1.25 million verdict. In a case so highly publicized the chances of an appellate court cutting the verdict were slim. But the gambit was partially successful: the Gastals were broke and willing to take less, rather than endure another long wait. They accepted $1,000,020—$230,000 less than the jury had awarded—with a third going to Simon, plus his expenses.

Over the next six years, as my reporting took me long distances from Louisiana, I would look back on that melancholy spring of 1986 with a looming mental image. One day I'd had lunch with Raymond Blanco, searching for some final insight from the bishop's trusted lay adviser. "What made the greatest impact on you?" I asked.

Blanco's normal ebullience dissolved. Shaking his head, he mentioned the ad hoc tribunal work done with Sigur and Reggie, screening problem priests. One night after they had finished he left late, filled with pity for a wayward priest—"I won't say his name, but trust me, he was abused as a kid like so many of them"—and, driving home, the totality of it all blew into him and Blanco suddenly felt terror, raw terror, the kind that made you think of the devil, and he began trembling. At home he jumped out of his car and ran into the slumbering house with fear pushing behind him like a sixty-mile-an-hour wind. He checked the rooms and, after making sure his wife and kids were safe, Raymond Blanco began to pray, and he kept on praying till the cloak of fear fell away.

PART TWO

The Political Dynamics of Celibacy

◆

Finally, brethren,

whatsoever things are true,

whatsoever things are honest,

whatsoever things are just,

whatsoever things are pure,

whatsoever things are lovely,

whatsoever things are of good report;

if there be any virtue,

and if there be any praise,

think on these things.

PHILIPPIANS 4:8

xi.

Homosexuality, Birth Control, and the Celibacy Crisis

There is an awareness that some priests are committing themselves to noncelibate relationships. This happens among both heterosexual and homosexual priests. Of more recent and urgent concern is the increasing number of priests who have a homosexual orientation. The heterosexual priest worries because he fears that the church will gradually become equated with homosexuality, and such identification frightens him. On his side, the homosexual priest sees this reaction as homophobic and is asking for acceptance of his priest brothers. The scene is confusing, with more questions than answers, but bishops need to be aware that this, too, is part of any honest reflection.

—National Federation of Priests' Councils newsletter, 1982

Only one graduate of my 1967 class at Jesuit High School became a priest. With hindsight one sees the same quiet drama of attrition unfolding at Catholic high schools and parishes across the country. Bishops expect priests to inspire young men to enter priestly life. That expectation began eroding when church authority experienced uncommon criticism from within.

At Jesuit High, bonds between students and clerics were strong; a masculine religiosity permeated the place. Ignatius Loyola, the sixteenth-century Spaniard who founded the Society of Jesus, loomed above in the large painting in St. Ignatius Hall: a bearded warrior with a wounded leg and penetrating gaze, his conversion and service to the Pope was a story told by our teachers, who personified four centuries of Jesuit history.

There is, for some, the temptation to satirize a culture fraught with saints. But Ignatius was *real*. So was St. Anthony, to whom my mother and grandmother prayed when things were lost. Saints were forces of the imagination, intercessors with God, models of morality to young people considering a vocation. The celibacy of many saints rarefied their aura; it was a spiritual sacrifice of sexual activity.

Like all cultures, Catholicism exaggerated its myths; however faith's durability dwelled not only in Father, Son, and Holy Spirit but also in the Virgin Mary and in many saints who enlarged Christ's passion and added color to the mystery of redemption. One dark day Father Roy Schilling entered our class and said: "President Kennedy has died in Dallas. Go directly to the Chapel of the North American Martyrs." There we gathered, 900 strong, at a requiem Mass for the first Catholic President in a chapel named for brave Canadian missionaries who died planting seeds of our faith.

The Second Vatican Council (1962–65) had a profound impact on my high school years. We discussed words like "metanoia"—from the Greek, meaning "radical conversion of will"—which seemed to encapsulate the church's moment in time. Few of us realized how epochal the moment was, though I suspect now the priests who taught us did.

Vatican II was the casting off of a fortress-church mentality that in modern times owed most to Pius IX; his was the longest papacy, from 1848 to 1876. In 1860 republican Italy annexed territories known as the Papal States, leaving only Rome and tiny Vatican City to the papacy's control. At Pius's request the French sent garrison troops to protect him. But in 1870 the garrison withdrew as Italian nationalists took Rome. In that imperiled setting Pius IX summoned the world's bishops to the First Vatican Council. The last Pope supported by an army, he had to redefine a power base. Pius had the Council declare that the church was the foundation of truth, "untouched by any danger of error or falsehood." He also declared the infallibility doctrine: that the Pope cannot err on definitive matters of faith and morality. (Many people think it means the Pope can never make a mistake.) Infallibility has been invoked only twice: in 1854, when Pius IX announced that the Virgin Mary was born free of original sin, and in 1950, when Pius XII defined her bodily assumption into heaven.

Papal infallibility was politically strategic, creating a realm where politicians could not compete. In 1871 Italy pledged to defend the Vatican and the Pope from alien forces. Refusing to concede the loss of the Papal States, Pius IX in his last seven years never crossed the Tiber bridge into Rome proper. Among the "principal errors" of the time, he said, was that "the Pope can or should reconcile himself to, or agree with, progress, liberalism, and modern civilization." A self-cast prisoner of the Vatican, he won global Catholic sympathy and carved out scores of dioceses, enlarging a religious monarchy.

His successor, Leo XIII, known as "the workers' Pope" for championing social justice, opened Vatican archives to scholarly research but maintained a fortress sensibility. Lester R. Kurtz writes that the Vatican "defined Catholic orthodoxy in terms of what it was not." Scholastic theology influenced by a dryly rationalist interpretation of the medieval works of Thomas Aquinas became a bulwark against modern thought. The early twentieth-century papacy of Pius X used the magisterium, or teaching office, in campaigns against selected enemies within the church. Claiming that Scripture was under attack by science and history, Pius X cast the issue in terms of defending his supreme prerogative to teach the truth of the Scripture. The magisterium demanded unity. A great wall of moral teaching went up with papal inerrancy as its mortar.

Pius X persecuted intellectuals and called Modernism a heresy. The *Index of*

Prohibited Books signaled Rome's supremacy over scholarly works that threatened it. Rome destroyed the career of Alfred Loisy, a French priest who sought a historical model for theology, and excommunicated George Tyrrell, an English Jesuit who scored a mentality in which "science and religion are mutually hostile." The progressive *New York Review,* launched in 1905 at St. John's Seminary in Westchester County, was snuffed out, dashing hopes of an American theological revival.

But the works of those discredited thinkers planted seeds which quietly and firmly took root. By the 1950s a new generation of clergy scholars had become established skeptics of Rome's architecture of power. These scholars argued that the church was not a fortress but a home and a community. French theologian Yves Congar broached the People of God concept; he saw monarchical structures sealing off spiritual growth. This line of thought flowed back to the early church fathers who accepted the *sensus fidelium,* or mind of the faithful, as a gift of the Holy Spirit which posited an authority—the entire believing church—which the Pope should faithfully consider.

In his famous encyclical *Pacem in Terris (Peace on Earth),* Pope John XXIII had written of faith fostering a "community of peoples based on truth, justice, love and freedom." As a Vatican diplomat and outsider to Curial politics he had been, at sixty-seven, a compromise choice for Pope: his cardinal electors correctly believed he would not reign long. Three months into his reign he startled them by issuing the call for Vatican II.

By the time of Pope John's call for the Council, the papacy had evolved from a fractious nineteenth-century monarchy into a wealthy religious state seeking its role in an age of ships being sent into space. Influential bishops at Vatican II echoed the thought of Congar, Karl Rahner, and other progressive theologians, celebrating the *sensus fidelium* and shifting the focus of Catholicism from papal authority to the warmth of the human family. The Catholic people were asked to embrace new roles for the church in the world. That was the promise held up to us by our Jesuit teachers, who now stressed social justice and tolerance of other races and faiths.

But changes that exhilarated the church shook the centuries-old institution of a celibate priesthood.

In 1966 there were about 60,000 U.S. priests, of whom 35,000 were diocesan clergy. By 1990 there were 26,000 diocesan priests, or a loss of 26 percent. According to sociologist Richard Schoenherr, an expert in church demographics, by the year 2005, surveys project a decline, including resignations and deaths, signifying a 40% drop from 1966. Religious orders have also experienced steep losses.

The American priesthood is getting older—median age, fifty-seven—without a new generation filling the ranks. The number of seminarians has dropped more than 80 percent since 1966. At the same time, the Catholic population has risen to 60 million, or 26 percent of the U.S. population. Schoenherr reports that 1300 U.S. priests resign yearly, 90 percent of them to marry. The forces behind this organizational decline, says Schoenherr, are "poor recruitment and poor retention rates, which are two sides of the same coin."

What caused the exodus? Pressures were building on clerical culture in 1972 when Andrew M. Greeley and the National Opinion Research Center at the

University of Chicago conducted a study of the priesthood. "The desire to marry is the strongest predictor of plans to leave the priesthood," Father Greeley wrote. "The principal reason for the desire to marry is loneliness."

With Vatican II the church of universal Latin had given way to a new openness in the Mass itself: where for centuries the faithful watched the back of the priest on the altar, now he faced his flock, speaking their own language. Greater lay participation in parish councils and religious education had broad appeal in the United States, where Catholic life was marked by accelerated wealth and professional standing. But as new roles opened for the laity, many priests and nuns waited as well for new ways of service. After the Council's first session, the influential Jesuit theologian John Courtney Murray predicted a marriage option for priests within five years. Polls in 1966 found 50 percent of U.S. clergy, and 80 percent of younger ones, favoring the option to marry.

One of them, Tom Peckham, ordained in 1960 in Detroit, left the clergy eleven years later to marry. When we spoke in 1986, Peckham was a substance abuse counselor in Chelsea, Michigan. "I saw the church closing the door on dialogue," Peckham recalled. "I lost friends and classmates in the late sixties. I respected the caliber of guys who were leaving—holy, prayerful men on the upper half of the intellectual end. When I left it wasn't in agony. I was making a statement. I didn't think marriage was something that would make you unholy and incapable of being a priest. I believe in the principle that I am still a priest."

As frustrations with celibacy mounted, Peckham continued, "the Detroit Priests Association wrote a letter to Cardinal [John] Dearden, protesting mandatory celibacy. Forty-four of us signed it. He was on his way to Rome; we wanted it discussed."

A civil rights advocate, Dearden supported greater independence for national bishops' conferences. Peckham: "He always listened and knew how to settle the troops, but Dearden was like smoke. We had a joint meeting with priests of Illinois, Michigan, and Indiana, pleading with him to present our case [to Rome]. People were getting more and more disheartened. He remained staunch. I presume it was in obedience to the papal letter."

"The letter" was a 1967 encyclical, *Sacerdotalis Caelibatus* (*The Celibacy of the Priest*) by Pope Paul VI. In one sense a social visionary, Paul wrote in *Populorum Progressio* (*On the Development of Peoples*) that rich nations must uplift poor ones or face "the judgment of God and the wrath of the poor." He encouraged Third World bishops to work with the poor; he transformed the College of Cardinals, historically Italian, into a more truly catholic institution by adding Africans, Asians, and Pacific Islanders. And yet, as British historian Paul Johnson writes, after the death of Pope John XXIII, Paul VI "inherited a democratic spirit but an autocratic machine"—the Roman Curia, which had opposed John's reform agenda. "Which should be allowed to prevail? Pope Paul attempted a compromise. He allowed the council to continue and complete its work. But he withdrew from its competence two subjects which he reserved for himself"—celibacy and birth control.

His 1967 encyclical called celibacy the church's "brilliant jewel"—that which "evidently gives to the priest, even in the practical field, the maximum efficiency and the best disposition, psychologically and clerically, for the continuous exercise of a perfect clarity." No psychological or empirical studies were cited in support of "maximum efficiency" because none existed. In reference to the decline in vocations then beginning, the Pope observed darkly "that individuals and families have lost their sense of God and all that is holy, their esteem for the Church and the institution of salvation through faith and sacraments."

Before his death in 1963, Pope John had convened a seven-member Pontifical Commission for the Study of Population, the Family and Birth Control to advise him on the morality of artificial contraception. Years later, a prelate of his inner circle, Igino Cardinale, told author Robert Blair Kaiser, "John's intent wasn't only demography. He wanted to see how solid the doctrine really was." European theologians were asking why the contraceptive pill should not be condoned. In 1944, Pope Pius XII had declared "procreation and education of children" to be the primary function of marriage, with the secondary end "mutual love of husband and wife." In a famous address to Italian midwives, Pius advocated restraint from intercourse during a woman's fertile period, if a couple did not wish to have children.

No device was to bar the flow of sperm or prevent a woman's potential to conceive. This was religious belief in a biological order, ordained by God, with procreation the sacred function of sex. But was that ancient view compatible with the modern family? Moreover, the controversy wasn't only a moral one. Paul VI also faced an epic political question: to uphold papal supremacy on *all* moral matters, or to concede one dimension to a democratic mechanism of consultation? If Paul VI reversed Pius XII, what would it mean for the historic power of the papacy?

After Pope John's death, Paul VI expanded the Population and Family Commission to sixty-eight members, including several married couples. While the Commission held its secret sessions, the matter of birth control also occupied the Council fathers, then meeting often in Rome. Aware that child rearing was no longer cheap nor large families a guarantee of marital harmony, the cardinal of Montreal fretted in Vatican II's last session about "the fear of conjugal love that has so long paralyzed our theology. . . . We must affirm that the intimate union of the couple finds its legitimate end in itself, even when it is not directed toward procreation."

An eighty-seven-year-old Greek Orthodox patriarch went further, asking of marriage whether "certain possibilities are not the outcome of outmoded ideas and, perhaps, a *celibate psychosis* on the part of those unacquainted with this sector of life?" (Emphasis added.) As the Pontifical Commission studied the demographics and ethics of the pill, Paul appointed a panel of twenty bishops and cardinals to give him further advice on birth control.

In October 1965, before leaving for New York (where he spoke eloquently at the United Nations on peace and the value of life), Paul offered a glimpse into his anguish over birth control. "The world asks what we think and we find ourselves trying to give an answer," he told an Italian journalist. "We can't keep silent. And yet to speak is a real problem. . . . The church has never in her history confronted such a problem." He hesitated. "This is a strange subject for men of the church to be discussing . . . even humanly embarrassing." Acknowledging the anticipation building over what Rome might say, he spoke a language of existential detachment. "And in deciding we are all alone. . . . We have to say something. But what? God will simply have to enlighten us."

All alone? Surrounded by advisers, he had a greater stock of facts than did John XXIII with which to assess positions little changed in centuries. And yet he felt embarrassed discussing this "strange subject"—suggesting that he sensed how volatile it would be for a celibate to define the morality of childbearing.

ii.

How did celibacy arise? What explains its hold—morally and politically—on the Roman Catholic hierarchy?

Buddhist monks practiced chastity before Jesus' birth; the temples of pagan Rome had vestal virgins. Sex was considered unclean; bodies had to be pure for rituals. The Greek philosophers known as Stoics advocated restraint of passion and praised celibacy. The Jews, of course, emphasized family and children. But among them the Essene sect fled Jerusalem to caves along the Dead Sea in the first century B.C. Sharing property, eschewing marriage, the Essenes rebelled against the Jewish leaders then in collusion with pagan rulers. Essenes vowed to celibacy became holy warriors for Israel. John the Baptist spent time among them.

Jesus brought a radical message to Palestine: "Repent, for the Kingdom of God is at hand." Singling out poor people as worthy of love, He forgave sins of prostitutes and preached a new ethic of individual responsibility. As accounts of the resurrection story spread, many of Jesus' followers believed that the world was about to end. Small groups met in private homes to share ritual bread and wine in recollection of the body and blood of Christ offered up at the Last Supper. Eschewing the Roman ideal of noble citizenship that endowed monuments and revered power, Christians welcomed slaves and fed the poor.

The apostle Paul was the great protagonist in Christianity's spread; he taught that Jesus was "Christos," or Messiah, the Son of God, whose death was an atonement for humanity's sins. Accepting Christ held promise of the afterlife. Paul's letters and relentless travel across Asia Minor turned an offshoot Jewish sect into a faith that slowly spread across the Roman Empire.

In his First Letter to the Corinthians, St. Paul wrote: "It is good for a man not to touch a woman." In the same letter he wrote, referring to his celibate state: "I wish all men were as I myself am." He also wrote: "It is better to marry than be aflame with passion." Neither condemning marriage nor demanding celibacy, the apostle was advocating a personal road of moral probity.

Many early Christians sought to emulate the angels by returning to an Edenesque state of purity. Convinced that time was ending, small groups abandoned sexual activity. "For them," writes Princeton historian Peter Brown, "the continent body stood for a principle of reversibility; the flow of life itself could be halted." In a world like ours, drenched with sexual images, celibacy may seem repressive. However, to early Christians, pagan culture was repressive. Public nudity, prostitution, and sexual trafficking in boys were tolerated in Greco-Roman cities and offended Christians, who were a distinct minority.

For Christians, sexual restraint was a form of freedom—affirming the Kingdom over pagan mores that subjugated women and granted men access to slaves, prostitutes, boys, or other men. Christianity did not introduce the concept of fidelity into marriage but the faith gave it greater credence and standing. Although monogamy eventually gained respect among the Greeks and Romans, the usual Greco-Roman nobleman did not see his wife as a spiritual partner—as Christians were to—but rather as one figure in a domestic environment including his children, slaves, and employees. Christian women who refused to wed, thus remaining virgins, or widows who chose celibacy over remarriage, could detach from the larger culture and devote themselves to the church. With life expectancy at thirty, continence held the potential for a longer, less fettered life. Total celibacy was impossible, lest the faith die with its final childless members. But widows, virgins, and older, abstaining couples practiced moderation and restraint in what Brown calls a "morality of the socially vulnerable." Without arms, wealth, or civic might, Christianity built a new social order using chastity as a cornerstone. Married couples pledged to fidelity, like the unmarried who renounced sexual activity, stood apart from pagan mores.

An idea of primitive democracy marked Christianity's growth. Paul wrote that the baptized were "neither Jew nor Greek . . . slave nor freeman . . . male nor female. For you are all one in Christ Jesus." (Galatians 3:28.) But his egalitarian message inspired no such structure. To survive, Christianity submitted to certain strictures; slavery was one, subservience of women another. Public roles for women would have clashed with the dominant Greco-Roman and Judaic standards that influenced the early church. Patriarchal thought considered that menstruation made women ineligible for the rabbinate. Christianity inherited such taboos and denied ordination to women. What ministering women could do was relegated to what theologian Elisabeth Tetlow calls "the inferior, but socially more acceptable, office of deaconess."

In a faith committed to helping the poor, the flock chose their bishops to oversee education of orphans and resolve disputes with "the gift of discernment." A bishop, wrote Paul, "must be blameless, married but once, prudent, of good conduct, hospitable, a teacher. . . . He should rule his own household, keeping his children under control and perfectly respectable. For if a man cannot rule his own household, how is he to take care of the church of God?" (Timothy 3:1–5.) Married bishops led the first-century diaspora churches. As Christian morality took root, so did a "postmarital abstinence from sexual relations," writes Peter Brown, "usually adopted in middle age [which] would later be imposed on priests after the age of thirty. This form of celibacy came to be expected as the norm for the average urban clergyman in the late antique period."

Survival grew more perilous in the late third and early fourth centuries as pagans put Christians to gruesome deaths in public arenas. As martyrdom inspired the faithful so, too, did virginity animate the Christian psyche as a continuing ideal of sacrifice. Ascetic groups in the desert practiced strict chastity, beginning a monastic tradition that would have far-reaching influence.

Christian attitudes toward sex and celibacy grew out of a culture surrounded by adversity and wracked by inner strife. As the faith grew, conflicts about sexuality swirled within it.

When Spanish bishops convened the Council of Elvira in the year 305, pagans were slaughtering Christians in the arenas of Rome. Canons drafted at Elvira codified thinking about sex: penalties for pederasts; marriage forbidden to those seeking holy orders; a call on married priests to cease sexual relations with their wives. Children born in a priest's home could be excommunicated. Celibacy gave clerical identity higher canonical standing than marriage.

And yet Jesus had said comparatively little about sexuality. His condemnation of divorce and praise of marriage gave humanity a code of mutual responsibility. Injustice was His greater concern. Jesus did not demand celibacy; the rule came from church fathers, but it was not universally enforced. Some priests and bishops continued to marry or live with women and sire children.

In 313 the Emperor Constantine converted to the faith and Christianity slowly supplanted paganism as the religion of the state. This was no simple power shift. Canonical concerns over the sex lives of Christians were added to Roman imperial law. Bishops assumed judicial roles in legal disputes. With congregations swelling, doctrinal disputes became political disputes.

The clash between Jerome and Jovinian in the early fifth century is a classic case of the skewed valuation of marriage and celibacy. Both men were monks. Jerome recalled his early desert years as "this prison house, where my only companions were scorpions and wild beasts, I often found myself surrounded by bands of dancing girls. My face was pale with fasting; but though my limbs were cold as ice . . . the fires of lust kept bubbling up before me while my flesh was as good as dead." Jerome eventually landed in Rome as a secretary to Damasus I, the son of a priest who fought his way into the papacy after three days of pitched battle that left 137 dead.

As mentor to a circle of aristocratic celibate women, Jerome counseled a twenty-year-old distraught after her husband's death. He insisted that she fast, sleep on the ground, and pray. She died two months later. Crawling out from an avalanche of criticism, Jerome fled. Five years later, in a Bethlehem monastery, he read an essay by Jovinian, in which celibacy was considered no more sacred than marriage. "Do not be proud," wrote Jovinian to his fellow priests. "You and your married sisters are equally members of the same church."

Elaine Pagels, a leading scholar of religion, writes that Jovinian "accused certain fanatical Christians of having invented—and then having attributed to Jesus and Paul—this 'novel dogma against nature.'" Jerome distorted Paul's writings when he wrote a female follower:

> *If after nakedness, after fasting, after prison, beatings and torments, Paul still used to cry:* Oh, wretched man that I am, who will deliver me from this body of death, *do you think that you, dear lady, can feel secure? What human being is not terrified by the Apostle's line of argument?*

Jovinian was a dutiful monk who drew scriptural inspiration from Matthew 19:6—"What God has joined together, let no one put asunder"—and from Genesis 1:28: "Be fruitful and multiply." He was excommunicated by Pope Siricus after protests by Jerome, Ambrose, and Augustine—each of whom became a saint. Deriding Jovinian for allegedly "wantoning with his favorites of both sexes," Jerome was upset over Jovinian's support among Romans with whom he had lost favor after the widow's death. But Jerome's militant attitudes impressed Pope Siricus, who considered priests with wives "masters of sin . . . enslaved to lust." Jerome's scriptural fabrications bolstered the papal power structure that had Jovinian tortured to death.

St. Augustine shared Jerome's dark view of sex. As a young Manichean he lived with a concubine who bore him a son. In *Confessions*, his autobiographical masterpiece, Augustine says little about them after he describes his conversion. He saw man as trapped by Adam's fall into sin: women were inferior, sex a necessary evil. "By insisting that humanity, ravaged by sin, now lies helplessly in need of outside intervention," writes Pagels, "Augustine's theory could not only validate secular power but justify as well the imposition of church authority—by force, if necessary—as essential for human salvation." Augustine's symbiosis of sex and sin gave a supremacy to the celibate state of life and fortified the power of an unmarried male hierarchy in the governance of the church. That one of the most lucid writers of early Christianity should hatch such a fateful view of human love remains the Catholic heritage's saddest irony.

When the Goths sacked Rome in 410, darkness descended on the Empire. Through the next several centuries the church preserved law and learning. Bishops took control of local economies and salvaged cities. Although church canons called for celibacy, the evolution of the papacy in these centuries ironically mirrored the struggle for familial claims over which monarchies fought. "The list of popes who fathered future popes reads like an Old Testament lineage recitation," writes Baltimore psychotherapist and celibacy scholar A. W. Richard Sipe:

> *Anastasius I (399–401) begat Innocent I (401–417); Hormisdas (514–523) begat Silverius (536–537); Sergius III (904–911) begat John XI (931–935).*
>
> *Other popes were the children of lesser clergy: Theodore I (642–649) was the son of a bishop; Damasus I (366–384), Boniface I (418–422), Felix III (483–492), Anastasius II (496–498), Agapitus (535–536), Marinus I (882–884), and John XV (985–986) were the sons of priests. . . . Many future popes were not necessarily born into the office but were groomed for it as children, growing up in Rome's Lateran Palace.*

Amassing fiefdoms, local feudal lords controlled abbeys and appointed their own bishops. European abbots and clerics who were married sought to pass church property to their sons. Church leaders also, to protect offices and land, sought protection from kings. Not surprisingly, simony—the selling of ecclesiastical offices—occurred frequently, a bustling commerce alongside clerical marriage.

By the mid-eleventh century, landed lords were threatened by the prospect of a hereditary religious caste. The church, in turn, was threatened with loss of property by clergy heirs—and by the control over bishops by temporal powers. In 1073 a German monk was elected Pope by popular acclaim, breaking the yoke of royal appointment. This was Gregory VII, a man on a mission to restore a celibate clergy.

He envisioned celibacy as a force of moral regeneration from below—celibate clergy serving as an example of restraint to the semi-Christianized people of Europe—while a papal theocracy would rule over kings and princes. Gregory's other strategic goal was halting the appointment of bishops by civil rulers, a practice called lay investiture by which feudal lords consolidated their power. But Gregory clashed mightily over these matters with Henry IV, who rallied the German bishops to his side. Gregory excommunicated Henry, who traveled to

Italy in penitential garb, pledging fealty to the Pope. Gregory was then plunged into a conflict between Henry and one of his rivals. When the Pope recognized the rival as king, Henry installed his own Pope. Gregory died amid dwindling support. But later popes upheld his reforms of clerical life, which became known as the Gregorian Reforms.

Peter Damian, a Benedictine abbot of the time, called clerical marriage a heresy. The newly restrictive celibate climate, writes historian James A. Brundage, "created something akin to a reign of terror among clerics and their families during the late eleventh and early twelfth centuries." Long after Damian and ` Gregory VII had died (both were canonized) the campaign enforcing celibacy ventured far from the early church's ideal of voluntary abstinence. And beyond spiritual or moral motives, other factors inspired the crackdown. Celibacy was also emphatically political: the church could not exert primacy over kings if it could not rule its own clergy.

When the archbishop of Rouen at the time laid down the law forbidding clerical marriage, his priests rioted. Another bishop was almost killed. Yet the campaign ground away, with wives who were themselves daughters or descendants of clerics and bishops "shorn of social position, driven from their homes, their marriages denounced as immoral from the pulpits, their honor ruined, their families broken, and their commitment to husband and children denounced as scurrilous and sinful," writes Brundage. Lateran decrees of 1123 and 1139 made clerical marriage a crime, reduced wives to the status of concubines or prostitutes, and rendered clerics' children illegitimate.

Sexual segregation became the foundation of a homosocial structure—all power invested in men. One result of the enforcement of celibacy was an increasing homosexual presence in clerical life. Yale Historian John Boswell quotes homoerotic literature that flourished in medieval monasteries and writes of a general tolerance toward gay people that marked the era. "The more the church suppressed priestly marriage," adds sociologist David F. Greenberg, "the stronger must have been the homosexual drive it aroused within its ranks." One other result of the enforcement of celibacy was a victory for the hierarchy in the politics of property. "Homosexual relationships," continues Greenberg, "did not result in progeny, and therefore did not threaten the preservation of church property."

An authoritative account of homosexual clerical life since the Middle Ages has yet to be written. But the fear of women embedded in that culture is clear. The strain of sexual paranoia in Jerome and Augustine carried into the Middle Ages: Albert the Great called woman "a misbegotten man," and Thomas Aquinas opined that woman needs man "as her personal master."

With the Council of Trent in the 1560s, the Counter Reformation consolidated the supremacy of celibacy. Rebutting Martin Luther's call for a married clergy, council fathers at Trent deemed "anathema" anyone who might argue "that the married state surpasses that of virginity or celibacy [or] that it is not better and happier to remain in . . . celibacy than to be united in matrimony."

Celibacy was destined to undergo recurrent abuses, as Henry Lea chronicled in a late nineteenth-century history. How could the suppression of intimacy not encounter failures? But this paradoxical institution also led to remarkable achievements. Celibacy gave immeasurable human capital to a faith whose childless nuns and priests required little pay; it fostered a kind of clerical civil service. Religious orders, a major force in the post-Reformation revival of the European church, were catalysts in church expansion to Latin America, Canada, and the United States. Celibacy produced generations of priests and nuns whose selfless toil as ministers, teachers, *de facto* social workers, and models of modesty and restraint gave the church a moral center.

iii.

Dissent over birth control exploded in April 1967, when Charles Curran, a prolific moral theologian at Catholic University of America in Washington, was fired by university trustees for advocating a couple's right to abide by their consciences in choosing to use artificial contraception. Father Curran's sacking triggered a five-day strike by students and faculty until he was reinstated. That July, Paul VI issued the celibacy encyclical (the encyclical on birth control, *Humanae Vitae [On Human Life]*, was to come a year later). His idea of celibacy as "the exercise of a perfect moral clarity" was emblematic of a medieval church turning its back on the church of the space age.

In the spring of 1968, Pope Paul requested advisory briefs on contraception from Italian bishops. Albino Luciani, bishop of Vittorio Veneto, took a sounding of physicians, theologians, sociologists, and married couples, including his own brother, who had a family of ten. Luciani's report not only advocated contraception but endorsed a specific anovulant pill. (Ten years later, when Paul VI died, Luciani was elected Pope, taking the name John Paul I, only to die after a month in office. Some believe he would have seriously reconsidered if not reversed *Humanae Vitae.*)

On July 29, 1968, nearly two years after the Pontifical Commission's report, Pope Paul issued *Humanae Vitae*, lessening the extreme gravity of its statements by deleting "with our infallible authority" from the draft. The letter contradicted his commission and ecclesiastical consultants in condemning all forms of artificial contraception. The encyclical's reception was an awesome spectacle.

In Washington, Curran and ten theologians drafted a response. When they held a news conference announcing their dissent, the list of sponsors who supported them had grown to 87 U.S. theologians. CUA's bitter strike of the previous spring moved its trustees to restraint in taking action against the dissidents. Meanwhile, in Britain, Cardinal Heehan stated that those using banned methods need not abstain from the sacraments. "Part of the controversy has visibly shifted to the issue of freedom of conscience," the *New York Times* noted. In late August seven priests were fired from the faculty of St. John Viannay Seminary in East Aurora, New York, for opposing the letter. The *London Times* reported that "secret instructions" in a cover letter to the encyclical had urged a united front among bishops, priests, and Catholic organizations.

I was working in a New Orleans steel factory that summer, before my sophomore year at Georgetown University. That fall I watched a religious fabric split alongside a divisive presidential contest among Hubert Humphrey, Richard Nixon, and George Wallace. Religious polemics were unheard of in the New Orleans of my youth. The Jesuits taught us to balance questioning with loyalty.

In Washington, I watched Cardinal Patrick O'Boyle, who had been an advocate of civil rights, threaten to punish forty-four archdiocesan priests if they did not recant opposition to *Humanae Vitae.* The National Federation of Priests asked the cardinal for an impartial panel to consider his ouster of the dissidents' leader.

Meanwhile, at St. Louis University, a Jesuit institution, the medical faculty announced that it would continue research on artificial contraception. On September 16, Pope Paul told the world that "selfishness" exaggerated the burdens of a large family for many couples. Six days later Cardinal O'Boyle's letter to Washington Catholics urged support of the Pope—the same day the cardinal of Vienna stated that Paul VI had "suffered for two years" before deciding on the letter. On Sunday, September 23, a group of Catholics stood up and walked out of Mass as Cardinal O'Boyle read his sermon.

An October 1 *New York Times* editorial said that O'Boyle had erred by imposing sanctions on the dissident priests. The University of San Francisco, another Jesuit institution, released a study saying that seventy-one percent of Catholics polled approved of contraceptives and that a majority of those using them were staying away from the sacraments. On October 7, Georgetown's Jesuit community announced support for the dissident diocesan priests. The next day came a poll by the University of Notre Dame and *NCR* which found that half of America's diocesan priests disagreed with the Pope's letter. A *New York Times* survey found that most bishops did not support O'Boyle's sanctions. By November 10, Atlanta Auxiliary Bishop Joseph Bernardin was in Washington to assist O'Boyle, whose stance was opposed by seventy percent of local Catholics. *L'Osservatore Romano* accused dissenting priests of heresy.

The great wall of moral teaching was cracking open. Conservative theologians argued that a papal letter required obedience. As *Humanae Vitae* receded from the headlines, the Catholic psychological landscape was, in Yeats's words, "all changed, changed utterly." Today upward of eighty-five percent of Catholics reject the letter. The official teaching, wrote Andrew M. Greeley, was caught

> in the physical dimensions of procreation instead of the psychic dynamics of love, in the authoritarian structure of the peasant family instead of the democratic structure of the modern urban family. . . . While fundamental morality does not change with the centuries, the human context of moral behavior does.

In *The March of Folly,* historian Barbara W. Tuchman defined folly as "the pursuit of a policy by an elite against the self-interest of the governed." Tuchman examined political blunders as found in the story of the Trojan horse, the Renaissance popes, the British Parliament during the American war of independence, and U.S. leadership in the Vietnam War. Her theory well applies to *Humanae Vitae.* Tuchman argues that a flawed policy "must have been perceived as counter-productive in its own time, and not merely by hindsight." The 1967 protests supporting Curran foreshadowed a reception of the 1968 encyclical. Furthermore, the Pope rejected the counsel of his sixty-eight Commission members and his ecclesial advisers.

"A feasible alternative course of action must have been available," continues Tuchman. What was the Pope's feasible alternative? A couple's right to family planning had the support of many moral theologians; an endorsement by the Pope would have won the praise of leaders in poor countries with surging birth rates. Instead, Pope Paul's celibacy and birth control encyclicals caused countless priests and sisters to view the church as betraying its Vatican II charter of reform. Many priests were disillusioned by celibacy, which they saw as a mechanism of control, much akin to *Humanae Vitae's* authoritarian attitude toward lay people's sex lives.

iv.

Alongside the attrition rate of thousands of priests who left to marry, the numbers of homosexuals entering clerical life began to escalate. Dozens of priests over age fifty, in every region of the country, told me that in the 1970s homosexuals began pouring into seminaries and order houses. The 18 gay clerics I interviewed for 1987 articles in *NCR* insisted that the younger generation was a gay majority.

Behavioral scientists consider that the homosexual orientation is set in place in childhood; years can pass before a person acknowledges it, if he or she ever does. Catholic doctrine holds that sin stems from free will. But if one has no choice over sexual orientation, how free is the will not to express love in a homosexual manner? The church teaches that this orientation is morally neutral but that homosexual acts are sinful. In requiring a life of sexual abstinence for all homosexual men and women, the Catholic Church—and most churches—lays a heavy burden on them and their families.

In 1961 the Sacred Congregation for Religious in Rome had circulated a letter stating: "Advancement to religious vows and ordination should be barred to those who are inflicted with evil tendencies toward homosexuality or pederasty for whom the common life and the priestly ministry would constitute serious dangers."

Yet in practice most bishops considered a priest who was homosexual and celibate on an equal footing with a heterosexual celibate—so long as the homosexual did not announce his orientation. By the 1980s, in any case, a restive gay subculture was throbbing beneath the surface of priestly life. Numerous essays by gay clergy challenged the magisterium's moral prohibition of active homosexuality. Many homosexual priests felt a profound sense of victimization and even persecution by this official church teaching. But the increasing presence of homosexual priests in clerical life also raised hard questions for other priests, bishops, and the laity.

Polls, for instance, show that a majority of Catholics support civil rights for homosexual people but also disapprove of homogenital sex. Moreover, opinion polls don't register the likely shock of most Catholic parishioners upon learning that their priest, if gay, was involved in an active sexual relationship.

Many homosexual clergy regard the pressure from bishops to keep their orientation a secret as just one aspect of the church's general homophobia. And it is a particularly painful aspect for many, as it is precisely through their sexual orientation that many believe they have been called to be ministers. "Gay clergy many times feel that their most effective ministerial gifts flow from or are directly related to their unique experience of being homosexually oriented," writes the Rev. Robert Nugent, a scholarly advocate of gay rights within the church.

But if many gay priests believe this enforced silence is homophobic, many other priests believe a double standard is at work by which the sexual struggles of heterosexual priests are dealt with more harshly and publicly than those of homosexual priests. A New England priest, for instance, wrote to a friend:

> The situation in my section of the eastern United States seems to be the same as in the midwest. Many capable men, who want very much to remain, are being forced to leave the priesthood because they are not given the option to marry. In my diocese this is very true. The Archbishop of a nearby archdiocese refuses to allow his men to be laicized, although this is permitted by the Holy See. What a terrible injustice!
>
> At the same time, there is an increasing number of men who remain in the priesthood who are homosexuals. Nothing is done about them. For example, one, who visits the rectory, is always "on the make"—frequenting gay bars, "befriending" high school students, going to New York City on sprees. I know many others who do the same. The alarming fact is that the majority of the younger clergy seem to fit the homosexual category, see nothing wrong with it, even disclose it to others (and with pride!). My bishop, at least, is aware of the problem and states he wants "no more fruits in the diocese!" He meets regularly with former priests who have married to show his sympathy and support.

The Rev. Richard McBrien, a liberal theologian at the University of Notre Dame, said:

> I think a great majority of lay people would ask why the priesthood should be a haven for homosexuals. Bishops are caught in the middle and running scared. They live in a church with a very hardline policy on homosexuality yet they realize they're drawing from that population well beyond its presence in society, by default. Instead of discussing holy days of obligation, bishops should raise hell about this on the floor of their conferences when they meet twice a year.

No one knows how many priests are homosexual, but researchers agree that the numbers are much higher than in society. The groundbreaking Kinsey report on male sexuality estimated that six to thirteen percent of American males were exclusively homosexual. Kinsey's research method has met with much criticism by scholars; his interview base, while large, was not a random probability sample, the standard in opinion polling.

"Some of the younger men coming in are different," an older New York Jesuit told me. "I don't say they're all gay. But there is a suggestion, in mannerism and dress, in hours they keep. You notice the absences. This is going on around us, and the church refuses to acknowledge it. I sense a great malaise. Sexual secrecy and political secrecy go hand in hand. Covering up sexual behavior becomes part of the church's governing process and its institutional psyche."

Baltimore Auxiliary Bishop P. Francis Murphy told a reporter: "I cannot give you percentages of the number of priests or seminarians who are homosexual in orientation. But what I can say is, if you have a system that invites only celibate men into the priesthood, that opens up at least the possibility that a higher percentage of homosexual persons might be attracted to that than would be to some other professions."

Among the first priests to address homosexuality as a pastoral concern was John F. Harvey, who published his first theological essay on the topic in 1955. Years later, after a great deal of pastoral counseling, his aim was to help "homosexual persons"—he eschewed the popular term "gay"—to achieve sexual abstinence, as the church wanted. Although viewed as a reactionary by many gay clergy and members of Dignity, an organization of gay Catholics, Harvey was influential in getting bishops to accept that a homosexual orientation was not sinful, though homogenital activity was.

Harvey founded Courage, modeled on the principles of Alcoholics Anonymous, utilizing support groups and a stair-step process to achieve celibacy. When we spoke in 1987, Harvey was in his late sixties, short, sturdy, nearly bald, every inch the old school priest, right down to the long vowels of his Philadelphia accent. "I don't know what the numbers are," he said, "but I think there are more homosexuals in the priesthood secretly [than in the past]. There's no way of proving it to be true, for obvious reasons"—meaning that a reliable survey could not be conducted, lest respondents risk punishment from their superiors.

The fear is not far-fetched. Richard Wagner of San Francisco was dismissed from the priesthood after the controversy surrounding the 1981 publication of his master's thesis, *Gay Catholic Priests: A Study of Cognitive and Affective Dissonance.* Wagner conducted ninety-minute interviews with fifty priests (none of them named) and obtained follow-up questionnaires on their sexual histories. "There is an informal network of gay priests operating in just about every section of the country," wrote Wagner. Forty-two percent of his interviewees came from California; 34 percent from New England; the rest were sprinkled through the Northwest and Midwest.

Only two of Wagner's interviewees said they were abstaining from sexual activity. Sixty percent said they felt no guilt about breaking their vows, 90 percent strongly rejected mandatory celibacy, 60 percent reported having group sex, and slightly less than half reported that they engaged in sex in public toilets or parks. Wagner wrote that 34 percent of his interviewees said that their partners were "distinctly younger," but he did not say how young.

In April 1986 a broad though admittedly partial survey of the gay priest phenomenon was under way in Chicago.* I located a priest working on it, who spoke on condition of anonymity. Five gay priests (all of whom would remain anonymous) were collaborating with a married sociologist, James G. Wolf, who was concluding doctoral work at the University of Chicago and who edited the study. The initial plan called for a random national sampling; however, too many potential respondents feared being identified and refused to participate, the Chicago priest told me. Instead, the researchers settled on a target group of gay clergy who, in turn, distributed a detailed questionnaire to others—101 in all. "This is not an acceptable scientific sample," the priest told me, "but it was the only way to get enough returns."

* Later published as *Gay Priests.*

The priest, who was thirty-six when we spoke, estimated that 50 percent of American priests were homosexual, "a large number of them psychosexually arrested. Most priests over thirty-five went through a [spiritual] formation process that was anti-intimacy. They became more comfortable in relationships with men because they were taught not to develop relationships with women. People who are spiritually sensitive learn otherwise. The church almost forced these men into an arrested development with no affective relationships, so a lot got fixated on a fantasy level with patterns of eroticism. That's why so many visit pornographic magazine stores and movie houses. They'll cover over emotions with chemical dependency, using substances to mask eroticism. When I came to grips with my own spirituality, I tried to integrate healthy sexuality and spirituality, without denying either side.

"Gay priests are being branded as heretics," he reflected. "We are trying to articulate a positive gay spirituality. . . . We need to lovingly challenge the hierarchy's archaic standards with healthy values." By healthy values, he said, he meant allowing priests to marry or live openly with male lovers. One priest in the study wrote that many gay priests "have found their ministry aided and their road to sanctity illumined by intimate, relatively stable relationships." Later I learned that another priest working on the study had AIDS, which was not revealed when *Gay Priests* was published in 1989. In 1987 the *New York Times* reported "a dozen cases" of priests with AIDS nationwide. In 1990, *New York Newsday* reported that more than two hundred priests had died of or been stricken with AIDS. Most seminaries and dioceses now require mandatory HIV testing, meaning that men must prove they do not have the virus before they can become Catholic priests.

Dr. Jay Feierman, the psychiatrist-consultant to the Paracletes, wrote in the preface to *Gay Priests*: "If certain members of the Roman Catholic clergy are outraged by the publication of this book or are embarrassed by its content, those feelings must be considered self-inflicted wounds that must be dealt with compassionately." Many ordinary Catholics must have similar "wounds." Who inflicts them on whom? If men discover they are gay after becoming clergy and choose to remain priests, why is it unreasonable to expect them to honor their vows? The flouting of celibacy in *Gay Priests* was done in secrecy. The result is a psychological split between the person's actual life and what he must do to conceal it.

James Wolf compared the findings in *Gay Priests* with a 1970 survey on priests' attitudes, commissioned by the bishops, which did not ask about sexual orientation. Several comparisons are revealing:

• In *Gay Priests*, 42.6 percent reported that at some point they felt abandoned by God. In the 1970 NCCB sample, it was 21.1 percent.

• In *Gay Priests*, 21 percent felt a lack of personal fulfillment, compared with 8.4 percent in the 1970 survey.

• Two thirds of the NCCB sample felt that at some point they had been tempted by the Devil, as against half of the gays.

"The priests in our sample," writes Wolf, "seem more prone to feelings of spiritual isolation than priests in the 1970 sample." If celibacy, however strenuous, was an ideal for which to strive, its dismissal by some may explain the spiritual isolation of any priest—gay or straight—that comes with leading a double life.

Robert Nugent has made a career of work with gay clergy. Ordained a Philadelphia diocesan priest, his civil rights work led him to ministry with homosexuals. He joined the Salvatorian order, which is known for its gay sympathies, and earned a Master of Divinity from Yale. Nugent and Sister Jeannine Gramick founded New Ways Ministry, which fostered gay support groups. He had written:

> *Few people challenge the assumption that the percentage of gay clergy and male religious is somewhat higher than that of the population at large.*
>
> *There is much less agreement . . . [as to] how the Church must respond to gay clergy, and what kind of "support" is called for today. Some object to support groups, for example, because they might be interpreted as Church encouragement for an "alternative lifestyle" which is rejected by Church teaching. Others are concerned about scandal to the "image of the priesthood."*

A studious chap with a thatch of silver hair, Nugent had the geniality of many parish priests I had known. He and Gramick refused to discuss their sexual orientations; yet in a clerical world rife with stories about sexual antics from seminarians to bishops, I never heard anyone suggest that the two were not celibates. As for clerical homosexuality, Nugent said: "I don't think the number is higher than forty percent. I'd say it's closer to a third."

The Rev. John Yockey, who taught seminarians moral theology at the Washington Theological Union and at Catholic University, considered himself an orthodox Catholic. "I frankly think the range of incidence in the Catholic clergy would be from disproportionate to *overwhelming*," he said. "Forty percent would not be an unreasonable estimate. Many younger men coming out of seminary are homosexual; but that does not mean they are necessarily genitally active. I think a large majority of gay-oriented clergy struggle to live out chaste lives. I think a distinct minority leads a double life."

A. W. Richard Sipe had a seasoned overview of the complexities in the crisis of the American priesthood. A dark-haired man with glasses, Sipe had the thoughtful calm of a priest, which in many ways he still was. Born in 1932, he graduated from St. John's Seminary in pastoral Collegeville, Minnesota, thence to Rome for two years of theology at Collegio Sant' Anselmo. Back at St. John's in 1955 he was one of the first participants in the Institute for Mental Health, a visionary program at the abbey which brought psychiatrists and clergymen together. His mentor, Dr. Leo Bartemeier, was counseling clergy, which Sipe would take up in later years. In 1965 he earned a certificate in pastoral counseling from the Menninger Foundation, followed by a two-year residency at Seton Psychiatric Institute in Baltimore.

In 1970, Sipe recalled, "I found myself lying in bed one night, staring at the ceiling, thinking about suicide. And with my background, I knew it was time to leave." Later that year he married Marianne Benkert, a former nun who had done residency as a psychiatrist at Seton.

Sipe's early caseload was predominantly with priests or ex-priests. Working with Bartemeier, he studied psychodynamic patterns that fed the acting out of sexual fantasies by certain patients. After Bartemeier's death, with case studies of 500 priest-patients, 500 nonpriests (many of them women who had been sexually involved with clergy), and interviews with 500 priests who were not patients, Sipe had a data base which, while not geographically random, still afforded insights. *A*

Secret World: Sexuality and the Search for Celibacy, his book incorporating these data, was published in 1990.

"The estimates others give are higher," he said of the numbers of homosexuals in the priesthood. "I think bishops can fight estimates, so my figures are conservatively lower. The data through 1978 show 18 to 20 percent homosexual. About half of those admitted genital activity. This does not include the increase of gays in seminaries in the 1970s and eighties. Privately a number of bishops have told me they believe it's now 40 percent. The information I've gathered since 1978, while not as extensive, supports that number. But again we have to make the distinction between those who struggle to lead chaste lives and those who don't. I would still say that half of these men are not for the most part sexually active."

He found the same dichotomy between celibacy and sexual activity applying to the 60 percent of priests he estimated today were heterosexual. "If half of all priests are sexually active," he continued, "be they gay or straight, we must determine what is happening psychologically. It's a tremendously prolonged period of adolescence. You have people trying to work out sexual identities in situations that don't favor it. So there's a great deal of splitting. People have to live almost two separate, unintegrated lives. One is internal, trying to figure out a sexual identity; the other is very responsible, active, serving the life of the church.

"I'm going to say it again and again: the church demands celibacy but does not train for it. Priests are not prepared for celibate living and the church does not openly support sexual education of its clergy. The church has no theology of sex, which leaves the priest unprepared. He can just mouth pronouncements of 'thou shalt not,' but he cannot truly teach his parishioners."

Seven thousand former priests, now married, form CORPUS—Corps of Reserved Priests United for Service—and seek restoration of their clerical faculties. Sipe told a CORPUS convention:

> *The lack of a refined theology of sex has profoundly influenced the power base of the Church. The "Church" as defined prior to Vatican II justified itself in its homo-social organization (men central; women adjunctive) and the hierarchy was consistent in its homosexual structure (power reserved to one sex) based on its acceptance of the Male Matrix as fundamental to theology and to the authority structure of the Church.*

For the hierarchy to reverse patterns of homosexuality in the priesthood would mean threatening its own authority structure—a system of sexual segregation, ruled by celibate males.

William McMahon, a Cincinnati businessman in his early sixties, was a CORPUS member who said he left the priesthood in Rockford, Illinois, in 1973 because "gays were running the diocese" and because he and others struggled with celibacy. "In the early sixties," said McMahon, "we were confronted with the Christian Family Movement. Through close relationships with married couples, we [priests] had to confront our own sexuality, especially through pre-Cana conferences [for engaged Catholic couples]. This was during the years leading up to *Humanae Vitae*, and these married couples made us look like nickel-and-dime priests. We had all these security blankets—the car, the rectory, a cook, cleaning lady, and the great respect of our parishioners—and here were these couples, taking real economic risks and being holier than we were. As priests became involved in lives of their people, celibacy became a hindrance to our ministry. They'd go home to their families, and we'd go home to an empty bed. I saw many good men leave, while gays moved up the ladder."

Psychologist Eugene Kennedy, who left the priesthood after Sipe, recalls: "There were plenty of homosexuals among the old [pre-Vatican II] priests, but it was dealt with differently. The culture was intact; there was not the acting out you find today. The rewards of clerical life created defenses. When you have an all-male society, there's lots of sublimated eroticism. But I would say a majority were heterosexual.

"If there was a problem, the guy went into a mental hospital. Many were sent to Seton Institute in Baltimore. That hospital [since incorporated into another one] was like a minimum security prison. I was in on some horrendous cases, and I had titanic battles with bishops over matters of my confidentiality as a therapist with a patient. The hierarchy wanted homosexuality handled with compassion, and not publicly. The whole objective was rehabilitation—get them back into the priesthood. The idea of freeing those men was ruled out. Instead they were put back into the clerical culture, fixed up with great margins of toleration. That culture is now in shards."

xii.

Therapy: The New Confession

On February 20, 1986, Michael Peterson and I finally shook hands in the Johns Hopkins medical complex, at a conference sponsored by the Sexual Disorders Clinic. Many parole officers were in the audience. At the podium Dr. Fred Berlin, director of the clinic, said that under Maryland law some of the men on the stage could be arrested for crimes which they were about to discuss as patients. Seven pedophiles than recounted their sexual histories; among them were a radiologist, ex-military officer, portly grandfather, teacher, and civil servant. All were on Depo-Provera. As each discussed the compulsiveness of his "fugue state" (over which, said Berlin, none had had control) heads shook skeptically in the audience. "This is amazing," whispered Peterson, seated next to me. "Imagine what it takes for those poor men to sit on that stage and say these things to *policemen.*"

He wore a dark suit, white turtleneck, and temporary neck brace, a result of back surgery the previous fall. When he took the podium for the last lecture, people were tired. "I grew up in a fairly rich family," he began. "My grandmother was this supposedly Mormon lady who loved martinis and smoked cigarettes down to the filter. She kept a .38 under the pillow. She said something to me once about sex offenders: 'When the penis grows hard, the brain grows soft.'" People laughed; he grinned.

At St. Luke, he explained, "we have four men, pedophiles, who have never masturbated in their lives." He raised his eyebrows, as if to say, *Imagine that.* "The church has taught that sex is evil. We're talking about our long tradition: 'If it feels good, it's wrong.' That's the opposite of our popular culture mentality." Of St. Luke's patients, he said, "Fifty percent are alcoholic *and* pedophile. I know a missionary who was an alcoholic for thirty-five years. He'd find boys, poverty-stricken, and hug 'em for five minutes. When he had an orgasm, the child would leave. Is that child abuse? I don't know."

He spoke of visiting clerics in jail. "And they say, 'I don't know what I did wrong.' At first I was astonished: *They really don't know.* . . . I can generalize and say that most people we see are not involved with the law. That's probably because until ten years ago, if clergy were found by police, the judge would say,

'Bishop, take care of him!' We use Depo-Provera in one hundred percent of our treatment."

I thought of Gauthe, whose injections of the hormone begun here under Dr. Berlin had been halted in Louisiana, where it was not available for prisoners. Many pedophile priests, said Peterson, "grow up with thoughts constantly plaguing them, so [the drug] becomes natural to them. We don't see heterosexual pedophiles at all. I don't know why. . . . Fifty percent were abused as children. A high percentage are children of alcoholics."

The evaluation period at St. Luke lasted three weeks. "They come because bishops order them," he explained. "The Roman Catholic Church is not a democracy; it's a strange kind of ethos. . . . We make them write a sexual history. In a few weeks you have to help them overcome years of problems. The big question is, should priests go back into ministry? We find that those who can go back are the ones not recognized by the media or involved in a scandal, with their credibility gone."

Several days later, in his office, he told me that the church crisis was far greater than he had realized when collaborating with Mouton and Doyle the previous spring. "More and more bishops are asking if I can guarantee that this man will not touch another child—and I have to say no."

ii.

I had come to see pedophilia as part of a deeper ailment within a culture premised on celibacy. Dr. Robert J. McAllister, a psychiatrist who had treated priests and nuns for thirty years, concluded that religious communities do not foster the affective bonds of healthy families. "Psychiatrists hear the confessions that cannot be told anywhere else," he wrote. McAllister's focus was on religious orders, vowed to poverty in communities, unlike diocesan clergy, who live in rectories and take no vow of poverty. He wrote:

> *Therapists frequently see religious whose attraction to the religious life appears to have originated in their adolescent sexuality. . . . Religious celibates who disclose sexual difficulty are often dismissed too casually. They usually come to the spiritual adviser asking one question: "Is this behavior morally wrong?" A yes or no answer to that question may provide moral guidance but deny psychological assurance. Other questions need consideration: What are the emotional components of this behavior? What are the psychological and interpersonal components of this behavior?*

Linking morality and psychology was indicative of a historic—and hesitant—shift on the part of many in the church. For much of this century the Vatican took a negative view of psychoanalysis. In line with that view, the influential American Bishop Fulton J. Sheen observed of psychology in 1949, "A man who has been told that everything is a symptom never need accuse or judge himself or ask to be judged." Confessing sins was central to Catholicism—especially so during the heyday of Bishop Sheen. One stood in line beside the pews, made an examination of conscience, then knelt in the confessional box, revealing sins to the priest, who sat behind a curtain; he listened, offered guidance, absolved the penitent of his or her sins, giving prayers for penance. The sacrament of confession bonded believer and priest in a molding of conscience. The sacrament's roots lay in early Mediterranean communities where sinners made public confession to the bishop. In contrast Irish churches of the Dark Ages considered the solitary priest as agent of each sinner's reconciliation. Penitential books advised the priest, listing sins and recommending absolutions. The more private Irish approach supplanted the Mediterranean ritual in which sin was seen more clearly in its social implications.

Clarence Thomson, a former priest who served in a North Dakota parish, recalls a turning point in his ministry: "In 1965, my custom was to spend four hours in the confessional Saturday afternoon, and another three hours at night, especially during Lent. The following year, instead of having two priests for seven hours, one priest for an hour in the afternoon and evening was enough. In October 1966, I met Father François Houtard, a religious sociologist, in Fargo, North Dakota, and mentioned this to him. He said the same thing had happened in Australia and all over Europe and America. It was like one huge voice coming down in 1965, saying, 'You don't have to do it any more.' "

Whether confession declined so ubiquitously is unclear. But a melding of psychology and Christian morality had begun to raise questions about the reflexive confessing of sins and to prompt a frank look at the deep psychological springs beneath human behavior. In the 1970s bishops across America were approving psychological screening of seminarians; many priests and nuns sought therapy; Catholic social services began utilizing therapists, some of whom were clergy or religious. Therapeutic models aimed to serve people by modern means; yet they also came at the expense of confession.

But if the use of therapeutic models began to supplant confession, psychological findings helped change Catholicism's moral emphasis from the realm of private sins to a broader social context. In a 1985 *Commonweal* essay, theologian James Gaffney saw behind "the widespread neglect of sacramental confession" a structural shift in moral attitudes. In the past, he wrote, confessed sins

> *offended and injured other people, sometimes great numbers of other people and in extremely complicated ways. Yet, because none of those people was heard from, their moral perspective could scarcely be introduced. Not surprisingly, then, Catholic moral thinking habitually understood sin in relation to sinners more than in relation to the victims of sins.*

Traditional moral thinking reflected an "ignorance of typical female and conjugal experience, intensified by . . . attitudes of authoritarian paternalism." For Gaffney, the greatest change to have come about of late was "the centering of moral assessment not on rules but on virtue." This idea of virtue was shaped "not by [one's] record of unbroken regulations, but by the cultivation and integration of certain basic habits, attitudes and outlooks." These new ethical concerns had begun to shift a Catholic focus from "the realm of sex . . . [to] the realm of justice." One effect of this new moral view—a view more concerned with active love and less with a self-conscious adherence to rules—was an awareness of suffering: "The closer one gets to the sufferer," wrote Gaffney, "the harder it becomes to refuse help."

A similar sensibility infused therapy and support groups, which foster personal self-discovery in order to overcome suffering. Alcoholics Anonymous members beseech God to help each person sustain sobriety. All therapeutic models seek a healing of victims, the sinned-against—those who, in the long tradition of penance, had not been heard. But therapy alone does not explain why so many Catholics rarely make confessions. They are at odds with ancient teachings about human sexuality. Officially, the church considers masturbation, fornication, homosexual activity, and bestiality as mortal sins. The equality presumed by the grouping begs the indulgence of a modern mind. And yet, in a culture cheapened by sexual images, Catholicism also affirms a moral responsibility for sexual behavior. The great theological efforts today seek bridges between tradition and individual dignity.

iii.

By virtue of his clinical services at St. Luke, the Rev. Dr. Michael Peterson was uniquely situated in the clerical milieu. He heard confessions of priests that could not be told elsewhere; his ministry was designed to heal the healers. "A priest who comes in here deserves a full battery of neurological tests, nothing less," he told me. He spoke of an older priest, arrested for selling child pornography, who had long been a severe alcoholic. Michael's concern was that no tests had been performed to determine brain damage from alcohol. With proof of impaired mental faculties, the judge might be more lenient.

I asked Peterson what his Mormon parents had thought of his conversion to Catholicism. "When I called to say I was going to be baptized [my mother] said: 'Don't bother. You were baptized at birth.' My mother came from a rigid Irish background. She was divorced and remarried in a matter of months to the only father I knew. She left the church because [her] family basically rejected her."

A Catholic all those years he was a Mormon, and his mother said, "Don't bother." He seemed detached, wry, emotionally aloof.

"When did you learn you were adopted?" I asked.

"When I was four or five. I never knew my biological father. I was confirmed at nineteen, the day after my baptism, which was canceled." He chuckled. "I walked down the aisle with a bunch of twelve-year-olds."

He had a strong social conscience. "I can't stand to see people on grates outside the White House. People are dying outside, people drive by in chauffeured limousines, and all we have to do is have a shelter for them. I have always had this sense of incredible injustice. When I had just begun psychiatry, I used to go home and feel terribly guilty after a racist would give a lecture and have some obviously bigoted view toward blacks or Jews or gays and I wouldn't stand up and walk out of the room."

"This would happen in lectures by psychiatrists?"

"Oh, they are rigid sons of bitches. If you don't fit whatever model they're buying into at the time, they're some of the most rigid people you'll ever meet. They're not the liberals everyone portrays them to be. Maybe they are compared with the rest of the population. My point is, I've always had feelings about injustice and an intellectual curiosity that guided me along."

"You became a priest relatively late in life."

"I was ordained eight years ago [1978] when I was thirty-five. I went in at thirty-two."

"Had you experienced many deep, loving relationships with women before that?"

"Mmm, yeah." He pondered for a moment. "I was engaged when I was real young, in college. But it's almost like I didn't have time for any of that. I've never been a social person. I don't go to parties. I never go out. I have friends, and I cultivate friendships, but I don't have time. I'm just driven."

"Prior to seminary, was it difficult for you being a doctor, a workaholic, not having a social life: was it something you had to suppress?"

"No. There was never enough time. I used to complain about that. It's strange. It's not that you don't sit down when talking to people. But every workaholic has a part that doesn't let you feel comfortable. I never think about money, and I'm always six months late for the IRS. It's like *you don't deserve* any time off—and that's perverted. But it drives a lot of people in our culture. I'm gonna die earlier than anyone else. I know that. Physicians die earlier. People with Type A blood die earlier."

Only on replaying the tape did I notice his intermittent coughing. In early 1986, I had no inkling of the disease that was stalking him. (In retrospect, I'm sure he knew; why else did he say, "I'm gonna die earlier"?) He smiled when I turned to church teaching about sexuality; he was enjoying the intellectual exercise. "I never thought of masturbation as a sin, so I never told about masturbatory fantasies in confession," he said. "The whole system of moral theology is so bizarre. Take purgatory. That was a way the church raised money: by selling indulgences. I think what most impressed me from my religious studies is that we are truly an Irish church. The Irish are some of the oldest people to agonize over sex. If you go back to France or Italy, the attitudes were more lenient.

"I'm not saying the church hasn't evolved," he continued. He mentioned an old film, *Robin Hood*, he had seen the other night and spoke of the church at that medieval time. "The church was the law and governing body. I don't think people examined their conscience and thought about masturbation. . . . I'm sure people did not do that until Irish monks brought the penitential books to Europe. Nobody thought about it. And I think our inheritance in this country is absolutely phenomenal. The hierarchy is at least fifty percent Irish and they bring a strong tradition of sex being bad."

"Which is why they can't handle gays."

"Right," he laughed. "Or know what to do with women."

A booklet on St. Luke Institute explained that Peterson's interest in alcoholism had come with discovery "that alcoholism was in his own family." I asked about that. "My mother was an alcoholic," he said, adding that she was in poor health. Sensing the subject of his family unnerved him, I said: "Let's talk about homosexuality."

He frowned. "I thought your assignment was pedophilia."

That was the starting point, I explained. But so many priests had abused teenage boys; and so many questions were being raised about gay priests. He checked his watch. Time was up. I asked if we could meet again. He proposed dinner three days later. But that morning his secretary called apologetically to say that Father had a scheduling conflict and was due in New York.

Many of the priests St. Luke treated were ACOAs—adult children of alcoholics. The alcoholic parent falls into a zone apart from spouse and children; the family may hold but affective bonding suffers—hence the term "dysfunctional family." Some ACOAs grow up meek and shorn of confidence; others become compulsive risk takers, or project exaggerated self-images to compensate for inner shame. Most struggle to sustain their relationships.

The confidence Ray Mouton had seen the previous spring as Michael departed for lectures in Australia was part of the persona. The inner man, I later learned from a St. Luke staffer, "was afraid he would make some kind of awful mistake. He had an arrangement: if things were not going well, he would get in touch and we would place an overseas call, frantic, had to have him back for an emergency—in reality, to get him off the hook." But he did well in Australia, as he always did in public.

After meeting Michael, my impression was of a hard-working, well-balanced clinician. But the frown on his face and abrupt termination of the interview made me wonder. When I asked Mouton whether he thought Michael might be gay, he replied, "It crossed my mind. I asked him once if homosexuality was a problem in the priesthood. He laughed, and said, 'If they kicked out all the gays, they wouldn't have enough priests left to say Mass.'"

iv.

Peterson believed that homosexuality is "shaped in utero"—the mother's womb—an orientation into which people are born, a position more than a few experts share. Others consider environmental factors in early childhood the dominant cause. The "nature vs. nurture" debate is unlikely to be resolved soon. In fact there are many homosexualities, varied forms of same-sex behavior. An influential 1951 study found that homosexuality was generally accepted in sixty-four percent of nonindustrialized cultures investigated. Attitudes toward same-sex behavior have varied through history. Western resistance to homosexuality is shaped by Judeo-Christian thought. Today major denominations struggle with the moral implications of whether to accept gay or lesbian ministers. Michael Peterson's career spanned two decades of upheavals over the relationship of religion and homosexuality.

Protest movements succeed to the degree that they build empathy with the middle class. The civil rights struggle gained outside the South because its goals of suffrage and desegregation touched primal tissues of democracy. The movement also had a profound religious character. Martin Luther King, Jr., wanted whites to see a black Christian morality guided by love rather than hate. Dr. King and other key leaders were ministers; churches were bases; stirring orators compared blacks to the children of Israel, searching for a promised land of freedom.

Homosexuals' demands for fair treatment in jobs and housing extended a civil rights legal ethic and emboldened men and women of many professions to unshackle their fears and proclaim their orientation. Others chose to blend anonymously into society. Gay liberation did not emerge from a vacuum. In the McCarthy witch hunts of the early 1950s, homosexuals were subjected to mass arrests, while FBI agents spied on those with government jobs. After the 1964 Civil Rights Act, heterosexual women and gays of both sexes began filing discrimination suits against the government. In 1969 police raided the Stonewall Inn, a gay bar and cultural enclave in Greenwich Village; from the three days of rioting that followed a protest movement was born.

Unlike the early civil rights quest, gay liberation had a distinct antireligious strain. Militants advanced a critique of "heterosexism" with the nuclear family (of Judeo-Christian tradition) seen as controlling agent. If society suppressed gays, then homoerotic sex would be a force of political witness. "In practice, most gay males accept that fidelity to a relationship is not to be measured in sexual terms," gay theorist Dennis Altman wrote in 1982, before the impact of AIDS.

Gay liberation challenged laws against sodomy that were rooted in religious beliefs. That meant changing attitudes. The watershed conflict came in the early 1970s, when gay protesters disrupted meetings of the American Psychiatric Association. At that time homosexuality was classified as an illness in *The Diagnostic and Statistic Manual of Psychiatric Disorders*, otherwise known as *DSM*, the reference text for treating mental patients. Protesting that such views betrayed a cultural bias, gays mounted an aggressive campaign against the psychiatric establishment over *DSM*.

Freud considered homosexuality "no vice . . . [and] it cannot be classified as illness"; rather, he said, it was a "variation of the sexual function produced by a certain arrest of sexual development." Freud believed that all people are inherently bisexual. Conservative psychoanalysts of the 1960s rejected that position, arguing that heterosexuality was the cultural and biological norm.

By the 1970s, however, more liberal psychiatrists were having second thoughts about homosexuality as an illness. A critic of his own profession, Thomas Szasz, wrote: "Psychiatric preoccupation with the disease concept of homosexuality conceals the fact that homosexuals are a group of medically-stigmatized and socially persecuted individuals. The noise generated by their persecution and their anguished cries of protest is drowned out by the rhetoric of therapy—just as the rhetoric of salvation drowned out the noise generated by the persecution of witches and their anguished cries of protest."

In late 1973 the APA board announced that homosexuality "by itself does not necessarily constitute a psychiatric disorder." Other psychiatrists cried foul. The board called for a referendum by mail to resolve the dispute. Of 10,000 who responded, 58 percent approved a change of classification in *DSM II*, the new manual to be approved by the APA. Thirty-seven percent were opposed, and the rest abstained or did not vote on the issue.

DSM II also included a compromise category, "ego-dystonic homosexuality"— for one whose sexual orientation caused conflict and mental suffering—to accommodate psychiatrists treating those who wanted to be heterosexual, or homosexuals struggling to come to terms with their orientation, or adolescents experiencing sexual identity problems. (In 1986 the category was dropped.) Although many practitioners disliked a ballot as a means of resolving a scientific dispute, homosexuality was no longer, officially, a mental illness. The U. S. Civil Service Commission soon ended its employment ban on gay people and various cities and states began to repeal sodomy laws.

Although it was by no means a goal shared by all homosexuals, activists in San Francisco and New York championed public bathhouses which afforded endless sexual contacts. Promiscuous behavior patterns, at least in the public eye, often overshadowed the movement's political agenda. A layer of gay culture went wild; people who had been repressed all of their lives surged out in an orgiastic release, with AIDS a lethal shadow.

As gay liberation's financial and voting clout registered with big-city politicians, its message to democracy at times grew muddled. When militants representing an extremist gay fringe invade St. Patrick's Cathedral in New York, shouting obscenities during Mass, or pelt worshipers with condoms as they leave a Boston ordination service, which political right takes primacy: freedom of religion or freedom of expression? After demonstrations like these, cries of homophobia and victimization fall on deaf ears.

Although the APA supported gay rights measures, many psychiatrists had a bitter aftertaste of the *DSM II* controversy. Perhaps that is what Michael Peterson meant in referring to some psychiatrists as "rigid sons of bitches." And yet just when medical orthodoxy was cracking, allowing Michael to join other professionals in coming out of the closet, he chose instead, in 1975, to embark upon a career that would shroud his homosexuality from the public. However deep his religious calling, Michael Peterson walked into the priesthood in the middle of its own sexual revolution. That, I suspect, was part of its appeal. His brilliance and wit made for a charismatic priest; as a gay psychiatrist, he might well have been pigeonholed.

As a psychiatrist-priest, he found exalted status in a clerical culture primed on therapy as a new confession. Penance still existed, but the examination of conscience was readily adaptable to patient-therapist dialogue in a larger search for causes and effects of psychological pain.

Therapy relies on a grasp of who or what has caused one's hurt. Gays frequently cite the pained early awareness of feeling different from one's peers. "Coming out" is meant to affirm one's orientation over the guilt wrought by cultural determinism. Therapy offered a way of approaching religious tenets that shaped Western thinking.

Ironically, as psychodynamic theories of homosexuality diverged, a rapprochement was building between psychology and Christianity. In 1950 a prominent psychiatrist wrote: "Every physician must heed the patient's religious attitudes and needs." A generation later, Alan Stone, the APA president, stated: "Psychiatry does not stand outside history or morality, but how do we decide which history and morality to accept?"

Attempts to graft psychological concepts onto scripturally based religious beliefs are among the major cultural conflicts of our time. Some denominations, for instance, accept what it means to be gay while others condemn homosexuality outright. Between these poles a vast theological debate is raging.

One vanguard approach to gay religion emerged in 1968 in Los Angeles' nondenominational Metropolitan Community Church, which attracted many ex-

Catholics. Founded by a Florida-born former fundamentalist preacher who left his wife and sons, MCC had eclectic rituals and standards with borrowed Christian strands. In the 1970s, MCC mushroomed, with churches in San Francisco, Boston, Atlanta, Philadelphia, and Salt Lake City, center of the Mormon Church, which views homosexuality in strongly negative terms.

MCC was one voice of a movement; as a religion it groped for definition. Some people hugged and kissed during services. Two sociologists who studied MCC in its formative years found magazines with ads for sex next to devotional literature. One congregation member referred to its youth ministry as "the Chicken Coop" because it attracted predatory older men, "chicken hawks." A moral ambiguity was at work, as the sociologists noted:

> Gay Christianity perhaps reaches the peak of inconsistency in its ethics. There is no doubt that MCC struggles with this problem. Given the gay theologians' handling —or discarding—of the Scriptures, the gay church has difficulty finding something to rely on as a standard for moral behavior. The question to be decided is whether to accept traditional fundamentalistic morals (minus the homosexual prohibitions) or to abandon them completely in favor of a new homosexual ethic.

While mainstream denominations weighed scriptural standards in trying to accept gays, the Unitarian-Universalist Association instituted the equivalent of a homosexual marriage rite. By 1986 at least forty such ceremonies had reportedly been performed. In 1978, New York City's Episcopal bishop ordained a lesbian to the priesthood, which sent shock waves through traditionally minded followers, including a small number of married priests who converted to Catholicism and were later given parishes as married Catholic priests. Episcopal priest Malcolm Boyd has written:

> Certain bishops were gay. One knew who they were, but the subject was never discussed with them. A rigid, pervasive code of priestly gentlemanly behavior governed the situation: always remain discreet, minimize risks of disclosure. . . . Some sources within the church claim that at least a third, if not more, of the hierarchy and clergy are gay.

As in the Catholic Church, no hard data support Boyd's estimate.

By the 1980s, with some 20,000 MCC adherents nationwide, Protestant and Reform Jewish congregations sponsored Bible-study groups for homosexuals, with an estimated 30,000 members across the country. Michigan had fifteen groups, wrote Detroit News religion editor Kate DeSmet, "with a combined membership of 150 to 200 people. The groups, which convene weekly or monthly, often serve to meet gays' religious as well as social needs, replacing bars and bathhouses as gathering places."

With the psychiatric establishment's new position on homosexuality, theologians began reexamining Catholic teaching on the topic. Charles Curran had broached a theory of compromise, or lesser-of-evils approach: heterosexuality was the biological and spiritual norm, but for those unable to change their orientation, even with therapy, abstinence was an unreasonable expectation. "There are many

somewhat stable homosexual unions which afford their partners some human fulfillment and contentment," he wrote. "Obviously, such unions are better than
homosexual promiscuity."

John J. McNeill, S.J., a World War II veteran, was a founder of New York's
Dignity chapter, an organization of gay Catholics. When Jesuit superiors in Rome
learned that McNeill was writing a book on homosexuality, they ordered him to
halt publication and cease his lectures. A commission of theologians empaneled to
review his work did not accept all of McNeill's conclusions but deemed the work
important. The Jesuit Superior-General Pedro Arrupe in Rome asked to read the
manuscript. McNeill obliged, was told to make revisions responding to the theologians' critique, and did so. In 1976, with the Society of Jesus' permission (but
not endorsement), *The Church and the Homosexual* was published.

The waiting period guaranteed the book's notoriety. On NBC's "Today
Show," McNeill said that he was homosexual. (Years later he spoke of an ongoing
sexual relationship at the time.) New orders came from Rome to cease speaking
and writing on the topic. Living in a Jesuit community on Manhattan's West Side,
McNeill counseled gays as a therapist, maintaining a long public silence.

His book asked why the homosexual had to see himself as "essentially in
contradiction to the divine will for man." McNeill considered Currran to be con-
signing the homosexual "through no fault of his own to a life in which every
expression of human sexual love will only serve to deepen the hold of an objectively sinful condition."

In different ways, McNeill and Curran questioned why the homosexual must
be a victim, as one more sinned against than sinning. McNeill further asked what
biblical authors really meant in judging same-sex acts. Genesis 19, for instance,
contains the famous story of Sodom, the wicked city eventually destroyed by two
angels sent from God. At the gates of the town the angels meet a virtuous man,
Lot, who invites them to stay in his home. Scripture continues:

> *The men of the city, both young and old, all the people to the last man,*
> *surrounded the house; and they called to Lot, "Where are the men who came to you*
> *tonight? Bring them out to us, so that we may know them." Lot went out of the door*
> *to the men, shut the door after him, and said, "I beg you, my brothers, do not act so*
> *wickedly. Look, I have two daughters who have not known a man; let me bring them*
> *out to you, and do to them as you please; only do nothing to these men. . . ." But*
> *they replied, "Stand back!" And they said, "This fellow came here as an alien, and*
> *he would play the judge! Now we will deal worse with you than with them." Then*
> *they pressed hard against the man Lot, and came near the door to break it down. But*
> *the men inside reached out their hand and brought Lot into the house with them, and*
> *shut the door. And they struck with blindness the men who were at the door of the*
> *house, both small and great, so that they were unable to find the door.*

McNeill notes: "There is no evidence elsewhere in the passage or in the Old
Testament to show that homosexual behavior was particularly prevalent" in
Sodom. Surrounding cultures, he argues, had legends "of a stranger (sometimes a
divine being in disguise) who visits a prosperous city and is refused hospitality."
McNeill says that the prototype of a sexually debauched city comes from a first-

century A.D. text written centuries *after* Genesis. Most of the references to Sodom in Jewish texts "stress the Old Testament themes of pride, arrogance, and inhospitality," he states. Reviewing scriptural passages in which homogenital sex is associated with fertility cults and temple prostitution, McNeill writes that the sin of Sodom was "primarily one of inhospitality," not homosexuality. Inhospitality implies passivity—not welcoming, not extending friendship. Then why did the angels blind the mob? Would inhospitality alone justify the extreme act of angels blinding the eyes of men bent on gang rape? Lot's offer of his virgin daughters to placate the mob was also appealing to a code of male supremacy. Does that mean that gang rape was considered more evil when done to men than women? Perhaps the angels were making a statement about that code as well by protecting Lot's daughters.

McNeill argues that homosexuality as a permanent condition was unknown to ancient Jews or early Christians. Rather, homosexual acts by heterosexual men were the great perversion—a betrayal of one's true nature. What then did scriptural authors think of sexual behavior patterns in the pagan world?

The ancient Greeks extolled homoeroticism in art works and verse. Certain gods practiced man-boy love, as did the bisexual male aristocracy; armies of Thebes and Sparta were charged with homosexuality as a fire of the male power drive. McNeill writes that the melding of self-centered lust and idol-worship incensed Scripture writers. Although St. Paul recoiled from "the rampant homosexuality he observed in Greece," writes McNeill, "his main point was always that the prevalence of homosexual activity was a sign of alienation from God"—in other words, of idolatry. Perhaps Paul did see homosexuality as a face of idolatry. Some revisionist theologians suggest that Paul was actually objecting to people who engaged in homosexual activity but who were in reality heterosexual and thus betraying their natural state; in other words, so this theory goes, Paul was making no judgment on people who are homosexual by nature and on the morality of their acts. This scholarly view relies on an anachronism, applying contemporary knowledge of homosexuality to a time when such findings did not exist. And finding these scholars' modern distinctions in Paul's words is not easy. In another epistle, he wrote:

> God delivered them up in their lusts to unclean practices; they engaged in the mutual degradation of their bodies; these men who exchanged the truth of God for a lie and worshiped and served the creature rather than the Creator. . . . Their women exchanged natural intercourse for unnatural, and the men gave up natural intercourse with women and burned with lust for one another. Men did shameful things with men, and thus received in their own persons this penalty for their perversity (Romans 1:24–27).

How could Paul have approved sexual contact between committed male lovers and condemned the same acts by men whose culpability lay in betraying their heterosexual orientation? Proposing a radical ethic of sexual restraint, Paul promoted a moral order that was in conflict with and victimized by the pagan status quo. Paul's focus was on social behavior that threatened Jesus' mission to found a family of faith. Theologians should not ignore the presence of homoeroticism and how it conflicted with early Christian life. Pagans in the late Empire adulated gods like Zeus, who abducted and raped the boy Ganymede—a living myth that one Christian philosopher denounced for influencing those men who ran "marketplaces of immorality and . . . infamous resorts for the young for every kind of corrupt pleasure." In statues to pagan deities, the Christian martyr Justin saw images that God had cast down from heaven: "Evil demons, effecting apparitions of themselves, both polluted women and corrupted boys . . . terrifying visions to people."

The gods were quite real to the pagan majority in the first three centuries of Christianity. Shrines to Zeus, Pan, and others "lay beside caves and chasms, high up on hilltops, in groves or out by the haphazard seats of the Nymphs and gods of healing," writes historian Robin Lane Fox. Cults flourished in cities too. People dreamed of their gods, often erotically; the gods appeared to people in waking visitations recorded by temple scribes.

Sexual plunder ran through Greek myth and charged its belief system. Sexual energy was value-neutral and enjoyed dominating, mocking, hurting, and tricking people, as the gods did in tales that have come down to us through time. Men dressed as Mercury and Pluto poked dying Christians with hot rods in the amphitheaters. Moral principles enunciated by the martyred Paul were a dissent from Greco-Roman culture that considered Christians to be atheists. That is not to say that homosexuals or bisexuals conspired out of their orientations to hurt Christians. The world of pagans, Christians, and Jews was more complex than that. Surely some homosexuals were Christian, too. But homoeroticism was part of the value system with which Christianity clashed.

John McNeill's more persuasive argument bore not on gay apologetics but on free will—that homosexuals do not have the power to change their sexual orientation. How, then, can homosexual relations that sustain genuine, faithful love *not* be morally just? It is, to me, the most powerful argument against a blanket condemnation of homosexuality. If people are not homosexual by choice, can all such love be inherently bad? Is a monogamous, dysfunctional couple who fight for years, psychologically scarring their children, morally superior to lesbian lovers who live for years in fidelity and kindness? Are genital mechanics a fair standard? McNeill writes:

> [M]any homosexuals have not only avoided the traps of promiscuity but have grown as human beings. They have learned to integrate their sexual powers in a positive way into their personality, with the result that these impulses become no longer a negative, compulsive and destructive force, but an instrument within their control for the expression of human love. There does not seem to be a clear condemnation of such a relationship in Scripture.

And yet the Bible clearly condemns homosexual acts. Adam and Eve symbolize the primordial image of a fertile human love. Even Father Bob Nugent, an ardent gay rights advocate, was unable to accept the idea of gay marriages. "I have problems going beyond Genesis," he reflected, meaning Adam and Eve as paradigms, and heterosexuality as the biological norm.

Yet how many gay people had I known, and who was I to judge their efforts to find happiness? How do loving parents who nurtured their young, only to confront a grown child's homosexuality, reckon with a harsh Bible? How should society respond? One approach rests on the nature of privacy. Many Catholics are sympathetic to the victimization of gay people, supportive of their individual rights, and not obsessed with how they make love. But they don't like confronting political protests or displays of a gay agenda in their churches. Churches are sacred spaces where people gather to worship as a community, not to accentuate their differences.

V.

At thirty-two, Michael Peterson was older than most seminarians when he began seminary studies in 1975. Cardinal William Baum of Washington allowed him to live at St. Anselm's Abbey, a monastic community founded by Thomas V. Moore, the first American psychiatrist to become a priest. Michael counseled priests and taught at Georgetown University Medical School during his religious studies. "He was driven, an achiever," recalls an older priest who taught him at DeSales Hall School of Theology. "He was constantly behind on assignments, getting to bed at 2 A.M., getting up at dawn. He was constantly tired. I don't know whether he took pep pills but it wouldn't surprise me. I wish he had come clean with me about his homosexuality. I think I could have helped him. He didn't take a psychological screening test."

In the 1970s another psychiatrist-priest from St. Anselm, Jerome Hayden, was the director of Marsalin Institute, a home for emotionally disturbed boys in Holliston, Massachusetts, near Boston. William H. Mann, a wealthy New York businessman and board chairman of Marsalin, considered Hayden "brilliant . . . an immensely complex, impractical and fascinating man." By 1977, though, Marsalin had a number of empty beds; Mann realized that the facility needed new direction. Than Father Hayden suddenly died.

At St. Anselm's Abbey the day of the funeral, Mann met Michael Peterson, about whom Hayden had raved. The moment seemed providential: Mann offered him the job, and Peterson took it. Peterson converted Marsalin into a facility for alcoholic clergy and within six months had a waiting list. He raised $85,000 to launch a bigger program at an old religious complex in Suitland, Maryland. Michael told me that after several years of shuttling between Boston and Washington he decided to consolidate the two facilities. Cardinal Baum was elevated to a Vatican post and in August 1980 James Hickey became archbishop. Hickey saw St. Luke Institute as a pioneering effort and was impressed that Peterson traveled with recovering alcoholics to their dioceses or religious communities, assisting their return to ministry. By 1985, St. Luke had begun "changing the market mix" by accepting pedophiles in addition to alcoholic clergy, according to a staffer who worked there at the time.

St. Luke clergy workshops screened films about intercourse, masturbation, and homosexuality. "It was done with great clinical care and group discussion," recalls a religious order staffer at the hospital. "These were men and women who had needs, areas of life never addressed in a clear healthy way. We had older priests who entered seminary as eighth-graders, with hang-ups restricting their personality structure. Therapeutically, we addressed questions in an open manner."

"It was Masters and Johnson stuff," Michael told me in a long telephone interview after it had been announced that he had Hodgkin's disease. "But this older priest wrote a letter complaining about the films to everyone he could think of, including Cardinal [name withheld: a Vatican prefect]. He's the one who said about pedophiles, 'Clip off their balls.' Anyway, I got a call from the nunciature. One of Laghi's aides [name withheld], this real asshole—he's so proud, can't even tell primary colors—said to me: 'There's been a complaint from Rome that your pedagogical techniques are not in keeping with the church. Now, we're not criticizing you—' I said: 'Well, yes. But you weren't there.'

" 'The nuncio would like an explanation of the way you teach.' So this psychologist and I wrote a straightforward explanation, why we use films to try and help people. Many people have never seen a vagina. They accepted the paper, told me, 'Thank you very much: the nuncio has decided he's not going to do anything about it himself.' 'Does that mean I can still teach?' 'You'll be informed.' Within a day or two Archbishop Hickey called. He was very understanding: 'Mike, it's foolish to play around with this stuff. It's just safer not to do it at seminary or diocesan workshops.' I assumed, reading between his lines, that I was free to do it if a religious order wanted. There was no formal censure—unless you're Charles Curran."

Hickey's conflicts with Peterson and Curran are a study in the hierarchy's divided mindset on sexual issues.

A dentist's son, born in 1920 into a pious Michigan family, James Hickey entered seminary at thirteen. Ordained in 1946, he ministered to Mexican farm workers before heading to Rome; he took doctorates in canon law and theology, later serving as rector of the North American College. The Latin American bishops' "preferential option for the poor" made a deep impression on him.

In 1974, Hickey became bishop of Cleveland. In parish after parish of the city's ethnic quilt he preached against racism and supported school busing. He opposed U.S. military involvement in El Salvador, where two Clevelanders—Ursuline Sister Dorothy Kazel and lay missionary Jean Donovan—worked among the poor. In March 1980 he joined them in San Salvador for the funeral of Archbishop Oscar Romero, who had been murdered while saying Mass in the cathedral. Twenty mourners were shot at the funeral as Hickey and others took refuge in the church. He asked Sister Dorothy to continue her work. In December 1980, five months after he became archbishop of Washington, the two women were murdered. Sister Dorothy "would have been home in June of 1980," he told a reporter. "She would be alive except that I asked her to stay."

Hickey became a critic of Reagan administration policy in Central America. He also became a point man in the Vatican campaign to restore orthodoxy in the restless American church.

Michael Peterson was anything but orthodox. But where Curran was a public figure, Peterson was largely unknown outside of church circles. Moreover, a psychiatrist treating priests was valuable to the hierarchy. As the pedophilia scandals grew, bishops and religious order superiors sought his expertise. His medical standing gave Michael a freedom of speech that few theologians had. In 1981 he told a gathering of U.S. and Canadian bishops that "the Christian church has had an exclusive focus on the genitals as comprising all of human sexuality. . . . The chasm between the biological sciences and theological sciences continues to cause, rather than heal, much human suffering."

At that time Curran was encountering new Vatican pressure to recant his views on homosexuality, birth control, masturbation, and abortion. (Curran was supportive of a woman's choice in the event of rape or incest.) Although other theologians held dissident views, Curran's role in the *Humanae Vitae* revolt made him a victim of his own celebrity, small though it was as a Catholic scholar. Curran lived in a book-lined flat two floors above the CUA theology department. Known as "Charlie" to students and faculty, his amiable personality was such that even faculty adversaries liked him. Rome's questions involved sexual ethics but the real issue was power: did a theologian have the right to disagree with Rome?

An ugly spat was brewing between American standards of academic freedom and Vatican theological hegemony. The papacy of John Paul II, so inspiring to Catholics in Communist Eastern Europe, was mounting a campaign against Latin American liberation theology exponents, who asked whether God wanted masses of people to be poor and how unjust societies could be changed. Rome also set its sights on elements of the U.S. church that questioned sexual issues. In both cases, theological research threatened Rome as the seat of power. Meanwhile, a sea of sexual behavior teemed beneath the surface of American clerical life.

In 1980 seven Jesuit psychiatrists produced a 192-page paper, "The Problem of Homosexuality in Religious Life," at the behest of a General Congregation of the Society of Jesus. The precipitating event was the refusal by superiors of the New York Province to approve the ordination of a young homosexual scholastic who was celibate. The *New York Times* reported that the "vice-provincial in charge of priestly preparation attributed the dismissal to inadequacies in [his] 'total personality, including alleged flaws in [his] ability to relate to other people.'" Another factor was the young man's "adoption of certain forms of behavior characteristic of a homosexual lifestyle." Seventeen Jesuits in the man's community signed a letter of protest.

The psychiatrists' report tracked the analytical view of those who considered homosexuality a mental disorder. They wrote:

> *A vocation decision should not follow immediately upon the discovery or disclosure of overt homosexual behavior. That should await the outcome of psychiatric evaluation and treatment. . . . An individual who is either unable or unwilling to resolve this problem, for whatever reason, should be regarded as unsuitable for life in the Society.*

When Peterson heard of the study he called Bob Nugent of New Ways Ministry, whose prodding of the church to openly discuss homosexuality was not popular with bishops. Nugent had long sought a dialogue with Peterson, whose workaholic pace was the stuff of clergy legend; the most Nugent could manage was the errant appointment sandwiched into business hours at St. Luke's. Now Michael was on the phone, anxious for the Jesuits' paper. Nugent was going out that night but offered to leave it on his doorstep. Peterson returned it by mail, thanking Nugent in a July 5, 1980, letter "for the opportunity to peruse the document.

. . . I am afraid that I did not have sufficient time to render a comprehensive analysis of the document. If that were ever desirable in the future, I would be happy to try and do that for you."

He scored the "rather traditional views" of research and criticized their ignoring "the biological basis of human sexual behaviors" and sociological data on gays. "Logical consistency was never an ideal of this type of moralistic thinking." Nugent agreed, but was disappointed over a natural ally avoiding him.

Nugent and Sister Jeannine Gramick were planning a New Ways symposium on homosexuality. They invited Archbishop Hickey to join theologians in presenting the magisterium's teaching. Curran, among others, would discuss pastoral alternatives. Such as: a gay asks his pastor if his monogamous relationship is immoral. Must Father tell him he is living in sin and therefore to desist? Or may Father counsel that such a relationship, as a lesser of two evils, is preferable to a lonely life of episodic sex?

On September 30, 1981, Gramick and Nugent went to the archbishop's residence. Monsignor John Donoghue, the chancellor, and the Rev. John Connery, S.J., a theologian, joined the prelate. "Had we known they were going to be there," recalled Nugent, "we'd have brought a canon lawyer and moral theologian." Hickey was gravely concerned that church teaching would be compromised at the New Ways symposium. Nugent and Gramick assured him they would present both sides. Two other bishops had agreed to participate. "If you were dealing only with priests, that would be different," said Hickey. He feared that lay people would accept views at odds with the magisterium as authentic. "It sounds like you're having a meal, and some of the food is good but some of it poisoned," he brooded.

Hickey blocked the bishops from appearing but the conference was held anyway. Over the next three years Hickey pressured Nugent's and Gramick's respective superiors in Rome to remove them from his archdiocese. He called New Ways' work a "scandal . . . ambiguous and unclear with regard to the morality of homosexual activity." Nugent and Gramick took residences on the East Coast, with frequent visits to New Ways' house in Mount Rainier, Maryland, where staffers planned projects. The pair traveled the country, raising the issue of homophobia, promoting Dignity's alternatives to magisterial teaching, encouraging gay clergy to join support groups and to strive for celibacy. Gramick called resistance to homosexuals in some religious houses "as bad as communities that won't accept blacks." The duo lobbied for gay rights and, as the AIDS plague grew, for pastoral help to the dying.

In response to Nugent's activism, Hickey denied him clerical faculties—the right to celebrate Mass and to hear confession. Nugent explained: "A chancery aide told me, 'We couldn't give you faculties because all the homosexuals would go to you for confession.' I was stunned. Wouldn't it be good if they came to me to confess sin?"

Peterson was able to avoid a turf war with the archbishop over his work at St. Luke, says Nugent, who added: "Mike fought with Hickey over the sexual films, saying, 'I am a professional and I need this.' Michael said Hickey finally told him: 'Okay, but you must tell these people that they must be celibate.'"

When Peterson sent him a dossier of information that St. Luke was distributing, Nugent was surprised to see materials from New Ways and Dignity. If it was okay for St. Luke to disseminate the literature, why was the archbishop trying to drive out Nugent and Gramick? When Nugent asked Peterson to speak at a meeting of religious formation directors, he begged off, saying that he wasn't qualified. Michael, not qualified? "He was distancing himself from New Ways because of our conflicts with Hickey," said Nugent. "He wanted to maintain a credible, professional reputation—not one of an advocate, and in the end I had to empathize with that."

As Peterson built his program and Nugent occupied a clerical limbo, Charles Curran's problems with Rome reached a crest.

At a press conference in March 1986, Curran disclosed a letter from Cardinal Ratzinger asking him to retract disputed positions. "The church claims the freedom to maintain her own academic institutions in which her doctrine is reflected," wrote Ratzinger.

One of the most powerful cardinals, a theological alter ego to Pope John Paul II, Ratzinger was a progressive theologian at Vatican II who turned rightward in the 1970s. As archbishop of Munich he quarreled with theologian Hans Kung of Tübingen, a liberal critic of the postconciliar church. When John Paul named Ratzinger prefect of the Congregation for Doctrine of the Faith, he gave him great latitude as a theological spokesman.

On March 8, Curran met with Ratzinger in the Vatican. Curran cited past admissions of errors by the Holy Office, such as its revision of its allowance of slavery and the burning of witches. He offered to stop teaching sexual ethics (which he hadn't taught in ten years) and to accept an official statement calling his views "at variance with existing official hierarchical teaching." The noted European theologian, Bernard Haring, a Redemptorist, urged Ratzinger to compromise. Ratzinger smiled enigmatically and ended the meeting with a prayer.

That same month, still weak from his back surgery, Peterson flew to Rome and discussed the pedophilia crisis with Cardinal Silvio Oddi of the Sacred Congregation of the Clergy, among others. Having logged 200,000 miles of air travel in the last year, he returned to Washington tired, and despondently told Tom Doyle that the meeting had achieved little.

Theologically, Michael was a flaming radical. But his therapeutic standing was that of a high confessor. When he translated the sinfulness of pedophilia into medical language—that such men lacked free will to curb their compulsions—the idea of such priests as themselves victims, more sick than sinful, softened the blow to ecclesiastical officers. Scandal and financial loss they could absorb: the church, after all, would go on. But a threat to clerical superiority the hierarchy would not tolerate. Politically, Peterson's limits were almost endless compared to a Charlie Curran or Bob Nugent, who sought dialogue, respectively, about sexual ethics and clergy homosexuality. Breaking the wraps on those issues challenged a clerical control mechanism: secrecy. Peterson's private briefings upheld that code of silence. Curran and Nugent violated it as figures in the public world.

A year after Michael's death, a staffer told me that at a St. Luke's clinicians' meeting, "he used to talk about 'Peterson Park'—where sexual activities of all kinds would be acceptable. He said it kiddingly, but I thought there was more to it than fantasy. He was threatened by people who had inklings of his private life, so people kept quiet. The self-destructive part never spilled into his professional life."

Until he fell ill with AIDS.

vi.

By April 1986, the Mouton-Doyle-Peterson report was experiencing an odd resurrection. At NCCB offices in Washington there was no policy; but with fifty cases surfacing across the continent, bishops and order superiors were calling authors of the controversial document for back-channel advice. At Doyle's behest, Mouton agreed to speak at an East Coast Canon Law Society conference in Morristown, New Jersey, on April 29.

Before that, on Good Friday, Peterson collapsed and was rushed to George Washington University Hospital. Mouton flew in from Louisiana, joining Tom Doyle at his bedside. "I'm dying," Michael said. "My lymphatic system has broken down." He told them he had Hodgkin's disease.

Mouton was crying. "It's not fair."

Michael whispered, "You're right, Ray. It's not fair—because you guys have to stay behind."

He asked for a rosary, which Doyle promised to get.

A handful of St. Luke staffers learned the true diagnosis and were sworn to secrecy by Peterson, who feared that scandal would destroy the program he had built. He went home to his house adjacent to St. Luke, and gave a black woman hired to care for him money to buy choir robes for her church. Shivering and coughing though he was, as president and medical director of St. Luke he kept close tabs, soon returning to his office for several-hour stretches each day or as often as possible.

Ray Mouton was depressed when he checked into his hotel in Morristown. Michael had befriended him during the dark months when Lafayette church officials had scorned his advice. The diocese and its insurers had now paid $10 million in settlements to Gauthe's victims, with more cases pending. Attorneys for the boys abused by Lane Fontenot in Spokane had added the Lafayette diocese to their list of defendants. Now the priest who had befriended Mouton's wife and children and in whom Ray had confided was slowly dying. Although Mouton suspected AIDS, Michael had given him a detailed explanation of Hodgkin's.

When the canonists convened in New Jersey, Mouton was surprised to see reporters. "Don't worry," Doyle told him. "The guys who planned this know what they're doing."

Like Peterson, Tom Doyle had tried privately to persuade bishops to confront the problem. Here now was a rare public opportunity for his passion for truth. He told the one hundred assembled priests that, although the number of pedophilia cases involved a "minuscule" percentage of the nation's 44,000 clerics, "It is the most serious problem that we in the church have faced in centuries." Fear of publicity, combined with "extreme moral judgmentalism in matters of sex," posed serious risks, he continued. And the first priority should be to extend the pastoral hand to afflicted families. "You don't send some imperious cleric out there to show them how bad they should feel about dragging the church's name through the mud," said Doyle.

Steve Montana, a therapist at St. Luke, spoke in place of Father Peterson. According to the *New York Times*:

> [*Montana*] *said sexual abuse of children was no more common among priests than it was among many groups that dealt with children. He said that among priests it was commonly homosexual rather than heterosexual and it was usually linked to other behavioral problems, including alcoholism.*
>
> *He said there were no effective techniques to screen out potential abusers of children before they are admitted to a seminary. He added that . . . priests who were sexually attracted to children should never be allowed to work with them.*

When Mouton's turn came, he said, "The Roman Catholic Church cannot credibly exert moral authority externally in any area where the public perceives it as incapable of maintaining moral authority internally."

On May 29 the Washington archdiocesan weekly *Catholic Standard* published a guest editorial by Monsignor Owen F. Campion. President of the Catholic Press Association and editor of a Tennessee church paper, Campion cited the *Times* story and Doyle's comments in arguing that

> *the commercial press has a responsibility to report [cases].* . . . *Their duty is to society, so that society can know and can judge those who seek to influence it.* . . .
>
> *No individual is above the civil law in this regard—nor beyond its sanctions.* . . . *The Church competes in society for loyalties. It will enjoy no such respect unless that respect is earned.*
>
> *Reporting these situations is distasteful. But it is a duty—and indeed can be an advantage.*

It was a remarkable essay for a diocesan paper, to which *Standard* editor Edgar Miller alluded in a column recalling his own years as managing editor of a Southern daily. At times, back then, Miller wrote, he had withheld information, convinced that "premature publication would do more harm than good. It's always a tough decision to make, and if I've erred it has probably been on the side of caution." He continued: "Most prior censorship is stupid, motivated out of fear and insecurity and not from a genuine concern that it would be harmful to the public."

Miller drew a contrast between the propaganda of a house organ and "trying to make a diocesan publication a newspaper rather than a mouthpiece for the diocese that owns it."

> *For the past three years, Archbishop James A. Hickey has given* The Standard *such free rein. We have published the news in many controversial situations in which people have used our columns to criticize him and his actions.*
>
> *I believe that in doing so Archbishop Hickey and the Church in Washington*

have been strengthened. . . . At the same time, we have been true to the teachings of the Church, showing that the Church, founded on the truth of the Gospel, has nothing to fear from contemporary truth.

It has been a noble experiment. It has provided an example. . . . I sincerely hope that it does not fail now.

Hickey fired Miller the day the issue was published. A week later, on June 4, the *Washington Post* quoted a church spokesman who said that the editorials "had absolutely nothing to do with it. . . . He had offered his resignation." Miller told the *Post:* "I don't dispute their right to fire me. But I think they are playing dirty pool with me by implying that I resigned the job."

The next day the *Post* reported the arrest of the Rev. Peter M. McCutcheon, thirty-four, a parish priest in suburban Maryland, for molesting two teenage boys. McCutcheon went to St. Luke. A lawsuit was filed against the archdiocese. At a late September meeting on outpatient evaluations, Peterson was coughing, and reportedly mixing up data. The next day he gave a deposition in the McCutcheon criminal case. By then other priests in the archdiocese knew he had AIDS—but not his archbishop, who became a defendant in a civil lawsuit related to Mc-Cutcheon.*

---

* McCutcheon was subsequently convicted; the lawsuits were settled after lengthy litigation.

xiii.

Labyrinths of Secrecy

My interviews with gay priests evinced a strange paradox. Frustrated by the hierarchy's moral stance, most considered themselves victims of homophobia. Bishops were obsessed with secrecy: fearing scandal, the crucial issue for them was that priests not publicly identify themselves as homosexual. Few did. But within clerical ranks many gay priests, especially those ordained after 1970, found reinforcing friendships and a culture more protective than society.

Celibacy comes from a Latin word meaning "alone." In 1974 a young Dominican, Donald Goergen, published a book called *The Sexual Celibate.* "There is a priceless solitude in celibate life," wrote Goergen, who had studied psychology at the Menninger Institute. "Solitude is found in interior peace and quiet. Silence itself is social. It is a form of human communication . . . with self, others, and God. There is the silence of listening . . . the silence of awe—for art, for nature, for God."

Rejecting Freud's notion of sexual repression as the root of neurosis, Goergen found in psychoanalyst Abraham Maslow's concept of the self-actualizing person —self-accepting, focused outside himself, not saddled with shame or guilt—a model for the celibate. "[He] has a sense of mission [and] is not as dependent upon the culture in which he finds himself for his own identity. He enjoys a greater degree of freedom from the environment and is motivated interiorly." Using psychodynamic theories to examine sexuality, Goergen told celibates not to fear themselves as sexual beings. He also told them to be patient. "Virtue is defined as an acquired disposition," he wrote, offering a theory not unlike AA's stair-step process. He continued:

> *Chastity then is acquired; it does not come all at once. It is acquired only by repeated action. It is renewed every day in our daily choices. We can in one act take the vow of chastity or commit ourselves to a life of celibacy, but we cannot in one act acquire virtue. . . . Chastity is not a state one enters but a lifelong task one chooses to live.*

Affirming the need for friendship, Goergen stressed that one's sexual identity should not be feared or renounced by the choice of celibacy. But neither of his core definitions—of celibacy and chastity—spoke of sexual *abstinence*. Celibacy is "a positive choice of the single life for the sake of Christ in response to the call of God." Chastity, he continued,

> *integrates the totality of sexuality into our lives as Christian men and women, which strives to unify the sexual and spiritual dimensions whether single or married, which universalizes affectivity in the direction of compassion and sees genitality as a sign of God's love for man by limiting it to a faithful and sustained commitment.*

The definition reflects Catholic thought as to marriage but evades the traditional premise of clerical celibacy: that a priest emulates Christ by sacrificing sexual activity for a higher plateau of love and human service.

Goergen outlined phases of homosexuality: denial and guilt, a gradual coming to terms with one's orientation, then sharing this realization with others. "Celibate homosexuality, in the positive sense, remains nongenital," he wrote. A celibate environment strengthened the homosexual orientation by bringing people together to "the exclusion of the other sex. There is no reason to fool ourselves about this. . . ." Goergen goes on:

> *When affectionate and genital feelings enter homosexual friendship, one should recognize and accept their presence. This does not mean the relationship is unhealthy. . . . Friendship between people of the same sex involves affective and erotic aspects. Limitations need to be placed on homosexual friendships lest they too become genital. These relationships as well as others require honest communication. . . . The ideal of celibate love is to be pursued.*

In addressing one of the church's taboo subjects, however compassionately, Goergen failed to consider the impact that "recognizing and accepting" homogenital feelings have on religious communities. How psychologically healthy is it to have some chaste priests and others—heterosexual and homosexual—sexually active? How should a community resolve gay-straight tensions? As the atmosphere of religious communities and seminaries changed in the 1970s, these were very real questions to which *The Sexual Celibate* seemed impervious.

Goergen himself was elected superior of the St. Albert the Great Province in Chicago. A middle-aged Dominican of Goergen's province told me of a friend who quit the order during the time of Goergen's leadership, saying, " 'Wake up. This place is as queer as it can be.' " My source continued: "It's when celibacy is flouted that charity is overpowered. . . . This goes on all the time. It's part of the ho-hum corruption that we've got to face." The solution, he said, was to "close up the seminaries. Knock out the gay vocational and formation directors. Neutralize [religious order] elections, go to Rome, and get someone appointed."

I felt sympathy for most of the gay priests I interviewed; I also found myself troubled by things some of them said. Of eighteen priests (and two who had recently resigned) I interviewed on an *NCR* assignment about gay clergy, only two claimed to have honored celibacy. (Several named bishops who they insisted were gay.) After my *NCR* report appeared in 1987, I had conversations with some two dozen other gay priests. With assurances of anonymity, some priests will confide to a journalist things they would never tell a bishop. Consider interviews by Doug Struck of the *Baltimore Sun* on the East Coast and in San Francisco:

> *"The pope has a right to disagree with me,"* shrugged one priest, who took a *two-year leave of absence to ponder the issue and decided not to give up the priesthood or his gay lover. "I had long talks with Jesus and found that anyone else he sends me is him, too."*
>
>   . . . *"I am still chaste,"* said [another] *sexually active gay priest. "I define chastity up here,"* he said, *pointing to his head and his heart, "not at the genitals."*

I was searching for a core of common values in clerical culture. The sources were unfailingly polite; after all, they were priests. As the church's liberal voice, *NCR* supported gay rights, and certain contributors were gay. My source network grew because they trusted the paper. Moving on to assignments for other publications, in hotels or friends' homes in far-flung cities, I reviewed notes and replayed tapes, trying to understand what I felt.

Richard Wagner wrote in his 1981 study about gay priests: "The sexually active priest is faced with a paradox. The same circumstances that guarantee secrecy also perpetuate the need for secrecy."

This paradox thrived in *Communication,* a newsletter for gay priests and lesbian nuns. Begun in 1977 in Philadelphia, its publisher moved to a diocese in West Virginia. In 1986 it had 400 subscribers. The anonymous letters and essays sought to draw people together for retreats and support groups. "The people we are trying to serve are often wounded and frightened," a *Communication* board member told me. Being "wounded" was part of a new cultural vocabulary. The newsletter goals were listed in a *Communication* brochure:

> • *to provide a forum for examining how to live as fully sexual persons within a religious/priestly lifestyle.*
> • *to develop a network of persons for ministry among gay and lesbian religious and clergy.*
> • *to liberate the Church toward living a whole, credible and life-giving sexual/ spiritual theology.*

As for celibacy, the editors had a caveat:

> *Experiences, insights or opinions may sometimes appear contrary to the moral teaching of the Church. They are published here, without censure, as the personal and sometimes difficult inner dialogue of our readers, in order to foster a realistic and honest exchange. They cannot be taken as the opinion of Communication Ministry Inc. or of its editors.*

"I am a layperson," wrote one reader to *Communication:*

My priest is in love with me also. However, he is in love with his priesthood as well. At the beginning, I was terrified . . . frightened of being hurt. When I stopped resisting and let this love come into my life, I began to understand a meaning, a dimension of faith, of peace, that would never have been possible without my lover. I consider myself very, very fortunate. The point is, he needs me, and I need him, and that about sums it up. And my faith has never been stronger or more meaningful.

The correspondent was unlikely to be very popular among his lover's parishioners if their relationship were known. What of the priest's honesty toward his flock?

A priest with *Communication* told me: "I believe my sexuality is part of my personality involved with the doing of love. If I am to be a healthy person, my sexuality needs to be integrated in a healthy way. We believe in a God of love. Celibacy is the absence of genital expression and I do not believe I have that gift." A few months later he spoke on the record in another paper and discussed his plight quite candidly. Booted out of the diocese by his bishop, he left the priesthood. *Communication* could not have flourished in a clerical culture which had a coherent grasp of what celibacy was and why it was necessary—and which honestly appraised sexuality.

Interviews with a range of priests demonstrated the incoherence of this clerical culture. A faculty member at a seminary near Detroit told me that, of the priests in his diocese under age forty, "comfortably one third, and maybe more are gay. . . . It becomes problematic when priests make clear in gay bars that they are gay priests. It can prove damaging to the priesthood when a priest dies of AIDS.

"I'd lie if I didn't say I'd like to go to bed with another person and hold that person," he reflected. "So how do we have significant friendships? Often people don't have the tools to live a good, deep celibate relationship. Celibacy is an attitude. I've seen gay men coming out who lose discretion. We're in the business of building people's faith lives, and because we're public witnesses to those people, tampering with that role is something I take very seriously. It concerns me."

A middle-aged man in a Washington suburb, recently resigned from the priesthood, said that he had been sexually active for years. "I was happy ministering to families, and I believe I did it well. I never thought of [sexually] approaching a kid. There was duplicity, though, and I got tired of it. I wanted to live as a free person. I had to address that I am who I am. I couldn't stand up there and tell the parish something else. The church is a haven for homosexuals. Older priests in the closet tend to be envious of younger priests who are more out front about it. Every gay priest I know is sexually active, without exception. I would estimate in this archdiocese that forty percent are gay, forty percent straight, and twenty percent are nonsexual."

A woman who grew up in his parish and knew him well said: "When I was a kid we were crazy about him. He was a very good priest and I consider him a good friend."

He still celebrated weekly Mass, wearing vestments, in his living room or at a country house he shared with his lover.

"It's a club," opined a young man who quit a Northern seminary, as we ate in a

Washington restaurant on a warm June day in 1986. "They have a come-on line: 'You'll never have to worry about anything as long as you're with me.'" He gave me names of several priests in what he called the local club.

"By 'club' you mean a subculture of gay priests?"

"That's another way of putting it, yes." He mentioned a black priest, George Stallings, whose rectory was a showplace of antiques. Adolescent boys were said to be overnight guests. I asked if church officials knew. "Maybe not." He shrugged. "But other priests do."

A priest who had known Stallings for years told me that his flamboyant life-style was well known among gay priests in the archdiocese. In the mid-seventies, under Cardinal Baum, Stallings had been a vocational director, recruiting young men for seminary. The priest did not know whether Stallings had molested two young people (as the *Washington Post* would later report) or how much Archbishop Hickey knew about Stallings. "Nothing about George would surprise me," the priest chuckled.

By June 1986 some fifty sex abuse cases involving priests had surfaced nation-wide. "I think it has to do with isolation in a rectory," the priest said. "Some of them have left. They become like names on a roster. I was with one who was literally run out of the diocese for his involvement with teenage girls. It was very strange indeed. They shipped him to a Midwestern parish. After two years he suddenly resigned because the church wasn't sympathetic to homosexuals. He used to tell me about his sessions at night with young men on the road. He was my pastor."

"What would you say to him about this?" I asked.

"I was working out my own problems. I said, 'You know, I have to live in peace. I cannot live in tension.' The number one source of tension is rectory life. The biggest problem in priestly personnel is who to place with whom." He mentioned a priest in the suburbs, "an outstanding man, who studied in Rome. He couldn't get along with his pastor, so he just left. The pastor is a guy picking up truckers at a truck stop, getting beat up. What is happening here? There is no incentive for doing anything. All I have to do is say Mass. There is no account-ability. There are so many priests with deep-seated problems."

"Are you celibate?" I asked.

He paused. "I don't know what to consider myself. I'm not very sexually active now. I go out several nights a week to gay places. I lost two good priest friends over this. They were very active sexually, with pickups or erstwhile lovers. They said, 'You're the one causing scandal, by publicly associating [with gays]. We're *quietly* active.'"

I had met few men so disillusioned and felt sorry for him. He said: "The best priests, they say, supposedly left during the *Humanae Vitae* controversy. That left a huge leadership vacuum.

"Officially," he continued, "there are no Dignity chaplains in D.C. A few do it unofficially. But that takes its toll. You become too hot. Baltimore is light-years ahead of us in terms of gay ministry. Many of our priests are sexually active, gay, closeted, alcoholic, but they won't be caught dead in a gay ministry be cause it involves being exposed. This diocese is homophobic. Nothing is said. Everything is secret. There've been some priests spying on me, spying on Dignity—who attends Mass, who celebrates—compiling files to give people in the chancery."

Evidence of this tattered trust reached Hickey in late 1985, when a survey of archdiocesan priests found "widespread dissatisfaction with work and living conditions and some estrangement from their bishop," as reporter Vincent Golphin wrote in *NCR*. Hickey invited priests to a February 1986 meeting to "sit down as brothers and see how tensions [can] be resolved. . . . Some of us feel overwhelmed with work, some not fully appreciated. Some find parish or archdiocesan structures heavy; others, perhaps, wish simply to 'go it alone.' " The survey impetus came from priests. All but ten of the archdiocese's 250 priests attended the meeting. One of them told Golphin: "Priests were saying [to Hickey], 'We want to know you, know who you are, and we want you to know us.' "

Golphin continued:

> *Some said Hickey merely inherited clerical unrest. . . . Major complaints at the meeting, sources said, ranged from priests' personal feelings of loneliness and inadequacy to what one priest described as "a residue of bitterness and resentment" concerning a 1968 archdiocesan dispute about the encyclical* Humanae Vitae.

As Cardinal O'Boyle had defended the birth control ban, it was Hickey, via Cardinal Ratzinger in Rome, who took up the task of guarding church ramparts against a host of sexual questions that wouldn't go away. After the 1968 debacle, a group of U.S. bishops drafted a document defending theological dissent "only if the reasons are serious and well-founded, if the manner of dissent does not impugn the teaching authority of the church and is such as not to give scandal." In his March 6, 1986, visit with Ratzinger, Father Curran had offered not to teach sexual ethics and conceded that his work was "at variance" with the magisterium. On August 18 the Vatican stripped him of his teaching license as a theologian. Curran announced that he would appeal the decision to CUA's board of trustees. The next day Archbishop Hickey (who was also university chancellor) stated that the bishops' norms on dissent were "simply unworkable," provoking outcries from Catholic theologians across North America, 750 of whom supported Curran on grounds of academic freedom. A number of bishops voiced misgivings about Hickey's statement.

How many Catholic colleges would welcome a theologian so denounced by Rome? CUA offered Curran a position in another department, which he refused. After his internal appeal failed, Curran sued CUA for unfair employment practices. The Court ruled that it had no jurisdiction. In 1991, after visiting-scholar positions at Cornell, Southern Cal, and Auburn, Curran accepted a tenured chair at Southern Methodist in Dallas. (No Catholic university would hire him.)

The same week Curran was sacked, Terrance Sweeney of Los Angeles was ordered by his Jesuit superior to destroy results of a survey he had taken of the U.S. hierarchy. Sweeney resigned from the priesthood and released his findings: almost a fourth of responding bishops approved of optional celibacy, and thirty percent supported the ordination of women deacons.

Ecclesiastical culture was driven by secrecy, from Vatican officials who would brook no dissent to gay priests willing to tell all, provided their identities were shrouded. Contraception, marriage for priests, ministerial roles for women, even roles for altar girls were being proscribed by members of a male hierarchy busy covering up the swelling homosexuality in its own ranks.

Ironically, for some bishops homosexual activity by priests posed an ambiguous threat to celibacy, as evidenced by civil depositions taken in 1985. Michigan attorney Mark Bello brought suit against the Detroit archdiocese on behalf of a young molestation victim. In discovery, Bello asked if homosexuality violated celibacy. The late Cardinal John Dearden, who was then the city's retired prelate, gave the official position that homosexuality "would be immoral for any person, at least objectively," and "would be a violation of [a priest's] obligation of celibacy in a sense over and above, if you will, the immorality of the act itself."

Auxiliary Bishop Thomas Gumbleton gave Bello a different answer: "Active homosexuality would not violate the vow of celibacy or the promise of celibacy. It violates the sixth commandment [Thou shalt not commit adultery]."

Bishop Joseph Imesch of Joliet, Illinois, had been a Detroit auxiliary when the crimes occurred. Bello asked if homosexuality violated the promise of celibacy, and he said: "Sure."

> Bello: What do you feel, or do you know, is the penalty for violation of these promises?
>
> Imesch: Eternal hellfire. I—you know, what's the penalty? Put in that I laughed.
>
> Bello: At the question or the answer?
>
> Imesch: There is no penalty. The penalty—that's the moral failing or fault with the person.

A fourth deponent, Father William Costigan, answered that "violating the oath of celibacy I understand to be that [a priest] would consort with some person who is not his partner, a person of the opposite sex."

In the definitive 1151-page Code of Canon Law: Text and Commentary (Paulist Press, 1985), I found but two references to homosexuality—as grounds for marriage annulment. Never has Vatican concern for homosexuality outweighed the perception of women as the greater threat to priestly service. Perhaps this attitude has encouraged the rising number of homosexual clergy. Nevertheless, any priest —homosexual or heterosexual—could fall from his pledge of chastity, pick up, and carry on, so long as he did not cause grave scandal. It was left to each bishop to decide what constituted scandal.

Of course, no one has been more responsible for the church's hard-line stance on matters of sexuality than John Paul II. Acknowledged now by many as one of the great heroes who helped bring about the collapse of Communism in Eastern Europe, he has been unbending in his opposition to changing the sexual teachings of the church. Was his ethos irreconcilably split between an adherence to political liberty and an adherence to rules governing sexual intimacy little changed in centuries?

Anthony Kosnik, a Detroit theologian fluent in Polish, offered insight on John Paul II's papacy. In 1976, as dean of Sts. Cyril and Methodius Seminary, Father Kosnik visited Cracow for Poland's mid-decade theological congress. He was a guest of Cardinal Karol Wojtyla, who would become Pope two years later. "I expected fifty people," Kosnik recalled in a 1986 interview. "When I arrived, there were eight hundred priests from all disciplines. Cardinal Wojtyla offered Mass each morning. Two thirds of the Polish hierarchy was there. All questions were submitted in writing. The cardinal was clearly in charge. He was also chief of dialogue with the Communist Party."

That uniformity of discipline, so different from the sprawling U.S. church, partially accounts for John Paul II's rigidity on matters of personal morality. Kosnik considered Poland "a success story when you look at how much they have endured under Communism. The Polish church didn't change much after Vatican II. Under opposition from the government, they couldn't afford to tolerate the diversity. John Paul's greatest concern is the confusion people have about faith. It's his conviction that he was chosen by God to bring unity to the church and to restore certainty of faith."

"There is no questioning of authority," he continued. "But no one could undermine church authority as well as they're doing it themselves. They're forcing people to take initiatives of their own, as in birth control, and now other issues. The magisterium feels very justified because of studies that show cancer can be caused by the pill and IUD problems. . . . The idea that we're special because we're celibate is terribly damaging. That isolationist mentality creates a clerical preserve. It gives people grounds for thinking they're superior. The Roman Curia has no real contact with the real world. That's the deformation."

ii.

During the early and mid-1980s, Archbishop (later Cardinal) Hickey of Washington, D.C., battled issues related to homosexuality on many fronts. In 1980, students called Gay People of Georgetown University began demanding recognition as a campus group. This meant the right to advertise in student publications and to use student funds for outside lecturers. Georgetown President Timothy Healy, S.J., refused "because it would be an inappropriate endorsement for a Catholic university." The District of Columbia, however, had passed a Human Rights Act which barred discrimination, including that based on sexual preference. A gay group at the GU Law School joined the campus group in a suit before D.C. Superior Court that accused Georgetown of violating the city ordinance. Which constitutional right held precedent: a Catholic university's exercise of religion, or the gay group's freedom of assembly and speech?

In October 1983 a judge ruled that the D.C. act denied Georgetown's religious freedom. In July 1985 a three-judge panel reversed the lower court 2–1 but vacated its own opinion and referred the case to the entire appellate court for consideration. Father Healy eventually decided to halt litigation. GU agreed to pay the other side's attorney fees, absorbed a total of $750,000 in legal expenses, and allowed the group to function on campus, with tangible benefits, while not endorsing its position. Archbishop Hickey had wanted Georgetown to pursue its appeal to the Supreme Court. But the constitutional issue was never resolved.

At about the same time Hickey also began pressuring Vatican superiors of Robert Nugent and Jeannine Gramick to expel them from his diocese. But since New Ways Ministry, which they founded, had no canonical standing, Hickey had no control over the modest frame house in the Maryland suburb where New Ways staffers planned projects and disseminated literature. "The institutional church has a lot of restitution to make for its sins and prejudices and for the guilt it has heaped on lesbians and gay people," Gramick charged. "Lesbians and gays are willing and eager to have a reconciliation." To Hickey, reconciliation with New Ways' agenda meant appeasement. "We believe that gays can express their sexuality in a manner that is consistent with Christ's teaching," stated Dignity literature which New Ways disseminated. "We believe that all sexuality should be exercised in an ethically responsible and unselfish way." This was dangerously open-ended language to Hickey. As Dignity members met for weekly Mass at the Georgetown campus, Nugent and Gramick were drawing media coverage of their lectures. Meanwhile, Hickey was sending information on Dignity to Ratzinger, who was at work on a document about homosexuality.

And although it was not publicly known then, Hickey in 1985 was experiencing a painful erosion of his once benevolent relationship with George Stallings. Hickey had come to Stallings's aid in 1972, when the twenty-four-year-old seminarian at the Pontifical North American College went home to North Carolina on summer break and ran afoul of his local bishop for sporting a mustache. Born poor, Augustus George Stallings, Jr., was only the third black in the college's 111-year history. When the bishop refused to allow his return to Rome, Stallings appealed to Hickey, the college rector, who arranged his transfer to the Washington archdiocese and allowed the resumption of his Vatican studies.

Ordained in Washington in 1974, Stallings proved a charismatic orator. As his inner city parish flourished, Stallings filled the rectory with antiques. When parish council members protested he flew into a rage. He also held back a portion of Sunday collections which was due the archdiocese. In 1985, when he stopped making the payments altogether, the parish's debt was approaching six figures. That summer he paid $60,000 for an old two-story house and began an $80,000 restoration. *Washingtonian* dubbed it the "Jewel of Anacostia." Stallings privately referred to his home as Augustus Manor, publicly claiming that he purchased the house out of his earnings as a visiting evangelizer on a national circuit of black parishes.

In a 1990 series in the *Washington Post,* reporters Bill Dedman and Laura Sessions Stepp found that in 1979 a parishioner complained "that Stallings held parties at St. Theresa rectory and had men visit at odd hours." An archdiocesan official said that "the source of complaints was unable or unwilling to specify allegations regarding possible sexual misconduct." In 1982, a pastoral assistant had quit after finding Stallings and a fourteen-year-old boy naked in a rectory bedroom. Stallings claimed they were taking a bath after jogging. His pulpit charisma made Stallings a commanding figure to his flock. When Hickey twice asked him to take a new parish, parishioners protested and he remained pastor. Exactly how much Hickey knew about Stallings's sexual activities is unclear; but in 1985 Hickey twice asked him to pursue further studies in Rome, a convenient way of pulling him out of his environment while keeping him within Hickey's canonical authority. Stallings would have none of it. He also accepted into his rectory a priest who had been suspended from his religious order for making sexual advances to adolescent males. In 1989, when Hickey ordered Stallings to enter the Paraclete monks' hospital in New Mexico, Stallings blasted the church for being racist and launched the breakaway Imani Temple. The *Post* subsequently reported statements by two young men that Stallings had molested them when they were altar boys. Accusing the *Post* of racism, Stallings trumpeted his support of Marion Barry in the then mayor's unsuccessful battle against drug charges and emerged as a folk hero to many embittered blacks.

Moreover, in mid-November 1985, Hickey, who was about to call his priests for a plenary meeting, experienced an open rebuke on the matter of homosexuality from twenty-seven religious orders. "Against [Hickey's] fierce objections," Religious News Service reported, the orders

> *have set in motion a nationwide discussion of what they say is a growing number of homosexuals among communities of priests, sisters and brothers.*
>
> *"The communities are dealing with gay and lesbian people within their own orders already, or among those who are applying for admittance, and non-gays ministering to gays," said John Gallagher, [New Ways] spokesman for a conference held here on the subject last weekend. . . .*
>
> *Of the 43 sponsoring groups, about 16 have chosen not to identify themselves publicly because of the sensitive and controversial nature of the topic, Gallagher said. . . . [G]roups openly endorsing the effort include regional branches of the Leadership Conference of Women Religious, which represents the superiors of women religious orders, provinces of the Sisters of Mercy and Sisters of Notre Dame, Friars of Atonement, and the National Conference of Religious Vocation Directors, a group of seminary and vocation counselors.*

Hickey sent a letter to area clergy, nuns, and seminarians, forbidding Mass at the conference, reiterating his opposition to New Ways. The conference went ahead anyway. With so much confusion about the moral meanings of sexual intimacy, little wonder morale was low among priests.

Two strains of clericalism were crawling along edges of a psychosexual fault line. In Hickey, a hard, Irish, sex-negative tradition of celibacy sublimated sexual energy into a power dynamic more medieval than antidemocratic. Steeped in spiritual life and splendors of ceremony, in sixteen-hour days of executive toil, planning, raising money, building, preaching, fueling the infrastructure and support system of priests and nuns, Hickey's leadership was a Roman tradition premised on obedience to authority. Moral teachings came with the territory, and homosexuality was a front-line dispute. Under Washington's microscopic media eye, Hickey was Rome's messenger and the church as he saw it was under attack.

The terrain of gay clergy, much murkier, teemed with unresolved erotic impulses and bitterness toward the church's stance on gay lifestyles, on the very meanings of homosexuality. Yet the same homophobic church allowed ample freedom to gay clergy provided they not publicly act out. Secrecy dominated both sides. Hickey, with a public line to defend, wanted to avoid scandal. So did Bob Nugent and Jeannine Gramick, who had serious concerns about promiscuity and felt that affirming the homosexual orientation would help gay clerics maintain celibacy. Rome and the U.S. bishops saw the gay issue in starkly different terms.

iii.

"Baltimore is light-years ahead of us in terms of gay ministry," a Washington priest had said. Fifty miles away, the nation's oldest archdiocese had 500,000 Catholics. In Baltimore the eighteenth-century Jesuit, John Carroll, was elected by fellow priests as the first archbishop born on American soil.

In the mid-1970s a handful of gays made regular trips to Washington for Dignity meetings. At the time the late Cardinal Sheehan had refused to let "those people" meet on church property. As the group grew, they began meeting in Father Joseph Hughes's home in a blue-collar Baltimore neighborhood. By 1986, Dignity was holding a weekly Mass at a downtown church whose pastor (not gay) told me that when he had asked his parish council, no one objected.

Don Miller, a housing activist, helped establish the Dignity chapter. Miller was fifty in June 1986. He had Kaposi's sarcoma, the dreaded cancer associated with AIDS that gives the skin purple lesions. "We established the official ministry in response to Archbishop Borders's letter saying no to a gay rights ordinance," said Miller. "That was in 1980. I sent an open letter to the archbishop, and at first he wouldn't meet with me."

Father Hughes asked Borders to meet with Miller, who pitched his case for an archdiocesan ministry to homosexuals. Although he maintained his opposition to the ordinance, the prelate authorized a task force, chaired by Hughes, out of which was formed Archdiocesan Gay and Lesbian Outreach (AGLO) in 1981.

Borders had solid precedent for his gesture. In 1976 the U.S. bishops issued a pastoral letter, "To Live in Christ Jesus," which recognized homosexuals in a more Christian light:

> Some people find themselves, through no fault of their own, to have a homosexual orientation. Homosexuals, like everyone else, should not suffer from prejudice against their basic human rights. They have a right to respect, friendship and justice. They should have an active role in the Christian community. Homosexual activity, however, as distinguished from homosexual orientation, is morally wrong.

AGLO provided spiritual counseling designed to strengthen ties between gays and lesbians and the church. Dignity was AGLO's alter ego. "When I was a Dignity chair," said Miller, "and someone wanted a priest, I'd refer them to priests who were supportive of the human person—in deeper spiritual life, in terms of self-worth. Some clergy still carry that attitude of, 'Here is a great sinner'—implying that a person has to rid himself of homosexuality. . . . Dignity is trying to develop a code of sexual ethics. Can you be gay, [sexually] practicing and a member of the church in good standing? Bishops officially say no. If someone is having an affair or sexual encounter, who is to judge whether it's not more caring or meaningful than some people have in long-term relationships? The argument is, Do gays want to model themselves on heterosexual relationships? The church has always reacted. But once it gets involved, it moves. That's why I always said, locally, we've got to work with the archbishop."

Joe Hughes was a tall, mild-mannered priest with graying sandy hair. I asked how he counseled gay people about sex. "The same as with women about birth control," he replied. "I explain the church teaching, and then offer theological alternatives. Church teaching is in many ways one of ideals—the best you can do. It's not infallible doctrine; it's official teaching. Not practicing birth control could be hindering the value of human life. What is more important: the value or the rule? You can't handle something like this in the pulpit. I don't think the church has made use of the findings of sciences. She locks up the rules; you have to have a license to be a sexual person. When the church speaks of homosexuality, she's always speaking of genital sex. There's more to being a homosexual than genitals. Most of the outreach I do has nothing to do with sexual acts."

He mentioned a young man "extremely upset because he was gay. He was going out at night, picking up people. He was really looking for acceptance, affection, not just sex. Being promiscuous was making him unhappy. Once he began to accept himself as a person who was looking for a very normal thing, someone of the same gender, he worked through it.

"A lot of people who are promiscuous have never dealt with their sexuality. Until I was almost forty, not only did I not realize I was gay, I didn't give any respect to the fact that I was a sexual person. Good Catholic boys didn't think about sex. You had dirty thoughts and you said three Hail Marys. I've seen *so many* religious who at age forty are preadolescents because they have completely repressed anything sexual. Adolescence is adolescence, whether you're fourteen or forty."

"It seems that, for a lot of gay priests, part of their pressure is not being able to identify themselves as gay," I said.

"I don't think it's different from any gay person," said Hughes. "Part of their stress is not being able to come out."

"A gay priest can come out within the gay community, secure that he will never be identified," I said. "I'm wondering whether a subculture becomes a competing lifestyle with what most Catholics expect of priests."

"Well, no. Gay people are as varied as straight people. I hate the term 'gay lifestyle' because there are many lifestyles gay people have. My gay friends are not part of the bars. They have their jobs, their professions; sitting around a room with gay and lesbian people is no different than sitting with straight people. Being gay does not have to permeate a person's life."

"I wonder, though," I said. "I interviewed a priest in Washington the other day who spent a long period going to bars. Does this compete with the traditional lifestyle of a parish priest, to be a role model to youngsters and an integral part of families?"

"Well, I don't know. It depends on what he's going to the bars for. I spend time in gay bars. It's professional for one thing: that's where gay people are. Straight priests go out to parties, wedding receptions, theaters, and it doesn't mean anything. So why can't a gay priest go out with people he can relate to? It used to be said that one of the safest places in Washington for a terminally ill Catholic to be on a Saturday night was the Lost and Found—a gay bar—because there were more Catholic priests there than any place else in the world"—and thus available to anoint the dying man with last rites.

"Why is the percentage of homosexuals so much higher among priests than in the general population?"

"I think the religious life *attracts*. In my day a good Catholic boy either got married and had a bunch of kids or he went into religious life. I was twenty-seven when I went in. I had obligations at home. But I'd always wanted to be a priest. Never went all the way"—meaning intercourse with a woman; he smiled—"now I realize I never *wanted* to go all the way. You feel like you're good, you're not drawn to that. And this doesn't have to be conscious or erotic, but if you're same-sex oriented, you're drawn to a life surrounded with guys. Sooner or later, the church is going to have to face up. Why can't a person be gay and a good seminarian, a good priest, a good religious? They don't want to sneak around keeping their mouth shut."

I asked what he thought of homosexually active priests. "The same thing about straight priests who have relationships. I don't make moral judgments. My biggest problem is the hypocrisy. The sexuality of it doesn't bother me in the least. The real perversion is mandatory celibacy. It's unnatural. The church says genital sex is a gift from God, meant to express love; then she says we can only do it if we're male and female. Something's wrong here." For Hughes, the celibacy issue involved what parishioners would think. "I would very much like a relationship," he reflected, "but I would have a great problem in dealing with that."

If gaining acceptability in Christian culture propelled Dignity and the gay clergy movement, what ideals and images, what moral witness and acts of renewal did they offer Catholics? In my travels I met another priest, who was in his late forties and held a good church post in an Eastern city. We met in his office. "Historically, I think a lot of gay men have gone into priesthood as a way of sublimating particular drives," he said. "The first time I went into a gay bar I saw four other priests: *here for the same reason I am*, I thought. I don't think it's anything to be ashamed of. They're as chaste as heterosexual priests."

After a five-year relationship with another man, he was currently "practicing celibacy—lest I scandalize you," he chuckled. Then he turned serious. "If our homosexual priests don't keep vows, isn't it great that we can be leading the church toward a married clergy? We need human, intimate relationships. It's much easier for the gay priest to throw off celibacy because he's learned to hide his orientation, be affirmed in the gay community, whereas the nongay priest experiences greater guilt with women. He can't throw off church teaching so easily."

I asked how the gay community viewed its sexually active priests. "The gay community does tend to affirm priests who have known relationships with others. I don't think that should be distorted out of context. A nongay priest—I prefer nongay to 'straight,' which implies that gay people are bent—is going to be affirmed also, but he doesn't have a community to support it."

His own sexual awakening had come through his involvement with Dignity. "The priest celebrating Mass was unprepared, so I offered my services. I got in touch with feeling very comfortable with my orientation. I eventually fell in love with someone outside the city and had to decide did I want to leave the priesthood. And I decided to do both. [Dignity] people were affirming; some were upset. But we discussed it. If it was going to be a source of scandal I would have broken off the relationship or discontinued my priesthood. But I worked through with them my being a priest and a lover in a genital relationship. It enhanced my priesthood. I became an alive person. When I went to funeral homes or jails or hospitals, I could empathize with people. I knew what it meant to lose a wife or husband." The relationship broke up "for various reasons. One of them, that for thirty-five years I'd lived a bachelor lifestyle. There was also the problem of distance."

I asked about the significance of sex abuse cases involving priests and adolescent boys. "It's often said that too many people in the gay community are too youth-oriented," he said. "But heterosexual men are drawn to nubile young women. I've only run up against a chicken hawk once in ten years. I'm not saying I don't admire a young kid. I might five years from now." He smiled. "I think most want relationships with peers." He winked.

"I don't see anything wrong with forty-five-year-olds having relationships with twenty-five-year-olds," he continued, comfortable with his topic. "When you get down into teenage years, it's a question. On the other hand, it's sometimes young people coming on to the older person."

"The parish priest has always been a role model for young boys. Do you think there's a conflict?"

His eyes flashed angrily. "Thank God there's finally a gay priest who can be a role model to gay boys in that school! We've got to worry about them, that ten percent. Those heterosexual boys have fathers, uncles, other priests. Who does the homosexual boy have? They need healthy, homosexual role models. So you ask what parents and grandparents will think—that's a problem, sure. But it's gonna solve other problems.

"That's why we need education—to tell people homosexuality is not something to be ashamed of, not a sickness, that it's natural. And if we teach people, they don't have to get upset. . . . My God, it would have been so much more helpful to me when I was growing up if there was someone I could have looked up to and said, 'Hey, this man is attracted to persons of the same sex and there's nothing wrong with that.' You've gotta be in touch with those feelings. When you're raised to think of yourself as sick, you don't root it out of your thinking, out of your feelings, out of your emotional response to life. So even though I've changed drastically in the last ten or eleven years, there's a little corner inside me saying, *You're no good.*

"If I had to do it over," he continued, "I would not have joined the priesthood because I do not feel called to celibacy."

"Why don't you leave?"

"Because I'm a darned good priest! I'm doing excellent work. I'm valuable, and they're losing too many priests as it is. I'm able to judge that even though I'm not called to celibacy. Right now it's not an issue because I'm not in a loving relationship."

The circles of his logic had knotted around my thoughts as the sun began to set. Exhausted by our talk, I thanked him and walked in the heat to a taxi stand, brooding about his casual concept of celibacy. And that wink and smile: was the guy really making a pass at me? What a stupid thing to do in an interview with a reporter. Should I have confronted him about it? Then what . . . Out of my memory floated the sonorous cadences of Deacon Frank Lastie, a jazz patriarch who introduced drumming into spiritual churches of New Orleans in 1929, and in a moving sermon on the human condition many years later said: "My, my, my! *What's about us today?"*

xiv.

The Vatican Crackdown

In early September 1986, as bishops awaited Cardinal Ratzinger's document on homosexuality, an ailing Michael Peterson flew with Tom Doyle to upstate Michigan, for a clergy conference day on pedophilia. Now a military chaplain and commissioned officer, Doyle had not seen the gaunt Peterson in weeks. *He's really strung out,* he thought. At the hotel Michael retired early.

Unable to read, Doyle kept thinking about Michael. When Doyle's Air Force physical exam showed high blood pressure, Michael sent him to a specialist who outfitted him with a monitor strapped around his bicep that deflated every fifteen minutes like a fart. Never worried about his own skin, Michael always cared about other people. *What the hell's going on?* Tom Doyle said to God. *This is Your church and it's all screwed up. I am looking for something that will help make some sense out of this.* A priest who said the rosary every day, Doyle prayed that Michael would live. *He's as much a part of the system as archbishops.*

Ray Mouton arrived the next morning, elated to see his friends. Doyle's calls had grown less frequent since their urgent work on the 1985 report, now buried between the NCCB and USCC in Washington. Peterson was in good form for his first speech.

Doyle, who had duties at the military vicariate in Silver Spring, Maryland, gave Mouton a Celtic cross and departed with the usual "I'll be in touch." Doyle realized that this was the last time they would work as a threesome. In the airplane, sipping tomato juice, he got a lump in his throat. *This is a hell of an ending to what we have started,* he thought. Then he wept.

Peterson slept through the afternoon. After dinner he gave Mouton medals depicting St. Luke, one for each member of his family; these were the same medals given to priests who completed the Suitland program. He began trembling; Mouton helped him to his bedroom. The next morning they flew to another clergy conference, in Gaylord, Michigan. At the podium, Peterson's hands trembled as he spoke. *It's AIDS,* Mouton thought. He was spent, fever-chilled, with sores like insect bites. "Hodgkin's is like AIDS," Peterson had said and

Mouton chose to leave it at that. No priest had done more for his faith as his bitterness had grown toward the church.

As Mouton spoke, the blank stares of priests gave him the impression that they were bored. On impulse he said something that he had never said before: since none of them had children, the thought of a child being sodomized was more horrific to him, a parent. Even the most empathetic priest could not feel the outrage of a parent whose son had been violated. "You were too tough on them, Ray," said Peterson after the session.

"I don't give a damn, Michael," came the cynical chuckle.

Ray's wife Janis, who adored Michael, was sure he was gay and Ray realized that subconsciously he had known it too. It made no difference. Michael's friendship had been a bright lining throughout their disillusioning experience with the church. Mouton believed that men surrounded by homosexuality—and hence without children—become desensitized to the way families live. Even Michael showed signs of that. His first concern had been the quality of tests run on Gauthe. Then he had asked about church officials' depositions. Only after that had he focused on how the boys were being treated. He approached victims in an abstract way, insisting that he did not know enough about them: it was not his field.

Mouton experienced a stabbing sense of loss. However sick he was, at least Michael sought solutions. The previous March, after his return from Rome, Peterson had told Mouton of Cardinal Oddi's promise that "a document is being prepared"—and Mouton wondered whether in this document Rome would acknowledge the crisis. Now the rumor mill was buzzing about an imminent letter from Cardinal Ratzinger. Mouton realized that, where Peterson viewed the bishops' cover-up mentality as a normal psychological product of Byzantine ecclesiastical ways, Doyle viewed the cover-up with increasing anger. Tom *believed* in the church, believed that bishops should confront evil as true spiritual shepherds. Time and again they had let him down. As Peterson sank into chilly sleep Mouton felt a piece of himself ebbing away. His family rarely attended Mass. He was sick of long-distance calls from defense attorneys, while cover-ups abounded. Doyle wanted him to continue these clergy presentations. To what end? Bishops had set themselves on a collision course with the courts.

On October 30, 1986, Rome released Ratzinger's global letter to bishops, "Pastoral Care of Homosexual Persons." The church, wrote Ratzinger, was "in a position to learn from scientific discovery but also to transcend the horizons of science and to be confident that her more global vision does greater justice to the rich reality of the human person. . . ."

Disputing new scientific approaches to homosexuality, the third paragraph carried a sonic boom: "Although the particular inclination of the homosexual person is not a sin, it is more or less a strong tendency ordered toward an intrinsic moral evil; and thus the inclination itself must be seen as an objective disorder." Ratzinger contradicted the U.S. bishops' 1976 letter that had welcomed those "who through no fault of their own" found themselves to be homosexual. The sexual faculty was "morally good only in marriage," he wrote. Homosexual activity was "self-indulgent" and could not "transmit life." Though not named in the letter, Dignity, the gay Catholic group at odds with church teaching, was the focus of an unmistakable message:

The movement within the Church, which takes the form of pressure groups of various names and sizes, attempts to give the impression that it represents all homosexual persons who are Catholics. As a matter of fact, its membership is by and large restricted to those who either ignore the teaching of the Church or seek somehow to undermine it. It brings together under the aegis of Catholicism homosexual persons who have no intention of abandoning their homosexual behavior. One tactic used is to protest that any and all criticism of or reservations about homosexual people, their activity and lifestyle, are simply diverse forms of unjust discrimination.

Ratzinger also said it was "deplorable" that homosexuals "are the object of violent malice in speech or in action. Such treatment deserves condemnation from the Church's pastors whenever it occurs." Then he dropped another bomb, faulting gay rights laws for gay bashing:

But the proper reaction to crimes committed against homosexual persons should not be to claim that the homosexual condition is not disordered. When such a claim is made and when homosexual activity is consequently condoned, or when civil legislation is introduced to protect behavior to which no one has any conceivable right, neither the Church nor society at large should be surprised when other distorted notions and practices gain ground, and irrational and violent reactions increase.

The letter hardly hinted at the possibility of care and loving affection among gays and lesbians. If God saw fit to imprint homosexuality on the fabric of humankind, how could a church of love demand, as Ratzinger did in the letter, that all homosexuals carry a cross denying what for them was the most profound expression of love?

Within weeks of the letter's publication, various bishops ordered Dignity chapters to cease holding Mass in Catholic churches unless the chapters accepted church teaching. In response Dignity members called the document the "Halloween letter" because of its October 30 release. The Jesuit author John McNeill broke his ten-year imposed silence, calling the document "almost diabolical. . . . Part of the issue has always been [church officials'] own fear of being unwilling to deal honestly and openly with their own fears of their own sexuality." McNeill thus violated an order from Peter-Hans Kolvenbach, S.J., the Superior-General in Rome, who on Ratzinger's orders had warned him to remain silent. He was expelled from the Jesuits after forty years in the order. "What is most likely to disturb the broadest segment of the Catholic community," editorialized *NCR*, "is the document's uncharitable and, therefore, unbelievable character."

Ratzinger's letter was part of a larger Vatican crackdown. On September 4, Auxiliary Bishop Donald Wuerl of Seattle announced that he was assuming authority over Archbishop Raymond J. Hunthausen in such key areas as the marriage tribunal, formation of seminarians, and ministry to homosexuals. Rome's unprecedented move was humiliating to the popular prelate, "Dutch" Hunthausen, whose problems apparently began with his 1980 pastoral letter advocating a greater role for women "in all forms of service, especially in the uniquely ecclesial areas of word and sacrament."

An outspoken critic of U.S. nuclear arms, Hunthausen withheld part of his 1982 taxes in protest, infuriating conservatives in a regional economy that relied on defense industries. "Like most American bishops, he lacked the guile and desire to play politics in the Vatican style," wrote *NCR* correspondent Penny Lernoux. But Hunthausen's maverick streak was tempered by piety. Although the Pacific Northwest had one of the nation's lowest rates of religious worship, two thirds of the archdiocese's Catholics attended Mass regularly, compared to fifty-three percent nationwide.

Conservative Catholics blasted Hunthausen for failing to uphold moral teachings. They sent letters to Rome, with editorial backing from *The Wanderer*, an ultra-right Catholic weekly published in St. Paul, Minnesota. On the crucial gay issue, Hunthausen was caught between competing forces: traditional Catholics opposed to any approval of homosexuals, and a gay community that considered him a protector, of sorts. Privately, a friend says, Hunthausen was troubled by the gay priest culture; yet he felt compassion for homosexuals.

Ratzinger had sent Archbishop Hickey of Washington, D.C., to investigate the Seattle archdiocese in 1983. But it was Bishop Wuerl's arrival in Seattle in 1985 that signaled the punitive manner in which the Vatican wished to handle Hunthausen. At forty-five, Wuerl was a generation younger than Hunthausen and otherwise his opposite. A skilled careerist with three degrees from Rome, he was invested as a bishop in 1985. Soon after, he was dispatched to Seattle where Hunthausen loyalists sized him up as an agent of the Vatican's persecution. "The broad governance of the archdiocese is still my primary responsibility," Hunthausen told reporters when the deal was announced, "shared in collegial fashion with Bishop Wuerl." But there was nothing collegial about it and everyone knew it.

With Hunthausen in mind, Eugene Kennedy, writing in the *NCR* edition covering Ratzinger's letter on homosexuality, remarked on the pain felt by "the great moderate center" not from "uncovering hard truths" but by being "spiritually debased" at the hands of Rome's arbitrary exercises of power. He continued in a description of the manner of such increasing power moves, whether coming from Rome or from local bishops:

> *[A]n underlying dynamic, recognized or not, is indeed that of asexual assault, marked by strategies of degradation, on good people.*
>
> *Asexuality connotes a lack of personal development, an immaturity characterized by a failure to achieve adequate differentiation of sexual identity. It is observed in many persons who use power to dominate others. The gratification experienced from this asexual mode of functioning is in some sense a substitute for mature sexual gratification.*
>
> *The assault is asexual because its term is not enlarged human relationship as much as the exercise of self-referent power. Asexuality is blind to family values, to the generativity that is the hallmark of a sound community. . . .*

ii.

When the NCCB convened in Washington on November 10, 1986, the Pope sent a rare seven-page letter, expressing "fraternal solidarity," with the sharp reminder that they were "and must always be, in full communion with the successor of St. Peter." Bishop James W. Malone of Youngstown, Ohio, the conference president, said that the closed session was "simply . . . to offer fraternal support to Archbishop Hunthausen and Bishop Wuerl. . . . We look to this as constructive expression of the collegial experience which unites us one another with the Holy Father."

As the bishops met in Washington, I was at a troubling crossroads in my research. I had a joint assignment from the *Cleveland Plain Dealer* and a daily paper in another state. Because of the legal threat surrounding my report on the information that follows, I cannot name the second newspaper, or the archbishop, quoted below, in a deposition.

My inquiry was triggered by a private detective who shared information on a Midwestern priest; he received a six-month sentence in 1978 for a single count of child molestation. The thirteen-year-old boy's parents had recently divorced when the priest entered his life as a paternal figure. After serving his time, the priest moved to Cleveland where then Bishop James Hickey accepted him for parish work. Meanwhile, the boy washed out on drugs, attempted suicide, and was hospitalized for psychiatric care. In 1986 a lawsuit was settled out of court for $325,000. The victim's attorney gave me depositions and I interviewed the young man. Facts unearthed in the litigation went far beyond the original criminal charges.

The priest had molested the plaintiff and his older brother. Unbeknownst to police in 1978, he had also become a father figure to four brothers in another broken family, molesting each in turn. The second family moved South with a $60,000 settlement for one of the four boys; they did not press criminal charges. When the attorney for the first family found them, the mother and two sons gave pretrial testimony for the boy in the first family. When the priest gave his deposition, in a Cleveland law office, he took the Fifth Amendment more than twenty-five times when asked about sexual activities with minors. At one point he said, "Haven't been any acts, you know, since the time of the conviction"—without elaborating. He also said he was homosexual.

The archbishop who asked Hickey to accept the priest testified: "We were making every effort to see to it that if he were given an assignment, it was going to be done with . . . surveillance is too strong a word, but some proper supervision." That decision was made before pedophilia recidivism rates became an issue. Was Father a safe risk? The man who had molested six teenagers said in deposition that he received no drug treatment, other than "sleeping pills"—ruling out use of Depo-Provera. The criminal judge ordered him not to "associate with any minor without the presence of a responsible adult" for five years. In that time he made trips back for psychological counseling. "I forget whether it was once a month or every other month," he stated.

The *Plain Dealer* was interested that such a priest was in Cleveland. In March 1986, another man, Brother Paul Botty, who taught at a local high school, had been given a seven-and-a-half-year sentence after admitting that he had molested four teenage boys. The other newspaper had reported Father's arrest and conviction in another state in 1978. I secured an assignment from the respective Sunday magazines, whose editors would run my story concurrently.

On November 15, a chilly Saturday, I parked outside the rectory of the suburban parish where he was assistant pastor. *Think of the kids,* I told myself, and pressed the buzzer. "Who is it?" came an intercom voice. I gave my name and asked for Father. The door opened: I recognized him from photographs, the hair grayer now, the face more worried. "What can I do for you?" he said.

"I'd like to speak with you about a private matter."

He ushered me into a parlor and we sat opposite each other. I explained that an article was under way. "I do not want to be interviewed!" he blurted. "I don't want my name to appear at all." I said that I understood but that the report would be published and if he agreed to an interview, perhaps he could convey himself in a new light. His face went white; he refused to talk. I explained that if he was truly rehabilitated, then his account of that struggle might make him a more sympathetic figure. Again he refused. "All right," I said. "Everything from here is off the record. I give you my word. I won't take notes."

I heard papers rustling in the next room, presumably the pastor, who wanted me to know that he was listening.

Father and I talked.

Forty-five minutes later he escorted me to the door. A chill crawled up my spine as I walked down the steps to tolling church bells. At the motel I wrote a detailed account of the conversation, which was unusable unless he went on the record. My pity for the priest mingled with outrage over what he had done to six young lives. One youth, already hyperactive, ended up in prison. How many such tragedies had the church effectively buried?

That night I read an analysis of the NCCB's Washington meeting by the *Plain Dealer* religion editor, Darrell Holland.

> *About 200 reporters covered the meeting, twice as many as usual for a bishops'*
> *conclave. They were attracted by the bitter controversy over the prospect of a mod-*
> *ern-day reform fight with an ancient institution that has bitterly fought change.*
>
> *Some bishops at the meeting, and others, blamed the media for the controversy.*
> *That is hardly the case. The controversy has been sparked by what many believe to*
> *be an unjust move by a good and gentle man.*

The secrecy involved in the Cleveland priest's transfer stemmed from a mentality about sex and power that was unraveling in reverse ratio to the Vatican crackdown. Holland continued:

> *Hunthausen defended himself publicly for the first time at the meeting. He said he*
> *was not a dissenter and that he was blameless of the charges. His defense was*
> *impressive. He swore his loyalty to the pope and the church's teachings.*
>
> *Hunthausen said he had tried to serve the needy and sinners, promote peace and*
> *justice in the world and the church, and that he . . . "often paid a price for*
> *speaking out honestly and without concern for our own selfish interests."*

He did not sound like a renegade disloyal to the church. He asked the U.S.
bishops conference for intervention to help bring peace to his archdiocese and to help
have his full duties restored. . . . [The bishops] pledged their unity with Rome and
expressed concern for Hunthausen, walking a tightrope to remain loyal while express-
ing concern for one of their own.

Diane Carmen, the *Plain Dealer* magazine editor, assigned a reporter to question parishioners about the priest I had tried to interview as part of a general story
about priests; to get an unbiased sounding, she did not tell the reporter about my
assignment. Weekend editor Jack Murphy wanted me to interview Bishop Anthony M. Pilla, who had succeeded Hickey, and to try again for an interview with
Father. The diocesan press officer told me that Pilla would respond only to questions submitted in writing, that a reply would take at least a week, that Father
would not talk, and that "your story will wreck his ministry." When I called Father
he again refused to talk. He had no arrest record in Ohio. That did not prove that
he had not reoffended; only that he had never been reported.

Curious about the secrets of Cleveland, I telephoned Michael Peterson in his
bedroom. He not only knew about Father but said, "There've been other cases in
Cleveland." However, he could not remember names. "I'm certain there were
others," he coughed. "The whole fucking thing is crazy—this mindset of institutional denial. Bishops keep recycling these guys."

"At least four cases," he said. *His immune system is going,* I told myself. In a
previous conversation he had said, "I have come to accept the inevitability of my
death—soon." The bronchial bursts made me feel that inevitability even more. He
had given me so much information, and he was dying. Yet he wanted me to know
more. I sensed that in some way he was trying to atone for what his death would
bring: public knowledge of the disease, a scandal to the church. I wanted to say I
knew he had AIDS, that his reputation was safe with me, but I could not bring
myself to do so. "It's awkward to say this, Michael, but is there anything I can do
for you?"

"I dunno. Pray for me. And just do what you're doing."

Praying for him was the easy part.

If Cleveland church officials were shielding other child molesters, then an
interview would leave Bishop Pilla vulnerable to such questioning. In New Orleans, I drafted the letter to Pilla, which consisted of questions about Father.
Among them:

Why did the diocese agree to accept the priest? Were any parishioners informed of his
criminal past? Will you state that he has had no relapses, no recurrences, has had no
involvement with youngsters since arriving in Cleveland?

Pilla had a master's in history and political science from John Carroll University, with an emphasis on European history under Communism. When journalist
Jim Castelli was writing a book about the bishops' peace pastoral, he asked Pilla
what he emphasized in his role as a teacher. "The whole question of peace and
the whole question of the poor," reflected Pilla. "If you want peace, work for

justice." Pilla worked hard to subsidize inner city parish schools which educated many black Protestant youngsters.

The response to my questions came from Auxiliary Bishop A. James Quinn— the Vatican trouble-shooter dispatched to Lafayette, who had approved the 1985 report of Mouton, Doyle, and Peterson.

"The tone of your questions is perceived to be offensive and biased," Quinn wrote to me. "Thus it is my judgment at this time that neither religion nor responsible journalism would be well served by responding to the specific questions as proposed."

Quinn defended the priest:

> I do not perceive the negative hopelessness that your questions imply in regard to Father. . . . I respect the moral repentance exhibited by Father. . . . I recognize that Father has paid the criminal and civil consequences that the Court and the Church imposed on him. The victim has been compensated to the satisfaction of the Court. . . . [The priest] has undergone extensive psychological counseling and has been recommended as an individual who can begin anew to function as a parish priest. Father continues to cooperate with this diocese through periodic reviews. To date, Father has ministered successfully in the parish to which he is assigned.

The *Plain Dealer* learned that Father took parish kids skiing and on camping trips. I submitted the article. Cleveland editors asked Pilla to meet with them. Pilla balked. Meanwhile the Sunday magazine editor at the second newspaper called to say I would be paid in full, but the story would not run. "Why not?" I asked.

"The editors here are saying, 'Why should we publish this?' It happened eight years ago." But the civil suit had only recently been settled, I argued, and its findings revealed crimes the paper had never reported. "Sorry," said the editor.

The *Plain Dealer* decided to publish after New Year's. In January, Diane Carmen called to say that her superiors had taken it from the magazine, with its long lead time for printing, to the news side, allowing late edits. Assistant managing editor Robert Snyder became my contact. "The bishop is willing to meet with us off the record," said Snyder, "but we've refused. We want him on the record, and if he refuses, the story will say that." At Snyder's request I participated in a conference call with editors and the paper's attorney. They asked if I had ever had sex with a priest (no) or been sexually abused as a child (no again). Snyder apologized for the questions, but I understood: the paper had a sensitive story from a nonstaff writer and was taking no chances.

Soon thereafter I was told that Cleveland church attorneys were threatening that if Father was named he would sue for invasion of privacy. How could a man once imprisoned for child molesting sue over a story about those crimes? By legal lights, if an ex-convict paid his debt to society and his crimes were re-reported eight years later, the reason had to be convincing. Because Father had no arrest record in Ohio, he could not only file suit, but the paper's counsel felt that no judge in the state would dismiss the case outright. Snyder cited estimates for such a case of a half million in legal fees with no guarantee about what a jury would do.

Convinced that the move was a bluff, I told Snyder that a lawsuit would give the paper discovery power to depose the bishop about other cases. But such suits are filed with numbing frequency and, although most are dismissed, even frivolous ones cost money to defend. The second paper's decision to punt suddenly made sense: the priest was Cleveland's problem, let Cleveland deal with it. I had little leverage. My story identifying Father was removed from the *Plain Dealer's* computer system, the original copy destroyed. Were a suit filed, said Snyder, subpoenas were valid only for existing material. The story was being refashioned into a lengthy editorial commentary. "Whatever we publish will appropriately credit you and your reporting," he said assuringly.

In mid-February, with the *Plain Dealer* working through a legal thicket, *Pittsburgh Post-Gazette* religion editor Eleanor Bergholz called me about a case there, which *NCR's* June 7, 1985, issue on pedophilia had described as "pending." This was the suit to which Minos Simon had alerted me in late 1984. I gave her the name of the Pittsburgh lawyer who had refused to give me details.

Ellie Bergholz was coming off the trial of Roger Trott, a priest in the town of Delmont, Pennsylvania, who had admitted molesting twelve boys. She was shocked by the plea bargain that gave Trott a five-year suspended sentence, beginning with treatment at St. Luke Institute. "If he was a football coach somewhere, would a judge have been that lenient?" she asked rhetorically.

On February 25, Ellie Bergholz called back. She had discovered the identity of the Pennsylvania priest whose case Minos Simon had told me about in 1984: Dennis Dellamalva. The civil suit had been filed in 1983, after Dellamalva went to the Institute for Living in Hartford, but the judge had sealed the docket. The *Post-Gazette* attorney filed a request to unseal depositions of Dellamalva and then Bishop William Connare of the Greensburg diocese. At hearings on the newspaper's motion to unseal the record, Bergholz was put under oath in judge's chambers and answered questions from church attorneys. "I felt I was being dragged into the cover-up," she told me. "The thrust of the questioning was, What is your story about? My point was, until we have information, we don't know what we're going to write."

The judge would not unseal depositions but gave the paper access to petitions and settlement figures. In May 1986 the church had paid $375,000 on behalf of three teenage boys molested by Dellamalva. Dellamalva's departure predated passage of a Pennsylvania law that required reporting abuses to civil authorities; he left the priesthood without being prosecuted. Bergholz wrote:

> *"We prepared a criminal complaint but we did not officially file charges," [prosecutor John Driscoll] said, adding that his office was guided by the feelings of the families and their attorney who wanted to protect the boys' privacy. . . .*
>
> *Dellamalva failed to stop his deviant behavior after being confronted by one family, the complaint states, and the now-retired Bishop William Connare "failed to discharge Dellamalva from his duties after having been confronted by the plaintiffs and others."*

"We still don't know how much the bishop knew and when," assistant city editor Eileen Foley told me, "or whether Dellamalva's transfers were related to his behavior. Without his deposition or Connare's, we just don't know the truth."

Bergholz discovered four cases involving Monsignor Francis McCaa under seal in Altoona. The families and their attorneys wanted to talk, but the seal order prevented them. Prosecutor Gerald Long, a member of McCaa's parish, was elected county judge and in that capacity ordered the records sealed. Diocesan officials told Bergholz that McCaa was a hospital chaplain in another state— which, they would not say. "I think the seal orders are a national strategy," Bergholz continued. "Keep it secret rather than face scandal or loss of credibility. When a priest is quickly dispensed with in a prosecution, that's maybe four [column] inches in a newspaper. When you get into all this secrecy it becomes a major story."

iii.

By January 1, 1987, 135 priests or brothers had been reported to the nunciature for molesting youths, in most cases boys. Meanwhile, the concealment of Michael Peterson's illness was straining his clinical colleagues. "He was running St. Luke from his house, which was crazy," a staffer later told me.

In November 1986, Richard Sipe, at a psychiatric meeting in Baltimore, learned that Peterson had AIDS. Because of his clerical background and his research on celibacy, Sipe had recently accepted an appointment to St. Luke's board of directors. He promptly informed the executive committee; by January, Peterson was still in charge. Sipe then told Bishop David Foley of Richmond, who told Archbishop Hickey, who days earlier had told the *Washington Post* that no priest in his archdiocese had AIDS.

In February 1987, Hickey met with the St. Luke board. Peterson, still CEO and medical director, was too sick to attend. "Once I started to ask," Hickey told the board, "people in my office knew Michael had AIDS." The board felt an announcement was necessary; however, one physician argued that Peterson had a patient's right to privacy. Board chairman William H. Mann wrote Peterson, assuring him that St. Luke's would continue operations. Michael then resigned. (The board's posthumous statement said he had resigned the previous fall.) It thus became Archbishop Hickey's lot to make daily visits to the sickbed, telling Michael that a letter from the two of them, advising bishops and area priests of his true illness, was the best way to deal with the illness. Hickey later stated that on February 27 (after the board meeting) when he visited Peterson

he shared with me for the first time that he was dying of AIDS. He expressed the fear that the fact of his illness might be used as a sensational way to undermine his work or attack the church he served. I reached out to him and offered my support, assistance, love and prayers as his bishop, as his friend, as his brother. I shared with him my conviction that the truth about his illness would bring forth support and compassion, not judgment and rejection.

At first, Peterson apparently felt his privacy would be compromised. "It was like being put in a sack, beaten with a stick, and told to sign, sign, sign," he told a St. Luke friend. Ray Mouton recalled: "Michael said he didn't want to sign that letter, but Hickey visited him every day until he agreed to it." Michael's letter to bishops, many of whom sent St. Luke's their problem priests, said: "I hope that in my own struggle with this disease, in finally acknowledging that I have this lethal syndrome, there might be some measure of compassion, understanding and healing for me and for others with it—especially those who face this disease alone and in fear." The letter strengthened Hickey's hand by allowing the church to break the news, averting implications of a cover-up. Had the news of AIDS leaked out, a brief scandal would have touched Hickey's fringes, with Michael dying in disgrace. Instead he received consoling letters from bishops and priests, praising his work, sparking optimism that St. Luke's would live on, as it did.

On Friday, March 13, Bob Snyder read me the commentary that would lead the *Plain Dealer's* Sunday "Perspective" section. It did not identify Father but put the onus on Pilla to do so. "The threat of a lawsuit was very real," Snyder said. "The question was, how do we get it out without putting ourselves in court? This was not easy. We are clearly forcing the Catholic Church to act. I think the [second paper] faced the same problem, and look what they did."

"Yeah," I grunted. "And they know his name. So if this thing hits the wires—"

"Which we expect it to."

"And someone calls me, asking his name, what do I do?"

"We're trying to cover ourselves, Jason. I know you've worked hard. My thought is that Bishop Pilla will i.d. him."

"I wouldn't bet my back pay on that, Bob."

"In a way this puts a cloud on all priests in the diocese. Pilla is stonewalling. That's their problem. I wish we could have published your story as written. Thom Greer, the managing editor, really pushed for this." The March 15 commentary by publisher-editor Thomas Vail, executive editor William J. Woestendiek, and Greer (who later succeeded Woestendiek) credited me, summarized the reporting, and said, "Editors have wrestled for weeks with a decision" about the story. They cited Father's deposition and reliance on the Fifth Amendment; quoted my questions to Pilla and Quinn's response; quoted a psychiatrist and pedophilia expert who called psychotherapy "disappointing—the success rate is not more than one in three." The commentary continued:

> *The parishioners may choose to allow their children to associate with him or not, but that choice can be theirs only if they are fully informed. . . . The diocese has suggested to us that by publishing the full story we will destroy the priest's ministry. . . . But we are concerned about the children of this parish and their parents and about our social and moral duty to warn them of any potential danger.*
>
> *It is the church's responsibility to act. The diocese brought this priest here and put him back in contact with children by assigning him to regular parish work. Diocesan officials allowed the parishioners to believe this man was a priest like any*

other; to be trusted and followed as a man of God. But he is not a priest like any other.

The Plain Dealer *calls on Bishop Pilla to resolve this problem by telling the parishioners about this priest and his past.*

That night a man from Cleveland telephoned me, asking if his parish had the priest in question; I apologized for not being able to answer. On Monday an ABC producer in Chicago called and I had to give the same answer. The producer asked why the paper hadn't identified him. "Call the paper," I said. It was distasteful for an investigative reporter to keep the lid on his story but I did not want myself or the *Plain Dealer* hauled into court. Pilla's letter to the paper appeared on St. Patrick's Day:

> *The ministry of the priest in question has been closely monitored since his assignment to the diocese nine years ago, and this supervision will continue. The procedures in place satisfied the diocese and the court system that the priest could fulfill the assigned ministry. The conduct that preceded the transfer of this priest to the diocese occurred 10 years ago. There have been no further allegations of misconduct in this 10-year period. In fact, his ministry has consistently received positive reaction from the community and colleagues.*
>
> *As you know, I agreed to discuss this matter with the* Plain Dealer, *but I did state that such conversations must be off the record. It was then, and continues to be, my belief that the newspaper is not the proper forum for a dialogue about the concerns expressed.*
>
> *While taking the necessary safeguards, we must remember that the church calls us to be a compassionate and forgiving people.*

When newspapers cover hard topics, the incensed minority usually calls or writes letters, with the approving majority more silent. Readers did not know what legal pressure was behind the publishing decision. "We would not rule out the possibility that he would be moved to another ministry in which he would not have contact with young people," a church spokesman stated in editions of March 18. Had the diocese known more about pedophilia when the priest was accepted, "it was likely the priest would have been placed in another kind of ministry." The story went on:

> *J. Jerome Lackamp, another diocesan spokesman, said yesterday the diocese had received about 50 calls, with many callers charging the newspaper was trying to tell the bishop how to do his job.*
>
> *Lackamp said some callers urged a boycott of the paper. He said a few callers questioned the wisdom of putting a priest with a sexual disorder in a situation where he would work with young people.*
>
> Plain Dealer *Executive Editor William J. Woestendiek said calls to him had*

been divided in support or opposition to the story. A log at the newspaper switch-board tallied 56 calls against the story and 34 in favor yesterday afternoon.

The story quoted a local pastor claiming to have heard from twenty parishio-ners, all critical of the paper. Another pastor called the editors "presumptuous" for thinking Pilla was unconcerned about the laity. But a third pastor voiced "dismay that such a person would be assigned to pastoral ministry. I would be crazy to accept a person like that on my staff." Pilla stood firm.

On April 7 reporter Darrell Holland quoted Auxiliary Bishop Quinn's an-nouncement that Father would be transferred in the upcoming rotation of priests to a nonparish position, at his own request, "for his own good and the good of the diocese." Holland wrote:

> *Quinn said making the priest's identity public would destroy his ministry and cause great harm to him and make him vulnerable to "the crazies."*
>
> *Because of the danger to children and the liability risk to the diocese, the priest would not have been assigned to a parish had the diocese not been convinced he was rehabilitated, Quinn said. "The* Plain Dealer *made us appear to be heedless of the welfare of children," he said. . . .*
>
> *"Just because someone molests a child does not mean he is a pedophile," he said. He said the PD commentary appeared to make rehabilitation seem impossible for a person who has molested children. Quinn said there was "a pretty good rate of cure."*
>
> *"The fact that the priest has been clean for 10 years is a very good sign of his rehabilitation," Quinn said.*
>
> *"It is a terrible crime but it is a disease that can be cured," he said. Quinn is also a lawyer.*
>
> *No priest who is a known, active pedophile would be assigned to a parish, Quinn said.*

The church succeeded in shielding Father. But the news coverage moved sev-eral young men to call the paper with traumatic stories of their own. Michael Peterson was right: other Cleveland priests had molested minors. Reporter Karen Henderson began investigating and on July 12 reported that in 1981 the diocese had paid $50,000 in "hush money" to the family of a fourteen-year-old boy who had been abused by the Rev. F. James Mulica. "The diocese assigned Mulica to two churches despite telling parents he would not be returned to family parishes," Henderson wrote. "He was transferred to a nonparish position after the *PD* began inquiring about him." The diocese offered a condominium, van, and job to the mother of a boy molested by the Rev. Joseph Romansk, a pastor. When the woman filed suit she was fired and lost her health coverage.

> *In a third case [wrote Henderson], the PD found the Rev. Allen F. Bruening, pastor of Ascension Church in Cleveland, was involved in the molesting of two brothers 20 years apart. In spite of pressure by the parents, the diocese delayed transferring Bruening for several months until the parents threatened legal action.*

In late 1987, after spending months probing cases across the country, *San Jose Mercury News* reporter Carl M. Cannon reported that church officials in Cleveland had dealt with seventeen cases of minors sexually abused by clerics.

By asking questions, Henderson caused the church to remove three priests. Five days before publication, Pilla sent out a letter for priests to read at Mass. "We stay in constant contact with the experts in the fields that relate to [sex abuse] problems," it said. "Each allegation of misconduct which is brought to my attention is investigated and dealt with in consultation with professionals." When the stories ran, protests to the newspaper intensified. Several priests called for a boycott of the newspaper; Henderson was physically barred from Pilla's press conference the day after her story appeared. A July 15 editorial stated:

> *If officials representing the church or any other organization refuse to talk to reporters, or simply respond with terse statements, how can they hope to have their views fully represented in the story that results? Nor is it responsible for church officials to rely on such limp and incredible excuses that priests somehow are on their own as "independent contractors."*
>
> *More important than finding a better way to deal with the media, the diocese must adopt a more responsible way to respond to victims, their families and persons of the parish who may have been reluctant to report problems of such incidents. It also must make sure that the victims understand that they are not at fault.*

When Ellie Bergholz's investigation of Pittsburgh-area priests appeared in the *Post-Gazette* the following month, letters poured in, attacking the paper and attacking the church. "My attitude at such times is to let the critics have their say," editor John G. Craig, Jr., wrote in an August 29 column. "I am going to make an exception to that personal guideline."

> *All of us were very sensitive to the fact that certain readers would be unable to accept publication of such news no matter how careful and balanced the presentation. . . . These readers are not interested in seeing such material in the newspaper. Period. This is because they find the subject distasteful, which it is, or because they believe it does not reflect favorably on the church, which it does not, or both.*
>
> *So why print the story? The quick answer is that the subject is an important one. The abuse of children is a topic about which readers wish (and need) to be informed. It is clear, on the basis of the evidence, that the Roman Catholic Church, in this part of Pennsylvania, is still unsure about how to deal with the problem. . . .*
>
> *At a gut level, some of us were also offended by the double standard. A guidance counselor at a Pittsburgh public school is accused by the parents of several students of making sexual advances and city police call him into the Station House, book him and fingerprint him—only to discover later that there was inadequate evidence to sustain the complaint.*
>
> *A Murrysville priest sexually abuses at least three boys, but when the parents complain to the powers that be, both clerical and temporal, nothing happens. No criminal charges are filed, no transfer is effected. Nothing. Only when they file a civil*

suit that is impossible to quash is there action. The parents are given money on condition that they speak to no one about the case and the priest is transferred and given medical help.

As in Lafayette, the church in Cleveland and Pittsburgh employed a strategy of concealment. In a letter to Bishop Pilla released to the media, Andrea Gorman, youth services coordinator of Cleveland's rape crisis center, explained some of the most damaging consequences of this strategy.

The first step in halting abuse is to "tell the secret." The impression you have conveyed is that you want to "keep it in the family." It is exactly this motive that binds the incestuous family together and perpetuates the system. You failed to give your people permission to break the silence, to act independently to terminate the abuse.

In early April Mouton called. "Michael told me he was gay," he sighed, "and admitted he had AIDS. Hickey has some kind of statement ready. I kidded Michael that he would get a hero's burial. He wants to know if St. Luke will survive. I told him sure: the church doesn't have enough places to put pedophiles."

On April 9, 1987, in George Washington University Hospital, with Bonnie Connor, a devoted friend and former nun, resting her hand on his forearm, Michael Peterson quietly expired.

At the wake, Dr. Fred Berlin of Johns Hopkins, who had treated pedophile priests, paid his respects, as did the pro-nuncio, Pio Laghi. In a tender eulogy, Washington Auxiliary Bishop Eugene Marino spoke of his treatment at St. Luke for alcoholism, calling Peterson "compassionate, understanding and gentle. . . . He touched my life profoundly. He came to the realization that men and women suffer not only mental illness, but ˜ deeper spiritual malady."

The funeral Mass in St. Matthew's Cathedral, with a procession of 150 white-robed priests, transformed the first acknowledged death of an American priest from AIDS into a virtual affair of state. "His last gift to us," said Hickey, "was the stark reminder of the human dimensions of this terrible epidemic, that those who suffer from it are our brothers and sisters who deserve our care, respect, and support."

Sadness welled within me, yet I could not help wondering about the priest who had revealed so many inner workings of the church. How much had I known about him? I felt guilty thinking that, and prayed for his peaceful rest. After the service Ray Mouton snapped that he did not want to talk. I watched Tom Doyle, face red with misery, as his white robes were swallowed in the crowd: he seemed so alone. Washed-out priests in black garb climbed onto buses heading back to St. Luke's. On the sidewalk a television reporter was interviewing a white-robed cleric. Tom Fox hurried off to interview Archbishop Hickey. I said a final prayer for Michael and walked to the Hilton to meet Richard Sipe for lunch.

iv.

The week that Peterson died, New York Cardinal John O'Connor, Chicago Cardinal Joseph Bernardin, and San Francisco Archbishop John Quinn, functioning as
an ad hoc Vatican team, met with Hunthausen in Chicago to resolve the Seattle
dispute. On April 19 the *National Catholic Register* reported: "Rome hopes to defuse
tensions by promoting Auxiliary Bishop Donald Wuerl . . . to his own diocese
and eventually retiring Hunthausen." A Seattle spokesman denied the story; but
Wuerl soon returned to Pittsburgh, where he later became bishop, and Archbishop Thomas Murphy of Montana, a longtime friend of Hunthausen, arrived in
Seattle as coadjutor, his designated successor.

Hunthausen salvaged his pride in the face of a crude Roman power play.
Many American Catholics admired him for it. A shadow triumph in the affair
went to Archbishop Hickey, who subsequently became a cardinal. The *Washington
Times* reported that Hickey's handling of Curran was important, but that his inquiry of Hunthausen had been a key loyalty test.

Who was Michael? I resisted the question for nearly a year, as leads from new
sources and legal documents rained into my life from distant places. Then I discovered people who had worked with him early in his priesthood. In 1977, when
Peterson converted the Marsalin home for troubled boys near Boston into a facility for alcoholic clergy, he hired staff therapists and was simultaneously raising
money for the Suitland complex. As he shuttled between Boston and Washington,
St. Luke took shape. His administrative alter ego was Stephen B. C. Johnson II.
Johnson was awed by Peterson's intellect. "Michael didn't have any boundaries or
sense that he could not do things," a clinician who worked for him states. Johnson
facilitated that sense, and in return Michael gave him power. As Dan Fredian, a
young priest-therapist who was hired to work at Marsalin, put it: "Michael had no
interest in money and relied on Johnson for everything."

"Put Steve in a roomful of people with money and in half an hour they'd
butter his hands," said a Suitland staffer. "He was the best salesman I've ever met
—as long as Michael was the product." A nun who traveled to conferences with
Johnson was put off by the lavish meals and expensive wines he charged to St.
Luke. Others heard him boast of investments and Eurodollars, wondering why
such a privileged man felt the need to work in a psychiatric hospital for priests.
Of the many sources in Boston and Washington, all concur that Michael's clinical
program helped scores of alcoholics into recovery. But the internal dynamics
grew bizarre. Michael Kennedy, who was Marsalin's director of operations, recalled: "Father Peterson was clearly homosexual. Our concern was that he was
abusing drugs. A private indulgence might not matter, but his behavior became
erratic."

Marsalin needed money for repairs, computers, and payroll. Peterson went
after adjacent properties. "Can you believe he's buying another house?" Johnson
asked Kennedy, who saw that Marsalin bank loans were getting harder to obtain.
Marsalin was licensed as a halfway house. Kennedy grew suspicious that patients
sent to the newly acquired houses "had nothing to do with our mission; yet they

could roam at will in a neighborhood with children." He said that Peterson told neighbors the men were visiting bishops and superiors. "Possibly one or two pedophiles stayed in the houses," a former Marsalin therapist said. "We were treating thirty-six clergy and were licensed for twenty."

Kennedy said: "Michael used his position as a priest to get power, a lifestyle without having to make explanations. He'd say, 'I'm not worried about Bishop So-and-so, not with what I know.' Whether he would act on that I don't know. But power brokers don't have to use their power. Michael knew a lot of sins of the church. He never forgot anything. His mind was like a computer."

St. Luke opened in 1982. "I knew he was drinking more," said Fredian. "I saw a man who was very, very tired, relying on his board instead of his staff. His difficulty was not in getting friends but sustaining relationships. He made many trips to San Francisco. He was vulnerable. That's probably why he got AIDS."

The wit and brilliance he manifested to Mouton, Doyle, and bishops was one part of Michael; the compulsiveness and vulnerability lay in a more secret compartment that Fredian and others saw. Eventually the contradiction between persona and personality broke down.

His mission as a priest was to help other priests. When a pregnant nun gave birth, he performed the baptism of the infant and had to be helped through the prayers because he didn't know them. Baptizing infants, so common to most priests, was uncommon to Michael. He had too many priests on his mind. In 1983, Kennedy begged him to get help for substance abuse. "I appreciate your concerns," Peterson told him, "but there's nothing wrong." Was the healer who helped others achieve sobriety now in denial? When Kennedy and a therapist told several St. Luke board members about Peterson's problem, he fired them. Six other staffers were then abruptly dismissed; security guards prevented Kennedy from removing his papers.

"The counseling goal was to create a bond with patients," Fredian reflected. "This was violated by the terrible firing process. When I resigned I felt it hurt Michael. To have someone say to his face, 'You're wrong,' was very confusing to him."

Married with three sons, Kennedy went six months looking for work, which wiped out the family savings. A therapist was unemployed ten months. In all, nine Marsalin staffers filed a wrongful employment termination suit. Attorney Alice Richmond of Boston, who represented the plaintiffs, told me: "Personnel files were removed under cover of darkness to Suitland. When we filed the request [for discovery], the files were destroyed."

With the plaintiffs scrambling to find jobs and unable to bankroll lengthy litigation, Marsalin filed for bankruptcy. In October 1984 the suit was settled for a modest $30,000. While Marsalin was in Chapter Seven proceedings in Boston, Michael Peterson, who was living in Suitland, next to St. Luke, was searching for adjacent property—just as he had done at Marsalin.

In 1985, St. Luke administrator Chris Bowman took title to a house on Peterson's block. "For about six months I owned the house," Bowman explained. "But St. Luke paid the $17,000 down payment and mortgage straight to my account. Unless you're IBM, it's way too much work for a bank to assess business income for a lousy house mortgage. Other houses were purchased in the same way." Peterson sold yet another house in the neighborhood to St. Luke for $55,000 in

March 1984. Steve Johnson sold another nearby house to St. Luke for $68,738 in May 1985. The Marsalin estate was closed the following month. The bankruptcy files show the final check cut on Marsalin's account in 1985 as $35,137—to St. Luke Institute, which had the same board of directors.

In 1986, St. Luke was admitting more and more pedophiles to a hospital with twenty-four beds. Unbeknownst to neighbors, Peterson began using the nearby houses for patients who had molested youths. It was a dicey move, and a zoning violation, yet it typified his idea of power. "What would you do?" he told a friend. "Put a thirty-foot fence around the houses? Where's a good place to put a pedophile?" He argued that priests were fear-stricken because they might be caught, knowing that even after treatment they might go to prison.

According to this source, "Michael maintained such control that no one was allowed to move into a position of authority at St. Luke. When he died, a scramble for power began."

The night before Michael died, Steve Johnson fired an accountant who objected to a $5000 expense receipt for meals submitted after one of Johnson's trips. As acting CEO, Johnson fired Bowman, who had been concerned about zoning of the houses; then he fired another longtime staffer who had been a confidant of Peterson. A psychiatrist with excellent credentials was hired, then fired, allegedly for poor record-keeping. When that happened, Richard Sipe, Dr. William F. Minogue (medical director of George Washington University Hospital), and another physician resigned from the board. An April 5, 1988, resignation letter from one of the doctors to board chairman William Mann stated:

> *I have become progressively uncomfortable with the moral tone of the Institute and its therapeutic programs. In my opinion, the Institute has been used as an outlet for the psycho-pathology of its founder and . . . for other members of the staff from its inception. I am not convinced there is agreement on the Board about this issue and I do not sense a strong commitment to reverse this trend.*

In December 1987, Johnson returned to the administrative staff and Monsignor Robert Batcher, a former seminary rector in Cleveland, became St. Luke's CEO. In an interview the following August, Batcher stressed that the turmoil "happened before I got here" and refused to discuss personnel disputes. I asked if pedophiles were still in the neighboring houses. "I don't know," he replied, taken aback. "I'd have to ask the attorney."

"Look," said a frustrated Batcher, "I got hit blind with these problems. Father Michael is dead. He left an excellent program with a mission to serve the church, and we are doing that."

Between 1983 and 1987, St. Luke claimed a remarkable five percent recidivism rate among alcoholics. In 1990, Dr. Frank Valcour, medical director, wrote that "55 child molesters had completed treatment by September 1989. Of those in follow-up (most of them), there were no reported instances of relapse and no new allegations. . . ." Follow-up procedures were not detailed.

Valcour's article continued:

> *Can the recovering perpetrator of child abuse ever minister again? Well, approximately 32 of the 55 mentioned above are productively engaged in some form of*

ministry. It is usual to have some strictures imposed which honor public sensibilities as well as to help the individual steer clear of risk situations. Of those who are not in ministry, their inactive state is usually not of their own choosing.

Who was Michael? A physician who could not heal himself. But that is not so rare. Perhaps the addictiveness that concerned Marsalin staffers drove him to sexual encounters that resulted in his contracting HIV. He told Tom Doyle he contracted AIDS from a cut while examining contaminated blood. Others who knew him well doubt that. His back operation in fall, 1985, was probably the turning point for an immune system already in jeopardy. The relentless travel became a race against time; the advancing shadow of his mortality pushed him on a harder, redemptive effort to help others and square himself with God.

A therapist who knew him believes that Michael's flaw was a conflict of ego and impulse, psyche and compulsion: hence the double life, the twisted power drive. It remains to be said that Michael Peterson helped many more people than he hurt. At root he was a good man, and in the time of the Vatican crackdown his life and death were an apt metaphor for the troubled clerical culture which buried him with honors due a priest in service of the church.

San Diego: The New Gay Clericalism

Homophobia implies victimization—that homosexuals suffer because of igno-rance, injustice, even irrational hatred. Violent assaults on gay people are the cruelest sign of this mentality, which permeates society in many subtler ways, much like racism. In raising the issue of homophobia at religious workshops, Bob Nugent and Jeannine Gramick tried to ease the suffering of gay people in secular as well as clerical life—a message with resonance. Although the church officially condemns homogenital sex, many pastors take a more nuanced attitude toward gay people, welcoming those who come as individuals of faith.

A congregation's acceptance of gay priests is something else. By the mid-eighties, signs of a once hidden subculture were sprouting like sedge through cracks of the immigrant church. In the June 19, 1987, *Commonweal,* the liberal Notre Dame theologian, Rev. Richard P. McBrien, posed more than forty ques-tions about this phenomenon, and offered few answers. Among his questions:

> Does [*sexual orientation*] *affect the gay priest's ministerial relations with hetero-sexual males, with women, with families, and with children? How does his homosexu-ality affect his relationship with heterosexual priests? Does the nature of these various relationships differ if the gay priest is sexually inactive rather than sexually active?*
>
> *If there is, in fact, a large body of gay priests in the United States, is there any relation between this phenomenon and the increasing visibility of child-molestation cases involving Catholic laity?*
>
> . . . *Do gay seminarians create a gay culture in seminaries? To what extent are seminary faculty members part of this culture? Are heterosexual seminarians "turned off" by existence of such a culture?*

The word "clericalism" refers to the control mechanisms and increase of power for its own sake in a religious hierarchy. It is rarely associated with gay priests; those who publicly identify themselves as homosexual court their bishops' wrath. But within the folds of ecclesiastical culture, some have said, lies another variant of clericalism. What happens when a clique of gay priests in a diocese or religious order become power holders, rather than victims? Two years after McBrien's article, Andrew Greeley fumed in *NCR* about gay clergy:

> *Blatantly active homosexual priests are appointed, transferred and promoted. Lavender rectories and seminaries are tolerated. National networks of active homosexual priests (many of them church administrators) are tolerated. Pedophiles are reassigned (despite the legal risks) and sometimes subjected to compulsory treatment with drugs to control their passions.*
>
> *If a heterosexual priest engaged in a blatant love affair with a woman, he would be suspended as quickly as a phone call could be made to the chancery.*

Few dioceses felt the gay clericalist impact more deeply than San Diego, California. On paper, Bishop Leo T. Maher was orthodox down the line. A staunch pro-lifer, Maher was also an early critic of Dignity, forbidding his priests to say Mass for the local chapter well before Ratzinger's 1986 letter on homosexuality. Yet Maher in the mid-eighties was like a boxer on the ropes, careening from one scandal to another involving money, pedophilia, and gay clericalism.

In fairness to Maher—who declined my interview requests—some problems were not unique to his diocese. But the accumulation of disturbances set Maher apart, prompting a well-placed cleric in the East to call San Diego "the most messed-up diocese in America." In August 1987, I spent two weeks in San Diego. On the return flight, gazing down on sinuous roads through Western mountains and desert, I paused while reading Willa Cather's historical novel, *Death Comes for the Archbishop*, set in the mid-nineteenth century, a story of westward expansion. "The old mission churches are in ruins," a missionary tells a bishop, calling the priests "lax in religious observance, and some of them live in open concubinage. If this Augean stable is not cleansed . . . it will prejudice the interests of the Church in the whole of North America."

In September 1987, on his second American journey, Pope John Paul II made several Western stops, but not in San Diego, where Father Junípero Serra founded the first California mission in 1769. "When you think of this diocese's historical significance," a priest told me, "the fact that Father Serra is being considered for canonization, the omission on the Holy Father's schedule says a lot." San Diego's disarray echoed Cather's novel; however, the sexual conflicts were different and her bishop was a hero.

In 1984 a scandal rocked the diocese when Mark Brooks filed suit against the church in San Diego civil court, essentially charging that he was driven out of St. Francis Seminary by hostile gays. Brooks later sent a detailed, 56-page account of his experiences to Pope John Paul II. The report identified certain faculty priests as having sexual relationships with seminarians. Brooks received a January 1987 letter from a papal secretary saying, "His Holiness is praying for you." Thus ended his communication with Rome.

Born in 1954, Mark Brooks grew up in Baltimore. His father was an alcoholic who deserted the family. His mother worked hard to support her son and three daughters. They moved often. "As a kid," recalled Brooks, "I made altars and said Mass in my bedroom. Those priests were surrogate fathers—played ball with us, put an arm on your shoulder, never in a threatening way." Out of high school he served four years in the Marines, ending his duty in San Diego, where he began working with autistic children.

Mass was a staple of his life, and in August 1980 he entered St. Francis. At twenty-six he was one of the oldest seminarians. That concerned him; some students were barely out of high school. But the rector, Monsignor Henry F. Fawcett, said that his maturity could make him a role model to younger men.

It gradually dawned on Brooks that at least a third of the seventy-five seminarians were homosexual. In itself, that did not bother him. But as coming-out stories proliferated, seminarians spoke of being "wounded" by homophobia. They needed "healing." The church needed healing. Mark needed healing to understand how heterosexist culture had wounded him. He thought these were trite terms, bordering on psychobabble; but he knew that the emotions among those who used them were real. As time passed Brooks became confused about spiritual direction, the mentor-student relationship of religious training.

In Brooks's first semester, the Rev. Vincent Dwyer arrived as a guest lecturer. A mesmerizing speaker, Dwyer espoused a theory of moral development influenced by the psychologist Lawrence Kohlberg. A style of spiritual formation known as the "Dwyer Program" stressed counseling, psychological testing, and Kohlberg's theory that people advance through distinct stages of moral growth— from parental influence and the conformity of peer associations as children, up a ladder of rewards and punishments in a given social order. At its summit, morality achieves a universal ethic, such as Gandhi and Martin Luther King espoused.

In the document he sent the Pope, Brooks wrote that Dwyer advised seminarians "not to fear intimacy. [We] were urged to take the 'risk' to enter into such friendship." Dwyer condemned gossip about "significant relationships"—an ironic twist on the prohibited "particular friendships" of old seminary life, when men were forbidden to walk in twos. At St. Francis they were told not to report relationships to faculty; that relationships were growing experiences. Celibacy acquired a more casual standing as sexual activity proliferated. Brooks wondered: *Is this preparation for priestly life?* He complained to Fawcett but the rector said to be patient; things would change the following year.

"I had trouble believing that," recalled Brooks, "because Fawcett seemed completely snowed by Dwyer."

A former Cistercian monk, Dwyer's program had its roots in Minnesota. In 1971, Lou Martinelli, a senior at St. Mary's College in Winona, helped conceive a human development program for freshmen. Now an educator and writer, Martinelli was influenced by Kohlberg and heading for graduate school. "The college embraced my idea," Martinelli told me. "They needed a director. Dwyer came for an interview. He was a very articulate, charismatic guy; we felt he could put the college on the map. Six months later I visited campus and found disillusioned students and faculty. Dwyer seemed to insist on a form of authority in which people were made to feel guilty if they did not agree with him."

Rick Scott, who later became a union official in Minneapolis, was academic dean at the time. He likened Dwyer's first lecture on the moral growth theory to "the wonderful world of Oz opening up. I made Vince chair of an interdisciplinary program. I would say his contribution was his initial lecture. That was my greatest disappointment. He used St. Mary's as a launching pad to sell this idea to other institutions. He'd go to high schools and present mini-programs. He didn't have success convincing Father Brown, who ran the Winona seminary, that Vince Dwyer should redesign the program. I wasn't that impressed with Vince intellectually. But he was a great pitch man. I thought his goal was to have a little plastic statue of himself in every church in America."

Dwyer left Winona to establish another program at Notre Dame, in South Bend, Indiana. There he gave clergy retreats but ran into budget problems and left after a dispute over a computer purchase, according to a priest who observed the situation. By 1980 his program had relocated in Washington.

Dwyer's lectures in San Diego that autumn left a local widow concerned about her son, a classmate of Brooks. Mary Jones* recalled: "Kids came over here until two in the morning, so confused they started crying. In the extreme, this Dwyer Program was honed down to mean you had to be gay."

In a telephone interview, Dwyer told me that he had seen no homosexuality at St. Francis. I asked about his encouraging men to "enter into intimacy." He replied: "Yeah, *spiritual* intimacy. Not physical intimacy. There's a big difference. One is in terms of being able to share one's life; the other is referring to genitalia, which I'm not talking about."

Why would Brooks criticize his program in a document sent to the Vatican? Said Dwyer: "That guy is—I think he had a lot of personal problems, which he was definitely involved in, in terms of alcohol and drugs. In my estimation he shouldn't have been in seminary to begin with." Dwyer's Center for Human Development was on the CUA campus in Washington, D.C. When I asked him to discuss it, he said: "I'm not going to make any other statements. In fact, I think it's foolish"—thus terminating the interview.

Mary Jones's first inkling that something was amiss came in autumn, 1980. She left a check for her son Bob* at the seminary, and looked in the piano room. "Cushions were on the floor. Guys were in togas, with wine goblets, not all wearing underwear . . . I started crying. A priest came over and said gently, 'This is not a time when parents are welcome.' " She said she complained repeatedly to Fawcett. "He would say, 'You don't understand. It's not what it seems.' I was very concerned about the alcohol. Some of these kids were getting smashed. I'd ask, 'Why is this allowed to take place? You guys are surrogate parents.' No one ever gave me a straight answer."

Why did she let Bob continue in the seminary? "I wanted to preserve our relationship at all costs. It's like these cults. Once you lose communication, you lose it all. When Bob told me he thought he was gay I went to his spiritual director, and I practically tore his apartment up." Crying, she said: "It's not that he's gay—it's whether he became gay because of seminary. I was the best mother I could be! I educated him in Catholic schools."

In a separate interview, Bob recalled his freshman year at the seminary with Brooks: "The Dwyer Program was positive, but it almost brainwashed people to overlook things. It definitely caused divisions; it all stemmed from an individual's maturity level. Dwyer's mindset was fed through the faculty, a program saying 'brave new world' and [faculty] telling students, 'We'll trust you to talk to us if you need to.' "

Nicholas Reveles, a priest who taught music at the University of San Diego, would visit the seminary. "It was no secret that he was gay," Bob continues. "I remember gently telling Fawcett: 'I know first hand of four people, including myself, that he has had.' Fawcett said, 'What are we supposed to do? Tell him never to come to the seminary? Do we go to the bishop?'

"I had problems with self-esteem in high school. Reveles was an artist, with long stories about his postconcert depression. He'd call at eleven at night. I'd walk to the other side of the earth for this guy. First he's holding your hand, then hugging, then unzipping your pants. It was my first homosexual encounter. But 'seduction' is an iffy word. I could have said no at any point. I don't know how to describe that cold, dirty, empty feeling after it happened. I went into chapel and started crying. Those of us who had been through it with him would see the next class of freshmen and he'd pick out one he liked; they're together in chapel, then he's driving Nick's car. Then all of a sudden the guy is dropped. They were very methodical episodes. And how do you say to someone, 'Be careful'?

"I may have been [homosexually] predetermined before seminary. Things in high school confirmed that. But seminary provided the atmosphere where it was acceptable." He had two gay relationships in seminary. After four years he chose not to continue studies for the priesthood and left San Diego.

When I spoke with Reveles, he said of Bob's statement: "It's just ridiculous. Simply not true. I am a public minister and a celibate priest, period."

In November 1980, Brooks discovered his father in a San Diego skid row hotel. "I was shattered," he recalls. "I prayed every night. Fawcett said, 'One of the hardest things to do is minister to your own family. Your father has to pay the consequences of his actions.'" Stephen Dunn, a young priest and vice-rector, counseled Brooks. According to Brooks, "He kept edging closer; he put his arm around my waist. He told me I needed affection and love, to put the family behind me. I pulled away. Over the next two years he propositioned me a dozen times."

Dunn did not return my calls requesting an interview. He also declined to be interviewed by *San Diego Catholic News Notes,* an independent conservative monthly, for a 1991 article assessing events at the seminary during his tenure there.

Reveles was going away for a weekend and offered Brooks use of his apartment. A sign affixed to the VCR said: "Play me." Next to it was a stack of pornographic tapes. In his document to the Pope, Brooks wrote of Reveles: "Later he wept, admitting that he was unable to pray or even administer the sacraments. I believed him to be a good man in reality. He attempted to convince me of the 'goodness' of homosexuality. He confided that many clergy were gay"—twenty-seven of whom Brooks named in his report, in addition to twenty-three seminarians.

Later, after filing suit, Brooks spoke of his conflicts with Reveles on a local radio show and in a television interview. When I asked about Brooks's accusations, Reveles said: "It's just not true. Absolute fabrications. Every time we hear his story it grows. To do something like that would be spiritually suicidal, and that's just crazy." Why would two former seminarians say such things about him? Reveles said: "Why do rumors grow? Any number of reasons. We know of rumors that aren't true."

Brooks grew miserable. In line for communion he saw students grabbing buttocks. Affairs blossomed. A seminarian in his late thirties took a sixteen-year-old boy to live with him. Bob Jones was troubled by that too. The boy eventually left, and in time so did the man. Brooks complained to Steve Dunn about the climate of promiscuity.

The night the Baltimore Orioles won the 1983 American League pennant, Brooks got plastered and began yelling war whoops. The next day he faced an intervention by six seminarians telling him he was an alcoholic. The six, he said, were a gay clique with whom he had repeatedly clashed. Fawcett ordered him to undergo alcoholism rehabilitation or face expulsion. Dunn imposed conditions on his hospitalization: no visitors, phone calls, or correspondence—clearly at odds with substance abuse treatment. Brooks entered a VA hospital in La Jolla.

"Mark was a heavy drinker," says Bob, "but why at that point did they come down hard and heavy? We were told we'd be expelled if we talked to him. Half of us wanted to rush over."

Brooks was released three weeks later; the diagnosis was not alcoholism but post-traumatic stress syndrome. Dunn expelled him. Brooks lived in his car until he found work. In January 1984 one of Bishop Maher's aides offered him a plane ticket out of San Diego; he refused. Brooks finally got a meeting with Maher, who listened, and promised a thorough investigation. "One thing he did ask me," said Brooks, "was if it was true that I had been living in my car. I told him, yeah, for a while. He was troubled by that, and said he was sorry. I felt at the time he was being shielded from the facts by people around him."

When St. Francis officials refused to give him a recommendation to another seminary, Brooks filed a civil damage suit on October 12, 1984, against the seminary, the diocese, and Maher. In November the rector, Fawcett, left for substance abuse treatment.

"Maher grew up in a hierarchy used to the type of power corporate people have," a lay person close to the bishop told me. "His style is no different from executives his age who came up from immigrant stock. As Irish, you have to build a fiefdom, and at the top you protect yourself. But the pluses are many. He's very supportive of the university, especially in creating scholarships. This is truly a spiritual man."

Born in Iowa in 1921, the fifth of nine children whose father came from Ireland, Maher was ordained in 1943, and four years later became secretary to the archbishop of San Francisco. In 1962 he became bishop of the new Santa Rosa diocese and began to build—schools, churches, gymnasiums, mausoleums.

The San Diego diocese was founded in 1936 as an offshoot of the Los Angeles archdiocese. Founding Bishop Charles F. Buddy called it "the rim of Christendom." In 1949 he launched the University of San Diego, envisioned as "the shining jewel to crown the diocesan education structure." He built it on a plateau above the city with a sweeping view of Mission Bay, and in 1954 established St. Francis de Sales Collegiate Seminary in the university complex. The diocesan chancery was also located there.

In 1971, two years after Maher became bishop of San Diego, the *San Francisco Examiner* reported that he had left Santa Rosa with a $12 million debt. Funds borrowed from a boys' center in Sonoma County prompted a state attorney general's probe, but no indictment. Maher lived well. In 1964 he purchased a twelve-room home in the elite Montecito Hills section of Santa Rosa, with swimming pool, guest house, and cabanas, later adding a library, chapel, wine cellar, and bar. The next bishop sold the estate to pay off the debt.

San Diego had a $15 million debt when Maher arrived. Thus he established the Stewardship Program, which assessed each parish a yearly fee. By 1987, with the diocese finally solvent, some priests resented the program, which they felt forced them to stress money in sermons. And they felt that Maher's predecessor, Bishop Francis Furey, had a tendency to take in "the walking wounded" from other dioceses—priests with emotional, sexual, or psychological problems.

In 1984 the *San Diego Reader*, a weekly, reported that Monsignor William Spain was in treatment for cocaine addiction, after a love affair with a male addict. Spain, who was independently wealthy, reportedly loaned Maher $100,000 and paid for trips the bishop made to Hawaii and Europe. After treatment, Spain's "new parish wouldn't accept him," a priest said. Spain moved to Hawaii.

A second *Reader* story quoted a diocesan accounting employee who charged that Maher withheld key information from diocesan financial statements: value of land and buildings was "horribly understated"; annual reports had no profit-and-loss statements; Maher's personal expenses were charged to departmental budgets. Maher issued a statement: "I have always tried to treat the clergy of this Diocese with kindness. . . . I can only pray that these accusations against me, unfounded as they are, have not hurt anyone else." The diocese began issuing regular financial statements. "After the articles," a priest said, "people thought someone from the Vatican Embassy encouraged Leo to retire." But such encouragement, if there was any, was to no avail.

Maher appointed a new seminary rector and removed Dunn as vice-rector. Two seminarians were also expelled in the aftermath of Brooks's complaints. In 1985 an investigator for the Vatican study on seminaries visited San Diego; no Vatican representative contacted Brooks, even after his 56-page report to the Pope. Members of Maher's staff, in conversations with lay people and other priests, portrayed Brooks as out to milk the church of money.

In April 1985 the diocese paid a Vietnamese family $75,000 to drop civil action against Monsignor Rudolph Galindo, rector of St. Joseph's Cathedral, for molesting their teenage son. Maher sent Galindo to a parish in the desert city of Calexico. The following month attorney Robert Woods negotiated a $15,000 settlement for Brooks to drop his suit, with $9000 back tuition waived.

When the news about his suit broke, Brooks was approached by several men who said they wanted to clean up things: Ed McCrink, Henry Fischer, and Willis Carto—the last of whom, Brooks would later learn, was the founder of the Liberty Lobby in Washington, which Jewish leaders consider the most anti-Semitic organization in the country. "They claimed to be friends of Cardinal Gagnon and Cardinal Ratzinger," said Brooks. "They offered to take me to Rome, the last place I wanted to go. All I wanted was to get information to the right people. The information I gave Henry Fischer became a story by Henry Thompson, his pen name."

In a telephone interview, McCrink said that he had met with Brooks but denied having Vatican contacts. Fischer said he had heard of Brooks but "I'm the wrong Henry Fischer." In any event, the "Henry Thompson" story ran that September in the *Spotlight*, a weekly paper hostile to Israel that Carto helped launch in Washington, with distribution boxes in San Diego. Taking credit for the Brooks "exposé," the story named fifteen parishes as having homosexual priests, but identified only one priest, Spain.

Jean Liuzzi read the *Spotlight*. A partner in Trident Investigative Services, she kept tabs on fringe groups. Ebullient and shrewd, Liuzzi worked well with policemen and lawyers. She was a devout Catholic, married, with three grown children, products of parochial schools. On Sundays she served as a Eucharistic minister, giving communion to the faithful at Mass.

Liuzzi sat up with a start when she saw her parish on the *Spotlight* list. She had gay friends; she also took priestly celibacy seriously and was already suspicious of a priest at her church and his relationship with another cleric who had come from a Midwestern diocese and was counseling seminarians. Calling priests she trusted, she found them confirming certain names on the list. She called Brooks, wondering if he was orchestrating a tale. To her office came a troubled young man who told his story in measured tones, the anger building slowly, while both of them smoked too many cigarettes. Paid by no one, Liuzzi spent weeks tracking leads. McCrink and Fischer offered payment if she would organize a march with banners denouncing "faggots." No way.

Confirming the thrust of Brooks's allegations, Liuzzi saw a promiscuous subculture as one strand in a larger web of problems. Her greater concern was a systemic abuse of power. Meanwhile, *San Diego Union* reporter Jon Standefer was investigating financial and sexual questions surrounding Monsignor William A. Kraft, the diocese's director of stewardship or deferred giving.

On her own Liuzzi learned that Kraft had left his last parish in 1978 after parishioners protested his handling of funds raised in bingo games. She also located a couple who claimed that Kraft had molested their son, an altar boy, in the mid-sixties. When Jean Liuzzi met with Maher, the bishop admonished her for causing scandal by her inquiries. "I wouldn't be here if there wasn't scandal already," she replied. She said she felt intimidated by him as her spiritual leader, but not by his power.

"We have a corrupt leadership," she said. "You are responsible." Maher turned red. Liuzzi pushed: "How do we know what is recorded for cash flow?" When he offered her access to diocesan books, she said that he had sole access to *all* financial records.

"Why did you make Father Kraft a monsignor?" she hammered. "You know the scandal this man has caused!" Maher asked what scandal. The altar boy at St. Therese, she countered, and a trail of questions about bingo games at his last parish. Maher told Liuzzi she couldn't document her charges. She asked why Galindo, after molesting the Vietnamese boy, went to a parish in Calexico. Maher said he was in treatment. "That's like letting an alcoholic work in a bar!" she said. Liuzzi named the gay priest in her parish: was he involved with the seminary counselor? Maher said she was causing scandal. "We need a committee to investigate *all* of this," she said. Maher asked for three months to do his own investigation. Soon thereafter the priest in her parish was transferred to another one.

Liuzzi wrote Calexico police about Galindo. A month later he was retired. She wrote Pio Laghi about San Diego's scandals. A polite staff-written letter from the nunciature acknowledging her concern made her realize it was time to quit. Besides, after hundreds of hours in unpaid time her business needed tending.

On December 29, 1985, Jon Standefer's long *San Diego Union* report shed light on Elvia Aguilar, the bishop's attractive secretary, to whom he had deeded a four-bedroom home belonging to the diocese. Standefer wrote that church officials, discovering the transaction before it was made public, told Maher it would look bad and, at the bishop's request, a wealthy layman granted Aguilar an after-the-fact loan, which entered diocesan coffers and balanced the books. Aguilar also paid $50,000 for a condominium valued at $160,000 from a developer who bought the land from the diocese for a swank real estate project. "An aura of scandal has attached itself to the diocese," Standefer wrote.

Some clerics felt heartened by the article. "The priests here are long suffering," one told me. "I'm convinced that information we tried to get to the Holy Father has not gotten to him." Others rose swiftly to the bishop's defense. At a January 1986 priests' meeting, Louis Copestake, editor of the diocesan newspaper, questioned whether publisher Helen Copley of the *Union* and *Tribune* newspapers should remain on the USD board of trustees. "I will not be compromised as a publisher," said Mrs. Copley, one of USD's largest benefactors, and she resigned from the board.

In 1972 a drifter arrested for assaulting Copestake claimed it was in response to sexual advances. The man passed a polygraph test. Copestake did not press charges. In 1988, Copestake left the diocese.

ii.

Summer, 1986, found Mark Brooks in Baltimore while a disruption was brewing at Holy Trinity Parish in the San Diego suburb of El Cajon. That spring, Maher ordered the longtime pastor, a beloved man, to retire, and in his place appointed Stephen Dunn, the former seminary vice-rector. One of Brooks's classmates, Jim McCaffery, who continued seminary studies for several years before leaving, later told *San Diego Catholic News Notes*: "[Dunn] and I had major philosophical differences, but he got crucified in this whole thing. He's a brilliant scholar, a prayerful man, who took a ton of grief and never said a word, for the sake of anybody else involved. I admire him for that."

Actually, Dunn made one statement about Brooks, and it backfired on him. It grew out of problems at Holy Trinity Parish that began in spring, 1986. Before arriving, Dunn sent word that the altar rail would have to go; he wanted a new, closer atmosphere in the church. Although removal of altar rails was a product of Vatican II's refocusing of the liturgy on lay people, there was no hard rule that they *had* to go. The rail in question was a treasured symbol in the parish. Dunn's larger designs for change clashed with the values of parishioner Liz Williams Reilly.

In 1962, when she was eighteen, the hills north of the city were laden with trees. El Cajon was like a rural town. Raised Methodist, she hungered for something more. It eluded her at other churches she visited—Baptist, Lutheran, even a Sunday with Holy Rollers in Marline. Something touched her at Holy Trinity, the oldest Roman Catholic parish in El Cajon, established in 1903. There was a dignity to the Latin Mass, a solemnity she found breath-taking. In 1963 she converted to the faith; four years later she married Bill Reilly, whom she met singing in the choir. Raising five children, they poured themselves into the church. Choir practice on Thursday nights; Tuesday nights Liz attended novena services. They taught catechism, worked at the parish fair, befriended priests and sisters.

The Reillys were upset by Father Dunn's announcement that the tabernacle, symbolic of Christ's presence, would be shifted from the main altar to the side of the church. This too was an option afforded priests by Vatican II. Reilly bridled at Dunn's style of authority. The previous pastor had invited seven Latino nuns for the fall semester. Dunn said their English was poor and they were not needed. Volunteers had raised $40,000 to prepare the convent for the sisters; but Dunn turned the convent into a parish center. When Liz Reilly and Millie Pietrzak [pronounced Peeter-zak] complained, Dunn accused them of slander and threatened to excommunicate them. "What you people are doing is evil," he said. "I invite you to *leave* this church."

The old pastor asked them to give Dunn a chance. Dunn invited Nicholas Reveles to refocus the choir, which Bill and Liz had quit by then. Reveles did not become a parish mainstay. Pietrzak also held strong traditional beliefs. When a visiting priest allowed five girls in leotards to dance at the offertory of Mass she thundered from her pew: "This is a desecration!"

Reilly listened to Dunn's sermons, taking notes, even taping some. In one he spoke of a "new age in what we do" and in another, "I am God. You are God"—a far cry to Reilly and others from the concept of God as the Supreme Being and maker of men. Whatever the source of his sermon, Dunn's conflict with parishioners was more than one of personalities. His authority and their faith tradition were clashing. The Reilly-Pietrzak group gathered 660 signatures asking Maher to reinstate the old pastor. When the core group met with Maher, he said that pastors often had different ways of doing things and asked them to accept Father Dunn.

In August 1986 an anonymous caller told Pietrzak about the seminary lawsuit, a copy of which she obtained from the court. The dissidents held a press conference in Pietrzak's home, calling Dunn's changes "creeping Protestantism." Without knowing more about the now settled lawsuit, they chose not to mention homosexuality. "Frankly, the subject scared me," says Pietrzak.

In reporting the El Cajon dispute, San Diego papers mentioned Dunn's role in the lawsuit. On August 16, Dunn told a reporter that Brooks's "charges were false. . . . I have not done anything to violate my vows in the priesthood and I have forgiven the man who made those charges."

People called Pietrzak, saying, "Don't give up." She also got a few obscene calls. She was jittery enough, challenging a pastor.

When a friend telephoned Brooks in Baltimore and read him the story, he was incensed that Steve Dunn, whom he blamed for destroying his vocation, should forgive *him*. He called Millie Pietrzak; they spoke for nearly an hour. He flew back to San Diego, and when he laid out his story in the Reillys' living room, awestruck people asked if he had documents. He showed court papers, his hospital release; he also advised them to meet with Jean Liuzzi.

The El Cajon group spent an afternoon in Liuzzi's office, asking lots of questions. Was Brooks credible? Did she know of many gay priests? Yes, said Liuzzi, who sensed their fears. "If you want to make an impact," she said, "don't just focus on your immediate problems. Your priest is one of many disruptions. When you encompass the whole situation—the seminary, financial problems, pedophilia— it's a stronger message."

But the fight in Reilly and Pietrzak was wearing thin.

Novena services were canceled. Bishop Maher came to say Mass—and asked parishioners to formally pledge their backing of Father Dunn. A third priest arrived but none lived there. The rectory became office space, with late calls taken by an answering service. The atmosphere was remote from what had attracted Liz Reilly at eighteen. When she called the chancery to request a meeting with the bishop, a priest "told me I was a troublemaker, called me a liar, over and over, and said the conversation was being taped."

On St. Patrick's Day, 1987, Reilly and five others met with Maher. They asked why confessions had been moved to the open altar from confessional compartments; people in line could overhear others' words to the priest. They complained of the priests' using their own words in the Nicene Creed. Maher agreed that such a confession practice was "not right" but otherwise stood by the priests.

Says a priest who knew Dunn: "Steve felt hurt because the bishop didn't support him." Yet Maher supported him over parishioners who protested an unraveling spiritual environment. The Reillys began attending Latin Mass at another location.

During a long evening at the Reillys', as the group recounted their thwarted efforts (including letters to Laghi and Rome), I found a form of dissent quite different from that found in the writings of Curran. These lay people saw the gay priest subculture as part of a post-Vatican II breakdown. Devotees of *The Wanderer*, an ultra-conservative Catholic weekly published in St. Paul, they admired Ratzinger. What struck me was their powerlessness in struggling to keep faith in a church that had changed. One man shared his letter to San Francisco Archbishop John Quinn, complaining of "sodomites," a term I would never use. But to dismiss them as mere reactionaries did not do justice to their disillusionment at the hands of a clericalist mentality. They believed in the rules about birth control, premarital sex, homosexuality—and in light of those rules the decay they saw was a product of disobedience to Rome. I was offended by the lengths to which Vatican officers were going to enforce those rules, punishing a devout theologian like Curran. Meanwhile, Rome seemed curiously unmoved by the abuses of gay clericalism.

Liuzzi's complaints, and news reports about gay priests (including several with AIDS), affected the bishop. "There is so much fear in San Diego," a celibate homosexual told me. "In support groups, how many guys share their struggle? People are afraid it gets back to the bishop. . . . They don't feel they can confess their orientation without being sent to the furthest corner of the diocese."

Diocesan clergy take no vow of poverty. But the *Code of Canon Law* is explicit: "Clerics are to follow a simple way of life and avoid anything which smacks of worldliness." Monsignor Kraft's career was a study of contrast to Canon 282. A native of Rochester, New York, he moved west and became pastor at St. Therese in the mid-sixties. "We were young families," a parishioner recalled. "He was very critical of us spending money on houses. That hurt; he said the money should go to the church. He built a rectory with a swimming pool."

In 1966, San Diego police were clamping down on cheating at bingo games in churches and VFW halls. Kenny O'Brien, who was on the vice squad then, responded to complaints in Kraft's parish. "We thought it was rigged. People were given cards making them sure to be winners. With fewer winners, more money was going back to the house. We made a preventive visit. Father Kraft became rude. He said he'd call the chief and have my job. I told him to call. I'm a Catholic and I've never seen a priest act like that." O'Brien's raid was a preventive measure; no charges were filed. The complaints stopped. In a lengthy telephone interview, Kraft told me that the bingo games "were held at arm's length from parish administration. Lay people ran it. No officer ever confronted me."

During that period, a couple complained to the chancery that Kraft had sexually molested their son. This was the family Jean Liuzzi located. The father told me that his son "responded very badly. His future was completely changed. I don't understand how [Kraft] got his honor [becoming a monsignor]. Those priests all hang together. It's all based on money. Nowadays one files a lawsuit. We just left the parish."

Kraft responded to the allegation: "Have they said that under oath? That's twenty-one years ago. I don't recall any such thing. Bishop Furey and I were the very best of friends. He never told me that. Nothing on my records would indicate any such activity you're speaking of. It sounds like a fairy tale. I was very beloved by the people there. I founded St. Therese and left it debt-free. I went to Mira Mesa to found Good Shepherd Parish."

In 1972, Kraft purchased a pair of newly built tract homes on Gold Coast Drive near Good Shepherd for $44,500, with a $9000 down payment. His salary then was $4200 per year. He rented each house for $145 monthly, which he said covered the mortgage. In 1974 he purchased a third house for $34,000, with a $16,000 down payment, renting it out as well. I asked how he got the initial $9000 for down payments. "I can't answer that," he replied. "I don't know. My father was a chief executive at Eastman Kodak. My family was always in a position to help me."

In 1983, with real estate booming, he sold the third house for $98,500, turning a $63,000 profit. In December 1986 he sold the Gold Coast houses for a combined total of $223,000, or a profit of about $179,000. I asked if many priests bought property as he did. "I cannot speak for other priests," he replied. "I'm not responsible for them. I've always been known to be an astute person for the church and if I can do it for the church I can do it for myself in any legal way possible."

By 1978, Kraft was pastor at St. Charles Borromeo, where parishioners sent affidavits to Maher accusing Kraft of berating people who questioned him. "[Kraft] was upset about parish finances," a teacher wrote, and "severely criticized" the Stewardship Program. "It also seems that Father Kraft is driven to destroy anyone he finds threatening . . . by carefully planned schemes against good and dedicated people."

An attorney in the parish wrote the bishop: "I warned Fr. Kraft of the slander laws for his statement of vicious parents spreading false rumors." The attorney's review of parish records showed an $88,197 drop in bingo revenues. "The finances appear to be handled in a highly unusual manner"—five bank accounts, the attorney observed. Sunday collections dropped that year from $100,000 to

$65,000. Reliable sources said that Maher told Kraft to leave the parish after New Year's. When Maher left for a meeting in Washington, Kraft called a parish council meeting, leaking word that he would answer his accusers. Word reached Maher, who telephoned Kraft and ordered him to vacate the rectory that night.

Michael Higgins, the diocesan canonist, took Kraft's place. Sifting through Kraft's records, Higgins* was disturbed to find an account calling for checks to be honored to any bearer without identification. Why would the pastor write checks to people who could not be traced? In a move that floored diocesan priests, Kraft sent a 1978 Christmas letter: "I have accepted our Bishop's assignment as fulltime Director of the Stewardship Program for the Diocese." When I asked Kraft about the events leading to his appointment, he said that Maher appointed him in June 1978 but that he delayed taking the position until December. He said that an outside audit of the parish left the bishop "more than happy. There were no improprieties."

For his *Union* article of December 29, 1985, Jon Standefer examined Kraft's bizarre financial dealings, including the use of various accounts. The reporter showed Kraft copies of checks he had written on bingo accounts. "I can't recall writing those checks," Kraft replied.

"Kraft did not stay in limbo long," wrote Standefer, of the time between Kraft's removal as pastor and his subsequent promotion:

> He made a contribution, which Maher characterized in a thank-you note as "a most generous gift," and was shortly thereafter named director of the stewardship program. Last year Kraft was made a Knight of the Holy Sepulcher; this summer he was elevated to the rank of monsignor.
>
> "He's great at fundraising," says a diocesan source. "That's one of the qualities Maher values most highly."

Kraft told me that he never saw the parishioners' affidavits, that allegations were "fictionated" by a parishioner to whom he had loaned money. "I did not write checks on a bingo account," he stated, oblivious to the checks Jon Standefer showed him. "It was a church account," he insisted. What about his 1978 "gift" to Bishop Maher? "I have at least forty-five different communications with the bishop," he said. "He's a very gracious person and acknowledges any little thing. That [letter] referred to nothing specific that I know or could identify."

Kraft lived in a two-story house with a swimming pool deeded to him by his late mother, and owned a condominium valued at $118,000 in Rancho Mirage, which he had purchased in 1981. I asked about that. "Why does anyone want a second home?" he replied. "That again is another investment that's being rented."

I asked when he had last spoken with Michael Bang. He said: "*Who?*" "Michael Bang." Kraft said: "I don't know who that is."

---

* In 1987, Higgins sued Maher for invasion of privacy, infliction of distress, and breach of employment contract. Higgins claimed that, for insisting that Kraft repay funds to the parish, Maher dismissed him, and agreed to reinstate him only after psychiatric care. Higgins charged that Servants of the Paracletes misdiagnosed him and used electroshock treatment. He was unable to sue the Paracletes because the civil statute of limitations had lapsed. The Court ruled it had no jurisdiction in a clerical dispute.

Jon Standefer had told me about a July 1987 warrant issued for Bang's arrest because of misuse of student government credit cards at a local college. In December 1987, two months after I spoke with Kraft, Bang turned himself in. The Court agreed to a work-release program. Bang fled. In autumn, 1988, he was arrested in Houston and brought back to San Diego. Washed out on alcohol and drugs, he began serving a three-year sentence for grand theft. In a psychologist's report, filed in municipal court, Bang stated that Kraft began molesting him in the fifth grade. At seventeen, Bang attempted suicide in Kraft's home. In the November 30, 1988, *San Diego Union,* Standefer wrote:

> *Bang's sister, a stepmother and his grandmother recently confirmed . . . that Bang had disclosed his relationship with Kraft to them at least 10 years ago, while it was allegedly happening. His stepmother, who was then living in the Bay area, recalled receiving a letter from Kraft, in which the priest warned her that she might hear rumors of homosexual conduct between himself and Bang, and assuring her that the rumors were untrue. Kraft says he never sent such a letter.*

"I emphatically deny any improprieties, sexually or otherwise, in my limited association with Michael Bang," Kraft told the *Union.* "Michael Bang has exhibited emotional imbalance and his untrue accusations are in keeping with this behavior."

Bang's attorney requested the psychological evaluation in hopes of reducing the jail term. Therapist Katherine DiFrancesca characterized Bang as a manic-depressive with a borderline personality who "blames his homosexuality on Father Kraft."

Maher told priests that Bang's story was "hogwash."

Bang's mother committed suicide before he was two. He was shuttled between grandparents and his father, who twice remarried and beat him regularly. The first stepmother, he told the psychologist, hit him "with wire hangers but usually she had dad go after me . . . with a leather belt. . . . He never just took me somewhere. He never talked to me." At the second stepmother's request, he was baptized a Catholic in 1970, at age nine, by Kraft in Good Shepherd Parish. The wreckage of his childhood left the boy vulnerable and in Kraft he seemed to have sought a surrogate parent. The alleged sexual abuse began shortly after that.

In 1972 he moved with his family. In 1975, sexually confused, a high school sophomore at odds with his father, he went to live with Kraft, where the sexual molesting resumed, according to DiFrancesca's report. Bang said Kraft gave him money, clothes, and covered his bank overdrafts during high school. Kraft denied it but told Standefer that Bang spent "a week or two" with the priest's parents. Bang left for Iowa to visit grandparents but returned two weeks later. Kraft met him at the bus station and dropped him at home. A short time later Kraft found Bang on the bathroom floor; he had swallowed pills belonging to Kraft's mother.

According to Kraft, Michael left a suicide note saying "that he could not be separated from a male friend that he met in Iowa." On release from the hospital, he left Kraft forever. The memories would endure like a cross upon the soul.

He worked as a medical assistant, restaurant manager, and cashier until 1983 when he joined the Mormon church. After eighteen months in Paraguay as a

Mormon missionary he returned with growing concern about his attraction to men, confessed it to a Mormon bishop, and was excommunicated. He enrolled in Grossmount College, plunged into campus politics, and got elected student body president. In July 1987, at a conference in Beverly Hills with other students, his entourage began running up $29,000 in charges on Student Government Association credit cards—hitting nightclubs and swank restaurants—while Bang stayed in the hotel drinking vodka and snorting cocaine. That night he wrecked his car, checked into a hospital for several hours, then caught a night flight to Utah to see his lover. He returned to San Diego just before Christmas of 1987 and turned himself in. The Court agreed to a private work-furlough program. On August 13, 1988, the day he was to begin, he left to see his lover in Utah.

"He is the only person who ever loved me unconditionally," Bang told the court psychologist of his lover. "I just didn't want to lose him."

Two weeks later he was arrested in Houston with his friend, brought back to San Diego, and sentenced to three years. Therapist DiFrancesca wrote:

When asked what he thought was wrong with him that he would be so stupid [as to flee], Mr. Bang mainly cried. "Is it so stupid to want to be loved? I've been looking for this all my life." Mr. Bang indicated that he has never been happy or felt that he belonged any place.

The seminary scandal, the rifts in the El Cajon parish, the diocese's unorthodox financial dealings, Maher's unswerving support of Kraft—these examples leave the image of a diocese run amok. "The San Diego diocese is out of control," a well-connected Western Jesuit told me in 1987. "It is replete with elements of materialism, worldliness, and leadership corruption in the area of Kraft. The most benign interpretation is that the bishop is naive, and has not given the clergy and laity a vision of what Christian life should be. The more devastating interpretation is that the bishop has personal liabilities to conceal, and to protect his own situation, he's got to protect some of his henchmen."

"The institution will live with scandals," remarked Eugene Kennedy, "but not with Charlie Curran. It's no secret San Diego has had problems for years."

When Maher spoke at a clergy retreat, gays in the back snickered at him; they resented his refusal to accept a gay priest unless he passed an AIDS test. Two local priests (one a high school chaplain) had just died of AIDS. Ironically, Maher's old-boy network mentality, of standing by his priests, offended traditional laity who otherwise would have supported him. In Maher the old clericalism, premised on orthodoxy and monetary clout, was subsumed by a gay clericalism which yawned at tradition and wielded power behind a wall of sexual secrecy.

Michael Bang was apparently the final straw for the Vatican. On April 22, 1989, the Vatican announced the appointment of Robert H. Brom of Winona, Minnesota, as coadjutor bishop of San Diego. Maher had the diocese purchase a $500,000 home for Brom. The new bishop said no thanks, sell the house. He was taking up quarters in the seminary, which had plenty of room.

On July 7, 1990, after twice undergoing surgery for a brain tumor, the seventy-five-year-old Maher officially passed the miter to Brom. In February 1991, Maher died of cerebral cancer. Nicholas Reveles left the priesthood. Kraft moved to Hawaii. Dunn began working with AIDS victims.

After the 1985 seminary scandal, enrollment was reduced to a trickle. But, by 1991, Brom had a new administration in place, with 27 students at St. Francis.

Mark Brooks abandoned his lifelong desire to become a priest and went to work for a company providing security systems. "I often looked toward the priesthood and the priests I knew at seminary for guidance based on the supernatural quality of their office," he reflected in a letter to me. "It was established by Christ and used to be known for holiness, humility, and yes, even piety. Instead I saw men under great pressure. Some blame celibacy. Others, the rigidity of Rome. I attribute the failure to a lack of faith—faith in God, faith in the holiness of their office. I think that above all a priest is supposed to be a man of prayer. They were not. I was hard pressed to find any of them praying in chapel, or reading their daily office.

"As a priest I would have loved to work with families that have been broken like mine. To reassure them of this reality: no matter how many times human love fails and fidelity is forsaken, there is one who never forgets, one who never fails to love."

xvi.

Wounded Seminaries

In a 1985 address to the Catholic Press Association, the Rev. James Burtchaell, a conservative theologian at Notre Dame, remarked that seminaries were once known "for the fresh and healthy people that studied there. . . . Today there is a dominant culture in many seminaries which is given to indulgence and effeminacy. . . . Many years ago the common pathologies afflicting priests in this country emerged from fatigue and showed themselves in eccentricity and alcohol use. Today there are pathologies involving sexual maturity and materialism that may be even worse." Ironically, Burtchaell left Notre Dame in 1991 under a cloud of scandal, accused of having made sexual advances to male students.

American bishops who built cathedrals knew that the spread of faith lay in vocations, the call of young people to religious life. As bastions of discipline, seminaries educated young males for holy orders. Shaped in the 1560s at the Council of Trent, the system sought a stronger reliance on discipline as a response to the Protestant Reformation. Seminaries forged a hierarchical worldview, with obedience and prayer meant to foster sexual sublimation.

In the United States seminary enrollment peaked in the mid-sixties, and since then has dropped *eighty-nine* percent. From 1969 to 1987 the number of high-school-age seminarians dropped from 15,737 to 2448. Major seminary, or college-age, enrollment dropped from 13,261 to 3934 in the same span. Enrollment in the theologates, or postgraduate study houses—which sociologist Dean Hoge calls "the most crucial" because they are the last step before ordination—dropped from 8885 in 1965 to 3698 in 1989.

For every 100 priests who die, retire, or resign, only 59 new ones are ordained. Opposition to celibacy alone does not explain the plunge in numbers. "When you look around the Church today," the Rev. James L. Caddy, president of Borromeo College in Cleveland, has written, "when you see overworked and often unhappy priests, when you see laity that continually raise their expectations and seldom seem pleased, what is there externally to attract vocations? When a perceptive young man observes such behavior, why should he want to join such an organization?"

American Catholic families produced a stream of vocations that peaked shortly after Vatican II. In interviews or conversations with priests over age fifty-five, I found broad consensus on the two vital sources of that current: the priests' mothers and the priests who influenced them as boys. Large families encouraged children drawn to religious life. Before women joined the work force, mothers volunteered for parish projects that brought them closer to priests. The more popular a priest, the more apt were women to encourage sons considering a vocation. Better educated than most of their parishioners, priests were esteemed. But by 1965 children of a prospering church were graduating from Catholic universities, embarking on careers unavailable to many of their parents. Priests were still respected, but a mystique was diminishing.

Cardinal Hickey, who entered a Michigan seminary at thirteen, recalled his altar boy service with a priest in the Saginaw diocese. "We talked about a lot of things," he told reporter Charlotte Hays. "I was impressed with his happiness, his dedication to the church. That struck a responsive chord. And you have to remember I was raised in a very pious home."

At the great moments priests were there to baptize infants, marry the young, anoint the dying, bury the dead. Many formed friendships with families in the parish. Women who confessed their sins to such priests could entrust their sons to seminaries known as strict training grounds for the soldiers of Christ. The mother anticipated the day when her son would become Father, with souls of his own to shepherd, like saints of the mythic past.

In 1981 Pope John Paul II ordered studies of seminaries in the United States, South America, and the Philippines. The Vatican chose Burlington, Vermont, Bishop John Marshall to head the study of U.S. seminaries. Bishop Donald Wuerl, former rector of a Pittsburgh seminary, was chief investigator. The study was never made public. In September 1986 (as Wuerl assumed his short-lived control over Hunthausen's authority in Seattle), Cardinal Baum issued a statement that "a few [seminaries] have one or more serious deficiencies," but offered little detail. He cited concerns over "weaker" scholarship and the presence of nonclerics in seminary classes.

In September 1984 a committee of the NCCB proposed a seminary policy in which men with "a public patterned lifestyle reflecting homosexual orientation" not be admitted. "Lifestyle" was not defined. A Boston auxiliary bishop called the policy "impossible to implement" because seminaries could not separate celibate homosexuals from those "active and totally without personal control." In June 1985, Youngstown, Ohio, Bishop James Malone, then president of the NCCB, discussed questions of homosexuality in seminaries with Cardinal Baum in Rome. On July 9, Baum issued a memorandum warning that "a homosexual lifestyle, whether one is actively gay or not, is unacceptable." Should orientation then be grounds for dismissal? If so, chaste homosexuals would have to lie about themselves.

The stake in these concerns was not small, according to Father Richard McBrien, a well-known liberal theologian at Notre Dame. "If the bishops honestly confronted the seminary crisis, they'd have to close them down," he said. "They're fraught with gays. Celibacy provides a cover for lots of homosexuals who are running away from sexuality. It also discourages healthy heterosexual males who would be terrific priests."

In *Seminary*, a fine account by Paul Hendrickson, the *Washington Post* reporter looks back on the religious life that might have been, and an environment that has vanished. In 1958, at fourteen, Hendrickson left home in Illinois for an Alabama seminary known as Holy Trinity. He stayed until 1965. Of the 21 boys in his class, one became a priest. In 1958 there were 381 American seminaries. By 1978, 259 had closed, including Holy Trinity. A curtain was lowering on a way of learning, a way of life.

> *The seminary was so focused [he writes] in the direction of books and prayer, it was hard sometimes to remember you were a teenager. Saturday afternoon was free . . . and so was Sunday afternoon after Vespers. Sunday night, following Benediction, the paper chase began all over again.*

Hendrickson also wrote of the sexual dynamics in those older times. "We still talked an awful lot about girls," he said.

> *Generally my attention seemed directed toward a select three or four seminarians every year; my subconscious must have done the preselecting. Sometimes they were seminarians older than I, though more often they were younger boys who tended to the fair-skinned and slight-framed. By turns I could feel jealousy, ardor, anger, and protectiveness for them. The prefects knew about such hidden emotions in us, I believe, and watched us like cats from a perch. No one talked about it. And I could stop neither my feelings nor my shame.*

Apart from adolescent impulses—an erotic stimulation caused by brushing against another; "mooning" jokes about flashing one's butt—Hendrickson records no homosexual behavior.

> *At its repressive worst, I suppose it could be said that the "system" led to some voyeurism, some morbid preoccupations, certain passive-aggressive dysfunctions. You could say our behavior was too imitative and conditioned by fear. Too often, I think, we were given to understand our sexuality as the enemy of chastity. The myth was that the body could be overcome. The body was for chastising. And while all of this may be true, more or less, it is also probably irrelevant. . . . No amount of amateur hindsight will explain how and why one hundred boys coped, dug in, got by. Got by? Most of us were nuts for the place. The school was strange in certain ways, yes, and it was also spiritual and mystical, deeply so. There was awe there. . . . I know dozens of priests and brothers from my old religious community and from other communities in the Church who seem to me neither unhappy nor maladjusted.*

In the old seminaries, "particular friendships" was a term of warning against homosexuality. William X. Kienzle, ordained in Detroit in 1954, left the priesthood in 1974. He went on to publish *The Rosary Murders* and a string of detective novels. "When we were going through seminary," Kienzle recalled, "exquisite precautions were taken against anyone of a homosexual leaning. The old seminaries turned out macho, asexual beings who had an absolute and unparalleled fraternity.

On weekends off, guys played golf, swam, shot billiards. As far as I could tell, it was extremely rare and definitely covert if any sort of [homosexual] behavior took place. I think there's been a drastic change. It's almost patently obvious now that a healthy percentage, if not the majority of new priests are not the same kind of people."

"It's more common than I ever thought," remarked theologian Anthony Kosnik, former dean of a seminary outside Detroit, of homosexuals in the seminaries. Besides homosexuality, Kosnik spoke of other factors that had also changed in seminaries. "The standards were higher in our day because seminaries were full, ergo competitive. Now, with less numbers, there's less quality. . . . The big problem in seminaries is that they're isolated from real life. The result is an inability to relate to other people, and worse, an attitude of superiority that allows the church to continue its dominating attitude. It bothers me when priests coming out [of seminary] attempt to tell more mature people how to run a parish. They have the power because the church gives it to them. Formation of ministry should be open to all people."

The seminary culture through which Kienzle and Kosnik passed certainly had homosexuals. But the cultural conditioning was heterosexual. "Macho, asexual beings" considered celibacy hard sacrifice but not a betrayal of manhood. Homosexuals in the pre-Vatican II seminaries, like those in society, were subtle about their orientations. The regimented milieu meant to restrict young men from women was sex-negative; and yet, whatever its flaws, the tradition generated vocations.

Amid the search in the 1970s for new formation policies, psychosexual pressures began to grow. When William Quigley was studying at St. Meinrad Seminary in rural Indiana in 1967, students no longer had to wear cassocks; women were on the faculty. Today a civil rights attorney, Quigley, who left St. Meinrad in 1970, says that open discussion of sexuality "wasn't even on the agenda." He continues: "I remember a psychologist gave a talk to us after he had done attitudinal testing. The results showed more of a 'feminine' interest in things—arts, music, literature—as opposed to more masculine things, like engineering and math. This caused a fair amount of controversy. As far as [gay] acting out, I'm sure it went on, but no more than on any college campus. When I was at St. Meinrad, you wouldn't dare say you were gay but celibate."

In 1976, twenty-two-year-old Len Cooper, a tall, lanky Alabamian, began studies at St. Meinrad, the first black seminarian from Birmingham. In a 1986 *Washington Post* essay, Cooper, a pressman at the paper, recalled experiencing racial slurs and fending off sexual advances from seminarians, and even from a monk in the library. "Homosexuality led to anger among heterosexual students, who would sometimes arm themselves with sticks," Cooper wrote, "and go out on what they called 'queer beatings.' They didn't actually attack the gays in the school, just made an effort to scare the hell out of them."

When Cooper told a seminary official of the gay-straight tensions and his own problem, he was reprimanded. After two years he was dismissed because of a "vocation crisis"—in fact, he says, because he complained about the sexually charged environment. The story of his departure first appeared in a 1979 *Post* article by a reporter who found him working as a lifeguard in Washington. St. Meinrad's then director, Father Thomas Ostick, denied that the seminary had a homosexual problem and called Cooper "an enigma." After Cooper's more detailed article of 1986, the *Post* published a reply from a St. Meinrad representative:

> *Our priestly formation programs are subject to very close scrutiny. . . . If there were any evidence to suggest the kind of gross negligence alleged in the article, it would have been noted by one or more of these formal reviews. As a matter of public record, we have not received any such notations.*

When I met Cooper, he brooded about the aftermath of his seminary crisis and about his loss of Catholic faith: "It wasn't the homosexuality, as much as the outright denial by St. Meinrad's authorities that what I encountered actually happened."

In his study of celibacy, Richard Sipe writes that more than one hundred priests—approximately one tenth of his selected sample—"reported problematic sexual approaches" during seminary years. Of these, "a few [incidents] had the force of real sexual abuse where the betrayal of the generational barrier was severely traumatic."

In 1986 an adult seminarian at Notre Dame in New Orleans invited a high school boy into his room, plied him with drinks, and molested him. The boy went home and destroyed property in his neighborhood before telling his parents. The seminarian was expelled. The family sued; the archdiocese settled with them for more than $600,000.

In another case, a young man identified in litigation as F.J. was fourteen in 1973 when he was expelled from St. Joseph's, a seminary in Edgerton, Wisconsin, operated by Redemptorist Fathers. The seminary had closed when attorney Jeffrey Anderson of St. Paul, Minnesota, brought suit in 1987 against Brother Newman Moore, two priests who ran the seminary, the school, the religious order, and the companies that held the seminary's insurance policies during the years in question.

"I represent the downtrodden, the underprivileged, the disempowered, those who have been stomped by the powerful," Anderson has said. In the late 1980s he negotiated claims exceeding $10 million for clients in more than fifty abuse cases involving ministers, most of them Catholic clergy. The foremost plaintiff attorney in the field, Anderson was instrumental in drafting a Minnesota law allowing child abuse victims to file suit as adults within two years of consciously discovering cause of injury.

The sixth of ten children, F.J. was the fourth male sibling to attend the seminary. All of the brothers eventually left. The suit charged that Brother Moore, who ran the carpentry shop, sexually molested F.J. "two to three times per week over a period of six months." As word of the liaison spread, several students ganged up on F.J. The suit charged that the rector expelled the boy, "using the untrue excuse [that he made] sexual advances toward other boys."

In deposition, a defense attorney asked, "You had been made the scapegoat, so to speak, is that what you're saying?"

"Well," replied the plaintiff, "I knew that I had done something terrible in my family's eyes."

He thought his parents had been told that his sexual relations with Moore caused the expulsion. His parents thought that he had been a discipline problem. When Moore sent letters and cassette tapes, they thought he was trying to help their troubled son. The summer after F.J.'s expulsion, Moore took him on a camping trip. "I was feeling guilt all the time about the sexual end of it," F.J. recalled. "The friendship part of it, no. I wanted to go back [to him] something awful."

Further testimony revealed that F.J. developed intense hostility toward his mother, whom he subconsciously blamed for not protecting him. The parents, meanwhile, entrusted F.J. to their parish priest for spiritual guidance. The seminary's preoccupation with secrecy spun a web of denial over all concerned. In his deposition Moore denied the sexual activity, only to grope for an explanation of the love letters and taped messages that Jeffrey Anderson put in evidence. Moore's personnel records showed frequent changes of assignment. He was later removed from the seminary after a priest saw another boy leave his room at an odd hour and reported him to superiors. Moore stayed in the order and sought ordination; however, it was denied.

In 1975, F.J. spent five days in a psychiatric hospital after threatening a girl who spurned him. Shortly thereafter he was seduced by a male disc jockey. Later, he sought counsel with a diocesan priest—who paid him $25 to masturbate. Yet another priest—a family friend his mother asked to help the youth—became intrigued with F.J.'s pornographic films; eventually they masturbated together. Married and divorced by eighteen, F.J. testified that his ex-wife listened to the tapes Moore had sent. F.J. procured men to have sexual encounters with his wife, while he watched "about a hundred times," he testified. The voyeurism continued into his second marriage. Defense attorneys questioned F.J. about his sexual patterns:

> Q: You have had affairs with between fifty and eighty males?
> A: Roughly.

When questioned about his heterosexual affairs, he stated: "I would say closer to eighty females. . . ."

> Q: Do you intend to continue threesome relationships with your second wife?
> A: There is a cycle every time when it happens, and then for two or three days I get very depressed, and then I start building towards it again. It's an obsession. . . .
> Q: During all those years that you were having these, what I would refer to as unusual sexual relations, you never once thought that your propensity to have those types of relations were related to your earlier experiences [with clerics]?
> A: I think towards the end of my marriage, I realized that the attraction of threesomes was the humiliation and degradation that those situations caused me, and I think I started to put two and two together.

The lawsuit was settled for $400,000.

Although most dioceses require seminarians to pass HIV tests before ordination, the changing sexual mores do not appear to have touched all seminaries. The diocesan seminary in Peoria, Illinois, to cite one, enjoys a reputation as a solid, celibate environment, committed to church tradition. Likewise, St. Joseph's Seminary in New York (called Dunwoodie, for the Yonkers neighborhood where it lies) is strongly traditional, as one would expect from Cardinal John O'Connor's archdiocese.

But if these seminaries appear to be free of sexual difficulties, they are not problem-free. A four-story structure of Renaissance design, Dunwoodie was built to house 240 men. "Hollow echoes on the gleaming terra-cotta floors call attention to the diminishing numbers," writes Paul Wilkes in the *Atlantic*. "About seventy-five [are] in training at Dunwoodie, ten or so of them sent from dioceses like Lincoln, Nebraska, and Gallup, New Mexico—staunch Catholic bastions that appreciate the classical, directed education." Men wear traditional clerical garb. No women study here. Falling enrollment fed a loss of

> *faculty members cherished by most institutions . . . those who publish and are known in their field. They have left complaining that an unimaginative curriculum and loyalty to Rome produce neither good priests nor good scholarship, and that the school does not pay enough attention to the psychological deficiencies and the immaturity of those students who otherwise do well in classes, and who reflexively profess orthodoxy.*

Sexual dynamics alone do not explain the failure of the pre-Vatican II generation of priests to inspire their successors. Rome's unbending insistence on *Humanae Vitae*, the crackdown on progressive theologians, and the denial of ministerial roles for women signal a fearful failure to embrace Vatican II's call for the church to embrace the modern world.

Some believe these disturbing patterns of seminary life will not change unless a greater value is placed on truthfulness. "Where vocations are concerned," a celibate homosexual reflected, "even with all the psychological testing, until we see *integrity* as a prerogative, until we ask them to define it, we're not going to get good men. Sexually active men, pedophiles, and closeted men will continue getting through the system as long as the emphasis is on quantity versus quality. The issue for me is not sexual preference but how they've integrated it into their experiences. The priesthood is a great place to hide."

And, in the opinion of some experts, there are built-in factors of church governance that work against these calls for integrity. Therapists Richard Sipe and Sister Fran Ferder, who have both treated many priests for a range of problems, consider the Vatican mindset that condemns all sexual activity outside of marriage to be locked in an adolescent stage of psychosexual development. This mindset is marked by passive-aggressive impulses toward woman and by a denial of acting-out behavior by both gays and straights that is going on under the bishops' watch. Trying to hide its sexual secrets, the ecclesiastical power structure, grounded in sexual segregation, then attacks those who expose or seek the truth.

ii.

Seminaries require psychological testing of applicants, with therapy usually available for students. The Rev. John Yockey, a professor of moral theology at Washington Theological Union, said of a typical student: "As he struggles to sort out important growth issues like his sexual identity and the quality and authenticity of his interpersonal relationships, if a seminarian works with a professional counselor, rather than looked upon as a stigma, such a decision is a real 'badge of health.'"

And yet the reliance on therapeutic models can become warped when used to advance an agenda. An anonymous seminarian writes in *Crisis*, a conservative Catholic journal, of "numerous seminarians and priests who are sexually active both with women and men." He also complains of faculty pressure to "conform to substandard or heterodox notions in order to avoid ridicule or, a worse weapon, the MX missile of the modern seminary: psychological accusations." He continues:

> *[A] faculty member at one seminary . . . spoke on the subject of homosexuality nearly all the time. This was also the subject of his graduate work. His obsession was well-noted by students and the source of wry amusement. But the real danger was that the faculty member was involved in rather intensely domineering (though not necessarily sexual) relationships with particularly impressionable students. The rector and other faculty were well-aware of this but failed to do anything about it.*

The Rev. Richard McGinnis, rector of Mount St. Mary in Emmitsburg, Maryland—the nation's second oldest seminary, founded in 1808—told me that seminarians of the late 1980s "resemble the generation of which they are a part—more conservative, they look for clear structures. As part of our screening, we look at a man's sexual behavior. The orientation is not problematic if he lives a celibate lifestyle. I look for a staying pattern in celibate living, also solid, meaningful relationships that are not marked by sexually acting out."

The Rev. Robert Levitt, rector of St. Mary's in Baltimore, was also upbeat. "The diocese is screening much more carefully, both psychologically and in terms of moral history," he told me in 1986. "At rectors' meetings I have attended, [homosexuality] has been a major item. But I see less problems than a few years ago, when the issue was really burning. Whenever an institution like the church is in flux, there's a sense of old ways falling apart. In the seventies, there were patterns of sexual ambiguity, suggestions of living with celibacy-redefined. We don't find that any more. We're getting older candidates who are more like the church that is out there. The average age here is twenty-seven. Their motivation in the sense of vocation is much clearer."

In a 1986 interview, Kevin Gordon, a former Christian Brother and gay activist in New York, told me that seminaries had a role in the pederasty phenomenon, which he called "a boomerang coming back from a repressed system." Gordon argued that priestly formation which did not affirm homosexuality forced men into lives of denial, with child molesting the worst manifestation of this acting out. Gordon later died of AIDS. The homophobia which he and others denounced was real. But the same system that condemned homogenital behavior and opposed the use of condoms to prevent transmission of the disease had ordained thousands of gay priests, established AIDS hospices, and quietly buried its own priests with AIDS, even as its public stance opposed use of condoms as one barrier to the lethal virus.

This same system has also reassigned countless pederasts. *Time* reported that ninety-five percent of priests at the monastic hospital in New Mexico (which reportedly treated some 230 child molesters) were put back into clerical life. Although *Time* did not examine the kind of ministries to which they returned, or post-treatment tracking of the offenders, the article reflected a clear ecclesiastical policy: recycle child molesters whenever possible.

iii.

If pederasty among priests was a reaction to a repressed seminary culture, the reaction occurred along a twisted line of narcissism. It is important to say again that I am speaking of seminary culture—not wider society. It is the effect of this culture on the acting out of homosexuals and heterosexuals that is at issue. As has been noted before, in the wider society studies show that the vast majority of homosexuals, like most heterosexuals, do not molest children. At the same time it would be irresponsible not to note that a strain of gay culture is taken up with youth-love and has been noted in the church for centuries. Many gay bookstores feature books celebrating man-youth (if not man-boy) sex, with covers depicting a kind of eternal male youth—he could be twenty-five or fifteen. Manhattan's Gay Pride parade includes the North American Man Boy Love Association, a pedophile club that advocates repeal of laws governing the age of sexual consent.

"A homosexual and a pedophile are not synonymous," states Sister Fran Ferder, a therapist who treats clergy with pedophilia and other problems in the Seattle archdiocese. "A true diagnostic pedophile does not necessarily have a good grasp of his sexual orientation. There can be a lot of crossover between little girls and little boys. . . . One could speculate that there is a tendency among many homosexual men, particularly in their twenties, to experience a delayed adolescence. When they have no way of engaging in homosexual dating while living at home, sexual exploration gets put on hold and acted out later on, in college, or in one's twenties. I think some Catholic gay men delay it altogether and choose seminary as an acceptable way of not having to deal with sexuality. And then it comes out when they're in their twenties or thirties, emotionally at an age of fifteen or sixteen—a regressive homosexuality."

Dr. Jay Feierman, a psychiatrist who has treated scores of clergy child molesters at the Paracletes' monastic hospital in New Mexico, does not accept the notion of regressive homosexuality, but echoes Ferder on the reasons for the attractiveness of seminary to some: "If you show adult men slides of male children, less of them are aroused than heterosexual men looking at slides of young girls. The typical homosexual has no interest in pubescent boys. Ones who are involved with boys are rarely involved with men. Celibacy tends to attract people who have no socially acceptable outlet for their proclivities."

According to experts, the pedophile or ephebophile returns, through his victims, to the point where his psychosexual aging process stopped. Thus, in the case of pederasty, the older man's narcissistic urges seize on a self-image buried in his psychic past as he seeks sexual fulfillment with a youth.

There are also some homosexuals who are drawn to an age zone of young manhood that hovers close to the age of legal consent. An account of this phenomenon appears in *States of Desire: Travels in Gay America* by Edmund White. "A young man of twenty who had arrived in L.A. only a month before has already been offered a dozen situations," he writes. "Wealthy men compete with one another for the privilege, no matter how short-lived, of supporting an attractive newcomer."

White then writes of a gay man who was slow to accept his orientation:

> *He never had a lover until last summer, when he met a Beautiful Boy in New York. The Boy returned to Los Angeles with him—and was instantly met by a big rush. At parties, right under his lover's nose, the Boy has received offers of everything from dinner or jewelry to plane trips to Egypt (accompanied, of course) to a ranch, deed and all. . . .*

"In fact, he's no boy," writes White. He's a young man, albeit "kept." But when age-of-consent laws are at issue, the youth obsession becomes a potentially criminal matter. Published in 1980, before child molestation became a national concern, White's book was celebrated in the gay press and favorably reviewed by mainstream critics. The last chapter is an apologia for sex with minors that would be unlikely to elicit the same level of praise in the nineties.

> *If there are two areas of gay life likely to outrage the straight community they are sex with minors and sex in public places [notes White]. Many gay theorists contend that the age of consent should be lowered to fourteen. Critics of pedophilia contend that children are easily manipulated by adults—through threats, through actual force, through verbal coercion, through money. A kid who wants extra spending money might be lured into sex by an unscrupulous adult [and] ruined.*

In defending man-boy love, White portrays youngsters as victims of their parents, because of whom "They can't vote, they can't drink, they can't run away, they can't enter certain movie theatres . . . can't refuse to go to school." He gives no sense of the power imbalance in adult-child sexual contact, no consideration to the fact that good parents try to protect, nurture, and raise children in a society that often seems to have lost its moral bearings. Instead, White records his sympathetic dialogue with a pedophile who speaks warmly of his "lover"—a boy twelve years of age. White then reflects:

> *I told him my own experiences. I had been a sissy boy constantly hankering for the affection of an adult man (anyone over seventeen—a soldier, say—seemed adult.*

> . . . *When I was thirteen I did sleep with an adult Indian in Acapulco and at*
> *fifteen I had a brief affair with a man in his forties. . . . When I was a child and*
> *wanted an older lover, he was envisioned as a savior, someone who would free me*
> *from the tyranny of my parents, who would* value *me.*

Whatever the parental tyranny he sought to escape, White's equation of self-value with sexual contact exposes a pathetic notion of dignity, as if a youth achieves integrity more through sexual contact with an elder than by the guidance of a teacher and the kindness of responsible mentors.

Some time later he expanded on his theory, telling an interviewer:

> *Many gay men have a fantasy about having an affair with their fathers; it*
> *seems to be a persistent but seldom mentioned theme. But if you become intimate with*
> *gay men you find that many of us have had this fantasy (sometimes it gets trans-*
> *ferred to an uncle or older brother, but it tends to stay within the family). . . .*
> *Sufficient time had gone by since my adolescence that I could write about it from a*
> *new, different point of view. Some sort of relationship of attraction, even affection,*
> *existed between the I (the middle-aged narrator looking back at this adolescent self)*
> *and the boy himself—a relationship I call "the pederasty of autobiography."*

Pederasty is another term for man-boy love, which was idealized in the bisexual male aristocracy of ancient Greece. Modern democracy, with its premium on individual rights, rejects the power imbalance and narcissism that pederasty entails. "The true narcissist is as familiar with self-hate as he is with self-love," writes John Crewdson in *By Silence Betrayed: Sexual Abuse of Children in America.* "No matter what he pretends to others or even to himself, deep inside he knows that his exalted self-image is a sham." Gay men who cannot sustain relationships with adults and so seek out youths are regressive homosexuals. Those who have this condition—as well as gay men who are simply unhappy about being homosexual —would qualify as ego-dystonic, or those in conflict with their orientation; the category that *DSM III* dropped in 1986.

The dominant pattern of American priests reported for abusing minors falls into the category of ephebophilia, sexual involvement with adolescents as opposed to prepubertal victims. Data in society show that most child molesters prey on girls. The seeming reversal of this pattern among priests is partially, most experts agree, the product of a segregated male culture that restricts sexual maturity at one extreme and, at the other, tolerates sexual rebels, some of whom are regressively focused on young people.

Of pedophilia in general, Dr. Fred Berlin has written: "Biological pathologies such as structural brain damage, hormonal dysfunctions, genetic anomalies, or electrical disturbances of the brain seem to play a role." Common, too, is a history of childhood abuse among adult offenders. Not infrequently one finds that a child molester priest was himself abused by a priest and thus suffers a distorted sexual identity. These patterns pass through clerical environments like incest through a kin-line.

History shows persistent fears of pederasty among early church leaders. As Christianity shaped new thinking about sexuality, the Greco-Roman sexual mores, which were permissive toward pederasty, slowly lost favor. The Council of Elvira in 305 prohibited "corrupters of boys" from ever receiving communion. St. Basil issued rigid penalties governing adult treatment of children in monasteries, where many priests literally grew up, arriving as oblates, or "gifts" of wellborn parents. Others entered as orphans. "Oblates assumed the duty of minding one another's morality," writes scholar Patricia Quinn of medieval French monastic life. "[U]nder the supervision of the masters, [moral reciprocity] deepened the boys' understanding of social interaction and the virtues that ought to regulate the relations of monks—charity, obedience, and above all, humility."

Segregated from the men, oblates still had sexual urges, which abbots apparently viewed with measures of tolerance. Boys who kissed "licentiously" leading to "pollution" (ejaculation) received a penance of ten special fasts. Those who masturbated together were denied communion for twenty to forty days. Yet in an all-male environment passionate attachments were inevitable, and some became sexual. Although a series of canons condemned sodomy, the response of ecclesial authorities toward homogenital acts was more tolerant than persecutorial until the Middle Ages.

In a respected history of attitudes toward homosexuality from early Christianity to the Middle Ages, John Boswell quotes an abundance of homoerotic literature that flourished in monasteries. The poems contain many images of youth. But, writes Boswell,

> Most used terms which suggested erotic attraction for young men and for older males interchangeably, clearly implying that age was not a consideration. The term "pederasty" frequently has no more relation to the age of the objects of desire than "girl chasing."

In the eleventh century, however, Peter Damian, a Benedictine reformer, wrote an urgent tract, *Liber Gomorrhianus*, condemning clerical homosexuality, with a sharp focus on pederasty:

> A cleric or monk who seduces youths or young boys or is found kissing or in any other impure situations is to be publicly flogged. . . . When his hair has been shorn, his face is to be foully besmeared with spit and he is to be bound in iron chains. For six months he will languish in prison-like confinement and on three days of each week shall fast on barley bread in the evening. After this he will spend six months under the custodial care of a spiritual elder, remaining in a segregated cell, giving himself to manual work and prayer, subject to vigils and prayers.

Damian wanted all homosexual clerics ousted. Pope Leo IX took a more restrained course, giving clergy opportunities of self-reform. A subsequent Pope, Alexander II, "an ardent and determined reformer," writes Boswell, "actually stole the *Liber Gommorhianus* from Peter and kept it locked away."

Although it is unclear whether clerical homosexuality was widespread in Damian's time, his concerns arose when monasteries were becoming overcrowded. Entry age was raised to eleven years; these boys lived amid many men who had had sexual experience in society. Love poems by monks in the late tenth and early eleventh centuries included celebrations of *paederastia,* influenced by Greek verse. Perhaps in response to this phenomenon, writes Patricia Quinn, a sculptural arch in the monastery of Vézelay depicts the Greek myth of the boy shepherd Ganymede seduced by the god Zeus. In this monastic rendition—"strategically placed in a zone where monks and children would have come together frequently to play and sing"—a leering devil looks down at the horrified boy. Probably a warning to oblates, the sculpture reflects Damian's perspective and "equates child seduction with rape," writes Quinn. Eventually monasteries stopped accepting boys.

iv.

The impact of changes in seminaries of the 1970s and eighties began surfacing in the 1990s. Dean Hoge studied priestly morale and found it low. "Putting it simply," writes Hoge, "seminary training in the past did not emphasize institutional leadership, and probably the majority of priests today feel inadequate to the task."

Training in leadership relies on mentors who imbue their followers with durable values. The bishops' concerns about acting-out behaviors underscore the immaturity of a learning environment presumed to mold men healthy enough to balance mature identities and the promise of chastity. That mandate is hard enough under the best of circumstances. Is the old idea of woman-as-temptress being supplanted by concerns of men-attracted-to-men? A deeper ill lies beneath such fears.

Seminaries should be centers of scholarship, where moral teaching is strengthened by interdisciplinary research. Rome's attack on liberal theologians reveals the ecclesiastical mind closing in on itself, afraid of outside learning. And the numerical decline of seminarians mirrors the Catholic laity's detachment from a hierarchy walled in by Rome's calcified politics. How can seminaries train men for leadership in a clerical culture at odds with its own moral code?

Theological College in Washington, D.C., is run by Sulpicians, an order founded in France that has a long history of educating seminarians. Located on the Catholic University campus—also known as the "little Vatican"—TC was once considered a premier American seminary. A therapist who had counseled seminarians there told me that all too many of them had "character problems—not only in terms of sexuality but also in terms of values. Some are beautiful people; others are corrupt. . . . The institutional church is desperate to keep them unmarried. The church is going to destroy itself if this doesn't stop."

The most impressive TC student I met was in his final year and has since been ordained. In his initial class of thirty, thirteen lasted. Said he: "I would say sixty to seventy percent of them are gay, and in the seminary an equal figure. I have a friend—a homosexual—who would say ninety percent."

What was it like for a heterosexual in a gay environment? "I'd known homosexuals before and accepted them as people. It was my first time in an all-male situation. I felt some demoralizing—a demythologizing of ministry. I feel that I struggle with my sexuality in a different way. They notice it when a woman comes into seminary or a cleric's life. That is a cause for raising of questions and observations, whereas a homosexual can bring someone into his life and it's not frowned upon. . . . My first year I found a lot of [sexual] overtures, but as time goes on it hasn't occurred as much. I was aloof in some ways because I did not want to be sexually attractive. I have a couple of women friends, but it is not like dating.

"Some [seminarians] do hit the gay bars. Some abstain and see the vow through; others are acting out in ways not characteristic of priestly life. At a social, people let go. Drinking leads to more drinking, and drives take over. Guys might start dancing, maybe leading to other actions. I have thought, *What's going on here? Where is the faculty? Everyone can see this.*

"I believe in the presence of Jesus in the Eucharist," he reflected. "There's a lack of respect for tradition. I also worry about the violence of language that is used, not only cuss words but in attitudes toward women. I question why [such men] can go through and be ordained. I see others struggle with vocational life and celibacy, or the church-as-seminary, and leave. I find that sorrowing."

Another seminarian, homosexual and celibate, with whom I spoke in 1986 said that TC was like North American College in Rome, taking a "more clinical approach than the behavior-mod[ification] thing they use at Mount St. Mary's. In the clinical model, your spiritual adviser is like your analyst. He asks you questions he thinks are relevant, takes your statements about yourself and tries to find out what's underneath that, gradually tries to grow into your privacy. The behavior-mod model says, we can't get that far in any scientific manner, so we will limit ourselves to evaluating your behavior and teach you a pattern of living that will nourish the inside."

He disliked the clinical approach, believing that faculty had neither the time nor the necessary skills. "Many clergy believe they're psychologists with a collar. You see a lot of that in our training; it's the de-Catholicizing of the church. There's a difference between being psychologically well and spiritually well."

Hostility to the image of a loving father also concerned him. "There is a real contempt for the hierarchic church. Using inclusive language at Mass is a biggie: 'it is right to give *God*'—rather than Him—'thanks and praise.' Our first-year class was more conservative. We said Him. And there was a big fight over it. So two Scripture scholars did a document on inclusive language. It took them six months. Then the liturgy committee did an evaluation. And everyone ended up saying what they want. There's no unity in prayers. Who decides how we pray—this individual church or the *universal* church? I'd say we get seventy percent at daily Mass. Some go to Dominican House or places where they're not exposed to folk Masses or sermons about woundedness. You don't meet many dumb Dominicans."

In 1988 the anonymous *Crisis* writer observed:

> *There is a blurring in these particularly parochial worlds of the distinction between friendships and teacher-student friendships. Often, faculty members are not that much older than students. The relationship between some faculty and some students takes on big-brother characteristics. The faculty member has the power. He can be manipulative given his dual role with the student—and the results can be disastrous.*

The most warped mentor-student bonds in a seminary degenerate into pederasty. A 1988 lawsuit alleged that in St. Joseph Seminary, a Benedictine abbey in lush woods sixty miles from New Orleans, a seminarian entered under auspices of a priest who had molested him since he was thirteen. A nearby pastor was accused of showing the student pornographic films in his rectory and a third priest of counseling him approvingly on sexual contacts. The victim was nineteen and showing signs of suicide when he quit. Attorneys, led by Raul Bencomo, sued the seminary, the New Orleans archdiocese, and individual priests, eventually settling out of court.

Many of the behavior patterns in seminaries during the seventies and eighties registered gay liberation's impact on clerical culture as well as great confusion among heterosexual seminarians. The tensions in seminaries also reflected fear and hostility toward women, an attitude fostered by sexual segregation. The climate in today's seminaries is hardly conducive to inspiring new vocations. As numbers dwindle, the celibate tradition erodes, and Rome avoids the great question: when will the church find a model of study and ministry faithful to the Vatican II ideal of the church as the People of God?

PART THREE

Tragedy and Hope

◆

"For our boast is this,

the testimony of our conscience,

that . . . we have behaved in the world. . . ."

2 CORINTHIANS 1:12

xvii.

The Bishops' Tragic Flaw

How should we account for bishops who proclaim the sanctity of life in the womb and recycle priests who molest children?

A therapeutic analogy offers one approach: the church-as-dysfunctional family. Catholicism is steeped in familial imagery—Holy Mother the Church, priests as fathers of a parish. Harboring child molesters is akin to the dynamics of an incestuous family. Concealment assaults the truth, with silence perpetuating the pain and degradation of victims.

Bishops are more than symbolic patriarchs. As regents of a moral order they teach the laity, govern the clergy, raise funds, tend infrastructures, and speak out on a host of issues. A bishop's moral authority suffers incalculably when the courts or the news media expose a cover-up of sexual abusers. As this pattern grew, the final stage of my reporting witnessed an epic tragedy.

In ancient Greek drama the tragic figure violates cosmic boundaries by thrusting himself into conflict with the gods. The chorus plays a crucial role, cautioning the actors to listen, be prudent, avoid strife. Shakespeare eliminated the chorus and cast evil in a psychological mold: the tragic hero's fatal flaw precipitates his downfall. In *King Lear* the flaw is hubris, or excessive pride; in *Othello* it is jealousy; in *Macbeth*, great greed.

Tragedy is alien to the democratic mind. In a society primed on personal freedom, the character-as-fate drama loses meaning. Man's conflict is with himself, not with rungs of higher power.

The Roman Catholic Church exists in democracy yet it also stands apart as a centuries-old religious monarchy. The hierarchy upholds moral boundaries between God and His people. When church superiors violate those limits, the hierarchy's own moral values bear deeper scrutiny.

As the molestation scandal widened I was interviewed on network television programs, and abuse survivors began calling me from distant places. They wanted to be heard; they wanted to halt the course of events that had damaged their own lives; they wanted assurance that others would not be hurt by the same priest— assurances I often could not give.

The women had the most profound impact on me. Some were reacting from adult relationships with priests. One woman, seduced and dropped by her pastoral counselor, disfigured herself with scissors. Another, molested in ninth grade, now married with children and immersed in church life, was frigid. Two ladies, worried about their pastor's overtures to teenage boys, discovered that he had come to their town from a treatment center after a plea bargain. A boy he had molested in a previous parish cut off a finger and received a settlement. When the ladies asked that Father be removed, the bishop not only refused their request but threatened a slander suit if they made a public issue of it.

Media coverage did not interest these women. They wanted healing, balance, to make things right. Litigation was not reform. These were "People of God" trying to repair broken scales of justice. In late hours, gazing at the night sky, I wondered how bishops opposed to abortion could so callously treat abused women and children? Here were men trained in Scripture, ethics, values. Reporters can expect subterfuge, cover-up, and lying from government or corporations. Even if one viewed the bishops' behavior as corporate, was there not a deep moral flaw?

Reading bishops' depositions, searching for threads of a common character, I often reproved myself: *What right have you to judge?* Yet, in the victims a greater judgment was gathering force. There was too much suffering out there, too great a betrayal, too many sexual Watergates laced across the map of the domestic church. As in traditional tragedy, when something evil cannot be halted internally, a counterforce will rise.

No reliable data provide percentages of child molesters in society. Many cases, especially ones of incest, go unreported. In 1985 a *Los Angeles Times* nationwide telephone survey questioned 2627 men and women from every state. Twenty-two percent—27 percent of women and 16 percent of men—said they had been sexually abused as children. Only 3 percent of the cases were reported to police.

There is no firm numerical baseline on perpetrators in society against which to compare clergy. Ministers attract more media because they hold positions of higher trust. The phenomenon is by no means exclusive to the Catholic Church.

Lloyd Rediger, a Presbyterian pastor-therapist, cites consultations with 1000 main-line Protestant clergy in estimating that two to three percent are pedophiles —similar to Richard Sipe's findings—with boys five times more likely to be victims. Sipe, however, found an additional four percent attracted to youths, though not acting on the impulse.

Psychiatrist Jay Feierman, of the Paraclete facility in New Mexico, told me that Sipe's figures were "much too low" but that he was not allowed to discuss his data findings under orders of the Paracletes.

Rediger's estimates are skewed by the control group, people in therapy, not a general population sample. Nevertheless, according to Rediger, "Approximately 10 percent of clergy (mostly male) have been or are engaged in sexual malfeasance." Malfeasance he defines as "the hard-core stuff: sexual behavior that involves a violation of trust." Most of it involved adultery.

A doctoral study conducted at Fuller [Presbyterian] Theological Seminary in Pasadena, California, drew figures from 3000 questionnaires sent to main-line ministers. Of these, 13 percent admitted to an adulterous relationship with a church member, 38.5 percent self-reported having had some sexual contact with a church member, and 76.5 percent reporting knowing of another minister who had had sexual intercourse with a member. If *Humanae Vitae* was the Catholic Church's watershed event, Rediger sees the acceptance of divorce for Protestant clergy, about the year 1970, as a turning point.

"It was the breakdown of a strong barrier to sexual malfeasance," he says. "Clergy in a committed marriage knew the rules and expectations. Then they found they could get a divorce and not be defrocked. That seemed by implication to give permission for other things. It not only broke up families but changed moral perspectives on behavior."

In 1984 a Baptist pastor in New Jersey was sentenced to twenty-two years in prison for sexually assaulting two young girls. In Minneapolis a Lutheran minister sued her senior pastor for firing her after she complained to superiors about his sexual advances. A Methodist minister in Dallas who was having an affair tried to murder his wife and commit suicide. A Portland jury ordered a Presbyterian minister to pay $1 million to a divorced man after he had an affair with the man's ex-wife: the couple had gone to him for marriage counseling. In California an Episcopal priest was sentenced to six years for molesting a seven-year-old boy in his church office, and a Greek Orthodox priest was sentenced to nine years for abusing two teenage boys. On August 3, 1990, *Los Angeles Times* religion writer Russell Chandler reported:

> As many as 2000 cases of sexual abuse by clergy are pending in the courts, according to insurance agents who specialize in church matters, and a new specialty class of lawyers expert in suing, defending or counseling churches regarding sexual misconduct has sprung up. Most insurers have quit issuing coverage for such liabilities or have limited it.
>
> "Today the number of credible sexual abuse and misconduct cases is astounding," said John F. Cleary, general counsel for the Church Mutual Insurance Co. of Merill, Wisc., which insures 46,000 churches.
>
> "It has been a hidden problem for generations," acknowledged Evangelical Lutheran Bishop Robert Keller of Spokane, Wash.

Other institutions were also being hit with lawsuits and criminal actions because of custodial figures who abused children. Molesters seek out day care centers, youth programs, schools, or volunteer work providing them access to young people. Safeguarding against such people has become a major task for institutions. *Washington Times* reporter Patrick Boyle's coverage of how the Boy Scouts of America responded to this threat is a case in point.

Between 1970 and 1990 roughly 400 abuse cases were reported of men connected with Scout activities. Most allegations involved sexual fondling. The men were banned from BSA. In many instances criminal charges were not filed; but the institution was often sued. A case in Oregon resulted in a $4 million verdict that was reduced to less than $800,000 on appeal. Where Scouting officials once let sex offenders quietly leave town, today they have a computerized registry of men deemed unfit to work with local troops. In trying to rid the Boy Scouts of such men, the national policies of the Boy Scouts rely on local implementation.

How has the Catholic bishops' response compared with that of the Boy Scouts and with the leadership of other churches?

In a July 1987 internal report to the NCCB, Bishop Adam Maida of Green Bay, Wisconsin (who later became archbishop of Detroit), wrote that some priests "with proper medical care and psychiatric treatment, and counseling and ongoing supervision, can continue to function in the church in some capacity with limited risk to young people."

How limited was limited? And why take the risk?

Maida listed three conditions that could warrant laicizing, or defrocking, a priest—serious harm to innocent victims; potential for grave scandal to the church; and exposure of heavy liability "should negligence on the part of ecclesial authority be proven." But innocents had been harmed. "Serious" had been a matter of degree. The other factors—scandal and provable negligence—hinged on whether information could withstand legal discovery. The striking quality is how readily all three factors applied in so many cases, and how often they were ignored.

The wave of cases involving priests in the 1980s also paralleled sexual misconduct by therapists. A 1989 survey in Wisconsin of 961 licensed psychologists, in which 41 percent responded, found 4.4 percent who admitted having sexual relations with a client. Few therapists report others who exploit their clients. Like ministers, therapists have lost malpractice coverage by insurers, even though only a small fraction violate the bonds of trust.

Clinical psychologist Gary Schoener is executive director of the Walk-In Counseling Center in Minneapolis, which specializes in treating victims of therapists. Of 3000 women the Center has counseled, 300 were abused by ministers. Schoener consults with several denominations. "The Mennonites have put out an excellent packet of materials on clergy abuse," says Schoener. "Some areas of the Evangelical Lutheran Church are doing an outstanding job; others are not. The Episcopalians and Lutherans are trying to pull together the smartest teams they have to establish national protocols, whereas the Catholic Church is in disarray on this issue. I have never heard of any kind of national strategy from the Catholic Church, despite its centrality of control. Nothing.

"I know of at least forty cases of priests around the country involving women or girls that were settled out of court," Schoener continues. "Minnesota was the first state to make therapist-client sex a felony. The archdiocese was very supportive of that, and when they started reevaluating cases, they sent policies to victim advocacy groups. These are difficulties common to all denominations. There has also been a great failure of mental health people to properly assess cases in the past; they gave what we know in retrospect was bad advice. You should never refer someone for therapy until you've had an independent diagnostic assessment. Hand me a sociopath and we can't fix it."

As a consultant to the Minneapolis-St. Paul archdiocese, Schoener studied clergy treatment facilities, including St. Luke, the House of Affirmation, the Paraclete facility, and others. "All of them suffer the same disadvantage," he says. "They put the priest under a microscope, but the victim is not part of the assessment." The dominant approach in Catholic clergy treatment facilities was to rehabilitate the offender whenever possible. Why were church officials so resistant to dismissing them?

The Rev. Stephen J. Rosetti, a psychologist who worked at the House of Affirmation, and L. M. Rothstein, Ph.D., of Institute of Living, had a theory. Acknowledging the absence of hard data, they nevertheless estimated "that over ninety percent of priests and religious who sexually molest children are not true pedophiles . . . [but] ephebophiles." As a result, "The experience among the residential treatment centers is that these child sex abusers can be treated effectively." Rosetti had a philosophical overview.

> *As a society, we would like to believe that child molesters are different, perhaps even evil, and that they should be treated with contempt and removed from our midst. Indeed, their crimes cannot be minimized, but neither can our common, broken humanity. We must not forget our inner darkness which makes us resemble the "dirty old man" that stalks his prey in the night. The existence of our private darkness frightens us as much as the spectre of the active child molester.*

Is society really so afflicted with "inner darkness" and "broken humanity"—or do such images apply more to the clerical culture itself?

House of Affirmation in 1984 was ready to send Gauthe to work for an ambulance company. In 1987, the Rev. Thomas A. Kane, a founder of Affirmation, was fired after siphoning funds to buy resort property in Florida and Maine. Kane repaid an undisclosed amount and was not indicted. Affirmation never recovered and, on December 31, 1989, closed its doors.

On one level, the bishops' blunders with child molestation cases were symptomatic of society's failure. In 1987, writes journalist John Crewdson, physicians accounted for just 14 percent of U.S. child abuse reports; "fewer than half of the children in Los Angeles County found to have venereal disease are ever reported by doctors to that county's child protection agency."

In *The Battle and the Backlash*, which investigates how the courts respond to child victims, David Hechler faults doctors and other professionals who show

> *a willingness to believe and support their colleagues (and to discount the word of children), and a desire to protect their reputations as well as those of the institutions they represent. And it may also be attributable to their desire to believe it never happened.*

Minnesota bishops evinced an extraordinary example of this moral paralysis when St. Paul attorney Jeffrey Anderson began litigation in 1984 on behalf of a young man previously molested by Father Thomas Adamson. By 1990, Anderson had settled eight cases, at least one of which, according to reports, exceeded $1 million. Because criminal statute of limitations had expired, Adamson was never prosecuted. One victim, after receiving a settlement, was later arrested in an attempted murder of the suspended cleric. Adamson and church officials gave depositions in what became an ongoing news story in Minnesota.

Like many such men, Tom Adamson was himself molested for more than two years, by a hired hand on his parents' farm, starting when he was fifteen. In 1961, as a young priest and assistant principal in the town of Adrian, he molested a boy on the school basketball team. The liaison would continue for twelve years, as the boy moved through seminary and became a priest himself.

In 1962, Bishop Edward A. Fitzgerald of Winona transferred Adamson to a high school a hundred and fifty miles away in Rochester. There he abused a new boy and three from the old parish, whose families he continued to visit. In 1963 he went to a new town, as coach, religion teacher, and school administrator. A fourteen-year-old ballplayer reported his advances to two priests, who told Fitzgerald: the first record of institutional knowledge. Fitzgerald, who was deceased by the time litigation began, had sent him back to Rochester, where he propositioned two new boys, who also told other priests.

Again Fitzgerald had transferred him. A monsignor arranged for him to see a psychiatrist; he had fifteen sessions. In 1972, after three more transfers, Adamson returned to Rochester a third time—*as principal of the parochial school,* where he had sex with a twelve-year-old boy for several years, unbeknownst to Fitzgerald.

In 1969, Fitzgerald retired and Loras Watters became bishop of Winona. A former spiritual director of North American College, with a Ph.D. in education from CUA, Watters had been auxiliary bishop of Dubuque, Iowa. In April 1974, Adamson fondled a boy in a sauna bath; the boy told another priest. Watters sent Adamson to a psychiatrist, who recommended that he enter Institute of Living in Hartford (where Gauthe would later be sent). Adamson checked in on June 4. On August 9, with a diagnosis of "sexual orientation disturbance," he was discharged, listed as "slightly improved," with recommendation for outpatient therapy. A month later he resumed pastoral duties in Rochester, while seeing therapist Father Kenneth Pierre in Minneapolis at an archdiocesan treatment center fifty miles from his parish.

In November 1974 the boy Adamson had seduced years earlier in Adrian was now a priest, committed for substance abuse. The dam of tolerance broke. He told his parents and an older brother we shall call Sam* all about Father Tom, who had been an extended member of the family. Shortly thereafter, Sam learned that two of his other brothers had been molested by Father Tom. Sam taught at the school where Adamson was pastor. From a coach he learned the names of other victims. In a deposition taken by Jeffrey Anderson, Sam said he called Bishop Watters:

> *I told him I was getting sick of listening to my parents cry all weekend at my house. . . . I wanted it acknowledged that no one was at fault in this matter except Father Tom Adamson, and the only way they were going to believe that was to have the Bishop run him out of the church. . . . [Watters said] that he wasn't aware of all this past background with Father Adamson that I was reciting to him about other parishes and other youths and my brothers and so on.*

Sam stated that Watters told him Adamson "was going to resign but he had to do that on his own, the church didn't have the responsibility to require him. . . . I didn't agree with that." Sam added:

> *All of a sudden priests started calling us, giving my wife a bad time on the phone. [One] priest started telling my wife how wrong we were, trying to push and*

*force Father Adamson out of the church and so on. I called them back one at a time
and told them I really wasn't interested in their observations.*

The monsignor who got Adamson into therapy in 1964 called; Sam said:

> *And his general attitude was just who the hell I thought I was to be pushing this
> wonderful priest, the best accounting man who possibly was a potential Bishop.
> . . . I told Father my concern and he said, "Well, everybody knows about it. We
> had a youth here at our parish who was accosted by Father Adamson and we've
> taken care of this and he's been to treatment at least once, maybe twice." . . . I said
> I thought it was the church's responsibility and also that the Bishop was telling me
> he had no prior knowledge. And he said, "Huh. He's aware of the whole ten-year
> history. He knows which parishes he's been in [and] why he left certain parishes."*
>
> *[H]e said that when Bishop Watters took over for Bishop Fitzgerald, that he
> was well aware of the background of all the variety of problems. And then he
> proceeded to mention a couple [of victims] that I wasn't even aware of.*

Again Sam called Watters, who reiterated that it was Adamson's choice to
resign. Anger roiling, Sam went to Adamson and said if he didn't pack up that the
family would stand up at Sunday Mass and tell the congregation. He told a nun
that if Adamson didn't leave he would kill him; she testified that she drove to
Winona and told Watters of the family's plight. Sam called Watters a third time;
he was noncommittal. But on Saturday night, December 31, Watters met with
Adamson, who resigned as pastor. A monsignor testified that Watters told him
Adamson was being transferred because of a threatened lawsuit. Sam now called
Watters, demanding therapy for all of Adamson's past victims. He stated that the
bishop refused, saying, "Little boys heal."

In a 1987 deposition, Watters said of Sam's calls in 1974: "I'm not sure that the
person identified himself. . . ."

> *Anderson: It was a man when you say "he"?*
> *A: It was a man, yes. . . . And stating that Father Adamson should be
> removed from the parish or dismissed from the priesthood.*

The bishop said he received "two or three calls. . . . Apparently this person
had contacted Father Adamson in the meanwhile and called back to threaten
some kind of public statement." Watters said he took no notes. "I don't remember
any specific statement, except . . . that he was unfit for the priesthood."

> *Q: Do you remember that caller saying that his concern was for youth and
> particularly boys and the inappropriate sexual contact of Father Tom Adamson with
> boys in that parish?*
> *A: I don't recall that, no. . . .*
> *Q: Do you recall if that caller had some concern about a family member of his?*
> *A: I don't recall.*

On January 6, 1975, Watters sent Adamson to the archdiocese of Minneapolis-St. Paul, informing Archbishop John Roach that he was to continue therapy with Father Pierre. Roach testified that Watters did not inform him of Adamson's sexual activities. In a 1976 internal memo, Roach noted that Watters wanted Adamson to remain in the Twin Cities "[f]or reasons which Bishop Watters was unwilling to discuss on the telephone. . . . [He] assures me that Father Adamson is a good priest, who is a victim of a situation in Winona." Roach placed him in a St. Paul rectory, and while continuing therapy, Adamson took courses at the University of Minnesota—in family counseling. Watters refused to take him back. In April 1975, Pierre made such a request to Watters on Adamson's behalf, predicated on outpatient therapy. Watters wrote Pierre:

> I am convinced that he doesn't even begin to appreciate the numbers of people in at least five different communities across the entire [Winona] Diocese who have finally pieced together incidents occurring over a 15 year span and who now openly raise questions about the credibility of all priests. . . . You would only have to struggle through the painful sessions I've had with heart-broken and bewildered parents who only now have come to discover the source of some of the problems of their sons.

But in deposition with Anderson, Watters backed away from the claims in his letter, saying: "No parent has contacted me about any of these situations or rumored about any of the places where Father Adamson was assigned." In questioning Watters about his letter to Pierre, Anderson cited "the painful sessions that you had with heart-broken bewildered parents—"

> A: Well, yes, and those sessions were before I ever came to Winona and they were—in fact, there was one incident when I was principal of a school in Dubuque.
> Q: Are you saying that this sentence is not referring to heart-broken parents in the Diocese of Winona?
> A: Exactly . . . there was a parent, father and mother who came to me and expressed concern about a contact that a priest had with their son and that was back in 1945 . . .
> Q: It obviously involved a different priest.
> A: Yes, the priest, who is long since dead, and I would be hard pressed to give you the names of the parents.
> Q: Well, then I direct your attention to the language of the letter, Bishop . . . "heart-broken and bewildered parents who only now"—you use the word now— "have come to discover the source of some of the problems of their sons." Not son, sons. That's more than one and you're referring now to the year 1975.
> A: "Now" doesn't refer to 1975. That "now" refers to whenever bewildered parents came to discover those things.
> Q: Did the bewildered parents come to you in 1975 to discuss the 1945 problem?
> A: In 1945 they discovered it, at the "now" they came to talk to me.

Q: *You are not referring to parents in the diocese of Winona?*
A: *Exactly.*
Q: *And that's your testimony under oath here today?*
A: *That's my testimony under oath. . . .*
Q: *Why do you use the word sons here?*
A: *It could be a typing error or . . . I don't know.*

Anderson and attorney Mark Wendorf documented abuses by Adamson in five communities from 1961 to 1975, just as Watters wrote in his letter. In January 1976, Adamson stopped seeing his therapist. In February, Roach sent him to a parish where he abused a new boy. That summer he became an associate pastor at another parish and abused four other boys. In 1980 one boy's parents demanded Adamson's removal and threatened to file charges. Chancellor (later Bishop) Robert Carlson of the Minneapolis-St. Paul archdiocese assured them the church would take care of the priest. Roach wrote Watters, telling him to take Adamson back, and had the priest sign a resignation from the archdiocese. He was hospitalized four weeks for depression.

Watters wouldn't take him back. So, in February 1981, Roach sent him to a parish in Apple Valley, forty miles from his previous parish. A memo from Carlson and Roach ordered him not to have contact with youths or former parishioners and to tell his old congregation he was going to Winona. His transfer did not appear in the archdiocesan listing of clergy assignments. In Apple Valley he molested a new boy. And so the dirty pages turn with stories of wrecked lives until 1985 when, under darkening legal clouds, Roach sent him back to Bishop Watters. Over the next five years the two dioceses and their insurance carriers hemorrhaged millions of dollars as Jeffrey Anderson negotiated eight settlements.

Anderson's ninth set of clients in the Adamson affair refused a $1.25 million settlement offer. (Three previous trials of Gauthe victims in Louisiana averaged $1.5 million per verdict.) The trial began outside St. Paul in November 1990. The issue was not negligence but by how much church and insurers would have to compensate the victims and, more critically, whether church officials were willfully indifferent to the rights of the victims. That would mean punitive damages, for which Louisiana law did not provide.

The *Minneapolis Star Tribune* and the *St. Paul Pioneer Press Dispatch* had given extensive coverage to the scandal. Trial testimony revealed little new of factual substance—with one striking exception. On November 14 a Rev. Joseph Wajds testified that he had reported a youngster's accusations of Adamson's sexual advances to church officials in 1979. What the jury did not know—but the newspapers reported—was that Wajds was a defendant in two civil suits in which *he* was accused of child sexual abuse. One had been settled the previous May. (After the Adamson trial Wajds was removed from his parish.) On December 7, 1990, the jury awarded a staggering $3.55 million to Anderson's clients. Of that, $2.7 million was in punitive damages not covered by insurance. The trial judge subsequently lowered the amount to $1 million and Anderson appealed.

"The boys that Father Tom abused," reflects Anderson, "each one down the line, suffered a terrible arrest of personality development and sexual identities.

Some are now homosexuals; some don't know what they are; others have abused children themselves. Each one is at risk of repeating what was done to them. They suffered in silence and secrecy for years. None of them escaped the ravages —chemical dependency, suicide attempts, broken self-esteem, sexual compulsions that Adamson imprinted on them. I know of thirty-four boys he molested. Of the eleven I represent, eight served time in jail and all have been in trouble with the law. All the kids were vulnerable at the time Adamson got them. Plenty of families have troubled teenagers but work through those problems. These families never had the chance."

Over and above the bishops' negligence, the clerical culture defended itself by reattacking Sam. But Sam, who was married, had blood brothers to protect. Watters's "sworn" testimony is so at variance with his own letter and others' testimony as to give perjury an exalted meaning. In 1985, when he took Adamson back under orders from Roach, Watters used Father Tom as a substitute priest until the legal risk was driven home. And so the lawyers advance, step by step, exacting retribution from a sick system that has betrayed its own canons.

Countless cases across the country have exposed a warped elitism: priests and bishops above, shunning lay people below, which is precisely what Tom Doyle and Ray Mouton had warned against.

ii.

After his work on the 1985 pedophilia report, Tom Doyle published articles in clerical journals on pedophilia, lectured to clergy in New Zealand and Australia and, at the behest of bishops in those countries, wrote their national guidelines. He had much less success with the U.S. hierarchy.

On Sunday, November 15, 1987, the eve of the NCCB autumn conference in Washington, Karen Henderson of the *Cleveland Plain Dealer* wrote about the 1985 document that Doyle, Mouton, and Peterson had prepared:

> *The guidelines are being followed by some dioceses, Doyle said recently, "but unfortunately not by all of them."*
>
> *Archbishop John May of St. Louis, president of the National Conference of Catholic Bishops, said that although the report was not an official document of the conference, "it was good advice." He said issues raised in the report were dealt with at a couple of meetings, but the task force was never set up.*

That autumn the bishops held a closed-door session on the topic.

On December 11, 1987, a Louisiana jury awarded $1.8 million to one of Tony Fontana's clients. Losses to the Lafayette diocese and its insurers reached $10 million, and by 1990 would reach $22 million. "Criminal charges have been filed against priests in 16 states," wrote syndicated religion columnist Michael J. McManus on December 19, 1987. "At least $25 million has been paid." McManus went on:

*This general neglect is stupid, fiscally perilous, and immoral. . . . The negli-
gence here is two-fold: a lack of remedial action when problems surface—and the lack
of preventive aid for children.*

On December 30, 1987, the *San Jose Mercury News* began a two-part series by
Carl M. Cannon, a political reporter in the Washington bureau of the Knight-
Ridder chain. For more than four months Cannon tracked cases in two dozen
dioceses and found a systemic pattern of churchmen failing to report allegations
to authorities, attacking families despite "earlier complaints against the priest in
question," and securing seal orders. "The church's reluctance to address the problem is a time bomb waiting to detonate within American Catholicism," wrote
Cannon.

Via the Knight-Ridder wire, Cannon's reports appeared in the *Philadelphia In-
quirer, Detroit Free Press,* and *Miami Herald,* among others. The *Akron Beacon Journal*
caught the eye of Ohio Auxiliary Bishop A. James Quinn. On January 8, 1988,
Quinn wrote Papal Pro Nuncio Pio Laghi, assuring him that bishops were doing
everything possible and criticizing Doyle and Mouton for giving interviews and
for wanting bishops to pay for their expertise. But the church had weathered
worse attacks in the past, he assured the nuncio, and "so, too, will the pedophilia
annoyance eventually abate."

On January 18 Laghi sent Doyle a copy of Quinn's letter, with written assurance that while he did "not subscribe to the conclusions drawn in [Quinn's] correspondence," he wanted the canonist to get a sense of concern "in some quarters"
over media coverage about the problem. Ever the diplomat, he complimented
Doyle for his hard work and expressed hope that his "efforts on behalf of the
Church will continue to bear fruit abundantly."

On January 28, Doyle wrote Laghi:

> *I have never sought out interviews. On all occasions I have tried to be objective and
> have been successful in either persuading reporters that some of their conclusions are
> erroneous or that certain information they had would and should not be published. I
> have been both dismayed and shocked at the amount of factual information many of
> the reporters have gathered.*

Doyle wrote that "negative image" problems stemmed from the "manner in
which certain cases have been handled." He termed "preposterous" Quinn's remark that he and Mouton tried to sell their services and continued:

> *This same line has emanated from the USCC general counsel office and was told
> to several business leaders in Cleveland who in turn put pressure on the publisher of
> the Cleveland Plain Dealer to prevent further coverage of the problem existing there.
> . . . My aim, and I know I speak for [Peterson and Mouton], was simply to alert
> the Church leadership to the gravity of the problem and hopefully provide some ideas
> as to how to handle it. I never understood the reasons behind the negative attitude on
> the part of certain officials of the NCCB-USCC.*

To Quinn, who had approved early drafts of the 1985 document, Doyle wrote
that news reports tapped "information from police or court records or interviews
with persons directly involved." He continued:

> It is not a case of the press vs. the Church. It is, I believe, a case of the Church
> grappling with a very serious problem that is also prominent in the general popula-
> tion. The articles will continue as long as we have the problem in the Church. . . .
> I am both saddened and surprised at your characterization of what we have done,
> not only to Archbishop Laghi, but to others as well.

"The U.S. Catholic bishops are presiding over a scandal," editorialized NCR
on January 8, 1988, urging bishops to "take an unequivocal stand in identifying
and removing" pedophiles from pastoral work and to "develop a national policy."
With 140 cases reported to Laghi and 100 in legal action, Tom Fox was blunt:

> [D]o not fall back on the advice of lawyers. In the final analysis, this is a
> moral issue that cries out for moral and pastoral answers. . . . We are not talking
> here about cash settlements, but about justice in the church. Bishops may be seen to be
> condoning immorality in order to protect the institution. They will not succeed.

Mike McManus's column, Cannon's reports, and Fox's editorial signaled the
potential of a media chain reaction. Religion editors were now taking a hard look
at a problem many had once considered minor. On February 9, 1988, USCC
general counsel Mark Chopko issued the first official acknowledgment of the
problem. His statement bemoaned "the profound tragedy for all involved" and
called pedophilia "a direct threat to the future well-being and stability of our
society." It affected "men and women without regard to whether they are married,
single or celibate." Chopko went on:

> For their part, the Roman Catholic bishops of the United States are deeply
> committed to addressing such incidents positively, to making strong efforts to prevent
> child abuse, to repairing whatever damage has been done, to bringing the healing
> ministry of the church to bear wherever possible.

Avoiding the term "policy," Chopko's 1000-word statement noted that the
USCC was not a national governing board; individual dioceses were legally autonomous. This put the church bureaucracy on record as having no role in how
bishops handled cases. If the bishops did adopt a policy, the risk factor in a given
case might increase should plaintiffs prove their bishop ignored guidelines. The
church, Chopko continued, would suspend a priest "from active ministry where
appropriate . . . [with] commitment of the diocese to heal the victims and their
families, rehabilitate the offender and reconcile all involved in the ministry of the
church."

In an April 8, 1988, memorandum to bishops and diocesan attorneys, Chopko
emphasized "the need to involve parents and pastors. . . . Any plan to attempt
to break the cycle of child abuse must include prevention as its cornerstone."

In interviews Chopko repeatedly denied the existence of a church cover-up. In a legal workshop he derided the 1985 document as "infamous" and said it had no official standing (despite approval by the nuncio and key bishops). Ironically, in his memo Chopko endorsed the infamous report's intervention-team concept:

> *We are aware that in some cases diocesan or insurance attorneys, concerned that such efforts may be seen as a means to discourage potential civil actions, have counseled against contacting the victims or families. We are also aware that in one case a victim was contacted and urged to drop any consideration of civil action against the church. Nevertheless, the dioceses should continue to contact the victims and families in an effort to show their true concern, and should offer the assistance and comfort of the Church in this time of need. If a damage action is to follow inevitably from the incident, it is better human relations to reconcile the injured in the Church. In the courtroom, it is often too late.*

Yet even that document did not address the problem of recidivism, which among diagnosed pedophiles was so high that many experts considered it an incurable disease. With Depo-Provera and sustained outpatient treatment, some offenders could suppress the urge but not rid themselves of it. Many offenders were not diagnosed pedophiles. Yet how many youths did a man have to molest before he was deemed morally unfit for ministry? Such men needed medical and legal help; but that could be provided while easing them out of clerical life.

That's not how Father Nicolas Aguilar Rivera left Los Angeles in mid-January 1988, while Chopko's statement was in the works. Amid parishioners' accusations that he had molested twenty-six boys, Aguilar fled to Mexico. "Chose to leave" was the term used by a spokesman for Archbishop (later Cardinal) Roger M. Mahoney, whose social justice stands were admired by many. At least his archdiocese offered therapy to the families.

On assignment for the *Los Angeles Times*, I called psychotherapist Richard Sipe, who had discussed the crisis with several bishops. "There's an almost culpable ignorance at work," he said. "Situations have been explained but people think the larger problem will go away. They handle it in a confessional manner: why shouldn't the person be forgiven even though it's a grievous sin? I think that's also why they justify the silence, that we don't tell anybody about these things. They are not facing the fact that people are sexual beings, and what do you do with your sexuality? The more subtle support systems of the pre-Vatican II church have broken down. We need honest confrontation with the whole problem of sexuality. Several bishops recognize the importance of discussing things. The other response is to say nothing, which seems to be the majority. They are aware that neither theologians nor anyone in the hierarchy can even broach questions."

"Because they fear retribution from Rome?"

"That's right. So, nobody has the answers, and rather than recognize that, there's an appeal to blind authority. Authority is claiming that they know what is right and wrong about sexuality, but the point is, they don't. For political or disciplinary reasons, rather than reasons of theology or pastorship or just good sense, you have a Galileo situation without a Galileo."

When I called Eugene Kennedy, who was a confidant of many bishops on a range of issues, his words startled me: "Bishops have chosen to take the advice of lawyers on issues that cannot be resolved merely by making the church legally defensible. Lawyers are not intrinsically interested in morality, but in making their area no wider than a ledge on which to balance themselves and their clients. Nationally, responsible journalists are starting to interpret it as a cover-up story, which has a terribly negative potential for the church. It's the sweating surface of a culture that is corrupting. The church has failed to examine the conflicts about human sexuality that throb within it. Cover-ups won't work. Where there is darkness we need light."

Implications of the crisis were not lost on diocesan attorneys, most of whom are loyal Catholics with blue-chip firms. At an April 26, 1988, gathering of these lawyers, one participant advised bishops to be more directly involved in the local seminary, and complained that "some priestly circles" distinguished between celibacy and chastity, advocating that "homosexual affairs are okay for a priest." Suspending or expelling pedophiles was essential, the attorney maintained; but if a bishop was unwilling to enforce such a policy, the diocese was perhaps better off without one (thus not increasing its liability). Another attorney noted that bishops had a duty to warn parishioners before sending a priest from treatment to a new parish.

In April 1990, at a Midwest Canon Law Society conference in Columbus, Ohio, Bishop Quinn lectured on pedophilia and suggested another legal stratagem. An audio cassette of his remarks found its way to me. Of clergy personnel files, Quinn said that those subpoenaed "cannot be tampered with, destroyed, removed. That constitutes obstruction of justice and contempt of court. Prior, however, thought and study ought to be given if you think it's going to be necessary. If there's something there you really don't want people to see, you might send it off to the Apostolic Delegate [Vatican Ambassador] because they have immunity. . . . Something you consider dangerous, you might send it there."

International law prohibits search and seizure of embassies in host countries. Embassies are considered foreign soil, inviolable as sovereign states. When Manuel Noriega took refuge in the Vatican Embassy in Panama, U.S. forces surrounded the compound but waited several days for the dictator to surrender. Quinn's suggestion of sending sensitive files to the Washington embassy, thereby removing them from the reach of American courts, had specifically been warned against in the 1985 report that Quinn approved. "In all likelihood," Tom Doyle had written, "such action would insure that the immunity of the nunciature would be damaged or destroyed by the civil courts."

With an assignment from the *Plain Dealer*, I telephoned Quinn at his office. He was cryptic: "Whatever I said is my own opinion. It was never discussed with the nunciature."

What about potential problems for diplomatic immunity for the Vatican? "I suppose you could think about that," he said.

I asked if sending sensitive files to the embassy posed possible First Amendment complications for religious freedom. "I suggest maybe you think about that too," he replied dryly.

Discovery subpoenas for church documents had triggered defense tactics citing the Code of Canon Law. Attorneys representing a Michigan youth were told that sensitive information was privileged by the seal of the confession between the accused priest and his superiors. Although the church later settled, the tactic has been used in other cases, delaying proceedings. The courts eventually tended to favor plaintiffs seeking such files, but it was hardly open and shut. In February 1990, Judge Thomas M. McKittrick of Montana ruled that bishops in Great Falls and Helena need not surrender files of an accused priest because such an order would "compel the bishop to violate the privacy provision of canon law." The plaintiff appealed. His attorney, Jeffrey Anderson, accused the church of trying "to hide behind the First Amendment. The regularity and consistency of these defense arguments is based on religious privilege we don't think applies."

Quinn's suggestion would broaden the scope of that privilege. The Rev. Bernard Yarrish, an embassy spokesman, said that to his knowledge no files had been sent. "It's a possibility but they've never had to resort to that measure."

What if church authorities do? According to Thomas Buergenthal, a judge on the Intra-American Court of Human Rights and professor of comparative law and jurisprudence at George Washington University, "Once [files] are in the embassy they are protected by diplomatic immunity. A court would not have jurisdiction to obtain them. The Vatican cannot be subpoenaed. It could waive its immunity and provide files but cannot be forced to do so."

Church authorities who sent the files could be forced to answer questions about their contents, Buergenthal added. But attorneys would first have to know that files had been spirited away to the embassy. Alfred P. Rubin, professor of international law at Tufts University Fletcher School of Law and Diplomacy was more blunt: "If they want a first-rate donnybrook resulting in loss of diplomatic relations, it's ultimately possible, depending on how mad U.S. authorities get over what looks like an attempt to cover unspeakable acts with the cloak of diplomatic immunity. This is the wrong arena to play those games in."

Would such tactics constitute obstruction of justice? "I hesitate to use those terms," replied Rubin. "In a formal sense, yes, of course: the whole purpose is to frustrate the courts' process. This is not so much obstruction of justice in the abstract as it is a clash of two fundamentally different principles—one that requires that disputes over personal injury be amenable to our secular judicial process, and the other that gives privileges and immunities to diplomats so that they can carry out their diplomatic function. I don't see how the church could defend this on legal and moral grounds."

iii.

Hiding things was one stratagem in a psychology of power rooted in fear. For deception to succeed, civil authorities had to be duped or coopted. When such activity was exposed, the power mindset showed a striking tendency to counterattack. A raw display of that happened in a city where those involved knew better.

Born in Italy in 1941, the Rev. Dino Cinel earned a Ph.D. in history from Stanford in 1979 and landed a teaching job at Tulane in New Orleans. With recommendations from California church officials, Cinel was assigned by Archbishop Hannan to part-time duties at St. Rita's Parish near the university. He lived with three other priests in the large rectory, two blocks from the arch-bishop's residence, one block from the chancery. With dark hair drooping over his forehead, Cinel's learning and wit charmed parishioners; he also earned tenure at Tulane.

Just before Christmas, 1988, Cinel flew to Italy for the holidays. Linda Pollack, an academic colleague, drove him to the airport and accidentally locked the keys in his car. She called St. Rita's pastor, Father James Tarantino, asking if he had an extra set. Searching Cinel's room, Tarantino found a box with 51 porno-graphic videotapes covering 160 hours, most of them featuring Cinel in sexual acts with teenage boys; hundreds of lewd photographs; and commercial child pornography, the possession of which is a felony under Louisiana law.

Tarantino told Hannan, who on December 29 telephoned Cinel in Italy. Their conversation became a topic in litigation later brought by a victim of Cinel's. In a January 1991 deposition, Hannan said that he had suspended Cinel from the priesthood and told him, "I would never recommend him for any other diocese . . . that this would be a good opportunity for him to begin a new life."

"You are telling him to stay in Italy, and just start over as a lay person?" asked a plaintiff attorney, about the call.

Answer: Yes.

"He replied, to my great surprise, that he resented the invasion of privacy of his room, and didn't show any kind of remorse," Hannan later told Leslie Bennetts of *Vanity Fair*.

Hannan's efforts in the Gauthe crisis gave him a unique vantage point from which not to repeat past mistakes. But as Bishop Frey failed to level with Gauthe's parishioners in 1983, so Hanna kept St. Rita parishioners in the dark about Cinel in 1989. Cinel returned to New Orleans, resumed his classes at Tulane, and mar-ried Linda Pollack, by whom he had a child. Hannan told Leslie Bennetts that Tulane officials were apprised of Cinel's activities. The university press office de-nied it; but in 1989 the arts and sciences dean told the history department chair to say "No comment" should reporters ask about Cinel.

Two years passed before the media began probing. Meanwhile, Cinel's porno-graphic materials became a legal hot potato.

Church attorneys held them for three months while a lawyer hired by Cinel demanded their return. Father Tarantino viewed several of the tapes to see if any parishioners were depicted and, to his relief, found none. The full video record was staggering: Cinel had photographed eight males, apparently between ages sixteen and eighteen, in snapshots and videos. The priest engaged in anal inter-course, oral sex, group sex with two boys at a time, plied them with pot, had a dog lick their genitals. Cinel cuddled and cooed and tickled the boys while the stationary camera rolled.

Many of these encounters had been taped at a summer house in rural Missis-sippi that a parishioner loaned him. Later Cinel bought his own summer place and an apartment building in New Orleans. His Tulane salary was $44,000. Two of the youths in the tapes had stayed with Cinel in the rectory at different times for stretches of several weeks in the mid-eighties.

In Hannan's deposition, an attorney asked about church policy on overnight guests in rectories. Hannan said that priests' relatives with "adequate reasons" would be welcome. He continued:

If somebody thought that, say, at a time of a deep freeze that somebody should
have been given refuge in a rectory, I certainly would consider that—or somebody
who is considered to be a derelict or castaway or runaway or something like that.

Q: But certainly there would be no justification for having young teenage boys
staying at the rectory on a regular basis, is that correct?

A: Unless there was an extraordinary reason for it.

Q: Like what?

A: If somebody, for instance, were I'd say in danger of aggression, that could
possibly be a reason.

On March 29, 1989, an archdiocesan lawyer gave Cinel's boxes to George
Tolar, an investigator in the office of District Attorney Harry Connick (father of
the jazz musician), and said that Tolar would soon be contacted by an attorney
representing the person who had owned the materials. Tolar was astounded when
he looked at the stuff.

In hopes of identifying people in the tapes, Tolar called Gary Raymond, who
had put in sixteen years as a sleuth on Connick's staff before turning private
detective. Raymond was experienced in pedophilia cases; he knew how victims
lived with shame, he saw it in their strained body language when an authority
figure asked questions. He was gathering information in a civil suit against the
archdiocese and the pastor in nearby Mandeville, involving the alleged abuse of a
child in the parish school. (The pastor was also a defendant in the seminary
lawsuit cited at the end of the previous chapter.) A grand jury had not indicted
that priest, who remained pastor despite protests to Hannan from the child's
parents.

After looking at Cinel's pictures, Raymond told Tolar: "It doesn't involve my
case. But whoever it is, you got a bad motherfucker here."

"We know that," said Tolar. "And he's gonna be prosecuted."

Tolar's boss, Harry Connick, had been DA for fifteen years. Connick had
lobbied the legislature to pass one of the nation's strongest antipornography statutes. He was also a parishioner at St. Rita's. On April 14 archdiocesan attorney
Thomas A. Rayer—who, like Hannan, had witnessed the Gauthe ordeal up front
—sent a remarkable letter to Tolar:

I have been requested by the attorney for Dr. Dino Cinel to communicate with
you regarding the intentions and positions of our client, the Archdiocese of New
Orleans, with respect to the turning over to you of various films and materials which
the Archdiocese has had in its possession and which belonged to Dr. Cinel. . . .
[T]he Archdiocese could not appropriately either return these materials to Dr. Cinel
or retain their possession, or destroy them without some possibility of adverse conse-
quences resulting from any of these alternatives. Our review of these materials leads
us to conclude that possible violation of criminal statutes could be involved in the
disposition of these materials by the Archdiocese in any of these three ways without
first having sought consultation from the District Attorney, and without giving your
office the opportunity to review this material. . . .

This action on the part of the Archdiocese should therefore not be considered by your office as in any way seeking the initiation of criminal charges with respect to this material or any activities of Dr. Cinel in relation thereto.

Much later, in a court hearing, Connick said that he had learned of Cinel's material from none other than Father Tarantino "in late 1988 or early 1989"—before his own staff knew.

On May 9 the U.S. Attorney, John Volz, wrote Connick, saying that Postal Service agents suspected Cinel of importing pornography across state lines. For years, Volz and Connick had been in a bitter turf war over drug cases and white-collar crime. "If you decide that state prosecution is not viable," wrote Volz, in reference to Cinel, "we would appreciate the use of this material as evidence in support of potential federal prosecution."

Cinel's attorney gave Tolar affidavits from two young men, Chris Fontaine and Ronald Tichenor, stating that they were over seventeen when they had sex with the priest. Both were street-hardened teens from shattered families when Cinel took them under his wing. Tichenor now was in Florida and wanted to be left alone. But Fontaine, who was mildly retarded, agreed to meet with Tolar.

On July 12, Tolar, a second investigator on Connick's staff, and agents from the Postal Service and U.S. Customs met with Fontaine. He had met Cinel in 1983 in the French Quarter shortly after being released from Hope Haven, a church home for teenage boys. When he was arrested for petty theft, a local judge, with eloquent assurances from the priest, sentenced Fontaine to six months' community service at St. Rita's. During that time, for several nights a week, Fontaine slept in the rectory.

The investigators showed Fontaine a pornographic magazine, made in Denmark, with nude pictures of himself. He began crying. The authorities present decided that state rather than federal charges allowed for a stronger case against Cinel. They assured Fontaine that Cinel would be prosecuted.

Besides the videotapes he had a large collection of commercial child pornography. Tolar says he met with Connick several times. "I told him I felt we were dealing with a pedophile for possession of the magazines. He told me, 'We have enough to worry about with murders and robberies and drug cases than to be worried about a dirty-book case.' I couldn't get him to budge . . ."

In September 1989, Gary Raymond was visiting a friend's boat in the local marina when he recognized the deckhand from Cinel's videos. Raymond asked if he knew Cinel: the broken expression on Fontaine's face said it all. Raymond took Fontaine to plaintiff attorneys, who filed a civil suit against the church and Cinel. As discovery ensued, the church paid for Fontaine's therapy. His lawyers wanted Cinel's materials as evidence to show that Cinel had violated Fontaine's privacy. But the boxes were in the D.A.'s office. Fontaine's attorneys requested a civil subpoena to duplicate the materials. Just before the subpoena was served on the D.A.'s office, Connick asked Tolar for a memo. Dated February 22, 1990, it said that Fontaine and Tichenor were over the consenting age when the sex acts occurred, and, "As a result of our investigation we determined that no violation of law occurred."

Later, when asked about the surrender of Cinel's incriminating materials, Connick would cite the memo in attempting to make Tolar his scapegoat. Well before that, the upshot was that Gary Raymond became legal custodian of Cinel's materials. How many prosecutors allow incriminating evidence to leave their office? In the end, Connick never viewed Cinel's cache of child pornography. On August 9, 1990, when Cinel gave a videotaped deposition to Fontaine's attorneys, the prosecution was dormant.

On August 28, after weeks of screening tapes with mounting disgust, Raymond delivered a videotape of Cinel's testimony to the office of his old boss, with a letter that read in part:

> *[Cinel is] a dangerous pedophile, an admitted pornographer with international connections in the sordid multi-million dollar child pornography business. He is and will continue to be a threat to society. . . . You will see an arrogant, nonrepentent individual who for many years has knowingly violated many laws.*
>
> *. . . . It's only a matter of time before some sharp-eared member of the media gets a whiff of what he or she thinks is a newsworthy story. Many questions will be asked of many people. Because your office played a role in this matter as it unfolded, questions will undoubtedly be asked of you. The one I truly hope I never hear is the first one that comes to my mind: Harry, why didn't you prosecute Dino Cinel? The best possible answer you can have waiting, Harry, is, "I did."*

"Tolar called me just before Labor Day," says Raymond. "And he said, 'Boy, is Harry pissed about the letter.' He told me that Harry was going to reopen the case."

Seven months later the case was still buried when Raymond saw Connick at a St. Patrick's Day celebration. As politicians hoisted green beer with friends, Raymond buttonholed the tuxedoed district attorney. "How ya doin?" smiled Connick.

"I'm fine, Harry. When is this priest gonna be prosecuted?"

A scowl crossed Connick's face. He stuck his forefinger in Raymond's chest: "Never—while I'm district attorney."

A few days later, at a funeral, Raymond bumped into Richard Angelico, a veteran investigative reporter with WDSU-TV, the NBC affiliate. "Richie," he said, "I got something you oughta see."

Of the many stories Angelico had broken in his long career, one had used hidden cameras to expose a ring of predatory men and teenage male prostitutes in the French Quarter. Cinel's tapes, far more graphic and obscene, would need careful editing. And Angelico was amazed at Cinel's arrogance in the deposition, a narcissism he had never seen in criminals.

In that deposition, plaintiff attorney Darryl Tschirn asked Cinel about his transatlantic call from Hannan. "The agreement was that the church would not *use* [make public] some material of a pornographic nature," Cinel replied, pausing studiously, "which Father Tarantino had brought to the archbishop. And I would resign from the priesthood—although that was somehow left unclear. The immediate request was for me not to return to the United States." As if his stance was self-evident, he said, "And, of course, I said that my work is here [at Tulane]." He continued, as if lecturing a student: "The question of resignation can be done only in writing. And I told the bishop that I would think about it and . . . as soon as I return to the United States in two weeks, I might do so."

In point of fact, Hannan had the power to automatically suspend Cinel, which he did.

Of his relationship with Fontaine, Cinel pondered aloud: "Probably, considering the promiscuity in which he was living, I was the best person he could have sex with."

In reference to the photographs he said he had sent to one Michael Toubo of COQ magazine in Denmark (Cinel had only sent photos of Fontaine), Cinel stated: "Not one picture of Ronnie Tichenor went to Copenhagen. And I thought he was better looking, but Ronnie said he was not interested in that."

Attorney Tschirn questioned him further: "Did you say Mass during this whole period of time?"

> A: Sure.
> Q: You gave out communion?
> A: Uh-huh (affirmative.)
> Q: Heard confessions?
> A: That's correct.
> Q: Did you go to confession?
> A: No, I don't.
> Q: Now when did you first start sending photographs of Chris to be used in publications?
> A: They were sent only once, early February, 1984. Pictures were never sent. I sent two or three rolls of film.

Cinel told Tschirn he received no money for the film, but added, "I was doing all this because Chris wanted me to."

> Tschirn: That was nice of you.
> Cinel: Isn't it? But then he said—it's amazing that you don't believe it.
> Tschirn: I think it's sick. You call it whatever you want.

Cinel elaborated on his Danish connection:

> I had no further contact with them until 1988, when I went over there. And I didn't even know whether they had used the pictures or not because they stopped sending any kind of material of their own to this country way back, probably in '84, on account of the difference of age of consent, that the American government notified them they would not be allowed. . . .

Cinel stated that his first homosexual encounters came at age thirteen, in an Italian boarding school with an unnamed priest he claimed was a close friend of the Pope. He spoke of sexual encounters with men and women during his priestly years in other states. On arriving in New Orleans in 1979, he said, he called the district attorney's office to determine the age of legal consent. He also admitted videotaping sex encounters in his rectory room.

Angelico interviewed Fontaine, with his face in shadows; then the reporter drove to Florida and persuaded Ron Tichenor to do an interview in the same fashion. When Connick met Angelico for an interview the D.A. had no idea how much Angelico knew. It showed.

WDSU reports began airing on May 14, 1991, hours after the story broke in the *Washington Times*. The paper's Southern correspondent, Hugh Aynesworth (tipped by New Orleans law enforcement sources), termed it "the most documented case of pedophilia involving a religious figure."

By this time Dino Cinel was ensconced in a tenured chair in Italian history at the City University of New York, Staten Island campus, with a salary of $90,000. In hiring Cinel, CUNY was not told of his New Orleans problems. When the story broke he was suspended from teaching duty, with pay guaranteed by his contract until the legal situation was resolved.

The WDSU reports, featuring audio bites from Cinel's videotapes with the youths, shocked viewers. Angelico hammered at a nervous Connick about state pornography laws. Still, in questions about Cinel, a gently drawling Connick referred to him as "Father Dino" until Angelico asked if he had refused to prosecute so as not "to embarrass Holy Mother the Church?"

Mouth agape, Connick blurted: "That was an absolute consideration in my mind."

Connick's office soon announced that the investigation had been reopened; the D.A. left town on a scheduled vacation.

For three nights, viewers saw Cinel's cool arrogance, discussing in the video depositions his sex acts with boys. Then, at the end of the week, Cinel returned to New Orleans and gave an interview to WWL (the CBS affiliate). Thus unfolded a bizarre media drama—the remorseless Cinel, under oath on WDSU's segments, contrasting with the same man on the rival station, now saying, "I want to apologize to parishioners"—and saying that his compulsion was behind him. He also said that his privacy had been invaded by the apprehension of his tapes.

Cinel told WWL that Archbishop Hannan had lied about a deal with Connick to block prosecution. The seventy-seven-year-old Hannan—who had retired in 1989—was still an active presence in New Orleans, hosting a religious news show on the archdiocesan television station. After Cinel's interview, Hannan saw red.

On the afternoon of Friday, May 17, Angelico went to the archdiocesan studio to tape an interview with Hannan. "I'm going after you personally!" Hannan snapped as Angelico arrived. "If you worked for me I'd have fired you!"

"What's wrong?" said Angelico, taken aback.

"You never asked for my side of the story!"

But he had, replied Angelico—and one of the church attorneys, Don Richard, had refused the request because of the pending civil suit. Thus, Angelico had quoted from Hannan's deposition in his reports. Now Hannan was ready, and when cameras rolled, his Irish countenance telegraphed outrage—but not at Angelico. He targeted Cinel and said that criminal charges should be filed against him.

In attacking Cinel—and in a letter to the *Times-Picayune* denying any deal with him to thwart prosecution—Hannan adroitly reduced a complex, damaging story to one of his word against that of a fallen priest who admitted having sex with youths he said were over seventeen.

But on WDSU's 6 P.M. broadcast of May 17, Angelico put his own spin on events by inviting Hannan to respond to the latest story seconds after it aired. Seated next to Angelico, Hannan watched as the two young men, faces in shadows, spoke of their stays in the St. Rita rectory in the mid-eighties. Fontaine said that the housekeeper cleaned his clothes, "fed me, cleaned up [Cinel's] room with all that stuff . . . she had to know."

The second interviewee, Tichenor, had said in an earlier report that he was thirteen when his relationship with Cinel began. Now, as Hannan watched, Tichenor said, "I became emotionally depressed, and another resident priest at the church, Father [named beeped out], approached me and asked what was troubling me. I told him it was the relationship with Dino Cinel and myself."

Angelico: "Did he offer help?"

"No, sir. . . . [He] asserted the fact that I should accept that things were right, that this man was doing nothing."

As Hannan watched the tape, Angelico saw him mumble, "My God. . . . My God."

When the tape ended, the broadcast went live to Angelico and Hannan. "Were the boys lying, Archbishop?"

"No, they're not lying so far as I know," said Hannan, who defended the housekeeper and St. Rita's priests, saying that they thought Cinel's guests were homeless youths needing a place to stay. Hannan had justified his initial silence by saying that no boys from St. Rita's Parish were involved with Cinel.

A counteroffensive came that Sunday: a letter from Hannan's successor, Archbishop Francis B. Shulte, read at Masses, criticizing the media for sensationalist reporting. Although both bishops sought to deflect attention from deeper dimensions of the scandal, the problem was not the messengers.

Were the youths who slept in St. Rita's rectory less deserving of the church's concern because they were not parishioners? And how could Tarantino and the other priests not have known? The archdiocese has places where street kids can find refuge. Covenant House is just outside the French Quarter.

Had it not been for a private detective and the news media, Cinel never would have been criminally charged. When that happened Cinel hired Arthur "Buddy" Lemann, a high-profile criminal attorney. The case was assigned to a salty old judge known for harsh sentences; Lemann enlisted a cocounsel who had represented the judge's wife in a civil matter, so the judge recused himself. The case was allotted to another judge—who was a political enemy of Connick. On January 10, 1992, the judge ruled that the prosecution had promised Cinel he would not be tried, and threw out the indictment. Then Lemann filed suit against Connick, Tolar, Raymond, Angelico, and attorneys for Fontaine, charging them with conspiracy to deprive Cinel of his legal rights in the handling of his material. As this book went to press a federal probe of Cinel's pornography was under way, the dismissed criminal charges were supposedly under appeal, Cinel's countersuit had not been heard, and George Tolar, whom Connick blamed for mishandling the case, was out of the D.A.'s office and back on the police force.

iv.

What explains the deception of bishops confronted with child-molesting priests? What is it in the ecclesiastical mind that reaches out to lawyers rather than parents? To call these bishops venal is unfair; accusations of hypocrisy also miss the mark. For in other ways they were accomplished public figures.

Roach of Minnesota: an architect of the NCCB's letter opposing the use of nuclear arms. Quinn of Ohio: a civil lawyer and canonist who helped the papal nuncio understand the Lafayette debacle. Pilla of Cleveland: keeping inner-city Catholic schools open for children of black non-Catholics. Hickey of Washington: an impassioned critic of American policy in El Salvador. Hannan of New Orleans: a defender of American foreign policy, and a racial progressive, providing low-income housing for the elderly.

But recycling or helping child molesters, evading realities among gay clergy, failing to present Rome with a rational agenda for reform—these men—among many others I could name—expose a flaw in the bishops' moral authority. The common denominator is a by-product of celibacy: they don't have children. They do not know what it means to hold an infant with colic in late hours, or the elation when a child learns to walk. Their appreciation of these and the myriad other experiences that come with parenting is abstract, vicarious, and minimal at best.

Celibate governing is a tradition of sexual segregation. Women do hold more places in church administration today; but they are subordinate figures in a power structure passed down the generations by men who cannot marry. Caught between a discriminating laity and an eroding clerical environment, the bishops retreat into a male matrix, a cultural womb of men reinforcing men, while sexual conflicts debunk their moral authority.

In *Tomorrow's Catholics, Yesterday's Church*, Eugene Kennedy writes of a church caught between two cultures—one traditional, anchored in patriarchy, rules, and obedience; the other, influenced by Vatican II's vision of the church-as-People of God, embracing a more flexible moral code. What binds these cultures together is a sacramental essence. "True authority," notes Kennedy, "is ordered to the enhancement of human relationships between flesh-and-blood persons; it is, therefore, thoroughly generative. Authoritarianism remains static and barren. Authority wakens to, speaks to, and respects sexuality in persons, calling forth what is authentically masculine and feminine. . . ."

Shunning sexual victims was not an aberration of the ecclesiastical system; it was a trait—the way things had always been done. Even amid pressure from the legal system and a free press, the rooted fabric of this mentality reveals itself time and again. The bishops' tragic flaw was an accumulation of factors—the hubris and arrogance of power, a refusal to relinquish control, and deep fears covered by sexual denial. But the ultimate vanity of a clerical state that considers itself morally superior was its appalling indifference to children. This moral myopia caused otherwise decent men to betray the church's ethos of defending

human life. Despite a noble history of voluntary celibacy, too many bishops—
shut off from affective bonding, unlettered in the vocabulary of child raising,
swamped by homosexuality and pederasty, hiding behind lawyers, mired in
the muck of the media—were blinded by their flaw and disgraced the People of
God.

xviii.

Arenas of Justice

Cradled by the cold Atlantic, Newfoundland bears a rugged Irish stamp. An island province of Canada high in illiteracy and with no highway system until the 1940s, it was an isolated culture similar to that of French Louisiana. People relied on clergy for legal advice, accounting help, even to write letters. In 1876 men came from the Congregation of Irish Christian Brothers, which had been founded by Edmund Ignatius Rice. The order opened schools across North America, like Brother Rice High in St. John's, Newfoundland. "Many of the Brothers' students," writes Michael Harris in *Unholy Orders*, an account of the pedophilia scandals there, "took their place amongst Newfoundland's leading barristers, merchants, politicians and clerics."

In 1898, St. John's bishop donated land for an orphanage, named Mount Cashel after the site in Ireland where St. Patrick baptized a pagan king. In the 1950s government agencies began placing wards at Mount Cashel. Behind the yellow stone walls and high maple trees, a religious order was rotting at its core.

In 1973, Shane Earle and his two brothers entered Mount Cashel. A childhood snapshot of Shane shows a blond-haired boy with cherubic cheeks and an innocent smile. The twenty-three-year-old I interviewed in Toronto in September 1989 was small, with fair skin, brown mustache, and hazel eyes. "My mother had two marriages and seven relationships," he said, with a distant gaze. "I was physically abused by my father and went into the orphanage."

Five months before we spoke, he had fathered a son out of wedlock. "She wanted to get married right away," he sighed. "But she knew there was a deep dark secret. When I told her, she felt she had to separate. I have no visitation rights—her lawyer says I'm not stable enough. She's about to marry another guy. I don't want to go through the antagonism of a legal fight." He paused. "I'm expecting someday to fall apart. I abused eighteen people [who were] between the ages of seven and eleven at the orphanage. I was seventeen when that stopped. I left Mount Cashel at twenty-one."

"How badly were you abused by the Christian Brothers?"

"I had encounters with five of them within a month of my arrival at six years of age." Gazing at his unlined face, I felt as if I were peering down a telescope at a child's lost innocence. "At Christmastime"—he winced—"I had the most gifts. I thought I was well loved. I was given things after sexual encounters."

Nine Christian Brothers, two of whom were lovers, sodomized, whipped, punched, fondled, and degraded at least thirty Mount Cashel boys for more than twenty years. Testimony pointed to a ring of overlapping pedophiles and sado-masochistic homosexuals, including five men, living in the town, who had grown up in the orphanage and returned to molest boys.

The Mount Cashel superintendent, Brother Douglas Kenny, came from a prominent local family. Years later, a victim testified that he had stormed into Kenny's office and accused Brother Edward English, in his presence, of being "a pervert." As Kenny ordered them out of his office, English said: "If I go down, you go with me. You're gay too, Doug." Kenny replied: "Shut up, shut up."

In 1975 the local government, as a sign of its esteem for the Christian Brothers, gave $450,000 to Mount Cashel for renovations.

When Elizabeth and John Scurry, a childless couple who met Shane Earle, offered to adopt him he was overjoyed. But Kenny blocked the move. "Shane is going back with his parents," Brother Kenny told them. "You're upsetting him." Kenny did more than block the boy's escape into a world of kindness. The Scurrys had given Shane a bowl of goldfish. After they left Kenny slapped him so hard, the bowl went shattering, and he flushed the fish down the toilet, telling the child, "You won't be visiting that family!" Shane later stated that Brother Kenny had raped him in an open field. "He told me, 'Now you're broken in. I like my boys broken in.' I bled for two days. I was terrified of the man."

In Toronto, Shane said: "Brother Joseph Burke was very kind to me. I'd do anything he asked. I loved him like a father. He molested me very gently. With the others, once sex was over, that was it. Burke dressed me in mornings, tucked me in at night, made sure my homework was done. When I left for that four-month period to live with my mom and her new husband, I missed Burke."

That was in December 1975. When he lost a library book card, the gentle pedophile whipped his buttocks so hard with a belt that the scars looked like lines on a map. A maintenance man helped Shane and his brother flee to their mother's flat. She called a police officer, who interviewed the boy. Treated by a doctor, his wounds noted for the police record, Shane waited in limbo. When his father got the news, he drove up to Mount Cashel, drunk and ready to fight Burke. Brother Kenny told him Burke was gone and that the matter was under police investigation.

Indeed, twenty-two boys (and five former residents) interviewed by police made accusations against Burke, Kenny, and four other Christian Brothers. But in 1976, amid centennial celebrations of the religious order in Newfoundland, the Canadian provincial, Brother Gabriel McHugh, promised the Deputy Minister of Justice that he would remove the offenders—and that promise forestalled prosecution. (In 1979, Brother McHugh became superior-general of the Irish Christian Brothers in Rome.)

Luggage in hand, Brothers Edward English and Alan Ralph went to the police, admitted their crimes, and left on the spot—Ralph to a clergy treatment program in Ontario, English to House of Affirmation. In less than a year, both had new religious postings. Brother Kenny was reassigned to Vancouver. A fifth Mount

Cashel brother became principal at a Christian Brothers high school in British Columbia. Brother Burke, whose belt-whipping started it all, was transferred to a college a few miles away from the orphanage. After leaving the order, he landed in Vancouver as vice-principal of a Catholic boys' school. As wards of the state, Shane and his two brothers returned to Mount Cashel in March 1976.

The publisher of the *St. John Evening Telegram* killed the story in deference to "one hundred years of good" by the order. Like an incest family, local powers sealed away the crimes, silencing boys who literally begged for help, sending them back to pay hell in the orphanage across town from Signal Hill where Marconi received the first transatlantic telegram in 1901.

Not until 1988 did the cover-up unravel. James J. Hickey, fifty-five, a popular parish priest (and former seminary recruiter for the archdiocese), was arrested on charges of multiple sex crimes with teenage boys. Like Gilbert Gauthe, he had selected victims from a stream of altar boys for years. In December 1987 a priest in psychological treatment who, years earlier, had been abused by Hickey at Brother Rice High told child welfare authorities and Archbishop Alphonsus Penney. Hickey denied the accusations; at a hearing more than twenty men gave graphic testimony against him. In early 1988, two months after Mark Chopko issued the USCC pedophilia statement, which was nonbinding on dioceses, the Canadian Conference of Catholic Bishops circulated a working paper to its 165 members on how to handle such accusations. On March 27 the *Toronto Star* reported:

> *The document suggests that bishops: appoint a special team in their diocese to investigate any complaints of child molestation by priests; withdraw the priest from the parish until the investigation is completed; provide counsel; and if sex abuse is found, bring the priest to trial under canon (church) law.*
>
> *Those found guilty could face expulsion from the priesthood.*
>
> *Background interviews with canon lawyers indicate . . . 12 such cases have been before the courts in Canada. There are about 12,000 priests in Canada.*

According to the *Star*, no Canadian diocese had yet been sued. With less than two dozen cases, the CCCB was devising a policy. The United States had six times more cases, yet none had riveted media attention there as Newfoundland's did in Canada.

In April 1988 several parents of Hickey's victims called on Archbishop Penney to request counseling. Penney refused to meet with them; his vicar-general said that offering assistance was inappropriate until Hickey's legal status was determined. In September, Hickey pled guilty and received a five-year term. On November 7 a second priest was charged with child sexual assault and subsequently convicted. On January 27, 1989, two other priests (one a former vocation director) were charged with gross indecency, and three days later an ex-priest was arrested for sexual crimes against youths while a priest.

"I would much rather today have a hemorrhage in the church than the trickle of life's blood ebbing away and making the church weaker and weaker," the white-haired Penney said on February 13 in response to the arrests and convictions. On his own, training to become a waiter, Shane Earle wondered: if all of those priests could be arrested, why not the Brothers? Shane had twice tried to commit suicide at Mount Cashel; boys he had known had scattered to the winds. He went to the St. John's police and for seven hours told it again, adding years of new information which amazed investigators took down. Meanwhile, an upstart weekly in St. John's, the *Sunday Express*, was digging into the past. After reading an article by publisher-editor Michael Harris demanding a government probe, Shane asked to be interviewed. The series began on Easter Sunday, 1989, and hit the town like mortar fire. When the Scurrys, who had offered to adopt Shane in 1975, read the paper they immediately contacted him and renewed the offer. Shaky, depressed, and confused, he moved into their home.

Facing a media debacle, Archbishop Penney asked a former lieutenant governor of the province, Gordon Winter, to lead a church inquiry. On March 31, 1989, the provincial Justice Department launched a government inquiry, led by Samuel Hughes, a retired justice of the Ontario Supreme Court. Investigators began tracking down young men who had grown up at Mount Cashel. Canadian commissions of inquiry operate with broad powers. As Brothers and ex-Brothers were brought back to St. John's from points afar for arraignment, their attorneys argued that the work of the Hughes Commission would unduly prejudice their clients when they would later, as seemed likely, be tried in court. But the arguments were to no avail.

Douglas Kenny, now married and vice-principal of a Toronto parochial school, lost his marriage and was suspended with pay from work pending the outcome of his criminal adjudication.

Meanwhile, at the Winter Commission hearings held at Newfoundland churches, people in parish halls demanded Penney's ouster. "It's the priests themselves have brought the church to its knees," cried one woman, "not the people, nor the press, and certainly not the victims." By July 6, when the church commission held its fourth hearing, seventeen priests, brothers, or former clerics had been charged with sexually abusing boys. "Some people won't let their children go into the confession box," said the vice-chair of St. John's school board. "The very role models one could trust are being destroyed." An elderly man in Penney's parish said of the archbishop: "When he comes to the altar, I walk out."

That summer, as I exchanged news clips with the *Sunday Express*, I wondered about the boys of Mount Cashel. A producer for a Toronto talk show, hosted by Shirley Solomon, invited me on the program with six Mount Cashel survivors, among other guests, and I spent a long evening with them after the taping.

John MacIsaac, thirty-one, a blunt, square-shouldered government worker in Ontario, spoke of being forced with another boy to fondle the genitals of one Brother: "To say no was not an option when you knew the things they were capable of doing. . . . From 1965 to 1976 there were 250 kids and when I left there were 125. I'm sure eighty percent were abused." MacIsaac's fifteen-year-old brother escaped from Mount Cashel in 1969 with six dollars in his pocket. Years later, after serving in the Army, John found his sibling in Toronto. "I fight back now," said MacIsaac. All he wanted was a house with a yard and a river behind it, a wife and a child and a good job.

Jim Ghaney, a carpenter in Ontario, spoke in near whispers of a childhood bedwetting episode for which a Brother made him march around the dormitory

with his suitcase, saying goodbye, humiliated, frightened of being put out on the
street.

The testimony given by victims before the Hughes Commission in St. John's
was televised live, with lengthy excerpts airing nationally across Canada. Horrific
stories told by young men, some of whom wept openly in testimony, incited
newspaper coverage uncommonly critical of the Catholic Church. "We had part
of our life stolen from us," one victim told a reporter. "Our childhood, our innocence, our sexuality. . . ." By making Newfoundland's agony a national story, the
media moved CCCB president Archbishop James M. Hayes of Nova Scotia to say
on July 12, 1989: "First in our compassion must be those who have been sexually
abused. . . . All of us want a solution, an understandable explanation and a way
to prevent this from ever happening again."

No such candor had emanated from the U.S. hierarchy.

That September, Shane Earle flew to Chicago as a guest on the "Oprah Win-
frey Show"—herself a survivor of child sexual abuse. In the studio that day he met
a woman called Hilary Stiles, who had recently published *Assault on Innocence,* a
thinly fictionalized account of her family's ordeal with the Chicago archdiocese in
the early 1980s, trying to remove a pedophile priest in her parish. Mount Cashel
had barely registered in U.S. news coverage. As Shane spoke of legal efforts to
obtain reparations from the provincial government and the Christian Brothers,
Hilary Stiles flashed back to her own anguish and the battering her faith had
taken; in the modest young Canadian she felt her heart tearing again as it had for
her son.

ii.

Her real name was Jeanne Miller—she had taken the pen name to safeguard her
son's anonymity. Published in 1988 by an obscure New Mexico publisher, *Assault
on Innocence* was ignored by the Catholic press; however, it got Jeanne Miller on
media talk shows, allowing her to speak out.

From her apartment in a Chicago suburb she was amassing a computerized list
of child-molesting priests, drawn from legal records and news accounts. Trying to
gauge the dimensions of the crisis, I too was searching for names and information.
In that pursuit, Jeanne Miller became a valued source, along with an array of
church insiders and attorneys Jeffrey Anderson and Tony Fontana. Out of the
collective suffering, Miller conceived of a network of moral witnesses, an organized group to pressure the American bishops to change the church's twisted
ways.

I was highly skeptical of the idea; most adult survivors want anonymity, not
public attention, and a pressure group could only work with visibility. Miller was
also helping a family in Chicago with research for their suit against the archdiocese when a Washington, D.C., political activist asked her help in planning a
confrontation with the bishops.

Thirty-nine-year-old Michael Schwartz was a policy analyst at the Free Congress Foundation, a think tank founded by Paul Weyrich, an Eastern-rite Catholic

and confidant of Jerry Falwell and Pat Robertson. Schwartz had also been clipping articles about pedophile priests. His wife was from South Louisiana; they had four children. Free Congress opposed gay rights and sex education in schools, and trained right-wing organizers. When Schwartz called Jeanne Miller for insights, he never thought to ask her views on abortion, which were decidedly pro-choice.

Years of pro-life speeches had earned Mike Schwartz the admiration of bishops; so did his public praise of *Humanae Vitae*. As "Hilary Stiles" recounted her experiences, Schwartz felt a humbling pathos. Reading Canadian news accounts, he was appalled that U.S. bishops could be so cavalier.

I kept abreast of the Mount Cashel survivors through telephone calls to John MacIsaac in Ontario, who was bracing himself to give testimony at criminal trials of the Christian Brothers in Newfoundland. He sent me batches of Canadian news clippings. "We are *going* to get justice," he said. "There's too much heat coming from the Hughes inquiry and media." But attorneys for the accused Brothers were still arguing that the Hughes Commission testimony was essentially a trial of the accused men that would prejudice a jury. "I don't know what faith I have in the system," brooded MacIsaac. "But they can't get away with what they did to us."

Mike Schwartz was an unlikely candidate to put heat on the American bishops. In the early 1980s he had worked in Milwaukee as director of the Catholic League for Religious and Civil Rights, which kept tabs on anti-Catholic bigotry, and he had written a book on the topic, *The Persistent Prejudice*. With the NCCB due to meet in Baltimore on November 6, 1989, Schwartz wanted to stage a protest press conference, calling attention to the bishops' inaction in the child molestation crisis.

Events in Milwaukee had convinced him that the scandal was a real threat to parish life. In July 1984 three lay teachers wrote Archbishop Rembert Weakland and Pio Laghi about an assistant pastor inviting young boys into his bedroom, and complained of another priest who "signed an open document supporting homosexuality and has preached support of it from the pulpit." The parish was staffed by Salvatorian, or Society of the Divine Savior, priests. Three young priests had recently moved into the rectory. Father Bruce Brentrup, the longtime principal, confided to the lay teachers his concern about boys in the young priest's room. The new pastor dismissed Brentrup, who later filed suit, saying he was ousted for not condoning "the homosexual lifestyle supported by . . . defendants."

Weakland, an advocate of academic freedom and greater autonomy for the NCCB, wrote the teachers on August 13, 1984, that "any libelous material found in your letter will be scrutinized carefully by our lawyers." That fall the teachers resigned under pressure from the school system—during which time the assistant pastor of whom they had complained, Dennis Pecore, was molesting a teenage boy. On January 22, 1987, Pecore was charged with second degree sexual assault. That July, the Salvatorians, the archdiocese, and insurers negotiated a settlement with the victim's family. The *Milwaukee Journal* asked the Court, to no avail, to break the seal on settlement terms. Pecore pled guilty to a reduced charge and was sentenced to a year in a halfway house with day privileges to attend college classes.

In February 1988 a self-styled lay activist, Tom Phillips, lashed out at Weak-

land (who was not present) on a fundamentalist cable TV show: "You don't believe in heaven, hell and the righteous judgment of God." Phillips was furious at
Weakland for cochairing a community AIDS program that occasionally distributed condoms to high-risk groups; permitting a Capuchin Brother to lecture high
school students on AIDS with discussion of condoms and without condemnation
of homosexuality; and allowing Father James Arimond to serve as chaplain of the
local Dignity chapter. (In 1990, Arimond pleaded no contest to charges of sexually abusing a teenage boy and spent forty-five days in jail.)

Phillips sent a 28-page manifesto to Weakland, a fundamentalist tract with
scriptural references to homosexuality. Weakland called the criticism "witch hunts
through an obsession with sexual issues." Of his own celibacy, Phillips told Marie
Rohde of the *Journal* that where he had once thought sexuality "the be-all and
end-all" he now saw it as "fool's gold. Real sexuality, real fullness," he said, "is not
found outside the rules but inside the rules."

Pecore's eighteen-year-old victim sought out Phillips. The young man then
wrote the judge, asking him to revoke the seal that his family had originally
opposed. All he wanted was that his anonymity be preserved. "I am very disgusted
with all the secrecy and homosexuality in the Archdiocese," he said. The judge
complied. The *Journal* reported terms of the $595,000 settlement. By then Pecore
was directing a clergy retirement home. Father Brentrup, the ex-principal at the
parish school, was living alone, scraping at odd jobs. (His lawsuit was later dismissed, the Court ruling that it lacked jurisdiction in a church matter.) Weakland
published some final thoughts in the May 26, 1988, *Catholic Herald:*

> *Sometimes not all adolescent victims are so "innocent," some can be sexually very*
> *active and aggressive and often quite street wise. (We frequently try such adolescents*
> *for crimes as adults at that age.) Pastorally, such cases are difficult to treat: we must*
> *not imply that the abuser is not guilty of serious crime, but we could easily give a*
> *false impression that any adolescent who becomes sexually involved with an older*
> *person does so without any degree of personal responsibility.*

Circuit Judge John F. Foley wrote a letter, calling the remark "dead wrong.
. . . The relationship between priest and adolescent is one that is based on the
highest form of trust obtainable." A lady wrote the paper, echoing the judge: "I
cannot imagine a sexually active, aggressive, street wise adolescent being able to
bribe, coerce, trick, threaten or force a mentally and emotionally stable
priest. . . ."

Schwartz invited Phillips to join the Baltimore protest.

On learning that a Free Congress staffer was planning a protest, I wondered
what direction this force field of human energies would take. Although I did not
share Schwartz's conservatism, someone was at last targeting mechanisms of
power. The Catholic left, fixed on homosexuality as a human rights issue, seemed
unable to grasp that the abuse of power by gay clericalism was as valid an issue as
homophobia. In different ways, Brentrup and the Milwaukee teachers; Liz Reilly's
group in El Cajon; Mark Brooks, and the boys of Mount Cashel were abused by
forms of clericalism. Yet archconservative Catholics, hostile to dissident theologians, often *equated* homosexuality and pedophilia, and failed to question the effect

on priests' sexuality of a religious power structure rooted in sexual segregation. The idea that Catholicism would recover if believers returned to the old ways—to rote learning and obedience—could not account for the psychological and social factors that had driven thousands of good men out of the priesthood. It always amazed me how Catholics of strong conservatism could protest the presence of young girls as altar servers—and fume about homosexual networks in clergy. What did they expect in a church that shunted women to the ministerial margins and rewarded unmarried men?

For his protest, Schwartz also included Charles Wilson, a layman who directed the San Antonio-based St. Joseph Foundation, which assisted people in appeals through canonical courts. A convert and retiree, Wilson was a student of canon law, orthodox to his toes, and one of the nicest men I met in my journeys. "Many bishops seem to think they rule a diocese by personal whim," said Wilson. "I think Catholics of all sorts of theological persuasions are becoming disenchanted with this."

Schwartz was more Machiavellian. "Rome can't take action against bishops who deceive us unless there is a scandal. And Rome can't provoke a scandal. This event [the NCCB protest] says to the Vatican, 'Here's the problem. Now, you guys fix it.' "

The central figure of his event was a young man prepared to say that he had been abused as a youth by an American bishop.

Agreeing not to reveal the accuser's identity, I flew to Baltimore with an assignment for the *Plain Dealer*. On Saturday, November 4, at Schwartz's home I met David Figueroa, thirty, taut, with black crewcut and dark Portuguese eyes, who volunteered that he had turned tricks in San Francisco during the mid-eighties and had been diagnosed HIV positive. Smoking Marlboros, he said he was in good health so far. He had come from his home in Hawaii with Patricia Morley, a high-energy, chain-smoking housewife who wore her conservatism on her sleeve and engaged in theological warfare with Bishop Joseph A. Ferrario of Honolulu. Pat Morley had made a mission of David's spiritual rehabilitation.

"I came from a family of eight brothers and seven sisters," said David. "I was in the middle, and I kind of slid by. I didn't receive that much attention from my father." He said he was molested in kindergarten by his parish priest, one Father Henry; the sexual abuse continued until he was fifteen, when Father Henry died. David's mother did housecleaning at the rectory. "My father beat my mom quite a bit. They were getting a divorce when Father Ferrario came to St. Anthony's."

Father Henry paid him for raking leaves, "the only source of money I had. I told Father Ferrario about Henry molesting me. He asked if I told anyone else and I said no. We were moving the dead pastor's desk when he reached over and grabbed me. I worked there daily, odd jobs around the parish. I tried to avoid him. He'd hold the job over me. He'd say we have to talk about it in his office. Then he'd say he needed a hug. If I wanted money, we had sexual encounters. He paid me even if I didn't work." A twisted knot of money and sex entangled them for years, he contends. "I thought all priests were pedophiles until I got to high school, and then it started to hit me. Football players dated cheerleaders. I played football. I had a relationship with a girl for a while, but it just never worked. I felt I was living two lives."

Taking Ferrario's money was part of that double life as David described it. As he got older, the relationship made him bitter. "When I finally came out and told people the truth about being gay," he said, "I was pissed off at myself."

He wanted to live in San Francisco. He said Ferrario paid the plane fare, and periodically visited him there in the early eighties, with sexual liaisons at St. Patrick's Seminary in Menlo Park where the bishop stayed. "One day at the seminary I said, 'This is wrong.' And he said, 'Yes, it's wrong, but we're weak.'"

In San Francisco he worked different jobs along with stretches of selling himself for sex. He spoke of landing a job as a houseboy for a gay doctor, and of a strained relationship with his mother, who knew he was gay but did not understand why.

Pat Morley's conflicts with Ferrario began in 1984 when he ordered the statues removed from St. Anthony Parish, changed the tabernacle, and rearranged the altar. While these moves may have been canonically within his purview, Morley —like the El Cajon parishioners—resented the changes and denounced them at a parish meeting. David Figueroa's mother was at the meeting. Eventually, the woman began confiding in Morley. On her own, David's mother wrote to Pio Laghi, telling the pro nuncio about her son's plight.

According to David, Ferrario told him that Laghi had forwarded him the letter, that the letter could damage him, and he asked Figuero to refute the charges. David said that he did so in a letter to Laghi for which he said he received a $400 check drawn on the Bishop's Charity Fund. His mother was furious at him for taking money from the man he said made him gay. So David wrote a second letter to Laghi to correct the record, spelling out details on Father Henry and Ferrario. "My life has become so unbearable now that I wish it would end today," he wrote. On April 7, 1986, Laghi replied:

> *Due to the serious and sensitive nature of this matter, I have decided to search for an occasion to have a representative of mine visit with you in the near future. Such a meeting is designed to give you the personal attention you deserve. The only condition I would insist upon is that he speak with you privately and that the discussion be kept confidential. Such an arrangement will provide you with the absolute freedom to elaborate in detail on your charges. . . .*

That May, an emissary from Laghi, one Father Walsh, met with David and his mother. "He spent an hour with us together and then an additional hour alone with me," continued Figueroa, and told them to keep the meeting confidential. A few days later Ferrario told him that Walsh had been a guest at the bishop's residence, and that Walsh divulged everything he and his mother had said.

Mother and son wrote Laghi but never heard from him again.

Schwartz and Morley helped Figueroa draft a three-page statement to be read at the press conference on November 5, 1989, in the Lord Baltimore Hotel. To preserve his anonymity, David would sit behind a screen in back of the stage where Schwartz, Chuck Wilson, Tom Phillips, and "Hilary Stiles" would sit. Figueroa would use the pseudonym Damien De Veuster [sic]—the famous priest who lived among lepers in Hawaii and was eventually made a saint.

At dusk on November 4, when my interview with Figueroa was done, Pat Morley had volumes yet to say. About the priest back in Hawaii who consecrated pound cake at Mass. About the homosexual network of priests on the islands. About her community radio program and arguments with Ferrario over doctrinal and liturgical abuses. About the *Catholic Lay Press* in Hawaii which had exposed Ferrario as a Modernist. Exhausted after six hours of interviewing, I joined Schwartz on a drive to Washington, where he sent a fax to Rome, asking the Pope to remove the bishop of Honolulu.

A bleary-eyed Jeanne Miller flew to Baltimore early the next morning, Sunday the fifth, curious about the men she would join. She only knew Schwartz, and him only by phone. At the Lord Baltimore Hotel she met her fellow protesters in Catholics for an Open Church—the name Schwartz had chosen for incorporation papers to shield individuals (notably himself) in the event of a defamation suit. Miller soon realized that she was the only pro-choice member of the group, which somehow, ironically, made sense. And then she met David, whose life magnified the suffering she had seen in Shane Earle and others assaulted by the church that had caused her such pain, yet which she could never really leave. *This is one of the holiest moments in my life,* she thought. She prayed: *Here we are, coming together from different emotional spaces, crying out. Please, Lord, do something.*

Reporters waited in the conference room. A table contained press packets, with individual prepared statements; a copy of the 1985 Mouton-Doyle-Peterson report; a lawsuit recently filed against the Chicago archdiocese; and *Assault on Innocence.* David sat behind a screen; Pat Morley slipped into a middle row. Schwartz, Phillips, Wilson, and Jeanne Miller stepped onto the stage, turned their backs to the press, linked arms, and bowed their heads. Trembling, Schwartz whispered, "Lord, we are afraid. We ask for courage to do what is needed and face consequences we will have to suffer."

Then he addressed religion editors, many of whom he knew: "It grieves me that this should have come upon our church." He discussed the 1985 report and introduced each speaker on the stage. When they were done, "Damian" began reading in a controlled voice as Pat Morley quietly wept. He said that he and his mother met with a prosecutor in Hawaii, but "due to the passage of time criminal charges could not be filed. . . . I know justice will be done!" Then he sobbed: "Bishop Joe, you've taken a part of my life away from me and it's *killing me!"* Then, almost spitting the words, he said: "You are a *pedophile!"*

A cool pall settled over the room. Laura Sessions Stepp of the *Washington Post* spoke first: "You must understand the situation we're in. If your family already knows, why can't you come forward with the truth and say, 'I'm willing to stand on my name'? And, secondly, do you have any documentation?"

"People I work with don't know what happened," said the voice behind the screen. "If this ends up in court, I can identify marks, a mole, on Bishop Ferrario's body in places that people don't normally see."

"That would help in court but it doesn't help us for tomorrow's newspaper," said Stepp.

Schwartz addressed David: "The problem reporters have is that anonymous allegations are simply of no news credibility. It must be corroborated before it can be printed." *You're blowing your presentation*, I thought. To Laura Stepp, Schwartz said: "He has copies of letters he addressed to Archbishop Laghi that he would be willing to make public with his name removed."

Schwartz identified Pat Morley, and when the briefing ended, several reporters gathered around her. She said that other Catholics in Hawaii had expressed concerns about Ferrario to the Vatican, to San Francisco Archbishop John Quinn, and to Cardinal O'Connor of New York. She said that Laghi told O'Connor the dispute was out of his jurisdiction.

Ten blocks away some three hundred white-robed bishops filed into Baltimore's cathedral in the waning afternoon for a Mass celebrating the two hundredth anniversary of the nation's first archdiocese. On the altar, under a canopy, sat Cardinal Agostino Casaroli, the Vatican Secretary of State. At the Omni Hotel, adjacent to the Lord Baltimore, Bishop Ferrario, flanked by USCC attorney Mark Chopko, stood in the doorway of the media center, wearing black clericals with a gold chain on his chest, waiting to meet reporters who had just attended the protest event.

USCC press officers disseminated a statement saying the charges "have been examined by Church authorities and . . . determined to lack substance."

A short, tanned, stocky man of sixty-two, Ferrario had a seeming calm as reporters gathered next to him, everyone standing up. Someone asked if the charges surprised him. He said no, he had gotten wind of the accusations in 1985.

"Has it ever been made public the way it was today?" a journalist asked.

Hand against the doorway, he tried to maintain his smile: "Not in this—not as personally as this. But obliquely, but yet not obliquely. There's a group in Hawaii that's a concerned Catholics group. They have a radio station and a paper, the *Catholic Lay Press*. They have written things, as I say obliquely—they actually printed one letter from Archbishop Laghi with blacked-out names. So I'm sure our media in Hawaii has been on to this."

Asked if he knew who made the accusations, he said with a chuckle, "I know him and his family very well."

"What can you say about the allegations—are they totally false?" asked another reporter.

In a measured tone, he said: "The accusations of sexual activity, yes, I would deny them entirely. The fact that I helped him, and his family, that's true. The mother was the housekeeper . . ." He reviewed the family's plight—many children, little money, ultimately a divorce.

"There's a relationship here, a lot of things I can't say. I worked with him, tried to help him, and in the letter he wrote Laghi, denying the charges that had been made against me, he did say that I was truly a father to him and that I tried to help him with his homosexual condition."

He admitted meeting with David over his mother's letter to Laghi in 1985. "He came up. I said, 'Here's the letter your mother sent. I have to make a statement. It would be good if you did.' He wrote a letter there but I didn't see what he wrote until about two years afterward when Archbishop Laghi showed me."

Schwartz had disseminated copies of a handwritten note, dated April 4, with no year, allegedly from Ferrario to David:

I cannot get the money from the various funds here. I will have to work on
something when I get home this evening. Sorry. But you did not give me the proper
lead-time. [signed] Bishop.

I asked if he had given Figueroa money for writing a letter to Laghi. He
winced. "That's . . . that's . . . that's false."

What motivated his accusant? another reporter asked. "I don't know what's
going through his mind," said Ferrario. "A year ago he called me up, crying,
saying these people [Morley and others] were pushing him, pushing him."

"Have you ever had sexual relationships with a minor?" asked Laura Stepp.

"No," he replied, holding a thin smile.

"Are you a homosexual?" I asked.

Again he said, "No."

Stepp: "Do you think he's being used by this group that would like to get rid
of you?"

"I can say that without too much fear of being wrong. It's an ultraconservative
Catholic group. You can read their paper."

I asked who Father Walsh was. Ferrario laughed. "That's not my domain.
That's someone sent by Archbishop Laghi."

"Can you tell us his first name?"

"I don't think I should. . . . The man was staying with me, for my sixtieth
birthday. I didn't know he was coming to investigate me. He told me afterward."
Walsh, he said, was not the priest's name. "All I will say [is he was] a visitor sent
by Archbishop Laghi." In Rome, Ferrario said, he was assured by the Congregation of Clergy that the Holy Father had full confidence in him.

Pressed by another reporter, he admitted meeting with David at the San Francisco seminary but denied sexual activity took place. "Our young men study
there," he said. Asked about Morley, he said: "The only thing I would say about
Patricia Morley is you spend some time with her and try to reason about the
church and theology . . ." Why were conservatives so opposed to him? He said
he was following the spirit of Vatican II, that problems arose when he supported a
gay rights ordinance, even though he had met with Catholic legislators, most of
whom opposed the bill, and told them to vote for what they thought best.

I said: "Mrs. Morley said a priest named McNeely celebrated Mass—" Ferrario
grinned. I said: "Why do you laugh?" He stopped smiling and said, "I don't know.
Go ahead."

"She said she and her son attended New Year's night—"

"And he gave 'em cake?" he said, anticipating the question.

I paused. He said: "Go ahead."

"Yeah, that he consecrated pound cake, and there were strobe lights, and he
was speaking of New Age theories. I take it from your glibness that you don't
believe that allegation?"

"Yeah, because the woman, what she did do—I don't know if you're Catholic
—she went to communion, received the host in her hand; it was supposed to be
pound cake. And she sent it"—he paused for emphasis—"by mail—*to Rome*." Reporters chuckled. Smiling, Ferrario continued: "Then Rome wrote back to me to
investigate it, and I checked the recipe . . ." More chuckles. "And it came from
the Benedictines!" Reporters laughed.

Someone asked the bishop why his accuser had made the charges. Ferrario said simply, "I don't know."

Laura Stepp asked: "Are you angry? Are you mad?"

"I'm not angry," he chuckled.

"What do you feel?" someone else asked.

After a moment he said, "Hurt."

Another journalist asked if he was considering legal action against Schwartz. He replied that when the issue was raised with Laghi he met with lawyers. "They said there's not much you can do. You're in the public eye . . . people can say things."

A man stepped forward. "My name is Michael Schwartz, Bishop Ferrario, and I believe David." Ferrario's smile was frozen on his face; he blinked, nodded, and left the hall.

"For someone getting his name dragged in the mud, he didn't seem too upset," a reporter muttered.

The next day's *New York Times* made no reference to the accusations. Stepp's story in the *Post* summarized the charges but did not identify the bishop "because reporters were unable to interview the young man to determine his credibility." Frank Somerville's lengthy report in the *Baltimore Sun* on the welcoming Mass concluded with an account of the dispute and identified Ferrario. A *Washington Times* report also identified Ferrario and quoted him as saying the young man had AIDS.

But absent a story on the wire services, the event had merely made a ripple.

On Monday, after reading the papers, an incensed Figueroa returned with Schwartz and agreed to on-the-record interviews with individual journalists. A dozen met with him individually, more out of curiosity, apparently, than anything else. Standing behind the screen had not helped his credibility. Some stories made passing reference to the accusations without identifying Ferrario. I used the "Damian" pseudonymn in the *Plain Dealer* article the following Sunday. The one report identifying him came in *The Wanderer*. Without wire service copy, the *Honolulu Advertiser* and *Star Bulletin* printed nothing.

In preparing my article, I telephoned the *Honolulu Advertiser* and asked a reporter looking into the allegations why nothing was reported. I was told the allegations were being checked. "If it was a congressman, you guys would have reported the allegations," I said. The reporter then said that the conversation was off the record and could in no way be quoted, a clever demand as it turned out.

A dejected Figueroa went to a friend's house in Kentucky. Morley returned to Kailua and on November 14 interviewed David for two hours by telephone on her weekly program, "Catholicism in Crisis," on KWAI-FM. For more than thirty minutes he now told his story in Hawaii. Caller after caller praised his courage and offered sympathy. Some denounced the bishop. David also identified a young man who quit the seminary after Ferrario allegedly tried to seduce him. "What do I have to gain?" cried Figueroa. "He ruined my life. I don't want him to ruin others."

The daily media in Hawaii made no reference to the broadcast.

Ferrario sent a November 16 confidential memo to his pastors with a statement to be read at Mass "ONLY if there is an actual press release or media coverage." Since the late 1970s, it said, "certain groups of people in Hawaii have spread false rumors" accusing the bishop "of sexual offenses." It continued:

> *Archbishop Giovanni Re, Secretary of the Vatican Congregation of Bishops which investigated the charges and dismissed them in 1987, said, "There did not turn out to be anything against this bishop. For us, the accusations were baseless."*

In December a second radio station interviewed Figueroa after Morley and others had picketed the chancery. The rest of the news media still ignored the fact that accusations were made. Later, a Hawaiian media analyst told me: "Ferrario has an advertising agency that represents him, and they have major clients who place ads in the media. The market here is very tight, and if you can threaten withdrawal of advertisements it's like waving a red flag. This is also a very laid-back place. The editors don't want a fight with the Catholic bishop."

And so, by default, the paper of record on Ferrario was the *Catholic Lay Press*, a tabloid in Hawaii with 3000 subscribers published by John O'Connor, a retired Knights of Columbus employee. The *Lay Press* reprinted articles (mostly from conservative Catholic journals) and accused Ferrario of tolerating liturgical abuses, squelching Latin Mass, and promoting dissident theology. Such disputes pass through the prism of the secular media as "liberal vs. conservative" Catholic stories. But how many dioceses have a bishop accused of pederasty?

On March 1, Schwartz arranged for Figueroa to take a lie detector test, which found "no significant emotional disturbances indicative of deception." Schwartz sent copies to selected reporters, but apart from a Gary Potter article in *The Wanderer* (reprinted in the *Lay Press*) the story was dead.

Figueroa was not the least of Ferrario's problems. Faced with a soaring debt, he attempted to sell Honolulu's historic St. Augustine Church for $42 million to a group of Japanese investors. The mayor of Honolulu objected. So did the Vatican. And that was the end of that.

iii.

In June 1990, after more than a year's research and public hearings, Gordon Winter, the former lieutenant governor of Newfoundland, presented his commission's findings to Archbishop Alphonsus Penney. *The Report of the Archdiocesan Commission of Enquiry into the Sexual Abuse of Children by Members of the Clergy*, a three-volume document, just under 600 pages, concluded with fifty-five recommendations. Winter was an Anglican; his collaborators were Catholic—a social worker; a nun-physician; a canonist; and a philosopher.

Since the government commission under retired Justice Hughes was investigating events at Mount Cashel, the Winter Commission focused on the seven archdiocesan priests accused of sexually abusing minors. Four were convicted, one acquitted, and two awaited trial when the report was published.

Although Canadian law provides for financial redress of torts, the settlement and verdict amounts are much smaller than those in the United States, a much more litigious country. The whole question of payments to the Mount Cashel victims, who had suffered abuse far worse than most boys abused in American cases, had yet to be resolved in Newfoundland.

"Victims of child sexual abuse are not to blame for being victims," the Winter Commission stated. The report called on the archdiocese to acknowledge its guilt, financially compensate the victims, and establish a victims advocacy board "composed of knowledgeable and concerned members of the community, operating at arm's length from church administration." The recommendations covered thirty-six pages and envisaged a radical overhaul of the archdiocese, creating a power-sharing arrangement with lay leaders for all church governance. The report said Penney had failed to follow 1987 procedures recommended by the Canadian Conference of Catholic Bishops:

> *Because the archbishop did not act vigorously on the complaints and concerns of his priests, parishioners and concerned parents, children continued to be abused by some priests, even while under criminal investigation. . . .*
>
> *While the local church's attitude was sympathetic and treatment—however ineffectual—was offered, it showed little compassion toward those victims. Church officials aligned themselves with the accused; their response to victims was thus inappropriate and unchristian, and thus compounded the victims' initial sense of betrayal by the church.*

On July 18, Penney convened a press conference, offered apologies to the victims, and announced that he was tendering his resignation to Rome. At sixty-five he had ten years left before he was required under canon law to retire. "We are a sinful church," he said. "We are naked. Our anger, our pain, our anguish, and our vulnerability are clear to the whole world."

The Winter Commission members did not have access to the priests' medical files; but after reviewing ages of the victims, they wrote that the clerics were not "classic" pedophiles. Rather, the document referred to the men as "regressed homosexuals" and a "statistical anomaly." Regressive homosexuality can be stress-induced, or a state in which stunted sexual development retreats into acting out adolescent fantasies. But how could this analysis be sustained without medical files? The report also stated that "a number of priests" refused to send youths to an altar boy function because known homosexual priests

> *were holding the jamboree. Several priests told the Commission they would not send anybody to the jamborees. . . . Events during the early years of [Penney's] tenure signalled the possibility of homosexual activity by priests. . . . Yet both subsequently convicted and alleged offenders were known to be constantly in the company of adolescent males.*

The Newfoundland report echoed Andrew Greeley's argument in a November 10, 1989, essay in *NCR*, which triggered a spate of complaining letters. Greeley wrote of a double standard:

If a group of heterosexual priests used a rectory as a house of assignation, they would all be suspended from the ministry by sundown. If they kept a summer cottage together and engaged in trysts and seductions at it (especially of young women), they would be banished to the farthest reaches of the republic. Celibacy in the minds of church leaders is for heterosexuals, but not for homosexuals.

That scenario unfolded in the summer of 1990 when Dale Russell of WAGA-TV in Atlanta reported that Archbishop Eugene Marino, who had recently resigned, citing stress, had been having a two-year affair with twenty-seven-year-old Vicki Long, an emotionally troubled woman. Marino met Long after she filed a paternity suit against a priest whose blood tests ended up not matching her child's. But Marino's faults paled in comparison with the lengthening pederasty scandal. The archbishop fell in love. Had he been a bachelor Protestant minister the tale would have been far less sensational, if one at all. After exchanging marriage vows with Long in a New York hotel, Marino retreated into the clerical world and underwent psychological treatment after a reported suicide attempt, according to WAGA.

Greeley wrote of the agony that many fine priests felt:

> *As one who believes in the value of celibate witness, I resent the ecclesiastical policy that continues to support it verbally and then tolerates its erosion. . . .*
>
> *How can one not criticize the idiocy of the destruction of the priesthood? Or the hypocrisy of denouncing homosexual behavior and tolerating it within our own ministers, sometimes on your own staff or among your own favorites?*

The Newfoundland report and Archbishop Marino's departure came on the heels of a more shocking scandal, involving Bruce Ritter, the Franciscan priest who founded Covenant House, the national shelter program for runaway youths, based in New York City. Charles Sennott of the *New York Post* reported the first accusations by a young man who claimed Ritter had a sexual relationship with him after his arrival at the facility. Then the *Village Voice* and the *New York Times* recounted similar stories by other victims—one of whom, after to no avail informing Franciscan officials of Ritter's activities, called the *Times.*

Rumors of Ritter's sexual activities with youths had circulated for years. But he controlled Covenant House like a fiefdom, doling out hefty salaries and even low-interest loans to favored staffers or friends. The Manhattan district attorney's office, apparently confronted with a difficult case because of criminal statutes of limitation, decided not to prosecute with the understanding that Ritter would resign. Cardinal John O'Connor and Franciscan superiors pressured Ritter to resign, and the embattled cleric finally did. The day afterward the Manhattan DA ended the investigation. An embittered Ritter moved into a farmhouse in upstate New York, refusing requests by his religious superiors that he rejoin a Franciscan religious community and undergo psychotherapy. Instead he began writing bishops across the country, requesting that they grant him clerical faculties. For obvious reasons, none wanted him. But through a friend in charitable fund-raising work, Ritter found a bishop willing to accept him—in the diocese of Alleppey, in Kerala, India, on the southern tip of the Arabian Sea.

The Alleppey bishop wrote to Lonfranco Serrini, the Franciscan superior-general in Rome, who approved the transfer to India. "The Vatican Congregation for the Clergy, which oversees such transfers, gave the final blessing," wrote Sennott, in the August 12, 1991, *New York Daily News*, where he had taken a new job. The story effectively blocked Ritter's departure, as the Indian diocese announced that he would be barred from public ministry there. Sennott expanded his investigation of Ritter's career in a book titled *Broken Covenant*.

Why didn't Cardinal O'Connor, who has great influence in the Vatican, convince Rome to have Ritter laicized—that is, dismissed altogether from the priesthood?

Rome's attitude toward Ritter, and key findings in the Newfoundland report, were mirrored by the moral decay of the Honolulu diocese under Bishop Ferrario. In the months after the Baltimore protest, I spent a small fortune in long-distance calls, interviewing people who long before David Figueroa's mother wrote Pio Laghi had tried to stop Ferrario from becoming bishop. The story appeared in the *Cleveland Plain Dealer*.

Joseph Ferrario was born in Scranton, Pennsylvania, and ordained in 1948 as a Sulpician, the French order that for centuries specialized in teaching seminarians. After graduating from St. Mary's, Baltimore, he taught at St. Patrick's Seminary in Menlo Park, California. In 1959 he arrived in Honolulu to teach at St. Stephen's minor seminary.

The diocese of Honolulu is part of the archdiocese of San Francisco, whose archbishop, John Quinn, was a former rector of St. Francis Seminary in San Diego. The first tinge of seminary scandal surrounding Ferrario occurred in 1980, in Hawaii, after a young man quit St. Stephen's. The family would not provide me their son's unlisted phone number. His father, a businessman, told me: "My son left the seminary because of an environment of promiscuity. Seminarians in some instances became party to clergy in homosexual unions." Nearly a year later his son told him that Ferrario, then an auxiliary bishop, had made an advance to him.

"It's unfair to suggest that this is a matter of interpretation," the father continued, in a calm voice. "I don't know what Ferrario's intentions were. He came to see me, and with [my son] present, I told the bishop exactly my position: I believed my son. The bishop explained his side"—that a gesture of affection had been misinterpreted. "I was visited by a representative of the Holy See," said the father, "and took an oath not to divulge contents of that discussion." (That was before Laghi's arrival in Washington. Jean Jadot was the Apostolic Delegate until 1981.)

As Ferrario climbed the episcopal ladder, a curtain of silence lowered on the island diocese. Other Catholics heard unsettling stories about him, informed Vatican officials, and were also ordered to remain silent. Most did, and Rome ignored their pleas.

The first priest to challenge Ferrario was Monsignor Francis Marzen, a 1951 graduate of the Josephinium Seminary in Columbus, Ohio. Marzen had founded two island parishes and for thirty-one years edited the diocese's *Catholic Herald*. "St. Stephen's Seminary was flourishing when Ferrario arrived [to teach there]," Marzen explained. "We were sending a good number of students each year. Before we knew what happened, they were dropping out before Christmas. These were good men, recommended by pastors. Something was wrong. I had conversations about this with [former] Bishop John Scanlan. Only after the seminary closed did stories about homosexuality arise."

A seminarian of that time period, who quit, told me that homosexual activity was widespread in the facility.

Ferrario became diocesan vocations director. "Requests were coming in from priests with problems, who wanted a diocese," Marzen continued. "Scanlan turned requests over to Ferrario. He corresponded with problem priests throughout the country. Some men turned up on our doorstep without Scanlan [being] fully aware of their arrival. Scanlan did not have courage to say, 'Wait, I don't have background.' Ferrario would vouch for them."

One priest welcomed by Ferrario, after Scanlan retired, was Monsignor William Spain, who left San Diego in the mid-eighties following news reports [see Chapter 16] of his relationship with a male cocaine addict. Ferrario and Spain concelebrated Masses.

In 1979, when Ferrario was auxiliary bishop, Ted Waybright and Sue Mueller, Catholic executives of a department store chain, were taken aback by what the female secretary of a local parish told them. The woman's signed, two-page statement, as taken by Mueller, became the first document in a dossier on Ferrario that was eventually sent to Laghi and to the Vatican. It said that the pastor of the parish where the woman worked had confided that one of his sexual partners had been Ferrario. When the secretary confronted Ferrario she saw "a noticed change in his facial expression, almost as if he was frightened." Ferrario ordered the priest out of the diocese, according to the secretary.

The document also listed sixteen priests as "active gays within the diocese"— as given to the woman from the departed pastor.

"When you hear something like that, at first you can't believe it," Sue Mueller recalled. She and Waybright met with Bishop Scanlan about the accusations, "but he was an old Irishman and had a difficult time believing it." In 1981, with Scanlan retiring, Mueller and Waybright wrote Pio Laghi, the newly arrived Apostolic Delegate in Washington, asking him not to support Ferrario. Laghi wrote that their communication was subject to Pontifical Seal—they must keep silent about their findings.

In March 1981, Monsignor Marzen flew to the mainland for a Catholic Press Association convention and, at the request of a cleric who had gotten wind of rumors, visited Laghi at the embassy. "I explained that Ferrario was bucking Scanlan behind his back," said Marzen. "I said there were divisions in liturgy, teaching, and administration. I was trying to keep things on a high level." Laghi thanked him. As Marzen readied to leave, Laghi asked him to wait. Laghi said he had received information from lay people and asked about homosexuality in the seminary. Marzen said that parents had complained to him of sons who left the seminary, some of whom had become gay.

What about Ferrario himself? Laghi asked. "I said it was common knowledge among clergy that he's homosexual," Marzen recalled, "but that I [had] never personally experienced an expression of it. It was second hand as far as I was concerned. Laghi pondered. He said, 'Well, Monsignor Marzen, I promise you he'll not be the next ordinary.' I said, 'Thank you, Excellency.' He said, 'What do I do with him as auxiliary bishop?' I said, 'I don't know.' He drew a big smile. 'Ah, I have an answer. I give him back to John Quinn, the one who promoted him!' I laughed too."

Instead, Laghi sent Ferrario a report on the allegations and ultimately recommended his appointment to Pope John Paul II.

Why did the nunciature disregard Marzen and concerned laity from Honolulu? A source knowledgeable about the nunciature's inner workings told me that in 1981 Laghi's greater concern was Chicago Cardinal John Cody, who was immersed in a financial scandal. The material sent by Waybright and Mueller was not closely checked. Nor was there "the mechanism to carry out a really decent investigation. Laghi should have sent a couple of competent people out there, but he didn't. The Holy See automatically presumes that bishops are capable of [a thorough investigation]. Scanlan was not." Asked if Laghi made a mistake with Ferrario, the source said: "Yes."

Ferrario sacked Marzen from his editorial job, removed him from his pastorship in 1985, refused to give him a new parish, and cut his pension from $900 to $600 per month. Marzen went to work in the City of Honolulu Information Office.

In 1982, Waybright and Mueller wrote San Francisco Archbishop Quinn, entreating him to get Laghi to reconsider. "The matter has been determined by the judgment of the Holy Father," wrote Quinn. "Now the obligation remains of accepting that judgment and of working together in charity setting aside all hostilities."

So Mueller and Waybright appealed again to the nuncio. "We desperately feel the need to discuss with someone within church authority our concerns," Sue Mueller wrote Laghi on June 19, 1982. "Are we to be totally cut off and denied the right to defend what we believe?" Laghi ordered them to support their bishop and ceased correspondence. Mueller and Waybright also wrote to Ferrario, specifying their complaints, and asked to meet. He wrote that he would give the request his "undue consideration."

In Marzen's parish Ferrario installed a priest who, stated Mueller, "had been removed from the diocese [by Scanlan] once before with homosexual charges." Mueller and Waybright twice flew to Rome and met with Cardinal Silvio Oddi, then prefect for the Sacred Congregation of the Clergy. They hand-delivered an October 1, 1985, letter from Father John Butler, who had left Hawaii to become a military chaplain. Butler identified the pastor replacing him as "a homosexual priest . . . who drifted into the Diocese . . . from Los Angeles" and tried to molest a high school student. "To avoid prosecution Bishop Ferrario promised psychiatric treatment" for the priest but instead gave him another parish. Butler wrote:

> *Can the Holy See afford the risk of allowing . . . Ferrario to continue to administer a Diocese like Honolulu? . . . Ferrario and his homosexual clique plead their homosexual weaknesses as the pretext to persecute heterosexual clerics and drive them from their parishes. Who is to speak for the victims of this homosexual persecution?*

"Oddi was very kind to us," sighed Sue Mueller, "and promised to do what he could." But nothing happened.

In attempting to convince Rome that Ferrario was a mistake, Mueller and Waybright kept their distance from Pat Morley's group because, says Mueller, "They were sympathetic to Archbishop Lefebvre"—the schismatic French prelate. Lefebvre's brand of hard-shell orthodoxy, as practiced by the Society of St. Pius X, opposed Vatican II changes. In 1987, Morley and several others, including *Lay Press* publisher John O'Connor, founded Our Lady of Fatima Chapel, to celebrate Latin Mass; but Ferrario denied them permission to say such Masses.

Three months before the 1989 Baltimore protest, Morley clashed with Ferrario on her radio program in Kailua; he was calling to tell her "you're wrong in just about everything you do" and that she was "not a Catholic by any stretch of the imagination." As the exchange grew more hostile, Morley became tearful, and Ferrario read canons regarding schism over the air. "Bishop Ferrario, you have just calumniated me!" cried Morley. The tape is peppered with Ferrario saying to Morley, "*Listen* to me!" and telling her that her conscience is in error.

iv.

In late summer of 1990, as I was reading the Newfoundland report, Penny Price, a producer of the "Geraldo Rivera Show," invited me to a taping scheduled at the end of August. I don't watch talk shows; but when a media opportunity arose to speak my piece I took it. Price was lining up quite a cast: one of Ritter's victims; John MacIsaac from Canada; David McCaan, who had been abused in another facility run by clergy in Canada; attorney Jeff Anderson of St. Paul, among others. "Is there a big case I don't know about?" asked Price. I told her about Figueroa and Ferrario. "If there is a guy with AIDS who says he was molested by a bishop I want him on this show," said Price.

"Let me talk to him first."

Geraldo Rivera did not exactly stand on an equal footing with Peter Jennings or Dan Rather. Having admired his investigative work for "20/20," I was amused at his more glitzy persona as a talk show host. But I knew from a previous appearance on his show that the subject of pedophilia was one he took seriously. I told David that if he appeared it might force the media to report his allegations. "Why should I do it again?" he said from Kentucky. "It didn't do any good last time!"

"That was behind a screen in Baltimore," I replied. "This is a nationally televised program."

When I flew to New York I had not seen David since the previous November; he was nervous but seemed healthy. When the taping began he sat on the stage with other victims. Jeff Anderson sat next to me in the front row. Geraldo and Price arranged the sequence of guests like witnesses in a trial.

David gave a tight summary of how the abuse began, adding, "This relationship lasted until last year when I turned him in. Our sexual relationship lasted till I was twenty-one. . . ."

Geraldo: "Jason Berry, do you believe him?"

The question caught me off guard. "Well, he passed a lie detector test." Since Ferrario was not present (having refused to appear), I recapped the Baltimore events, explaining that Ferrario had denied the charges, at which point Geraldo cut in, reading the USCC's statement that the charges against Ferrario had been investigated and were determined to be "unfounded."

"They're calling you a liar," he said to Figueroa.

David's face shook. "They did not investigate. It was a cover-up. . . . I've finally come to realize how wrong it really was and I'm tired of holding it in. I think this person belongs behind bars." Rushing, he said that Ferrario had falsely distanced himself from Figueroa by saying he "was one of the kids who hung around the rectory. . . . Well, which one is it? Was he counseling me for homosexuality? Did he know me? Or was I vague to him, just one of the people who hung around?" Restless to say more, he was halted by an ad break.

When taping resumed a woman stood in the audience: "I am not taking the priest's side, but after you've been molested so long, now you say it's wrong: why wasn't it wrong all the time?"

A smattering of applause and approving voices surged, as David excitedly said, "There was a point in my life where I was so used to it that I believed I was gay myself!"

"You actually thought it was *right?*" the lady said.

"I thought I was *gay.* I didn't think it was *right.* I *still* don't think it's right."

"So what are you *now?*" she retorted sarcastically, as some people clapped.

"Right now," he piped, trying to gesture with his hand, trying to smile, "I'm just kind of in between—" He stammered. "I can't develop relationships . . . it's impossible . . ." People were talking. "I'm sort of in limbo."

Jeff Anderson whispered, "They're tearing into the poor guy."

A man in the audience said: "I have a li'l daughter who's three years old and she knows right from wrong, and you waited till you was twenty-one years of age. I think you enjoyed it just as much as the preacher did!"

Raising his voice over the applause, David said: "There came a time in my life that I was gay, that I was getting used to it, that I enjoyed it. You're one hundred percent right! I'm not saying I didn't—" The program cut to an advertisement.

Anderson muttered: "He doesn't know how to articulate the psychological bondage that grows out of sexual abuse. I want to represent that guy and sue that bishop."

At the end of the program Geraldo gave each victim a brief sum-up. Said David: "I've gone through most of my life thinking what happened to me was *my fault,* that *I* caused it to happen. And the reason I'm only coming forward now is 'cause I finally realized *I'm a victim.* . . ."

After the taping I caught up with David backstage. He was seething: "There was so much I wanted to say! Geraldo didn't give me time. That stupid guy in the audience didn't—"

"Sure he was stupid," I said, putting a hand on his shoulder. "The world is filled with stupid people blaming people like you. You stood up and made your points, David. That took guts."

When the program aired in Honolulu the news media there broke a ten-month silence and attacked David Figueroa. The September 12 *Star Bulletin* reported that his story "was received with skepticism by a studio audience" and quoted Ferrario's written statement citing the USCC denial of the year before. "[B]oth the Vatican and the U.S. Catholic Bishops Conference have since declared [the charges] to be baseless and false," the *Star Bulletin* said.

The article quoted three people who had been youths in the parish when Ferrario was pastor, stating that he did nothing improper with them. The story quoted me about Figueroa passing the lie detector test instead of reporting who administered it and why. The *Honolulu Advertiser* also defended the bishop against "unsubstantiated" charges. Although Pat Morley had provided abundant leads, neither paper covered Mueller, Waybright, Marzen, the seminary, or Butler's letter to Oddi. By the time my story appeared in the *Plain Dealer* two weeks later, the Honolulu dailies had put the issue to rest. In October the Vatican held a synod on the formation of priests, with celibacy ordered off the agenda by Pope John Paul II.

In winter and spring of 1991, five former Christian Brothers from Mount Cashel—Burke, Thorne, Ralph, English, and French—were brought back to Newfoundland, tried for abuse crimes years earlier, and given prison terms. By 1992 all nine men had been convicted. For each trial, the survivors flew back to testify. "The whole experience was pretty frightening," said John MacIsaac. "On the witness stand, we were made to appear as if we were lying. I looked at those men and I saw red—twenty-five years ago, then versus now. Representatives of the Irish Christian Brothers showed up at the trials. Only after the verdicts did they publicly apologize."

On May 2, 1991, Ferrario excommunicated Pat Morley, her nineteen-year-old son Christopher, *Catholic Lay Press* publisher John O'Connor, and three of their friends at the radio station and Our Lady of Fatima Chapel. Ferrario charged them with the canonical crime of schism. Charles Wilson of the St. Joseph Foundation drafted canonical appeals, which suspended the expulsion order pending approval in Rome. "Nowhere does the diocese cite specific words or deeds," said Wilson. "I'm not defending everything Pat Morley and her friends have said and done. But I see nothing here that makes a strong case for excommunication. It's so obviously heavy-handed."

"I was in Washington this spring," said *Catholic Lay Press* publisher John O'Connor, a retired Knights of Columbus employee, "and I went to the nunciature. I had previously spoken with a priest of the staff, whom I tipped off about Ferrario's attempted sale of St. Augustine Church. This time he wouldn't return my calls. So I went to the embassy, and got inside, but I couldn't get to see him. They're embarrassed, don't want to talk about it. I'm going to pray very hard for the bishop to come to his senses and take a job in the Sudan and reflect on his life. I have seventeen grandchildren. Do you think I'm going to allow them to be turned over to the likes of his associates?"

In the months following Figueroa's television appearance, Jeff Anderson met with him at length, flew to Hawaii to meet with prospective witnesses, and engaged a law firm on the island to serve as cocounsel. The civil suit, filed in August 1991 in federal court in Hawaii, sought to expand the time frame in which an adult survivor of child abuse can seek damages, as other states have done. To date no criminal charges have been brought against Ferrario.

The Court dismissed the suit, on grounds that Figueroa had waited too long to file his claim. In the final measure, it was one more legal footnote to the corruption of clerical life in a nation of 60 million Catholics, which sends more money to the Vatican than any other nation on earth.

xix.

Chicago: The Empowerment of Victims

With 2.3 million Catholics, Chicago is the nation's largest archdiocese, an image of the domestic church writ large. Irish priests of yesteryear forged bonds with politicians who rose from immigrant wards to harden the great urban muscle of the Midwest. In the fabled stockyards, men of varied European ancestry butchered livestock brought in by rail from the heartlands. There are still Irish taverns where talking stops when a stranger walks in.

Under Mayor Richard J. Daley, city and church shared a medieval equilibrium. Tough ward heelers paid fealty to mayor and cardinal. In 1984, six years after Daley's death, Harold Washington became the city's first black mayor in an election hostile even by Chicago standards. In 1989, after Washington died, Richie Daley, son of the machine builder, was elected mayor. By then Chicago had an aging infrastructure supported by property taxes twice those in affluent suburbs, where progeny of many immigrant families settled. Richie Daley did something the old man never would have dreamed of: he campaigned openly for gay votes. Once that would have stoked a prelate's ire. But, like Daley, Cardinal Joseph Bernardin was a pragmatist with some sizable problems.

With the archdiocese $25 million in debt, Bernardin began closing inner-city parishes, selling schools and property, terminating archdiocesan employees. Demographic shifts alone do not explain the financial crunch. According to Father Andrew Greeley, national Catholic giving to parishes and dioceses has declined by fifty percent since Vatican II, an era of unparalleled affluence among the laity: a quarter of the Fortune 500 CEOs are Catholic. Much greater giving goes to Catholic universities. Greeley contends that people are protesting archaic attitudes in ecclesiastical authority—particularly the 1968 birth control encyclical— by voting with their pocketbooks.

So too has the image of the priesthood suffered. At Trinity House, a Chicago outpatient clinic for priests with AIDS, one such cleric had infected eight other priests. But it was child molesters who presented Cardinal Bernardin with the foremost challenge of his clerical career.

An architect of the National Conference of Catholic Bishops' collaborative efforts, Bernardin was America's most influential prelate. His "consistent ethic of life" opposed abortion as well as capital punishment. Renowned for his diplomatic skills in forging compromises between factions of the NCCB, the cardinal offered advice to the Chicago Bar Association in 1983, telling the attorneys, "Discourage litigation. Persuade your neighbors to compromise whenever you can, point out . . . that the nominal winner is often a real loser—in fees, expenses and waste of time."

But, for Bernardin, pedophilia litigation was another matter.

James A. Serritella was the chief archdiocesan attorney. Raised on the city's West Side, Serritella was a seminarian at Gregorian University in Rome before returning to lay life. He earned a master's in economics and a 1971 law degree from the University of Chicago. "I wanted to work within the system to make it better," he told the *Chicago Lawyer;* he also likened "political freedom and democratic values" to a "very fragile flower," and stressed society's need to provide health services to the poor.

As a young lawyer, Serritella joined Reuben and Proctor, a big downtown firm. Chicago native Jonathan Turley, a graduate of Northwestern Law School, who teaches law at George Washington University, said that the firm had a "law of the jungle, Darwinistic attitude . . . using litigation as a trial by ordeal." Don Reuben's clients included the Chicago Bears and the *Chicago Tribune.* Serritella cemented ties with Cardinal John Cody, whose imperial aloofness was legendary. Cody performed few weddings. Two he did perform were those of Jim Serritella and Mayor Michael Bilandic.

In 1981 the *Chicago Sun-Times's* investigative reports on Cody's bizarre financial dealings, which included generous gifts to a lady friend, triggered a federal investigation. Reuben and Serritella advised Cody "to stonewall" the probe, writes Eugene Kennedy, "which they termed an outrageous breach of the separation of church and state." Cody's attorneys made quite a pair—Serritella, a large, heavy man rooted in the culture of the church, and Don Reuben, much smaller, a Jew who knew the city's legal labyrinth as a politician knows his wards. While Cody ignored subpoenas, the duo defended him before the grand jury. The federal probe halted when Cody died. After Bernardin became prelate he told the *Sun-Times* that his review of church finances found no wrongdoing on Cody's part. He said he told the lawyers, "You're working for me now, you've got to tell me the truth."

In 1986 the eighty-member Reuben and Proctor merged with a firm nearly twice its size that had been founded in 1872. Bitter infighting caused the megafirm's collapse. "They tried to merge a street gang with a bridge club," one attorney groused. Taking the lucrative archdiocesan account, Serritella became a partner at Mayer, Brown and Platt, a major downtown firm seeking new clients after the collapse of Continental Bank, one of its big accounts.

Serritella had impressive credentials. A board trustee of St. Xavier College, St. Mary of the Lake Seminary, and Mundelein College, he wrote on church legal issues and lectured other churches on the unenviable task of defending ministerial misconduct. In the mid-eighties at least four suits involving child molestation had been settled by the archdiocese. "Jim Serritella is a decent, humane guy," said Patrick Murphy, Chicago's Public Guardian, who negotiated settlements for boys abused by a priest in a home for youths.

In such cases the defense lawyer treads a sinuous moral line. Church-as-client has legal rights, especially when financial demands are made; but a community of faith also has moral values. How should a legal defense be balanced against the ethics of pastorship? Should attorneys use the same tactics they would in defending a drug manufacturer or hazardous waste dumper?

In spring of 1986, Bernardin wrote Tom Doyle, chastising him for his remark to the *New York Times* that pedophilia was the church's "greatest problem in centuries." Doyle shrugged it off; he had not invited press to the New Jersey event at which he spoke. That June, Doyle organized a closed conference at the Dominican priory outside Chicago in River Forest, where he had served as a novice. Several order superiors attended, as did Bishop Thomas Britenbach of Grand Rapids, Michigan. "Cardinal Bernardin did not attend, nor did his staff," said Ray Mouton, who gave a presentation at Doyle's request. "A number of seats were empty. I think they were mad because the *Times* had quoted Doyle."

Psychologist Richard Issle, who consulted with the archdiocese, reviewed clinical issues. Doyle discussed canon law. "In my comments," said Mouton, "I stressed the importance of doing the morally correct thing—reaching out to the families. My message was, we're the church, right? So let's act like the church."

Serritella arrived after lunch. Mouton: "Serritella said, 'What you people have to remember is that when one of these situations develops, those people'—meaning the families—'are the enemy, and I'm on your side'—meaning the church's.

"I took issue with him," continued Mouton, "and said we're supposed to be aligned with needs of the children."

Serritella spoke from experience. Shortly before the River Forest gathering he had dispensed with a nettlesome case, never dreaming that it would have so many repercussions.

The problem began in 1982 when Father Robert Mayer, an assistant pastor in suburban Arlington Heights, took several boys to a lake house and tried to fondle Jeanne Miller's fourteen-year-old. When the boy recounted what had transpired —adding that the priest had plied them with alcohol and pot—the Millers met with the pastor. "Pursue it," he said. "This man has a problem with young boys." They met with chancery officials but, says Jeanne, "We were stonewalled. Father Kenneth Velo [a chancery official] said there was nothing in his [personnel] records. He said, 'You're dealing with motherly instincts. Nothing happened. You can't prove it and even a court of law would not see it that way.'" The priest remained in the parish. Says Miller: "Kids kept visiting him. Parish staff wrote letters supporting us, and held raffles to help with our legal fees."

The Millers contacted police and engaged a civil attorney to help them remove the priest. According to Jeanne, prosecution faltered after two boys "supposedly had conflicting stories." The police detective, Portia Wallace, said that the family's civil suit marred a "verbal agreement with their lawyer not to file suit till we finished investigating. I believe the priest is a pedophile. My main beef was with the archdiocese. It looked as though every time there was a complaint they would move him. They just blew me off, man. . . . It was like three monkeys: hear no evil, see no evil, speak no evil."

For my reporting Miller provided documents that had been filed in court. The couple had gathered statements from other families on the priest's drinking and sexual overtures, asked the diocese to remove him and reimburse their $6500 in legal fees. Late in 1983, she continues, "Serritella offered us $1500, with no strings attached, if we would delay filing. When we refused, he offered to personally go to jail if we'd delay filing it." The suit, filed December 22, made Christmas headlines, then faded from media focus. But a private investigator followed her, she says, and someone rifled their garbage, in what she believed was a search for papers pertaining to the suit.

A crucial turn came when a fourteen-year-old boy who had visited the summer house with the Millers' son asked to meet the Millers' lawyer, Nancy Kaszak. With his parents' approval they met at a restaurant the boy chose. Though the thrust of the conversation was favorable to Mayer, the boy spoke of the priest's drinking and emotional outbursts. Kaszak drafted an affidavit and sent it to the boy to sign. He mailed it back, unsigned, with "take out" as marginalia on key points, contradicting his own story. Jeanne Miller claims that he made the changes in the priest's presence. Kaszak did not file the affidavit. But Serritella's team did file one, purporting it to be the boy's, saying that at the restaurant Kaszak told him to have "whatever I wanted," and that he had no dinner, but two cocktails—neglecting to specify, according to Kaszak's response, that they were *shrimp* cocktails. The affidavit said:

> [T]here was quite a bit of talk about smoking, swearing, drinking, being naked and sex. Nancy wanted me to be frank and open with her. She asked me a lot of very personal questions about myself and my relationships. I was very nervous.

The boy and his parents disavowed the second affidavit. The judge found it "not authentic or genuine" and ordered it expunged from the case file. "We had to go through an emergency pleading process to show it was a false affidavit," continues Miller. "It took two attorneys twenty-four hours to invalidate and cost us $1700 in attorneys' fees and court costs. That shoved us over the edge financially." To keep the suit alive, the couple spent their savings, mortgaged the house, and Jeanne sold her jewelry.

After eighteen months Mayer was transferred—three times, eventually. Twice, says Miller, policemen in new parishes visited her, seeking information. They kept surveillance on one of the rectories. "I know of two young men he molested before my sons," she said. "They have since committed suicide."

Finally, in 1985, with $35,000 gone in legal fees, the family accepted a $15,000 settlement and swallowed the rest. The church admitted no guilt. In view of six-figure losses in other states, Serritella had gotten the church off for a pittance. But as a condition of settlement, the judge ordered Cardinal Bernardin to meet with the plaintiffs. In his office that spring of 1985, says Miller, "Bernardin pointed to a stack of papers on his desk, and told us they were sexual complaints against priests and took time to investigate. We said the whole issue of pedophilia needed to be addressed. He said our case had forced them to do that. He told us, 'It's still a mystery how your case got out of hand.'"

The litigation took a more personal toll. "My husband wanted to put it behind us and reinvolve himself in parish life," continues Jeanne Miller, who plunged into writing the book, *Assault on Innocence*, using fictitious names and the pseudonym

Hilary Stiles. She also earned a master's in theology and then enrolled in law school. "We were both raised Catholic: it was the formation of our values and beliefs and morals. I discovered a lot of myths in the litigation process. I couldn't go back to Mass. I couldn't tolerate the hypocrisy. My husband became a Eucharistic minister. I separated myself from the religion; the structure is insane. I felt I had to go beyond the institution to resume my faith life." In 1988 the couple divorced.

In a brief telephone interview, Serritella declined to discuss any litigation involving the archdiocese. Asked about general issues that a given diocese faces in such cases, he told me: "There are a lot of issues. An issue of fact: did the person do it? Second is whether there was any prior knowledge on the part of a supervisor. Third is whether a person had been screened for his or her position." Asked to discuss the archdiocesan policy toward child abuse accusations, he said: "I am not authorized to speak on their legal matters. . . . Our firm is not a spokesman for any clients unless specifically authorized to do so."

When I embarked on a *Chicago Reader* assignment, Bernardin and other church officials declined my interview requests. But in the January 12, 1990, edition of the archdiocesan weekly paper, *New World*, Bernardin said of the archdiocese's attitude in such cases: "The child and family are handled with sensitivity and compassion." Detailed guidelines by the vicar for priests were promulgated in a February 28, 1990, letter to local clergy:

> [P]ainstaking efforts are made to get to the truth of the situation. Complete cooperation is given to civil authorities investigating such cases. Counseling is provided for the victims. Psychiatric evaluation of the accused is required. Depending on the findings, the appropriate remedial steps are taken.

On paper it looked good. But Jeanne Miller and the cardinal were destined to meet again.

Published by an obscure New Mexico press, *Assault on Innocence* was Miller's vehicle to survivors in other states. In May 1988 she flew to Seattle for KING-TV's "Good Company" talk show. A young priest had just been accused of molesting five minors, jolting that archdiocese. Using her pseudonym, Jeanne's story echoed powerfully in the lives of two women who had embarked on the same quest—to hold the church accountable.

Adele Doran, a research analyst for the Republican State Senate Caucus, lived in Federal Way, south of Seattle. Maryalyce Ebert Stamatiou, a nurse, lived north of the city in Snohomish.

Adele was raised in Illinois. Her father was not just an alcoholic. "My mother died without knowing that he molested me," she recalls. "I rolled up in a ball and pretended to be asleep. I was the middle child of five and didn't have a real good feeling about myself." In the third grade her parents divorced. She lived with her father until the ninth grade when he placed her in an orphanage run by a priest and nuns: "It was the happiest period of my life. I began to feel loved." Two years later she returned to her mother and never saw her father again.

At nineteen she moved to Washington State and, like many Adult Children of

Alcoholics (ACOA), she married another ACOA. By age twenty-five she had five kids. Once all were in school she became a paralegal. Over the years her husband's drinking worsened. She decided on intervention, a confrontation to break defenses and get the alcoholic into treatment. A priest friend made her promise to move out if her husband refused. The children were now grown.

When intervention failed, she left. "I tried so hard. For years I covered up for my children's dad. He didn't drink at home but he was never around. I never had family to help me. I had a great deal of faith, and prayed, *God, don't let me be bitter.* The kids didn't think I could do it on my own."

She read about a priest taking in street children in Colima, Mexico. "I went there as a way of thanking God for helping me on this difficult journey. Casa San Jose was a reconverted pig barn. I woke the kids, helped with breakfast, scrubbed the floor, got rid of lice, and worked with kids individually." A year later she returned to Seattle and landed a good job in politics. Then, in 1981, a teenager named Theresa committed suicide by throwing herself in front of Adele's car. Investigators found that Theresa was an incest victim. In the aftershock, Adele resolved that God wanted her to feel Theresa's pain for a reason. Just when she had found serenity as a Eucharistic minister, a girl died, a girl like the one she herself had been. What if someone had helped Theresa earlier? What if, what if, what if?

Plunging into research, she published a long report for the Senate GOP Caucus, "Child Sexual Abuse and Exploitation," and began organizing forums on the topic. After one, a dark-haired young woman confided that she had been abused as a child. Adele said that if she needed help, just call.

Maryalyce Ebert was also an ACOA. Her father's drinking left a dysfunctional family long after he found sobriety. And like Adele, Maryalyce was an incest survivor, repeatedly molested as a child by a brother, and later by an uncle. When the uncle died she began recovering suppressed memories. In 1986, married with five kids, she wanted to confront the brother she feared. One day at a hospital she bumped into a chaplain, James McGreal, who had once been a close family friend, taking her two brothers skiing. Although she had not seen him in years, Father Jim's photograph hung in her parents' home. Now he was remote. Only when she reminded him of her brothers did he ask about her parents.

She had severed ties with her brothers, John and Gregory, both of whom had molested kids. John was in San Diego, sunk in drugs. Therapy had taught Maryalyce about dealing with addictive behavior like John's. After listening to women at Adele's conference, she flew to San Diego and confronted John; he startled her with bitter talk of how Father Jim had molested him. Numb, she returned to Seattle and had a cathartic discussion with her parents: Greg had told them the same thing.

She believed that John had done to her what McGreal had sexually imprinted on him. Father Jim fired her rage. In autumn, 1986, her mother died. After the shroud of bereavement fell away she wanted to make sure McGreal was not preying on kids. He had left the hospital. A nun at the archdiocese said he was out of state on a continuing education program. In fact, he was at the Paracletes' facility in New Mexico. McGreal was fortunate: the criminal statute of limitations had expired, and the Seattle to which he returned had solid programs for pedophiles.

Tim Smith, a therapist experienced with offenders and victims, served with Lucy Berliner, research director of Harborview Medical Center's sex offenders unit, on a commission authorized by Archbishop Hunthausen to develop an archdiocesan policy for pedophilia cases—a pioneering effort, all things considered. But McGreal had never been criminally charged; what then was the church's obligation to his victims? None, a lawyer might argue, barring litigation. Sister Fran Ferder, who directed the archdiocesan counseling center, felt otherwise. Ferder had to approve a living arrangement for McGreal. Smith, his therapist, wanted a monitored environment with other clergy. Maryalyce told the chancery that if she couldn't see Father Jim the press would get her story. Smith and Ferder agreed that McGreal should face his past. At Smith's office in July 1987, Maryalyce took notes at the confrontation.

McGreal admitted molesting John but remarked of Greg: "I can't believe he would say something like that." She asked why her brother would lie about something like that. "I don't know," said McGreal. "Maybe he was angry at me." Denial was a sickness, so she told him how John, at thirteen, had begun molesting her when she was four, and how a childless uncle saw them and moved on her when John joined the Navy. She told him how Greg had run pornographic movie houses in a string of cities and was involved in filming some, how he molested both his kids and got John involved in the same theater chain for nine years until John's wife left him after he got shot in a porn-film dispute. "This is the legacy of sexual abuse in my family that you contributed to!" she shouted at McGreal.

Smith suggested that McGreal discuss his past. "Well," said Father Jim, legs crossed, eyes closed, "I was molested by a priest when I was thirteen. My mom and dad were having a lot of trouble with their marriage and went to him for counseling. They held him in very high regard. How could I tell them what he'd done to me? So I just kept all of the anger in and later projected that anger on my victims." Maryalyce asked if he saw parallels with her family. "Yes," he said, "all of it."

"You knew Dad was not a terribly affectionate man and you knew about his drinking."

"Yes, I was helping him with that," said McGreal.

"You took advantage of your knowledge, betrayed my parents' trust and respect, and you betrayed and violated those boys!"

"I've always had a problem rationalizing a parental role with children," he said. "There's been problems in the families and I've always had a problem stepping into an emotional vacuum, with how I interpret what others want from me. I can't keep my hands off them. They want one thing and I think they want something completely different."

Tim Smith told her: "Jim is very good at desensitizing himself. . . . He can be totally out of touch with what you're saying."

She asked when he started molesting and he said when he was twenty-seven. He was then sixty-four. He said he was dismissed from the hospital for fondling a young patient's thigh. As he discussed the Paraclete program she realized the chancery had lied to her about his "continuing education." Sensitive to her pain, Smith said Jim's treatment could not quickly undo a pattern of thirty years. He lived with a group where all knew of his addiction and defenses. "I sure am sorry for what I have done," said McGreal. "I know my actions have hurt people."

His apology seemed terribly hollow to her.

Not long after that she discovered that his treatment was not secluded: a priest told her that McGreal was living in the rectory of St. Theresa's in Federal Way and was a regular celebrant at Mass. Adele Doran: "After twenty-five conferences on child abuse, I knew it was a matter of time before I found a priest. When Maryalyce told me it was my parish, I cried for three nights. Then I asked the pastor, Joe Kramis, a personal friend, to come over. I told him parishioners had to know. He asked for time to discuss it with the priests' council." Kramis assured her that McGreal had no contact with children; but Adele knew he had befriended an older couple, who provided day care for their two grandchildren. On December 18, 1987, Maryalyce wrote Hunthausen:

> You have set an example to your people and the entire church on your stand against nuclear weapons . . . and then not once, not twice, but three times [referring to victims of McGreal], take this man, who has scarred God knows how many beautiful young boys' lives—you take him and reshuffle him around from one place to another. Sir, with all due respect, this is an atrocity . . . Please remove Fr. McGreal from his priestly duties . . . where he will never hurt another child.

On February 10, 1988, the week after the USCC issued its pedophilia statement, Hunthausen wrote back that sexual abuse of children was an area he was "just beginning to recognize in its totality."

The prelate expressed his sadness over the impact of McGreal's "disorder" on her family, and assured her that his current assignment—in "limited ministry" and not involved "directly with young people"—had been made after consulting with therapists. He offered consolation, saying, "I know my words can in no way make up for the deep wounds caused you and your brothers," and asked her prayers for him and his advisors, as he would be praying for her.

But his soothing words stopped short of what she wanted. Adele implored the Rev. George Thomas, the chancellor, to remove McGreal. After coadjutor Archbishop Thomas Murphy spoke at the parish, Adele and several friends followed him to his car. She had a memo requesting that McGreal be moved and parishioners be told. Murphy refused to take it. She continues: "Father Kramis called with a message from the archdiocese: they would sue me for breaking confidentiality if we made public disclosure about McGreal. I said, 'Nothing's ever been told to me in confidence.' "

Seven months after Maryalyce's letter, McGreal was still in the rectory when Father Paul Conn, in Port Angeles, was indicted on five counts of taking indecent liberties with young boys. (Conn later went to jail.) The archdiocese provided therapy for the victims. When Adele learned that KING-TV's "Good Company" was planning an edition on the topic, she told Maryalyce, who called the producer. Adele went to the rectory and told McGreal that, if he did not vacate, Maryalyce would go public. "She's out for revenge," McGreal fumed. "She's a victim," countered Adele. "I've never been challenged like this," said McGreal. Adele replied: "That's too bad. If you need someone to talk with, come see me."

Stomach churning, Maryalyce sat in the studio audience, listening to "Hilary Stiles"—as Jeanne Miller was identified. When the interviewer turned, Maryalyce stood and in a choking voice told her story about a priest in Federal Way—

omitting his name. Federal Way had two Catholic parishes and switchboards at both were bombarded with calls.

The onus now shifted to the church. Tipped by Adele, *Seattle Times* reporter Carol M. Ostrom attended Mass at St. Theresa's on Sunday, May 22. Neither parish, pastor, nor McGreal was named in Ostrom's first report. After communion, Kramis told the flock: "Father McGreal is a pedophile." Faces crumbled. A wide-eyed couple stared; an older couple gasped. "His really is a success story," continued Kramis, as waves of emotion rocked his flock. He told them counselors would be on hand after the service, and an upcoming parish meeting would be open to all. "Clearly, it's the secrecy that has angered many at Father Doe's parish," wrote Ostrom. She quoted the unnamed pastor (Kramis): "Because there's a small area of his life that's dysfunctional, I don't think you should take away his opportunity to give his gifts to others."

Back-to-back revelations about pedophiles now jeopardized Hunthausen, whose grace under Vatican pressure the year before had made him a hero to many. Hunthausen reached for high ground in a May 25 public letter, identifying McGreal, hoping "to break the cycle of silence that perpetuates abuse in the human family."

> *I want to express my deep concern and compassion for all those whose lives have been directly affected by this painful situation. I assure them that the Archdiocese will do all in its power to provide them with pastoral care in the days ahead. At the same time, we wish to create a new atmosphere based on education and dialogue. . . .*

With the parish in an uproar, Chancellor Thomas announced that McGreal would be moved. Emotions surged through a parish meeting. Kramis apologized. "Confidentiality was never intended to protect offenders from the consequences of their acts," declared one man. "Why do we have to send him away?" a woman tearfully cried. "I cannot see any reason . . . to turn our backs on Father Jim!"

That July, after McGreal's departure to a ministerial retirement center, Mary-alyce, Adele, and Maryalyce's father went to the chancery in hopes of achieving a sense of reconciliation with Hunthausen and Thomas. Adele continues: "Her father tried to explain his pain in trying to come to grips with his sons, calling Hunthausen 'Excellency,' groping to express himself. Hunthausen folded his arms over his chest and said, 'What do you want me to do about it?' I could have cried. This man is known for compassion and belief in world peace. When Maryalyce started talking about victims, there was no response. I said the archbishop should write a letter to be read at the pulpits apologizing to the victims. Hunthausen said, 'I have nothing to apologize for and will not write such a letter.'"

Hunthausen did, however, order all priests and archdiocesan staffers to attend a daylong workshop on child abuse by the Rev. Marie Fortune, a Universalist minister-therapist, and director of the Center for the Prevention of Sexual and Domestic Violence in Seattle. Moreover, the archdiocesan treatment program for offenders, under therapists Sister Ferder and Father John Heagle, became a model of its kind.

Says a knowledgeable insurance source: "Seattle did not have many lawsuits

because their archbishop had the guts to do the right thing." The greater courage
lay in Maryalyce Ebert Stamatiou and Adele Doran, whose bittersweet victory
came in a climate of public opinion Jeanne Miller helped foster. In pressing reform on the church, the three women shared a profound common denominator:
collectively, they had brought fourteen children into the world.

                                    ii.

Back in Chicago, Jeanne Miller continued to gather information on pedophilia
cases, which she was sharing with a couple identified in court papers as John and
Jane Doe.* Their seven-year-old son was the central figure in a lawsuit against the
archdiocese, charging that a suburban pastor had molested and beaten the boy in
concert with the school principal, a former nun. Of the many lawsuits I followed,
this was like no other. John and Jane Doe were using litigation to force Cardinal
Bernardin to change the way the archdiocese handled child molesting priests.

     You might say that nothing in the Does' lives prepared them for the haunting
story of their son, and the way the church and legal system responded to the
shocking charges the Does forced them to confront; then again, everything the
Catholic faith taught the Does, every lesson in morality, had shaped them for the
ordeal.

     "It was a very simple life, and a good life that we had," John Doe reflected as
we followed the Adlai Stevenson Expressway into the glinting sun of a February
afternoon. "South Side Irish in this city have always been a different breed: you
took your identity from your neighborhood, parish, and school."

     He had buddies who had stayed in the old neighborhood, but Doe wore a
fine dark suit and his home in the suburbs was a world removed from the Chicago
his forebears found three generations ago. He was an attorney, with a guarded
quality to his speech, as if to keep memories of the recent past at bay: "My
mother and father grew up next door to each other. In the Depression, I've been
told, when people didn't know what they were gonna eat, neighbor would help
neighbor with a slab of bacon, a piece of this, a piece of that. My mother took
care of four older people in two next-door houses. Nobody got medals for it.
That was the way people lived. I'm the first in my family to finish high school. I
bought my mother a house a few years ago, but she spends a good deal of time at
our place."

     We drove past row upon row of trim bungalows. As darkened brick and medi-
eval spires of churches emerged and receded, Doe grew animated. "The guys who
really ran things, the figures you looked up to, were the old monsignors. Just
about every parish in the 1950s had the man who came out thirty years earlier
when it was nothing but farmland and he built the church and built the school
and was himself a cornerstone of the neighborhood.

     "People would say, 'That's Father Green, he built St. Rita's. . . . There goes
Monsignor Hishen, he built St. Gall.' A guy who built one of those parishes could
have built a factory, could have practiced law or been a doctor. These guys had
dough; they knew everybody, they were named in people's wills. So the first

thing [Cardinal] Cody did was break those old patriarchs. He pushed through a rule saying you couldn't be a pastor if you were over seventy. There were a lot of hale and hearty septuagenarians and Cody made 'em retire. It was a power play, because the next thing he did was make every parish start sending money down-town [to the chancery], where before each pastor had more control over his parish funds.

"By the time I was coming up, the older priests who were power brokers had seen the boom times, the Depression, the war, and now they had married that generation off. Kids were expected to go to school, keep your mouth shut, don't make waves. I went to St. Rita's. The school was a three-story building with 2400 kids, about 60 kids per room. We were taught by nuns. There was no such thing as insubordination problems. There must have been eight priests in the rectory. . . . The neighborhood's changing now. Latinos and blacks moving in, the Irish moving out. Recently an old woman was raped on the church doorstep before seven-thirty Mass in the morning. That stuff was unheard of when I was a kid."

We stopped at St. Rita's, a huge structure of pale yellow Indiana limestone slab. The parish high school a few blocks away had recently been sold to the city's public system, one more footnote to the flight of Irish progeny to suburbia. The church is locked, because of crime. Doe gazed up. "This church was built in 1948 for $2 million and it was paid for in three years. Everyone made good dough during the war. There's a pipe organ inside that's a hundred feet wide—all brass . . . and a white marble altar with huge pillars and a marble canopy fifty feet above the altar. You build a place like this today and it'd cost $50 million."

He cast a final glance at the old stomping grounds. "See that closed-circuit TV antenna on top of the school? Cody wasted a big bundle with the idea that he wanted his own television station. They built the studios downtown and every parish had to ante up its share. Then it flopped and they sold it all to a local public broadcasting channel for ten cents on the dollar."

A scowl crossed his face. "What Bernardin has done is worse. It's one thing to waste money. It's another thing to entrust your kid to a system that protects child molesters."

Doe's wife Jane, also an attorney, was born into a wealthier family on the North Side. They met in law school. Later, in her office, framed by a radiant view of the Chicago skyline, she smiled: "Just say I am a product of Catholic schooling with none of the memories of horrendous discipline situations that some Catho-lics carry from their student days." She recalled a nun who taught her in high school. "She's dead now, God rest her soul. She and her brother, who was a Jesuit priest, spoke to each other in Latin. She was such an impressive woman, logical and very clear of thought—the closest thing to a counselor I had. Growing up, I never met a priest or nun I didn't love or trust."

Early in her legal career, Jane Doe had occasion to represent indigents in juvenile court, and helped prepare abused children who gave testimony. Well into her thirties when their only child was born, she took time off from her legal career until he entered grade school. The boy, identified as Richard in the court papers, was in second grade at St. Norbert's School in Northbrook when life's smooth surface began to crack.

It was the spring of 1987; his grades were suffering and he had become quiet and withdrawn. On the teacher's advice Jane had his vision and hearing tested; no impairments were found but the testing specialist said she had never seen such a depressed child. Then Richard told his parents, "I'm getting beaten up every day on the playground." They had noticed bruises before, but thought little of it. The boy was no sissy; John Doe bought boxing gloves and headgear, told him to defend himself if attacked—and call him from school if more fights erupted. But they wondered: why was this happening in affluent Northbrook?

In July they made an appointment with the principal, Alice Halpin, a former nun whose contract had been voted down by the parish school board; but the pastor, Robert Lutz, overruled the board and saw that Halpin's contract was renewed. Before meeting with Halpin, the Does visited Lutz at the rectory.

Three years earlier, in 1986, lay leaders of the parish had written Auxiliary Bishop Timothy Lyne, complaining of poor morale and "lack of leadership" under Father Lutz, who struck them as being "under great stress since his appointment here . . . [and] continues to look tired and drawn." Lyne dismissed their complaints. A lay leader told me that Lutz was "ineffective and does not interact with people. . . . It's like he's numb. Alice Halpin is an excellent math teacher but she is a very difficult person to deal with. She is *never* wrong. We had a very good parish. The strong lay people have left. Lutz and Halpin's misery rubbed off on the whole community."

In the rectory that July night the Does complained of the playground fights. They recall Lutz saying that school could do little to overcome deficiencies of children who were not given proper training at home. "I've seen older kids fighting in the schoolyard, but I've never seen the younger kids doing it," he said—an admission that surprised them.

"The buck stops here," said John Doe. "It's your parish and your school." Lutz didn't see it that way, and told them to take it up with Miss Halpin. "I won't discuss this with her until after you've met with her," Lutz said. He repeated the statement as they departed, which left them puzzled and uncomfortable.

When they met with Halpin, she immediately volunteered that she had discussed the matter with Father Lutz. They brought up the fights. She said their son was oversensitive. They asked why she didn't stop the fighting. "A principal's place is not on the playground," she replied. John Doe told her that his son complained of four boys ganging up on him. Halpin called it "a figment of his imagination." John Doe wanted to know why his son had not been allowed to call him after such fights. Halpin said that she had denied the boy's request; her rules were her rules.

They withdrew the child from the school on the spot.

As summer wore on, the boy told his parents that Halpin had cursed him in her office, where other boys had also been brought after fights. In late July 1988 the Does wrote to the parish school board and archdiocesan authorities, complaining of "this atmosphere of abuse, both physical and verbal"—but without mention of Miss Halpin's alleged profanities.

Safe in a new school, the boy told his parents that Halpin had slapped him several times in her office. From her work with abused kids, Jane Doe realized that youngsters often reveal painful information in gradual stages. She was worried he might say more; a psychologist advised the Does not to pressure Richard, to let him come forward with information at his own pace.

In September 1988 the Does were invited to a reconciliation meeting at archdiocesan offices with church officials and Miss Halpin. It did not go well. Halpin denied the accusations. She remained as principal. Soon thereafter, a nun who was at the meeting wrote the Does, saying that the church had, as required by law, informed DCFS—the state Department of Child and Family Services—of their charges, and that attorney James Serritella would be contacting them.

Meanwhile, they discussed the situation with the psychologist who had advised them, Dr. Anne Brown of Evanston, who had done extensive work with perpetrators and victims of child abuse.

"Initially I thought it was a school problem," Anne Brown told me. "Then as the parents started telling me what the boy was saying about the principal, I got concerned. The [Does] didn't want to hear this stuff. They spent thousands of dollars [on testing], trying to find another explanation. I cannot tell you how sick they were—sick at heart, sick at soul."

Safe in his new school, Richard was racked with nightmares. He wrote a will giving away his toys and notes and saying his death was imminent. On October 18, 1988, he doubled over in pain, urinated blood, and was rushed to the hospital. After medical tests, physicians said the probable cause was a torn urinary tract. A few days later Richard told his dad that while he was at St. Norbert's Father Lutz had kicked him in the groin, stomach, and back.

Anne Brown advised the parents to go to the police, and only after the boy gave his statement would she begin counseling him; this would preempt any potential charge—as is often made by defense attorneys for child abusers—that his story was shaped by a therapist. Doe took his son to the Northbrook station where he gave a statement. The police subsequently told Doe that Lutz and Halpin had denied the accusations.

Several days later John and Jane Doe met with Jim Serritella at the downtown offices of Mayer, Brown and Platt. "He told us there were no prior problems with Lutz or Halpin, that he couldn't understand it," says Doe. Serritella asked the Does to let a psychologist of his choosing screen the boy. Anne Brown told the parents it would be harmful for another stranger to pry into the boy's troubled life; they refused Serritella's request.

On November 1, 1988, Serritella wrote the Does to say that the church had made a supplemental report to DCFS, as required by law, based on their most recent charges. Lutz and Halpin, he added, "have been restricted in their contact with children pending the outcome of our investigation"—without saying how this could be done in a grammar school. DCFS sent case workers to the school, but they, like the police, could not find other children to corroborate Richard Doe's charges.

In abuse investigations children are often terrified of telling people what happened to them. Bewildered and embarrassed, they retreat into a cocoon of secrecy, the unraveling of which can be painful and protracted. Some parents never file charges out of fear that the victim will be retraumatized by police, social workers, and courts. It had taken Richard Doe more than a year before he told his parents.

John Doe, a believer in systems, was beginning to feel betrayed by his church. Not long after the meeting in which Jim Serritella had told them otherwise, Doe learned that Lutz had left his previous parish after accusations that he struck and sexually harassed a female principal. Her civil rights suit against the archdiocese also said the priest had denied her recommendation for a new job in the parochial system, where she had worked for twenty years. Lutz had arrived in Northbrook in 1984, just as Robert Mayer, the priest who abused Jeanne Miller's son, went to his new parish.

In late November 1988 the Does handed out a letter before a St. Norbert's Parish school board meeting, calling on members to investigate "the striking of our son by Miss Halpin, and her allowing Father Lutz to strike him in her presence." Some parishioners reacted angrily; but the board president wrote the Does to say, "[A]s a parent myself I feel bad for you and your family" and wished them well in the new school.

In January 1989 the boy told his father that Lutz had sexually molested him. A distraught John Doe discussed the boy's plight with his wife. They agreed to meet again with the police. After John went to bed, Jane sat alone, sobbing. *Don't let my son be what he might become,* she prayed. *Help us to rectify this as much as we can. Help us to protect other children, and God forgive me for what I want to do to those people.*

Cook County had 700 assistant state's attorneys, or prosecutors. Dan Jordan, the one assigned to the Doe case, overruled requests by the parents and police for a single, videotaped interview with the boy. Only later did the Does learn that Jordan's decision not to videotape violated a protocol between LaRabida Children's Hospital and the state's attorney's office for screening children who say they have been abused. When I called Jordan he said he could not speak without the approval of Mary Ellen Cagney, head of the state's attorney's sexual crimes prosecution division. She refused to let him be interviewed. When I asked why Jordan's sessions with the boy were not videotaped, she said: "For very good and sound reasons. I don't intend to be interviewed by you. . . . The case was investigated by a number of agencies."

On three occasions, while the parents waited in another room at the station, Jordan grilled the boy, asking and reasking questions as a policeman took notes. Richard said that in Halpin's office he also encountered Lutz. The officer's transcript reads:

> *Richard was asked if, when Lutz started to disrobe, he tried to leave the office. Richard related that he had, but Lutz (now naked) reached through the doorway and pulled him back inside . . . kicked him in the middle of his back with a bare foot and that before kicking him, Lutz had said, "you fucking asshole." . . . Lutz and Halpin then proceeded to roll about on the floor. . . . Did not attempt to leave because he was stunned and did not know what to do. 4:26 P.M. (Richard is admonished that these events are not his fault and it's okay to tell all—as long as it's true.) Lutz then kissed Halpin on the mouth—both still naked. Richard is asked if he has seen this type of behavior (naked adults rolling on the floor, kissing) before on TV, movies, magazines, etc. Reply: No.*

The boy said that Lutz showed him photographs of "penises and butts" and "pee-pee'd on my shoes"—which were on the floor, not his feet. The boy was then put through a drill.

Question: "Would you repeat the sequence of events again?" Answer: "I went to the office and Lutz said bad things to me." Question: "What?" Answer: "Shithead and asshole." Question: "How many times, total, ever—have you seen Lutz and Halpin naked?" Answer: "Once." Question: "And this was when they rolled around naked on the floor, took your clothes off. . . ." Answer: "Yes."

Jordan also pressed a line of questioning the purpose of which seemed to have been to humiliate the boy. He asked Richard about his visit with the doctor that Jordan insisted he make, over the parents' objections. "What did the doctor ask you yesterday?" Richard: "I don't know." Jordan: "What did the doctor do to you yesterday?" Richard: "He just put his finger in my butt and left." The physician found no tearing of the rectum.

The notes taken by the police officer read: "5:06 P.M.: Interview concluded as Richard appears emotionally drained."

At the end of the third session the child begged to see his father and threw himself in his arms, sobbing, "They think I'm lying." As Jane Doe comforted the child, John Doe confronted Dan Jordan: "What are you doing to my kid?"

"This is like the way the Romans treated the soldiers," replied the prosecutor.

"What the hell does that mean?"

"They swung a sword three times heavier than the one they used in battle. Our approach is to make it three times harder than in the trial."

Richard M. Daley was state's attorney at the time, running for mayor. His office decided not to prosecute. The reason given to the Does was that the boy had fabricated the story to please his father, whom he feared and who he knew disliked Lutz.

"They really harassed that kid," said therapist Anne Brown, of the authorities. "They treated him like a criminal. They attacked him, as much as accused him of lying, didn't help him speak. If they had done this to a child accused of committing a crime, the child's attorney would have been all over them for violating his rights. The first thing I had to deal with was not the kid's feelings of what happened with the priest, but what happened with these police and state's attorneys people who had been presented to him as good guys. They just shut him down.

"There is no doubt in my mind that this kid was traumatized spiritually, physically, psychologically," she continued. "There is no doubt in my mind that it happened in school in the context of the relationship with Lutz and Halpin. Children do not store experiences in a logical sequence. This [becomes clear] in cases where the law says, unless we can get the child to say on six different occasions that it happened on such-and-such a day, and the kid doesn't say it consistently, it's not the truth. Seven-year-olds just don't think that way. Two kinds of realities clash."

Unlike most plaintiffs in civil suits alleging child abuse, the Does were both attorneys. With their son in a new parochial school, seeing an excellent psychologist, the church refused to reimburse their medical bills. So the Does hired a seasoned plaintiffs' counsel, Thomas D. Decker, who also had considerable criminal defense experience. They invested thousands of hours of their own time researching the pedophile priest crisis. Beyond help for their son they wanted reform: an independent board of lay experts to handle accusations against priests and help victims.

In the spring of 1989, with the two sides at stalemate, John Doe was casting lines for help. A member of the archconservative Cardinal Mindzenty Foundation referred him to Father John O'Connor, a Dominican in his sixties who offered to introduce him to Cardinal Edouard Gagnon of the Pontifical Council for the Family. Gagnon would be arriving from Rome to join O'Connor, a religious lecturer, at a conference in Mitchell, South Dakota.

On June 22, 1989, the Does and O'Connor met Gagnon's plane at the Sioux Falls airport. The following account is based on individual interviews with the Does and O'Connor, and detailed correspondence between Gagnon and John Doe, who took notes immediately after the drive.

A balding man who spoke English with a flattened French Canadian accent, Gagnon stepped off the airplane with a yellow straw hat and gold chain across his black shirt. Father O'Connor made the introductions; they put the cardinal's bags in the car and set forth on the seventy-five-minute drive, John and Gagnon in the front, Jane and O'Connor in the back. Doe discussed his son and said he wanted to meet Pope John Paul II. "There is no need for you to go," said Gagnon. "We already know about the pedophilia problem. It is particularly an American and Canadian problem."

"You mean to tell me you've known about it and haven't done anything about people who entrust their kids to priests?"

Gagnon replied that Rome had received "hundreds of letters. It is beyond the power of the Holy See to control."

"They exercise more control over a McDonald's franchise than you exercise over bishops," John Doe snapped.

"That is unfair," said Gagnon. "The church is in a schism. American bishops will not obey the Holy Father where he has sought to intervene. It only makes matters worse."

Schism means that a group formally breaks away from the authority of Rome. When the word dropped from Gagnon's lips, years of tutelage under nuns made Jane Doe sit forward: "Pardon me, Cardinal, did you say schism?" Yes, replied Gagnon. John said, "If we're in a schism why don't you tell the laity?"

"They have no right to know."

John Doe's Irish wrath was rising: "I don't give a damn about altar girls or doctrinal points! I've only got one issue: protecting children from their priests!"

"You're trying to right all the wrongs of this world," said Gagnon. "You talk about bad priests. What about bad lawyers?"

Doe cited recent convictions of Cook County judges and attorneys for bribery. "The people who put them in jail are lawyers. We clean up our mess, not like you priests."

"Then you should pursue a lawsuit," said Gagnon.

Jane Doe was amazed: a Vatican cardinal was telling them to sue. Did he know that meant naming another cardinal, the archbishop Joseph Bernardin, as a defendant? But what difference did it make? Suing the church was—*suing the church.*

A bitter silence filled the car. Then, gently, Gagnon asked: "Is this your only child?" "Yes," said the parents. "It's terrible what happened," the cardinal brooded. "I am sorry. When I was a boy in Canada, we had ways of dealing with men like this. They must feel the lash. Then they won't do it."

Soon thereafter, John Doe wrote Gagnon in Rome, recounting their exchange, and sent an impassioned, respectful letter to the Pope. Gagnon wrote back: "I understand your suffering and your worries and I shall do my best to convince the Holy Father that he should do something urgently." A papal secretary replied: "His Holiness . . . invokes God's blessings upon you."

The suit prepared by attorney Tom Decker charged that the boy's abuse was "reasonably foreseeable" to Bernardin because of the pending lawsuit against the archdiocese by the previous school principal, whom Lutz had fired and who had accused him of sexual harassment. In July, Doe called Mayer, Brown and Platt as a courtesy to ask if they would accept service of legal papers for the cardinal. Says Doe: "Attorney Bob Finke told me the suit was worth more to them if we didn't file it"—suggesting that the church would pay to keep it out of court, a not uncommon device in sensitive cases with high-profile defendants. This was essentially the same offer Serritella made to Jeanne Miller and her husband at Christmas, 1983.

At Finke's request, the Does and Tom Decker went to the Mayer, Brown offices and met with Serritella, Finke, and Auxiliary Bishop Lyne. The Does refused settlement overtures; they wanted Bernardin to empanel a lay board to handle abuse accusations. The archdiocese was "on the cutting edge," said Serritella. "The rest of the country looks to Chicago for leadership on this issue." He gave them copies of archdiocesan policies which, says Doe, dealt mainly with school personnel. Serritella said that a known priest-pedophile would be closely supervised. Tom Decker asked how this was done and how many were under supervision, but received no reply. John Doe said: "I know of cases in this archdiocese where that policy is honored only in the breach."

Finke asked for information on such cases. Doe said that Decker would reveal it at the appropriate time. "If it comes to litigation, we are hard-nosed lawyers," said Finke.

The lawsuit charged that Lutz "threatened the plaintiff Richard Doe with death or grave bodily injury, and threatened to kill his family members, if he disclosed" the alleged acts. The suit said that priest and principal,

acting in concert, verbally abused [the boy] and struck and kicked him in the head and body in the [principal's] office . . . sexually molested the plaintiff Richard Doe by touching and fondling his genitals and other body parts, by touching him with their hands and body parts (including their genitals), by disrobing and photographing him, and by forcing him to look at lewd photographs of naked children.

When the lawsuit was filed a Northbrook police official said that the charges had been deemed unfounded after an investigation in which more than forty people were interviewed. Lutz and Halpin strongly denied the charges as well. An archdiocesan spokeswoman said: "The matter has now been referred to legal counsel for defense and preparation for counterclaims"—signaling a return-strike.

Having failed to halt the suit, the church would bunker in for the fight. Whether Mary Dempsey and Patricia Bobb, the attorneys for pastor and principal respectively, were part of that decision, or enlisted by Serritella's firm, is unknown. Neither attorney would say how she entered the case or who was paying her fees. Lutz and Halpin sued the Does for defamation because of the letters criticizing them that the couple had given to the parish school board. This claim of defamation attacked the factual substance of the correspondence sent by the Does to the school board and disputed all of the allegations pertaining to abuse in the Does' lawsuit.

As in the Millers' suit and in the five-year-old case against the archdiocese by the principal Lutz had fired, the church responded with a corporate defense of ordeal by litigation.

In such cases the defendant typically pays heavy legal fees in order to reduce greater financial exposure. A large industry accused of polluting a community can mount an aggressive defense costing several million dollars; but it could save millions more if the result is an out-of-court settlement, instead of a trial with attendant news coverage that provokes further litigation. A belligerent defense that prolongs litigation can also wear down the plaintiffs, forcing them to settle for a smaller amount, rather than wait years for a larger settlement or verdict.

For the archdiocese of Chicago, facing a $25 million debt, the outlay of attorneys' fees became a topic of speculation in the city's legal community. Blue-chip firms charge $200 to $300 an hour. With three attorneys staffing a case, one day of depositions could cost a client $4000, not counting the bill for research and preparation. As the Doe lawsuit proceeded, Cardinal Bernardin continued to close schools and sell off property.

As I followed these events, I watched John Doe's rage settle into cynicism about church officialdom. I had seen the anger eat up other people in such situations. Unlike Jeanne Miller, whose divorce left her with a feminist theological sensibility, the Does held to a traditional faith. "I went to Mass every Sunday with my old man when I was a kid," John Doe told me. "Now I go and think of those jerks in control and wonder why I go. . . ."

In his spiritual agony John Doe began reaching out to priests he thought might help him. He wrote to Andrew Greeley, who kept a busy schedule writing novels and sociological studies, alternating semesters between the University of Chicago's National Opinion Research Center and the University of Arizona. Greeley also wrote a Sunday column in the *Chicago Sun-Times*. On July 13, 1986, he had written, "The leadership of the church continues to pretend that the [pedophilia] problem does not exist despite the national publicity." He continued:

> *No problem is ever solved discreetly any more, especially in the Catholic Church. The problems are only solved when the Catholic people say out loud and on the record what a lot of them are thinking privately, and aim their message directly at the religious leadership.*
>
> *Stop it. Now.*

When he received John Doe's letter Greeley replied immediately and befriended the family.

On December 17, 1989 (before Greeley and I met), Greeley's column cited an article of mine in the *Baltimore Sun* about Serritella's statements at the River Forest priory in 1986 with Ray Mouton and Tom Doyle present. Wrote Greeley:

> *To make the families of the victims of priests the enemy is evil, damnable.*
> *If Mr. Serritella really said what the Sun quoted him as saying (and there has never been a public denial of the quote) he should be fired. If the cardinal will not fire him, then Rome should appoint a bishop who will fire him.*

Some time later, over breakfast in Chicago, Greeley and I discussed the Does' bitter standoff with the church of Serritella and Bernardin. Without an indictment, the Does would have to prove criminal negligence, and in Cook County's byzantine courts that would be painstaking. I asked Greeley what made him decide to be an ally of the Does. "I got to know them," he said. "I went to their home for dinner. I watched how they interacted as a family. They were good, stable people. What they wanted made perfect sense—an independent review board to clean up the mess."

John Doe found another ally in Tom Doyle.

After the suit was filed, Doyle answered the messages Doe had left at the military vicariate in Silver Spring, Maryland. The canonist listened as Doe related the chain of events. He questioned Doe about the archdiocese's response—and apologized on behalf of the Catholic Church. Doe asked if he would consider being a witness in their behalf; Doyle said he'd think about it.

On October 11, 1989, attorneys Decker and Doe took Doyle to lunch at the Attic Club in the LaSalle Bank Building, where Decker's office was located. As they discussed the case, Doe noticed the figure of a heavy man across the room, staring at them. It was Jim Serritella. The next day, by messenger, Serritella sent a letter to Decker:

> [I]t is our position that all priests of the Archdiocese of Chicago are representatives of our client, the Archdiocese. Accordingly, you should direct any and all communications to them through our office. . . . As a result of the foregoing, I ask you to identify the priest and the contents of the conversation involving the case.

A bemused Tom Decker wrote back, explaining that he and his client had not spoken "with an Archdiocesan priest on the day you mention." Decker continued:

> [M]y clients and their son are practicing Catholics and, without notice to you, plan to continue associations with priests in observation of their faith.
> In regard to contacts with priests about violations of the criminal law, which is a context in which we may wish to confer, a priest is free to decline to speak with me or my representatives and I would honor the written expression of any priests of such a desire. I know of no principle, however, that I may be restricted in speaking with anyone about crimes that may have occurred. If you have authority for your position, however, please let me know.

Serritella did not reply. Shortly before the incident, however, in a speech to 400 parochial school teachers on the South Side, he discussed church policy regarding child abuse allegations. According to people who attended, he said: "Don't touch a kid for any reason." What if a child fell down? a teacher asked: can't we reach out? "No." They asked about children with learning disabilities, who often have special problems. Serritella reportedly replied that if a company cannot service its customers it goes out of business. A school should not accept students who need services it cannot provide. Someone mentioned a diabetic child whose mother gave the teacher hard candy and 7-Up in case of an attack. Serritella said that the principal should not have allowed the student to enroll. Referring to an unnamed suburban teacher who had been accused of sex abuse, he said that archdiocesan policy was automatic suspension without pay. The audience groaned. Someone asked if the archdiocese provided legal support. There was no guarantee, Serritella reportedly said, adding that, if the accused was acquitted, he or she would be reinstated with back pay. Suppose such a case took five years? "You're out of work," he reportedly replied.

On February 25, 1990, Greeley struck again in the *Sun-Times:*

> *Before the laity of Chicago contribute to the collections designed to get the cardinal out of the financial mess he has created (money to be "squeezed" out of them, according to his financial aide Jack Benware), they must demand that he clean out the pedophiles, break up the active gay cliques, tighten up the seminary and restore the good name of the priesthood.*

Three months later, in May, Serritella spoke to officials of the Evangelical Covenant Church and gave this advice:

> *If there's something dangerous on your property, you better get that thing off your property and analyze whether it's dangerous or not before you let people have contact with it.*

He recommended an intervention team with a psychiatrist "knowledgeable about sexual disorders. . . ." His taped comments continued:

> *The first step is that you remove the accused from the situation in which the situation arose. And that's a hard thing to do. If it's a pastor, you say you're suspended from pastoral duties and may not come near the church, pending the investigation of the accusation.*

But Father Lutz and Miss Halpin remained on the job. Why were they not removed? Was the archdiocese operating under a new, enlightened attitude espoused by the cardinal's attorney? Or were church officials and their attorneys confident that the new state's attorney, Jack O'Malley, would, like his predecessor Richie Daley, not prosecute the priest? If Lutz and Halpin were innocent, why remove them? If, on the other hand, the archdiocese was operating under the old ethos of secrecy, denial, and counterattacking victims, then the pastor and principal remained in their positions because the church did not want to appear to be admitting that the charges could be true. Put another way, the legal defense might be strengthened by leaving them in place.

Apart from Greeley's columns, the Chicago news media largely avoided the topic of pedophile priests throughout 1989 and 1990. I was preparing a lengthy report for the *Chicago Reader*, a muckraking weekly, when Tom Doyle gave a deposition in the Doe case on February 18, 1991. In it, he named two Chicago-area priests who had been accused of child molesting but not prosecuted, and a third who was sentenced to four years' probation in 1986 for abusing a fourteen-year-old boy at Maryville Academy, a foster home—the only such case that Daley had prosecuted.

Deposed by Bettina Getz of Mayer, Brown and Platt, Doyle said that in 1985 he discussed pedophilia with the archdiocesan chancellor, Father Robert Kealy, and gave him sections of the report he was writing with Mouton and Peterson. In a letter Kealy said he would be back in touch; however, the next time they spoke was at a wake five years later. On paper, said Doyle, the archdiocese now appeared to have adequate procedures. "But there is a big difference . . . [in] the way they are applied."

> *Q: Did you make any independent investigation as to what policies and procedures were in place in the Chicago Archdiocese in 1989?*
>
> *A: Yes. . . . I asked another priest who is a member of my same order who works in the Archdiocese as vice-chancellor if he was aware of any policies and procedures used by the Archdiocese in a uniform fashion when allegations of sexual abuse [by] clergy were made, and he replied in the negative.*

The priest was David Hynous—"a canon lawyer like myself"—with whom Doyle recalled having a conversation in 1987:

> *[He] said that when something like that comes down they close ranks at the top. . . . I was given to understand, and this was an opinion, that anything that was handled was handled secretly at the top.*

Getz asked if he had any other basis for his opinion that the archdiocesan policy was inadequate. Doyle said:

> *I know for a fact that there were certain priests who had been accused who remained in place with no evaluations having taken place or to my knowledge no investigation.*

He named Robert Mayer, the priest accused in Jeanne Miller's 1984 suit, adding: "I began hearing stories about him in the late seventies when I was working down at the chancery."

> *Q: Do you know how these accusations of child abuse were handled internally by the Chicago Archdiocese?*
>
> *A: Yes, I do. . . . I know that then chancellor and Vicar General, J. Richard Keating, conducted the investigation.*

Q: *How do you know that?*

A: *He told me.*

Q: *What else did he tell you?*

A: *That they thought that the only thing parents were interested in was money. . . .*

Q: *[I]s it your opinion that that investigation was handled improperly?*

A: *Yes.*

Q: *Why?*

A: *There seemed to be a lot of evidence that there had been misconduct on the part of this priest, a lot of stories, a lot of talk.*

Q: *Hearsay?*

A: *On an ongoing basis. He had a widespread reputation among the Diocesan priests, and as I said, he was transferred from one parish to another.*

At the time of the deposition, Mayer was pastor of St. Odilo in the working-class neighborhood of Berwyn, where he was under a "mandate" by Cardinal Bernardin—an order forbidding him to spend time alone with anyone under twenty-one. As with the "restriction" under which Lutz was operating in Northbrook, Mayer's "mandate" was to police himself. Questioned further about the inadequacy of archdiocesan policy, Doyle stated that in the Doe case "the accused person or persons were left in place."

> *I have consistently advised ecclesiastical people, when you are dealing with something like this that is emotional and explosive, one thing of primary importance is that there be a sensitive pastoral intervention with the parents. . . . In asking what kind of pastoral assistance the [Does] received, I believe it was woefully inadequate and nonexistent. . . . Because in the past there have been and continue to be documented incidences of cover-ups, stonewalling, things of this sort. . . .*
>
> Q: *When Mr. [Doe] asked you about this lay board in [their initial] telephone conversation, what was your response?*
>
> A: *Well, I said I think it's a good idea. . . .*
>
> Q: *Is it necessary to have some lay members on the board in order for the policies and procedures to be effective?*
>
> A: *I believe that it would be the most effective if it was a majority of lay persons.*

After my article appeared on May 24, 1991, in the *Chicago Reader*, the defense secured a gag order preventing interviews. Meanwhile, Father Greeley in his column stepped up his criticism of Bernardin:

> *No one in authority in the church would talk to the author of the Reader article. That's one way to stonewall the media. . . .*
>
> *Doesn't anyone tell the cardinal that to the average citizen such silence looks like an admission of guilt?*
>
> *Cannot the cardinal take the case out of the hands of the lawyers and intervene*

to end the suffering of all concerned? Can he not develop a policy that will make it most unlikely that such cases will ever happen again?

Can he not show that the church cares and cares deeply about the victims of pedophile priests and their families?

I beseech him to do so before it is too late.

For new legal tides were turning against the church, as Jeffrey Anderson prepared a lawsuit naming the Rev. William Cloutier, pastor of a church in Skokie; the suit was on behalf of a young man who claimed that in 1979, when he was thirteen, Cloutier had molested him in an Oak Forest parish and had been removed by the archdiocese. The church promised the family that Cloutier would "never function as a priest again." At the time police allowed the archdiocese to handle the matter. No arrest was made. (Anderson negotiated a settlement for the victim with the archdiocese.)

Meanwhile, reporter Mary Ann Ahern of WMAQ-TV, the NBC affiliate, decided to investigate priests who had been accused but never prosecuted. She found a rare source in Jeanne Miller, who in late August learned that Robert Mayer had just been yanked from St. Odilo. The priest she had implored Bernardin to remove ten years earlier had been spotted by neighbors on the roof of the rectory garage, in the nude, sunbathing with a man of twenty and a fourteen-year-old boy. Police were called; Mayer wouldn't respond; they barged in. When the archdiocese got word, Bernardin himself went to St. Odilo and ordered Mayer out. Parishioners were told that Mayer was resigning for "personal reasons." Mayer went to St. Luke Institute.

On October 10 a confidant of Bernardin, *NCR* columnist Tim Unsworth, revealed to Jeanne Miller that the religion columnists of the two Chicago dailies, and a few selected parties, had been invited to a background briefing by the cardinal over tea at the Drake Hotel. The topic: archdiocesan policy in handling pedophilia charges against priests. Miller called Mary Ann Ahern, who promptly aired a story outside the archdiocesan office noting that "Channel 5 has not been invited" to the closed meeting. The next day embarrassed church officials opened the meeting to Ahern and others. It was held at the archdiocesan offices, with Bernardin absent.

Auxiliary Bishop Raymond Goedert admitted that several priests were being reviewed because of past problems, but when asked how many, he refused to engage in "a numbers game." The church had no reason to apologize, said Goedert. However, he added: "The cardinal is torn apart by this."

The press conference was a public relations disaster. That night, Ahern on WMAQ broke the news of why Mayer had left St. Odilo. She also spotlighted the cases of Cloutier, Lutz, and a fourth priest. The WMAQ report hit St. Odilo, a heavily blue-collar parish, like a ton of bricks.

Bernardin sent Goedert and several assistants to meet with parishioners. On October 22, 1991, with a small tape recorder, Jeanne Miller sat down, unrecognized by Goedert, who had once met with her, trying to mollify her in the aftermath of the 1982 lawsuit to have Mayer removed from their parish in the suburbs. Speaking of that suit now, Goedert dismissed "a mother's" overreaction to some "horseplay" between her son and Mayer. "All we found was smoke, but there was no fire," Goedert told the parishioners.

As Miller simmered, Goedert said that Mayer had undergone psychiatric testing three times but had not been diagnosed a pedophile, rather a "narcissist." He also revealed the terms of Mayer's "mandate" and said that the archdiocese "made a mistake."

Parishioners were not impressed. One mother revealed that Father Mayer had given eighth-grade boys a sex education lesson in the rectory in which he approvingly discussed homogenital practices, including "fisting"—simulating sodomy by burrowing one's fist into another man's anus. At a break, a woman told Miller that her son had gone to Mayer's Fox Lake cottage with Father Henry Slade. Jeanne was flabbergasted: Henry Slade had been convicted of child molestation in the adjacent Joliet diocese in 1990 and was on probation after serving six months in prison. When the meeting resumed, the St. Odilo lady confronted Goedert about Slade's joining Mayer and the boys at the lake house.

"Father Slade is from Joliet and has nothing to do with the archdiocese of Chicago," said Goedert, which provoked new angers.

"Do you really understand the feelings of a sexually abused child?" said a woman who identified herself as the foster parent of an abused child. "Do you understand the emotional scarring that these children have?"

Like so many bishops in other states, Goedert had no way to respond adequately. The following night, October 23, a second meeting was held at St. Odilo. As tempers flared, a fourteen-year-old girl shakily announced that Mayer had molested her. After a police investigation, the state's attorney's office indicted Mayer on four counts of sexual activity with a minor.

On October 20, Greeley unleashed a new offensive in his *Chicago Sun-Times* column. Bishop Goedert, he wrote, "missed the point that each 'number' represents a child victimized by the church and family suffering because of [it]. . . ." He continued:

> State's Attorney Jack O'Malley should appoint a special prosecutor to investigate clerical pedophilia and possible obstruction of justice.
>
> Among the questions a special prosecutor should ask are the following:
>
> • Have Chicago area police forces routinely covered up such cases?
>
> • Have honest and diligent cops been punished or threatened with punishment by their superiors for trying to pursue professional investigations of these cases?
>
> • Have personnel in his own office been responsible for obstruction of justice?
>
> • Has the Department of Child and Family Services followed its own rules when abuse charges are filed against priests?

Greeley asked whether "the church [has] repeatedly and persistently reassigned priests that it knows have been guilty of sexual abuse?" Of Bernardin, he wrote: "He needs a lay review board—including at least one member of the family of a victim—to determine whether a priest ought to be reassigned."

Attorneys for Father Lutz then issued a subpoena for columnist Greeley to give a deposition about his relationship with John Doe.

In his complex relationship with Cardinal Bernardin, nothing like this had ever happened. Greeley's priestly relationship to John Doe was protected by a confidentiality guaranteed in Illinois statutes as well as in the Code of Canon Law. In 1981, Greeley had championed Bernardin as Cardinal Cody sank into a financial scandal before his death. The Chicago-bred Greeley was delighted when Bernardin got the appointment. But the relationship soon went sour over, among other things, Greeley's offer to give the archdiocese $1 million for inner-city schools, which Bernardin declined because the novels that had made Greeley rich contained steamy sexual scenes involving women, priests, and a cardinal or two. Although the religious imagination permeating those works was decidedly Catholic, Bernardin thought they hurt the image of the church.

Bernardin had the power to withdraw Greeley's clerical faculties. But even with the critical attacks in Greeley's columns, the cardinal made no move to intimidate him into silence. Greeley arrived unannounced at the cardinal's mansion early one morning and said: "Joe, what the hell is going on here?" Bernardin was puzzled. Showing him the subpoena, Greeley said, "Joe, neither one of us needs this. It would be most unseemly if my attorney had to defend me against your attorney to preserve the seal of the confessional."

Nodding wearily, Bernardin agreed. "Andy, why don't you come in?" Thus began a halting truce between two sons of the church with quite different compositions.

The debacle surrounding Mayer caused Bernardin to apologize in a pastoral letter and to announce the formation of a three-person commission to report back to him with policy recommendations. In an interview with Ahern, the cardinal spoke in a measured baritone, with a gentle smile, saying, "The principal mistake was the assignment at St. Odilo, which I regret very much. I'm going to do everything I can to make sure that this kind of mistake is not made again."

Greeley praised Bernardin in print for his courage.

He also began giving the cardinal advice on people he should meet if he wanted to avoid being sucked into the patterns of scandal that had soiled many other ecclesial high brethren.

For his advisory commission, Bernardin chose a juvenile court judge, his vicar-general, and a printer who had served as chairman of the advisory council to the Department of Child and Family Services. Their mandate was to conduct closed hearings, review priests' files, and present the cardinal with a report outlining policy recommendations.

On October 29, the *Chicago Sun-Times* published a blunt editorial, directed at prosecutor Jack O'Malley, entitled "Enforce the Laws on Child Abuse," which read in part:

> *Sexual abuse of children is more than an internal matter to be handled by the Catholic Church. . . . The Church's dispatching of an accused priest for therapy to some out-of-town clinic does not settle the matter. Nor does a conclusion by an internal, Church-appointed committee that the charges are insufficiently backed up by evidence. . . . Joseph Cardinal Bernardin's promises to take a more rigorous look at such cases may or may not reassure Catholics themselves. But more needs to be heard from secular authorities so that the rest of the community can be reassured that no individual, no institution, is given a pass on these kinds of horrible allegations.*

In late November, Jeanne Miller and her ex-husband attended a meeting at their old parish in Arlington Heights, from which they had tried to have Mayer removed. Bishop Goedert and other church representatives were trying to make amends with parishioners. Near the end, Jeanne stood up and told Goedert: "At St. Odilo's six weeks ago I expected you to ask me how my son was after all this time, and you didn't."

With those words Goedert began to cry. He embraced the Millers and publicly expressed his apology.

The next morning when Jeanne arrived at work, a telephone call came from Joseph Bernardin. "I've wanted to call you for several weeks," he said nervously. "I'd like to meet with you."

iii.

When his parents left Italy by boat in 1927, his mother was pregnant with the son who would grow up to become the cardinal. The Bernardins settled in Columbia, South Carolina, where Joseph was born April 2, 1928. His father died when he was six; his mother worked as a seamstress to support the boy and his sister. In 1948 he graduated *summa cum laude* from St. Mary's Seminary in Baltimore, followed by advanced studies at Theological College in Washington, D.C. As a young priest he rose through ecclesiastical ranks, becoming auxiliary bishop of Atlanta, then archbishop of Cincinnati, and then Chicago, where he arrived to pick up the broken pieces that Cardinal Cody had left.

On the night of November 25, as Jeanne Miller walked up the steps of the cardinal's mansion on North State in downtown Chicago, she sensed a golden opportunity to persuade Bernardin to institute a meaningful reform mechanism.

Although Halpin (admitting no guilt) had resigned as principal, Lutz was still pastor. Bernardin was lurching toward the review board concept, and he could always order his legal advisers to reach a financial agreement. But the latter move would only work if Lutz were out. Miller respected Bernardin's abilities, in the National Conference of Catholic Bishops, at forging compromises and shaping pastoral letters. His call to her seemed to bode well. But a ten-year obsession with the hierarchy's duplicity on child abusing priests had left her with a steely pragmatism. She had her answers down; she hoped for honest dialogue.

Now Jeanne Miller sat alone with Cardinal Bernardin in his residence. A slender man of medium height, balding with gray sideburns, he told her that the commission would be short-term, reviewing personnel files for past allegations. He wanted their work to be "as certain as humanly possible" so no children would be put at risk.

Then he said, "What would you do in my position?"

Tell the truth, she said: identify the priests who had abused youths, remove them, settle all pending civil cases.

The Lutz case was a tough one, he replied. Four investigations had decided it was unfounded—Northbrook police, DCFS, state's attorney, and an evaluation of Lutz at the Isaac Ray Center, a psychiatric facility. "You also have a kid who passed a polygraph and was videotaped by his own psychologist," she said in reply.

"Look at the competence of the people you rely on," she added, arguing that law enforcement had botched its probe. "Mayer was cleared by the Isaac Ray Center three times," she continued. "He was misdiagnosed. If you win this case, and Lutz stays in the parish, ten years from now you'll have another Mayer situation on your hands." Bernardin asked her to visit the Ray Center and give him a report on her findings.

"I can do it," she said. "But I don't have a degree in psychology. I'm just responding from my own research."

Again he asked her to visit the Ray Center; she agreed.

"Let's look at Jim Serritella," she said. "Here's a man who has said that when people bring these allegations, they become the enemy." Did he really say that? the cardinal asked. Yes, she replied: ask him. (The statement was also a matter of legal record—in Tom Doyle's deposition.)

"I don't have faith in Serritella's credibility or honesty," she said. She used the analogy of a person with a cancer diagnosis seeking a second opinion before deciding on treatment. Why not get another legal opinion about the Doe case and others? "It's a good idea," he said, jotting a note on a small pad.

Other bishops were displeased with his public stance, he averred. When he mentioned the media coverage she saw the distress in his face; he hated the news onslaught.

"Your image is deteriorating," she said. "I would love to help you. The church needs a national policy. You could be a national hero." She told him he was tremendously admired for his world peace initiatives, he had been a leader then, but now, "You've lost it."

"You don't pull any punches," he said. "I guess if I want your opinion you'll give it straight."

"Yeah, I don't play games."

He said he would be in touch. Coatless, he walked outside, into the bitter, freezing wind, accompanying her to her car. "How is your son?" he asked. Doing well, she replied: he had graduated from college with an engineering degree and landed a good job in Texas. He would soon be visiting for Christmas. "I'd like to see him," said Bernardin. "I'll ask," she said; however, her son subsequently said no.

On December 4, an assistant state's attorney announced the indictment of Robert Mayer on four counts of sexual assault. That night on television, WMAQ's report had Ahern ask Jeanne Miller for a comment. "I think the cardinal should be investigated for obstruction of justice," she said. Watching the broadcast, Greeley groaned.

On January 6, 1992, Jeanne Miller met with psychiatrists and staffers at the Isaac Ray Center. She was impressed with the psychological testing, the focus on a patient's sexual history, therapeutic programs, use of Depo-Provera, and general psychiatric care. Because the archdiocese had granted permission for them to speak with her, they explained that the church did not allow them to assess priests with the penile plethysmograph—a device by which a thread-thin ring attached to the penis measures responses to slides of naked individuals (men, women, children) interspersed with nature scenes. A second attachment to the finger simultaneously gauges mental responses to the stimuli. The patient sits alone in a room. The physician reads computerized graphs like a heart monitor. Isaac Ray physicians considered it state-of-the-art testing for deviant behavior. They also told her that they could not apply the tests to priests because canon law prohibited it.

Puzzled, she contacted Bernardin. "Isaac Ray assured me they could make an accurate diagnosis without it," said Bernardin. But that had nothing to do with canon law, she said. He agreed. It was *moral* law that prohibited him from allowing any test device that might cause a priest to achieve an orgasm. She then learned that plethysmographs do not in fact cause patients to ejaculate. When she told Bernardin, he thanked her and promised to review the matter.

As the archdiocesan commission continued its work, five more priests, making a total of nine, not counting Lutz, were removed from parishes because of past sexual problems with youths.

iv.

In mid-1991 Judge Jerome Lerner imposed a gag order in the Doe vs. Lutz case. By late winter of 1992, I was in New Orleans when the situation took an abrupt turn, affording new information that did not fall under that order.

A St. Norbert's parishioner identified for legal purposes as Mrs. A was married with several children—a passing acquaintance of John and Jane Doe. In 1989, Mary A's youngest son was acting strangely: sleeping with his windows shut during hot weather, keeping a baseball bat by his bed. In a chance conversation with Jane, Mary recounted an argument she had had over the phone with Alice Halpin concerning the principal's treatment of her son when he had returned to school after a bout of chicken pox. The principal demanded that the boy leave school because of a mix-up involving a doctor's note. Halpin held him out of two classes for several hours and interrogated him until Mary fetched the boy and left him with a family friend for the afternoon.

"You should ask him what happened in those two hours," John Doe told her.

That night she asked her son Sam: "When Miss Halpin was checking you for chicken pox, was Father Lutz there?"

"Mom, I put that way back here," he said, pointing to the back of his head, "and I'm not going to bring it up here," pointing to the front of his head.

Sam was a year older than Richard Doe; the two boys did not know each other. Mary discussed the conversation with her husband Bill. Their concerns grew when Sam later said that he had been alone in a bathroom with Father Lutz, who checked his arms and legs for chicken pox. When they asked if anything else happened, the boy said, "I don't want to talk about it now." Mary knew about the state's attorney's interrogation of Richard Doe and she did not want her son put through the same grinder. She placed an anonymous call to the Northbrook police station, which she later learned was taped.

"The [boy's] story continued to unravel," she stated. "He told us he had been fondled by Father Lutz. . . . he said Father Lutz called him an 'asshole.' . . ."

When a state policeman arrived at her home (tipped off by a Northbrook officer who recognized her voice on the recording) she asked if he was a "mandated reporter"—i.e., bound by state law to report anything she said to the Division of Child and Protective Services. Yes, he said. She replied only that they were consulting a psychologist. "We felt [DCFS] had a reputation as an abusive and badly managed organization," she later explained. They moved the child to another school.

The boy was still sleeping with baseball bats and toy guns, hiding kitchen knives under his pillow. In a statement given to her attorney, she continued:

> In first grade he drew pictures of people with bodies. But by the third grade the bodies had disappeared—only legs, arms and heads. The psychologist at [the new school] suggested his drawings were abnormal and showed a lack of body integrity . . . [and] showed anger and frustration at himself. When he started fifth grade . . . the teacher introduced herself and said, "A teacher will never hurt a child," and Sam turned to me and said, "Well, mom, we know that's not true."

Yet even with a therapist, the boy was reluctant to speak about his experiences at St. Norbert's. He began making suicidal statements, and at a celebration for an aunt in the family, who had been a nun for many years, the boy saw a priest and began shaking all over. But whenever the Does inquired, Mary told them the boy had no problem, everything was okay. "We were afraid of the system abusing Sam," she said in a legal statement. It continues:

> We were afraid of the archdiocese suing us. In 1991 Sam admitted [that there had been] three separate incidents with Father Lutz. This came at the height of his behavior problems. He described an instance where Sam had his clothes off and a second incident where Lutz had his clothes off . . . "all except for his black socks." He told us Lutz took him in the back of church to wash dishes. Lutz asked the teacher if Sam could help him clean up. Sam said Lutz called him a "son of a bitch."

In the spring of 1991, Mary received a subpoena to give a deposition in the Doe lawsuit. The family attorney learned that the defense's decision to subpoena her had come after John Doe, in deposition, had revealed information about his conversations with her. A deposition was the last thing Mary and Bill wanted. But church attorneys had forced her into it. Her testimony stretched over two days that July. Defense attorneys asked about the order of events, how the boy gave details. A key passage reads:

> Q: What specifically did your son say in describing how Father Lutz supposedly touched him?
> A: "Grabbed my penis."
> Q: He said Father Lutz grabbed his penis?
> A: Yes.
> Q: Did he describe any other action that Father Lutz allegedly did in relation to your son's penis?
> A: No.

The week after Mary's deposition, Sam was home with a bout of intestinal flu. Mary recalled: "He said, 'Mom, what if I don't have the flu? What if I have some other disease?' It seems like kids with this problem drop you little hints that let you know you haven't heard it all. He wanted us to find out. At that instant I thought, *This kid thinks he's got AIDS.*" Reassuringly, she said that everyone gets the flu. The next day Mary and Bill sat with the boy. She asked what had been on his mind in asking about the disease. "What followed," she stated, "was the rest of the story that he was too disgusted to talk about before. He told us about oral sex both ways and masturbation."

Now the parents found themselves being drawn deeper into the legal nightmare they wanted to avoid. Like the Does three and a half years earlier, they had to decide about filing criminal charges. Through their attorney, John Dienner, they requested a victim-sensitive interview at LaRabida Children's Hospital. Mary: "The only fly in the ointment was the state's attorney's office. They did not want to go to LaRabida; they wanted to interview Sam themselves without a two-way mirror." This was the same process employed with the Doe child, even though the prosecutor's office had an established agreement with LaRabida to use its services for such an interview only with a two-way mirror. Mary and Bill refused. Diane Ramza of the state's attorney's abuse unit relented; but the session was not videotaped. The interview was conducted at LaRabida by a social worker, Mark Parr. Among those observing the interview through the two-way window were Ramza, two Northbrook police officers (including the one who took notes on the Doe child's sessions), and a DCFS representative.

After the session, according to Mary, the interviewing social worker told her that he believed her son, that he had done well. Ramza said that, although she believed the boy had been traumatized, such allegations were difficult to prove and could not always be prosecuted.

Northbrook police commander Randy Walters, having botched the Doe case, wanted to interview Sam. Mary and Bill refused but met with Walters and several other policemen. The policemen said that the Doe boy kept changing his story each time he took a break from the sessions to see his parents—a statement which is not borne out by the police digest of those sessions. They assured her their interview of the boy would only take a half hour. "I asked them if they had read my deposition," continues Mary. "They said no, but Sue Stone [an attorney for Lutz] had given them a chronological order of events. They told us the depositions in the Doe case were not going well and that [the Does] would lose the case for lack of proof. They also said our story was nothing like the Doe case. . . . Because of the way Richard Doe behaved in questioning, they said, Sam would be considered the first victim and what we really needed was a third victim [to make the case stronger]."

The law enforcement system that had failed before exposed its own mendacity. Prosecutor O'Malley, through his subaltern Ramza, would not prosecute; the defense assured police that the first victim's case was foredoomed; the police conveniently argued that they needed more victims to make an arrest.

Mary did agree to accompany her son to the old school, with police officers and Ramza, to locate the bathrooms where the molestation was alleged to have occurred. Ramza assured her that Sam was "a very good witness" but "we knew there was no evidence from the beginning."

After the meeting Mary told her son, "We've done what we can do."

"Yeah, Mom, but he's still there and I went through all this for nothing," said her son.

The rage that gathers in parents whose children have been violated moves inexorably toward those figures of authority who, as lawyers say, "knew or should have known." Having read Father Greeley's columns, Mary asked if he could possibly arrange a meeting with the cardinal. Greeley jumped at the idea: he advised Bernardin to read Mary's deposition and to meet with the couple. When the cardinal agreed, Greeley felt that a crucial corner was about to be turned.

In mid-January, Bernardin met with Mary and Bill. "In setting up the meeting," related Mary, "Father Ken Velo told us, 'Don't worry. We're really with you on this.' My husband and I walked into a big conference room. Bernardin listened carefully to everything we said. He was very cordial; he took notes. We emphasized that we weren't working with the Does and I would not have testified if [the defense] hadn't sent me the subpoena.

"He told us that he'd give the [advisory] commission my deposition, and that he'd ask the state's attorney to investigate. The commission also had a letter I wrote Jack O'Malley, which he never answered. We met with the cardinal for two hours; I kept emphasizing that we were not part of the Does' suit.

"We told him everything Sam had said. I sat next to the cardinal and eyeballed him, touched his forearm when I made my points. At the end he said, 'I'm really between a rock and a hard place. If I take Lutz out, he is subject to an ecclesiastical court within the church. And that's what makes this so difficult.' As we left I thought about Velo's comment—'We're really with you'—when we saw sitting outside the cardinal's office this huge fat guy, wearing a suit, who looked like an oversized Velo. He said to my husband, 'Why don't you take your wife across the street for a pizza?' We got on the elevator. My husband said, 'He had to be a lawyer.' And I thought, *Where do they find these people?*"

She began talking with Mary Ann Ahern. Unwilling yet to go on camera, she waited to see what Bernardin would do. Ahern meanwhile talked with Northbrook police commander Randy Walters by phone, asking about the new accusations. "Oh, there's nothing to that case" he told Ahern. "Those two families are just working together."

When Ahern told her what Walters had said, Mary called Walters, who said, "I just told her, 'No comment.'"

On January 23, Cardinal Bernardin wrote the couple, thanking them for meeting with him and sharing "the experiences . . . as they have impacted your son . . ." Nevertheless, he explained, "appropriate investigative bodies" had reported her son's allegations to be "unfounded." But, since the couple had provided "what you identify as new information," the church had passed that information to the prosecutor, Office of Catholic Education, and DCFS. "We will await [their] response," he noted, expressing confidence that the Lord would help "us sift through this difficult matter."

Mary's patience snapped. On January 28, she wrote Bernardin:

Dear Joe,

I found your letter of January 23, 1992, to be inappropriately short. I would have hoped that since my husband and I spent two emotionally draining hours telling

you of the hell that our Sam has been through, you would have had more compas-
sion and substance in your letter. We do not need a letter that merely repeats the word
"unfounded" and amounts to nothing more than covering yourself legally. . . .

Joe, when we sat with you, Bill and I told you we felt that your lawyers were
running the investigation. . . . It doesn't take a legal genious [sic] to realize that
this makes the investigation biased and one sided at best.

It seems to us, Joe, that the Lord is already helping you "sift" through this
matter. In fact He is literally tearing down your door saying "DO SOME-
THING"!!

On February 3, Bernardin wrote the couple, expressing an apology "if the way
in which my letter was written gave the impression that I lacked compassion."
Assuring them that he was "most sensitive" to their concerns, he reiterated in
slightly gentler words that the investigation had proved unfounded—but added
that Lutz remained "under a mandate never to be alone with a minor." He also
told them that he had passed the new evidence (what the boy told Mary after her
testimony) on to appropriate channels. On one point he was firm: "Our attorneys
are not 'running' the investigation of these official bodies . . ." And if the couple
thought that, the cardinal continued, then they should inform the authorities.
And, because he did not want the archdiocese "or any of its agents" to be seen as
"inhibiting an objective investigation," the cardinal stressed that he would personally bring their concerns to the authorities involved. He assured them that his
waiting for official responses should in no way be taken as a "lack of compassion
for you and your son."

The couple wrote back, with a respectful salutation, proposing that their son
and the priest be given polygraph tests. Bernardin responded with a letter saying
that the Employee Polygraph Protection Act of 1988 prohibited lie detector tests
"except in limited circumstances not applicable here."

With Greeley, Jeanne Miller, and Mary Ann Ahern keeping me abreast of Chicago developments, I wondered if Bernardin might agree to an interview. The
year before, in preparing the *Chicago Reader* report, I had been told by a church
press officer that the cardinal could not discuss matters in litigation. But now he
had given interviews to Ahern and other journalists about his efforts to resolve
the crisis.

The archdiocese had removed nine priests when I broached the possibility of
an interview to Greeley, who promised to put in a word with the cardinal. I wrote
the cardinal, requesting an interview. After several weeks and no reply, I called his
office; his response came by fax, saying that he could not discuss Lutz and Mayer,
for legal reasons. He also wanted to know what kind of questions I would ask,
which was understandable, I suppose, given the nature of my reporting. I realized
that my option was a general interview or none at all. So I wrote back, listing a
few questions of a general nature; he agreed to meet me on April 8.

On April 2, Jeffrey Anderson filed suit against Lutz and the archdiocese on
behalf of Mary, Bill and their son. The Minnesota attorney had dozens of similar
cases in litigation across the country. After months of work by the cardinal's

advisory commission, and Bernardin's attempts to strike a more open posture with the media, Anderson told the *Chicago Tribune:* "We're hoping this action will cause [the church] to reexamine how they deal with these issues and these priests."

One of Lutz's lawyers, Mary Dempsey, told the *Tribune:* "The only reason these charges have been brought is to intimidate the archdiocese into paying money damages, and to intimidate an innocent priest."

Anderson, who was not bound by the gag order in the Doe case, sent me Mary's deposition, a lengthy statement she had prepared, and arranged for my interview with her. She also gave interviews to WMAQ and the *Chicago Tribune.*

On Sunday, April 5, Auxiliary Bishop Timothy Lyne, who had given last rites to old Mayor Daley, visited St. Norbert's and gave a sermon praising Father Lutz. The signal was unmistakable: the church was bunkering in for legal battle with not one but two families, as the Does headed toward trial. That meant destroying the credibility of two kids as witnesses if the church were to prevail.

New Orleans was abloom with spring greenery when I flew to chilly Chicago. With his international travels, speeches, and high standing in the NCCB, Bernardin had more of a reputation to protect than most bishops. He had taken a more public posture on the abuse scandal, even as events exploded around him, and now he was in the thick of it, groping to resolve an awful mess.

Lincoln Steffens in his early twentieth-century muckraking about big-city political machines found a common trait among the bosses he exposed. Corruption was systemic, but within that system the bosses honored their deals. The Catholic bishops of today were a different kind of fraternity. On most moral issues they were true to their religious heritage. Yet in policing the clerical brotherhood they had failed miserably; mendacity and denial were symptomatic of the sexual segregation in which the bishops lived.

I felt a strange ambivalence before the interview. Bernardin had taken a drubbing in the media; but he had also responded by removing nine priests, stalked by past accusations, from their parishes. The credibility of his reform agenda hinged on disposition of the Lutz cases. Before the interview I visited Andrew Greeley. With the exception of Tom Doyle, no priest had done more to hold the hierarchy accountable. Doyle had worked internally, unknown to most people; Greeley was a prominent writer who had devoted more than a dozen articles to the topic that ate at his conscience like a tumor.

"Joe's very nervous about the interview," remarked Greeley. "He hates getting bad press. I reminded him that you're both Southerners. I told him you were fair."

"I tell myself that too," I said. "But his decision to leave Lutz in the parish is destroying his reform effort. He's spent a fortune on attorneys' fees, and cases like this are never supposed to go this far."

Greeley nodded. "He's a victim of his attorneys. I think he's beginning to sense that. I also think Serritella's days are numbered, at least on these kinds of matters. The new in-house counsel will play a more decisive role. Joe knows that he's got a problem and he's determined to see it through."

"I don't see how he can do that until the Northbrook lawsuits are resolved."

Greeley smiled wryly. "Without an indictment, Joe doesn't see how he can remove Lutz. Ironically, the fate of the cardinal's reform agenda is tied to O'Malley."

And O'Malley, a Republican up for reelection in a heavily Democratic town, seemed in no hurry to indict priests.

Cardinal Bernardin met me in his downtown office with a firm handshake and a pleasant smile. Wearing black clericals with a gold chain across his chest, he introduced me to Sister Brian Costello, an aide who sat to his left in the interview.

I asked why the pedophilia crisis had reached such a magnitude in the church. "Most of the reporting laws as I understand it came into effect in the late seventies and early eighties," he replied. "I don't think—I *know* this is a problem in all professions, including the priesthood. As priests we've made a commitment to lead chaste lives. When people put trust in priests, and these abuses occur, it creates more consternation."

In his first letter, Bernardin had sent me a column published under his name in the archdiocesan paper, which included these strong words:

> *The human being is not a spirit imprisoned in a body but an embodied person. What one does to the body one does to the person. Hence our tradition has always proclaimed the dignity and the inviolability of the human body. We are horrified when the human body is violated, mutilated, and destroyed by those who assert power over it.*
>
> *Only slightly less evil than murder is the sexual abuse of the human body. Those who sexually exploit the body of another debase its most intimate dignity and inflict on it, both in the actual act and through the after effects, the worst of horrors.*

In his office I asked: "What is it in the church, and society, that devalues children?"

He frowned pensively. "I'm not sure I'd refer to it as devaluing. Rather, it's our living in a world where violence is too prevalent, and when that occurs, the first victims are those who are the most vulnerable. Traditionally that has been women and children. It's more a question of vulnerability."

"Do you think the NCCB needs a national policy?"

"It's been subject to debate for some time," he said. "The responsibility of each bishop is to work within the framework of canon law. Each diocese is—"

"Autonomous, according to [USCC attorney] Mark Chopko," I interjected.

"Well, some like Chopko would see [the pedophilia crisis] legally and others differ on a common policy. I'm not a lawyer. I don't know how to evaluate that dimension of the debate." He felt that bishops "should share our experiences and reach a common understanding. I think the Conference is moving in that direction.

"I've been a bishop twenty-six years," he continued, gesturing with his hands, "and this has been the most difficult thing I've had to face. I love the priesthood. I love the people of Chicago. Even though the percentage of priests doing this is small, one incident is too many. . . . I know that something needs to be done and I'm going to pursue it."

I said: "The image of the priesthood, and the Catholic Church, has suffered greatly because of the child molestation scandal. Rome has been silent. Do you have any insight into Rome's response?"

"The image of the priesthood is a concern of mine," he said pensively. "Priests generally feel that if these things are made public then all the rest of us are under a cloud." He cited a speech he had made to his clergy about these difficulties, and spoke more confidently: "Then I went to Mundelein Seminary—I didn't bring any colleagues with me—and made a presentation myself. I put it in a broader context about human sexuality, and I talked about sexual dysfunctions. It was the first time they had heard a bishop speak so candidly. I received sustained applause."

He then said that he had not mentioned the applause to brag, rather to emphasize how much it had meant to the seminarians. His concern about his own image was palpable. He could have been a politician trying to shore up his sagging standing in a public opinion poll.

The American bishops' autonomy, he explained, did not mean "that we're not accountable to the Holy See. It's our responsibility to deal with this problem. There's another point I'd like to make: I don't think the problem is quite the same in other parts of the world. I don't mean that these things don't happen—that's part of human nature. We live in a society that's very litigious. That's not the case in other parts of the world. Rome is looking at the whole world. The Holy See has intervened when there have been doctrinal disputes. Here we're not dealing with something that's doctrinal. We're dealing with an abuse, a sin.

"One item of dialogue between the Holy See and Bishops Conference has to do with the new Code of Canon Law: a bishop cannot dismiss a priest from the clerical state. It's only done in two ways—if the man himself seeks laicization, and we present the petition; or, if the local bishop thinks a priest should be dismissed, he sets up a tribunal to hear a case through a canonical trial."

Monsignor Larroque in Lafayette had discussed the same centuries-old procedure in his 1984 deposition. I knew of only one diocese that had used it— Phoenix, Arizona, in 1991—after the priest in question, George Brederman, was given a long prison term after extradition from Florida where he had fled while on probation.

"Even if I dismiss a priest after a trial," said Bernardin, "he is not dispensed from celibacy. That goes to Rome."

"But why would a man remain celibate if he was dismissed?"

Bernardin smiled. "I'm only telling you what canon law says."

I asked if it was true that Rome had agreed to accept adjudication in American courts as a condition allowing a bishop to dismiss a priest. "I think many of our bishops feel that if indeed a person is guilty of pedophilia then we should be able to dismiss him," the cardinal carefully replied. "There has been discussion with the Holy See on that."

He felt strongly that a priest found guilty of sexual abuse of minors "should not return to parish ministry." Perhaps some special ministry, he reflected, "if you can't reduce the risk."

But most such men were not prosecuted. What then were the criteria for removing a known child molester? Said the cardinal: "A lot depends on the nature of the offense, the number of times, the time span [after an occurrence], programs after treatment, whether you can provide adequate supervision. With proper supervision, a man might be able to function in some ministry not in contact with minors. If there is a person about whom we have a doubt, we're concerned enough about it to tell the priest, 'We'll keep you in this parish only if the parish leadership knows or agrees.'" That meant informing "eight or ten people. We've done that."

He drew a circle on the table, saying, "Sometimes we talk as if the laity don't understand. We have found our lay people are understanding, eager to help."

"And if they were to say no?"

"We'd remove him. Nobody can be a judge of his own case."

To my surprise he brought up the Northbrook impasse. "In the Lutz case, both sides are under a court order not to talk. Sometimes only one side of the story gets out."

"I sought interviews with you and all parties last year."

He nodded. "I will tell you what has been made public: these cases have been investigated by every law enforcement agency," he said, ticking off the list. "The Commission has received everything that exists. I also hired [retired] Judge [Nicholas] Bua to give us a second reading."

Bua had made no public statements.

"Why weren't there indictments?" I asked.

"I'm not the state's attorney." He shrugged. "Maybe it's because there's not enough evidence. All you can do is leave no stone unturned in trying to get at the truth. You wish things weren't complex. Am I happy that we have this suit? No."

"Jim Serritella gave a speech saying that families were the enemy."

"I don't see it that way. He told me he didn't say that. He was very stung by that. I must say this: I've been given no evidence of victims and families as adversaries."

Here was the bureaucratic mind retreating behind its own defenses: his lawyer denied having said what a roomful of people heard him say, and the tortured odyssey of two families from Northbrook did not mean they had been treated adversarially. Now the cardinal was exhibiting confidence—telling me of his renewed friendship with Andy Greeley ("We were alienated before."), and of his dialogue with Jeanne Miller.

"The whole business about Jeanne and Father Mayer was at the beginning of my administration and I've learned a lot since then," he insisted. "The allegations that we didn't deal with this at all, in general terms, that whenever we had a problem all we did was transfer, maybe with a little bit of counseling, our records will show that that's not true."

But there had been no set policy in years past; the whole tradition of sexual denial warranted against it. And what records contained was no guarantee of truth, for sexual information was often known but not recorded.

I asked what the new policy would entail. The cardinal said:

"One of the things I expect to come from the Commission is to propose to us a structure or a process to deal with these cases in the future. While I don't want to second-guess the Commission, one recommendation is that we have a body, a structure, that's independent of the chancery but answerable to me alone.

"I do foresee the possibility of that structure having two levels," he continued. "A board to address questions of probable cause, and another level, another group, to have hearings and then recommend to me their findings. This would be an objective, independent group, with laity and some priests, well defined, with a good mission."

That was what the Does wanted at the outset, I said.

"They were pleased that I took the first step in naming the commission," said Cardinal Bernardin.

And so in the seventh spring of my journey, with the Does and the second Northbrook family at a bitter impasse, I left Chicago with an image of Bernardin as Hamlet: torn by indecision, forced to acknowledge acts of terrible evil, his better impulses sacrificed to a system shaped by the wily ways of lawyers. In our meeting, Bernardin had spoken not of families and the suffering of children, but of structures, processes, and commissions. And yet, no other archbishop had a priest accused of pedophilia in two lawsuits still in his parish, with a well-paid legal team targeting the families as enemies of priest and church.

On May 1, attorneys for Father Lutz countersued Mary A and her husband for libel, invasion of privacy, intentional infliction of emotional distress. It was the same return-strike strategy used against the Does after they filed suit in 1989. This time the motion cited the Division of Child and Family Services position that the charges were unfounded "due to no credible evidence to substantiate the allegations" (since Richard Doe, and the principal at Lutz's former parish who accused him of sexual harassment, did not count). The defense lawyers added that Cardinal Bernardin's special commission and his advisor, retired Judge Bua, neither of whom had spoken publicly on this family before, both had "determined Minor A's allegations to be lacking in any factual support."

The parents said they had not met with Bua or the cardinal's commission.

The counter-suit, filed by attorney Susan Stone (a colleague of Mary Dempsey), stated that the allegations against Lutz were lodged "only after [the boy] was subjected to repeated and suggestive questioning by his parents" and that the boy had first denied such activity "despite being subjected to this repeated coaching by his parents." Furthermore, the boy "enjoyed the attention he received from his parents when he told the false stories about allegedly being abused by Fr. Lutz." The parents knew that the "false stories" were meant to deflect attention "from his own misconduct . . . participating in a theft from a neighborhood store, setting fires, vandalism . . . and other delinquent acts." The document also charged that the boy changed "crucial elements of his story"—the time, place, and nature of the abuse.

The counter-suit cited the parents' letters to Bernardin and other authorities as malicious and defamatory, adding that Greeley had written a column that damaged Lutz's good reputation and standing. Greeley, however, was not sued for libel.

"It's outrageous to counter-sue parents who have legitimately brought a complaint," said Jeffrey Anderson. "There's no doubt in my mind that it's hollow and brought to intimidate."

Church lawyers also sent a private detective to sniff around Northbrook. He contacted a lady whose son plays with "Minor A." The detective told her, "I have been hired to look for dirt on [that family]."

"I was shocked," the lady told me. "I don't think the [A's] are asking that much. It bothered me that my church would do this. I always figure they're supposed to offer us comfort. . . . Why don't they move [Lutz] and give everyone some peace of mind?"

Of the countersuit, Andrew Greeley reflected: "Whatever the church's intentions, the legal effects are to intimidate parents—have them think that they'll be beaten into the ground if you dare to accuse a priest."

As Cardinal Bernardin's advisory commission conducted closed hearings, revelations elsewhere jolted the Catholic Church. On May 7, a revered Irish bishop, sixty-five-year-old Eamonn Casey of Galway, abruptly resigned his position after the *Irish Times* reported that he had paid more than $115,000 to a Connecticut woman, Anne Murphy, forty-four, with whom he had had a son out-of-wedlock in 1974. "I acknowledge that Peter Murphy is my son and that I have grievously wronged Peter and his mother," Casey announced in a prepared statement. Casey was a charismatic speaker and impassioned advocate of social justice, one of Ireland's most popular bishops.

It was also on May 7 that a Boston television station, WBZ, aired portions of a taped telephone conversation in which Frank Fitzpatrick, an insurance adjuster and private detective, confronted James R. Porter who years earlier, as a priest in the Fall River–New Bedford area, had allegedly raped Fitzpatrick, who was then a child. In an interview with a television reporter, Porter admitted sexually abusing between fifty and one hundred youths. As victims came forward with anguished stories in New England, Porter, married with four children, was living in St. Paul, Minnesota. In 1967 he had gone to the Paracletes' New Mexico treatment facility; in the mid-seventies he left the priesthood. In 1989, when Fitzpatrick tried to locate Porter, Massachusetts church officials refused to help. "I asked what Porter's middle initial was, and his date of birth and social security number and they said, 'Sorry, we don't have any of that,'" he told the *Boston Globe*. "The monsignor who called me back said maybe it was best to leave it in the hands of the Lord."

With coverup accusations abounding in Massachusetts, the Chicago drama took a new, strange turn in early June. Norbert Maday—one of the Chicago priests removed from his parish months earlier by Cardinal Bernardin—had been the subject of a television report in which victims, their faces shadowed to preserve anonymity, accused him of various sexual acts. Nevertheless, State's Attorney Jack O'Malley declined to prosecute Maday, citing statute-of-limitation problems. An emboldened Maday convened a news conference to assert his innocence —only to be hit the following week with an arrest warrant by authorities from Oshkosh, Wisconsin, on charges that he committed sexual crimes with Chicago youths who had accompanied him to a summer place there. Maday was booked at a Chicago station; Bernardin posted the $5000 bond. The governor of Wisconsin sent an extradition request to the Illinois governor.

Maday's problem was notable because Wisconsin authorities developed leads from an Illinois state police report that had been given to Diane Ramza, the assistant state's attorney who declined to prosecute Father Lutz. Making good use of the document, Wisconsin authorities were puzzled by the failure of O'Malley's office to pursue Maday and build a criminal case.

Maday's plight formed an ironic prelude to the long-awaited release, on June

15, of The Cardinal's Commission on Clerical Sexual Misconduct with Minors. The Commission members were Julia Quinn Dempsey, an associate juvenile judge in Cook County Circuit Court; Bishop John Gorman, the archdiocese's vicar general; and John P. Madden, a professional printer, board member of a Catholic juveniles' home, and member of DCFS's Advisory Council.

The ninety-three-page document intelligently summarized literature in the field, and proffered the blueprint for a Permanent Review Board, with six of the nine members to be lay people, including a psychiatrist, social worker, attorney, and a victim of child abuse or the parent of a victim. This was similar to what John and Jane Doe had long advocated. The Commission called for a full-time nonclerical case manager to monitor accusations, direct investigations, and assist victims—in essence much of what John and Jane Doe had originally demanded, with a structure similar to what the Cardinal had told me he envisioned. The Commission said that it had reviewed files on fifty-seven cases of priests accused of sex abuse dating to 1963, and had found insufficient evidence in eighteen of these cases. "The overwhelming number of [verified] cases," the report stated, "involved homosexual ephebophiles, that is, priests sexually attracted to young teen-aged boys."

The report noted that five priests had been removed during its eight-month review at the Commission's request, with six priests removed by church officials just prior to that.

"There was only one founded case of pedophilia involving a priest-uncle with two six-year-old nieces," the report continued. "The other allegation of pedophilia . . . involved a priest who was accused by two different seven-year-old boys"—a clear reference to the cases in Northbrook. "After an extensive review of the evidence in both cases, the Commission concluded that the charges were unfounded."

That conclusion had been telegraphed several weeks earlier in the counter-suit filed against Mary A and her husband; that counter-suit had cited the Commission's finding before it was made public. How could an objective, independent body let itself be used by one side of such a controversial case? And on what did the Commission base its decision that the charges were unfounded? They did not interview the two boys. When Mary A requested a meeting with the Commission they refused. The three Commission members did meet with Jane Doe, but she says they declined to discuss specifics of her case.

The Commission's report did not address the concerns voiced by Greeley and Jeanne Miller about legal strategies that target families who file suit as enemies of the church.

In late May attorneys for pastor and principal added new charges to the defamation counter-suit against the Does, citing my report a year earlier in the *Chicago Reader*; however, the newspaper was not sued, nor was I.

The defense stated that a psychologist who had examined the Doe child wrote his parents that he was "a very troubled boy" with an "extreme potential for distorting reality." The defense charged that accounts of the alleged abuse given to police by father and son "differed dramatically" and that the accusations of sexual abuse were made after Northbrook police and DCFS decided that the physical abuse charges were "unfounded." The motion said that three doctors who examined the boy at the time of his hospitalization found "no objective evidence" that he had urinated blood. One physician "entertained the possibility" that the patient had faked his symptoms.

The suit also stated that a private investigator for the Does in 1989 interviewed more than a hundred people about Lutz and Halpin but turned up no incriminating evidence. The complaint further charged that the boy "changed his story about the purported abuse every time he told it" and that public authorities decided "there would be no prosecution due to the lack of any objective evidence to substantiate Richard Doe's ever-changing allegations."

In my review of the court records I found no medical documents on the boy. In the *Reader* article I cited the interviews by the private detective.

The pivotal accusation was that the boy had changed his story. The police reports do reflect changes, but given the number of times he was interviewed and the *way* he was grilled, is that so surprising? He was seven years old.

The amended claim stated that the Does "gave reporter Jason Berry copies of the Northbrook police reports with the express intention that Berry would selectively incorporate into this article certain portions of those reports . . ."

The police reports did indeed influence what I wrote. When I found them I considered it a stroke of luck: they were in the court record as part of a discovery request by the church. The Does never gave them to me. One of the police reports was missing from the court record. Whether it would strengthen or weaken the defense I cannot say.

Although the Cardinal's Commission did not directly address questions about legal tactics, its report stated that the police and state's attorney's office "often share information with the media [jeopardizing] the victim's privacy and confidentiality."

What should church officials do when they have knowledge of child-molesting priests? On this crucial matter the Commission followed an extremely narrow—and highly questionable—interpretation of Illinois law with regard to an institution's responsibility for reporting child molesters; the report also echoed bishops' mistakes of the past. It stated:

> *Civil authorities are often not interested in prosecuting cases involving events that happened many years ago. Moreover, the civil authorities do not necessarily get involved immediately when someone calls local law enforcement personnel.*
>
> There is no legal obligation to report all child sexual abuse to law enforcement personnel. No law requires a citizen to report crimes. Neither is there a moral obligation to report all child sexual abuse to civil authorities for the purpose of criminal prosecution . . . The decision to initiate a criminal investigation resides with the victim and/or the victim's parents, not with the Church.

Thus the church could wash its hands of any obligation to report child abuse by priests to the state's attorney. This point raised eyebrows in the Chicago press. The *Chicago Sun-Times* lead editorial of June 17, 1992, stated:

The commission, in short, believes the child's interests sometimes require that such cases not be turned over to the criminal justice system. This gives us pause. What the law requires and whether the law is wise are two different questions.

It is understandable when churches do not inform civil authorities of such misconduct at the request of victims or parents. But in the absence of such request, it is hard to understand the legal or moral basis for not involving law enforcement officials.

There exists a natural strain between public and church officials over such legal issues. Normally, our view is that what a church does is its own business.

But when children placed in its trust become its victims, it is no longer its own business. It is everyone's business to make sure that those children receive the full protection of the law that they deserve.

My research had found nine priests in the archdiocese who had recently been removed. The report stated that seven priests had been removed "in recent times," and referred to five more who had been removed after the Commission began its work. Furthermore, eight other priests "have been professionally evaluated and all are under close supervision"—by whom, the report did not say, nor did it reflect on the problems this internal approach had caused in the past. "Several [of the eight priests] are in the process of being reassigned to non-parish ministries," the report enigmatically noted.

This made a total of twenty priests.

In the final measure, after nine months of deliberation in Chicago, the church report decided that the church should handle child-molesting priests with its own internal mechanisms.

On June 16, the day after Bernardin made the report public, Mark Cavins, chief of the state's attorney's sex crimes unit, told the *Sun-Times* that priests in caretaker capacities with children did have an obligation to report abuses to the state under the law, and sheepishly revealed that he had asked not the archdiocese but the church's law firm of Mayer, Brown & Platt to provide files on the eight men. "We know about virtually all the cases," insisted Cavins—feeding new speculation about Jack O'Malley's unwillingness to indict such men. Was Robert Mayer the only priest who could be prosecuted among the twenty (including Maday) yanked for sexual contact with minors by the church?

But that was Jack O'Malley's problem. Cardinal Bernardin at last had a plan to implement, a structure, a process that would free him to focus on loftier realms of church governance.

Thus in the summer of 1992 the Northbrook cases were among many still pending in the United States involving priests and allegations of the sexual abuse of children.

In an interview more than a year earlier, Jane Doe had reflected on a fortress-church obstinate in its refusal to extend the healing hand. She gave voice to the passions of so many parents and children I had met: "I'm horribly disappointed at having gone up the ladder, starting with our Christian community school board, to the archdiocese, Bishop Lyne, on to Cardinal Gagnon, further appealing to Rome. Then we get a letter that the Pope is aware of our concern. The church of

Rome is either saying to the American church, 'Handle this yourself,' or is denying the problem and saying, 'We're not going to care for these children.' Jesus
knew that throughout time there would be people who would follow him and
people who would deny him. We follow Christ and don't deny him. This is our
test, and this is our time."

EPILOGUE

Prospects for Reform

Catholics and Communists have committed great crimes, but at least they have not stood aside, like an established society, and been indifferent. I would rather have blood on my hands than water like Pilate.

—*Graham Greene,* The Comedians

No Catholic can view the decay of ecclesiastical culture without an aching personal loss. Catholicism is a tissue of basic values—kindness; respect for individual life; responsibility of spouses toward each other and children; sexual moderation; a commitment to the poor; obedience to just authority; a spiritual sharing through Mass and sacraments. These values form the essence of community and when they are assaulted, especially by ecclesiastical leaders, the true church—the Mystical Body of Christ—absorbs a deeper suffering.

The icons, statues of saints, stained-glass windows, and altar rails bespeak a visual vocabulary in each believer, a spiritual mosaic fostering intimacy with God. This scenery is profoundly psychological—the pictures in our minds—and nurtures cultural memory. Priests hold a precious place in this collective memory, and parish life relies on priests at peace with themselves to extend this mental terrain. I regret that this book contains so few of these men. But it was not their story I set out to tell.

The failure of the Roman Catholic hierarchy to nurture a healthy clergy cannot be rationalized as the result of sin in the world or, as many conservatives contend, of a church divided by theological dissent. The corruption of ecclesiastical culture is part of a psychological and sexual crisis that has been building for years. The faithful have every right to demand that this situation, made all the more disgraceful by Rome's silence, be changed. What will it take to move the church to decisive action?

The Vatican thinks in terms of centuries, not in decades or even years. And today's clericalism refuses to acknowledge that the problems need a remedy. How else to explain the six-month lapse in which Alphonsus Penney remained archbishop of St. John's *after* his resignation was tendered, following two years of horrific media coverage and a church report highly critical of Penney? Rome's procrastination was an insult to Newfoundlanders. How else to explain the Vatican's failure to conduct a solid investigation of Joseph Ferrario as bishop of Honolulu, despite priests and responsible laity who conveyed authentic concerns to Washington and Rome? What is the moral reasoning behind legal tactics in Chicago under Cardinal Bernardin's watch? Or the Franciscan superior-general in Rome who approved Bruce Ritter's transfer to a diocese in India? Out of sight, out of mind? Such inertia stands in jagged contrast to the persecution of Charles Curran and Archbishop Hunthausen, who retired in 1991.

The *sensus fidelium*, or mind of the faithful, asserts its rights when the hierarchy, from Rome on down, tolerates the preventable corruption wrought by sexually abusive men. The failure of church governance was exposed by an imperative of democracy—that children, too, have rights.

A faith two thousand years old will not mature in wisdom without rejuvenating its moral authority. That cannot be achieved by the all-out embrace of democratic methods; but it does require clear, honest thinking. An ethos of defending human life by resisting abortion and the death penalty fulfills a requirement of moral reason; denunciations of contraception and artificial insemination reflect unfair strategies of control. But the great failure of church authority reveals itself in a power structure rendered morally sterile by its toleration of child abuse.

"Clericalism breeds a paranoidal secrecy," writes David Rice in a study of priests who left to marry. "Just as civil regimes use official secrets to cover up ineptitude or wrongdoing, citing state security, the clerical institution cites the danger of scandal and shrouds its every deed and misdeed in the deepest silence." Whom does "scandal" hurt? The faithful know that scandals are a part of church history. One does not abandon faith—or give up on democracy—because of institutional rot. True faith transcends the sins of religious governance.

Rome's response toward the clergy's sexual crisis shows how far ecclesiastical leaders have drifted from ideals they espouse. Families become the enemy.

Cardinal Gagnon called it "a schism"—when a group separates itself, breaking off communion with Rome. If, in fact, that is the case, why has there been no sign of moral outrage in the Vatican? As a bureaucracy, the Roman Curia—from the Latin *co-vir*, meaning "men together"—has shown scant concern about the molestation scandal in North America, just as the NCCB and USCC wanted no part of the 1985 Doyle-Mouton-Peterson report. This has far less to do with the inertia common to large bureaucracies than with a deep if tacit fear of what true reform would entail.

In the year following the hardcover publication of this book, a growing movement of adult survivors of clergy abuse triggered greater news coverage. Jeanne Miller's group, The Linkup, had four thousand members by early 1993, while a more activist group, SNAP (Survivors Network of Those Abused by Priests), led by Barbara Blaine, began staging public protests against the bishops. Blaine, abused by a Toledo cleric as an adolescent, ran a shelter for homeless women and children at the Catholic Worker House in Chicago. After a six-year struggle to have the priest who abused her (and others) removed from his ministry, she compared the hierarchy to "an incest family keeping a lid of secrecy on the children."

As the media bombardment worsened, the bishops turned to Rev. Canice

Connors for help. A Franciscan priest-psychologist who had become director of St. Luke Institute, Connors drew together some thirty therapists, canonists, and theologians, as well as Jeanne Miller, for a three-day think tank to provide recommendations for the bishops. Although Connors watered down the group's report, his presentation of the findings to the NCCB at its June 1993 convention was a small step forward. The recommendations called on the bishops to reach out to victims with pastoral and psychological care, to strengthen seminary standards, and to make sure that child molesters not be returned to ministry with children.

The NCCB formed an ad hoc committee to study the recommendations and open a dialogue with survivors groups.

A few days later Pope John Paul II broke his long silence on the issue with a prepared statement to the bishops, saying: "I fully share your sorrow and your concern, especially your concern for the victims so seriously hurt by these misdeeds." The Pope's concern was activated by a message he kept hearing from U.S. bishops on their visits to Rome: media coverage of the scandal was damaging the church, and the bishops wanted greater autonomy to summarily dismiss, or laicize, pedophile priests.

The Pope announced formation of a committee to explore the bishops' request for broader dismissal powers. He also scored the news media for sensationalism.

The deeper crisis in ecclesiastical culture has not been addressed. "You can kick out ephebophiles, but the [seminary] is constantly producing others to fill their shoes," notes Richard Sipe, "by favoring those who are emotionally immature and reject women."

Leslie Lothstein, a clinical psychologist at the Institute of Living who has treated many ministers and professional care-givers, adds: "The study that people in the church don't want done is comparing deviant sexual behavior among Protestants, Jewish, and Catholic clergy. [At the Institute] we've seen over one hundred priests involved with teens or children, compared to one Protestant minister and no rabbis. Ministers of other denominations are usually involved with adults."

And so a consideration of reform prospects must begin with a qualifier: what *should* be done has little relation to what will be done until influential lay people prevail on reasonable churchmen to confront the decay in authority so pronounced in the pedophilia scandals. Denying the existence of this decay is one symptom of a spiritual cancer. Arresting the illness requires a structural change in the ecclesiastical concept of church, and history suggests the Vatican will resist that to the bitter end. The erosion of seminary formation, gay behavior patterns in rectories and religious communities (the full scope of which this book has barely limned), changes in church administration as a new generation advances—these signal a decline that cannot be reversed so long as ministry is open only to unmarried males.

But changing this tradition cannot succeed without simultaneously affirming the validity of celibacy as a form of genuine moral witness for those who so choose it. A staunch proponent of celibacy, the Rev. Charles Fiore of Wisconsin—who is also one of the most outspoken critics of the American bishops' mishandling of the pedophilia crisis—puts it this way: "I am offended that many priests have broken their vows. Celibacy is counter-cultural in our society, where people make promises and break them all the time—in marriage, in business, in many venues. I am a priest. I was taught that from those to whom much has been given, much is expected in return. I consider my vocation a special grace."

Mandatory celibacy is a papal law and thus can be changed. Those who argue that, because Jesus was celibate, so must all priests be, ignore the example of married apostles. Nor did Jesus stipulate that only celibate males be granted the privilege of administering the sacraments. What Jesus did *not* say may well have greater impetus in this regard. What would Jesus have thought of the clerical families broken by medieval celibacy statutes? Today, CORPUS—an organization of priests who left to marry—has some seven thousand men yearning for ministerial work. Would Jesus approve of denying them sacramental roles, while an ecclesiastical culture harbors child molesters, tolerates homosexual activity, and turns a blind eye at priests living with women in Third World countries?

Peruvian missionaries estimate that eighty percent of local priests live with women. In Zaire, where tribal traditions of polygamy clash with the enforced status of celibacy, a missionary told Irish author David Rice that all local priests in his diocese had fathered children by various women: "The women usually stay on the mission, have little huts near the mission. Everyone knows it—the bishop, the chief—it's common knowledge."

Reports of this kind expose the deeper problem of celibacy: credibility. A church that insists on priestly service only from celibate males invites critical scrutiny of its institutional behavior. Optional celibacy will not be a panacea, but opening the diocesan clergy to married men and women will be a major step in refocusing the institutional church on the People of God—revitalizing parish life by putting families in the rectory, a shift away from today's clericalism. This transition will be fraught with conflicts. Celibates who have honored their vow may well wonder why they have done so.

But wrenching changes have already registered their impact. The church must change; the question is not when but how.

A married clergy will improve clerical life only to the degree that those priests who choose to remain celibate find affirmation from their married colleagues. A tradition that is many centuries old, and that has in other ways well served the church, should be strengthened in the process of reform.

The presence of a married clergy will not eradicate child sexual abuse. But as society grows in awareness, the spread of husbands, wives, and children in rectories will lay a different cultural foundation from the one today, fraught with pederasty.

Polls show that the laity are quite prepared for married priests. It is the men who rule the church who fear the loss of power. The driving factor may well be money: increased losses from civil litigation, and a continuation of lowered donations by lay people in the pews. The $400 million in losses due to child molestation in the last decade is nearly six times the Vatican deficit. This includes attorneys' fees, medical expenses for priests, therapy costs to victims, direct cash settlements, and portions of settlements shared with insurers.

The courts and various state legislatures are showing greater sympathy toward delayed discovery for survivors—meaning that an adult who was victimized as a child has a year in some states, more in others, after consciously understanding the impact before bringing a case. Those therapists from clergy rehabilitation facilities who give rosy assessments of ephebophiles should take a deep breath and hold it. One repeat offender in a diocese where money is tight could have a crippling financial impact. It is a gamble to return such men to a clerical milieu marked by homosexual activity and little sense of accountability.

Monetary pressure alone will not achieve reform. Groups like the Knights of Columbus must squarely face the crisis and not transfer blame from Rome to a "dissident" North American church. Many people (especially non-Catholics) have the image of an all-seeing Vatican, poised to dispatch inquisitors and pull things into line. In disputes with the magisterium that can be the case, depending on the visibility of the alleged perpetrator—a Charles Curran or a Leonardo Boff, the Brazilian exponent of liberation theology. Sexual corruption is another matter. Absent a whole-scale disaster, as in Lafayette or Newfoundland, the Vatican leaves its bishops to fend for themselves—a sort of "you got yourself into this, now pull yourself out" mentality.

Property concerns behind the enforcement of celibacy in the eleventh century no longer make sense. The church is losing huge amounts of money yet fails to institute reforms. Catholics will not contribute to dioceses where they see cover-ups and an image of priestly life that mocks their values and religious expectations. Alternatively, if married priests put their own stamp on parish life, the level of giving will likely increase, meaning more money to Rome. At some point the Vatican, perhaps under a future Pope, will bend to financial reality, relax the celibacy rule, and move toward a new manner of ministry.

A marriage option for priests could move Catholic theology to shift its emphasis from celibacy to family dynamics, from sexual renunciation to generative bonding; theology could begin to focus on what it takes to sustain marriages and to strengthen the nuclear family—profound concerns in times such as these.

Homosexuality is a great theological concern today. Moral thinking is a dynamic process. Theologian James P. Hanigan has written: "To exclude, in principle, a minority [homosexuals] from the possibility of living such a [faith] life . . . is simply unacceptable for a faith that is catholic or universal in principle and outreach." Another theologian, Lisa Sowle Cahill, notes that Jesus associated with people considered outcasts. She continues:

> *Forgiveness is mediated to all in Jesus, even those whom "the righteous" condemn and shun. . . . To the extent that homosexual love is characterized by fidelity and service, by repentance and reconciliation, it follows Jesus' teaching and example. The larger community also must include homosexuals in their attitudes of love, forgiveness, and reconciliation, as well as judgment . . . while Scripture specifically affirms a heterosexual norm, and prohibits homosexual acts, it also affirms qualities of relationship which can be achieved by homosexuals.*

Cahill concludes that "it is possible to judge sexual acts in other contexts as non-normative but objectively justifiable in the exceptional situation." If the magisterium is unlikely soon to endorse such a position it does not mean that gay people are unwelcome in the Catholic Church. But church is not a political forum. People seek serenity in religious rituals; prayer is inherently private, and sacred spaces must be respected. Homosexuality is not a clinical illness, but those gay behavior patterns that invade sacred spaces, or abuse religious traditions, fail to soften opinions of a skeptical majority.

The Catholic Church's homosexual crisis points up the greater dilemma in its treatment of women. For those who seek ministerial roles, whether they are called priests per se is perhaps less important than the sacramental functions they provide.

What the Roman Catholic Church so desperately needs is a domestic theology, a spiritual vision of life in the real world for heterosexuals and homosexuals in the context of family. Celibacy, as a political and theological model, has failed to give maternal grace her rightful role in ministry.

The hard times on which clerical life has fallen are part of a larger breakdown in society. The deterioration of our cities, cynical public attitudes bred by political corruption, the spreading imagination of violence and the poverty into which a quarter of American children are born—all reflect a loss of order, civility, and values.

I began this book by focusing on one community in French Louisiana, with no idea that what happened there was being replicated in so many other regions. In the ensuing years, as I followed the lives of abusers and survivors, my own faith sustained a struggle I have yet to fully comprehend. At this juncture I feel as if a great weight is lifting. Yet there is a sense of evil I know will haunt me to the grave. When I felt its awful chill I tried to pray, and found my thoughts returning to the Jesuit teachers of my youth. The survival of my religious belief owes much to those men and I can only hope that it endures.

Journalists routinely withhold sensitive information from what they finally publish for backup needs should some findings be questioned. In so doing I have also withheld personal reflections that were too painful to write about. There are angers that rise within a man from a volcano in the soul. Perhaps my reticence comes from a knowledge of those who shouldered greater weights in the uphill struggles of their lives. As a child I was taught that faith is a gift. I know now that faith is an odyssey, and in the darkness of this journey each of us must find a light.

Source Notes

Prologue

p. xix — "most serious problem . . . in centuries." Jonathan Friendly, "Catholic Church Discussing Priests Who Abuse Children," *New York Times*, May 4, 1986.

p. xix — "church's financial losses." A 92-page internal report to American bishops on pedophilia discussed financial ramifications: "The Problem of Sexual Molestation by Roman Catholic Clergy: Meeting the Problem in a Comprehensive and Responsible Manner." Unpublished, 1985. F. Ray Mouton, J.D., Rev. Thomas P. Doyle, O.P., and Rev. Michael Peterson, M.D.

Mouton predicted that, absent a responsible policy, U.S. dioceses would lose $1 billion over the next decade. He based his projection on more than a dozen Louisiana cases and others around the country at the time. Although some 400 priests or brothers have been reported to church or secular authorities in the last decade, the number of victims is much higher. The Orlando diocese paid $2.5 million to three youths molested by William Autenrieth, according to Carl M. Cannon in the Dec. 31, 1987, *San Jose Mercury News*. More than 25 suits involving victims of Gilbert Gauthe in Lafayette, Louisiana, were settled or tried at a cost of $22 million to the diocese and its insurers. Two Minnesota dioceses settled seven lawsuits brought by attorney Jeffrey Anderson on behalf of victims of Thomas Adamson. An eighth case went to trial, with a $3.5 million jury verdict in January 1991 that was lowered to $1 million by the judge and then appealed.

Estimating church losses necessarily involves some guesswork. The figures below are conservative by all standards I could find.

Diocesan liability policies prior to 1986—when the insurance industry retreated from coverage of clergy sex abuse—had deductibles in the 15 to 20 percent range. In a $1 million settlement, the church would pay $150,000 to $200,000, with insurance shelf coverage paying the rest. As coverage evaporated, some dioceses formed self-insurance risk pools; however Chicago, the nation's largest archdiocese, reportedly has no coverage. For all dioceses, the financial risks are much greater now. In Lafayette and Minneapolis/St. Paul, the dioceses and their insurers squared off against each other after paying settlements, over how much each side actually owed. Nationally, with insurers unwilling to absorb a prorated percentage of loss, church losses undoubtedly exceeded the 20 percent level.

Jeanne Miller, a paralegal who founded Victims of Clergy Abuse Linkup, has kept tabs on cases since the mid-eighties and calculates $500 million in court awards and settlements as of 1992.

Most dioceses now offer therapy to victims of priests, at least in principle. (A New Orleans archdiocesan attorney stated that medical expenses for a plaintiff suing the church and ex-priest Dino Cinel had been reimbursed to the tune of $40,000.) Most child molesters have multiple victims. It is much cheaper to provide open-ended therapy to an adult survivor than to litigate with that person. Of the Minneapolis/St. Paul archdiocese, consulting psychologist Gary Schoener says, "I would assume the cost [of victims' therapy] is in excess of $100,000. New victims keep surfacing, so they'll keep paying on a cumulative basis. The vast majority I'm aware of are women coming in with old cases. Outpatient treatment at $90 a session for fifty weeks is $4500; if a psychiatrist is involved, it's even higher. Some people are getting reimbursed for costs to date, with bills of $40,000 to $50,000."

As litigation mounted in the early 1980s, the insurance premiums escalated, according to a well-placed insurance source. If the church's overall share of settlements, direct payments, losses from arbitration, and rising premiums doubled, from 20 percent to 40 percent of the $500 million, the total loss comes to $200 million.

Two other areas involve direct church funds:

1. Legal expenses. Plaintiff attorneys in these cases usually work on contingency—a third of the settlement, plus reimbursement of costs. Such cases involve hundreds of hours in defense preparation, large portions of which are billed to the client. A three-hour civil deposition can easily require five times as much research by several attorneys, whose individual fees may range from $100 to $250 per hour. According to Ray Mouton, defense fees in criminal and civil cases in Lafayette by 1986 "exceeded $500,000"—of the $6.5 million in settlement or verdict judgments as of that February.

In the Adamson trial, Jeffrey Anderson estimates defense fees "in the range of $1 million." In the Doe litigation covered in the final chapter, the number of motions, known depositions, attorneys present for hearings, and information in the public record led Jeanne Miller to estimate $800,000 in defense fees.

Most dioceses retain blue-chip firms for a range of legal needs—real estate transactions, probating wills, investment portfolios, employee disputes, etc. In time-intensive litigation, when the retainer fee is exceeded, the church pays more. They also generally pay defense costs for the priest. Ancillary expenses are also steep. Court reporting services run $50 to $100 per hour. A 300-page deposition can cost $800 to $1000. Expert witnesses must be paid. In the Adamson trial, a psychiatrist who testified for the church was paid $26,000. A psychologist who bills 25 hours in the discovery phase of a lawsuit can add $5000 to a defense bill. Court filing fees add up—in Cook County, Illinois, it's $300 to file a complaint—as do the costs of serving subpoenas, and of private investigators, whose fees run from $40 to $100 per hour. Of $500 million in civil losses, I calculate 33 percent in legal expenses, amounting to $165 million.

2. Medical expenses. Criminal judges routinely order child molesters to undergo sustained treatment, with or without a jail term. Health insurance covers only medically necessary services—not a court-ordered or disciplinary situation. A month's stay at a monastic treatment facility in Jemez Springs, New Mexico, run by Servants of the Paraclete, averages $4500, according to a knowledgeable source. Only a small portion of those costs is covered by health insurance. For serious offenders, inpatient treatment runs at least five to six months, followed by outpatient therapy aftercare. Injections of Depo-Provera, the

synthetic hormone that suppresses the sexual appetite, run $1440 a year—$120 a month, according to Dr. Fred Berlin of the Sexual Disorders Clinic at Johns Hopkins Hospital.

The following costs for one man can be deduced. Inpatient care (90 percent of $4500 for six months), $24,300. Six months of outpatient therapy, $500 monthly, or $3000. Total $27,300. (If the patient is on Depo-Provera, the yearly total is $28,740.) Five years of outpatient aftercare is $21,000 per man. An important hidden cost is the priest's financial support while he is inactive as a minister. A reasonable subsidy is $20,000 a year, according to Gary Schoener. The overall cost of a clergy child molester for the first year, including subsidy, is $48,740.

Many such men incur greater costs. Adamson of Minnesota was twice hospitalized for different periods well before his suspension. Gauthe had sessions with a psychiatrist and a psychologist, years apart, before his suspension. He also spent a year in a New England psychiatric facility, at $9000 a month. Many priests are sent to private hospitals, which are much more expensive than church facilities. Three weeks at the Sexual Disorders Clinic at Hopkins runs $7000, according to Berlin.

Using a low-end figure, of $49,000 for a year's treatment and subsidy, the total for 400 men in the 1982–92 time span is $19.6 million. These men will require therapeutic aftercare once their inpatient treatment is done. Again, using a conservative gauge of a year's aftercare at $6000 per man, or $54,000 for the remaining nine years, the total for 400 men is an additional $21.6 million.

The total for priests' medical treatment is $41.2 million.

Grand totals: settlements (200), legal expenses (165), and medical expenses (41.2) come to $406.2 million.

p. xx — "Sipe estimates . . ." A. W. Richard Sipe, *A Secret World: Sexuality and the Search for Celibacy* (New York: Brunner Mazel, 1990), p. 162.

p. xx — Doyle, "3000 American priests . . ." Carl M. Cannon, "Hiding Molesters Insures More Victims, Experts Say," *San Jose Mercury News*, Dec. 30, 1987.

p. xx — "The evidence suggests . . ." David Finkelhor, *Child Sexual Abuse: New Theory and Research* (New York: The Free Press, 1984), p. 196.

p. xx — "gay clergy . . . medieval monasteries . . ." See John Boswell, *Christianity, Social Tolerance, and Homosexuality: Gay People in Western Europe from the Beginning of the Christian Era to the Fourteenth Century* (Chicago: University of Chicago Press, 1980).

p. xx — Sipe on homosexuality: op. cit., p. 107.

p. xxi — "requiring HIV tests . . ." Bill Kenkelen, "Dilemma for religious orders: to test or not to test for AIDS," *National Catholic Reporter*, Sept. 2, 1988. [Hereafter referred to as *NCR*.] Most dioceses now require HIV testing. See Robert Nugent, "Homosexuality and Seminary Candidates," *Homosexuality in the Priesthood and Religious Life*, edited by Jeannine Gramick (New York, Crossroad, 1989), p. 200.

p. xxi — "asexual dynamic." Eugene Kennedy, *Tomorrow's Catholics, Yesterday's Church* (New York: Harper & Row, 1988), p. 114.

CHAPTER 1   *Pleadings*

p. 5 — "wild horses roamed the Attakapas . . ." For regional information, see Harry Lewis Griffin, *The Attakapas Country: A History of Lafayette Parish* (Gretna, La.: Pelican, 1974), and Harnett Kane, *The Bayous of Louisiana* (New York: Morrow, 1943).

p. 5 — "*le grand dérangement* . . . [the great displacement]." I have relied on Carl A. Brasseaux, *The Founding of New Acadia: The Beginnings of Acadian Life in Louisiana, 1765–1803* (Baton Rouge: LSU Press, 1987); Jacqueline K. Voorhies, "The Acadians: The Search for the Promised Land," in *The Cajuns: Essays in Their History and Culture* (Lafayette: USL, 1978), edited by Glenn Conrad; and Barry Jean Ancelet, Jay Edwards, and Glen Pitre, *Cajun Country* (Jackson: University of Mississippi Press, 1991).

pp. 6 ff Account of Roy Robichaux (a pseudonym) is based on interviews with the source in late 1985 and early 1986; with attorney Paul Hebert in spring and fall of 1985; and an interview with the two men in December 1985.

p. 6 — *"protect ourselves . . ."* Account of Gauthe's sermon is drawn from interviews with Ted Campbell and a confidential source.

p. 11 — "case of misguided affection." Meeting in chancery is based on Hebert-Robichaux interviews. Larroque declined numerous interview requests.

p. 13 — "like three zombies." Benefiel, in a November 1985 telephone interview, described the trip to Bay St. Louis and said that Frey's "face crumpled like a paper bag." Frey's mood swing is referenced in his civil deposition of Jan. 18, 1985, with plaintiff attorney J. Minos Simon. [Gastal vs. Hannan, 15th Judicial District Court for Louisiana, 84-48175.] Frey declined numerous interview requests.

p. 14 — "bishop made him nervous." Gauthe, deposition with Simon, Oct. 31, 1984, said the bishop made him "quake in his boots."

p. 14 — "hundred here, a hundred there . . ." Interview with Gilbert Gauthe, Aug. 23, 1986, Wade Correctional Facility, Homer, La.

p. 14 — Gauthe-Larroque meeting is based on Larroque's testimony with Simon, Jan. 18, 1985, and interview with Gauthe.

p. 15 — Ted Campbell interviews in spring 1985; see also JB, "The Tragedy of Gilbert Gauthe, Part II," *Times of Acadiana*, May 30, 1985.

p. 21 — "Bouillion treated boys . . ." Bouillion declined interview requests but gave testimony in the Gastal case on same. Hebert discussed Bouillion's approach with me at length, as did two parents. For background I consulted David Finkelhor, *Sexually Victimized Children* (New York: The Free Press, 1979) and *Child Sexual Abuse*.

p. 22 — "sight of her husband in the nude . . ." Confidential source.

p. 22 — "Shwery requested . . ." My initial interviews with Bencomo were in spring 1985, with periodic follow-up discussions. Shwery declined a series of interview requests.

p. 23 — "rectal bleeding . . ." Dr. Perry Sudduth, the boy's physician, testified as to test results in the Feb. 1986 civil trial.

p. 23 — "treatin' us like criminals" and "Faye Gastal prayed . . ." Interview with Gastal parents, Mar. 1985. I spoke frequently with Faye Gastal in the year that followed.

p. 24 — "cart before the horse . . ." Telephone interview with Wright. "Anatomy of a Coverup," *Times of Acadiana*, Jan. 30, 1986.

p. 25 — On news coverage: interviews with Dee Stanley and Jim Baronet. See JB, "The Tragedy of Gilbert Gauthe, Part II," *Times of Acadiana*, May 30, 1985.

p. 25 — Reggie, ". . . excitement of having him back in again." Transcript, "60 Minutes," Vol. XVI, No. 14, Dec. 18, 1983.

CHAPTER II   *Ethics of an Exposé*

p. 27 — Re oil waste dumping: See JB, "The Poisoning of Louisiana," *Southern Exposure*, May 1984.

p. 28 — John Pope, "Church knew of abuses, sex case depositions show," *New Orleans Times-Picayune/States-Item*, Nov. 9, 1984. The *States-Item* name was later dropped.

p. 30 — The Associated Press story appeared in the *Times-Picayune* and *Baton Rouge Morning Advocate*, among other dailies.

p. 30 — "church has its own atonement . . ." Debby Abe, "Boise priest gets seven year prison term," *Idaho Statesman*, Jan. 24, 1985.

p. 31 — "I was an altar boy . . ." *Times of Acadiana,* "Tragedy of Gilbert Gauthe, Part I," May 23, 1985.

CHAPTER III   *Mouton for the Defense*

p. 34 — "Always I totally drown . . ." My initial interviews with Mouton in spring of 1985 focused on the criminal case. Lengthy interviews about his background, and events treated in later chapters, began in Nov. 1985 and continued into the following year.

p. 36 — "I would not like to have to extradite him." Interviews with Nathan Stansbury, Oct. 16 and 21, 1985.

p. 36 — "report on damage to the children." A copy of the Jan. 12, 1984, document provided to a reporter, without photographs of the boys and certain passages blotted out, reads in part: "The impact on that child is extensive when he is sexually abused during the week, and on Sundays, witnesses his parents bowing, kneeling, genuflecting, praying, receiving sacraments and graciously thanking the priest for his involvement in their lives. Such events have a powerful impact (in the child's mind) in believing that such sexual activities have been sanctioned by their parents."

p. 37 — "not a nesting place . . ." Rev. Thomas A. Kane, Ph.D., "The House of Affirmation," reprint from *Brothers Newsletter,* Vol. 17, No. 2 (undated).

p. 37 — "psycho-theological community." Ibid.

p. 42 — "Blanco began each day . . ." I interviewed Raymond Blanco several times in the spring of 1986.

p. 42 — "Catholics were a terrorized minority." See Michael Schwartz, *The Persistent Prejudice: Anti-Catholicism in America* (Huntington, Ind.: Our Sunday Visitor, 1984).

pp. 43–46 — Blanco, Mouton interviews.

pp. 43–46 — A letter by Paul Hebert on behalf of his clients, published in *The Daily Advertiser,* called Bishop Frey's statement "not an accurate and true reflection of what has occurred."

"In fact," wrote Hebert, "although Church leaders were told of this matter over one year and three months ago, this statement from the Bishop is the first expression by the Church as to the tragic and unfortunate situation involving our children, and those of many others. The extent of the sexual abuse by this priest and the fact that there were minor children involved was never told to the parents of the victims or the parishioners. . . . It is inaccurate and misleading to attempt to portray to the public that the Church leaders have always made themselves available, as it is more an obligation of going to the parents of all victims and giving them the true information about what happened to their children."

CHAPTER IV   *The Passion of J. Minos Simon*

p. 47 — "When you are raised . . ." I interviewed Simon in spring and fall of 1985, and twice in early 1986.

p. 47 — "what human dignity is about . . ." Opening statement in the Gastal civil trial, Feb. 5, 1986, Abbeville, La.

p. 49 — on Hartford, Gulfport: Gauthe interview.

p. 49 — "Did Father Gilbert Gauthe engage . . ." Interview with Stansbury. The prosecutor had the video tapes destroyed after the grand jury returned its indictment.

p. 51 — "carry a message to the bishop . . ." Stansbury interview.

p. 51 — "slept soundly . . ." Faye Gastal interview.

p. 52 — "Is my recollection . . ." *Gastal v. Hannan*, 15th Judicial District, Vermilion Parish, La. Docket No: 84-48175. Deposition quotations are taken from transcripts in the case.

p. 56 — "days of the jocks are over." The priest confirmed contents of the conversation in a background interview.

p. 58 — "a church court . . ." Historian Edward Peters, in *Inquisition* (New York: Free Press, 1988), p. 36, provides an antecedent of the canonical court. During the ninth-century rule of Charlemagne, Roman law was "still regarded as the personal law of those born Roman. . . . When an individual entered the Church as a cleric, however, most early medieval laws recognized him as having, in a sense, come under another personal law. . . . The subordination of clerics within a legally and canonically defined hierarchy was explicit, if not always meticulously observed . . . and the obligations of bishops, if not always or often observed, were widely known, including the bishop's responsibility for discovering heresy or schism, particularly among the clergy itself."

p. 59 — "Dear Bishop Frey:" The letter was attached to the deposition.

p. 62 — "Larroque's answers . . ." *Code of Canon Law: Latin-English Edition*, published by the Canon Law Society of America, Washington, D.C., 1983, is a standard text with facing pages in the two languages. The definitive text, 1152 pages, with footnotes, is *The Code of Canon Law: A Text and Commentary* (Paulist Press: New York, 1985).

p. 63 — Canon 392 was shaped by the *inquistio* procedure of the early medieval church. Peters writes: "Genesis 18.21 was invoked to remind bishops that God did not condemn the wickedness of Sodom from afar, but went down into the city himself to discover its offenses. Bishops, like God, should investigate their flocks. . . . When clerical purity and clerical independence from lay domination became a major theme of reformers during the eleventh century, the inquiry into clerical abuses grew apace, and [the] rules for episcopal visitation took on a new meaning" (Peters, op. cit., p. 37).

CHAPTER V   *Sexual Outcasts*

p. 66 — "carbon copy of Gauthe . . ." "Fallen Priests," *Times of Acadiana*, June 13, 1985.

p. 67 — Stansbury on Limoges. Ibid.

p. 67 — "law-and-order type." Ibid.

p. 67 — Autobiographical sketch. See Donald J. Hebert, *A History of St. Anthony Parish* (Eunice: Hebert Publications, 1983).

p. 68 — "who were pushing . . ." Frey/Simon deposition, Jan. 18, 1985.

pp. 68–70 — The account of the nuns and O'Connell appeared in the May 23, 1985, *Times of Acadiana* and *National Catholic Reporter*, June 7, 1985.

pp. 71–72 — Finkelhor, Money quotes: *Times of Acadiana*, May 23, 1985.

p. 71 — Re Jordan, Minn. Joe Rigert, David Paterson, and Josephine Marcotty, "The Scott County case: How it grew, why it died," *Minnesota Star and Tribune*, May 26, 1985. These reporters conclude that fabricated allegations by several children, prosecutorial blunders and a therapeutic "atmosphere of isolation, pressure and rewards" created a snow-ball effect. Two leading journalists in the field of child sexual abuse—John Crewdson, author of *By Silence Betrayed* (New York: Little, Brown, 1988), and David Hechler, author of *The Battle and the Backlash* (Lexington, Mass.: D. C. Heath, 1988)—are less convinced that abusive acts were minimal. Crewdson and Hechler contend that serious molestations oc-curred at the McMartin preschool. In 1990, after the longest and costliest criminal prose-cution in California history, none of the original defendants was convicted. A group of McMartin parents steadfastly claimed that their children were victims of a satanic cult.

p. 73 — Rev. Patrick Roemer was youth minister of St. Paschal Parish in Thousand

Oaks. Over protests by county prosecutors, a superior court judge sentenced him to confinement in a mental institution, from which he was subsequently released. Civil lawsuits filed by attorney Pamela Klebaum on behalf of four victims alleged that, between 1970 and 1978, Roemer several times "informed counselors, psychologists and other personnel of [his] tendencies toward pedophilia and . . . prior and continuing sexual molestations of minor children." The lawsuits were settled for an undisclosed sum. *[Names withheld] vs. Roman Catholic Archbishop of Los Angeles,* Superior Court of State of California, County of Ventura, No. 82750, filed June 5, 1984.

p. 73 — In 1986, Rev. William O'Connell pleaded guilty to 26 felony charges involving sexual abuse of boys and served a year behind bars, with a five-year probation. Attorney R. Daniel Prentiss, representing parents of a victim, filed suit against the Providence diocese and eventually settled out of court, after extensive coverage in the *Providence Journal,* which drew upon church officials' depositions.

pp. 73–75 — John Money interview supplemented by "Biographical Information," unpublished fact sheet, The Johns Hopkins Medical Institutions, May 1985. Money is Professor of Medical Psychology and Associate Professor of Pediatrics. His many books and articles are largely written for a professional audience; the work most accessible to the lay reader is *Lovemaps* (New York: Irvington, 1986), which examines forty forms of paraphilia.

p. 74 — "leveller . . ." and colleague dispute. Mark Bowden, "A squabble over sex operations: Doctors dispute value of gender changes," *Baltimore Sun,* Mar. 24, 1980.

p. 76 — "People do not . . ." Fred S. Berlin and Edgar Krout, "Pedophilia: Diagnostic Concepts." Monograph, The Johns Hopkins School of Medicine and the Johns Hopkins Hospital. Later published in *American Journal of Forensic Psychiatry,* Vol. 7, Issue 1, 1986.

p. 77 — "We try to . . ." *Idaho Statesman* Jan. 24, 1985.

pp. 82–83 — Bencomo-Larroque: *[Names withheld] v. Archbishop Philip M. Hannan, Et Al.* 15th Judicial District Court, Parish of Vermilion, State of Louisiana. Nos. 84-48174, 84-48176, 84-48177.

CHAPTER VI   Men in High Places

pp. 85–86 — On Pio Laghi's background: Penny Lernoux, "Blood taints church in Argentina," *NCR,* Apr. 12, 1985. In *People of God* (New York: Viking, 1989), Lernoux expanded her report on Laghi: "In 1976, in the early months of the military regime, he gave a speech to the army in which he cited the church's just-war theory to sanction the military's campaign against dissent. He then blessed the troops. Of course it was not the nuncio's job to supplant the Argentine bishops in denunciation of human rights violations—a task most of them refused. On the other hand, said Emilio F. Mignone, an Argentine Catholic writer and human rights activist, Laghi displayed considerable cynicism in his public embrace of the junta. According to Mignone, Laghi played tennis regularly with Admiral Emilio Massera, among the most bloodthirsty of the military leaders, and, said Mignone, he admitted giving communion to a general he knew to be involved in the massacre of five Irish-Argentine priests and seminarians—this at the funeral Mass for the slain priests" (p. 71).

p. 86 — My first interviews with Doyle were in Washington in February-March 1986, with telephone interviews thereafter.

p. 86 — "wrote the section on marriage." See also: "The Moral Inseparability of the Unitive and Procreative Aspects of Human Sexual Intercourse," in *Marriage Studies III: Reflections in Canon Law and Theology* (Washington, D.C.: Canon Law Society of America, 1985), Thomas P. Doyle, O.P., editor.

p. 87 — "The Dominicans . . ." Paul Johnson, *A History of Christianity* (New York: Atheneum, 1974), pp. 234–35.

p. 87 — "nothing resembling . . ." Eric O. Hanson, *The Catholic Church in World Politics* (Princeton University Press, 1987), p. 81.

p. 88 — "the chasm between . . ." Rev. Michael R. Peterson, M.D., "Psychological Aspects of Human Sexual Behavior," *Human Sexuality and Personhood* (St. Louis: Pope John Center, 1981), p. 109.

p. 89 — "But, Father . . ." Interview with Michael Peterson, Mar. 3, 1986, Suitland, Maryland. The biographical sketch of Peterson is drawn from this interview and St. Luke Institute literature.

p. 91 — John Money and Anke A. Ehrhardt, *Man & Woman Boy & Girl* (Baltimore: Johns Hopkins, 1972), p. 24.

p. 93 — "Communicating such risks." Virginia meeting account is based on interviews with Doyle and Peterson.

p. 97 — "Then they flew . . ." Account of dinner at the Foundry restaurant taken from interviews with Doyle, Mouton, and Peterson. Shwery declined several interview requests.

p. 99 — "The introduction focused . . ." "The Problem of Sexual Molestation by Roman Catholic Clergy: Meeting the Problem in a Comprehensive and Responsible Manner." Unpublished, 1985. The frontispiece explains: "The three major parts of the final draft were prepared in May of 1985 and this final draft was compiled on June 8–9, 1985, by Mr. F. Ray Mouton, J.D. and Rev. Thomas P. Doyle, O.P., J.C.D."

CHAPTER VII   Rumblings in the Fourth Estate

p. 103 — "notorious fact . . ." Richard Hofstadter, *The Paranoid Style in American Politics and Other Essays* (New York: Vintage, 1964), p. 8.

p. 103 — "Anti-Catholicism . . . Puritan." Ibid., 21.

p. 103 — "A typical Swaggart statement . . ." Jimmy Swaggart, *Catholicism & Christianity* (Baton Rouge: Jimmy Swaggart Ministries, 1986), p. 3.

p. 104 — "We didn't arrive . . ." Charles Lenox, "Citizens can stop the cancer by cutting off the money supply," *Sunday Advertiser*, Nov. 17, 1985.

p. 105 — Kane: "If someone breaks . . ." *Times of Acadiana*, June 13, 1985.

p. 106 — Wright's letter: "A press interview . . ." "Editorial Perspective," *Times of Acadiana*, May 23, 1985.

p. 107 — "Teaneck, New Jersey . . ." A detailed account of the family's tragedy appeared in the Apr. 24, 1988, *Asbury Park Press*, by reporter Bonnie Britt.

A 1984 civil suit of Richard and Margaret Schultz alleged that Brother Edmund Coakley of the Franciscans, as scoutmaster and parochial school teacher, abused the couple's two sons. The suit charged that Coakley "compelled the younger son, Christopher Schultz, when he was 11, to engage in sadomasochistic activities, including bondage, and threatened him so that he would not reveal what happened at the church, school, and at the Pine Creek Reservation Scout camp in Foresport, N.Y.," writes Britt.

Another parent stated in court papers that Coakley had been dismissed from a previous Scout position for improper conduct. On May 19, 1979, Christopher swallowed drugs from a medicine cabinet, saying, "It's not worth living," and died the next day. "His mother, a registered nurse, suffered a nervous breakdown, according to court papers," wrote Britt.

The New Jersey Supreme Court upheld the Archdiocese of Newark and the Boy Scouts of America's position that charities were immune from paying damage suits, and dismissed all claims in March 1984. An attempt to seek redress in New York courts failed because the family was domiciled in New Jersey.

The parents eventually divorced.

Legislative attempts to repeal the law failed. New Jersey is one of a handful of states with statutes barring civil claims against churches and nonprofit, charitable organizations.

p. 107 — On Norman Rogge. For his 1967 arrest, Rogge pled guilty to one count of contributing to the delinquency of a juvenile, for sexually fondling a youth. The Court ordered him on probation, stipulating that he must "continue medical treatment." At the time of his 1985 arrest Rogge's accomplice, Michael Betancourt, was serving a one-year sentence on an unrelated sexual offense. The two were part of a group called Child Search. An investigation by *Tampa Tribune* reporter Dan McLaghlin found that Betancourt also had a 1970 sex-abuse arrest and that the group's vice-president was on probation from a Texas conviction of illegally taking his own child from his ex-wife's custody. Another Child Search associate had spent time in a state mental institution as a sex offender. Rogge agreed to a plea bargain. After a jail sentence he returned to Louisiana, as an assistant pastor in New Orleans, purportedly in a supervised situation.

p. 107 — "These are serious . . ." "Pedophilia Problem Needs Tackling," *NCR*, June 7, 1985.

p. 108 — "Our reporter . . ." "Editorial Perspective," *Times of Acadiana*, May 23, 1985. [Jointly written by Matys, associate editor Geoff O'Connell, and the author.]

p. 110 — "My brother bishops . . ." Eugene Kennedy, *Re-Imagining American Catholicism: The American Bishops and Their Pastoral Letters* (New York: Vintage, 1985), p. 164.

p. 110 — "George Will accused . . ." and other press notices. Ibid., p. 162, 9.

p. 110 — "A 1970 survey . . ." Andrew M. Greeley, *Priests in the United States: Reflections of a Survey* (Garden City: Doubleday, 1972), p. 139.

p. 110 — "From his own case studies . . ." Eugene Kennedy and Victor J. Heckler, *The Catholic Priest in the United States: Psychological Investigations* (U. S. Catholic Conference, 1972).

p. 111 — "Gauthe's picture . . ." Kathy Sawyer, "Priest's Child-Molestation Case Traumatizes Catholic Community," *Washington Post*, June 9, 1985.

p. 111 — "Hoye made certain the pedophilia briefing was off limits to the press." An affidavit by Hoye in a civil suit filed against Vance Thorne, a priest in Jackson, Mississippi —*Spann v. Thorne*, No. J87-0114(B)—states: "My understanding was that the report, which was neither requested by nor presented to the NCCB/USCC was being surfaced by its three authors (and not by NCCB/USCC) for critical comment and reaction by certain key bishops, e.g., the corporate officers, but not itself intended for discussion at that time"— meaning Collegeville, Minnesota, in June 1985. The deadline pace in the writing of the document was precisely so that it would circulate at the NCCB meeting. Hoye's suggestion of a report offered to the bishops "for critical comment" carries little credibility when weighed against the involvement of two bishops—A. James Quinn, a civil attorney who was Laghi's emissary to Louisiana, and William Levada, a designate of Cardinal Law's committee—who participated in discussions during the drafting. Hoye was more candid with Tim McCarthy of the *NCR* in a May 30, 1986, report, in which the USCC general secretary said: "It is a pastoral problem that should not be debated in the press."

For an exegesis on the nonexistence of a cover-up, see Mark E. Chopko, "Liability for Sexual Conduct of Clergy," *Tort and Religion*, Tab N, American Bar Association, 1990.

p. 112 — ". . . twice the number reported in *Time*." "Painful Secrets: Priests accused of pederasty," *Time*, July 1, 1985.

p. 112 — Roach on "the consistency with which . . ." Jim Castelli, *The Bishops and the Bomb: Waging Peace in a Nuclear Age* (Garden City: Image Books, 1983), p. 40.

p. 112 — "Medical section was flawed." Eugene Kennedy, in conversation with the author.

CHAPTER VIII   Prosecution

p. 114 — "The child was caught . . ." Attorney Simon placed the deposition in the court record in Abbeville, which allowed reporters to make copies. (*Gastal v. Hannan*, 15th Jud. Dist., La. 84-48175.)

p. 116 — "The violence in nature gave Nathan Stansbury feelings of tranquillity." I interviewed Stansbury twice by telephone prior to the Oct. 14, 1985, trial date; the profile is based on longer interviews in his office, Oct. 14 and 15, 1985.

p. 121 — "Hannan had marching orders . . ." See Thomas J. Reese, S.J., *Archbishop: Inside the Power Structure of the American Catholic Church* (San Francisco: Harper and Row, 1989), pp. 308–9: "Archbishop Hannan became involved because the Vatican wanted to avoid the publicity that would surround a criminal trial. 'My job was to see that the right steps were taken to make sure that there wasn't any trial,' says Archbishop Hannan."

p. 122 — "kiss the . . . ring." Joan Cook, in conversation.

p. 123 — "sent a buzz through the staff." Staff member, Sexual Disorders Clinic.

p. 123 — "the priest fell to his knees." Interview with Gauthe.

p. 124 — "He'll be a guinea pig." Stansbury's remark about "chemical castration" was misinterpreted in several media reports of the plea bargain, which suggested that Depo-Provera was a condition of the agreement. Gauthe voluntarily agreed to the treatment, which is not chemical castration. The reports caused the New Orleans chapter of the American Civil Liberties Union to protest the sentence, until the plea bargain terms were clarified.

p. 126 — "Fontana did contract work . . ." "Church Faces New Suits," *Times of Acadiana*, Nov. 14, 1985.

p. 127 — "Unlike Monsignor Larroque . . ." Ibid.

p. 127 — Engbers's sketch. See *A History of Vermilion Parish, Louisiana* (Abbeville: Vermilion Historical Society, 1983).

p. 128 — "On November 7, 1985 . . ." "Listening to the Voices," *Times of Acadiana*, Nov. 14, 1985.

p. 132 — "On November 13, Fontana filed . . ." 15th Judicial Dist. of La., Docket No. 85-7412. Engbers later died in Holland; the lawsuits were pending as of May 1, 1992.

pp. 133–34 — Lenox's call for a boycott was ostensibly triggered by a satirical cover story on the opening of the Cajundome, a stadium which had experienced cost overruns and criticism over potential economic benefits.

CHAPTER IX   Monarchy vs. Democracy

p. 136 — Baudouin's preface. "New revelations about a priest who has been charged with sexual abuse," Nov. 21, 1985, *Times of Acadiana*.

p. 138 — "What these women . . ." *Times of Acadiana*, Dec. 12, 1985.

p. 139 — "I *want* to try this case." "Anatomy of a Cover-Up," *Times of Acadiana*, Jan. 30, 1986.

p. 139 — "According to one study . . ." Karen Henderson, "Church is up against critics," *Cleveland Plain Dealer*, Dec. 19, 1987.

pp. 139–40 — "Stephens also reported . . ." The final installment of Stephens's three-part series—"One case points to a greater tragedy. The Campbell Case"—appeared Jan. 7, 1986, in the *State Journal-Register*. In a rundown of cases that had recently surfaced in other states, Stephens included a summary of the Butaud allegations. "According to a diocesan lawyer," he wrote, "Engbers resigned because of heart trouble and failing vision—not child abuse charges."

p. 140 — "Oliver Houck . . ." *Times of Acadiana,* Jan. 30, 1986.

p. 142 — "They knew something was up . . ." Ibid.

p. 143 — "JUSTICE MUST BE DONE." Ibid.

p. 145 — "Bob Wright orchestrated . . ." No bylines given: "Bishop denies Gauthe cover-up, won't give up job," *Sunday Advertiser,* Feb. 2, 1986. (Managing editor Lenox and a staff reporter conducted the interviews.)

CHAPTER X   Verdict and Counterattack

p. 147 — "Abbé Megret . . ." Roger Baudier, *The Catholic Church in Louisiana* (New Orleans: Roger Baudier, 1939), pp. 347, 367. See also *A History of Vermilion Parish,* Louisiana.

p. 164 — "story hit the airwaves . . ." On Fontenot: articles by Michael Murphey in *Spokane Spokesman Review:* "Priest flees after charge he molested teens," Feb. 9, 1986; "Lack of record may hinder apprehension of priest," Feb. 9, 1986; "2 more boys claim molesting by priest," Feb. 11, 1986; "Deaconess kicked out priest after teen-ager complained," Feb. 11, 1986; "Statutory rape charge is filed against priest," Feb. 13, 1986; " 'Crisis of faith' strikes clergy," Feb. 23, 1986; "Priest's license returned," March 2, 1986; "Priest faces 2nd felony charge," March 4, 1986.

p. 168 — "I don't believe in God." Tim McCarthy, "Church still on trial in pedophilia crisis," *NCR,* May 30, 1986.

CHAPTER XI   Homosexuality, Birth Control, and the Celibacy Crisis

p. 171 — "There is an awareness . . ." National Federation of Priests' Councils, *News Notices,* Nov.–Dec. 1982, Washington, D.C., 1982.

p. 172 — "In 1860 republican . . ." J. N. D. Kelly, *The Oxford Dictionary of Popes* (New York: Oxford University Press, 1986), p. 309.

p. 172 — "untouched by any danger . . ." Lester R. Kurtz, *The Politics of Heresy: The Modernist Crisis in Roman Catholicism* (Berkeley: University of California Press, 1986), p. 36.

p. 172 — "principal errors . . ." Kelly, op. cit., p. 310.

p. 172 — "defined Catholic orthodoxy . . ." Kurtz, op. cit., p. 33. On Loisy, ibid., p. 68. On Tyrrell, ibid., p. 74.

p. 173 — "The progressive *New York Review* . . ." Eugene Kennedy, *The Now and Future Church: The Psychology of Being an American Catholic* (New York: Doubleday, 1984), see Chap. 2.

p. 173 — "*sensus fidelium* . . ." Patrick Granfield, *The Limits of the Papacy* (New York: Crossroad, 1988), pp. 134–36.

p. 173 — "In 1966 . . ." I have used data from Richard A. Schoenherr and Lawrence A. Young, *The Catholic Priest in the U.S.: Demographic Investigations* (Madison: Comparative Religious Organization Studies Publications, University of Wisconsin, 1990).

p. 173 — "poor recruitment . . ." Telephone interview with Richard Schoenherr, Jan. 30, 1992.

p. 174 — "The desire to marry . . ." Greeley, *Priests in the United States,* p. 139.

p. 174 — "John Courtney Murray . . ." A. W. Richard Sipe, "The Future of the Priesthood: Celibacy, Sex and the Place of Women." A paper given at the First National Meeting of CORPUS, American University, Washington, D.C., June 17, 1985. CORPUS (Corps of Reserved Priests United for Service) is an association of 7000 married men who left the priesthood and seek restoration of clerical faculties.

p. 174 — "I saw the church . . ." Tom Peckham, telephone interview, Detroit, Nov. 1986.

p. 174 — "judgment of God." Hanson, *Catholic Church in World Politics*, p. 47.

p. 174 — "transformed the College . . ." Kennedy, *Now and Future Church*, p. 108.

p. 174 — "inherited a democratic spirit . . ." Johnson, *A History of Christianity*, pp. 510–11.

p. 174 — "brilliant jewel." Pope Paul VI, *Sacerdotalis Caelibatus* (The Celibacy of the Priest), *The Papal Encyclicals* 1958–81, Vol. 5 (Ann Arbor: Piriam Press, 1990), pp. 203–21.

p. 175 — "John's intent . . ." Robert Blair Kaiser, *The Politics of Sex and Religion* (Kansas City: Sheed and Ward, 1985), pp. 38–39. The quotation from Pope Pius XII is also from Kaiser, as are quotations on p. 171 from the cardinal of Montreal and Greek Orthodox patriarch (pp. 64–65), and Pope Paul's statement to the Italian journalist on p. 171 (p. 108).

p. 176 — "Buddhist monks . . ." Henry C. Lea, *History of Sacerdotal Celibacy in the Christian Church* (1966 repr., University Books, Inc.), p. 6.

p. 176 — On the Essenes: Elaine Pagels, *Adam, Eve and the Serpent* (New York: Random House, 1988), p. 4. Peter Brown, *The Body and Society: Men, Women and Sexual Renunciation in Early Christianity* (New York: Columbia University Press), p. 38. Lea, op. cit., p. 8.

p. 176 — "For them . . ." Brown, op. cit., p. 64.

p. 177 — On marriage in the Roman Empire: Paul Veyne, "The Roman Empire," *A History of Private Life: From Pagan Rome to Byzantium* (Cambridge, Mass.: Harvard University Press, 1987), pp. 137–38.

p. 177 — "morality of the socially vulnerable." Peter Brown, "Late Antiquity," ibid., p. 261.

p. 177 — "What ministering women could do . . ." Elisabeth M. Tetlow, *Women and Ministry in the New Testament: Called to Serve* (Lanham, Md.: University Press of America, 1980), p. 129.

p. 178 — "In 313 the Emperor . . ." On Elvira canons: James A. Brundage, *Law, Sex, and Christian Society in Medieval Europe* (Chicago: University of Chicago Press, 1988), pp. 71–73.

p. 178 — "Bishops assumed judicial roles . . ." Robin Lane Fox, *Pagans and Christians* (New York: Knopf, 1986), p. 541.

p. 178 — "this prison house . . ." Brown, *Body and Society*, p. 383. On Damasus I: Kelly, *Oxford Dictionary*, pp. 33–34.

p. 178 — "accused certain fanatical . . ." Pagels, op. cit., p. 91.

p. 178 — "If after nakedness . . ." Brown, op. cit., p. 377.

p. 178 — "wantoning with his favorites . . ." Pagels, op. cit., pp. 93–95.

p. 179 — "By insisting . . ." Ibid., p. 125.

p. 179 — "The list of popes who fathered future popes . . ." Sipe, *A Secret World*, p. 38.

p. 179 — "Amassing fiefdoms . . ." Brian Tierney, *The Crisis of Church & State 1050–1300* (Englewood Cliffs: Prentice-Hall, 1964), pp. 23–26, 36.

p. 179 — "He envisioned . . ." Michael Goodich, *The Unmentionable Vice* (New York: Dorset Press, 1979), p. 23.

p. 180 — "created something akin to . . ." Brundage, op. cit., p. 216.

p. 180 — "When the archbishop of Rouen . . ." David F. Greenberg, *The Construction of Homosexuality* (Chicago: University of Chicago Press, 1988), p. 283.

p. 180 — "shorn of social position . . ." Brundage, op. cit., p. 219.

p. 180 — "Boswell quotes . . ." John Boswell, *Christianity, Social Tolerance, and Homosexuality;* see particularly, Chap. 7, "The Early Middle Ages."

p. 180 — "The more the church suppressed . . ." Greenberg, op. cit., p. 289. "Homosexual relationships . . ." Ibid., p. 288.

p. 180 — "anathema . . . that the married state . . ." Richard P. McBrien, *Catholicism*, Vol. 2 (Minneapolis: Winston Press, 1980), p. 791.

p. 181 — "Dissent over birth control . . ." Charles E. Curran, "Growth (Hopefully) in Wisdom, Age and Grace," p. 101, in *Journeys* (New York: Paulist Press, 1975), ed. Gregory Baum. John Deedy, *American Catholicism: And Now Where?* (New York: Plenum, 1988), p. 248.

p. 181 — "Albino Luciani . . ." David A. Yallop, *In God's Name* (New York: Bantam, 1984), p. 31. Unlike his section on Luciani's birth control research, Yallop's thesis that Pope John Paul I was murdered rests on speculation. John Cornwell debunks Yallop's thesis in *A Thief in the Night* (New York: Simon and Schuster, 1989). Cornwell (p. 15) writes: "In the late sixties, Luciani became interested in birth-control problems, interviewing doctors and theologians to form his own opinion, but he fell into line and defended Pope Paul VI's encyclical. Andrew M. Greeley, in *The Making of the Popes, 1978: The Politics of Intrigue in the Vatican* (Kansas City: Andrews and McMeel, 1979), reports that before the 1968 encyclical, "Some cardinals like Albino Luciani of Venice weighed in with memos of their own to the pope suggesting that nothing be done at the present time, that Paul simply remain silent on the issue. This would have been the easy way out and was probably all the curial opponents wanted in the first place" (p. 46).

p. 181 — "deleting . . . infallible . . ." Greeley, ibid., p. 47.

p. 181 — "Cardinal Heehan . . ." *New York Times*, July 30, 1968. "Part of the controversy . . ." *New York Times*, Sept. 3, 1968.

p. 182 — "St. Louis University." *New York Times*, Sept. 9, 1968. "selfishness." *New York Times*, Sept. 17, 1968.

p. 182 — On O'Boyle: *New York Times*, Sept. 22, 1968; "Bernardin." *New York Times*, Nov. 6, 1968; *L'Osservatore Romano*, cited in *New York Times*, Nov. 13, 1968.

p. 182 — "changed utterly." W. B. Yeats, "Easter 1916," *Selected Poems and Two Plays of William Butler Yeats* (New York: Macmillan, 1962), p. 85.

p. 182 — "The official teaching . . ." Greeley, *Priests in the United States*, p. 69.

p. 182 — Barbara W. Tuchman, *The March of Folly From Troy to Vietnam* (New York: Knopf, 1984), p. 5.

p. 183 — "Behavioral scientists consider . . ." For general history, theory, and reference on homosexuality, I have relied on Alan P. Bell and Martin S. Weinburg, *Homosexualities: A Study of Diversity Among Men and Women* (New York: Touchstone, 1978); John Boswell, *Christianity, Social Tolerance and Homosexuality*; Vern L. Bullough, *Sexual Variance in Society and History* (Chicago: University of Chicago Press, 1976) and *Homosexuality: A History* (New York: New American Library, 1979, David F. Greenberg, *The Construction of Homosexuality*; C. A. Tripp, *The Homosexual Matrix* (New York: McGraw-Hill, 1975).

p. 183 — "In 1961 . . ." Robert Nugent, "Homosexuality, Celibacy, Religious Life and Ordination," in Jeannine Gramick, ed., *Homosexuality and the Catholic Church* (Mount Rainier, Md.: New Ways Ministry, 1983), p. 92.

p. 183 — "gay clergy . . ." Robert Nugent, "Priest, Celibate and Gay: You Are Not Alone," *A Challenge to Love: Gay and Lesbian Catholics in the Church* (New York: Crossroad, 1984), ed. Robert Nugent, p. 257.

p. 184 — "The situation . . ." Confidential source.

p. 184 — "I think a great majority . . ." Telephone interview with Richard P. McBrien, Jan. 15, 1992.

p. 184 — "Some of the younger men . . ." Confidential source.

p. 184 — "I cannot give you percentages . . ." Frank Somerville, "Catholics See Benefit in Ending Ancient Celibacy Rules," *Baltimore Sun*, May 24, 1987.

p. 185 — "I don't know what . . ." JB, "Homosexuality in Priesthood Said to Run High," *NCR*, Feb. 27, 1987.

p. 185 — Richard Wagner, *Gay Catholic Priests: A Study of Cognitive and Affective Dissonance* (San Francisco: Institute for Advanced Study of Human Sexuality, 1980), p. 12.

p. 185 — "In April 1986 . . ." An abbreviated version of the interview appeared in my *NCR* report of Feb. 27, 1987.

p. 186 — On priests with AIDS: Robert Lindsey, "Catholic Church Tenets Are Shaken as Some of Its Clergy Contract AIDS," *New York Times*, Feb. 2, 1987. Rose Marie Arce and David Firestone, "Church Deals with AIDS—Among Priests," *New York Newsday*, Sept. 16, 1990.

p. 186 — "If certain members . . ." Jay Feierman, foreword. James G. Wolf, ed., *Gay Priests* (San Francisco: Harper and Row, 1989), pp. ix–x.

p. 186 — "The priests in our sample . . ." Ibid., pp. 21–22.

p. 187 — "Few people challenge . . ." Nugent, op. cit., p. 257.

p. 187 — "I frankly think . . ." *NCR*, Feb. 27, 1987.

p. 187 — I first interviewed Sipe by telephone in February 1987, followed by lengthy interviews in Baltimore in 1988 and 1989, and again by phone on other occasions.

p. 188 — "The lack of . . ." Sipe, CORPUS speech, pp. 14–15.

p. 188 — "gays were running . . ." *NCR*, Feb. 27, 1987.

p. 189 — Kennedy quotation: Ibid.

CHAPTER XII   Therapy: The New Confession

p. 191 — "Several days later . . ." Interview with Peterson, Mar. 3, 1986, Suitland, Md.

p. 191 — "Psychiatrists hear the confessions . . ." Robert McAllister, *Living the Vows: The Emotional Conflicts of Celibate Religious* (San Francisco: Harper & Row, 1986), pp. 3, 70, 75.

p. 191 — "A man who . . ." Fulton J. Sheen, *Place of the Soul* (New York: McGraw-Hill, 1949). See Chap. 7, "Psychoanalysis and Confession."

pp. 191–92 — On penance: Ladislas Orsy, S.J., *The Evolving Church and the Sacrament of Penance* (Denville, N.J.: Dimension Books, 1978), pp. 32–33.

p. 192 — Clarence Thomson, telephone interview, May 10, 1989.

p. 192 — "the widespread neglect . . ." James Gaffney, "Catholic Moral Teaching in Transition: Values, Victims & Visions," *Commonweal*, Aug. 15, 1986.

p. 194 — "A booklet on St. Luke . . ." St. Luke Institute (no date or author given; 2420 Brooks Drive, Suitland, Md. 20476), a 44-page booklet on the facility and its functions, p. 3.

p. 195 — "The inner man . . ." Confidential informant.

p. 195 — "nature vs. nurture." John Money, *Gay, Straight and In-Between* (New York: Oxford University Press, 1989), p. 23: "The best answer that can be given today to the question of causation is that homosexuality and heterosexuality develop in stages, and have more than one contributing agent. . . . No one has yet recaptured the prenatal history of adult homosexual men and women. There is no way of being able to measure or estimate prenatal hormones retrospectively. Direct evidence comes from animal experiments and from human beings born with a known prenatal history of abnormal hormone levels. From this direct evidence it is inferred that genitally normal boys and girls who develop as prehomosexuals had a prenatal hormonal history that produced a proclivity toward, but not a predestined certainty of developing a postnatal homosexual history."

p. 195 — "An influential . . . study . . ." Clellan S. Ford and Frank Beach, *Patterns of Sexual Behavior* (New York: Harper & Row, 1951). "The civil rights struggle . . ." Taylor Branch, *Parting the Waters: America in the King Years, 1954–63* (New York: Simon and Schuster, 1988); Pat Watters, *Down to Now: Reflections on the Southern Civil Rights Movement* (New York: Pantheon, 1971).

p. 196 — "In the McCarthy . . ." John D'Emilio and Estelle B. Freedman, *Intimate Matters: A History of Sexuality in America* (New York: Harper & Row, 1988), pp. 294, 310. Dennis Altman, *The Homosexualization of America, the Americanization of the Homosexual* (New York: St. Martin's, 1982), p. 188. See also Randy Shilts, *And the Band Played On: Politics, People and the AIDS Epidemic* (New York: St. Martin's, 1988).

p. 196 — "Freud considered . . ." Ronald M. Bayer, *Homosexuality and American Psychiatry: The Politics of Diagnosis* (Princeton: Princeton University Press, 1987), p. 27.

p. 196 — "Psychiatric preoccupation . . ." Thomas Szasz, *The Manufacture of Madness* (New York: Delta Books, 1970), p. 170.

p. 196 — "by itself does not . . . constitute . . ." Bayer, op. cit., p. 103. My account of the APA conflict is drawn from Bayer's study.

p. 197 — "Every physician . . ." and "Psychiatry does not stand . . ." Robert J. McAllister, "Psychiatry and Religion: Yesterday and Today," *Psychiatry, Ministry and Pastoral Counseling* (Collegeville, Minn.: Liturgical Press, 1984), A. W. Richard Sipe and Clarence J. Rowe, eds., pp. 31, 35, 36.

p. 198 — "Gay Christianity . . ." Ronald M. Enroth and Gerald E. Jamison, *The Gay Church* (Grand Rapids: Eerdmans, 1974) p. 77.

p. 198 — "Certain bishops . . ." Malcolm Boyd, *Gay Priest: An Inner Journey* (New York: St. Martin's, 1986), p. xiii.

p. 198 — "with a combined . . ." Kate DeSmet, "A Crisis of Conscience: Homosexuals and the Church," *Detroit News: Michigan* (Sunday magazine), Mar. 23, 1986.

pp. 198–99 — "There are many . . ." Charles Curran, *Catholic Moral Theology in Dialogue* (South Bend: Notre Dame, 1976), pp. 216–17. See also Charles Curran, "Moral Theology and Homosexuality," in Jeannine Gramick, ed., *Homosexuality and the Catholic Church*, p. 163. John Harvey, *The Homosexual Person: New Thinking in Pastoral Care* (San Francisco: Ignatius Press, 1987), is the definitive work on the church's official teaching.

p. 199 — John J. McNeill, *The Church and the Homosexual* (Kansas City: Sheed Andrews and McMeel, 1976), pp. ix–x.

p. 199 — "essentially in . . ." Ibid., p. 32.

p. 199 — "There is no evidence . . ." Ibid., p. 74.

p. 200 — "primarily one . . ." Ibid., p. 50.

p. 200 — "the rampant homosexuality . . ." Ibid., pp. 56–57.

p. 200 — "Some revisionist theologians . . ." See for example Vincent J. Genovesi, S.J., *In Pursuit of Love: Catholic Morality and Human Sexuality* (Wilmington: Michael Glazier, 1988), p. 264.

p. 201 — "marketplaces" and "Evil demons . . ." Pagels, op. cit., p. 40. "lay beside . . ." Fox, op. cit., p. 41.

p. 201 — "[M]any homosexuals . . ." McNeill, op. cit., p. 66.

p. 202 — "driven, an achiever." Confidential informant.

p. 202 — "brilliant . . . complex." Mann on Hayden: *St. Luke Institute* booklet, p. 5.

p. 202 — "Hickey saw St. Luke . . ." At an Apr. 11, 1987, press conference, Hickey said: "He would almost invariably go back with that recovering alcoholic to the diocese or to the religious house where the patient is to be housed, to make a nice transition. . . . He wanted St. Luke's to reach out as an institution of caring." Transcript courtesy of Tom Fox.

p. 202 — "changing the market mix" and "great clinical care . . ." Confidential informants.

p. 203 — "Masters and Johnson stuff." Peterson, telephone interview, Oct. 1, 1986.

p. 203 — Biographical material on Hickey: John M. Barry, "Power in the Kingdom," *Washington Post Magazine*, July 19, 1981. Marjorie Hyer, "New Direction: Archbishop Hickey Revitalizes the Church," *Washington Post*, Jan. 2, 1982. Charlotte Hays, "Straddling the Abyss Between Left and Right," *Washington Times*, June 28, 1988. The quotation on Sister Dorothy is from Hays.

p. 203 — "In 1981 he told . . ." Peterson, in *Human Sexuality and Personhood*, pp. 98–99, 108.

p. 204 — "The precipitating event . . ." "A Jesuit Candidate Dismissed by the Order," *New York Times*, Oct. 25, 1977. Cited in Ned H. Cassem; Angelo D'Agostino; James J. Gill; John T. Murray; Jon O'Brien; Louis Padavano: "The Problem of Homosexuality in Religious Life." Unpublished, 1980. Rev. Gill discusses the study in "Homosexuality Today," *Human Development*, Fall, 1980, p. 16.

p. 205 — "Had we known . . ." Interview with Nugent, Aug. 5, 1988.

p. 205 — "If you were dealing . . ." Nugent interview. The archdiocese released a one-page summary of the meeting, dated Sept. 31, 1981. New Ways issued statements recounting events as well. On expulsion of Nugent and Gramick: Frank Somerville, "New Canon Law Challenged: Nun, Priest Fight Order to Stop Gay Ministry," *Los Angeles Times*, Mar. 19, 1984, repr. of *Baltimore Sun* article. Somerville wrote that Nugent and Gramick "contend that Hickey has curtailed academic freedom as well by preventing open discussion of their books."

pp. 205–6 — The St. Luke dossier, "Sexual Attitudes Reassessment Workshop," included photocopies of various articles; lengthy extracts from Janet Shible Hyde, *Understanding Human Sexuality* (New York: McGraw-Hill, no date given), 2nd ed.; and questions that Peterson acknowledged as borrowed in part from Rev. Michael Foley and Rev. William Perri, Servants of the Paraclete, at their program in Jemez Springs, N.M. The New Ways Ministry material, 28 pages, constituted the last section (followed by quiz questions), entitled "Homosexual Catholics: A New Primer for Discussion." Nugent, Gramick, and Thomas Oddo, CSC authors, Dignity Inc. publisher, in cooperation with New Ways.

The "Sexual Attitude Reassessment Workshop" handbook explained its objectives: "1. Take advantage of educational aspects of sexual knowledge. 2. Become more comfortable with discussing sexual topics. 3. Become aware of your own thoughts, feelings and attitudes and those of others toward sexuality and intimacy. 4. Become aware of how unresolved sexual and intimacy issues interfere with quality sobriety and a healthy lifestyle. 5. Become aware of how the healthy fulfillment of sexuality and intimacy needs supports quality sobriety."

The literature continues: "Some of the audio-visual material may indeed be sensitive. As you watch these presentations, you will experience all types of sensations: arousal, disgust, pity, horror, nausea, fascination, interest, disinterest, boredom, somnolence, excitement, etc. No single reaction to the visual presentation is 'normal' or 'correct.' No two persons in the room will have the same sensations at the same time. . . . You may wish to be more objective about your feelings or you may even entertain your own fantasies. Again, no reaction is wrong, immoral or unusual. . . . it is our hope that you will learn to respect those reactions within yourself."

p. 206 — "At a press conference . . ." Ratzinger quote: *NCR*, Mar. 21, 1986.

p. 206 — "Curran met with Ratzinger at the Vatican . . ." Joan Barthel, "The Silent Spring of Father Curran," *Washington Post Magazine*, Mar. 22, 1987.

p. 206 — "he used to talk . . ." Confidential informant.

p. 207 — Doyle, Mouton, Montana quotes: Friendly, *New York Times*, May 14, 1986.

p. 208 — Owen F. Campion, "Pedophilia: Reporting Sex Abuse Cases Is Called a Duty, Advantage," *Catholic Standard*, May 29, 1986, p. 13. Edgar Miller, "Editor's notes: A noble experiment," p. 2.

pp. 208–9 — Marjorie Hyer, "Catholic Editor Says Diocese Fired Him," *Washington Post*, June 4, 1989. Matthew Daly, "Priest Charged in Teen Sex Case," ibid., June 5, 1986.

CHAPTER XIII   Labyrinths of Secrecy

p. 210 — "In 1974 . . ." Donald Goergen, *The Sexual Celibate* (New York: Seabury Press, 1974), p. 220. "Abraham Maslow's concept . . ." Ibid., p. 59.

p. 210 — "Virtue is defined . . ." Ibid., p. 97. "Chastity then is . . ." Ibid., p. 103. "Celibate homosexuality . . ." Ibid., p. 189.

p. 211 — "Wake up . . ." Confidential informant.

p. 212 — "The pope has a right . . ." Doug Struck, "Gay Catholic Priests Walk Narrow Line," *Baltimore Sun*, May 25, 1987.

p. 212 — "The sexually active priest . . ." Wagner, op. cit., p. 24.

p. 212 — *Communication* was published in Wheeling, West Virginia, under a restricted mailing list. Several back issues of its Philadelphia period are reproduced in Enrique Rueda, *The Homosexual Network* (Old Greenwich, Conn.: Devon Adair), pp. 549–70.

p. 213 — "I believe . . ." Telephone interview from Baltimore, June 1986. Interviews in Washington, Feb. and June 1986.

p. 215 — "sit down as brothers . . ." Vincent Golphin, "Hickey meets priests suffering 'low morale,'" *NCR*, Feb. 21, 1986.

p. 215 — "simply unworkable . . ." Barthel, *Washington Post Magazine.*

p. 216 — "The late Cardinal . . ." Depositions provided by Mark Bello of Southfield, Mich. Case No. 83-256-466-NZ, Oakland County Circuit Court.

p. 216 — "I expected fifty people . . ." JB, "A Pope Visits the Conflicts Facing Catholics," *Los Angeles Times Opinion*, Aug. 30, 1987.

p. 217 — "In 1980 . . ." On GU gay rights dispute: University President Timothy S. Healy, S.J., sent a ten-page letter to alumni, Mar. 28, 1988, recounting legal issues, explaining decision not to appeal.

p. 218 — "The institutional church has . . ." Christine Guilfoy, "Catholic Hierarchy: Stomping on Grassroots?" *Gay Community News*, Dec. 3, 1983, Washington, D.C. Repr. in *Bondings: A Publication of New Ways Ministry*, Winter 1983–84, Mount Rainier, MD.

p. 218 — "Hickey had come to Stallings's aid . . ." My account is based on reports in the *Washington Post* by Bill Dedman and Laura Sessions Stepp: "Years of Defiance: Roots of Stallings's Rebellion," Apr. 29, 1990; "Concerns About Stallings's Lifestyle Fueled Conflict," Apr. 30, 1990; "Stallings Builds a Black Church Far from Rome," May 1, 1990.

p. 219 — "Against Hickey's fierce objections . . ." William Bole, "Catholic organizations hold symposium focusing on gay clergy," Religious News Service, Nov. 12, 1985. See also Bole, "Catholic group brings issue of gay nuns and priests into open," RNS, Nov. 4, 1985.

p. 220 — Interview with Don Miller, Baltimore, June 4, 1986.

p. 220 — "To Live in Christ Jesus" quote appears in Nugent, op. cit., p. xi.

pp. 220–21 — Interview with Joe Hughes, Baltimore, June 5, 1986.

p. 222 — "Historically . . ." Confidential informant.

CHAPTER XIV   The Vatican Crackdown

p. 224 — "Unable to read . . ." Doyle, telephone interview, Feb. 25, 1991.

p. 225 — "in a position to learn . . ." The letter appears in: Jeannine Gramick and Pat Furey, eds., *The Vatican and Homosexuality: Reactions to the "Letter to the Bishops of the Catholic Church on the Pastoral Care of Homosexual Persons"* (New York: Crossroad, 1988), pp. 1–10. All subsequent quotations are from this edition.

p. 226 — "almost diabolical." Dick Ryan, "Jesuits to expel rebel gay priest," *NCR*, Nov. 14, 1986. "What is most likely . . ." *NCR* editorial, same issue.

p. 226 — "Rome's unprecedented move . . ." Penny Lernoux, *People of God* (New York: Viking, 1989), pp. 212–13.

p. 227 — "Like most American bishops . . ." Ibid.

p. 227 — "Conservative Catholics blasted . . ." See particularly Gary B. Bullert, "A Report on Conditions in the Archdiocese of Seattle, 1987." Unpublished. Courtesy of the author.

p. 227 — "A skilled careerist . . ." Wuerl became secretary to Bishop John Wright of Pittsburgh in 1967. In 1969 Wright left for Rome where he became Prefect for the Congregation of the Clergy. Wuerl went too. In 1970, as Boston Cardinal Richard Cushing lay dying, Wright, who had once served as Cushing's secretary, was rumored to be next in line. In *Common Ground* (New York: Knopf, 1984) J. Anthony Lukas writes on pp. 390–91: "Relations had rarely been smooth between Wright and Cushing [when told that Wright had his eye on the episcopal throne, Cushing growled, 'He may have his eye on it, but I've got my ass on it']. And Wright suffered another major liability: among insiders he was believed to be a homosexual, a trait tolerated in cosmopolitan Rome, but a severe handicap in puritanical Boston." Wright did not go to Boston; however he was made a Cardinal. Donald Wuerl's years of service to Wright put him on the inside track. After Wright's death Wuerl returned to Pittsburgh as a seminary rector. He became a bishop at thirty-eight.

p. 227 — "The broad governance . . ." Associated Press account in *New York Times*, Sept. 6, 1986.

p. 227 — "With Hunthausen in mind . . ." Eugene Kennedy, "Asexuality seen in power moves on U.S. church," *NCR*, Nov. 14, 1986. See also Eugene Kennedy, "A Dissenting Voice: Catholic Theologian David Tracy," *New York Times Magazine*, Nov. 9, 1986.

p. 228 — "simply . . . to offer . . ." Darrell Holland, "Sanctions of archbishop raise reform questions," *Cleveland Plain Dealer*, Nov. 15, 1986.

p. 228 — "Haven't been any . . ." Thomas Vail, William J. Woestendiek, Thomas H. Greer, "The parish must be told the truth, Bishop Pilla." *Cleveland Plain Dealer*, Mar. 15, 1987.

p. 229 — "That night I read . . ." Holland, op. cit.

p. 230 — "The whole question of peace . . ." Jim Castelli, op. cit., p. 31.

p. 231 — "The tone of your questions . . ." Vail et al., op. cit.

p. 232 — "We prepared . . ." Eleanor Bergholz, "Priests and Pedophilia: A new awareness," *Pittsburgh Post-Gazette*, Aug. 25, 1987.

p. 233 — "Hickey later stated . . ." Prepared statement to media. See also Marjorie Hyer, "Mourners Seek Meaning in Priest's AIDS Death," *Washington Post*, Apr. 14, 1987.

p. 234 — "It was like being put . . ." Confidential informant, Washington.

p. 234 — "The commentary continued . . ." Vail et al., op. cit.

p. 235 — "The ministry . . ." Pilla, letter to *Plain Dealer*, Mar. 17, 1987.

p. 235 — "We would not . . ." Darrell Holland and Ronald Rutti, "Catholic Diocese weighs alternatives for priest," *Plain Dealer*, Mar. 18, 1987.

p. 236 — "On April 7 . . ." Darrell Holland, "Priest with child molesting record granted transfer from parish," *Plain Dealer*, Apr. 7, 1987.

p. 236 — *Plain Dealer* continued coverage: Karen Henderson, "Diocese shields child-molester priests," July 12, 1987; "Pilla: Priests' sex problems dealt with," July 13, 1987; Holland, "Diocese denies shielding three priests," July 17, 1987; Henderson, "Complaints about priest date to '60s'," July 19, 1987; Henderson and Holland, "Panel to deal with sex abuse by priests," July 28, 1987.

p. 237 — "seventeen cases . . ." Carl M. Cannon, "The church's secret child-abuse dilemma," *San Jose Mercury News*, Dec. 30, 1987.

p. 237 — "My attitude . . ." John G. Craig, Jr., "Catholics are too sensitive about unflattering news," *Pittsburgh Post-Gazette*, Aug. 29, 1987.

p. 238 — "In a letter . . ." *Plain Dealer,* July 28, 1987.

p. 239 — "handling of Curran . . ." Hays, *Washington Times,* June 28, 1988.

p. 239 — "Then I discovered . . ." Interviews on Marsalin and St. Luke were conducted in Boston and Washington in July 1988.

p. 240 — "In all, nine Marsalin staffers . . ." *McCollough, et al v. Marsalin Institute, et al,* #83-5778, Middlesex Superior Court.

pp. 240–41 — "In 1985, St. Luke administrator . . ." Property records show that Bowman took title to 2409 Brooks Drive. Peterson sold 4723 Medora Drive to St. Luke in March 1984. Steve Johnson sold 4803 Medora Drive to St. Luke in May 1985.

p. 241 — "The bankruptcy files . . ." United States Bankruptcy Court for the District of Massachusetts. In re: Marsalin Institute. Case No. 84-352-L.

pp. 241–42 — "In 1990, Dr. Frank Valcour . . ." Valcour, "The Treatment of Child Sex Abusers in the Church," in Stephen J. Rossetti, ed., *Slayer of the Soul: Child Sexual Abuse and the Catholic Church* (Mystic, Conn. 23rd Publications, 1990), p. 45.

CHAPTER XV   San Diego: The New Gay Clericalism

p. 243 — "In the . . . *Commonweal* . . ." Richard McBrien, "Homosexuality and the Priesthood: Questions We Can't Keep in the Closet," *Commonweal,* June 19, 1987.

p. 244 — "Blatantly active . . ." Andrew M. Greeley, "Bishops paralyzed over heavily gay priesthood," *NCR,* Nov. 10, 1989.

p. 244 — "I paused . . ." Willa Cather, *Death Comes for the Archbishop* (New York: Knopf, 1962), p. 7.

p. 244 — "In 1984 a scandal . . ." *Brooks v. Maher,* Superior Court, San Diego County, No. 529114. A 21-page autobiographical statement, dated June 1, 1984, was part of the record. See also Blaine Townsend, "Vatican's Letter Against Homosexuality Hits Home with Former USD Seminary Student," *University of San Diego Vista,* Nov. 13, 1986.

p. 244 — "Brooks later sent . . ." Mark Brooks, "Report of Homosexuality and related activity within Seminary Formation, Priesthood and Diocese of San Diego," Feb. 6, 1986. To Pope John Paul II. Unpublished. Courtesy of the author. (Receipt of the document was acknowledged by letter, Jan. 13, 1987, from Monsignor G. B. Re of the Vatican Secretariat of State.)

p. 244 — "As a kid . . ." Interviews with Brooks, Aug. 1987, San Diego, and by telephone thereafter.

pp. 245–47 — "The college embraced . . ." Martinelli, Scott: telephone interviews, 1988. Dwyer, telephone interview, Sept. 1987. Mary Jones, interview in San Diego, Aug. 1987; Bob Jones, Nicholas Reveles, telephone interviews Aug. 1987.

pp. 248–49 — "rim of Christendom" and Maher biographical material: *1987 Catholic Directory Diocese of San Diego, Special Jubilee Edition,* pp. 7–8. Also, Robert Blair Kaiser, "San Diego's Bishop Maher has a double-sided mission," *San Diego Tribune,* Dec. 27, 1984. Jon Standefer, "Problems dog Leo Maher," *San Diego Union,* Dec. 29, 1985. Rev. Lester Kinsolving, "In Santa Rosa: The Diocese Owes $12 Million," *San Francisco Examiner,* Feb. 27, 1972.

p. 249 — "In 1984 . . ." Neil Matthews, "The Faith and the Fortune" and "On the Sudden Departure of William Spain," *San Diego Reader,* Aug. 23, 1984.

p. 249 — "Maher issued a statement . . ." David Hasemyer, "Catholic diocese under scrutiny," *San Diego Tribune,* Oct. 25, 1985. On Galindo: Standefer, *Union,* loc. cit.

p. 250 — "Jean Liuzzi read . . ." "California Catholics Crying for Help as Scandal Sweeps the Church," *Spotlight,* Sept. 20, 1985.

p. 250 — Interviews with Liuzzi, San Diego, Aug. 1987.

p. 251 — "questioned whether . . ." Mark Combs and Blaine Townsend, "Copley vows not to return," *University of San Diego Vista,* Apr. 10, 1986. On Copestake: Alan Ashby,

"Charges dismissed against man in priest beating case," *San Bernadino Sun-Telegram*, Oct. 20, 1973; "Priest's request for leniency clears assailant of charges," ibid., Oct. 26, 1973; "Hit priest after sex act, man claims in petition," ibid., Feb. 6, 1974.

p. 251 — "One of Brooks's classmates . . ." Tim Ryland, "It's Harder to Hear God's Voice: The Rise and Fall—and Rise—of Saint Francis Seminary," *San Diego Catholic News Notes*, Aug. 1991.

pp. 252–53 — Interview with Reilly, Pietrzak, Aug. 1987, El Cajon.

p. 252 — "Dunn told a reporter . . ." Rita Gillmon, "Protest starts at El Cajon church," *San Diego Union*, Aug. 16, 1986. Manny Cruz, "Church members mount campaign to block changes," *Daily Californian*, Aug. 15, 1986.

p. 254 — "In 1966 . . ." Telephone interview with Kenny O'Brien, in Los Angeles, from San Diego, Aug. 1987. O'Brien was working for L.A. Bar Association. "During that period a couple . . ." Confidential informants, San Diego, Aug. 1987. Kraft, interview by telephone, Sept. 1987.

p. 254 — Parishioners' affidavits provided by diocesan source.

p. 255 — "*In 1987 . . ." *Higgins v. Maher*, Superior Court, County of San Diego, 587931. I interviewed Higgins and his attorney, Glen Margolis, in August 1987, with the suit pending.

p. 256 — "In a psychologist's report . . ." Jon Standefer and Irene Jackson, "Priest molested Bang, reports psychologist," *San Diego Union*, Nov. 30, 1988. Biographical data on Bang drawn from Psychological Evaluation by Katherine DiFrancesca, Nov. 29, 1988.

p. 256 — Maher, "hogwash." Diocesan source.

p. 258 — "But, by 1991 . . ." Ryland, *San Diego Catholic News Notes*, Aug. 1991.

p. 258 — "I often looked . . ." Brooks, correspondence with the author, Mar. 5, 1988.

CHAPTER XVI   Wounded Seminaries

p. 259 — "In a 1985 . . ." Burtchaell's address appears in *Origins*, June 6, 1985. Pat Windsor, "Notre Dame's Burtchaell to resign, sources say," *NCR*, Dec. 6, 1991.

p. 259 — "In the United States . . ." Richard A. Schoenherr and Lawrence A. Young, *The Catholic Priest in the U.S.: Demographic Investigations* (Washington: USCC, 1990).

p. 259 — "When you look . . ." Caddy, quoted in *CARA Seminary Forum*, Vol. 15, Nos. 1 and 2, Spring and Summer, 1987 (Center for Applied Research in the Apostolate, Washington, D.C.).

p. 260 — "We talked about . . ." Hays, *Washington Times*, June 28, 1988.

p. 260 — "Baum issued . . ." Robert Nugent, "Homosexuality and Seminary Candidates," in Jeannine Gramick, ed., *Homosexuality in the Priesthood and the Religious Life* (New York: Crossroad, 1989), pp. 209–10.

p. 260 — "On July 9 . . ." Ibid., p. 208.

p. 261 — "The seminary was so focused . . ." Paul Hendrickson, *Seminary* (New York: Summit, 1983), p. 41.

p. 261 — "We still talked an awful lot . . ." Ibid., p. 161.

p. 261 — "At its . . ." Ibid., p. 166.

p. 261 — "When we . . ." JB, "Seminaries Seen to Spawn Gay Priesthood," *NCR*, Mar. 6, 1987.

p. 262 — "It's more common . . ." Kosnik, interview in Detroit, Nov. 1986.

p. 262 — "wasn't even on the agenda . . ." JB, *NCR*, Mar. 6, 1987.

p. 262 — "In 1976 . . ." Len Cooper, "Race, Sex, and My Failed Dream of Being a Priest," *Washington Post, Outlook*, Sept. 14, 1986.

p. 262 — "The story of his departure . . ." Neil Henry, "Priestly Dream Crushed," *Washington Post*, Aug. 20, 1979.

p. 263 — "Our priestly . . . programs . . ." Daniel Conway, "The View from St. Meinrad: How a Catholic Seminary Combats Racism and Sexual Harassment," *Washington Post Outlook*, Sept. 28, 1986.

p. 263 — "Richard Sipe writes . . ." *A Secret World*, p. 112.

p. 263 — "In 1986 an adult seminarian . . ." *NCR*, Mar. 6, 1987.

p. 263 — "In another case . . ." *F.J. v. Brother Newman Moore et alia.* State of Wisconsin, Circuit Court, Dane County. File No. CV 1759.

p. 263 — "I represent the downtrodden . . ." Virginia Rybin, "Tenacious lawyer carves out specialty," *St. Paul Pioneer Press*, June 17, 1990.

p. 265 — "Hollow echoes . . ." Paul Wilkes, "The Hands That Would Shape Our Souls," *Atlantic*, Dec. 1990.

p. 265 — "Where vocations . . ." Confidential informant.

p. 266 — "As he struggles . . ." Yockey, letter to the author, Sept. 23, 1986.

p. 266 — "An anonymous seminarian . . ." Francis Sullivan [pseudonym], "Meet Father Freud: An Eyewitness Account of Seminary Life," *Crisis*, July/Aug. 1988.

p. 266 — McGinnis, Levitt, Gordon: *NCR*, Mar. 6, 1987.

p. 267 — "This same system . . ." Anastasia Toufexis, "What to Do When Priests Stray," *Time*, Sept. 24, 1990.

p. 267 — "A homosexual and a pedophile . . ." Fran Ferder, telephone interview, Jan. 16, 1992.

p. 267 — "If you show adult men . . ." Jay Feierman, telephone interview, Jan. 17, 1992.

p. 268 — "A young man of twenty . . ." Edmund White, *States of Desire: Travels in Gay America* (New York: Plume, 1991 edition), p. 18.

p. 268 — "In fact, he's no boy . . ." Ibid., p. 19.

p. 268 — "If there are . . ." Ibid., pp. 307–9.

p. 268 — "I told him . . ." Ibid., p. 312.

p. 269 — "Some time later . . ." Larry McCaffery and Sinda Gregory, eds., *Alive and Writing: Interviews with American Authors of the 1980s* (Urbana and Chicago: University of Illinois Press, 1987), p. 267; pp. 263–64, interview with Edmund White.

p. 269 — "The true narcissist . . ." John Crewdson, *By Silence Betrayed: Sexual Abuse of Children in America* (Boston: Little, Brown, 1988), p. 62.

p. 269 — "Data in society . . ." Gene G. Abel et al., "Self-Reported Sex Crimes of Nonincarcerated Paraphiliacs," *Journal of Interpersonal Violence*, Vol. 2, No. 1, Mar. 1987, pp. 3–25.

p. 269 — "Of pedophilia . . ." Fred S. Berlin and Edgar Krout, "Pedophilia: Diagnostic Concepts, Treatment and Ethical Considerations," *American Journal of Forensic Psychiatry*, Feb. 7, 1986.

p. 270 — "Oblates assumed . . ." Patricia A. Quinn, *Better Than the Sons of Kings: Boys and Monks in the Early Middle Ages* (New York: P. Lang, 1989), p. 170.

p. 270 — "Most used terms . . ." Boswell, *Christianity, Social Tolerance and Homosexuality*, p. 30.

p. 270 — Peter Damian, *Book of Gomorrah*, trans. with introduction and notes by Pierre J. Payer (Waterloo, Ontario: Wilfrid Laurier University Press), p. 61.

p. 270 — "an ardent . . ." Boswell, op. cit., p. 213.

p. 271 — "strategically placed . . ." Quinn, op. cit., p. 186.

p. 271 — "Putting it simply . . ." Dean Hoge, "Psychological Pressures Impinging on Catholic Priests." A paper given to the American Psychological Association, Boston, Aug. 11, 1990.

For an interesting background reference, see Raymond H. Potvin and Felipe L. Muncada, *Seminary Outcomes: Perseverance and Withdrawal* (Washington: Catholic University Press, 1990).

p. 272 — Interview with therapist and seminarians, fall, 1986, Washington.

p. 272 — "There is a blurring . . ." *Crisis,* July/Aug. 1988.

CHAPTER XVII   The Bishops' Tragic Flaw

p. 278 — *"Los Angeles Times* . . . survey . . ." Crewdson, op. cit., p. 28.

p. 278 — "consultations with 1000 mainline Protestant . . ." G. Lloyd Rediger, *Ministry and Sexuality: Cases, Counseling, and Care* (Minneapolis: Fortress Press, 1990), p. 55.

p. 278 — "Approximately 10 percent . . ." Telephone interview with Lloyd Rediger, Mar. 11, 1992. Rediger provided data from the Fuller Seminary study cited.

p. 279 — "In 1984 a Baptist . . ." Russell Chandler, "Sex Abuse Cases Rock the Clergy," *Los Angeles Times,* Aug. 3, 1990.

p. 279 — ". . . 400 abuse cases were reported of men connected with Scout activities." Patrick Boyle, "Scouts Honor," *Washington Times,* May 20–24, 1991. A special reprint edition. The figures cited appeared in the May 20 report, "Scouting's sex abuse trail leads to 50 states."

p. 280 — "A 1989 survey . . ." Anthony Kuchan, "Survey of Incidence of Psychotherapists' Sexual Contact With Clients in Wisconsin," in Gary Richard Schoener et al., *Psychotherapists' Sexual Involvement With Clients: Intervention and Prevention* (Minneapolis: Walk-In Counseling Center, 1990), pp. 51–64.

p. 280 — "The Mennonites have . . ." Telephone interview with Gary Schoener, Mar. 12, 1992.

p. 281 — Stephen J. Rossetti and L. M. Rothstein, "Myth of the Child Molester," *Slayer of the Soul: Child Sexual Abuse and the Catholic Church* (Mystic, Conn.: 23rd Publications, 1990), p. 17.

p. 281 — "House of Affirmation . . ." Michael Harris, *Unholy Orders: The Tragedy at Mount Cashel* (Toronto: Viking, 1990), p. 240.

p. 281 — "physicians accounted for just 14 percent . . ." Crewdson, op. cit., p. 222.

p. 281 — "a willingness to believe . . ." David Hechler, *The Battle and the Backlash: The Child Sexual Abuse War* (Lexington, Mass.: Lexington Books, 1988), p. 20.

pp. 281–85 — On the Adamson cases, I have relied on chronological summaries by attorneys Jeffrey Anderson and Mark A. Wendorf, in the cases of: *Mary Doe and her son v. Diocese of Winona et alia.* Second Judicial District, Ramsey County, Minn. File No. 482278. Statement of Facts. *John T. Doe et alia v. Diocese of Winona.* Tenth Judicial District, Anoka County, Minn. File No. C6-89-012659. Statement of Facts. All quotations are from photocopies of deposition transcripts signed by the deponents.

p. 285 — ". . . a Rev. Joseph Wajds . . ." Jeff Baden, "Priest says he told of sexual allegations," Associated Press article in *St. Paul Pioneer Press,* Nov. 15, 1990.

p. 285 — "The boys that Father Tom abused . . ." Telephone interview with Anderson, Jan. 17, 1991.

p. 286 — "Criminal charges . . ." Michael McManus's column, "Ethics and Religion," appears in 130 newspapers. He is based in Silver Spring, Md. Quotation comes from the *Allentown Morning Call.*

p. 287 — "The church's reluctance . . ." Cannon, Dec. 30, 1987.

p. 288 — "His statement bemoaned . . ." USCC Pedophilia Statement (Washington: USCC), Feb. 9, 1988.

p. 289 — "In interviews . . ." Mark E. Chopko, "Liability for Sexual Conduct of Clergy: Institutional Overview," *Tort and Religion,* Copyright 1990, American Bar Association. Under subtitle C—*There is no "Cover-up"*—Chopko writes: "If misconduct complaints have not been correctly handled in the past, these are not mistakes of negligence as they are of ignorance." Chopko refers to the 1985 report as "a 90-page appendix" following a cover memo that Peterson wrote in sending the work to bishops. He neglected to mention that the "appendix" was written first.

p. 289 — "In a legal workshop . . ." Proceedings . . . Twenty-fifth National Meeting of Diocesan Attorneys, May 1, 2, 1989. Office of General Counsel USCC.

p. 289 — "We are aware . . ." Chopko, USCC memo, unpublished.

p. 289 — "Amid parishioners' accusations . . ." JB, "Priests: Escapes, Evasions," Los Angeles Times, Mar. 20, 1989.

pp. 289–90 — Sipe, Kennedy quotes, ibid.

p. 290 — "In April 1990 . . ." JB, "Immunity: A haven for sensitive files, too?" Cleveland Plain Dealer, June 17, 1990.

p. 292 — "would never recommend . . ." Deposition of Archbishop Philip M. Hannan, Jan. 2, 1991. Fontaine v. The Roman Catholic Church of the Archdiocese of New Orleans et al. Civil District Court, Parish of Orleans. No. 89-25790. Division L.

p. 292 — "He replied, to my great surprise . . ." Leslie Bennetts, "Unholy Alliances," Vanity Fair, Dec. 1991.

p. 294 — "Tolar says he met . . ." Former U. S. Attorney John Volz disputed District Attorney Connick's assertion that federal authorities were building the case, as did George Tolar, an investigator on Connick's staff at the time. JB, "Connick and Cinel," Gambit: New Orleans Newsweekly, Apr. 28, 1992. I interviewed Gary Raymond at length on several occasions in 1991 and 1992. My first story on the case, "Vows of Silence," appeared in Gambit, May 28, 1991.

p. 295 — "The agreement was that . . ." Cinel deposition, Aug. 9, 1990.

p. 297 — "WDSU reports . . ." Angelico's reports aired throughout the week and were fed to NBC affiliate stations. WDSU is owned by Pulitzer Broadcasting.

p. 297 — "The paper's Southern correspondent . . ." Hugh Aynesworth, "Sex tapes haunt pedophile priest," Washington Times, May 14, 1991.

p. 299 — "True authority . . ." Eugene Kennedy, Tomorrow's Catholics, Yesterday's Church, p. 111.

CHAPTER XVIII   Arenas of Justice

p. 301 — "An island province . . . high in illiteracy . . ." Michael Valpy, "Church Sexual Abuse Is Abuse of Power," Toronto, Globe and Mail, March 26, 1989.

p. 301 — "Many of the Brothers' students . . ." Michael Harris, Unholy Orders: Tragedy at Mount Cashel (Toronto: Viking, 1990), p. 22. I have relied extensively on Harris's account.

p. 301 — "My mother had . . ." Interview with Shane Earle, Toronto, Sept. 8, 1989.

p. 302 — "If I go down . . ." Harris, op. cit., p. 52.

p. 302 — "Shane is going . . ." Interview with Shane Earle.

p. 302 — "Shane later stated . . ." Interview with Earle.

p. 303 — "The publisher . . ." Philip Lee, "Evening Telegram publisher killed story on Mount Cashel," Sunday Express, Apr. 2, 1989. Lee wrote key stories on the scandal for the St. John's weekly.

p. 303 — ". . . across town from Signal Hill . . ." Sean Fine, "Mount Cashel hearings revive the past for men haunted by painful memories," Toronto, Globe and Mail, Nov. 13, 1989.

p. 303 — "The document suggests . . ." Gail Burns and Walter Stefaniuk, "Catholics study plan on abuses by priests," Toronto Star, Mar. 27, 1988.

p. 303 — "I would much rather today . . ." Canadian Press, "Church rocked by sex scandal," Toronto Sun, Feb. 17, 1989.

p. 304 — "Meanwhile, at the Winter Commission . . ." See The Report of the Archdiocesan

Commission Enquiry into the Sexual Abuse of Children by Members of the Clergy (St. John's: Archdiocese, 1990), Vol. II, pp. C2–7. [Also referred to as the Winter Commission.] See also Kevin Cox, "Young people shun RC Church in wake of sex cases, inquiry told," Toronto, *Globe and Mail,* July 7, 1989, and Canadian Press reports in *Globe and Mail,* Oct. 25, 1989, and *Toronto Star,* Oct. 31, 1989.

p. 304 — "To say no . . ." John MacIsaac, in conversation, Toronto, Sept. 9, 1989. "I fight back now . . ." and "We had part . . ." quotes come Cox, *The Globe and Mail,* Oct. 25, 1989.

p. 305 — Jeanne Miller, *Assault on Innocence* (Albuquerque: B&K Publishers, 1988). [Now available from the author, c/o VOCAL—see address in Acknowledgments.] I began communicating with Jeanne Miller in 1988, with formal interviews on trips to Chicago in 1990, 1991, and 1992. The lawsuit on which the book is based is *Michael Doe and Susan Doe v. The Catholic Bishop of Chicago,* Circuit Court of Cook County, No. 82 L 2493.

p. 305 — "Thirty-nine-year-old Michael Schwartz . . ." Schwartz provided information by telephone in Oct. 1989, followed by interviews in Washington and Baltimore the first week of Nov. 1989.

p. 306 — "Events in Milwaukee . . ." My account of events surrounding Pecore is drawn from ongoing coverage in the *Milwaukee Journal;* telephone interviews with Paul Niebler and Bruce Brentrup in fall 1988 and with *Milwaukee Journal* religion reporter Marie Rohde in Feb. 1991. Father Brentrup provided a detailed chronology of events in a Dec. 7, 1988, correspondence.

p. 307 — "You don't believe . . ." Marie Rohde, "Critics attack Weakland on sexual morality issues," *Milwaukee Journal,* Feb. 24, 1988. Background on Phillips comes from Rohde, "A bishop's critic: Conservative Catholic raps Weakland's stands," *Milwaukee Journal,* Feb. 27, 1988. Among Phillips's other complaints were Marquette University theologian Daniel Maguire's positions on homosexuality and abortion. Weakland supported academic freedom while disavowing Maguire's views.

Phillips included many articles in a thick compilation of printed materials that accompanied his broadside against Archbishop Weakland. He was selling the package for $15 in 1989. The materials include the archbishop's letter to priests refuting the accusations; correspondence of Pecore's victim with the Court in requesting removal of the court-ordered seal; and Phillips's correspondence with various church officials and conservative columnists. "Dossier on Rembert G. Weakland of Milwaukee," Catholics Serving the Lord. P. O. Box 1405, Milwaukee, WI 53201.

p. 307 — "(In 1990, Arimond . . .) On Oct. 4, 1990, the *Milwaukee Sentinel* cited the criminal complaint that "Arimond fondled a boy, who is now 18, in the summer of 1988." Arimond was quoted: "I'm extremely sorry as to what's taken place and I'm extremely ashamed." The 45-day sentence included work release privileges.

p. 307 — "Weakland called the criticism . . ." Marie Rohde, "Critics engaged in 'witch hunts,' Weakland says," *Milwaukee Journal,* Mar. 3, 1988.

p. 307 — "The *Journal* reported terms . . ." On May 6, 1988, the reported terms of the settlement, under structured payments spread over 32 years, were as follows: Of the $150,000 immediately awarded, none went directly to the victim. His mother received $25,000, the same amount to his father, the same amount to D. Michael Guerin, the attorney appointed guardian for the victim. The remaining $75,000 went to the family's law firm, Gimbel, Reilly, Guerin and Brown. The victim's scheduled payments were to begin in 1989 with $10,000 a year until 2000; then $12,500 a year until 2010; and $20,000 annually from 2011 until 2021. Aetna Insurance Co. paid the settlement based on a discounted annuity, "with an undisclosed amount contributed by the defendants." Case No. 531-098, Milwaukee County Circuit Court, Branch 2B.

p. 307 — "Sometimes not all . . ." Rembert G. Weakland, "Pedophilia and the Clergy," *Catholic Herald,* May 26, 1988.

p. 307 — "Circuit Judge . . . Foley . . ." Both letters appear on the June 9, 1988, "Mailbag" page of the *Catholic Herald.* Weakland replied in his June 23 column. In reference to his previous column, he noted:

> *I was speaking about adolescents—not about children. I was not talking, and that is clear from the text, about every case, but about real exceptions. I would add, if the priest is an adult, he's even more responsible before the law because of his special role of counselor and religious model. But the issue remains: Can it be that some adolescents must also assume some moral responsibility for their acts? . . . Although one can say that an adolescent is not legally responsible for a sex act with an adult, I doubt that Catholic teaching can be true to itself and say absolutely that in all cases such an adolescent never has any moral responsibility.*

p. 308 — "Many bishops . . ." Wilson, Schwartz quotes appeared in Nov. 4, 1989, *Baltimore Sun* and Nov. 5 *Cleveland Plain Dealer* opinion page articles by the author. The section draws on my follow-up article in the *Plain Dealer* of Nov. 12, 1990; the interview with Figueroa referenced in the narrative; correspondence between Figueroa, his mother, and Pio Laghi contained in the packet that Schwartz gave me in Baltimore.

p. 313 — "Stepp's story . . ." Laura Sessions Stepp, "Pedophilia Allegations Raised at Bishops' Conference," *Washington Post,* Nov. 6, 1989. Frank P. L. Somerville, "Catholic hierarchy marks 200 years of U.S. church," *Baltimore Sun,* Nov. 6, 1989. Larry Witham, "Youth accuses Hawaii bishop of pedophilia," *Washington Times,* Nov. 6, 1989.

p. 313 — "The one report identifying . . ." Gary Potter, "Bishop Accused of Sex Abuse," *The Wanderer,* Nov. 16, 1990. Ibid., "Man Who Accused Bishop of Sex Abuse Reveals His Identity," Nov. 23, 1990.

p. 314 — "On March 1 . . ." Gary Potter, "Bishop's Accuser Passes Lie-Detector Test," *The Wanderer,* Mar. 29, 1990.

p. 315 — "Victims of child sexual abuse are not to blame . . ." Winter's colleagues on the Commission were Frances O'Flaherty, M.S.W.; Sister Nuala P. Kenny, M.D., F.R.C.P.; Rev. Everett MacNeil, M.A., J.C.L.; and John A. Scott, Ph.D. Copyright by the Archdiocese of St. John's, 1990.

Recommendations of victims advocacy board, etc., are found in Winter Commission, Vol. 3, pp. 17–19.

p. 315 — "Because the archbishop . . ." Ibid., Vol. 1, p. 108.

p. 315 — "We are a sinful church . . ." Harris, op. cit., p. 332.

p. 315 — "regressed homosexuals." Winter Commission, Vol. 3, p. 12.

p. 315 — "a number of priests . . . jamboree." Ibid., Vol. 1, pp. 12, 24.

p. 315 — ". . . echoed Andrew Greeley's argument . . ." Greeley, "Bishops paralyzed over heavily gay priesthood," *NCR,* Nov. 10, 1989.

p. 316 — "involving Bruce Ritter . . ." Charles M. Sennott broke the story: "DA Probing Rev. Ritter," *New York Post,* Dec. 12, 1989. Sennott later moved to the *New York Daily News.* As this book was completed, Sennott's book on Ritter, *Broken Covenant,* was scheduled for autumn 1992 release.

Following Sennott's initial reporting, the key stories on Ritter were: Philip Nobile, "Body and Soul: New Allegations About the Secret Life of Father Ritter," *Village Voice,* Jan. 30, 1990. Ralph Blumenthal and M. A. Farber covered the story extensively in Jan. 1990 in the *New York Times.*

p. 316 — "Rumors of Ritter's sexual activities . . ." Sennott, in conversation.

p. 317 — "The Alleppey bishop . . ." Sennott, "Father Ritter chooses passage to India," Aug. 12, 1991, *New York Daily News.*

pp. 317–19 — "Joseph Ferrario . . ." The account is drawn from "Celibacy: An eroding cornerstone," *Cleveland Plain Dealer,* Sept. 16, 1990, by the author.

p. 322 — "The whole experience . . ." MacIssac, in conversation.

p. 322 — "I was in Washington . . ." Telephone interview with John O'Connor, June 25, 1991.

CHAPTER XIX   Chicago: The Empowerment of Victims

p. 323 — "According to Father Andrew Greeley . . ." See Chap. 7, "Money: Isotope for Anger," *The Catholic Myth: The Behavior and Beliefs of American Catholics* (New York: Scribner's, 1990).

p. 323 — "At Trinity House . . ." Rose Marie Arce and David Firestone, "Church Deals With AIDS—Among Priests," *New York Newsday*, Sept. 16, 1990.

p. 324 — "Discourage litigation." A. E. P. Wall, *The Spirit of Cardinal Bernardin* (Chicago: The Thomas More Press, 1983), p. 137.

p. 324 — "I wanted to work . . ." Donna Gill, "Beyond Linares: Questions plague health care system," *Chicago Lawyer*, 1989.

p. 324 — "law of the jungle . . ." JB, "Sins of the Fathers," *Chicago Reader*, May 24, 1991. Unless cited otherwise, quotations involving the Doe lawsuit and related events are taken from the *Reader* report, which I researched on trips to Chicago in 1990 and 1991.

p. 324 — "to stonewall . . ." Eugene Kennedy, *Cardinal Bernardin* (Chicago: Word, 1989), p. 238.

p. 324 — "You're working for me . . ." Roy Larson, Gene Mustain, and William Clements, "Bernardin discloses Cody use of funds," *Chicago Sun-Times*, Dec. 17, 1982.

p. 324 — "greatest problem in centuries." *New York Times*, May 4, 1986.

p. 325 — "Serritella arrived . . ." Mouton's quote first appeared in "Sending the Bishops a Message," *Baltimore Sun*, Nov. 4, 1989, by the author.

p. 325 — "For my reporting . . ." *Michael Doe and Susan Doe v. The Catholic Bishop of Chicago*, Circuit Court of Cook County, No. 82 L 2493.

p. 327 — "In a brief telephone interview . . ." *Chicago Reader*, May 24, 1991.

p. 327 — "Adele Doran . . ." Telephone interviews and correspondence with the author, Jan.–Feb. 1991.

pp. 327 ff — "Maryalyce Ebert Stamatiou . . ." First interview in June 1988, Seattle; telephone interviews June 1989, Jan.–Feb. 1991. She provided a written account of Mc-Greal confrontation based on notes taken at the time, and correspondence with church officials.

p. 331 — "Tipped by Adele . . ." Among the many press accounts of Seattle events, I found these to be particularly useful: Carol M. Ostrom, *Seattle Times*, May 25 and 28, 1988; Timothy Egan, *New York Times*, June 12, 1988; Wendy Culverwell, *Federal Way News*, May 29, 1988; Rick Jackson, *The Herald*, Aug. 25, 1990.

p. 331 — "Says a knowledgeable . . ." Confidential informant.

p. 332 — "John and Jane Doe." The lawsuit, *Doe v. Lutz*, was filed in Cook County Circuit Court, No. 89 1 10141. My interviews with the couple were conducted under agreement of anonymity.

p. 334 — "In July they made an appointment . . ." Attorneys Mary Dempsey and Patricia Bobb, who represented Lutz and Halpin, respectively, denied my interview requests.

p. 336 — "Her civil rights suit . . ." The grievance in question, *Nigrelli v. Archdiocese*, 84 C 5564, was under a protective order in federal court, sealing all but a skeletal chronology of motions; however a plaintiffs' motion in the *Doe v. Lutz* case included an affidavit by Mildred Nigrelli, plaintiff in the federal lawsuit, and a summary of allegations in that case by attorney Thomas D. Decker, representing the Does. Lutz was not a defendant in the suit.

p. 336 — "The officer's transcript . . ." The document was in the court record of the Doe case.

p. 338 — "The following account . . ." Doe provided photocopies of the correspondence with Gagnon and the Pope.

p. 340 — "The leadership . . ." Andrew Greeley, "Church time bomb: Pederast priests," *Chicago Sun-Times,* July 13, 1986.

p. 341 — "On December 17 . . ." Andrew Greeley, "Pedophile priests—clergy can't sweep them under the rug," *Chicago Sun-Times,* Dec. 19, 1989. My correspondence with Greeley began after I read the column. We met in Chicago several months later.

p. 342 — "Before the laity . . ." Andrew Greeley, "Catholic Church must clean out the pedophile priests," *Chicago Sun-Times,* Feb. 25, 1990.

p. 344 — "Meanwhile, Father . . ." Andrew Greeley, "Hardball not the answer," *Chicago Sun-Times,* June 2, 1991.

p. 345 — "For new legal tides . . ." The suit Anderson filed in Cook County Circuit Court, *Robert Bednars v. Catholic Bishop of Chicago and Reverend William Cloutier,* led to a negotiated settlement.

p. 346 — "Parishioners were not impressed . . ." Jeanne Miller taped the meeting.

p. 346 — "On October 20 . . ." Andrew Greeley, "A special prosecutor needed on pedophilia," *Chicago Sun-Times,* Oct. 20, 1991.

p. 347 — "Greeley praised . . ." Andrew Greeley, "Response on pedophiles welcome —but it's only a start," *Chicago Sun-Times,* Nov. 3, 1991.

p. 348 — "When his parents . . ." Kennedy, *Cardinal Bernardin,* p. 17.

p. 348 — "On the night . . ." I conducted several telephone interviews with Jeanne Miller in Jan. 1992; she also sent a detailed written account of the meeting, copies of her correspondence with Cardinal Bernardin, and a lengthy memorandum on her meetings with physicians and staff of the Isaac Ray Center.

p. 350 — "A St. Norbert's parishioner . . ." Telephone interview, Apr. 1, 1992. The account is based on her deposition in the *Doe v. Lutz* case, provided by attorney Jeffrey Anderson; her written statement made prior to filing suit; and copies of correspondence with Bernardin.

p. 354 — "But now he had . . ." See in particular Peter Steinfels, "Inquiry in Chicago Breaks Silence on Sex Abuse by Catholic Priests," *New York Times,* Feb. 24, 1992.

p. 354 — ". . . Anderson filed suit . . ." *Father A and Mother A vs. The Catholic Bishop of Chicago,* filed in Cook County Circuit Court.

p. 355 — "Anderson told . . ." and "Lutz's lawyer . . ." Michael Hirsley, "Northbrook priest faces sex lawsuit," *Chicago Tribune,* Apr. 3, 1992.

pp. 356–57 — "Cardinal Bernardin met me . . ." The interview took place on Apr. 8, 1992.

p. 356 — "In his first letter . . ." Cardinal Bernardin, "The horror of sexual abuse," *The New World,* Mar. 6, 1992.

p. 359 — "On May 1 . . ." JB, "A Crisis of Spiritual Trust Afflicts Catholic Church, *Los Angeles Times,* May 17, 1992.

p. 359 — "The counter-suit . . ." *Father Robert J. Lutz, Counterplaintiff, v. Father A and Mother A, Counterdefendants,* Circuit Court of Cook County, No. 92 L 004149.

p. 360 — "On May 7 . . ." Associated Press report, "Irish bishop resigns; reportedly paid woman," *Boston Globe,* May 8, 1992; telephone interview with attorney Peter McKay, June 18, 1992.

p. 360 —"It was also on May 7 . . ." Allison Bass, "Nine allege priest abused them, threaten to sue church," *Boston Globe,* May 8, 1992.

pp. 360–61 — On Maday's arrest: Leon Pitt and Daniel J. Lehmann, "Bernardin puts up bail for priest in sex case," *Chicago Sun-Times,* June 11, 1992.

p. 361 — "The overwhelming number of cases . . ." Hon. Julia Quinn Dempsey, Most Rev. John R. Gorman, Mr. John P. Madden, Rev. Alphonse P. Spilly, C.P.P.S., Secretary, "Report to Joseph Cardinal Bernardin, Archdiocese of Chicago: The Cardinal's Commission on Clerical Sexual Misconduct with Minors," June 1992, p. 21. Of the fifty-nine cases the Commission said that it studied, forty-three constituted cases of homosexual ephebophilia.

p. 361 — "There was only one . . ." Ibid., p. 21.

p. 361 — "In late May . . ." *Robert J. Lutz and Alice Halpin, Counterplaintiffs, v. John Doe and Jane Doe, Counterdefendants.* Circuit Court of Cook County, No. 89 L 10141.

p. 362 — "Often share information with the media . . ." "Cardinal's Commission," op. cit., p. 19.

p. 362 — "Civil authorities are often not . . ." Ibid., p. 19.

p. 362 — "Thus the church could wash its hands . . ." *Chicago Sun-Times* editorial, "Abused Kids Deserve Law's Full Protection," June 17, 1992.

p. 363 — "The report stated that seven . . ." "Cardinal's Commission," op. cit., p. 22

p. 363 — "On June 16 . . ." Daniel J. Lehmann, "Share Priest Files, Bernardin Urged," *Chicago Sun-Times*, June 17, 1992.

p. 363 — "I'm horribly disappointed . . ." *Chicago Reader*, May 24, 1991.

p. 363 — "Jane Doe had . . ." *Chicago Reader*, May 24, 1991.

EPILOGUE: Prospects for Reform

p. 366 — "Clericalism breeds . . ." David Rice, *Shattered Vows: Priests Who Leave* (New York: Morrow, 1990), p. 137.

p. 367 — "I am offended that many priests have broken their vows . . ." Telephone interview with Rev. Charles Fiore, Jan. 8, 1992.

p. 367 — "Peruvian missionaries estimate . . ." Rice, op. cit., p. 120.

p. 367 — "The women . . ." Ibid., p. 121.

p. 368 — "To exclude, in principle . . ." James P. Hanigan, *Homosexuality: The Test Case for Christian Ethics* (Mahwah, N.J.: Paulist Press, 1988), p. 23.

pp. 368–69 — "Forgiveness is mediated to all . . ." Lisa Sowle Cahill, "Moral Methodology: A Case Study," in *A Challenge to Love* (New York: Crossroad, 1984), ed. Robert Nugent, p. 78. See also Cahill, "Can We Get Real About Sex?" *Commonweal*, Sept. 14, 1990.

Index

University of Illinois Press
1325 South Oak Street
Champaign, IL 61820-6903
www.press.uillinois.edu